ISSUES IN CORPORATE GOVERNANCE AND FINANCE

ADVANCES IN FINANCIAL ECONOMICS

Series Editor: M. Hirschey, K. John and
A. K. Makhija

ADVANCES IN FINANCIAL ECONOMICS   VOLUME 12

ISSUES IN CORPORATE GOVERNANCE AND FINANCE

*HD
2741
I87
2007*

Web

EDITED BY

MARK HIRSCHEY

*Anderson Chandler Professors of Business
University of Kansas*

KOSE JOHN

*Charles William Gerstenberg
Professor of Banking and Finance
New York University*

ANIL K. MAKHIJA

*David A. Rismiller Professor of Finance
The Ohio State University*

ELSEVIER
JAI

Amsterdam – Boston – Heidelberg – London – New York – Oxford
Paris – San Diego – San Francisco – Singapore – Sydney – Tokyo

JAI Press is an imprint of Elsevier

*S/O
July 21, 2008*

KJ

JAI Press is an imprint of Elsevier
Linacre House, Jordan Hill, Oxford OX2 8DP, UK
Radarweg 29, PO Box 211, 1000 AE Amsterdam, The Netherlands
525 B Street, Suite 1900, San Diego, CA 92101-4495, USA

First edition 2007

British Library Cataloguing in Publication Data
A catalogue record for this book is available from the British Library

ISBN: 978-0-7623-1373-0
ISSN: 1569-3732

For information on all JAI Press publications
visit our website at books.elsevier.com

Printed and bound in the United Kingdom

07 08 09 10 11 10 9 8 7 6 5 4 3 2 1

CONTENTS

LIST OF CONTRIBUTORS

Rosenfeld Ahron	Ben-Gurion University of the Negev, Beer-Sheva, Israel
Ritab S. Al-Khouri	Yarmouk University, Irbid, Jordan
Scott Besley	University of South Florida, Tampa, FL, USA
Nalinaksha Bhattacharyya	University of Alaska Anchorage, AK, USA
Don M. Chance	Louisiana State University, Baton Rouge, LA, USA
Jean Jinghan Chen	University of Surrey, Guildford, UK
Peng Cheng	University of Surrey, Guildford, UK
Ei Yet Chu	University Malaysia Sarawak, Malaysia
Douglas J. Cumming	Schulich School of Business, York University, Toronto, Ontario, Canada
Stephen P. Ferris	University of Missouri-Colombia, Colombia, MO, USA
Bill Francis	Lally School of Management and Technology, Troy, NY, USA
Steve P. Fraser	United States Air Force Academy, CO, USA
Koresh Galil	Ben-Gurion University of the Negev, Beer-Sheva, Israel
Vijay Gondhalekar	Grand Valley State University, Grand Rapids, MI, USA

Christopher J. Green	Loughborough University, Loughborough, UK
Iftekhar Hasan	Lally School of Management and Technology, Troy, NY, USA
Kenneth A. Kim	State University of New York at Buffalo, Buffalo, NY, USA
Peter Kimuyu	University of Nairobi, Kenya
Pattanaporn Kitsabunnarat	Chulalongkorn University, Bangkok, Thailand
Hardjo Koerniadi	Auckland University of Technology, Auckland, New Zealand
Beni Lauterbach	Bar-Ilan University, Ramat Gan, Israel
Ming-Hua Liu	Auckland University of Technology, Auckland, New Zealand
Ronny Manos	School of Business, Rishon Lezion, Israel
Victor Murinde	Birmingham Business School, Birmingham UK
C.R. Narayanaswamy	Clayton State University, Morrow, GA, USA
Takeshi Nishikawa	St. John's University, Jamaica, NY, USA
Imants Paeglis	John Molson School of Business, Montreal, Quebec, Canada
Christos Pantzalis	University of South Florida, Tampa, FL, USA
Alexandros P. Prezas	Suffolk University, Boston, MA, USA
Fazilah Abdul Samad	University Malaya, Kuala Lumpur, Malaysia
Sridhar Sundaram	Grand Valley State University, Grand Rapids, MI, USA
Murat Tarimcilar	The George Washington University, Washington DC, USA

Dogan Tirtiroglu	John Molson School of Business, Montreal Quebec, Canada
Efrat Tolkowsky	Tel Aviv University, Tel Aviv, Israel
Alireza Tourani-Rad	Auckland University of Technology, Auckland, New Zealand
Ben-Zion Uri	Ben-Gurion University of the Negev, Beer-Sheva, Israel
Gopala K. Vasudevan	University of Massachusetts, Dartmouth, North Dartmouth, MA, USA
Xinrong Xiao	University of International Business and Economics, Beijing, China
Tung-Hsiao Yang	National Chung Hsing University, Taichung, Taiwan
Amzaleg Yaron	Ben-Gurion University of the Negev, and Sami Shamoon College of Engineering, Beer-Sheva, Israel
Abdul Hadi Zulkafli	University Malaya, Kuala Lumpur, Malaysia

PART I:
ISSUES IN CORPORATE
GOVERNANCE

MANAGERIAL POWER IN THE DESIGN OF EXECUTIVE COMPENSATION: EVIDENCE FROM JAPAN

Stephen P. Ferris, Kenneth A. Kim,
Pattanaporn Kitsabunnarat and Takeshi Nishikawa

ABSTRACT

Using a sample of 466 grants of stock options to executives of Japanese firms over the years 1997–2001, this study tests the managerial power theory of compensation design developed by Bebchuk, Fried, and Walker (2002) and Bebchuk and Fried (2004). This theory argues that managers of firms with weak corporate governance will use their "power" to design executive compensation that is "manager-advantageous." Using our option grants sample, we test to determine if any of the firm's governance mechanisms are able to limit managerial self-dealing with respect to executive stock options. We find that smaller boards and a higher percentage of independent directors are important governance mechanisms for the control of managerial influences in the design of stock-option compensation. An alternative hypothesis, that firms elect to grant advantageously designed options to encourage risk taking by managers, is not supported by our empirical results. Finally, we determine that the

Issues in Corporate Governance and Finance
Advances in Financial Economics, Volume 12, 3–26
ISSN: 1569-3732/doi:10.1016/S1569-3732(07)12001-6

market response to the announcements of such grants varies inversely with the extent to which the options are managerially advantageous. Overall, we conclude that managerial power effects are present in the design of executive stock options and that theory of managerial power advanced by Bebchuk et al. holds internationally.

1. INTRODUCTION

Recently, Bebchuk et al. (2002) and Bebchuk and Fried (2004) contend that the exercise of managerial power rather than the pursuit of optimal contracting best explains the process by which executive compensation is designed in the United States. Under Bebchuk et al.'s managerial power paradigm, executives have the ability to influence their compensation levels by the nature of their positions, their level of equity ownership, and the organizational structure of the board. The managerial power approach views executive compensation as part of the agency problem, with managers using their control over compensation to obtain economic rents.[1,2]

This managerial power model of compensation contrasts with the more familiar theory of optimal contracting. In that theory, compensation is seen as a tool to minimize the agency conflict that exists between senior managers and shareholders (e.g., Jensen & Meckling, 1976). The level and composition of compensation are established to provide managers with an optimal set of incentives to undertake those activities which maximize shareholder value. Executive compensation is viewed as a mechanism to help align the interests of managers and shareholders and thereby reduce agency conflict.

Bebchuk et al. (2002) and Bebchuk and Fried (2004) further observe that many of the current practices surrounding the granting of executive stock options can not be reconciled with the incentive alignment sought by optimal contracting. Rather, they argue such practices are indicative of a managerial power approach towards compensation. Among the practices that Bebchuk et al. claim are inconsistent with optimal contracting include the granting of options that are already in the money, short waiting periods prior to exercise, and incentive compensation representing only a small percentage of total compensation.

In this study, we test for the presence of managerial power effects over compensation in the world marketplace by examining the nature of executive stock options granted in Japan. We elect to examine equity options since they are the compensation component on which Bebchuk et al.

(2002) and Bebchuk and Fried (2004) focus their theoretical analysis and develop the empirical conjectures that we test. For every Japanese executive stock option granted, we measure its vesting period before it can be exercised, its duration term before expiration, its size relative to fixed compensation, and its moneyness. Like Bebchuk et al. (2002), we consider an executive option to be "manager-advantageous" if the option can be immediately exercised, has a long duration, is small relative to fixed compensation, and is closer to being in-the-money.

Further, following Bebchuk et al. (2002) and Bebchuk and Fried (2004) view of empowered managers, we consider those firms with "weak" internal governance as having empowered managers. According to Bebchuk et al., firms with weak or ineffectual governance allow empowered managers to emerge who are able to award themselves additional compensation, including advantageously designed options. This study proceeds to test whether or not such empowered managers enrich themselves through the award of options that are designed in a highly manager-advantageous fashion.

In addition to being one of the first to test Bebchuk et al.'s managerial power view of compensation design, this study makes two other contributions to the compensation literature. First, by studying Japan's experience with executive options, we are able to observe whether the managerial power view of compensation applies only to the U.S. or if it is also globally relevant. This determination is important because it can provide insight into the international usefulness of executive compensation and its design to mitigate the agency conflict inherent in the corporate organizational form. Given the extensive literature that has documented the existence of agency conflict worldwide (e.g., see LaPorta, Lopez-de-Silanes, & Shleifer, 1999; LaPorta, Lopez-de-Silanes, Shleifer, & Vishny, 2000; Denis & McConnell 2003), this study offers valuable insight into how the design of compensation can align the conflicting interests of shareholders and managers. Kato, Lemmon, Luo, and Schallheim (2005) also study Japanese executive stock options and their impact on agency conflict, but do not consider the cross-sectional differences in the design of executive stock options.

Second, using Japanese executive stock options to test Bebchuk et al. (2002) and Bebchuk and Fried (2004) thesis allows us to consider governance mechanisms that are less common or absent from the U.S. marketplace. For example, Japanese firms often maintain high leverage and close ties with banks (Kester, 1986; Hoshi, Kashyap, & Scharfstein, 1990). These banks can be large creditors and/or significant equityholders. If banks have a significant presence in the firm, then they possess a strong incentive to monitor the firm. Diamond (1984) argues that banks can be better monitors of firms' activities than other investors. Japanese firms might also belong to a keiretsu, which is a diverse group of firms interlinked through corporate cross-shareholdings and an extensive network of product–market and financial relationships (Nakatani, 1984; Prowse, 1990; Berglöf & Perotti, 1994). While the early literature reveals benefits to maintaining bank relations and business group membership, some of the more recent literature suggests the existence of costs resulting from these relations. Weinstein and Yafeh (1998) find that banks might extract rents from their client firms, while Ferris, Kim, and Kitsabunnarat (2003) and Khanna and Yafeh (2005) report little benefits to business group membership. This study thus contributes to the ongoing debate regarding the usefulness of bank relations and group affiliation. More specifically, our analysis examines how the existence of bank relationships and/or keiretsu membership can influence managerial power and compensation design.

Our study sample consists of 466 Japanese executive stock options granted during a 5 year sample period extending from 1997 to 2001. We test to determine if the presence of various internal governance mechanisms is able to limit the ability of managers to exploit the design of their option compensation. The governance mechanisms that we consider include ownership structure (managerial and institutional), board structure (independence and size), debt (total debt and bank debt), and keiretsu affiliation. We find that firms governed by boards with a higher fraction of independent members, but fewer total members are less likely to grant executive options that are highly advantageous to managers. We also test an alternative hypothesis – that firms grant favorably designed options to increase risk-taking by managers, but our empirical results are not consistent with such a process. Finally, we conduct tests on the market reaction to announcements of option awards. We find positive abnormal returns to the announcement of executive option grants, which is consistent with most U.S. evidence (e.g., Brickley, Bhagat, & Lease, 1985; DeFusco, Johnson, & Zorn, 1990). We then categorize these options according to the degree to which they are managerially advantageous. We find that the market reacts less favorably to the more managerially advantageous options.

Overall, our findings provide empirical support for Bebchuk et al. (2002) and Bebchuk and Fried (2004) managerial power view of compensation design, with powerful managers receiving options that are designed for their benefit. A firm's corporate governance structure, specifically its board of directors, can limit the ability of managers to self-deal in the design of their compensation. We determine that smaller boards and a higher percentage of independent directors are important governance mechanisms for the control of managerial influences in the design of stock-option compensation. We also find that the market response to the announcement of such grants varies inversely with the extent to which the options are designed to be managerially advantageous.

We organize the remainder of this study into three sections. In the following section we briefly discuss Japanese executive option programs, describe our data, and provide some descriptive summary statistics. In Section 3, we present our major empirical findings. We conclude in Section 4 with a brief summary and a discussion of our findings.

2. JAPANESE EXECUTIVE OPTION PROGRAMS, DATA SOURCES, AND SAMPLE CHARACTERISTICS

2.1. Japanese Executive Stock-Option Programs

Historically, Japanese firms were not permitted to use stock options as a component of executive compensation. On May 16, 1997, the Japanese Commercial Code was amended to allow such options for both executives and employees. This amendment became effective on June 1, 1997. Japanese stock-option grants must be approved at a general stockholder's meeting. The terms of the option must include the recipient's identity, the number of shares, the share price, time to exercise, the option's duration, and the exercise price. The duration of a stock option is limited to 10 years and the total shares contained in an option plan cannot exceed 10% of the firm's outstanding shares. Although these options are not presently expensed, there is a continuing policy debate about changing this.[3]

2.2. Data Sources

Our sample initially includes all executive options granted by non-financial firms listed on the Tokyo Stock Exchange over the period 1997–2001. The data used in our study are drawn from four different sources. Information related to stock-option grants, such as announcement dates, grant dates, exercise price, vesting and expiration periods, are obtained from Daiwa Securities. Data on the firms' block equityholders, number of board members, fraction of independent board members, and bank debt data are collected from various issues of Kigyo Keiretsu Soran. We should mention that although Kigyo Keiretsu Soran does not identify which directors are independent, it does provide information on directors' employment history and directors' current affiliation. Following Kang and Shivdasani (1999) and Miwa and Ramseyer (2005), we identify directors not affiliated with the firm as an independent director. The executive compensation data are taken from the Nikkei Economic Electronic Databank System (NEEDS) database developed by Nihon Keizai Shimbun America, Inc. Total compensation for executives is at the firm level. Finally, the financial statement data and stock return data are obtained from the PACAP Databases – Japan.

We initially identify 1,259 employee stock-option grants. We eliminate 274 grants approved for non-executives. Another 230 option grants are eliminated due to insufficient data regarding option characteristics. Of the remaining grants, we retain only those for which we have complete governance data for the granting firm. Application of these screens results in a final sample of 466 options that were granted by 255 different firms.

2.3. Firm Characteristics

The time series of our sample of option grants is presented in Panel A of Table 1. Our 466 observations are distributed over 5 years, with the majority of them occurring in the years 2000 and 2001. No firm, however, grant more than one option per year. This reduces concerns over repeated observations of a given firm within our sample. This clustering of observations over the last 2 years of our sample is also noted by Kato et al. (2005). The lack of observations early in the sample period probably reflects slowness by Japanese firms to exploit the regulatory change allowing the use of options in executive compensation.

Our analysis of the industry distribution of executive options shows that they are employed across most industry types, but with a heavy concentration in manufacturing and wholesaling/retail. Rather than representing any particular industry trend, this pattern corresponds to the distribution of Japanese business activity across these industries.

In Panel C, we provide a comparative analysis of the option-granting and non-granting firms. We observe a number of important differences between these two groups of firms. We find that the granting firms are significantly larger than those that do not grant options. This difference is robust to both market and book measures of size. The granting firms are also more profitable, use less debt, are less risky, and enjoy higher market valuations than their non-granting counterparts.

Table 1. Executive Option Grants: Sample Characteristics.

Panel A: Number of executive options granted by year

Year	Number of Observations	% of Sample
1997	12	2.58
1998	44	9.44
1999	48	10.30
2000	176	37.77
2001	186	39.91
Total	466	100.00

Panel B: Number of executive options granted by industry

Industry	Number of Observations	% of Sample
Agriculture, forestry, fishery, and mining	7	1.5
Construction	13	2.79
Manufacturing	300	64.38
Wholesale and retail	79	16.95
Real estate	3	0.64
Transportation and communication	10	2.15
Services	54	11.59
Total	466	100

Panel C: Characteristics of firms that grant executive options

Firm Characteristics	Granting	Non-Granting	Difference
Total book assets (in millions of yen)	416121.50	229852.20	186269.30***
	(87416.50)	(61481.00)	
Market value of equity (in thousands of yen)	468785.40	153249.80	315535.60***
	(59636.90)	(20855.30)	
Total debt/total assets	0.468	0.574	−0.106***
	(0.467)	(0.582)	
EBIT/total assets	0.046	0.029	0.017***
	(0.037)	(0.026)	
EPS = net income/shares outstanding	81.096	78.230	2.866
	(19.039)	(8.427)	
Beta	0.810	0.963	−0.153***
	(0.756)	(0.993)	
Market-to-book value of assets	1.472	1.154	0.318***
	(1.157)	(0.989)	
Number of observations	466	7664	

Notes: This table provides sample size information for a sample of 466 executive options that were granted by non-financial Japanese firms during the period from 1997 to 2001. The number of grants is presented by year (Panel A) and by industry (Panel B). The characteristics of firms that grant options and that do not grant options are also presented (Panel C). For all option granting firms, the firm-specific variables are measured at the fiscal year-end immediately preceding the option grant announcement date. Means, standard deviations (in parentheses), and difference in means, are reported.
***Significance at the 1% level.

Overall, the findings contained in these three panels suggest that the adoption of executive stock options began slowly in Japan after their legalization, but has accelerated in more recent years. Executive stock options are being used by firms in all industry groups in approximate proportion to their presence in the Japanese economy. The firms that elect to use them are large and profitable. Their low leverage ratios and high market valuations further suggest that these granting firms are also generally well managed.

2.4. Option and Governance Characteristics

In Table 2, we describe the characteristics of the options that serve as the focus of our analysis as well as the governance structure for our option-granting sample firms. We see that the number of options issued by these granting firms is small relative to the total number of shares outstanding. This is likely to be reflective of the relative newness of options and the desire of firms to be conservative in their initial use of them in Japanese compensation packages. The waiting period to exercise is approximately 20 months, while most options in our sample have a life span of about 4 years (46.5 months). In addition to a stock option, an executive might receive a bonus or an increase in their base salary. From Table 2 findings, we see that the value of the option grants relative to other forms of additional pay is fairly high at 70%. This suggests the existence of a strong pay-for-performance relation for those executives awarded these options. Finally, we observe that most options are awarded out-of-the-money. This contrasts with the U.S. experience where Bebchuk et al. (2002) note that most options granted are at-the-money.

In Panel B of Table 2, we provide an overview of the governance structure for our sample firms. These variables are important to our later analysis of the ability of the firm's internal corporate governance mechanisms to control the design of options awarded to executives. We find that, on average, corporate managers own $\sim 7\%$ of the firm's equity while financial institutions (34.4%) and other corporations (21.8%) are the other large equity investors. These ownership statistics are consistent with Prowse (1992) results concerning the equity ownership structure of Japanese firms. The boards of directors for our sample firms are large by U.S. standards and average over 19 individuals. A little over 14% of these directors can be classified as independent. These board characteristics are similar to those reported by Kang and Shivdasani (1999). Our sample firms finance about

Table 2. Option Characteristics and Governance Characteristics.

Variable	Mean	Median	Q1	Q3	Std. deviation
Panel A: Executive option characteristics					
Number of option shares/total shares outstanding	0.009	0.005	0.002	0.120	0.012
Waiting period to exercise (in months)	19.650	26.000	11.000	26.000	10.743
Length of time before option expires (in months)	46.554	36.000	36.000	58.000	20.625
Option value/(option + bonus + raise in salary)	0.700	0.940	0.000	0.996	0.604
(Current stock price−option exercise price)/current stock price	−0.138	−0.044	−0.152	0.000	1.085
Panel B: Governance characteristics and risk-taking of firms that grant executive options					
% ownership by managers	6.972	0.000	0.000	8.230	12.666
% ownership by financial institutions	34.395	35.545	22.612	46.339	15.179
% ownership by other corporations	21.797	17.445	9.723	31.827	15.577
% independent directors to total directors	14.282	9.091	0.000	22.727	14.695
Board size (number of directors)	19.496	17.000	14.000	23.000	8.776
Total debt/total assets	0.468	0.467	0.318	0.597	0.195
% of firms with bank loans	80.472				
% of firms that belong to a keiretsu	20.601				
Standard error from market model	0.105	0.093	0.074	0.119	0.050

Notes: Panel A provides summary statistics for a sample of 466 executive options that were granted by non-financial Japanese firms during the period from 1997 to 2001. In Panel B, the governance characteristics of firms that grant options are presented. All governance variables are measured at the fiscal year-end immediately preceding the option grant announcement date. The standard error is estimated from the market model in which the firm's monthly returns are regressed on the monthly returns of an equally weighted market portfolio for a 60-month period prior to the option grant.

half of their assets with debt (46.8%) while over 80% utilize some kind of bank debt. Approximately 20% of our sample firms are members of a keiretsu.[4] Finally, the panel also reports summary statistics on firm-specific standard errors from a market model. We use this variable to test the possibility that options are granted in an effort to increase managerial risk taking.

3. EMPIRICAL FINDINGS

3.1. The Relation between Internal Governance and Options

In this section, we conduct a preliminary examination of the relation between the characteristics of the option granted and the firm's corresponding governance structure. Bebchuk et al. (2002) and Bebchuk and Fried (2004) argue that weak or ineffectual governance allows managers to obtain more power or to become entrenched. Specifically, firms with disperse ownership or fewer institutional shareholders, weak or ineffectual boards, and anti-takeover provisions, are posited to have empowered managers. In this study, the governance characteristics that we consider are ownership structure (managerial and institutional), board structure (independence and size), financial structure (total debt and bank debt), and keiretsu membership. We ignore anti-takeover provisions because they are practically non-existent in Japan.

Firms with high levels of equity owned by managers might grant fewer manager-advantageous options because these managers are less likely to demand options that are harmful to share value. But it is equally likely that managers as large shareholders are more empowered to grant themselves advantageous options. Assessing the ultimate effect of managerial ownership on the nature of executive stock options remains an empirical issue that is addressed later in this study.

Concentrated ownership of equity by external investors is established in the literature as a monitor of firm activity (e.g., Demsetz & Lehn, 1985; LaPorta et al., 1999). In our sample, the large external shareholders are all institutions. Therefore, firms with high levels of equity ownership by financial institutions and other corporations might grant fewer manager-advantageous options.

Firms with boards that have more independent directors and fewer directors are usually described in the governance literature as more effective. Weisbach (1988) finds that independent board members are more effective monitors than insiders. Yermack (1996) determines that smaller boards are more active monitors, with board processes losing effectiveness as board size increases. Consequently, we anticipate that firms with a higher fraction of independent directors or smaller boards are better able to limit managerial self-dealing in the design of their executive stock options.

Jensen (1986) argues that debt service can offer a partial solution to the agency problem between managers and shareholders. Further, Hoshi et al. (1990) note that Japanese banks are active monitors of their client firms. Prowse (1990) contends that firms belonging to a keiretsu have multiple monitors through the many implicit contracts that exist among group members. Therefore, firms with more debt and/or a greater bank presence, and firms that belong to a keiretsu, are likely to be better monitored and thus grant fewer manager-advantageous options.

Previous studies examine the relation between a firm's corporate governance and its executive compensation. Hartzell and Starks (2003) find that CEO compensation is higher in firms with low institutional ownership. Core, Holthausen, and Larcker (1999) report that CEO compensation is greater when firms' boards are larger and less independent. Their studies are broadly consistent with Bebchuk et al. (2002) and Bebchuk and Fried (2004) managerial power view of executive compensation. Our study contributes to this literature by focusing exclusively on executive stock options as a device for managerial exploitation of entrenchment.

To conduct our empirical tests, we first create an options characteristics index which measures the extent to which an option grant possesses characteristics that are advantageous to managers. Our option characteristics index is the sum of four different dummy variables. The first dummy variable is equal to one if the option's time to exercise is below the sample median and zero otherwise. The second dummy variable has a value of one if the option's duration to expiration is above the sample median and zero otherwise. A third dummy variable is equal to one if the option value relative to fixed compensation is below the sample median and zero otherwise.[5] A fourth and final dummy variable assumes a value of one if the option's moneyness is above the sample median and zero otherwise. For each executive option, the value of these four dummy variables is summed to create an aggregate score. Index values range from 0 to 4, with higher values of the index being consistent with options that are more advantageous to the manager.[6] Of the 466 option grants in our sample, 19 have an option index score of 0, 121 have an index score of 1, 161 have a score of 2, 119 have a score of 3, and 46 have a score of 4.[7]

To determine whether the firm's governance structure affects the design of their executive option grants, we assign firms into subsamples based on ownership distribution (equity ownership by managers, financial institutions, and other corporations), board structure (size and independence), and the total debt ratio. Firms in the "high" and "low" subsamples are those firms whose governance measures are above and below the corresponding sample median, respectively. The subsamples for bank debt or keiretsu membership are constructed on the presence or absence of their characteristics rather than reference to a median value. For each subsample, we report the mean (median) value of the options characteristics index. Table 3 contains our corresponding statistical tests of differences between the various subsamples.

In Table 3, we observe statistically significant differences in the option characteristics index for three classifying variables. Firms with higher managerial-ownership grant executive options that are less manager-advantageous than compared to firms with low managerial ownership (1.61 mean index vs. 1.92 mean index). This finding suggests that the existence of significant managerial ownership can mitigate managerial power effects. Managers appear not to grant themselves self-serving options at the expense of their share value.

We further see that firms with more independent board members and smaller boards grant options that are less manager advantageous. The other governance characteristics do not seem to influence option design. Therefore, it appears that board structure is one of the most-important governance-related factors regarding the ability of managers to empower themselves and thereby extract favorably written stock options. This result is consistent with Bebchuk et al. (2002) and Bebchuk and Fried (2004) thesis that firms with relatively weak or ineffectual boards empower managers who can subsequently influence their compensation in self-serving ways. This result also contributes to the board literature which suggests that boards with a higher fraction of independent directors and fewer directors are "better" boards. The greater explanatory power of boards regarding compensation design relative to other governance mechanisms reflects its explicit responsibility for the design of executive compensation. Therefore, it is not surprising that "better" boards grant fewer manager-advantageous options.

In this study, we also test an alternative hypothesis – that firms grant options to managers to encourage risk-taking. Consistent with Demsetz and Lehn (1985), Prowse (1992), Himmelberg, Hubbard, and Palia (1999), and Holderness, Kroszner, and Sheehan (1999), we use the standard error from

Table 3. Option Characteristic Index Values and Measures of Firm Governance.

	High		Low		High–Low			
	Mean	Median	Mean	Median	Dif. mean	t-test	Dif. median	Z-test
% ownership by managers	1.6124	2.0000	1.9183	2.0000	−0.3059	−2.96***	0.0000	−3.04***
% ownership by financial institutions	1.8498	2.0000	1.7124	2.0000	0.1374	1.33	0.0000	1.41
% ownership by other corporations	1.7253	2.0000	1.8369	2.0000	−0.1116	−1.08	0.0000	−1.14
% independent directors to total directors	1.6435	2.0000	1.9153	2.0000	−0.2718	−2.64***	0.0000	−2.67***
Board size (number of directors)	1.8919	2.0000	1.6803	2.0000	0.2116	2.05**	0.0000	2.18**
Total debt/total assets	1.7253	2.0000	1.8369	2.0000	−0.1116	−1.08	0.0000	−0.95
Bank loan dummy	1.7413	2.0000	1.9451	2.0000	−0.2038	−1.56	0.0000	−1.44
Keiretsu dummy	1.8333	2.0000	1.7676	2.0000	0.0657	0.51	0.0000	0.54
Standard error of market model	1.7350	2.0000	1.7950	2.0000	−0.0600	0.58	0.0000	0.21

Notes: The sample consists of 466 option grant announcements made by non-financial Japanese firms from 1997 to 2001. We create a manager-advantageous option index as follows. We create four dummy variables, where the first dummy variable is equal to one if the option's time to exercise is below the sample median, a second dummy variable is equal to one if the option's duration to expiration is above the sample median, a third dummy variable is equal to one if the option value relative to fixed compensation is below the sample median, and a fourth dummy variable is equal to one if the option's moneyness is above the sample median. For each executive option, the values of these four dummy variables are added up to create a manager-advantageous option index from 0 to 4, where 4 denotes those options that are most manager-advantageous. The sample is divided into subsamples based on the firm's ownership distribution (equity ownership by managers, financial institutions, and other corporations), board structure (size and independence), total debt ratio, and standard error from a market model. Firms in the "high" and "low" subsamples are those firms whose governance measures are above and below the sample median, respectively. Firms that have bank debt and that belong to a keiretsu are also put into a "high" subsample. All governance characteristics are measured at the fiscal year-end immediately preceding the option grant date. Standard error is estimated from the market model in which the firm's monthly returns are regressed on the monthly returns of an equally weighted market portfolio for a 60-month period prior to the option grant. For each subsample, we report the mean and median manager-advantageous option index. We conduct t-tests for the mean differences in the index between the high and low subsamples and Wilcoxon Z-tests for the median differences in the index between the high and low subsamples.
*Significance at the 10% level.
**Significance at the 5% level.
***Significance at the 1% level.

the market model as a proxy for firm-specific risk. More specifically, our standard error is estimated from the market model in which the firm's monthly returns are regressed on the monthly returns of an equally weighted market portfolio for a 60-month period prior to the option grant. If firms are rewarding managers for risk taking, then we expect those firms with manager-advantageous options to exhibit more risk (i.e., higher standard errors). From the last row in Table 3, however, we see that such a relation does not hold.

3.2. Logit Model of the Relation between Internal Governance and Options

To better understand the cross-sectional variation of our option characteristics index, we present estimates from a multivariate ordered logit regression model using our option index as the dependent variable. The explanatory variables include all of our governance variables, including ownership structure (managerial and institutional), board structure (independence and size), capital structure (total debt and bank debt), and a keiretsu membership dummy variable. The summary statistics of these variables are reported in Table 2. The ordered logit regression results are reported in Table 4.

In Table 4, we again see that firms with boards having a higher fraction of independent directors grant fewer manager-advantageous options. The parameter coefficient on the independent director variable is negative and statistically significant at conventional levels. Firms with fewer board members also grant fewer manager-advantageous options. The parameter coefficient on the board size variable is positive and statistically significant. These board variable results confirm our findings from Table 3; "better" boards are able to limit managerial power effects in compensation design. Unlike Table 3, however, we see that the managerial-ownership variable is not significant when controlling for other governance variables. Interestingly, we see that when a large fraction of equity is held by other corporations, those firms grant more manager-advantageous options. This result suggests that other corporations serve as only weak monitors, allowing managerial power effects to influence compensation design. Our finding that corporate shareholders might be weak monitors is consistent with the conclusions of previous researchers. Lichtenberg and Pushner (1994) and Pushner (1995) find a statistically significant negative relation between firm performance and equity ownership by corporate shareholders. They argue that Japanese firms with large corporate shareholders are

Table 4. Ordered Logit Analysis of Equity Stock Option Grants.

Explanatory Variables	Parameter Coefficients		
Intercept 1	1.702***	1.521***	1.023*
Intercept 2	0.447	0.262	−0.236
Intercept 3	−1.127**	−1.317***	−1.820***
Intercept 4	−2.934***	−3.131***	−3.638***
% ownership by managers	−0.011	−0.008	−0.004
% ownership by financial institutions	0.007		0.960
% ownership by other corporations		1.065*	1.555**
% independent directors to total directors	−0.015**	−0.019***	−0.019***
Board size (number of directors)	0.030***	0.032***	0.029***
Total debt/total assets	−0.563	−0.754	−0.698
Bank loan dummy	−0.194	−0.154	−0.124
Keiretsu dummy	0.107	0.161	0.138
Standard error of market model	0.993	0.145	1.612
Pseudo R^2	0.078	0.080	0.082
Number of observations	466	466	466

Notes: This table presents parameter coefficient estimates using an ordered logit regression model. The sample consists of 466 option grant announcements made by non-financial Japanese firms from 1997 to 2001. The dependent variable is the manager-advantageous option index, which is calculated as follows. We create four dummy variables, where the first dummy variable is equal to one if the option's time to exercise is below the sample median, a second dummy variable is equal to one if the option's duration to expiration is above the sample median, a third dummy variable is equal to one if the option value relative to fixed compensation is below the sample median, and a fourth dummy variable is equal to one if the option's moneyness is above the sample median. For each executive option, the values of these four dummy variables are added up to create a manager-advantageous option index from 0 to 4, where 4 denotes those options that are most manager-advantageous. The explanatory variables are all measured at the fiscal year-end immediately preceding the option grant date. The bank loan dummy is equal to one if the firm has bank debt, otherwise the dummy is equal to zero. The keiretsu dummy is equal to one if the firm belongs to a keiretsu, otherwise the dummy is equal to zero. The standard error is estimated from the market model in which the firm's monthly returns are regressed on the monthly returns of an equally weighted market portfolio for a 60-month period prior to the option grant.
*Significance at the 10% level.
**Significance at the 5% level.
***Significance at the 1% level.

insulated from external discipline, allowing managers to consume perquisites rather than pursuing value maximization.

Finally, we see again that firms with higher levels of idiosyncratic risk (i.e., firms with higher standard errors) do not grant more manager-advantageous options. The statistical insignificance of the idiosyncratic risk proxy is inconsistent with the view that options are granted to encourage managerial risk taking.

An issue that raises concerns about the component of the option design, its vesting period, its duration term, its relative size, or its moneyness, is the primary explanatory factor in the logit models presented in Table 4. In unreported tables, where each option characteristic is an indicator dependent variable in a logit model or a continuous dependent variable in an OLS model, we find that the board variables have the most explanatory power, and with the hypothesized signs, when the option's relative size and its moneyness are dependent variables. In other models, the board variables have the hypothesized signs, but are statistically insignificant. Unlike Table 4, however, the total debt ratio is statistically significant and possesses the hypothesized sign in almost all of the models.[8] We choose not to report these results given the limited additional information they provide.

3.3. Announcement Period Returns

For each announcement of a stock-option grant, we calculate daily abnormal returns using a standard event-study methodology. We estimate market model parameters over a 200 trading day interval, beginning day −220 relative to the announcement day and ending on day −21. Our benchmark market return is the PACAP equally weighted market return.[9] Daily abnormal returns are used to obtain a cumulative abnormal return (CAR) from day −t prior to the option grant announcement to day +t following the announcement. Because of missing return data for our sample firms, CARs can be calculated for only 411 of our sample option grants. Table 5 presents CARs for various event windows.

In Panel A of Table 5, we observe that the cumulative abnormal returns are uniformly positive and significant across all estimation windows. For example, the mean CAR(−1,1) and CAR(−10,10) are 1.02% and 1.76%, respectively; both are significant at the 1% level. This result is consistent with previous findings for U.S. (e.g., Brickley et al., 1985; DeFusco et al., 1990) and Japanese (Kato et al., 2005) announcements of executive stock options. Our results indicate that the market favorably capitalizes the anticipated changes resulting from an increased use of executive equity incentive compensation.

We next conduct an initial analysis of how cross-sectional differences in option characteristics affect the magnitude of the announcement period returns. Using the options characteristics index, we use an index value of 2 as

Table 5. Stock Price Reaction Around Executive Option Grant Dates.

Panel A: CARs for all option grant announcements

	N	Mean	Median
CAR (−1,0)	411	0.0046**	0.0032**
CAR (0,1)	411	0.0112***	0.0053***
CAR (−1,1)	411	0.0102***	0.0037***
CAR (−5,5)	411	0.0140***	0.0101***
CAR (−10,10)	411	0.0176***	0.0145**

Panel B: CARs by "manager-advantageous" option index

	Index = 0, 1, or 2			Index = 3 or 4		
	N	Mean	Median	N	Mean	Median
CAR (−1,0)	272	0.0064***	0.0040**	139	0.0012	0.0007
CAR (0,1)	272	0.0061***	0.0128***	139	0.0082	0.0034
CAR (−1,1)	272	0.0121***	0.0047***	139	0.0066	0.0028
CAR (−5,5)	272	0.0148***	0.0129***	139	0.0125	0.0073
CAR (−10,10)	272	0.0214***	0.0224***	139	0.0102	0.0007

Notes: The sample consists of 411 option grant announcements made by non-financial Japanese firms from 1997 to 2001. We compute abnormal daily returns using the market model. We estimate the market model by using 200 trading days of return data ending 21 days before the repurchase announcement. We use PACAP equally weighted market returns as the benchmark. $CAR(−t, t)$ is the cumulative abnormal return from day $−t$ to day t where day 0 is the option grant announcement date. In Panel B, we split the sample into a high manager-advantageous option index and a low index. The index is created as follows. We create four dummy variables, where the first dummy variable is equal to one if the option's time to exercise is below the sample median, a second dummy variable is equal to one if the option's duration to expiration is above the sample median, a third dummy variable is equal to one if the option value relative to fixed compensation is below the sample median, and a fourth dummy variable is equal to one if the option's moneyness is above the sample median. For each executive option, the values of these four dummy variables are added up to create a manager-advantageous option index from 0 to 4, where 4 denotes those options that are most manager-advantageous. Panel B reports CARs for a subsample of firms whose option index is equal to 0, 1, or 2, and a subsample of firms whose option index is equal to 3 or 4.
*Significance at the 10% level.
**Significance at the 5% level.
***Significance at the 1% level.

our threshold value to divide the options into subsamples of more or less managerially advantageous options. Those options with scores of 2 or less are viewed as less managerially advantageous while those with scores of 3 or more are classified as more managerially advantageous.

In Panel B of Table 5, we separately estimate the announcement period returns across the two subsamples. For those options least favorable to managers, we observe statistically significant positive announcement period returns. This is consistent with a positive market response to options perceived to be designed from an optimal contracting perspective. The lack of statistical significance of the announcement period returns for those options that are more managerially advantageous probably reflects the market's uncertainty regarding their ability to adequately incent management and consequently impact firm performance. These options have characteristics that are suggestive of managerial influence over compensation design and thus are less likely to stimulate increased performance by managers. These results provide an initial suggestion that the market does not uniformly view the granting of executive stock options as a favorable development. Rather, the market's response is conditional upon the characteristics and terms of the option grant itself.

3.4. Multivariate Analysis of Announcement Period Returns

In this section, we use multivariate regression analysis to further examine the ability of the option characteristics index to contribute to an explanation of the cross-sectional variability in the daily returns surrounding executive stock-option grant announcements. The dependent variable in our regression analysis is the announcement period return. Our primary independent variable of interest is the manager-advantageous executive option dummy that equals one if the options characteristics index has a value of 3 or 4, and zero otherwise.

We also include a number of control variables in our model specification. Greater utilization of incentive compensation through option grants will likely have a more immediate impact on firms that are currently unprofitable or lack attractive internal investment opportunities because these firms require additional managerial effort. Hence, we include EBIT standardized by total assets and the firm's market-to-book ratio as regressors. Because larger firms are more likely to adopt and benefit from the incentive effects of stock-option linked compensation, we also include the log of total assets as a control value. Financial leverage controls for possible managerial monitoring by creditors and consequent substitution for the use of incentive compensation to reduce agency conflicts. Finally, we control for possible year and industry effects with appropriate dummies. Table 6 contains our regression results from this analysis.

Table 6. Cross Sectional Regression Analysis of the Stock Price Reaction.

Explanatory Variables	Dependent Variable				
	CAR (−1,0)	CAR (0,1)	CAR (−1,1)	CAR (−5,5)	CAR (−10,10)
Intercept	−0.0099	0.0343	0.0100	0.0232	0.0453
High mgr-adv option index	−0.0089**	−0.0123**	−0.0166**	−0.0133	−0.0241*
Log(total assets)	0.0013	−0.0013	0.0012	−0.0006	−0.0024
EBIT/total assets	0.1395***	0.2072***	0.2615***	0.3546***	0.8413***
Total debt/total assets	0.0284***	0.0222	0.0208	0.0421*	0.0823**
Market-to-book value of assets	−0.0058***	−0.0101***	−0.0125***	−0.0110**	−0.0313***
Year dummies	Yes	Yes	Yes	Yes	Yes
Industry dummies	Yes	Yes	Yes	Yes	Yes
Adjusted R^2	0.032	0.040	0.063	0.041	0.093
F-value	1.91**	2.15***	2.82***	2.17***	3.79***
Number of observations	411	411	411	411	411

Notes: The sample consists of 411 option grant announcements made by non-financial Japanese firms from 1997 to 2001. The dependent variable, CAR($−t$, t), is a cumulative abnormal return surrounding option grant announcement dates. We compute abnormal daily returns using the market model. We estimate the market model by using 200 trading days of return data ending 21 days before the option grant announcement. We use PACAP equally weighted market returns as the benchmark. The manager-advantageous option dummy is equal to one if the manager-advantageous option index is equal to 3 or 4, otherwise the dummy is equal to zero. The option index is created as follows. We create four dummy variables, where the first dummy variable is equal to one if the option's time to exercise is below the sample median, a second dummy variable is equal to one if the option's duration to expiration is above the sample median, a third dummy variable is equal to one if the option value relative to fixed compensation is below the sample median, and a fourth dummy variable is equal to one if the option's moneyness is above the sample median. For each executive option, the values of these four dummy variables are added up to create a manager-advantageous option index from 0 to 4, where 4 denotes those options that are most manager-advantageous. All other explanatory variables are measured at the fiscal year-end immediately preceding the option grant-announcement date. Parameter estimates using the OLS regression method are presented.
*Significance at the 10% level.
**Significance at the 5% level.
***Significance at the 1% level.

We observe in Table 6 that the manager-advantageous option dummy is inversely related to the announcement period return. This result confirms our earlier results that the market reacts differently to executive stock options, with the response depending on the option's characteristics. Executive options that are highly advantageous to managers have a negative effect on announcement period returns. This suggests that the market doubts the ability of such options to incent mangers to undertake value maximization activities. We find that this inverse relation is robust to a variety of announcement period return estimation windows.[10]

Finally, we observe that profitable firms and low market-to-book firms enjoy larger announcement returns. Although such a result might initially appear surprising for profitable firms, it is consistent with firms adopting executive options to mitigate the agency costs associated with the free cash resulting from their high profitability. Firms with few growth opportunities might benefit from adopting executive options to motivate their managers to more aggressively seek value-enhancing opportunities.

4. CONCLUSION

Bebchuk et al. (2002) and Bebchuk and Fried (2004) contend that the exercise of managerial power, rather than optimal contracting, explains executive compensation design. They argue that firms with weak internal governance have unchecked, and thus powerful, managers who are able to grant themselves compensation that serve themselves more than their shareholders. Therefore, executive compensation is likely to be part of the agency problem rather than a solution to it. In this study, we test the managerial power thesis of Bebchuk et al. (2002) and Bebchuk and Fried (2004). Specifically, we test to see if firms with weak internal governance enable managers to grant themselves executive stock options that are "manager-advantageous."

In our study, we use Japan's experience with executive stock options. Little is known about executive stock options outside the U.S., so a study of Japanese stock options contributes to the growing literature on international agency costs. Also, Japanese data offer us the ability to consider governance devices that are not pervasive in the U.S. In particular, Japan is a bank-centered financial system, with an economy where business groups (i.e., the keiretsu) are prevalent. Therefore, we are able to test the potential roles of banks and business group affiliation in influencing compensation design.

Using a sample of 466 executive stock-option grants, we first identify executive stock options that are "manager-advantageous." We consider an executive option to be manager-advantageous if the option can be immediately exercised, has a long duration, is small relative to fixed compensation, and is closer to being in-the-money. We then identify various internal governance characteristics to see if firms with "better" governance are able to mitigate managers' ability to grant themselves self-serving options. The governance characteristics we consider include ownership structure (managerial and institutional), board structure (independence and size), debt (total debt and bank debt), and keiretsu affiliation. Among these governance characteristics, we find that firms with boards having more independent directors, but fewer members are less likely to grant manager-advantageous options. An alternative hypothesis, that riskier firms grant manager-advantageous options to reward managers for their risk-taking, is not supported by our data.

We also find positive abnormal daily returns surrounding option grant award announcements, consistent with existing U.S. evidence. In univariate and multivariate regression tests, we find that those stock options that are manager-advantageous have lower announcement period returns. The market appears to be able to recognize the grant of a managerially advantageous option and does not react favorably to such an announcement.

Overall, our study contributes to the corporate finance literature in several important ways. Most obviously, our study tests whether Bebchuk et al. (2002) and Bebchuk and Fried (2004) argument of managerial empowerment and its implication for executive compensation is limited to the U.S. or has international relevance. More fundamentally, however, this study examines the limits of incentive compensation to serve as a mechanism to control agency conflicts within the modern corporation. Because of its focus on Japanese executive stock options, this study extends the literature on incentive contracting and compensation to one of the world's most-important capital markets outside of the U.S.

The final contribution of this study resides in its assessment of the ability of the firm's governance structure, specifically its board of directors, to mitigate or limit managerial rent seeking through the advantageous design of executive compensation packages. This analysis allows us to gain a better understanding of the relative effectiveness of governance mechanisms in aligning shareholder and managerial interests for the enhancement of firm value.

NOTES

1. Researchers that examine options as a way of reducing the agency problem include Jensen and Murphy (1990) and Yermack (1995). They find that options do not properly align interests between shareholders and managers. In fact, Yermack (1997) and others argue that options can increase agency problems as executives might act in ways to enhance the value of their options at the expense of firm value. Coles, Daniel, and Naveen (2006) provide a review of these issues.

2. Besides Bebchuk et al. (2002), Blanchard, Lopez-de-Silanes, and Shleifer (1994), Yermack (1997), and Bertrand and Mullainathan (2001) suggest that managers might be able to influence a component of their compensation. However, Bebchuk et al. develop a full account of how managers influence their compensation, with particular emphasis on the design of the executive options they are awarded.

3. One proposal being considered involves expensing stock options over the period from its granting date to its vesting date.

4. We use Dodwell Marketing Consultants (1985/1989) to identify which firms belong to a keiretsu. Their identification of keiretsu firms considers the ratio of group members' shareholding to the total shares held by the top ten shareholders. In addition, they also consider the following factors: (1) the characteristics and historical background of the group and the company, (2) the different sources and amounts of bank loans, (3) whether or not board members come from other group companies, (4) the company's attitude toward the group, and (5) the company's connections to nongroup companies and to other groups.

5. We recognize that managers would want large options, *ceritus paribus*. However, if given the choice between receiving an option grant worth one million dollars or being given a one million dollars raise in salary, note that the manager is likely to opt for the latter. Bebchuk et al. (2002) also note that options that are small relative to fixed salary represents a manager-advantageous compensation contract.

6. Rather than creating an index to measure the extent to which executive options are managerially advantageous, we could have valued the options using some pricing model. However, given that the time to exercise and the relative size of the options are also important to our study, we decided to create an index to incorporate all aspects of options that can be deemed managerially advantageous.

7. A potential problem with this index would exist if the four dummy variables are correlated. However, in correlation analysis, we find that only the first two dummy variables are statistically and significantly correlated, but that its correlation coefficient is only -0.15.

8. The finding that firms with higher debt ratios tend to be less likely to grant manager-advantageous options is consistent with Jensen (1986) who argues that debt can mitigate the agency problem between shareholders and managers, as managers must regularly service debt-related obligations and thus reducing the level of free cash flow subject to managerial discretion.

9. Using a value-weighted return yields results that are qualitatively identical.

10. In untabulated findings, we determine that the option's duration and moneyness are the primary explanatory variables of the announcement period's cross-sectional variability. The vesting period and relative size contribute only secondary explanatory ability.

REFERENCES

Bebchuk, L., & Fried, J. (2004). *Pay without performance: The unfilled promise of executive compensation*. Cambridge, MA: Harvard University Press.

Bebchuk, L. A., Fried, J. M., & Walker, D. J. (2002). Managerial power and rent extraction in the design of executive compensation. *University of Chicago Law Review, 69*, 751–846.

Berglöf, E., & Perotti, E. (1994). The governance structure of the Japanese financial keiretsu. *Journal of Financial Economics, 36*, 259–284.

Bertrand, M., & Mullainathan, S. (2001). Are CEOs rewarded for luck? The ones without principals are. *Quarterly Journal of Economics, 116*, 901–932.

Blanchard, O. J., Lopez-de-Silanes, F., & Shleifer, A. (1994). What do firms do with cash windfalls. *Journal of Financial Economics, 36*, 337–360.

Brickley, J. A., Bhagat, S., & Lease, C. (1985). The impact of long-range managerial compensation plans on shareholder wealth. *Journal of Accounting and Economics, 7*, 115–129.

Coles, J. L., Daniel, N. D., & Naveen, L. (2006). Managerial incentives and risk-taking. *Journal of Financial Economics, 79*, 431–468.

Core, J. E., Holthausen, R. W., & Larcker, D. E. (1999). Corporate governance, chief executive compensation, and firm performance. *Journal of Financial Economics, 51*, 371–405.

DeFusco, R. A., Johnson, R. R., & Zorn, T. S. (1990). The effect of executive stock option plans on stockholders and bondholders. *Journal of Finance, 45*, 617–627.

Demsetz, H., & Lehn, K. (1985). The structure of corporate ownership: Causes and consequences. *Journal of Political Economy, 93*, 1155–1177.

Denis, D. K., & McConnell, J. J. (2003). International corporate governance. *Journal of Financial and Quantitative Analysis, 38*, 1–36.

Diamond, D. W. (1984). Financial intermediation and delegated monitoring. *Review of Economic Studies, 51*, 393–414.

Dodwell Marketing Consultants (1985/1989). *Industrial Groupings in Japan.* Tokyo, Japan: Dodwell Marketing Consultants.

Ferris, S. P., Kim, K. A., & Kitsabunnarat, P. (2003). The costs (and benefits?) of diversified business groups: The case of Korean chaebols. *Journal of Banking and Finance, 27*, 275–297.

Hartzell, J. C., & Starks, L. T. (2003). Institutional investors and executive compensation. *Journal of Finance, 58*, 2351–2374.

Himmelberg, C. P., Hubbard, R. G., & Palia, D. (1999). Understanding the determinants of managerial ownership and the link between ownership and performance. *Journal of Financial Economics, 53*, 353–384.

Holderness, C. G., Kroszner, R. S., & Sheehan, D. (1999). Were the good old days that good? Changes in managerial stock ownership since the Great Depression. *Journal of Finance, 54*, 435–469.

Hoshi, T., Kashyap, A., & Scharfstein, D. (1990). The role of banks in reducing the costs of financial distress in Japan. *Journal of Financial Economics, 27*, 67–88.

Jensen, M., & Meckling, W. (1976). Theory of the firm: Managerial behavior, agency cost, and ownership structure. *Journal of Financial Economics, 3*, 305–360.

Jensen, M. C. (1986). Agency costs of free cash flow, corporate finance, and takeovers. *American Economic Review, 76*, 323–329.

Jensen, M. C., & Murphy, K. J. (1990). Performance pay and top-management incentives. *Journal of Political Economy, 98*, 225–264.

Kang, J.-K., & Shivdasani, A. (1999). Alternative mechanisms for corporate governance in Japan: An analysis of independent and bank-affiliated firms. *Pacific-Basin Finance Journal, 7*, 1–22.

Kato, H. K., Lemmon, M., Luo, M., & Schallheim, J. (2005). An empirical examination of the costs and benefits of executive stock options: Evidence from Japan. *Journal of Financial Economics, 78*, 435–461.

Kester, C. W. (1986). Capital and ownership structure: A comparison of United States and Japanese manufacturing corporations. *Financial Management, 15*, 5–16.

Khanna, T., & Yafeh, Y. (2005). Business groups and risk sharing around the world. *Journal of Business, 78*, 301–340.

LaPorta, R., Lopez-de-Silanes, F., & Shleifer, A. (1999). Corporate ownership around the world. *Journal of Finance, 54*, 471–517.

LaPorta, R., Lopez-de-Silanes, F., Shleifer, A., & Vishny, R. W. (2000). Agency problems and dividend policies around the world. *Journal of Finance, 55*, 1–33.

Lichtenberg, F. R., & Pushner, G. M. (1994). Ownership structure and corporate performance in Japan. *Japan and the World Economy, 6*, 239–262.

Miwa, Y., & Ramseyer, J. M. (2005). Who appoints them, what do they do? Evidence on outside directors from Japan. *Journal of Economics and Management Strategy, 14*, 299–337.

Nakatani, I. (1984). The economic role of corporate financial grouping. In: M. Aoki (Ed.), *Economic analysis of the Japanese firm*. New York: Elsevier.

Prowse, S. D. (1990). Institutional investment patterns and corporate financial behavior in the United States and Japan. *Journal of Financial Economics, 27*, 43–66.

Prowse, S. D. (1992). The structure of corporate ownership in Japan. *Journal of Finance, 47*, 1121–1140.

Pushner, G. M. (1995). Equity ownership structure, leverage, and productivity: Empirical evidence from Japan. *Pacific-Basin Finance Journal, 3*, 241–255.

Weinstein, D. E., & Yafeh, Y. (1998). On the cost of a bank-centered financial system: Evidence from the changing main bank relations in Japan. *Journal of Finance, 53*, 635–672.

Weisbach, M. (1988). Outside directors and CEO turnover. *Journal of Financial Economics, 20*, 431–460.

Yermack, D. (1995). Do corporations award CEO stock options effectively? *Journal of Financial Economics, 39*, 237–269.

Yermack, D. (1996). Higher market valuation of companies with a small board of directors. *Journal of Financial Economics, 40*, 185–211.

Yermack, D. (1997). Good timing: CEO stock option awards and company news announcements. *Journal of Finance, 52*, 449–476.

MARKET-VALUE-MAXIMIZING OWNERSHIP STRUCTURE WHEN INVESTOR PROTECTION IS WEAK

Beni Lauterbach and Efrat Tolkowsky

ABSTRACT

We hypothesize that in a country with lax corporate governance rules Tobin's Q is maximized when controlholders' vote approaches the supermajority level. In this holding range, controlholders do not possess extreme power (cannot pass supermajority decisions), nor do they feel a strong temptation to loot the firm (which largely belongs to them). Using a sample of 144 Israeli firms, we find that Tobin's Q is maximized when control group vote reaches 67%. This evidence is strong when ownership structure is treated as exogenous and weak when it is considered endogenous. Other ownership structure variables do not appear to have a significant valuation effect.

1. INTRODUCTION

In most of the world economies ownership structure is concentrated; that is every firm has its own control group that governs it – see Laporta, Lopez-de-Silanes, and Shleifer (1999).[1] Empirical studies such as Faccio and

Issues in Corporate Governance and Finance
Advances in Financial Economics, Volume 12, 27–47
Copyright © 2007 by Elsevier Ltd.
ISSN: 1569-3732/doi:10.1016/S1569-3732(07)12002-8

Lang (2002) describe the closely held governance structure in Western European firms. Typically, the control group comprises a single individual, a family, or a few business partners, with large holdings (frequently over 50% of the vote) that enable the controlholder(s) to dominate firm decisions.

The concentrated ownership structure is natural. Each business enterprise has a small nucleus of founders who often bequeath their shares so that control remains in the family. Large shareholding may also be rational and beneficial. Shleifer and Vishny (1986) argue that in dispersed ownership firms there is little monitoring of firm's operations and CEO actions by shareholders. When large shareholders exist they monitor the firm more closely and are keen on creating value for the firm because of their large equity stake in it.

The problem with large shareholders is that once they gain control they also have incentives and power to exploit the firm. Controlholders tend to extract private benefits for themselves at the expense of other shareholders (minority shareholders, hereafter) who are typically small investors from the public.

Some private benefits extraction is tolerated by the law. For example, Johnson, Laporta, Lopez-de-Silanes, and Shleifer (2000) show that courts in Europe protect "tunneling" (transfer of resources from the firm to its controlling shareholders) when it (tunneling) can be presented as a business decision. The "Invisible Hand", i.e., the natural forces operating in free economic markets, does not eliminate private benefits as well. Bebchuck (2002) shows that with lax minority defense laws it is optimal for control groups to get organized and extract private benefits.

Evidence on private benefits is abundant. For example, Barclay and Holderness (1989) find that in the U.S. large blocks of shares trade at a significant premium over the *post-block-trade* market price of the shares. The block buyers pay a higher than market price for the shares probably because they are able to extract some private benefits (enjoyed by them only) from the firm. Dyck and Zingales (2004) study 412 control transactions (large block sales) in 39 countries in 1990–2000. From the price premia paid in large block sales, they estimate that in these countries the ratio of private benefits to firm value is between 4% and 65% with a mean of 14%.

The existence of private benefits decreases the cash flows available for minority shareholders (small investors from the public) and reduces public belief in stocks, which hurts the shares' market value. Given that minority holders are interested and receive only the market value of the shares, the question becomes which ownership structure maximizes the shares' market valuation (minimizes the private benefits).[2] We examine this issue in Israel, a country with median investor protection (see Laporta, Lopez-de-Silanes, Shleifer, & Vishny (2002) Table III), and above-median private benefits (see Dyck & Zingales, 2004 Table 2).

Our main finding is that market valuation, approximated by Tobin's Q, is maximized when control group vote is $\sim 67\%$. This result is reasonable and appears to represent controlholders' incentive and ability to loot the firm. In countries with lax investor protection the ability to extract private benefits is high at almost every level of controlholders' ownership. In such economic environments, private benefits extraction decreases with controlholders' ownership percentage because as controlholders' ownership increases their incentive to steal diminishes – when controlholders own most of the firm the stolen private benefits come mainly from their own pocket. The decrease in private benefits with controlholder ownership percentage generates an increase in market valuation (Tobin's Q). However, this increase in Q has its limits. When controlholders ownership and effective voting power exceeds 75% (the majority needed for certain key firm decisions that require supermajority-vote), controlholders power to exploit the firm becomes extreme, and they apparently step up their private benefits extraction, which depresses market valuation and Q. The market-value-maximizing ownership structure in lax investor protection countries is attained, thus, when control group vote is somewhat below the super-majority level – at 67% vote in our sample.

Section 2 reviews the literature and develops our hypothesis. Section 3 describes the sample and empirical variables' construction. Section 4 presents the results of tests of our hypothesis when ownership structure is treated as exogenous and when it is considered endogenous. Section 5 concludes.

2. THE RELATION OF FIRM MARKET VALUE TO OWNERSHIP STRUCTURE

2.1. Previous Empirical Evidence

The effect of ownership structure on firm's market value has been extensively studied. In the U.S., Morck, Shleifer, and Vishny (1988) fit a piecewise linear regression of Tobin's Q on controlholders ownership. Firm valuation increases for management holdings of 0–5%, decreases in the range of 5–25%, and increases for management holdings greater than 25%.

McConnell and Servaes (1990) fit a quadratic relation between Q and insider ownership. Q increases with insider ownership, peaks at ownership levels of 40–50%, and then slightly decreases with insider ownership.

Recent European studies also document significant relations between firm's market value and its ownership structure. In Sweden, Cronqvist and Nilsson (2003) find a negative relation between Q and controlholders' vote. In Norway, Bohren and Odegaard (2003) report a quadratic relation between Q and insider ownership – firm's Q increases up to insider ownership of $\sim 60\%$; then it decreases. A quadratic relation is observed in Swiss firms too – see Beiner, Drobetz, Schmid, and Zimmermann (2006). It appears that the quadratic (inverted U) pattern of the relation between Q and insider ownership, first observed in the U.S. by McConnell and Servaes (1990), emerges in European economies as well.

Some studies consider the possibility that ownership structure is endogenous. According to Demsetz and Lehn (1985) there is no fundamental causal relation between ownership structure and valuation. Each firm chooses the governance structure that suits it most. As Himmelberg, Hubbard, and Palia (1999) suggest, in such circumstances (of no relation between ownership and valuation), spurious correlation between value and ownership might still emerge because of the "omitted variables" problem – some economic variables explain both Q and ownership but do not appear in the regressions that we (empiricists) used.

Empirical estimation taking into account the possible endogeneity of ownership structure, e.g. Cho (1998), Demsetz and Villalonga (2001), and Bohren and Odegaard (2003), does not find any significant effect of ownership on market valuation (Tobin's Q). However, Coles, Lemmon, and Meschke (2006) argue that the standard econometric corrections for endogeneity do not perform well in this case, and McConnell, Servaes, and Lins (2006) present evidence that changes in insider ownership do cause changes in Q. Thus, the effect of ownership structure on firm valuation is still unresolved and remains quite elusive. It is also possible, as Larcker, Richardson, and Tuna (2004) suggest, that the effect of governance on firm valuation is small and difficult to measure.

2.2. Theoretical Discussion and Hypothesis

Since Jensen and Meckling (1976) it is clear that the higher the percentage ownership of the entrepreneurs (or control group in our context) the less they consume at the expense of the firm. This is commonly known as the incentive effect. When the control group owns a majority of firm's equity, controlholders incentive to loot the firm is muted because in such cases they steal mainly from their own pockets. Given the cost of stealing, Laporta et al. (2002), LLSV (2002) hereafter, suggest (see their Equation (10)) that as controlholders' ownership increases, their private benefits extraction decreases and firm's Tobin Q increases.

LLSV (2002) also note that Tobin's Q measures the valuation of the firm from the perspective of a minority outside shareholder. Such an investor receives only the market price of the stock, thus considers only the market valuation of the firm. (In contrast, controlholders "enjoy" both firm's market value and the private benefits they extract.[3]) The realization that Tobin's Q measures minority shareholder valuation leads LLSV (2002) to the prediction that improvements in investor protection increases Q – see their Equation (9). When small investors are better protected, private benefits diminish, and firm's market value increases.

LLSV (2002) test their investor protection proposition across countries, and document that Tobin Qs are higher in countries with better investor protection. Claessens, Djankov, Fan, and Lang (1999) study of East Asian companies, and Black, Jang, and Kim (2006) cross-sectional study of Korean companies reach identical conclusions. Better minority shareholder protection increases firms' market value.

We note a simple form of minority shareholder protection common to many economies. Most firm decisions require a 50% majority in shareholders' meeting, but some more crucial decisions require a supermajority vote (75% in Israel). Thus, small investor protection is especially weak when controlholders' vote exceeds 75%. The 50% vote level also appears as a barrier for the control group. However, in countries with lax corporate governance codes we hypothesize that controlholders do not have serious difficulties in passing routine resolutions even when they control 25% of the vote only. Thus, we propose that in a country with lax corporate governance the power to expropriate is strong and increases rather slowly with controlholders' vote over a wide range of control group ownership. Only when controlholders' ownership approaches 75% which assures domination over supermajority decisions, controlholders' power to expropriate the firm significantly increases.

Combining the incentive and power effects leads to the tradeoff theory of private benefits (McConnell & Servaes, 1990) – the power of controlling shareholders to expropriate outside investors is moderated by their financial incentive not to do so. As controlholders vote increases, their power to expropriate increases, but their incentive to do so decreases.

Superimposing the tradeoff theory to a country with weak investor protection, our hypothesis is that up to 75% of the vote the incentive effect dominates, i.e., private benefits extraction by controlholders decreases. Beyond 75% vote (or maybe slightly less than it, given that some small investors do not vote), private benefits extraction increases because of the upgraded ability of controlholders to expropriate the firm.

The testable implication of our hypothesis is that (private benefits) Tobin Qs (decrease) increase with controlholders' vote up to somewhere below 75%. Above 75%, (private benefits) Tobin Qs start to (increase) decrease as controlholders power becomes almost absolute. Graphically, we predict an inverted-U shape relation between Q and control group vote with a peak slightly below 75%. This prediction can be tested by fitting a quadratic function to the Q – vote relation, as in McConnell and Servaes (1990).

The relation between Q and ownership structure might depend on other ownership characteristics as well. For example, institutional investors sometimes protect public interests against the controlholders (Hauser & Lauterbach, 2004). Thus, institutional ownership may trim private benefits and improve market valuation (Tobin Qs). Second, the control group composition may affect private benefits extraction. When the control group is cohesive (comprises a single individual or a family) cheating can be more easily coordinated and Tobin's Q should decrease (Cronqvist & Nilsson, 2003). We do not expect these additional factors to impact much the fundamental relation of Q to controlholders' vote. However, we will use institutional investor holdings and control group structure as control variables in some of our analysis.

Last, we note that private benefits extraction might also depend on future plans of equity offerings. When controlholders contemplate future equity offerings they may restrain their agency behavior (private benefits extraction) because looting the firm sometimes attracts press attention and can create bad public image to the firm. Dyck and Zingales (2004) highlight the corporate governance role of the press. The prospects and size of future equity offerings increase with controlholders' vote because when controlholders own a large majority they can dilute their holdings while still maintaining control. Thus, the larger the control group ownership, the more cardinal become the future offerings consideration, and the stronger is the press deterrent power. In short, besides the incentive effect that decreases private benefits extraction as control group vote increase, there are the public image and future equity offering plans that restrain controlholders' agency behavior, especially at high levels of controlholders' ownership.

3. DATA AND VARIABLE CONSTRUCTION

We examine Israeli data. Relative to other countries, Israel is an economy with median small investor protection – see LLSV (2002), closely held firms, and above-median private benefits – see Dyck and Zingales (2004). Thus, we expect our results to be relevant for and representative of many other lax corporate governance countries as well.[4]

The sample comprises firms whose stocks traded on the Tel-Aviv Stock Exchange (TASE) at the end of 2002 and belonged either to the TA100 or Yeter 150 indices. These are essentially the largest and most actively traded stocks on the TASE. We exclude: (1) firms operating in the financial sector such as banks and insurance companies because of the heavy regulation in this sector, and (2) firms that belong to small industries (industries with less than four firms traded on the TASE) because our inference is also based on industry-adjusted statistics. These exclusions leave us with 149 firms in nine industries: Electronics, Textile, Chemistry, Metal products, Computers, Food, Trade, Real Estate, and Services.

For each firm we collect ownership structure information from Article 24 of the company's annual report. This Article reports the names and holdings of large shareholders, specifies any family relations between them, and identifies the owners of companies that are large shareholders. With these data we are able to disclose the ultimate shareholding (see Laporta et al., 1999) for most sample firms. For 15 firms with complex pyramidal ownership structure we needed supplementary data, and collected it from the Company Registrar–a government agency where each company registers its Bylaws and reports its shareholders.

Based on Article 24 we construct the following variables: % vote of the control group, % vote of institutional investors, % vote held by the firm itself (treasury stocks), % vote of firm subsidiaries, and ownership type. Ownership type dichotomizes the controlholder(s) as either 1 (= a family or individual person) or 0 (= other). It is noteworthy that only 3 out of our 149 firms have dual class shares, that is, a difference between % in vote and % in equity.

To characterize more precisely the control group voting power we compute the Adjusted Controlholder Vote (ACV) as follows:

$$\mathrm{ACV} = \left[\frac{\text{conrolholders' vote}}{(100 - \text{Treasury stocks vote} - \text{subsidiaries vote})} \right] \quad (1)$$

The adjusted vote subtracts from total vote the non-voting shares – shares bought back by the firm and shares held by firm subsidiaries.

As a final adjustment we adopt Himmelberg et al. (1999) and Demsetz and Villalonga (2001) log transformation of controlholders vote, and define:

$$TCV = Ln\left[\frac{ACV}{(100 - ACV)}\right] \qquad (2)$$

This log transformation reduces the skewness of the ACV distribution, and serves in our regressions.

Reviewing the data we find 146 firms with controlholder vote above 25% and 3 firms with "controlholder" vote below 10%. We decided to drop these three dispersed ownership firms and focus on firms that have a solid control group. Our hypothesis pertains to firms with a control group. Thus, like LLSV (2002), dispersed ownership firms are excluded.

Accounting data on the sample firms are compiled from the Grafit data base of Tochna La'Inyan, a local data base vendor, and stock return data are from Predicta, another data base vendor.

Tobin's Q is estimated as the approximate market value of the firm divided by its book value:[5]

$$Q = Ln\left[\frac{\begin{array}{c}\text{market value of equity} - \text{book value of equity}\\ +\text{book value of total assets} - \text{tax reserves}\end{array}}{\text{book value of total assets}}\right] \qquad (3)$$

We also examine the industry-adjusted Q defined as:

$$Industry - adjusted\ Q = Ln\left(\frac{Firm\ Q}{Median\ Q\ in\ firm's\ industry}\right) \qquad (4)$$

This adjustment should neutralize the industry specific effect on Q.

4. EMPIRICAL RESULTS

4.1. Sample Description

Table 1 describes the 146 sample firms. The mean (median) total book value of assets at the end of 2002 is 1.3 (0.45) billion NIS (New Israeli Shekels) – ∼400 (1 0 0) million U.S. Dollars. The mean (median) 2002 sales is ∼900 (1 0 0) million NIS. Most of the firms are profitable with a mean ROA

Table 1. Descriptive Statistics.

	Number of Firms	Mean	Median	Standard Deviation	First Quartile	Third Quartile
Firm characteristics						
Book value of assets (million NIS)	146	1308	450	2491	199	1409
Sales (million NIS)	146	869	303	1954	120	578
Book value leverage	146	0.31	0.27	0.25	0.09	0.48
Return on assets	146	0.08	0.07	0.11	0.03	0.12
Return on equity	146	0.03	0.06	0.31	−0.02	0.14
Std. of daily stock returns	146	3.4%	3.2%	1.6%	2.5%	3.7%
Ownership structure						
Controlholders' vote	146	64.4%	64.5%	15.6%	52.9%	77.9%
Adjusted controlholders' vote	146	66.8%	68.6%	15.5%	54.9%	79.7%
Institutional vote	146	3.47%	0.00%	5.35%	0.00%	6.17%
Vote held by firm's subsidiaries	146	1.84%	0.00%	4.05%	0.00%	1.90%
Vote of treasury stocks	146	1.64%	0.00%	5.60%	0.00%	0.06%
Valuation ratios						
Q ratio[a]	144	1.01	0.95	0.36	0.81	1.07
Industry-adjusted Q ratio[b]	144	0.03	0.00	0.29	−0.11	0.13

Notes: The sample comprises firms whose stocks trade on the TA100 or Yeter150 indices of the Tel Aviv Stock Exchange at the end of 2002. Book value leverage is the book value of debt divided by the book value of assets. Return on assets is sales minus cost of goods sold minus selling general and administrative expenses divided by the book value of assets. Return on equity is net income divided by book value of equity. The standard deviation of daily stock return is computed during 2000 through 2002.
[a]Two firms with the highest and lowest Q ratio are excluded.
[b]Industry-adjusted Q ratio = ln [firm Q ratio/median Q ratio in firm's industry].

of ∼0.08 and a mean ROE of ∼0.03.[6] Book leverage (= book value of debt divided by book value of assets) is ∼0.3, and the mean and median standard deviation of a sample firm daily stock returns in years 2000–2002 are ∼3.3%.

Firm ownership is quite concentrated. In our sample, the mean and median controlholder vote is ∼64.5%. Adjusting for treasury stocks and shares held by firm subsidiaries increases the control group mean voting power to 66.8%. In 15% of the firms adjusted controlholders' vote is below 50%, in ∼47% of the firms it is between 50% and 75%, and in ∼38% of the firms controlholders vote is above 75%. Institutional investors (pension, mutual, and provident funds) invest in $\sim$42% of the sample firms. In the sample of firms with institutional investor ownership the mean (median) institutional vote is 8.7% (8.0%).

The mean (median) Q ratio at the end of 2002 is 1.01 (0.95). In calculating these statistics we have omitted two outliers: the firm with the highest Q and the firm with the lowest Q. The reported Q values are low relative to historic Q levels in Israel, and reflect the recession in the Israeli economy and TASE after the 2000 worldwide stock-market crash.

4.2. Preliminary Observations on the Effect of Ownership Structure

Table 2 presents results of ANOVA and non-parametric Kruskal–Wallis tests of the effect of various ownership structure parameters on Tobin's Q. The mean Q is lowest (0.89) when ACV is less than 50%, medium (0.98) when ACV is above 75%, and highest (1.07) when controlholders' vote is between 50% and 75%. This finding is consistent with our hypothesis that firm market valuation (Tobin's Q) is maximized when controlholders' vote approaches

Table 2. Ownership Structure and Firm Market Valuation – Preliminary Analysis.

	Number of Firms	Mean Q	Mean Industry-Adjusted Q
Controlholders' vote			
Less than 50%	21	0.89	−0.01
50%–75%	68	1.07	0.07
More than 75%	55	0.98	0.00
p-value of ANOVA test		0.13	0.37
p-value of Kruskal–Wallis test		0.08	0.39
Controlholders' type			
Family or individual control	71	1.04	0.03
Others	73	0.98	0.02
p-value of ANOVA test		0.34	0.80
p-value of Kruskal–Wallis test		0.80	0.60
Institutional investors' ownership			
Firms without institutional ownership	61	1.02	0.03
Firms with institutional ownership	83	0.99	0.02
p-value of ANOVA test		0.61	0.84
p-value of Kruskal–Wallis test		0.78	0.75

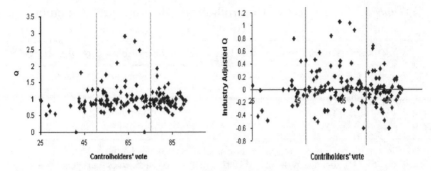

Fig. 1. Market Valuation (Tobin's *Q*) as a Function of Controlholders' Vote.

75%. Nevertheless, the difference in *Q* across our three controlholders vote levels is only marginally statistically significant at the 10% level, and when industry-adjusted *Q*s are examined the results weaken considerably. Thus, the evidence in Table 2 offers only weak support to our hypothesis. Fig. 1 graphs the firms' *Q* and industry-adjusted *Q* against adjusted controlholders' vote.

Table 2 also reports that Tobin *Q*s are insignificantly higher when a family or a single individual control the firm and insignificantly lower in firms with institutional investor ownership. Institutional investor ownership and control group type appear to be of secondary importance (if at all).

4.3. The Effect of Controlholders' Vote on Market Valuation

Table 3 examines the effect of controlholders' vote on firm *Q* when controlholders' vote is considered exogenous. LLSV (2002) argue that ownership structure is exogenous and largely shaped by the histories of the companies and their founding families. In support of their argument LLSV point at the fact that ownership patterns are extremely stable.

We fit a quadratic relation between *Q* and controlholders' vote, similar to McConnell and Servaes (1990). The alternative is to fit a piecewise regression as in Morck et al. (1988). The quadratic formulation is preferred because it suits better our purpose of finding the controlholder vote percentage that maximizes firm market value. If we fit the quadratic relation: $Q = a \cdot \text{TCV}^2 + b \cdot \text{TCV} + c$, then maximum *Q* is achieved when $\text{TCV} = -b/2a$.

Table 3.   The Effect of Controlholders' Vote on Firm Valuation
(Tobin's Q).

	Q Regression with Industry Random Effect		Industry-Adjusted Q OLS Regression	
	Coefficient	t-Statistic	Coefficient	t-Statistic
Constant	1.007	23.3	0.045	1.31
TCV	0.185	2.4	0.109	1.78
TCV^2	−0.123	−2.7	−0.084	−2.34

Notes: The sample comprises 144 firms whose stocks trade on the TA100 or Yeter150 indices of the Tel Aviv Stock Exchange at the end of 2002. The Q ratio is defined as market value of equity minus book value of equity plus total book value of assets minus tax reserves divided by book value of assets. Industry-adjusted Q is the log of the ratio of firm's Q to industry median Q.

$$^a TCV = Ln\left[\frac{ACV}{(100 - ACV)}\right]$$

$$\text{where } ACV = \frac{\text{Controlholders' vote}}{100 - \text{Subsidiaries' vote} - \text{Treasury stock vote}}$$

ACV is controlholders' vote adjusted for the non-voting treasury stocks and shares held by subsidiary firms. Transformed control vote (TCV) is a log transformation of ACV suggested by Himmelberg, Hubbard, and Palia (1999) in order to reduce skewness.

The first regression in Table 3 uses raw Q as the dependent variable, and adjusts for industry effects by allowing a random industry effect (random effect estimation). We estimate that $a = -0.123$ and $b = 0.185$, which implies a maximum Q at a TCV of $0.185/(2 \cdot 0.123) = 0.75$. Using the definition of TCV in Eq. (2), a TCV of 0.75 implies an ACV of 0.68. Thus, our random effect Q regression indicates that market valuation (Q) is maximized when adjusted controlholders' vote reaches 68%.

The second regression in Table 3 uses the industry-adjusted Q as the dependent variable and a simple OLS regression technique. Using this method we estimate that $a = -0.084$ and $b = 0.109$. Thus, Q is maximized at a TCV of 0.68, which translates into an adjusted controlholders' vote of 66%.

Our findings regarding Israel are not that extreme compared to existing international evidence. McConnell and Servaes (1990) show that in the U.S. market valuation peaks at ∼40–50% insider ownership, and Bohren and Odegaard (2003) who use Norwegian data identify a peak in Q at ∼60% insider ownership.

The evidence in Table 3 supports our hypothesis that market valuation (Q) is maximized when controlholders' vote approaches 75%. At this vote level, controlholders do not have excessive power (cannot dominate supermajority decisions) nor do they have a strong incentive to expropriate the firm. From our hypothesis' perspective, the maximum Q at a control-holders' vote of $\sim 67\%$ suggests that even with less than 75% of the vote controlholders can dominate even the most cardinal firm decisions, namely the supermajority decisions. This may be a result of small investors' indifference or non-voting behavior. If the controlholders (small share-holders) hold 67% (33%, respectively) of the vote, and 1/3 of small shareholders do not vote even on the most crucial firm decisions, then the control group has an effective supermajority of $67\%/89\% = 0.753$ even when it (the control group) retains only 67% of total vote.

4.4. Does Controlholders' Vote Affect Q When Vote is Considered Endogenous?

Demsetz and Lehn (1985) suggest that ownership structure is endogenous. When both firm valuation (Q) and ownership structure (controlholders' vote) are considered endogenous, studies such as Cho (1998) and Demsetz and Villalonga (2001) find no relation between ownership structure and market valuation. Demsetz and Villalonga (2001) conclude that there is no fundamental economic relation between valuation and ownership structure – each of these variables is independently determined by firm characteristics and business environment.

To test this proposition we follow Demsetz and Villalonga (2001) (DV, hereafter), and construct the following simultaneous equation system:

$$Q = a_0 + a_1 \cdot \text{TCV} + a_2 \cdot \text{TCV}^2 + a_3 \cdot \text{rnd\_to\_sale} \\ + a_4 \cdot \text{fix\_to\_sale} + a_5 \cdot \text{leverage} + \varepsilon_1 \tag{5}$$

$$\text{TCV} = b_0 + b_1 \cdot Q + b_2 \cdot \text{std\_ret} + b_3 \cdot \text{ln\_sale} \\ + b_4 \cdot \text{leverage} + b_5 \cdot \text{dual\_listing} + \varepsilon_2 \tag{6}$$

where, in addition to the previously defined Q and TCV (see Eqs. (2) and (3)), rnd_to_sale is the ratio of R&D expenses to sales; fix_to_sale is the ratio of fixed assets to sale; leverage is the book value of debt divided by the book value of assets; std_ret is the standard deviation of daily stock return during 2000 through 2002; ln_sale is the natural logarithm of sales in thousands NIS; and dual_listing equals 1 when firm's stock is also listed on the Nasdaq of NYSE and zero otherwise.

Our explanatory variables are somewhat different than those of DV. We use vote and vote squared as explanatory variables whereas DV use only vote. This modification is required in order to test our hypothesis that the Q–Vote relation is non-linear. Second, we do not have a measure of industry concentration (DV use such a measure in their Q equation). Third, we use the stock return standard deviation as an instrument in the Vote regression, while DV use beta and non-systematic risk – the standard deviation of the residuals. Fourth, we use Ln(sales) as the firm size variable (similarly to Himmelberg et al., 1999) instead of Ln(assets) that DV use.[7] Last, we add dual_listing as an instrument in the vote regression because Israeli firms that also list abroad tend to have lower ownership concentration. (Eighteen of our 144 sample firms trade also on the Nasdaq or NYSE.)

The above system is estimated using three stage least squares (3SLS). DV use two stage least squares (2SLS). However, we find some significant correlation between Eqs. (5) and (6) residuals which suggests 3SLS estimation. Anyway, as in Cho (1998), the 2SLS and 3SLS estimates are similar and lead to identical conclusions.

Table 4 presents the results of the 3SLS estimation for raw and industry-adjusted Qs. Similarly to previous studies we find that controlholders' vote does not affect Q significantly. Thus, we cannot resolve the existing puzzle in empirical literature. When vote is considered exogenous controlholders' vote affects market valuation. But, when controlholders' vote is allowed to be endogenous, it does not appear to have any significant relation to market valuation. Noteworthy, the insignificant "endogeneity-corrected" results may be due to some malfunctioning of our standard endogeneity correction procedure – see Coles et al. (2006). Thus, the question of whether or not there exists a fundamental relation between market valuation and ownership structure remains unresolved.

Interestingly, the signs of the vote coefficients in Table 4 remain as in Table 3. In the fitted Q equation, the point estimate of the vote coefficient is positive (0.587) and the point estimate of the vote-squared coefficient is negative (−0.439). These point estimates imply that Q is maximized at a controlholders' vote of 66%. When industry-adjusted Q is the dependent variable – see Panel B, the fitted vote coefficient is 0.21 and the fitted vote-squared coefficient is −0.15, which imply a maximum Q at a controlholders' vote of 67%. Thus, even when both Q and vote are considered endogenous, our data (weakly) suggest 67% controlholders' vote as the maximum Q ownership structure.

We also attempted to augment the equation system by adding two other ownership structure variables to it. AIV is institutional investor vote

Table 4. Controlholders' Vote and Firm Valuation – 3SLS Estimation.

Panel A: Systems with Raw Q

	Basic system		Augmented system	
	Q equation	TCV equation	Q equation	TCV equation
Constant	**1.16**	−0.9	**1.15**	−0.43
TCV	0.587		0.547	
TCV²	−0.439		0.4137	
rnd_to_sale	−0.35		−0.35	
fix_to_sale	−0.002		−0.002	
Leverage	−0.22	−0.16	−0.21	−0.18
Q		1.66		1.42
std_ret		7.58		7.49
ln_sale		−0.007		−0.013
dual_listing		**−0.78**		**−0.8**
ct_dum			0.04	
AIV			−0.004	**−0.036**

Panel B: Systems with Industry-Adjusted Q

	Basic system		Augmented system	
	Industry-adjusted Q equation	TCV equation	Industry-adjusted Q equation	TCV equation
Constant	0.062	0.735	0.082	0.98
TCV	0.1339		0.237	
TCV²	−0.15		−0.167	
rnd_to_sale	−0.29		−0.29	
fix_to_sale	−0.001		−0.002	
Leverage	−0.03	−0.34	−0.04	−0.33

Table 4. (Continued)

Panel B: Systems with Industry-Adjusted Q

	Basic system		Augmented system	
	Industry-adjusted Q equation	TCV equation	Industry-adjusted Q equation	TCV equation
Industry-adjusted Q		1.58		1.40
std_ret		5.27		5.6
ln_sale		0.003		0.006
dual_listing		**-0.89**		**-0.89**
ct_dum			-0.01	
AIV			-0.0008	**-0.036**

Notes: Panel B: The same systems as in panel A with industry-adjusted Q replacing raw Q. This table examines the effect of controllers' vote on firm market valuation (Tobin's Q) when controllers' vote is considered endogenous. Q is defined as market value of equity minus book value of equity plus total book value of assets minus tax reserves divided by book value of assets. Industry-adjusted Q is the log of the ratio of firm's Q to industry median Q. TCV is a measure of controllers' vote (see Table 3). Rnd_to_sale is the ratio of R&D expenses to sales. fix_to_sale is the ratio of fixed assets to sale; leverage is the book value of debt divided by the book value of assets; std_ret is the standard deviation of daily stock return during 2000 through 2002; ln_sale is the log of sales in thousands NIS; dual_listing equals 1 when firm's stock is also listed on the Nasdaq or NYSE and zero otherwise; ct_dum equals 1 when the control group comprises a single individual or a family, zero otherwise; AIV is a measure of institutional investor's vote (institutional vote adjusted for non-voting shares). Coefficients significant at the 5% level are shown in bold characters. Panel A: systems with raw Q. Basic system is:

$$Q = a_0 + a_1 \cdot TCV + a_2 \cdot TCV^2 + a_3 \cdot rnd\_to\_sale + a_4 \cdot fix\_to\_sale + a_5 \cdot leverage + \varepsilon_1$$
$$TCV = b_0 + b_1 \cdot Q + b_2 \cdot std\_ret + b_3 \cdot ln\_sale + b_4 \cdot leverage + b_5 \cdot dual\_listing + \varepsilon_2$$

Augmented system (with additional ownership structure variables) is:

$$Q = a_0 + a_1 \cdot TCV + a_2 \cdot TCV^2 + a_3 \cdot rnd\_to\_sale + a_4 \cdot fix\_to\_sale + a_5 \cdot leverage + a_6 \cdot ct\_dum + a_7 \cdot AIV + \varepsilon_3$$
$$TCV = b_0 + b_1 \cdot Q + b_2 \cdot std\_ret + b_3 \cdot ln\_sale + b_4 \cdot leverage + b_5 \cdot dual\_listing + b_6 \cdot AIV + \varepsilon_4$$

adjusted for non-voting shares. AIV is constructed in an analogous way to ACV – see Eq. (1). The second new variable, ct_dum, is a dummy variable that equals 1 when the control group consists of a single individual or a family (and equals 0 otherwise).

We expect institutional investor ownership to improve market valuation (Q) because institutional investors may monitor the control group. This prediction is not supported by the data. In Table 4, institutional ownership has an insignificant effect on Q. Perhaps there are reasons for institutional investors to prefer lower Q stocks, a tendency that is not neutralized by our set of control variables. Such an explanation basically argues that institutional investor holdings are also endogenous.

Similarly, ct_dum is insignificant in our fitted equation systems – see Table 4. We expect lower Qs in firms where the control group is in the hands of a single individual or a family because in these cases the control group appears relatively cohesive and can more easily "agree" on extracting private benefits – see Cronqvist and Nilsson (2003). Again, as is the case of institutional ownership, a possible reason for the insignificant effect of ct_dum is that family ownership is itself endogenous. In short, a well-developed analysis of the effect of ownership structure on market valuation should possibly include several simultaneous equations. We leave this issue for future research.[8]

4.5. The Effect of Controlholders' Vote on Firm Profitability

It is also interesting to examine the effect of controlholders' vote on firm profitability. Inference on firm profitability is subject to the same problems as our valuation (Q) analysis. For example, if we find a positive correlation between controlholders' vote and firm profitability, it could be that higher controlholders vote promotes excellent leadership which improves firm profitability. Or, causation may be reversed, i.e., it could be that in firms with better profitability controlholders sell (issue) to the public a smaller proportion of equity.

We replicate the analysis of Tables 3 and 4 using firm Return on Assets (ROA) and Return on Equity (ROE) in place of Q. ROA is defined as sales minus cost of goods sold minus selling general and administrative expenses divided by the book value of assets, and ROE is net income divided by book value of equity. Further, we industry-adjust ROA and ROE by subtracting the industry median from the firm ROA and ROE.

The fitted regressions are:

$$\text{Industry} - \text{adjusted ROA}_i = \underset{(0.9)}{0.011} + \underset{(0.4)}{0.008}\,\text{TCV}_i + \underset{(0.1)}{0.001}\,\text{TCV}_i^2 + e_i, \text{ and}$$

$$\text{Industry} - \text{adjusted ROE}_i = \underset{(1.3)}{0.016} + \underset{(0.2)}{0.005}\,\text{TCV}_i + \underset{(0.2)}{0.003}\,\text{TCV}_i^2 + \varepsilon_i$$

where TCV_i is a measure of controlholders' vote – see Eq. (2), and t-statistics are shown in parentheses. Statistically insignificant relations are also found when fitting a simultaneous equation system of profitability and control-holders vote, an analysis that parallels Table 4. Thus, firm profitability appears unrelated to firm ownership structure.

It is possible that firm control structure is related to market valuation (Q), while firm profitability is not. This can happen when cash flows to shareholders are not well represented by accounting profitability, and/or when the cost of equity (required stock return by public investors) is higher for firms with corporate governance problems. Future research should examine these alter-natives.

5. SUMMARY AND CONCLUSIONS

Does ownership structure affect firm market valuation? We suggest that in an economy with lax corporate governance laws, the controlholders ability to expropriate small shareholders is high at all levels of control group vote. Thus, private benefits extraction is affected mainly by the incentive effect. As controlholders' vote increases they exploit the firm less because they are increasingly stealing from their own pockets. However, we also propose that as controlholders' vote approaches 75%, their power is significantly upgraded because with 75% of the vote controlholders can dominate even the most crucial firm decisions (that require a supermajority vote). Thus, with a vote that assures control over supermajority decisions, control group power becomes almost absolute, and their private benefits extraction might step up considerably.

The testable implication of our hypothesis is that firm's market valuation, approximated by Tobin's Q, increases with controlholders' vote up to a point where controlholders amass close to 75% of the vote; then Q starts to decrease with vote. This inverted-U pattern of Q evolves as a mirror image of private benefits extraction – private benefits decrease with controlholders' vote until vote reaches a level of close to 75%; then private benefits increase.

We test the hypothesis on a sample of 144 Israeli firms traded on the Tel-Aviv Stock Exchange at the end of 2002. Israel scores about median in Laporta, Lopez-de-Silanes, Shleifer, and Vishny investor protection index. Hence, our empirical results might be of relevance to many economies.

Using a variety of estimation techniques (random effect regressions, industry adjustments, and three-stage least squares) we fit a quadratic relation of market valuation (Q) to control group vote and find that Q is maximized at a control group vote of $\sim 67\%$. This finding appears consistent with our hypothesis. Some of the small investors do not vote even on the most crucial firm decisions. Thus, effective control of supermajority decisions can be obtained even with less than 75% of the vote. We note though that our evidence is strong only when controlholders' vote is treated as exogenous. When both Q and controlholders' vote are considered endogenous, the quadratic relation of Q to vote becomes statistically insignificant (yet maximum Q is still obtained at a controlholders' vote of $\sim 67\%$).

The practical implication of our study is that firms with more than 75% controlholders' vote should be encouraged (by regulation?) to dilute controlholders' holdings. We also call regulatory attention to firms with "no majority," where controlholders' vote is 20–50%. In such firms, controlholders might be tempted to expropriate the firm. Last, because of insufficient sample size, we could not study firms with controlholders' vote below 20%. Thus, we cannot conclude about the optimality or deficiencies of disperse ownership firms.

Future research should replicate our study in other economies, and attempt to investigate more thoroughly what exact corporate governance features affect private benefits extraction and firm valuation.

NOTES

1. Even in the U.S. and U.K., where exchange-traded firms tend to have dispersed ownership, most other firms have concentrated control structures.
2. This question should interest regulatory agencies as well. This is because private benefits extraction is most probably dissipative, i.e., destroys value. Thus, minimizing private benefits may increase economic efficiency.
3. The considerable value of private benefits is revealed in control transfer transactions, as we mentioned before.
4. Previous evidence on Israel includes only Ber, Yafeh, and Yosha (2001) who show that the accounting profitability of Israeli firms increases with the % ownership of large shareholders.

5. This is the formula used by LLSV(2002).

6. We define ROA as sales minus cost of goods sold minus selling general and administrative expenses divided by the book value of assets. ROE is computed as net income divided by the book value of equity.

7. We attempted also Ln(assets). The main results and conclusions are not sensitive to this choice.

8. We have also attempted adding accounting profitability measures, Return on Assets – ROA and Return on Equity – ROE, to the Q and TCV equations. Superior ROA and ROE affect positively the firm's valuation (Q). However, the relation between Q and controlholders' vote (TCV) remains statistically insignificant.

ACKNOWLEDGMENTS

The paper has benefited from the comments of Yakov Amihud. Any remaining errors are our own. Financial assistance from the Sapir Fund at Tel-Aviv University is gratefully acknowledged.

REFERENCES

Barclay, M. J., & Holderness, C. G. (1989). Private benefits from control of public corporations. *Journal of Financial Economics*, *25*, 371–395.

Bebchuck, L. A. (2002). *Asymmetric information and the choice of corporate governance arrangements*. Discussion Paper 398. Harvard Olin.

Beiner, S., Drobetz, W., Schmid, M., & Zimmermann, H. (2006). An integrated framework of corporate governance and firm valuation. *European Financial Management*, *12*, 249–283.

Ber, H., Yafeh, Y., & Yosha, O. (2001). Conflict of interest in universal banking: Bank lending, stock underwriting and fund management. *Journal of Monetary Economics*, *47*, 189–218.

Black, B., Jang, H., & Kim, W. (2006). Does corporate governance predict firms' market values? Evidence from Korea. *Journal of Law, Economics and Organization*, *22*, 366–413.

Bohren, O., & Odegaard, B. (2003). *Governance and performance revisited*. Working Paper. Norwegian School of Management.

Cho, M. H. (1998). Ownership structure, investment, and the corporate value: An empirical analysis. *Journal of Financial Economics*, *47*, 103–121.

Claessens, S., Djankov, S., Fan, J., & Lang, L. (1999). *Expropriation of minority shareholders in East Asia*. Working Paper 2088. World Bank.

Coles, J., Lemmon, M., & Meschke, F. (2006). *Structural model and endogeneity in corporate finance*. Working Paper. University of Utah.

Cronqvist, H., & Nilsson, M. (2003). Agency costs of controlling minority shareholders. *Journal of Financial and Quantitative Analysis*, *38*, 695–719.

Demsetz, H., & Lehn, K. (1985). The structure of ownership: Causes and consequences. *Journal of Political Economy*, *93*, 1155–1177.

Demsetz, H., & Villalonga, B. (2001). Ownership structure and corporate performance. *Journal of Corporate Finance*, *7*, 209–233.

Dyck, A., & Zingales, L. (2004). Private benefits of control: An international comparison. *Journal of Finance, 59*, 537–600.

Faccio, M., & Lang, L. (2002). The ultimate ownership of Western European corporations. *Journal of Financial Economics, 65*, 365–395.

Hauser, S., & Lauterbach, B. (2004). The value of voting rights to majority shareholders: Evidence from dual class stock unifications. *Review of Financial Studies, 17*, 1167–1184.

Himmelberg, C., Hubbard, R. G., & Palia, D. (1999). Understanding the determinants of managerial ownership and the link between ownership and performance. *Journal of Financial Economics, 53*, 353–384.

Jensen, M., & Meckling, W. (1976). Theory of the firm: Managerial behavior, agency costs, and ownership structure. *Journal of Financial Economics, 3*, 305–360.

Johnson, S., Laporta, R., Lopez-de-Silanes, F., & Shleifer, A. (2000). Tunneling. *American Economic Review Papers and Proceedings, 90*, 22–27.

Laporta, R., Lopez-de-Silanes, F., & Shleifer, A. (1999). Corporate ownership around the world. *Journal of Finance, 54*, 471–517.

Laporta, R., Lopez-de-Silanes, F., Shleifer, A., & Vishny, R. (2002). Investor protection and corporate valuation. *Journal of Finance, 57*, 1147–1170.

Larcker, D., Richardson, S., & Tuna, I. (2004). *Does corporate governance really matter?* Working Paper. Stanford University.

McConnell, J., & Servaes, H. (1990). Additional evidence on equity ownership and corporate value. *Journal of Financial Economics, 27*, 595–612.

McConnell, J., Servaes, H., & Lins, K. (2006). *Changes in equity ownership and changes in the market value of the firm.* Working Paper. London Business School.

Morck, R., Shleifer, A., & Vishny, R. (1988). Management ownership and market valuation: An empirical analysis. *Journal of Financial Economics, 20*, 293–315.

Shleifer, A., & Vishny, R. (1986). Large shareholders and corporate control. *Journal of Political Economy, 94*, 461–488.

CORPORATE GOVERNANCE AND PERFORMANCE OF BANKING FIRMS: EVIDENCE FROM ASIAN EMERGING MARKETS

Abdul Hadi Zulkafli and Fazilah Abdul Samad

ABSTRACT

Corporate governance is regarded as a major issue during the post-financial crisis period in Asia. These countries have implemented corporate governance reforms to enhance the protection of shareholders and stakeholders interests. Such reforms have affected the conduct of business of all corporations in the region as it allows for greater monitoring especially by the shareholders. Unlike earlier studies which focused on non-financial firms, this study analyzes the corporate governance of listed banking firms in nine Asian emerging markets. Corporate governance mechanisms that serve to monitor the banking firms can be classified into Ownership Monitoring Mechanism, Internal Control Monitoring Mechanism, Regulatory Monitoring Mechanism, and Disclosure Monitoring Mechanism. This paper suggests that there are differences in the monitoring mechanisms of banking firms and non-bank firms.

Issues in Corporate Governance and Finance
Advances in Financial Economics, Volume 12, 49–74
Copyright © 2007 by Elsevier Ltd.
ISSN: 1569-3732/doi:10.1016/S1569-3732(07)12003-X

1. INTRODUCTION

Corporate governance has received wide attention in the financial community ever since the Asian financial crisis in 1997 and further enhanced by corporations scandals such as Enron and WorldCom, and recently Royal Ahold in the Netherlands. At the initial stage, the corporate governance implementation in Asian countries was focused on measures taken as resolution to the crisis such as restructuring, mergers, and acquisitions exercises as well as government intervention in the private sector. Later, the Code of Corporate Governance which recommended various governance elements in ensuring its effectiveness towards protecting the shareholders as well as stakeholders interest was formulated and used as a guideline for the corporations in formulating their governance-related matters.

With appropriate reforms being put in place, episode is now focused on the effectiveness of such reforms in improving performance. Attention is being made on the implications of the reforms in improving corporate governance at the national and firm's level and how it leads to improve corporate performance. Though it is generally agreed that effective corporate governance assures protection on investment and generates return, studies have found differences in corporate governance practices across industries.

Nevertheless, study on corporate governance and performance relationship has so far been focused on non-financial firms since financial firms are considered as unique as compared to other non-financial corporations. Earlier studies indicated that corporate governance mechanisms for banking firms are different from the non-financial corporations since both groups operate under different environments. The significant difference can be explained through the regulatory environment where they are subjected to various regulatory requirements. There is also an issue of moral hazard in the operation of banking firms where there is an expropriation of bank resources in the form of theft, transfer pricing, asset stripping, hiring family members, and credit allocation that enriches the bank insiders and hurt the bank. In addition, banking firms are exposed to information asymmetry problem that requires a higher disclosure of information to their shareholders and creditors (depositors). Information asymmetry is larger in the banking firms compared to the non-financial firms. As such, it is crucial to examine the disclosure in banking firms and whether it is beneficial to the shareholders and the banks. Based on corporate governance mechanisms that serve to monitor the banking firms such as Ownership Monitoring Mechanism, Internal Control Monitoring Mechanism, Regulatory

Monitoring Mechanism, and Disclosure Monitoring Mechanism, this paper attempts to identify whether there exist any differences in the monitoring mechanisms of banking firms and non-banking firms.

2. CORPORATE GOVERNANCE LITERATURE REVIEW

2.1. Issues of Corporate Governance in Banking

Bank is classified as an intermediary that pools money from investors/depositors, lends it and monitors on their behalf. Levine (2003) concluded that heavy reliance on banking sector is an engine of economic growth in developing economy while Arun & Turner (2004) argued that in an underdeveloped financial market, banks are the most-important source of finance for majority of the firms as well as the main depository for the economy's savings. It is further argued that there are important roles played by the financial intermediaries in an economy classified as the role in monitoring non-financial firms, the role in producing allocative efficiency, and the role in providing intertemporal smoothing of risks (Emmons & Schmid, 1999). Given the importance of banks in an economy, failure in the banking system would directly affect the financial health of the country (Banerjee, 2004).

There are important facts regarding the importance of corporate governance of banking firms. According to Caprio, Leuven, and Levine (2003), governance mechanisms would be able to reduce the expropriation of bank resources and promote bank efficiency. The expropriations are inclusive of theft, transfer pricing, asset stripping, hiring family members, and credit allocation that enriches the bank insiders and hurt the bank. The concept of efficiency can be viewed from the flow of funds in the form of debt or equity to the corporations producing goods and services in the most-efficient manner with the highest rate of return. The banking institutions have in fact been positively contributing to companies' performance (Eldomiaty & Choi, 2003). Banks in Germany as characterized by its "Universal Banking System" are more heavily involved in financing corporations as compared to capital markets thus the need to assume much larger role of corporate governance due to their position as lenders, share underwriters, major equity holders, stock exchange market maker, holder of corporate board positions and exercising proxy votes held by small shareholders (Lowengrub, Luedecke, & Melvin, 2003). As major creditors to the corporation and in some countries as major equity holders, banks play a role in influencing the corporate governance of firms as well (Caprio et al., 2003). Chirinko, van Ees, Garrestsen, and Sterken (1999) argued that in a situation of large creditorship where firms rely on credit from financial institutions, bank is able to play governance role by monitoring the firm activities, demand audits, and impose penalty payments. As such, sound governance of a bank increases the likelihood that bank will exert sound governance over the firms they fund.

Studies generally reached a consensus that there are indeed significant differences in corporate governance practices between banking firms and corporations in other economic sectors. The differences are attributed to the special nature of the banking institutions that warrants for broader view of corporate governance for banks compared to non-financial firms (Adams & Mehran, 2002, 2003; Levine, 2003; Macey & O'Hara, 2003).

Corporate governance mechanisms in the banking industry are largely explained by the nature of the industry itself. First, there is a conflict between claimant and shareholders of a banking firm. Crespi, Garcia-Cestona, and Salas (2003) argued that there is a conflict between the shareholders' and depositors' interest. Shareholders are disposed to take high-risk projects that maximize the shareholders wealth at the expense of the value of the deposits. Such activity will not give benefits to the depositors even if the high-risks activity succeeds. In fact, they will suffer some portion of losses should the bank fail due to excessive risk-taking. In such situation, the regulation is needed to protect the depositors' interest. Macey and O'Hara (2003) argued that a broader view of corporate governance should be adopted in the case of banking institutions that include depositors as well as shareholders.

Second, banks are operated with greater opaqueness since opaqueness is one of the special attributes of banks that require different treatment of its corporate governance (Levine, 2003). The issue of opaqueness is related to information asymmetries, which is more pronounced in larger banks compared to non-financial firms. In a banking business, loan quality is not readily observable and can be hidden for long periods. On the other hand, banks can alter risk composition of their assets more quickly than most non-financial industries. Furthermore, banks can readily hide problems by extending loans to clients that cannot service previous debt obligations. As the information is incommunicable, depositors do not know the true value of the bank's loan portfolio (Bhattacharyya & Rao, 2004). Those instances reveal the severe difficulties in acquiring information about bank behavior and monitoring the ongoing bank activities that hinder traditional corporate governance mechanisms.

Third, banks have a unique capital structure as distinguished by its liabilities and equity. Berger, Herring, and Szego (1995) concluded that banks have the highest leverage as compared to other firms in any industry. Bank is characterized by heavy reliance on debts that typically amounted to 90% of its total liabilities and equity. This is largely in the form of deposits which are available on demands. On the other hand, bank's assets take the form of loans and advances. Thus, bank is creating the liquidity for the economy through the holding of illiquid assets (loans) and issuing liquid liabilities (deposits). This situation allows for a bank run where the depositors rush to be among the first to withdraw their money before the bank's cash reserves are drained.

Levine (2003) further argued that government may improve the governance of the banking institutions by privatizing banks with substantial government ownership since heavy government involvement changes the corporate behavior of banking institutions. Nevertheless, it is also recommended that greater ability and incentive should be induced to the private investors to exert governance rather than relying heavily or excessively on government regulations.

However, consistent with political view, government ownership is regarded to be detrimental as it may induce political intervention in the banking firm (Arun & Turner 2004). The extensive government ownership of banks that are mainly found in developing economies (La Porta et al., 2000) led to the governance problem of conflict between government/ taxpayers as owners and the bureaucrats/managers who control the bank. These include the acts of managers which are unfavorable to the owners in the issues of incentives, prerequisites, leisure time, staff numbers, undertake less risk than the optimal standard as well as using their position to serve special groups as a platform for political career.

Nonetheless, there is still another option that may force the banks to adopt good corporate governance practices instead of focusing on the removal government ownership. Stiglitz (1999) argued that competition in the product or service market acts as a substitute for corporate governance mechanisms. Competition can partially be intensified with the entrance of foreign bank and may act as a substitute for corporate governance mechanism. Arun & Turner (2004) suggested that governments should allow for the opening up of banking sector to foreign banks. The idea behind such strategy is that domestic banks are forced to adopt with new management technique, mechanisms, and information technology brought about by foreign banks in order to be competitive in the industry.

2.2. Corporate Governance Monitoring Mechanism

2.2.1. Ownership Monitoring Mechanism
2.2.1.1. Large Shareholders.
Large shareholders are often referred as block shareholders and can benefit the minority shareholders because of their power and incentive to prevent expropriation (Mitton, 2002). However, these controlling shareholders may also pursue objectives that are inconsistent with those of minority shareholders'. The expropriation of minority shareholders by controlling shareholders involved with the transfer of resources out of firms for the benefits of the controlling shareholders and it is termed as "tunneling". This is confirmed by Baek, Kang, and Park (2004) who reported that acquisitions by business group (chaebols) in Korea is used to increase their own wealth through tunneling.

2.2.1.2. Government Ownership.
The extensive government ownership leads to the conflict between government/taxpayers as owners and the bureaucrats/managers who control the bank. According to Bai, Liu, Lu, Song, and Zhang (2003), the controlling government may use the listed company as a vehicle to meet the policy goals that may conflict with shareholders' interests. On the other hand, government ownership of banks would make the managers act unfavorably to the owners in certain issues, undertake less risk, and use their position to serve special groups as a platform for political career (La Porta et al., 2000b).

2.2.1.3. Foreign Ownership.
Foreign ownership or shareholding is exercised through the holdings of shares in a particular firm. At the extreme level, the mechanisms of either domestic merger or cross border may induce better-governance practices from one bank to another. Micco, Panizza, and Yanez (2004) conclude that the entry of foreign banks in developing countries plays a useful role by making domestic banks more efficient in terms of overhead cost and spreads, although there is no effect on profitability of domestic banks. It was concluded that industry performance measured by Tobin's Q increases when the firms within the industry acquired by foreign firms coming from countries with stronger corporate governance practices (Bris & Cabolis, 2003). It was further argued that the value of the acquiring industries in poor protective countries increases when they buy firms coming

from countries with greater shareholder protection. Findings from Baek et al. (2004) revealed that firms with ownership concentration by unaffiliated foreign explain the smaller reduction in the share value during the financial crisis.

2.2.2. Internal Control Monitoring Mechanism

Shareholders who are owners of companies elect a board of directors to monitor the running of the company. Board of directors is designated for the purpose of ensuring the alignment of firm activities and its specified objectives. The board has the duty to make sure that top managers behave in a way that will provide optimal value for shareholders (Coles, McWilliams, & Sen, 2001). Keenan (2004) highlighted three major duties of board which deals with developing the business strategy, appointment of senior management, and ensuring the availability of information, control, and audit systems for observing company's performance and making decisions. In the other perspective, Sussland (2005) viewed board of directors as a referee and a coach. As a referee, they approve or disapprove major decisions and the final reports by applying the prescribing rules. As a coach, they must sufficiently get involved with top management and be proactive to take appropriate measure when problems arise. According to Jensen (1983), there are at least three characteristics used to explain the board structure of a firm.

2.2.2.1. CEO Duality.
Leadership structure of a firm can be divided into combined leadership structure and separated structure (Coles et al., 2001). This has something to do with the position of the chairman of the board and the manager (the CEO in the American setting or the Managing Director in British style organizations). Efficiency in monitoring management could be enhanced through CEO–Chairman duality, where a single person assumes the position of Chairman and CEO simultaneously because less contracting is needed and information asymmetry is reduced (Haniffa & Cooke, 2005). However, it was found that there is a negative relationship between CEO duality and corporate performance. The argument is that the CEO who is also a board chair will have a concentrated power base that will allow him/her to make decisions in their own-self interest and at the expense of shareholders. Jensen (1983) maintained that the combined structure is an inappropriate way to design one of the most critical power relationships in the firm. In a study involving 348 Australia public listed firms, Kiel and Nicholson (2003) reported a negative relationship between CEO duality and Tobin's Q after controlling for firm size. As such, the views supported

the use of separate leadership structure where the titles are separated into two positions held by two separate individuals and the power spreads out in a way that allows the boards to completely perform its fiduciary duties.

2.2.2.2. Board Size. There are conflicting ideas about the appropriate size of a board of directors in both financial and non-financial firms. In terms of figures, Vafeas (1999) documented a board size of 12 while Xie, Davidson, and Dadalt (2003) recorded a mean of 12.48. Jensen (1983) suggested that having a small board can help improve performance as the board is less likely to function effectively when it gets beyond seven or eight people. For non-financial firms, board size may be negatively related to performance. Jensen (1983) further argued that any increase in board size will make it less effective at monitoring management because of free-riding problems amongst directors as well as increased decision-making time. Meanwhile, a study by Eisenberg & Sundgren. (1998) on Finnish firms identified the same correlation but using different performance measures, i.e., operating performance, return on assets (ROA) and operating margin. Consistent with Yermack and Eisenberg, Mak and Kusnadi (2002) found that there is an inverse relationship between board size and Tobin's Q for firms in Malaysia and Singapore. They combined firms from the two countries in a pooled regression and obtained similar results. However, Dalton, Johnson, and Ellstrand (1999) in another analysis involving 131 samples discovered a positive relationship between board size and performance. Following previous studies in non-financial firms, Cornett, Hovakimian, Palia, and Tehranian (2003) found that the number of board members is negatively and significantly related to abnormal return in bidding bank involving diversifying acquisitions. He further concluded that board size as corporate governance mechanism is effective in reducing the managerial incentive to enter value-destroying bank acquisitions.

In another perspective, contrary to the evidence for non-financial firms, there is a positive relationship between board size and Tobin's Q of bank holding company (Adams & Mehran, 2002, 2003). In addition, they found that there is no significant negative effect of board size on ROA but constraints on board size in the banking industry may be counter-productive as bank holding company may have a larger board than the manufacturing firms.

2.2.2.3. Board Independence. Board independence refers to the entry of outsiders into the board. Increase in the proportion of outside directors on the board should increase firm performance as this could provide a more effective monitoring of managers (Adams & Mehran, 2003). The rational of having independent directors is to reduce agency cost, to gain access to the capital market as well as to ensure accountability in executive remuneration (Lawrence & Stapledon, 1999). The positive aspect of having board independence is evidenced in a study by Cook, Hogan, and Kieschnick (2004). They highlighted that the survival of firms in the thrift (which is similar to banking firms) crisis is due to greater proportion of independent directors in the board. Petra (2005) argued that independent directors may play a role in controlling management in aspects such as takeover threats, CEO compensation, and nominations of directors. Cornett et al. (2003) in a study on intrastate bank acquisitions also found that greater proportion of outsiders on the board leads to greater acquiring bank returns. Chhaochharia and Grinstein (2004) studied the announcement impact of governance rules in U.S in response to 2001–2002 corporate scandals. The rules require firms to have majority of independent directors, independent audit committee, independent nominating committee, and independent compensation committee. They found that large firms who changed their governance structure in order to comply with the rules enjoyed significantly higher returns that vary between 14% and 23% in the year the rules are announced.

Adams and Mehran (2002, 2003) conducted a study on the banking sector and found no significant relationship between the proportion of outsiders on the board and firm performance based on Tobin's Q, although they found some evidence of a positive correlation between Tobin's Q and majority-outside board.

2.2.3. Regulatory Monitoring Mechanism
The banking industry often requires a careful analysis of its risk management function due to its high leverage and high-risk characteristics. Berger, Herring, and Szego (1995) and Saidenberg and Schuermann (2003) argued that capital regulation particularly in banks protects consumers and depositors and reduces systemic risk. Meanwhile, Gersbach and Wenzelburger (2003) stressed that capital adequacy serves as an indicator of the banking system and suggested a strict enforcement of capital adequacy rules as one of the policy measures in banking crisis.

The banking capital regulatory requirement is related to the risk management of the banking firms. From the capital management perspective, there are three financial approaches used to explain risks (Lin, Penm, Gong, & Chang, 2005), i.e., State Preference Theory, Option Pricing Theory, and Portfolio Theory. Early studies suggested that the first two theories affirm the effectiveness of capital management and that stricter capital management is likely to decrease bank's level of risks exposure. It means that when capital adequacy is high (low), the insolvency risk index is low (high). An unregulated bank will take excessive risks in order to maximize shareholder value at the expense of deposit insurance. Capital adequacy requirement can reduce these moral hazard incentives by forcing bank shareholders to absorb a larger part of the losses, as such, it may lead to more capital and less risk-taking and this would lower the bank's default probability (Rime, 2001).

Regulatory monitoring through capital adequacy requirement serves as a governance mechanism tool that used to ensure that the banks are well capitalized. Lindquist (2004) argued that as the other forms of regulation disappear, and with the experience from the banking crises, capital adequacy regulations become relatively more important. In a study involving unbalanced bank-level panel data from Norway, there is evidence to support that having buffer capital defined as the ratio of excess capital to risk-weighted assets serves as an insurance against failure to meet the capital requirements. According to Das and Ghosh (2006), the capital adequacy ratio (CAR) is positively related to the technical efficiency. In most cases, it is observed that the higher the CAR of the bank, the larger is the magnitude of technical efficiency estimates. They argued that well-capitalized banks are perceived to be relatively safe, which in turn lowers their cost of borrowing and consequently is efficiency enhancing.

With regards to profitability, reviews by the Basel Committee concluded that there are mixed results in terms of market expectations concerning the announcement of minimum regulatory requirements on the profitability of the banks measured by its share price performance (Bank for International Settlement (BIS), 1999). However, the empirical results from Lin et al. (2005) indicated that there is a significant positive relationship between capital adequacy and various financial performances, i.e., ROA, Return on Equity, Profit Margin, and Earnings before Income Tax.

2.2.4. Disclosure Monitoring Mechanisms

The financial transparency and disclosure are important mechanisms that provide depositors, creditors, and shareholders with credible assurances that banks will refrain from fraudulent activities. According to La Porta, Lopez de Silanes, Shleifer, and Vishny (1999), disclosure and accounting rules provides investors with the information they need to exercise their rights while financial reporting or disclosure quality had been determined as one of the mechanisms in assessing corporate governance of a firm (Mitton, 2002; Coles et al., 2001). La Porta et al. (1999) also argued that accounting standards play a critical role in corporate governance by making contracts more verifiable. It is also evidenced that change in firm value during a financial crisis is a function of firm-level differences in corporate governance measures (Baek et al., 2004). In a comprehensive study involving banking fragility and disclosure in 49 countries, Tadesse (2005) concluded that banking crises are less likely in countries with financial-reporting regimes characterized by comprehensive disclosure, informative disclosure, timely disclosure, and more stringent auditing.

Information asymmetry is identified as one of the unique characteristics in the banking industry. In dealing with asymmetry problem, information disclosures have always played an important role to serve the purpose of monitoring by depositors. In a situation of asymmetry problem, it is important for the stakeholders especially the depositors to be supplied with sufficient information in helping them to monitor the financial institutions. However, their ability to monitor is not only subjected to the availability of such information. It is more important that they have a good quality of institution-specific information available to determine their ability to monitor financial institutions effectively.

2.2.4.1. Big 4 External Auditors. The role of external auditors is very important in bank disclosure. According to Niinimaki (2001) an auditor plays an important role as a bank supervisor to ensure that depositors are informed on financial difficulties that may lead to bank runs, the role is further enhanced in a situation where the deposits are insured as the depositors would have less incentive to monitor the banks.

Higher disclosure quality may be achieved by appointing reputable external auditors (Mitton, 2002). With regard to Asia, evidence from Fan and Wong (2001) suggested that Big 5 auditors in Asia do have a corporate governance role as they are more likely to ensure transparency and eliminating mistakes in firm's financial statements because they have a greater reputation to uphold; may be more independent than local firms; face greater legal liability for making errors, and may offer higher perceived disclosure quality (in the case in which actual disclosure quality is not higher) due to their prominent and recognizable names.

2.2.4.2. Big 3 Rating Agency. Rating announcement conveys informa- tion to financial markets about the financial health of a bank and this is being reflected by appropriate valuation of bank's stocks. Firms' overall credit ratings reflect a rating agency's opinion of an entity's overall creditworthiness and its capacity to satisfy its financial obligations. Nier and Braumann (2002) argued that investors have more information about a bank if the bank is rated by a major rating agency. Acting as intermediaries in the disclosure process, they gained access to information that is not publicly available to investors and that information is then incorporated into the rating. According to Kliger and Sarig (2001), the reason for a particular firm to pay for the rating service is due to the fact that it allows firms to incorporate inside information into the assigned ratings without disclosing specific details to the public at large. On the other hand, Boot and Milbourn (2003) argued that rating agencies could be seen as information-processing agencies that may speed up the dissemination of information to the financial markets. In the end, all investors may make rational decision on their investment based on such ratings.

If rating agencies convey new and useful information about the financial health of a bank, it is expected that the bank's stock prices will increase following upgrades or decrease following downgrades (Richard & Deddouche, 1999). This implies that ratings changes that are good (bad) news for bondholders will also be good (bad) news for stockholders. As such, rankings by reputable agencies can also explain the reputation of a firm.

3. DATA AND METHODOLOGY

A total of 157 listed banks were identified in the nine countries of Asian emerging markets but only 107 were included in the study due to data completeness. This represents 68.15% of listed banks in the selected Asian emerging markets. This study involves cross-sectional data sets of emerging markets consisting of nine countries; and different number of banking firms in each cross-section or cluster ranging from 3 to 21 observations.

There are four dimensions of monitoring mechanisms used to study the relationship between corporate governance and performance. In addition, control variable is also included to account for the firm level differences among the listed banks in Asian emerging market. The definitions of each variable are summarized in Table 1. This study assumed a direct relationship between corporate governance monitoring mechanisms (independent variables) and corporate performance of banking firms (dependent variable).

Using a Pooled Estimated Generalized Least Squares (EGLS) regression model, the relationship between corporate governance mechanisms and

Table 1. Description of Variables.

Variable	Description	Sources
Tobin's Q	The ratio of the firm's market value to its book value. The firm's market value is calculated as book value of assets minus the book value of equity plus market value of equity	Author's calculations based on Bloomberg
ROA	Accounting return computed by pre-tax income to total assets	Author's calculations based on Bloomberg
Largest blockholders	Equals one if there is a single shareholder owns at least 5% or more of the stock in the bank, and zero otherwise	Author's calculations based on annual reports
Government	Equals one if the government shareholding in the bank is at least 5%, and zero otherwise	Author's calculations based on annual reports
Foreign	Equals one if the foreign shareholding in the bank is at least 5%, and zero otherwise	Author's calculations based on annual reports
Board size	The number of directors appointed by the shareholders on the board	Author's calculations based on annual reports
Board independence	The fraction of number of independent directors to total number of directors	Author's calculations based on annual reports
CEO duality	Equals one if the position of Chairman and CEO is held by one person (combined leadership), and zero otherwise	Author's calculations based on annual reports
Capital adequacy	A measure of the amount of a bank's capital expressed as a percentage of its risk-weighted credit exposure	Bloomberg database
Big 4 auditor	Equals one if the bank is audited by one of the Big 4 international external auditors, and zero otherwise	Annual reports
Big 3 rating	Equals one if the bank is rated by one of the Big 3 international credit rating firms, and zero otherwise	Information from Moody's, S&P and Fitch; and annual reports
Firm size	Book value of total assets	Bloomberg and annual reports

bank's performance is analyzed based on the following equations:

$$CP_{i,k} = a + \beta_1 OWN_{i,k} + \beta_2 CEO_{i,k} + \beta_3 SZB_{i,k} + \beta_4 INDB_{i,k}$$
$$+ \beta_5 CAR_{i,k} + \beta_6 BIG3_{i,k} + \beta_7 BIG4_{i,k} + \beta_8 SIZE_{i,k} + e_{i,k} \qquad (1)$$

$$CP_{i,k} = a + \beta_1 GOV_{i,k} + \beta_2 FOR_{i,k} + \beta_3 CEO_{i,k} + \beta_4 SZB_{i,k}$$
$$+ \beta_5 INDB_{i,k} + \beta_6 CAR_{i,k} + \beta_7 BIG3_{i,k} + \beta_8 BIG4_{i,k}$$
$$+ \beta_9 SIZE_{i,k} + e_{i,k} \qquad (2)$$

for i = 1, 2, ..., N and k = 1, 2, ..., K

where:

i	=	Country
K	=	Banking firms
CP	=	Corporate performance measured by Tobin's Q and ROA
OWN	=	Large blockholders/shareholders
GOV	=	Government ownership
FOR	=	Foreign ownership
CEO	=	Duality
SZB	=	Number of Director in bank t
INDB	=	Number of independent Directors in bank t
CAR	=	Capital adequacy ratio
BIG 3	=	Rating of banks by reputable rating agencies (Big 3)
BIG 4	=	Auditing by reputable external auditor (Big 4)
SIZE	=	Size of banks measured by total assets
e	=	Random error
β_i	=	Parameters to be estimated

4. RESULTS AND DISCUSSIONS

4.1. Descriptive Statistics

The descriptive statistics for all variables are presented in Tables 2 to 4. It is found that 93.46% or 100 banks in the sample are having at least 5%

Table 2. Descriptive Statistics on Ownership.

Emerging Markets	N	Large Blockholders		Foreign Shareholding		Government Shareholding	
		At least 5%	Less than 5%	At least 5%	Less than 5%	At least 5%	Less than 5%
Malaysia	12	12	0	0	12	10	2
Thailand	8	8	0	1	7	7	1
Philippines	18	18	0	11	7	4	14
Indonesia	21	21	0	9	12	7	14
Korea	6	6	0	4	2	2	4
Singapore	3	3	0	0	3	1	2
Hong Kong	9	9	0	5	4	0	9
Taiwan	12	8	4	1	11	4	8
India	18	15	3	5	13	12	6
Total	107	100	7	36	71	47	60
Percentage	100	93.46	6.54	33.6	66.4	43.9	56.1

Table 3. Descriptive Statistics on the Categorical Variable.

Emerging Markets	N	CEO Duality		Big 3 Rating		Big 4 Auditor	
		Separated	Combined	Big 3	Others	Big 4	Others
Malaysia	12	12	0	7	5	12	0
Thailand	8	7	1	6	2	6	2
Philippines	18	15	3	8	10	14	4
Indonesia	21	21	0	13	8	13	8
Korea	6	2	4	6	0	6	0
Singapore	3	2	1	3	0	3	0
Hong Kong	9	7	2	8	1	9	0
Taiwan	12	12	0	6	6	9	1
India	18	7	11	8	10	0	18
Total	107	85	22	65	42	74	33
Percentage (%)	100	79.44	20.56	60.7	39.3	69.16	30.84

shareholding by a single shareholder ranging from 0 to 99.99%. In terms of the type of large shareholders, foreign shareholdings can be found in 36 banks (33.6%) while there is an existence of government's shareholdings in 47 banks (43.9%). In terms of board structure, the average board size and board independence are 10.39 persons and 32.29% respectively. On the other hand, the number of banking firms, which falls into Separated Leadership, is 85 (79.44%) while Combined Leadership has 22 banks (20.56%). The study also discovers that the CAR for all banks is above the 8% requirement. It is found that there are 65 (60.7%) banks with Big 3 rating agencies while 42 (39.3%) banks are either rated by other rating agencies or not rated at all. There is also a significant presence of Big 4 auditors where 74 (69.16%) banks are audited by Big 4 External Auditor while 33 (30.84%) are audited by other categories of external auditors. In terms of size, banking firms in Singapore, Korea, and Hong Kong are categorized as the largest banks with mean asset value of more than US$25,000 million. Their mean values are greater than the overall means of US$16,974.96 million.

4.2. Corporate Governance Monitoring Mechanisms and Corporate Performance

The result for the regression analysis of all corporate governance monitoring mechanisms is presented in Tables 5 and 6. It presents the regression results

Table 4. Descriptive Statistics on the Continuous Variable
for the Full Sample.

Emerging Markets	N	Dependent Variables		Independent Variables			
		Corporate performance		Board structure		Regulatory monitoring	Firm size
		Tobin's Q	ROA	Board size	Board independence	Capital adequacy	Total assets
Malaysia	12						
Minimum		0.96	0.47	5	27.78	9.06	3877.56
Maximum		1.21	2.61	11	100	22.40	47,238.80
Mean		1.05	1.26	8.08	47.45	15.15	15,972.07
Median		1.04	1.13	8.00	38.75	14.85	10,838.72
Std. deviation		0.08	0.64	1.68	20.54	3.51	12,833.74
Thailand	8						
Minimum		1.00	0.23	9	18.18	10.72	4212.40
Maximum		1.07	2.39	18	55.56	14.56	36,178.60
Mean		1.03	1.15	12.5	34.19	12.46	17,960.13
Median		1.03	1.08	11.50	31.67	12.20	17,226.85
Std. deviation		0.03	0.71	3.51	12.67	1.66	11,059.13
Philippines	18						
Minimum		0.89	0.09	7	13.33	11.02	24.04
Maximum		1.16	3.17	16	57.14	51.22	9494.19
Mean		0.99	1.30	12.11	27.59	22.28	2476.37
Median		0.98	1.07	11.00	27.28	20.60	1248.81
Std. deviation		0.08	0.87	2.37	10.69	9.91	2774.38
Indonesia	21						
Minimum		0.93	−9.18	2	0.00	9.44	125.43
Maximum		1.23	5.97	10	69.23	40.19	26,733.73
Mean		1.07	2.05	5.38	31.15	17.95	4748.60
Median		1.07	2.35	4.00	33.33	15.11	2014.91
Std. deviation		0.08	3.97	2.77	20.58	7.26	6907.11
Korea	6						
Minimum		0.99	0.44	5	37.50	9.47	4504.28
Maximum		1.04	0.98	13	70.00	11.17	176,560.36
Mean		1.01	0.72	8.33	60.47	10.68	58,459.56
Median		1.00	0.72	8.00	63.07	10.82	39,727.92
Std. deviation		0.02	0.44	2.88	14.62	0.63	63,909.21
Singapore	3						
Minimum		1.03	1.23	10	40.00	15.60	73,416.42
Maximum		1.05	1.41	14	64.29	17.70	107,509.95
Mean		1.04	1.34	12.33	54.21	16.37	87,842.33
Median		1.05	1.38	12.00	58.33	15.80	82,600.63
Std. deviation		0.01	0.32	1.53	12.66	1.16	17,640.83
Hong Kong	9						
Minimum		0.97	0.74	10	0.00	12	5417.62
Maximum		1.30	2.42	20	90.91	20.5	102,505.60
Mean		1.08	1.46	13.29	36.71	16.94	26,501.86
Median		1.07	1.48	12.00	30.00	17.13	10,750.95
Std. deviation		0.10	0.74	3.26	27.36	2.88	35,052.37

Table 4. (*Continued*)

Emerging Markets	N	Dependent Variables		Independent Variables			
		Corporate performance		Board structure		Regulatory monitoring	Firm size
		Tobin's Q	ROA	Board size	Board independence	Capital adequacy	Total assets
Taiwan	12						
Minimum		0.98	−0.92	7	0.00	3.76	4773.65
Maximum		1.06	1.63	25	83.33	13.30	41,311.75
Mean		1.02	0.32	14.09	9.09	10.38	14,906.14
Median		1.02	0.34	14.00	0.00	10.88	9040.05
Std. deviation		0.98	0.92	5.32	25.12	2.45	11,927.90
India	18						
Minimum		0.98	0.55	9	0.00	9.48	731.97
Maximum		1.19	2.71	18	75.00	16.88	126,372.57
Mean		1.02	1.70	11.78	23.57	12.70	16,994.73
Median		1.01	1.63	11	0.00	12.77	6794.99
Std. deviation		0.05	0.52	2.34	29.00	1.88	28,768.48
Total	107						
Minimum		0.89	−9.18	5	0.00	3.76	24.04
Maximum		1.30	5.97	25	100	51.22	176,560.36
Mean		1.03	1.37	10.39	32.29	15.68	16,974.96
Median		1.02	1.32	10.00	33.33	13.79	7771.64
Std. deviation		0.07	1.50	4.17	24.40	6.64	28,060.68

for both performance measures, i.e., Tobin's Q and ROA, and corporate governance monitoring mechanisms. The first two columns include ownership monitoring mechanisms without controlling for size while the next two columns incorporated size in the model specifications. The R^2 in all models are found to be very consistent with and without the control variable. For example, in the first table, the adjusted R^2 for model without size effect are 0.481542 and 0.494008, respectively. When it is incorporated with total assets, the R^2 are almost at the same rate of 0.479495 and 0.495596. On the other hand, the adjusted R^2 for model with ROA is lower than model with Tobin's Q as a dependent variable. The adjusted R^2 are 0.306985 and 0.334674 (without the inclusion of total assets) and 0.277279 and 0.281678 (with the inclusion of total assets).

4.2.1. Ownership Monitoring Mechanism
The results in all of the models indicate that measures of ownership monitoring mechanisms are best explained only when Tobin's Q is used as the performance measure. Columns (i) and (iii) of Table 5 indicated a

Table 5. Regression Result Using Tobin's Q as the Dependent Variable.

Independent Variable	(i)	(ii)	(iii)	(iv)
Constant	0.299292	−0.079800	0.274305	−0.079800
	(0.5590)	(0.8360)	(0.5915)	(0.8360)
Large blockholder	−0.410928		−0.398665	
	(0.0524)*		(0.0610)*	
Foreign shareholding		−0.337224		−0.608680
		(0.0003)***		(0.0006)***
Government shareholding		−0.629793		−0.364106
		(0.0005)***		(0.0013)***
Board size	−0.019699	0.003951	−0.012543	0.000309
	(0.3177)	(0.7736)	(0.5756)	(0.9812)
Board independence	−0.001750	0.000372	−0.002195	0.000106
	(0.5704)	(0.8759)	(0.4602)	(0.9659)
CEO duality	0.095488	−0.026795	0.047133	0.010616
	(0.4776)	(0.8773)	(0.7346)	(0.9535)
Capital adequacy	0.078428	0.082210	0.077504	0.083024
	(0.0001)***	(0.0001)***	(0.0002)***	(0.0001)***
Big 3 rating agency	0.328859	0.316252	0.317983	0.302426
	(0.3217)	(0.2763)	(0.3426)	(0.3010)
Big 4 external auditor	0.382500	0.407833	0.398793***	0.398047
	(0.0097)***	(0.0030)***	(0.0081)	(0.0039)***
Total assets			−1.43E-06	1.55E-06
			(0.1123)	(0.3165)
Adjusted R^2	0.481542	0.494008	0.479495	0.495596
Number of observations	107	107	107	107

*Significant at 10% level.
**Significant at 5% level.
***Significant at 1% level.

significant negative relationship between large blockholders and Tobin's Q, with and without controlling for size. However, an accounting based measure as shown on Table 6 does not provide a statistically significant result even though opposite signs are obtained in a model involving ROA. As such, we conclude that market-based measure is better than accounting-based measure to capture the relationship between ownership concentration and bank's performance.

The same pattern is generated when foreign shareholdings are included as proxies for ownership. As presented in columns (ii) and (iv) of Table 5, both models showed that foreign ownership is negatively related with Tobin's Q and statistically significant at 1% significant level. Using ROA as the dependent variable, foreign ownership is still significantly negatively related

Table 6. Regression Result Using ROA as the Dependent Variable.

Independent Variable	(i)	(ii)	(iii)	(iv)
Constant	0.949951	0.954549	0.949001	0.955236
	(0.0000)	(0.0000)	(0.0000)	(0.0000)
Large blockholder	0.007661		0.007797	
	(0.3425)		(0.3447)	
Foreign shareholding		0.018895		0.016705
		(0.0155)**		(0.1127)
Government shareholding		0.004586		0.001252
		(0.3171)		(0.8255)
Board size	0.000147	0.000195	0.000508	0.000475
	(0.8400)	(0.7715)	(0.5313)	(0.5610)
Board independence	−4.54E-06	−0.000121	−5.17E-05	−0.000165
	(0.9802)	(0.6007)	(0.7776)	(0.4814)
CEO duality	−0.029733	−0.020736	−0.028184	−0.020941
	(0.0008)***	(0.0022)***	(0.0106)**	(0.0206)**
Capital adequacy	0.002861	0.002797	0.002883	0.002858
	(0.0297)**	(0.0154)**	(0.0249)**	(0.0110)**
Big 3 rating agency	0.024727	0.020696	0.023337	0.020024
	(0.0726)*	(0.1374)	(0.0825)*	(0.1350)
Big 4 external auditor	0.032548	0.031650	0.032347	0.032341
	(0.0001)***	(0.0007)***	(0.0001)***	(0.0002)***
Total assets			−5.72E-08	−5.02E-08
			(0.5658)	(0.5680)
Adjusted R^2	0.306985	0.334674	0.277279	0.281678
Number of observations	107	107	107	107

*Significant at 10% level.
**Significant at 5% level.
***Significant at 1% level.

with Tobin's Q without controlling for size. Anyway, it is not consistent with the remaining models where none of them generates any significant coefficients. Again, it is market-based measure that successfully depicts the relationships.

Using government shareholding as another proxy for ownership also depicts the same results as far as relationship with Tobin's Q is concerned. In the model with and without controlling for size, we found that government shareholding is significantly negatively related with Tobin's Q also at 1% significant level. Again, accounting-based measure failed to identify any significant relationship between government ownership and Tobin's Q.

4.2.2. Internal Control Monitoring Mechanism

Results on Table 5 showed that board size is negatively related to Tobin's Q using large shareholders/blockholders in the specification but not statistically significant. However, the sign of the relationship changes when both foreign and government shareholdings are treated as proxies for ownership monitoring mechanism. None of the model successfully indicates significant relationship when ROA is substituted as a proxy for corporate performance.

Board independence is also found to have the same relationship with board size with and without controlling for size. The results in Table 5 revealed that CEO Duality is not significant in explaining corporate performance when Tobin's Q is used as performance measure but showed a statistically significantly negative relationship when ROA is used as performance measure for all models.

4.2.3. Regulatory Monitoring Mechanism: Capital Adequacy Ratio

The regression results showed that there is a statistically positive significant relationship between Capital Adequacy and Tobin's Q as well as ROA, with and without controlling for size.

4.2.4. Disclosure-Monitoring Mechanism

Similarly, the disclosure-monitoring mechanism is found to have a statistically significant relationship with both Tobin's Q and ROA. There is also a statistically significant positive relationship between Big 4 external auditors and Tobin's Q as well as ROA at 1% significant level albeit a lower coefficients for ROA as compares to Tobin's Q. Nevertheless, none of the models indicate any statistically significant relationship between the Big 3 credit rating agencies and Tobin's Q. However, the variable is found to have a statistically significant positive relationship with ROA only in the ownership concentration model at 10% significant level.

4.3. Corporate Governance Monitoring Mechanisms of Banks and Non-Banks

Table 7 provides a more interesting finding in that we are able to identify many similarities as well as differences between the relationship of corporate governance mechanisms and corporate performance between banking firms and non-banking firms.

Table 7. Comparative Results between Banks and Non-Banks.

Variables	Relationship	
	Bank	Non-bank
Large blockholders	Negative	Negative
Foreign shareholding	Inconclusive	Positive
Government shareholding	Negative	Negative
Board size	No relationship	Negative
Board independence	No relationship	Positive
CEO duality	Negative	Negative
Capital adequacy	Positive	Not applicable
Big 3 rating agency	Positive	Not applicable
Big 4 external auditor	Positive	Positive
Total assets	No relationship	Positive

In terms of ownership monitoring mechanism, our study confirmed that the presence of large blockholders leads to poor performance for the banking firms, which is consistent with previous studies on non-banks firms. We segregated the large blockholders into different shareholders category and we found that the presence of government ownership is detrimental to corporate performance, and this confirmed previous findings between government shareholdings and corporate performance in all industries. Nevertheless, the same cannot be said for foreign shareholding. While it has a negative effect with Tobin's Q, the positive relationship with ROA might give some support to the evidence in non-banks study where the presence of foreign shareholders improve the performance of the firms. The positive relationship might be an indication of initial success of the liberalization of the banking industry in Asia whereby the foreign players with larger capital are moving aggressively to tap into the new markets.

In terms of internal control monitoring mechanisms, we found that CEO Duality is detrimental to corporate performance for both banking and non-banking firms. Thus, recommendation of having separate leadership by the Code on Corporate Governance by the authorities in the affected countries proves to be a suitable governance mechanism across all firms.

Finally, the disclosure-monitoring mechanism through the appointment of Big 4 external auditors by the banking firms is found to be consistent with previous studies on non-bank firms where it is significantly positively related to corporate performance. Thus, having Big 4 External Auditors will benefit the shareholders across different industries since it provides credibility to information for shareholders when making investment decision.

5. CONCLUSIONS

The objective of this paper is to identify whether there exist any differences in the monitoring mechanisms of banking firms and non-banking firms and our findings have generated a perspective on corporate governance monitoring mechanisms in the banking sector. In summary, we found that all ownership monitoring mechanisms are significantly negatively related with corporate performance measures in the banking firms in Asian emerging markets. However, between the two corporate performance measures, Tobin's Q is able to explain the relationship better in all the models while ROA is able to yield a significant relationship only when large shareholder is used as the independent variable.

We also found that none of the Internal Control Monitoring Mechanisms displayed any significant relationship with market-based corporate performance but one aspect of internal monitoring mechanism which is CEO Duality provides evidence that accounting measure is able to explain the relationship better. However, our results confirmed that the Big 4 External Auditors played a more significant role in delivering information as compared to the Big 3 Rating Agencies, but Big 3 may also partially contribute to the disclosure monitoring mechanism of the banking firms in Asian emerging markets based on the statistically significant positive relationship between Big 3 and ROA in two of the four models.

In terms of ownership monitoring mechanism, our study confirmed that the presence of large blockholders leads to poor performance for the banking firms, which is consistent with previous studies on non-banks firms. In terms of internal control monitoring mechanisms, we found that CEO Duality is detrimental to corporate performance for both banking and non-banking firms while the disclosure monitoring mechanism through the appointment of Big 4 external auditors by the banking firms is found to be consistent with previous studies on non-bank firms where it is significantly positively related to corporate performance.

Thus our results displayed some similarities between bank's and non-bank's corporate-governance monitoring mechanisms. However, the nature of the banking firms itself exposed certain differences in the monitoring mechanisms between the two groups. We also found that banks in the Asian emerging markets are well governed in some aspects as a result of key governance reforms since the 1997 financial crisis. Our study further highlighted that in certain aspects, banking firms in the Asian emerging markets appreciate the importance of good governance in terms of separating the positions of CEO and Chairman as well as effort on improving the quality of corporate disclosure. Comparing the outcome from corporate governance studies in banks and non-banks proves that both banks and non-banks are similar in certain aspects yet each group has its own unique features that differentiate their corporate governance monitoring mechanisms. However, it is important to note that the findings are generated during the early stage of the adoption of good corporate governance in Asia.

The study is being hampered by data completeness. The researcher managed to collect a full set of data for 107 banks or equivalent to 68.15%, which is closed to the population of listed banks in Asian in emerging markets. Data on the rest of the banks are either incomplete or the annual report which is the main source for corporate governance information is not available. The implication of having such a number of observations is reflected with limited diagnostics tests in the regression. The study uses information in one point of time, which is 2004. As such, generalization made in this study may not be appropriate for the other period of study. In addition, the study limits the ownership identity to the foreign and government shareholders only. Apart from the limited number of observations, the family and individuals ownerships of the banks are not included since there is no access on such information especially when the shares are registered under private firms or nominees. The ownership identity is only limited to the available information contained in the annual reports and other published information. On the other hand, the study ignores accounting standard adopted in the different countries. This is consistent with the other study on Asian firms such as Mitton (2002), Claessens and Fan (2002), Fan and Wong (2001). In effect, the calculations of corporate performance measures are based on unstandardized accounting information.

There are number of recommendations can be made for the future research. Acknowledging the limitation of data in this study, the first and foremost is to propose that a larger pool of observations is used in the future study. Longer time-period can be included so that performance and monitoring mechanisms relationship can be evaluated over a large number of observations. Having a longer period can be also associated with the future benefits of the ongoing bank reforms of which the importance of corporate governance is better appreciated and understood, thus appropriately adopted by the banking firms. In terms of ownership, future research may treat ownership concentration; and government and foreign ownership according to percentage instead of dummy when more data is available. The advantage of having such form of data format would allow the analysis to capture the appropriate level of ownership, which may contribute to a better or poor corporate performance of banking firms.

REFERENCES

Adams, R., & Mehran, H. (2002). *Board structure and banking firm performance.* Working Paper. Federal Reserve Bank of New York, http://papers.ssrn.com/paper.taf?abstractid = 302593

Adams, R., & Mehran, H. (2003). *Is corporate governance different for bank holding companies.* Federal Reserve Bank of New York Economic Policy Review, Federal Reserve Bank of New York.

Arun, T. G., & Turner, J. D. (2004). Corporate governance of banks in developing economics: Concepts and issues. *Corporate Governance: An International Review, 12*(3), 371–377. Available at SSRN: http://ssrn.com/abstract = 557319.

Baek, J-S., Kang, J-K., & Park, K. S. (2004). Corporate governance and firm value: Evidence from the Korean financial crisis. *Journal of Financial Economics, 71*, 265–313.

Bai, C., Liu, Q., Lu, J., Song, F., & Zhang, J. (2003). *Corporate governance and market valuation in China.* Working Paper. University of Hong Kong.

Banerjee, A. (2004). *Corporate Governance: A relook into the Indian banking system.* Working Paper Series. Available at SSRN: http://ssrn.com/abstract = 631681 or DOI: 10.2139/ssrn.631681

Bank for International Settlement (BIS). (1999). *Capital requirements and bank behaviour: The impact of the Basel accord.* Basel Committee for Banking Supervision.

Berger, A., Herring, R. J., & Szego, G. P. (1995). The role of capital in financial institutions. *Journal of Banking and Finance, 19*, 393–430.

Bhattacharyya, A. K., & Rao, S. V. (2004). *Economic impact of regulation on corporate governance: Evidence from India.* Working Paper No. 486/2004. Indian Institute of Management Calcutta.

Boot, A. W. A., & Milbourn, T. T. (2003). *Credit ratings as coordination mechanisms.* Working Paper No. 457. William Davidson Institute, Business School, University of Michigan.

Bris, A., & Cabolis, C. (2003). Adopting better corporate governance: Evidence from cross-border mergers. EFA 2003 Annual Conference Paper No. 237.

Caprio, G., Leuven, L., & Levine, R. (2003). *Governance and bank valuation.* Working Paper No. 10158. National Bureau of Economic Research.

Chhaochharia, V., & Grinstein, Y. (2004). *Corporate governance and firm value – The impact of the 2002 governance rules.* Unpublished Manuscript.

Chirinko, B., van Ees, H., Garrestsen, H., & Sterken, E. (1999). *Firm performance, financial institutions and corporate governance in the Netherlands.* CESifo Working Paper Series No. 210.

Claessens, S., & Fan, J. P. (2002). *Corporate governance in Asia: A survey.* Working Paper. International Review of Finance, Vol. 3, pp. 71–103.

Coles, J. W., McWilliams, V. B., & Sen, N. (2001). An examination of the relationship of governance mechanisms to performance. *Journal of Management, 27*, 23–50.

Cook, D. O., Hogan, A., & Kieschnick, R. (2004). A study of corporate governance of thrifts. *Journal of Banking and Finance, 28*, 1247–1271.

Cornett, M. M., Hovakimian, G., Palia, D., & Tehranian, H. (2003). The impact of the manager–shareholder conflict on acquiring bank returns. *Journal of Banking and Finance, 27*, 103–131.

Crespi, R., Garcia-Cestona, M. A., & Salas, V. (2003). *Governance mechanisms in Spanish banks: Does ownership matter.* Finance Working Paper No. 19/2003. European Corporate Governance Institute.

Dalton, D. R., Johnson, J. L., & Ellstrand, A. E. (1999). Number of directors and financial performance: A meta analysis. *Academy of Management Journal, 42*(6), 674–686.

Das, B. A., & Ghosh, T. S. (2006). Financial deregulation and efficiency: An empirical analysis of Indian banks during the post reform period. *Review of Financial Economics*, *15*(3), 193–221. (article in press).

Eisenberg, T. S., & Sundgren, M. W. (1998). Larger board size and decreasing firm value in small firms. *Journal of Financial Economics*, *48*, 35–54.

Eldomiaty, T. I. & Choi, C. J. (2003). *Bank's orientation and performance in stakeholders– shareholders business systems.* Working Paper Series. Available at SSRN: http://ssrn.com/ abstract = 462600

Emmons, W. R., & Schmid, F. A. (1999). *Corporate governance and corporate performance.* Working Paper 1999-018A. Federal Reserve Bank of St. Louis.

Fan, J. P. H., & Wong, T. J. (2001). Do external auditors perform a corporate governance role in emerging markets? Evidence from East Asia. EFA 2001 Barcelona Meetings. 3rd Annual Fin. Mkt. Dev. Conference, Hong Kong. Available at SSRN: http://ssrn.com/ abstract = 270641 or DOI: 10.2139/ssrn.270641

Gersbach, H., & Wenzelburger, J. (2003). *The workout of banking crisis: A macroeconomic perspective.* Working Paper Series. Available at SSRN: http://ssrn.com/abstract = 408380 or DOI: 10.2139/ssrn.408380

Haniffa, R. M., & Cooke, T. E. (2005). The impact of culture and governance on corporate social reporting. *Journal of Accounting and Public Policy*, *24*, 391–430.

Jensen, M. C. (1983). The modern industrial revolution, exit, and the failure of internal control systems. *Journal of Finance*, *48*(3), 831–880.

Keenan, J. (2004). Corporate governance in UK/USA boardrooms. *Corporate Governance*, *12*(2), 172–176.

Kiel, G. C., & Nicholson, G. J. (2003). Board composition and corporate performance: How the Australian experience informs contrasting theories of corporate governance. *Corporate Governance*, *11*(3), 189–205.

Kliger, D., & Sarig, O. (2001). The information value of bond ratings. *Journal of Finance*, *55*(6), 2879–2902.

La Porta, R., Lopez de Silanes, F., & Shleifer, A. (2000). *Government ownership of banks.* Working Paper 7620. National Bureau of Economic Research, Massachusetts.

La Porta, R., Lopez de Silanes, F., Shleifer, A., & Vishny, R. W. (1999). *Investor protection and corporate governance.* Working Paper Series. Available at SSRN: http://ssrn.com/ abstract = 183908 or DOI: 10.2139/ssrn.183908

Lawrence, J., & Stapledon, G. P. (1999). *Is board composition important? A study of listed Australian companies.* Working Paper Series. Available at SSRN: http://ssrn.com/ abstract = 193528 or DOI: 10.2139/ssrn.193528

Levine, R. (2003). *The corporate governance of banks: A concise discussion of concepts and evidence.* Discussion Paper. Global Corporate Governance Forum, World Bank.

Lin, S. L., Penm, J. H. W., Gong, S. C., & Chang, C. S. (2005). Risk-based capital adequacy in assessing on insolvency-risk and financial performances in Taiwan's banking industry. *Research in International Business and Finance*, *19*, 111–153.

Lindquist, K. (2004). Banks' buffer capital: How important is risk. *Journal of International Money and Finance*, *23*, 493–513.

Lowengrub, P., Luedecke, T., & Melvin, M. (2003). Does corporate governance matter in the market response to merger announcements. Financial Management Association Annual Meeting.

Macey, J. R., & O'Hara, M. (2003). *The corporate governance of banks.* FRNBY Economic Policy Review, Federal Reserve Bank of New York.

Mak, Y. T., & Kusnadi, Y. (2002). *Size really matters: Further evidence on the negative relationship between board size and firm value*. Working Paper. NUS Business School. Available at SSRN: http://ssrn.com/abstract = 303505 or DOI: 10.2139/ssrn.303505

Micco, A., Panizza, U., & Yanez, M. (2004). *Bank ownership and performance*. Working Paper Bank, No. 518. Inter American Development.

Mitton, T. (2002). A cross-firm analysis of the impact of corporate governance on the East Asian financial crisis. *Journal of Financial Economics, 64*, 215–241.

Nier, E., & Braumann, U. (2002). Market discipline, disclosure and moral hazard in banking. EFA Annual Conference, Paper No. 664.

Niinimaki, J. P. (2001). Intertemporal diversification in financial intermediation. *Journal of Banking and Finance, 25*, 965–991.

Petra, S. T. (2005). Do outside independent directors strengthen corporate boards? *Corporate Governance, 5*(1), 55–64.

Richard, R. J., & Deddouche, D. (1999). *Bank rating and bank stock returns: Puzzling evidence from the emerging markets*. IMF Working Paper No. WP/99/151.

Rime, B. (2001). Capital requirements and bank behaviour: Empirical evidence from Switzerland. *Journal of Banking and Finance, 25*, 789–805.

Saidenberg, M., & Schuermann, T. (2003). *The new Basel accord and questions for research*. Working Paper No. 03-14. Wharton Financial Institutions Center.

Stiglitz, J. E. (1999). Reforming the global financial structure: Lessons from recent crises. *Journal of Finance, 54*(4), 1508–1522.

Sussland, W. (2005). The board of directors: A referee or a coach? *Corporate Governance, l5*(1), 65–72.

Tadesse, S. (2005). *Banking fragility and disclosure: International evidence*. Working Paper No. 748. William Davidson Institute, Business School, University of Michigan.

Vafeas, N. (1999). Board meeting frequency and firm performance. *Journal of Financial Economics, 53*, 113–142.

Xie, B., Davidson, W. N., III., & Dadalt, P. J. (2003). Earnings management and corporate governance: The role of the board and the audit committee. *Journal of Corporate Finance, 9*, 295–316.

ON THE DUTY OF CARE OF INSTITUTIONAL INVESTORS: EVIDENCE ON PARTICIPATION OF MUTUAL FUND MANAGERS IN SHAREHOLDER MEETINGS IN ISRAEL

Amzaleg Yaron, Ben-Zion Uri and Rosenfeld Ahron

ABSTRACT

This paper analyzes Israeli mutual fund managers' decisions regarding participation in shareholder meetings. The evidence suggests that the decision is affected by both the institution's and its beneficiaries' interests. Consistent with the beneficiaries' interest, the odds of attending are higher when the proposals to be voted upon could harm the fund's beneficiaries, than in other proposals, and the odds decrease with board independence. Consistent with the institution's interests, the odds that mutual funds managed by commercial banks will participate in shareholder meetings are found to be negatively related to the corporation's bank debt level. Surprisingly, despite their legal obligation, only 27% of the mutual fund managers expected to attend a meeting actually do so.

Issues in Corporate Governance and Finance
Advances in Financial Economics, Volume 12, 75–90
Copyright © 2007 by Elsevier Ltd.
ISSN: 1569-3732/doi:10.1016/S1569-3732(07)12004-1

1. INTRODUCTION

Voting in shareholder meetings is an important mechanism used by shareholders to exercise their controlling rights and affect corporate governance. Individuals holding shares through institutional investors cannot exercise their voting rights directly. Under the duty of care, institutional investors are expected to vote for them. If institutions perform this duty, an increase in public holdings through institutional investors is expected to improve the voting process by reducing the free rider problem.[1] Evidence over the last decade shows an increase in institutional investors' holdings and in their active involvement in corporate governance, but the motives and ability of institutions to influence firms' decisions are still not fully understood.[2]

Facing a management-sponsored proposal, institutional investors have to decide whether to attend the meeting (the "participation decision") and how to vote (the "voting decision").[3] This paper analyzes the participation decisions made by Israeli mutual fund managers and addresses the following issues: (a) to what extent do mutual fund managers actually fulfill their fiduciary duty to participate in shareholder meetings; (b) and what are the factors that affect the fund manager's decision whether to attend a meeting. Inconsistent with the duty of care, we find that only 27% of the mutual fund managers who are expected to attend a meeting actually do so. However, we do find that the probability of attending a meeting is significantly related to the topic of the proposal and the strength of corporate governance in the firm. Specifically, we find higher tendency for mutual fund managers to participate in potentially harmful proposals such as related party transactions and compensation issues, than in other proposals, and that the odds of participation decrease with board independence. We further find that mutual funds managed by commercial banks tend to participate more frequently in shareholder meetings than non-bank funds, although their participation is found to be negatively related to corporate bank debt level.

The remainder of the paper is organized as follows: in the second section, we outline our main hypothesis. In the third section, we describe the sample design, and provide statistics describing the data. The empirical tests and results are presented in the fourth section, and the last section concludes the paper.

2. HYPOTHESES

An institutional investor is expected, under the duty of care, to exercise the voting rights of its beneficiaries and vote according to their best interest.

In the absence of monitoring costs this duty means attending every share-holder meeting. For a diversified mutual fund this obligation may result in having to attend hundreds of meetings every year. Since participating in a meeting is costly, a mutual fund manager acting in the best interest of the fund's beneficiaries is more likely to attend meetings where the expected benefits exceed expected costs,[4] while in other cases he will tend to free ride on other shareholders' voting.

The benefits from attending a meeting and voting are greater, the larger the expected damage to its beneficiaries from the proposal to be voted upon. This depends on the likelihood that the proposal is damaging, the magnitude of such damage, and the ability of the institution to affect the outcome by attending. A management-sponsored proposal is more likely to be damaging in corporations with weaker corporate governance. We, therefore, hypothesize that the probability a mutual fund will participate in a shareholder meeting is higher the weaker the corporate governance in the firm. Following Hermalin and Weisbach (1991) and many others, we use board independence to measure the strength of corporate governance in the firm.

Some proposals are expected to be more harmful to shareholders than others. Examples of such proposals include related party transactions[5] and compensation issues.[6] We therefore hypothesize that the probability a mutual fund will participate in a shareholder meeting is higher for shareholder meetings with potentially harmful proposals than in meetings without such proposals.

The ability of the fund to affect the voting is strengthened by the special majority rule which is part of the law requiring mutual funds to attend.[7] Even if the fund manager does not expect to affect the outcome by his attendance, a strategic advisory effect, as suggested by Maug and Rydqvist (2004), can motivate attendance.[8]

Agency theory suggests that the participation decision is driven by the interests of the institutional investor and not its beneficiaries.[9] The stronger the business relation between the institution and the corporation, the less likely the institutional investor is to attend a meeting. Some of the mutual funds in our sample are managed by commercial banks, while others are managed by private investment companies. Following Brickley, Lease, and Smith (1988), we expect bank-owned funds to have more business with corporations than mutual funds managed by private investment companies. Further, we use bank debt leverage, i.e., the ratio of book value of bank debt to book value of equity, as a proxy for the strength of business relations between bank funds and corporations. We hypothesize that bank-managed funds are less likely to attend and increasingly less so the higher the bank debt of the firm.

3. THE DATA

Under section 77 of the Mutual Investment Law of 1994, mutual fund managers in Israel are obligated to vote and file a report on their vote to the Israel Security Authority (ISA), for every significant proposal that has the potential to affect the wealth of fund beneficiaries.[10] Such proposals include, for example, the approval of related party transactions, changes in the firm's charter, and compensation plans of major shareholders employed by the firm. The report to the ISA contains the following information: the name of the fund manager, level of holdings, the type of meeting (i.e., regular or special), the topic of the proposal, and the way the fund voted. Data on a fund's assets, the proportion of total assets held in stocks, and the identity of fund managers, are drawn from the fund's annual reports as well as from the PREDICTA database. Data on each firm's ownership structure, board structure, accounting performance, capital structure, market value, and main industry are taken from the firm's annual reports and from the TAKLIT-HON databases.[11]

Failure to attend a meeting in which the mutual fund manager had to vote could result in a personal lawsuit. In order to determine whether mutual funds fulfill their duty and participate in shareholder meetings, we need to establish the population of meetings which they should have attended. That is, we need to know if a mutual fund held shares at the time of the meeting, but chose not to participate. Unfortunately, specific data on the funds' holdings is not available on a large scale.[12] We thus concentrate only on the largest firms in Israel (top 100) and assume that fund managers hold shares in all of these firms.[13] The final sample includes 254 proposals in 64 firms during the period from December 1999 to December 2001.[14]

4. EMPIRICAL RESULTS

4.1. Summary Statistics

The distribution of proposals and the participation of mutual fund managers over the topic of the proposal and over time is shown in Table 1. More than

Table 1. Participation of Mutual Funds in Shareholders' Meetings by Topic and Time during 1999–2001.

Panel A: Participation by topic

Topic of Proposal	Number of Proposals in Sample (Percentages of Total)	Participation Ratio Average (Standard Deviation)
Change in firm charter	24 (9.4%)	22.5% (41.8%)
Compensation to insider (major shareholder employed by the firm)	65 (25.6%)	38.8% (48.7%)
Personal lawsuits insurance for officers and directors	43 (16.9%)	28.5% (45.1%)
Related party transactions	35 (13.8%)	34.6% (47.6%)
Restructuring of options held by insider	5 (2.0%)	23.2% (42.3%)
Duality in CEO/COB position	4 (1.6%)	23.7% (42.7%)
Nomination and payments to outside directors	30 (11.8%)	18.0% (38.4%)
Dividend distribution	14 (5.5%)	7.3% (26.1%)
Other "Regular" proposals	34 (13.4%)	14.6% (35.4%)
Total	254	27.0% (44.4%)

Panel B: Participation by quarter

	1999		2000				2001			
	Total	Q4	Q1	Q2	Q3	Q4	Q1	Q2	Q3	Q4
Number of proposals	254	13	9	25	12	7	40	56	65	27
Average participation ratio (%)	27.0	26.7	27.8	16.9	37.7	33.8	27.8	33.1	24.1	22.4

Notes: This table describes the participation of mutual fund managers in shareholders meetings by the topic of the proposal and over time. The average participation ratio is the average ratio of proposals attended by the funds to the total proposals on each specific topic (quarter). The sample consists of 254 management-sponsored proposals in 64 of the largest (top 100) firms in Israel.

25% of the 254 management-sponsored proposals in the sample deal with compensation issues. An additional 17% of the proposals include insurance against personal lawsuits to managers and directors of the firm, and about 14% include the approval of related party transactions. A small part of the

Table 2. Distribution of Proposals by the Participation of Mutual Funds in Shareholders' Meetings in 64 of the 100 Largest Corporations in Israel during 1999–2001.

	N	Proportion of Funds that Voted from the Total Funds that had to Vote (X)			
		$X < 10\%$	$10\% < X$ $< 30\%$	$30\% < X$ $< 50\%$	$X > 50\%$
Number of proposals	254	58	83	87	26
(% of total)		(22.8%)	(32.7%)	(34.2%)	(10.2%)

Note: Distribution of 254 proposals in 64 of the largest 100 corporations in Israel during 1999–2001, by level of participation of mutual funds.

proposals seems quite natural by nature. These proposals include dividend distribution (5.5% of the proposals) and other regular proposals (13.4% of the proposals).

Defining the participation ratio to be the number of proposals attended to the total number of proposals, we find the participation ratio to vary across topic and time.[15] High participation is found in compensation issues (funds participate on average 39% of the meetings), and related party transactions (funds participate 35% of the meetings) and low participation is found in dividend (average participation ratio of about 7%) and regular proposals (average participation ratio of about 15%).[16] The distribution of proposals and participation ratio over time is presented in panel B. Although it shows an increase in number of reported proposals in the last year of the sample, there is no clear trend in the participation ratio over time (Table A2).

The distribution of the proposals by participation level is reported in Table 2. The average number of mutual funds that participate and vote any given proposal is 10.3, which accounts for about 25.5% of the funds that were required to attend. Moreover, in $\sim 33\%$ of the proposals, the number of funds attending is less than 30%, and only for 23 proposals (8.4% of all the proposals) did the number of funds participating in the meeting exceed the 50% level (more than 19 funds). These findings are consistent with previous findings of Hauser, Rosenberg, and Ofir (1999) as well as with the report of the ISA (see Table A2 in the appendix), which shows a low level of participation by mutual fund managers in shareholder meetings.

4.2. Participation of Mutual Funds in Shareholders meetings – Regression Analysis

We estimate the following logit model:

$$PARTICIPATE = \beta_0 + \beta_1 TOPIC + \beta_2 FUND + \beta_3 FIRM$$
$$+ \beta_4 MEETTYPE + \beta_5 TIME$$

where the dependent variable is a dummy variable equal to one when the fund participates in the meeting and zero otherwise. The independent variables include a set of variables designed to capture the effect of the topic of the proposal, fund specifics, and firm characteristics. We also include a dummy variable for the type of meeting (i.e., special or regular annual meeting) and time fixed effect. The total number of observation is 9,652.[17]

The estimation results presented in Table 3 suggest that mutual funds participate more frequently in special meetings where the odds of including a potential harmful proposal are greater than in regular (annual) meetings. Participation of funds also varies across the topic of the proposals. Consistent with the univariate findings we find high participation in compensation issues, approval of related party transactions, and approval of duality in the CEO-COB position, and low participation in "regular" proposals and dividend distribution. These findings support our first hypothesis of higher participation in potentially harmful proposals.

The estimated results presented in Table 3 also support the second hypothesis. Both the negative coefficient of the ODIR variable (i.e., proportion of outside directors) and the positive coefficient of the duality in the CEO-COB position [DUAL], suggests that the funds tend to participate less frequently in firms with a more independent board where there is less need for monitoring.[18]

4.3. Potential Business Relationships and Fund Participation

As participation and voting is public information, the funds are expected to be absent more frequently from meetings in firms with which they have business relations compared to firms with which they have no relations. This view suggests that the variation in participation of funds across firms is significantly greater than the variation of participation across different proposals in same firm. To test this hypothesis, we use an ANOVA test, and

Table 3. Logistic Regression on Participation of Mutual Funds in Shareholders' Meetings during 1999–2001.

Independent Variable	The Dependent Equals One when the Fund Participates in the Meeting and Zero Otherwise	
	(1)	(2)
CONSTANT	10.22^b (0.02)	1.10 (0.76)
MEETTYPE	0.41^a (<0.01)	0.39^a (<0.01)
FUNDBANK	1.42^b (0.02)	1.08^b (0.03)
FUNDSIZE	0.23^b (0.04)	0.31^a (0.01)
FUSTTOAST	0.18 (0.78)	0.13 (0.75)
FIRMSIZE	−0.84 (0.17)	0.73 (0.26)
ROA	7.08^b (0.02)	6.11^b (0.03)
STCKRT	0.12^c (0.10)	0.11 (0.11)
MRTBK	0.32^a (<0.01)	0.29^a (<0.01)
LEVERAGE	$−1.10^a$ (<0.01)	$−0.94^a$ (<0.01)
INHOLD	$−8.62^a$ (<0.01)	−2.54 (0.46)
BOARDSIZE	$−0.12^c$ (0.10)	−0.07 (0.27)
DUAL	1.41^b (0.02)	−0.10 (0.91)
OUTDIR	$−3.32^a$ (0.01)	−1.59 (0.27)
TOPIC*	+	−
Personal lawsuits insurance	2.03^a (<0.01)	
Change in firm charter	1.49^a (<0.01)	
Related party transactions	2.66^a (<0.01)	
Restructuring of options	0.92^a (<0.01)	
Compensation to shareholder	2.85^a (<0.01)	
Compensation to outside directors	1.01^a (<0.01)	
Duality	2.21^a (<0.01)	
"Regular" proposals	0.32^a (<0.01)	
Year	+	+
N	9,652	9,652
Pseudo R^2	0.413	0.351

Notes: The dependent variable is a dummy variable equal to one when the fund attended the meeting and zero otherwise. MEETTYPE equals to one for special meeting and zero otherwise. FUNDSIZE is the log of value of assets of the mutual fund. FUSTTOAST is the ratio of the mutual fund stock assets over its total value of assets. FIRMSIZE is the log of asset value of the firm. FUNDBANK is a dummy variable equal to one when the fund is managed by a bank and zero otherwise. ROA is the firm's return on assets. STCKRT is 1 year of firm stock return prior to the meeting. MRTBK is the ratio of firm's market value of equity plus book value of debt to book value of assets. LEVERAGE is the ratio of long-term debt to book value of equity. INHOLD is the proportion of firm equity held by insiders. BOARDSIZE is the number of directors. OUTDIR is the proportion of outside directors in the board. DUAL is a dummy variable equal to one when the CEO is also the chairman of the board and zero otherwise. In both models, we control for time fixed effect. *P*-values are in parentheses. Superscript letters a, b, c indicate statistical significance at the 1, 5, and 10% levels, respectively.
*The missing category is proposals to approve dividend distribution.

find the average variance of participation ratio between firms to be significantly higher than the average participation ratio within firm (*F*-statistic of 9.85). Based on this finding, we cannot reject the hypothesis that potential business relations do not affect fund participation.

Following Brickley et al. (1988), we divide the funds into banks and non-banks and categorize the former group as more sensitive to pressure by corporate management, since they potentially have more business relationships with the firm. We expect bank funds to take a more passive role in monitoring (i.e., to participate less).[19] The 38 fund managers in the sample by banks (9) and non-banks (29) are described in Table 4. It shows that, on average, a bank fund (average value of assets 1,184 million USD) is significantly larger than a non-bank fund (average value of assets 44.1 million

Table 4. Participation of Bank and Non-Bank Mutual Funds in Shareholders' Meetings in Israel during 1999–2001.

Independent Variable	All Mutual Funds	Non-Bank Mutual Funds	Bank Mutual Funds	Difference Non-Bank Versus Bank Funds
	(A)	(B)	(C)	B–C
Panel A: Descriptive of bank and non-bank mutual fund managers				
Average value of fund assets in millions USD (standard deviation)	353.7 (53.8)	48.2 (32.7)	1,184.6 (908.4)	−1,290[a]
Average proportion of fund assets held in stocks (standard deviation)	40.3% (29.6%)	47.9% (39.3%)	19.5% (8.7%)	32.1[a]
Number of mutual fund managers	38	29	9	
Panel B: Participation of banks and non-banks fund managers				
Average participation ratio (standard deviation)	27.0% (44.4%)	22.8% (42.0%)	40.2% (49.0%)	−17.4%[a]
Number of observations	9,652	7,366	2,286	

Notes: Panel A provides some descriptive statistics of mutual fund managers in Israel by bank and non-bank fund managers. Panel B describes the participation of mutual fund managers by bank and non-bank managers. Super script letter 'a' indicates statistical significance at the 1% level.

Table 5. Logistic Regression on Participation of Mutual Funds in
Shareholders' Meetings during 1999–2001.

Independent Variable	Non-Bank Mutual Funds	Bank Mutual Funds
CONSTANT	3.49 (0.42)	2.98 (0.71)
MEETTYPE	0.37[a] (<0.01)	0.46[b] (0.02)
FUNDSIZE	0.28[b] (0.02)	0.19 (0.70)
FUSTTOAST	0.52 (0.28)	−1.55 (0.32)
FIRMSIZE	−0.90 (0.27)	−1.27 (0.37)
ROA	8.18[b] (0.02)	14.33[b] (0.04)
MRTBK	0.09 (0.42)	0.23 (0.23)
BANKLEV	0.06 (0.13)	−0.08[a] (<0.01)
STCKRT	0.20[b] (0.03)	0.28[c] (0.10)
INHOLD	−8.39[b] (0.05)	−3.51 (0.60)
BOARDSIZE	−0.17[b] (0.02)	−0.10 (0.41)
OUTDIR	−0.45 (0.79)	−5.61[b] (0.04)
DUAL	−1.76 (0.11)	2.00 (0.28)
PROPOSAL_TOPIC*	+	+
Personal lawsuits insurance	2.31[a] (<0.01)	2.29[a] (<0.01)
Change in firm charter	1.31[a] (<0.01)	1.95[a] (<0.01)
Related party transactions	2.64[a] (<0.01)	2.74[a] (<0.01)
Restructuring of options	1.71[a] (<0.01)	1.67[a] (0.01)
Compensation to insiders	2.85[a] (<0.01)	2.61[a] (<0.01)
Compensation to outsiders	1.51[a] (<0.01)	0.14 (0.29)
Duality	0.96[a] (<0.01)	−0.14 (0.70)
"Regular" proposals	2.43[a] (<0.01)	2.72[a] (<0.01)
Year	+	+
N	7,366	2,286
Pseudo R^2	0.394	0.449

Notes: The dependent variable is a dummy variable equal to one when the fund participates the meeting and zero otherwise. MEETTYPE equals one for special meeting and zero otherwise. FUNDSIZE is the log of asset value of the mutual fund. FUSTTOAST is the ratio of the mutual fund stock assets over its total value of assets. FIRMSIZE is the log of asset value of the firm. ROA is the firm return on assets. STCKRT is the 1-year firm stock return prior to the meeting. MRTBK is the ratio of firm market value of equity plus book value of debt to book value of assets. BANKLEV is the ratio of book value of firm's total liabilities to banks to book value of equity. INHOLD is the proportion of firm equity held by insiders. BOARDSIZE is the number of directors. OUTDIR is the proportion of outside directors in the board. DUAL is a dummy variable equal to one when the CEO is also the chairman of the board and zero otherwise. In all estimations we control for time-fixed effect. *P*-values are in parentheses. Super script letters a, b, c indicate statistical significance at the 1, 5, and 10% levels, respectively.
*The missing category is proposals to approve dividend distribution.

USD), and has significantly less of their assets in stocks compared to non-bank funds. Information about the participation of bank and non-bank funds is also provided in Table 4. The average participation of bank funds (40.2% of the meetings) is found to be significantly higher than the average participation of non-bank funds (22.8% of the meetings).

Both the univariate findings presented in Table 4 and the positive significant coefficient of the FUNDBANK dummy variable in the estimation results presented in Table 3, suggest that mutual funds managed by commercial banks participate more frequently in shareholder meetings than non-bank funds. These findings are inconsistent with Brickley et al.'s findings and with our hypothesis. A possible explanation of the inconsistency with the classification of Brickley et al. is the differences between the Israeli capital market and the US regarding the market power of banks. Israeli banks are hardly pressure sensitive. The banking industry is concentrated in the hands of large banks that are active in all aspects of the capital market including investment banking, commercial banking, brokerage, as well as individual banking.[20] In the next section we further analyze the factors that affect the participation of bank and non-bank fund managers separately.

In Table 5 we divide the sample of funds into bank and non-bank funds and estimate for each group a logit model where the dependent variable equals one if the fund attended the meeting and zero otherwise. Comparing the participation of bank and non-bank fund managers we find that all funds tend to participate more frequently in special meetings taking place in firms with relatively good past performances. The estimation results presented in Table 5 also show that both bank and non-bank mutual funds tend to participate more frequently in meetings with potentially harmful proposals, such as related party transactions and compensation, than in meetings without such proposals. Consistent with our hypothesis, the negative significant coefficient of the BANKLEV coefficient in the second estimation shows that bank mutual funds participate less in firms with higher bank debt, suggesting that bank funds tend to participate less in meetings taking place in firms with which they have more business relations than in firms with less business relations.

5. CONCLUSIONS

Since 1994, Israeli law obligates mutual fund managers to attend shareholder meetings in which a significant proposal, one that has the potential to affect the wealth of fund beneficiaries, is raised. This obligation is monitored by the Israeli Security Authority, and reports of attendance rates are published yearly. This study explores the extent to which mutual funds attend shareholder meetings and the factors that affect this decision.

This paper analyzes the participation of Israeli mutual funds in 254 management-sponsored proposals. Inconsistent with the duty of care, we find that only 27% of the mutual fund managers who are expected to attend a meeting actually do so. However, we do find that the probability of attending a meeting is significantly related to the topic of the proposal and the strength of corporate governance in the firm. Specifically, we find a higher tendency for mutual fund managers to participate in potentially harmful proposals such as related party transactions and compensation issues, rather than in other proposals, and that the odds of participation decrease with board independence. Consistent with agency theory, the evidence presented in this paper further suggests that the participation of mutual funds managed by commercial banks is negatively related to corporate bank debt level.

The evidence presented in this paper suggests that even in the presence of a legal obligation, a large part of outstanding shares are not voted upon, as institutional investors are absent from the majority of shareholder meetings. These conditions increase the ability of the firm's controlling owners to expropriate the rights of minority shareholders and affect the efficiency of the capital market. Surprisingly, despite the very low attendance rate, not even a single lawsuit has been filed to date against a mutual fund manager that failed to meet his legal obligation.

NOTES

1. As a long-term player, the institutional investor might help management improve long-term performance (Gillan & Starks, 2000). Jarrell and Poulsen (1987) argue that sophisticated, well-informed shareholders, such as institutions, are likely to vote more consistently in accordance with their economic interests than less-informed shareholders. On the other hand, others such as Black (1997) and Romano (1993) argue that the institutional investor lacks the expertise to properly evaluate management decisions. Further arguments are that an institutional investor may be subject to internal agency problems (Scism, 1993), pressure from the firm's management (Hwang, Nachtmann, & Rosenfeld, 1997), and even political and public pressure (Smith, 1996).

2. See, for example, Smith (1996) which analyses the negotiations of pension funds and management. Others, such as Del Guercio and Hawkins (1999) and Wahal (1996), analyze more confrontational forms of activism such as raising proposals in

annual meetings. Black (1997) and Karpoff (1996) provide surveys of evidence and conclude that institutional investors have little effect on firm performance.

3. For a complete analysis of voting decisions of mutual funds in Israel, see Amzaleg, Ben-Zion, and Rosenfeld (2005). For recent evidence on voting decisions of the 10 largest mutual funds in the US, see Davis and Kim (2005) and Rothberg and Lilien (2005).

4. For a discussion and modeling see: Admati, Pfleiderer, and Zechner (1994) and Pozen (1994).

5. See, for example, Gordon, Henry, and Palia (2004).

6. See, for example, Amzaleg and Mehrez (2004).

7. About 95% of all public firms in Israel have a controlling shareholder. In these conditions, most of the management-sponsored proposals have the necessary majority votes. Section 275(a) of firm law determines any special majority needed in order to approve potentially harmful proposals (i.e., related party transactions). The special rule requires at least one-third of all outside votes (e.g., pension funds, mutual funds, insurance companies) to vote in favor of the proposal.

8. Moreover, if other outside shareholders follow the same rationale, the institutional investor can increase both the actual and the advisory effect of voting on management decisions.

9. Davis and Kim (2005) and Amzaleg et al. (2005) find evidence that mutual fund managers use their voting rights to promote current (or potential) business relationships with the management of the firm, at the expense of their beneficiaries. See also Ingley and Van-Der Walt (2004).

10. The Israeli market consists of about 600 mutual funds, managed by about 40 mutual fund managers. Although we analyze the voting by fund managers, we use the term "fund" for the sake of simplicity.

11. PREDICTA and TAKLIT-HON are databases managed by commercial firms that collect all public information on all Israeli mutual funds and firms.

12. We have complete data of holdings by three fund managers: Lahak, Piya, and Analyst. On average, they hold shares in over 90% of the 100 largest firms (and similar percentages in the top 100 firms in the sample). Although they cannot be considered representative of all mutual fund managers in terms of size and level of involvement in the capital market, this gives us some idea about mutual fund managers' holdings in the top 100 firms. Another fact that supports our assumption is that all the fund managers have at least one mutual fund that specializes in the equity market. Due to diversification needs and the low trading in stocks of small firms, the assumption that they all had some level of holdings in the 100 largest firms in the Israeli market seems to be reasonable. For the frequency of meeting and proposals by firms, see table A1.

13. We do not find any significant differences between the distribution of proposals in the initial sample and final reduced sample across topic and time (not reported).

14. Note that we only consider significant proposals in which more than two other fund managers reported their attendance at the meeting to the ISA. The sample period was primarily dictated by data availability. Mutual Investment Law was enacted in 1994. Section 77 was issued in 1994 and was reasonably enforced only a few years later. In those years, the reports were issued on hard copy and destroyed after about a year. The sample period includes the earliest data available.

15. Using one-way ANOVA, we estimate an F-statistic of 63.1 which is statistically significant at the 1% level. Employing a similar test to analyze participation over time, we find that the average variation in participation ratio between quarters is significantly higher than the average variation in participation ratio within quarters. The F-statistic for this test is 18.2.

16. The definition of the proposals as regular is a self-definition. These proposals include, for example, approving the firm's annual report and renewing the contract with the accounting firm.

17. The sample includes 38 mutual fund mangers. Each one had to vote in all 254 proposals.

18. For further discussion on board effectiveness as a controlling mechanism see: Hallock (1997) and Hermalin and Weisbach (1991).

19. Brickley et al. (1988) consider mutual funds as a group to be non-sensitive. However, even Brickley et al. (1988) acknowledge that: "Individual institutions within a category are likely to have different ties with the management."

20. The capital market in Israel is highly concentrated with massive involvement of banks in all aspects. The two largest banks in Israel actually control a large portion of the mutual funds industry and other aspects of the capital market. There is an ongoing debate in Israel about the reduction of involvement of banks in the capital market. A national committee was formed exactly for that purpose and its main recommendation (2004) is to separate banks' activities from mutual investment, obligating banks to sell their mutual funds.

REFERENCES

Admati, A., Pfleiderer, P., & Zechner, J. (1994). Large shareholders activism, risk sharing, and financial market equilibrium. *Journal of Political Economy, 102,* 1097–1130.

Amzaleg, Y., Ben-Zion, U., & Rosenfeld, A. (2005). *On the role of institutional investors in corporate governance evidence from voting of mutual funds in Israel.* Working paper. Ben-Gurion University of the Negev.

Amzaleg, Y., & Mehrez, A. (2004). The "One Million Club": Executive compensation and firm performance. *The Israeli Economic Review, 2,* 107–147.

Black, B. S. (1997). *Shareholders activism and corporate governance in the United States.* Working paper. Columbia University.

Brickley, J., Lease, R. C., & Smith, J. R. (1988). Ownership structure and voting on anti-takeover amendments. *Journal of Financial Economics, 20,* 267–291.

Davis, G. F., & Kim, H. (2005). *Would mutual funds bite the hand that feeds them? Business ties and proxy voting.* Working paper. University of Michigan.

Del Guercio, D., & Hawkins, J. (1999). The motivation and impact of pension fund activism. *Journal of Financial Economics, 52,* 293–340.

Gillan, S. L., & Starks, L. T. (2000). Corporate governance decisions and shareholders activism: The role of institutional investors. *Journal of Financial Economics, 57,* 275–305.

Gordon, E. A., Henry, E., & Palia, D. (2004). *Related party transactions: Association with corporate governance and firm value.* Working paper. Rutgers Business School.

Hallock, K. (1997). Reciprocally interlocking board of directors and executive compensation. *Journal of Financial and Quantitative Analysis, 32*(3), 331–344.

Hauser, S., Rosenberg, J., & Ofir, S. (1999). *Testing the benefits of imposing the participation of mutual funds in shareholder meetings.* ISA publication (Hebrew).

Hermalin, B. E., & Weisbach, M. S. (1991). The effects of board compensation and direct incentives on firm performance. *Financial Management, 20*(4), 101–112.

Hwang, C.-Y., Nachtmann, R., & Rosenfeld, A. (1997). Ownership and acquiring firm performance. *Advances in Financial Economics, 3,* 187–209.

Ingley, C., & Van-Der Walt, N. T. (2004). Corporate governance, institutional investors and conflicts of interest. *Corporate Governance: An International Review, 12*(4), 534–551.

Jarrell, G., & Poulsen, A. (1987). Shark repellents and stock price: The effect of antitakeover amendments since 1980. *Journal of Financial Economics, 19,* 127–168.

Karpoff, J. (1996). *The impact of shareholders activism on target companies: A survey of empirical findings.* Working Paper. University of Washington.

Maug, E., & Rydqvist, K. (2004). *Do shareholders vote strategically? Evidence on the advisory role of annual general meetings.* Working paper. Humboldt University of Berlin.

Pozen, C. R. (1994). Institutional investors: The reluctant activists. *Harvard Business Review* (Jan./Feb.), *72*(1), 140–149.

Romano, R. C. (1993). Public pension fund activism in corporate governance reconsidered. *Columbia Law Review, 93,* 795–853.

Rothberg, B., & Lilien, S. (2005). *Mutual funds and proxy voting: New evidence on corporate governance.* Working paper. Zicklin School of Business.

Scism, L. (1993). Relationship investing shows strains. *Wall Street Journal* (November 26), C1, C5.

Smith, M. (1996). Shareholders activism by institutional investors: Evidence from CalPERS. *Journal of Finance, 51,* 257–262.

Wahal, S. (1996). Pension funds activism and firm performance. *Journal of Financial and Quantitative Analysis, 31,* 1–23.

APPENDIX

Table A1.   Frequency of Meetings and Proposals by Firms during
1999–2001.

Number of Proposals/ Meeting over the Entire Sample Period	Number of Companies Receiving this (First Column) Many Proposals	Total Number of Proposals
1	13	13
2	9	18
3	13	39
4	9	36
5	6	30
6	4	24
7	2	14
8–10	5	43
>11	3	37
Total	64	254

Note: This is a distribution of the 254 proposals, with over 64 firms included in our sample of top 100 firms in Israel during 1999–2001.

Table A2.   Distribution of Meetings by Participation of Mutual Fund
Managers.

Year	Total Number of Meetings	Less than 30% of the Managers	Between 30 and 70% of the Managers	More than 70% of the Managers
1998	296	44 (15%)	154 (52%)	98 (33%)
1999	291	30 (10%)	142 (49%)	119 (41%)
2000	435	49 (11%)	206 (47%)	180 (42%)
2001	330	16 (5%)	141 (43%)	173 (52%)

Note: This table describes the distribution of all shareholder meetings in any given year by the level of participation of mutual fund managers.
Source: ISA annual report of 2001. The report is available on the ISA Website at the: www.isa.gov.il

GOOD MANAGERS INVEST MORE AND PAY LESS DIVIDENDS: A MODEL OF DIVIDEND POLICY

Nalinaksha Bhattacharyya

ABSTRACT

This model explains dividends as a component of a contract set up by an uninformed principal. I start from a well-documented empirical fact that there is a relation between dividends declared and executive compensation. I find that when hidden information is about the productivity of the agent then dividend – conditional on cash available – bears a negative relationship to managerial type. That is, for a given level of available cash, the lower type manager declares a higher dividend than that declared by a manager with higher productivity. The result is robust under different model extensions. I also discuss empirical implications of the model.

1. INTRODUCTION

Explaining dividend policy has been one of the most-difficult challenges facing financial economists. Despite decades of study, we have yet to completely understand the factors that influence dividend policy and the

Issues in Corporate Governance and Finance
Advances in Financial Economics, Volume 12, 91–117
ISSN: 1569-3732/doi:10.1016/S1569-3732(07)12005-3

manner in which these factors interact. Three decades ago, Black (1976) wrote, "The harder we look at the dividend picture, the more it seems like a puzzle, with pieces that just don't fit together" (p. 5). The situation is pretty much the same today. In a survey of dividend policy, Allen and Michaely (1995) conclude that "[m]uch more empirical and theoretical research on the subject of dividends is required before a consensus can be reached" (p. 833). The fact that a major textbook such as Brealey and Myers (2002) lists dividends as one of the ten important unsolved problems in finance reinforces this conclusion.

The seminal paper of Miller and Modigliani (1961) establishes that in a perfect capital market, given an investment policy, dividends are irrelevant in determining share value. Empirically, however, we have observed that a change in dividend policy does have a significant impact on the share price. Different researchers have concentrated on different types of imperfections in the market in order to understand the role of dividends. The two types of market imperfections that have been investigated are differential taxes on dividends and capital gains, and asymmetric information.

Considerations of differential taxes on dividends and capital gains have led to the clientele theory of dividend policy. The clientele theory says that shareholders face different tax rates with respect to dividends and capital gains. Shareholders sort themselves into clientele groups based on the established dividend policies of firms in such a manner that the individual shareholder has the optimum or near optimum dividend income for his/her marginal tax rates. Recently Allen, Bernardo, and Welch (2000) have advanced a theory based on the clientele paradigm to explain why some firms pay dividends and others repurchase shares.

Consideration of the second type of market imperfection, asymmetric information, has led to two classes of theories: signaling theories and the free cash flow hypothesis. Signaling theories (see for example Heinkel, 1978; Bhattacharyya, 1979; Miller & Rock, 1985; Williams, 1988; John & Williams, 1985; Bernheim, 1991) posit dividend policy as a vehicle used by managers/insiders to transmit private information to the market. The free cash flow hypothesis (see for example Jensen, 1986 and Easterbrook, 1984), on the other hand, postulates that dividends are used to take away excess cash from mangers and put it in the hands of shareholders.

The empirical evidence on the three current paradigms of dividend policy are mixed, as can be seen in Table 1. Dividend policy thus continues to remain a puzzle and the search for an answer to this puzzle continues. In this paper, I try to provide a tentative partial answer by developing an alternative theory of dividend policy.

Table 1. Findings of Empirical Research vis-a-vis the Three Current Hypotheses of Dividend Policy.

Research	Dividend Clientele Hypothesis		Signalling Hypothesis		Agency Hypothesis	
	Do not reject	Reject	Do not reject	Reject	Do not reject	Reject
Aharony and Swary (1980)			✔			
Bernheim and Wantz (1995)			✔			✔
Black and Scholes (1974)		✔				
Chaplinsky and Seyhun (1990)	✔					
Chen, Grundy, and Stambaugh (1990)		✔				
Christie (1994)				✔		✔
Denis et al. (1994)	✔		✔			✔
Dhillon and Johnson (1994)					✔	
Downes et al. (1982)				✔		
Kao and Wu (1994)			✔			
Lakonishok and Vermaelen (1986)	✔					
Lang and Litzenberger (1989)				✔	✔	
Lewellen et al. (1978)		✔				
Litzenberger and Ramaswamy (1982)	✔					
Long et al. (1994)						✔
Manuel et al. (1993)			✔			
Michaely (1991)		✔				
Penman (1983)			✔			
Poterba (1986)		✔	✔			
Sant and Cowan (1994)			✔			
Smith and Watts (1992)					✔	
Yoon and Starks (1995)						✔

The basis of my theory lies in the empirical observation of a link between dividends and executive compensations (Ferreira White, 1996; Healy, 1985; Lewellen, Loderer, & Martin, 1987; Lambert, Lanen, & Larcker, 1989) and between executive compensation and accounting earnings (Healy, 1985; Pavlik, Scott, & Tiessen, 1993). I model the link between dividends, outputs, and compensations identified in the empirical studies cited above and try to understand the impact of such linkages on the dividend policies followed by firms. If the compensation contract is a monotonically increasing function of dividends alone, then the rational action for the manager is to have a 100% dividend payout ratio. Having both dividends and outputs as components of compensation contracts ensure that managers try to achieve a proper balance between dividend payments and investments.

When managers are of different productive qualities (which are privately known to managers but are essentially unobservable attributes), then, in equilibrium, compensation contracts will be set up in a way such that managers with the lowest level of acceptable quality will be paid the reservation wage ex ante and managers of higher quality will be paid information rent ex ante. The amount of rent will depend, inter alia, on the probability distribution of managerial quality. In equilibrium, the optimal compensation contract will be such that, ceteris paribus (and in particular for a given amount of available cash), managers of highest quality get the most rent and invest the most in productive projects, while managers with least-acceptable productive quality will get just the reservation wage and will invest the least.

It therefore follows that compensation contracts will ensure that, for a given amount of available cash, managers with higher quality will get more information rents (i.e., more compensation), will invest more in productive enterprises and, as a result, will have less money to distribute as dividends. Similarly, managers with lowest acceptable quality will get the participation wage and invest less, thereby leaving more cash for distribution as dividends. Therefore, for a given level of available cash, the manager with lower level of acceptable productivity declares a higher dividend than that declared by a manager with higher productivity.

In this paper, I explain dividend policy by using the asymmetric information paradigm. However, unlike the signaling models (where the informed manager/insider uses the dividend as a signaling device), I posit dividend policy as a component of a screening contract set up by an uninformed principal. In the game-theoretic classification of information games, my model is a screening game, i.e., a game where the uninformed party moves first; in contrast, signaling models are games where the informed party moves first.

Some empirical implications of this model are quite different from the implications of signaling models and implications of the free cash flow hypothesis. Under the signaling theories, higher firm value is signaled by higher dividends. Therefore, under the signaling paradigm, dividend increases should result in positive abnormal returns on the announcement of dividends. The free cash flow conjecture (Easterbrook, 1984; Jensen, 1986) posits that higher dividends are better because higher dividends remove free cash from hands of managers; consequently, managers have less money to waste. According to this conjecture, announcement of higher dividends would also lead to higher abnormal returns. Thus under both signaling theories and free cash flow conjecture, dividend increases are positively related to the abnormal announcement returns. By contrast, my theory says that higher dividends, *conditioned on cash available*, is an indication of lower agent type. Therefore, according to my theory, announcement of higher dividends should result in negative abnormal returns once we condition for the level of available cash. Another empirical implication for my theory is that dividends, conditioned on cash available, should be negatively related to managerial compensation.

The paper is organized as follows. Section 2 motivates the paper by discussing the need to understand the linkages between dividends and executive compensations. Section 3 develops the model. Section 4 discusses extensions of the model. Section 5 deals with empirical implications of the model. Section 6 discusses some relevant issues and Section 7 concludes. All proofs are given in the Appendix.

2. MOTIVATION – DIVIDENDS AND EXECUTIVE COMPENSATION

Empirically, it has been well established that for large publicly traded firms, executive compensation is influenced by dividends, either directly, or indirectly through the linkage of dividends to stock price. Ferreira White (1996) examined the compensation contracts of 62 large companies in oil and gas, food processing, and defence/aerospace industries. Twenty-eight of these had a dividend provision. Pavlik et al. (1993) report that in 1991, base salary was 33% of executive compensation, while stock options, restricted stock, and performance shares were 36%. These components are affected by dividend decisions.

We also have evidence that short-term compensation is linked to dividends. Healy (1985) mentions that often the upper limit on the amounts to be transferred to a bonus pool is related to cash dividend payment on common stock. Consistent with Healy's work, Lewellen et al. (1987) find a statistically significant positive relationship between the short-term component of executive compensation (i.e., salary and bonus) and dividends. They write "[t]he findings further support the notion that firms seek to prevent tendencies toward over-retention of earnings by linking salary and current bonus payments to dividend payouts" (p. 301).

The other important determinant of executive compensation is accounting earnings (Pavlik et al., 1993; Healy, 1985). For example, Healy (1985) finds that "[b]onus contracts have a similar format to performance contracts

except that they specify annual rather than long-term earnings goals"
(p. 87). Pavlik et al. (1993) state that "[a]ccounting and stock returns are the
performance measures that have been consistently associated with changes
in compensation"(p. 155).

The linkage of executive compensation to dividends, accounting earnings,
and stock prices needs to be understood. Executive compensation is
typically determined by solution to agency issues. To quote Jensen and
Murphy (1990)

> The conflict of interest between shareholders of a publicly owned corporation and the
> corporation's chief executive officer (CEO) is a classic example of a principal agent
> problem. If shareholders had complete information regarding the CEO's activities and
> the firm's investment opportunities, they could design a contract specifying and
> enforcing the managerial action to be taken in each state of the world. Managerial
> actions and investment opportunities are not, however, perfectly observable by the
> shareholders; indeed, shareholders do not often know what actions the CEO *can* take or
> which of these actions will increase shareholder wealth. In these situations, agency
> theory predicts that compensation policy will be designed to give the manager incentives
> to select and implement actions that increase shareholder wealth. (pp. 225–226 –
> emphasis in original)

In this paper, I apply the principal-agent paradigm to understand the role of
dividends as a control device. Given a particular level of cash, shareholders
will want this to be apportioned between dividends and further investment
in the activity of the firm. However, the actual apportionment of this cash
into investment and dividends is decided by the manager. The productivity
of the manager (the "type" of manager) is private knowledge. We
investigate dividend/investment in this setting using the principal-agent
paradigm. Two papers most cited by empirical researches on dividend policy
in an agency paradigm are by Easterbrook (1984) and by Jensen (1986).
Neither of these papers formally models the agency relation. This paper will
contribute to explanations of dividend policy by rigorously modeling the
dividend decision in an agency theoretic setting.

3. THE MODEL

I start with a simple model and see what insights are offered by this simple
model. Later, I extend my model to see if these insights remain valid under
more complicated scenarios. My basic model contains one principal
and one agent; both are risk-neutral. The risk-neutrality of the principal
is representative of shareholders who hold well-diversified portfolios.

The assumption of agent risk neutrality does not permit the first best solution because (as we shall see later) the model involves pre-contract private information. Furthermore, the principal owns an investible resource C. C can be conceptualized as cash available which can either be invested or which can be paid out as dividends.[1]

There are two factors of production: skill and investment. The agent supplies the first of these factors of production – namely skill and decides on the level of investment, the second factor. The agent has a skill which is necessary to make the asset productive. This skill is represented by a parameter θ. For our purpose, we assume that it can only have two values, L(ow) and H(igh) and $\theta_H > \theta_L$. We should emphasize here that demand exists for both the types. Before entering into the contract, the agent knows his/her level of skill, although he/she cannot alter it; the principal, however, is not aware of the agent's skill level. Later I extend the model by allowing skill to follow a continuous distribution.

The agent also selects I, the amount to be invested. We assume that the parameter values are such that $I \leq C$. The excess of C over I is paid off as a dividend D. That is $D = C-I$. Subscripts H and L are used to indicate the choice for a particular type.

Note that this budget constraint (namely, that the sum of dividend and amount actually invested is equal to C) implicitly assumes that the agent cannot lend or borrow in the capital market. In our model, compensation is a function of dividends and output. We want to understand how such a compensation function impacts on dividends when different agents have different productivity. The realized production $\tilde{Y}$ is observed by both principal and agent. The production function is given by $\tilde{Y} = \theta \ln(I) + \tilde{\varepsilon}$ where $\tilde{\varepsilon}$ is random noise with zero mean. In this basic model, we assume that the compensation contract offered to the agent is linear and is of the form $\tilde{\omega}_j = \beta_0(\hat{j}) + \beta_D(\hat{j})D_j + \beta_Y(\hat{j})\tilde{Y}$ where $\hat{j}$ is the type reported by the agent. Later in my generalized model, I assume a generalized compensation function. The sequence of the foregoing events is shown in Table 2.

In all my subsequent analyses I also assume that the efficient investment choices are interior solutions for the appropriate optimization problems. I do this because I want to model dividend policy and specifically I am trying to understand the impact of executive compensation on dividends. If the efficient investment choices are corner solutions then there are two possible investment choices – either the agent will invest all the amounts available and pay no dividends (i.e. set $I = C$ which necessarily means $D = 0$ in our case) or invest nothing and pay all available cash out as dividends (i.e. set $I = 0$ which by construction implies $D = C$). We want to understand

Table 2.   The Sequence of Events. *C* is the Initial Cash Endowment and
D is the Dividend Declared.

1	2	3	4	5
C is observed by all. Agent privately observes his/her own type.	Principal offers a menu of wage contracts	Agent declares his/her type and selects from menu	Agent declares *D*, and invests the balance of *C* over *D*	The final output is realised and observed by all. Principal receives the payoff and agent receives the wage.

dividend policy and these two corner cases do not increase our understanding and do not lead to any testable predictions.

Proposition 1. No pooling contract exists in equilibrium.

Proof. See Appendix.

The implication of Proposition 1 is that the equilibrium contact must be separating. Therefore by observing dividends declared it must be possible to infer about the types of agents. It should be reiterated again that this is a single period model and revelation of agent type cannot lead to any further action by the principal. In other words , the principal, on observing the dividend decision, will learn about the type of the agent but cannot terminate the contract. Also, as I have said earlier, demand exists for both types of agents.

Proposition 2. The H-type agent will declare a smaller dividend than the L-type agent.

Proof. See Appendix.

The result is intuitive. Cash is available for apportionment into investment and dividend. Shareholders want agents with higher productivity to invest more than that by agents with lower productivity. They achieve such an end by offering two separating contracts. An agent with lower productivity picks the contract with higher weight on dividends and declares a higher dividend. An agent with higher productivity, on the other hand, picks the efficient contract and invests more in the production process. As a result, an agent with higher productivity declares a smaller dividend than that declared by an agent with lower productivity.

4. ROBUSTNESS CHECK-EXTENSIONS
OF THE MODEL

In my model, I have assumed that managerial effort is not a factor in the production of output. I have further assumed that there are two types of agents – a L-type and a H-type. In order to examine the robustness of the model, I have extended the model to include privately costly managerial effort in the production function and I also allow managerial type to be distributed continuously. In addition I also generalize the model by using a generalized production function, a generalized cost of effort function, and a general managerial compensation function (as opposed to the linear compensation function used in the basic model).

In the extension of the model, where in addition to having the necessary skill, the agent also needs to exert effort in order to make the asset productive, the effort exerted by the agent (represented by e) is not observable by the principal. The agent chooses the level of effort supplied and incurs a private cost of effort. The cost of effort is represented by $1/2\ Me^2$ where M is a positive number. The production function is given by $\tilde{Y} = \theta e \ln(I) + \tilde{\varepsilon}$ where $\tilde{\varepsilon}$ is random noise with zero mean.

In the extension, where I generalize the model, I use generalized forms for production function, cost of effort function, and managerial compensation function. I also allow the managerial type to be distributed continuously. I had to impose some restrictions on the functional properties in order to have a tractable model. The detailed analysis for these two extensions are not included here for reasons of brevity. They are available from the author.

These extensions show that my results in Propositions 1 and 2 are generally valid. In other words, conditioned on cash available the dividends declared are negatively related to managerial type.

5. EMPIRICAL IMPLICATION

I find that, for a given level of cash availability, a manager with lower productivity declares a higher dividend than that declared by a manager with higher productivity. The intuition is that given a particular level of cash, the manager with higher productivity would be induced to invest more than the manager with lower productivity. As a result, the manager with lower productivity will disburse more cash as dividends compared to the manager with higher productivity.

I have developed my model of dividend policy by positing dividends as devices to discriminate between agents of different productivity. Productivity of an agent is an unobservable variable. However, for a given level of cash available, the uninformed principal learns about managerial productivity from the dividend decision. Since dividend level is publicly observable, and level of cash available is also known to a large degree of confidence (through the use of publicly available, audited financial statements), the market would also be able to deduce the productivity of managers by observing dividend decisions. Therefore, market prices would react to dividends.

I would expect that a rational market would observe the dividend decision and infer that a higher level of dividend, *conditioned on cash available*, is an indicator of lower managerial type. I would therefore expect that, *conditioned on cash available* the abnormal return on dividend announcement would be *negatively related* to the level of dividend. Therefore the empirical implication of my theory is that the abnormal stock return on dividend announcement for a stock should be negatively related to the fraction of available cash paid out as dividends. It would be useful here to highlight the differences between the empirical implications of my theory and the empirical implications of the signaling theories of dividend (e.g. Heinkel, 1978; Bhattacharyya, 1979; Miller & Rock, 1985; John & Williams, 1985; Ambarish, John, & Williams, 1987) as well as the hypotheses based on free cash flow paradigm as enunciated in Easterbrook (1984) and Jensen (1986).

Under the signaling theories, higher firm value is signaled by higher dividends. Therefore, under the signaling paradigm, dividend increases should result in higher abnormal return on dividend announcements. My theory opposingly states that, *conditioned on cash available*, higher dividend is an indication of lower agent type and should result in lower abnormal return on dividend announcement.

Free cash flow conjectures of Easterbrook (1984) and Jensen (1986) posit that higher dividends are better, because higher dividends remove free cash from the hands of managers, and managers then have less money to waste. Also according to these conjectures, the announcement of higher dividends would lead to higher abnormal returns on dividend announcement. In contrast, my theory suggests that higher dividends, *conditioned on cash available*, result in lower abnormal returns on dividend announcement. However, I should point out that my concept of free cash flow is different from the way Easterbrook and Jensen used it. Jensen considers free cash flow to be the cash remaining with managers after all the positive NPV opportunities have been exhausted. In my model C is the cash available *before* the investment decision.

There is another empirical implication for my theory. According to my theory managers with lower productivity maintain higher ratio of dividends paid to available cash compared to managers with higher productivity. Also, according to my theory, managers of higher quality will earn higher total compensation. In the light of my model, I therefore expect to see a negative association between the fraction of available cash paid as dividends and managerial compensation.

Testing the model empirically will be the subject of future research. However I would like to note that results from some earlier research are consistent with the empirical implication of this paper (e.g. Cole, 1980; Downes & Heinkel, 1982; Divecha & Morse, 1983; Bajaj, 1988; Johnson, 1995).

6. DISCUSSIONS

I have used principal-agent paradigm to explain dividends, and I find that, when productivity of agents are private information, then dividends *conditioned on cash available* are negatively related to managerial productivity. That is, for a given level of available cash, a lower type manager declares a higher dividend than that declared by a higher type manager. This is intuitive, because a higher type manager has higher productivity, and, therefore, it makes sense to induce the higher type manager to make higher investment and thus pay less dividends. Signaling models, like Miller and Rock (1985) and Heinkel (1978), have underinvestment as a cost, and the higher type manager underinvests. In contrast, in my model the higher type manager achieves the first best investment level and the lower type manager underinvests so as to limit the information rent paid to the higher type manager.

In discussing empirical implications for my model, I have implicitly assumed that the market does not observe the selection of the contract by the agent. There are two reasons for this. Firstly, executive compensation data is typically obtained from the proxy statements and the annual reports and these statements give the compensation data for the past year and *not for the coming year*. Secondly, the contract is often implicit. Consider the following quotation from Murphy (1999).

An executive's wealth is *explicitly* (and mechanically) tied to the principal's objective (creating shareholder wealth) through his holdings of stock, restricted stock, and stock

options. In addition, CEO wealth is *implicitly* tied to stock-price performance through
accounting-based bonuses (reflecting the correlation between accounting returns and
stock-price performance) and through year-to-year adjustments in salary levels, target
bonuses, and option and restricted stock grant sizes. (p. 2522 – emphasis in original)

Other researchers have also made the assumption that the information on
compensation contract is private and not available to the market. For
example Persons (1994) assumes that "the compensation contract is the
private information of the manager and the board" (pp. 426–427). Persons
also writes the following as an elucidation.

Within the model, the assumptions of private contracting and lack of commitment may
seem strained – why not just make the contract public and require large penalties if the
contract is changed? In reality, there are several factors that, in my view, make these
assumptions reasonable. They include competitive considerations, nonpecuniary and
unobservable compensation, the limited length of employment contracts, and the
complexity of the environment in which firms operate. First, a manager's compensation
plan may reflect strategic considerations; considerations the firm does not want its
competitors to know. This argues against a public contract. Second, one should view a
manager's compensation broadly. In addition to a periodic pay-check, compensation can
be nonpecuniary (plush office, corporate jet, directing corporate donations as the
manager desires) and even unobservable (autonomy, cooperativeness from the board).
(p. 437)

7. CONCLUSION

In this paper, I have developed a theory to explain dividends. I use the
empirical finding that there is a relationship between executive compensation and dividends to model managerial compensation as a function of
dividends and output. In the paper I have used a linear compensation
contract. I find that these compensation contracts entice managers to
declare dividends (thereby revealing the level of investments) in such a
manner that the most-efficient manager gets a first best efficient contract
and the other managers get less-efficient contracts. As a result dividends,
conditional on cash available, are inversely related to the managerial type.
These conclusions are found to be robust because they hold when I extend
the model by introducing costly managerial effort as a factor input in
production. I also find that these conclusions hold when I use general forms
(with some restrictions for tractability) of production function, cost-of-
effort function, and managerial compensation function. Details of these
extensions to the model are available from me.

The result is intuitive. Cash is available for apportionment into investment and dividend. Shareholders want agents with higher productivity to invest more than agents with lower productivity. They achieve so by offering two separating contracts. An agent with lower productivity picks the contract with higher weight on dividend and declares a higher dividend. An agent with higher productivity, on the other hand, picks the efficient contract and invests more in the production process. As a result, an agent with higher productivity declares a smaller dividend than an agent with lower productivity. The proof of the pudding is in eating, and the validity of a theory is the degree of its congruence with empirical reality. Future research directions would include testing my model empirically and extending this model to a multi-period set up. In my model, I have assumed that the budget constraint (namely, that the sum of dividends and amounts actually invested is equal to C) is binding and the agent does not raise funds in the capital market. In the real world, however, managers issue shares, borrow money, and pay dividends. To take into account all the three actions simultaneously in an agency-theoretic setting we would require a much richer model – possibly a multi-period game-theoretic model. My conjecture is that in such a set up the information content of the action would be based on the net financing (issue minus dividend) which, when added to initial cash, gives investment. The market would have to price the new shares based on what they learn from this net financing. Incentive conditions become more interesting as the manager considers both investment distortions, that arise from the non-linear production function, and the pricing implications, for the new issue that results from truth telling or mimicking. Such a model would be a very intricate and interesting subject for future research.

NOTES

1. Payout to shareholders can be in the form of dividends or share repurchase. My objective is to understand what determines the payout to the shareholders. So for the purpose of this paper we focus on the payout and not on the form of the payout. The form of the payout – dividends or share repurchase – is a matter of considerable puzzle in itself and has been investigated by other researchers (as for example see Brennan & Thakor, 1990; Bagwell, 1991). I am not considering forms of payout for reasons of tractability.

2. I have used the revelation principle to simplify the analysis. Revelation principle as enunciated in Rasmusen (1994) states that "(f)or every contract ... that leads to lying ... there is a contract .. with the same outcome ... but no incentive for the agent to lie" (p. 198).

3. The single crossing criterion is also known as the Spence–Mirrless criterion or the sorting criterion. It implies that the indifference curves for two type of agents can cross only once. For details see Tirole (1988) and Fudenberg and Tirole (1991).

4. The result that the more productive type is offered an efficient contract (i.e. one which achieves first best outcomes) and the less productive type is offered an inefficient contract so as to reduce the information rent paid to the more productive agent, is a standard result in the principal-agent literature. For example, see Varian (1992) and Laffont and Tirole (1993).

ACKNOWLEDGMENTS

This paper resulted from my doctoral dissertation at the University of British Columbia. I have profited enormously from discussions with my supervisor Prof. Ron Giammarino and with the other members of my committee, viz. Prof. Jerry Feltham, Prof. Rob Heinkel, and Prof. Burton Hollifield. Prof. Amin Mawani and Prof. Mitch Farlee were always ready with supportive advice. My thanks are also due to the seminar participants at the Northern Finance Association conference.

REFERENCES

Aharony, J., & Swary, I. (1980). Quarterly dividend and earnings announcements and stockholders' returns: An empirical analysis. *Journal Of Finance, 35*, 1–12.

Allen, F., Bernardo, A., & Welch, I. (2000). A theory of dividends based on tax clienteles. *Journal of Finance, 55*, 2499–2536.

Allen, F., & Michaely, R. (1995). Dividend policy. In: R. A. Jarrow, V. Maksimovic & W. T. Ziemba (Eds), *Handbooks in operations research and management science* (pp. 793–837). Amsterdam, New York: Elsevier.

Ambarish, R., John, K., & Williams, J. (1987). Efficient signalling with dividends and investments. *Journal of Finance, 42*, 321–343.

Bagwell, L. S. (1991). Share repurchase and takeover deterrence. *The Rand Journal of Economics, 22*, 72.

Bajaj, M. (1988). *Rational dividend policy: Theory and evidence.* Unpublished doctoral dissertation. University of California, Berkeley.

Bernheim, B. D. (1991). Tax policy and the dividend puzzle. *The Rand Journal of Economics, 22*, 455.

Bernheim, B. D., & Wantz, A. (1995). A tax-based test of the dividend signaling hypothesis. *American Economic Review, 85*, 532–551.

Bhattacharyya, S. (1979). Imperfect information, dividend policy, and "the bird in the hand" fallacy. *Bell Journal of Economics, 10*, 259–270.

Black, F. (1976). The dividend puzzle. *Journal of Portfolio Management, 2*, 5–8.

Black, F., & Scholes, M. (1974). The effects of dividend yield and dividend policy on common stock prices and returns. *Journal of Financial Economics, 1*, 1–22.

Brealey, R. A., & Myers, S. C. (2002). *Principles of corporate finance* (7th ed.). Boston: Irwin/ McGraw-Hill.

Brennan, M. J., & Thakor, A. V. (1990). Shareholder preferences and dividend policy. *Journal of Finance, 45*, 993–1018.

Chaplinsky, S., & Seyhun, H. N. (1990). Dividends and taxes: Evidence on tax-reduction strategies. *Journal of Business, 63*, 239–260.

Chen, N.-F., Grundy, B., & Stambaugh, R. F. (1990). Changing risk, changing risk – premiums, and dividend yield effects. *Journal of Business, 63*, S51–S70.

Christie, W. G. (1994). Are dividend omissions truly the cruelest cut of all. *Journal of Financial and Quantitative Analysis, 29*, 459–480.

Cole, J.A. (1980). *Theory and evidence regarding the information content in dividends.* Unpublished doctoral dissertation. The University Of Michigan, Michigan.

Denis, D. J., Denis, D. K., & Sarin, A. (1994). The information content of dividend changes: Cash flow signaling, overinvestment, and dividend clienteles. *Journal of Financial and Quantitative Analysis, 29*, 567–587.

Dhillon, U. S., & Johnson, H. (1994). The effect of dividend changes on stock and bond prices. *Journal of Finance, 49*, 281–289.

Divecha, A., & Morse, D. (1983). Market responses to dividend increases and changes in payout ratios. *Journal of Financial and Quantitative Analysis, 18*, 163–173.

Downes, D. H., & Heinkel, R. (1982). Signalling and the valuation of unseasoned new issues. *Journal of Finance, 37*, 1–10.

Easterbrook, F. H. (1984). Two agency-cost explanations of dividends. *American Economic Review, 74*, 650–659.

Faynzilberg, P. S., & Kumar, P. (1997). Optimal contracting of separable production technologies. *Games and Economic Behavior, 21*, 15–39.

Ferreira White, L. (1996). Executive compensation and dividend policy. *Journal of Corporate Finance, 2*, 335–358.

Fudenberg, D., & Tirole, J. (1991). *Game theory.* Cambridge, MA: MIT Press.

Healy, P. M. (1985). The effect of bonus schemes on accounting decisions. *Journal of Accounting and Economics, 7*, 85–107.

Heinkel, R.L. (1978). *Essays on financial markets with asymmetric information.* Unpublished doctoral dissertation. University of California, Berkeley.

Jensen, M. C. (1986). Agency costs of free cash flow, corporate finance, and takeovers. *American Economic Review, 76*, 323–329.

Jensen, M. C., & Murphy, K. J. (1990). Performance pay and top-management incentives. *Journal of Political Economy, 98*, 225–264.

John, K., & Williams, J. (1985). Dividends, dilution and taxes: A signalling equilibrium. *Journal of Finance, 40*, 1053–1070.

Johnson, S. A. (1995). Dividend payout and the valuation effects of bond announcements. *Journal of Financial and Quantitative Analysis, 30*, 407–423.

Kao, C., & Wu, C. (1994). Tests of dividend signalling using the Marsh–Merton model: A generalised friction approach. *Journal of Business, 67*, 45–68.

Laffont, J.-J., & Tirole, J. (1993). *A theory of incentives in procurement and regulation.* Cambridge, MA: MIT Press.

Lakonishok, J., & Vermaelen, T. (1986). Tax-induced trading around ex-dividend days. *Journal of Financial Economics, 16*, 287–319.

Lambert, R. A., Lanen, W. N., & Larcker, D. F. (1989). Executive stock option plans and corporate dividend policy. *Journal of Financial and Quantitative Analysis, 24*, 409–425.

Lang, L. H. P., & Litzenberger, R. H. (1989). Dividend announcements – cash flow signalling vs. cash flow hypothesis? *Journal of Financial Economics, 24*, 181–191.

Lewellen, W. G., Loderer, C., & Martin, K. (1987). Executive compensation and executive incentive problems: An empirical analysis. *Journal of Accounting and Economics, 9*, 287–310.

Lewellen, W. G., Stanley, K. L., Lease, R. C., & Schlarbaum, G. G. (1978). Some direct evidence on the dividend clientele phenomenon. *Journal of Finance, 33*, 1385–1399.

Litzenberger, R. H., & Ramaswamy, K. (1982). The effects of dividends on common stock prices – tax effects or information effects? *Journal of Finance, 37*, 429–443.

Long, M. S., Malitz, I. B., & Sefcik, S. E. (1994). An empirical examination of dividend policy following debt issues. *Journal of Financial and Quantitative Analysis, 29*, 131–144.

Manuel, T. A., Brooks, L. D., & Schadler, F. P. (1993). Common stock price effects of security issues conditioned by current earnings and dividend announcements. *Journal of Business, 66*, 571–593.

Michaely, R. (1991). Ex-dividend day stock price behaviour: The case of the 1986 Tax Reform Act. *Journal of Finance, 46*, 845–859.

Miller, M. H., & Modigliani, F. (1961). Dividend policy, growth and the valuation of shares. *Journal of Business, 34*, 411–433.

Miller, M. H., & Rock, K. (1985). Dividend policy under asymmetric information. *Journal of Finance, 40*, 1031–1051.

Murphy, K. J. (1999). Executive compensation. In: O. Ashenfelter & D. Card (Eds), *Handbook of labor economics* (pp. 2485–2563). Elsevier Science.

Myerson, R. B. (1982). Optimal coordination mechanisms in generalized principal-agent problems. *Journal of Mathematical Economics, 10*, 67–81.

Pavlik, E. L., Scott, T. W., & Tiessen, P. (1993). Executive compensation: Issues and research. *Journal of Accounting Literature, 12*, 131–189.

Penman, S. H. (1983). The predictive content of earnings forecasts and dividends. *Journal of Finance, 38*, 1181–1199.

Persons, J. C. (1994). Renegotiation and the impossibility of optimal investment. *Review of Financial Studies, 7*, 419–449.

Poterba, J. M. (1986). The market valuation of cash dividends – the citizens utilities case reconsidered. *Journal of Financial Economics, 15*, 395–405.

Rasmusen, E. (1994). *Games and information: An introduction to game theory* (2nd ed.). Cambridge, MA: Basil Blackwell.

Sant, R., & Cowan, A. R. (1994). Do dividends signal earnings? The case of omitted dividends. *Journal of Banking and Finance, 18*, 1113–1133.

Smith, C. W., & Watts, R. L. (1992). The investment opportunity set and corporate financing, dividend, and compensation policies. *Journal of Financial Economics, 32*, 263–292.

Tirole, J. (1988). *The theory of industrial organization*. Cambridge, MA: Massachusetts Institute of Technology.

Varian, H. R. (1992). *Microeconomic analysis* (3rd ed.). New York: W.W. Norton & Company.

Williams, J. (1988). Efficient signalling with dividends, investment and stock repurchases. *Journal of Finance*, *43*, 737–747.

Yoon, P. S., & Starks, L. T. (1995). Signalling, investment opportunities, and dividend announcements. *Review of Financial Studies*, *8*, 995–1018.

APPENDIX – PROOF OF PROPOSITIONS

For the sake of easy reference, notations used are summarized below.

C	Cash available for investment
I_j	Investment level chosen by agent of type j, when agent truthfully declares type to be j
$I_{\hat{j}j}$	Investment level chosen by agent of type j, when agent declares type to be $\hat{j}$, $j \neq \hat{j}$
D_j	Dividend level selected by an agent of type j, when agent truthfully declares type to be $j = C - I_j$
$D_{\hat{j}j}$	Dividend level chosen by agent of type j, when agent declares type to be $\hat{j}$, $j \neq \hat{j}$; $D_{\hat{j}j} = C - I_{\hat{j}j}$
θ_j	Productivity parameter for agent of type j. For our purpose, we assume that j can only have two values – L(ow) and H(igh) and $\theta_L < \theta_H$
$\tilde{Y}_j$	Stochastic production. Production function is given by $\tilde{Y}_j = \theta_j \ln(C - D_j) + \tilde{\varepsilon}_j$, where $\tilde{\varepsilon}_j$ is random noise with zero mean. Note that $(C - D_j)$ and $(C - D_{\hat{j}j})$ are investments
P	Probability that the agent is of type L
ω_j	The wage function (assumed to be linear in D and $\tilde{Y}$) offered to an agent of type j, when agent truthfully declares type to be j
$\omega_{\hat{j}j}$	The wage function (assumed to be linear in D and $\tilde{Y}$) offered to an agent of type j who reports his/her type to be $\hat{j}$, $j \neq \hat{j}$

Thus

$$\tilde{\omega}_j = \beta_0(j) + \beta_D(j)D_j + \beta_Y(j)\tilde{Y}, j = \hat{j}$$

$$\tilde{\omega}_{\hat{j}j} = \beta_0(\hat{j}) + \beta_D(\hat{j})D_{\hat{j}j} + \beta_Y(\hat{j})\tilde{Y}, j \neq \hat{j}$$

Where

$\beta_0(j), \beta_0(\hat{j})$	are constant components of the wages,
$\beta_D(j)D_j, \beta_D(\hat{j})D_{jj}$	are components of the wages proportional to dividends,
$\beta_Y(j)\tilde{Y}, \beta_Y(\hat{j})\tilde{Y}$	are components of wages proportional to outputs,
$\tilde{Y}$	is stochastic output
ω_0	The reservation wage below which no agent will enter into a contract

We use a caret (ˆ) to indicate parameters as reported by agent about its type. Thus, $\hat{j}$ represents the type reported by agent. We shall use the generalized revelation principle as enunciated in Myerson (1982) and Faynzilberg and Kumar (1997) so that in equilibrium the agent tells the truth, i.e., $j = \hat{j}$.[2] Also note that dividends are contractible information in our model. That is principal can design contracts for pre-specified levels of dividends.

We also assume that $\beta_D \neq 0$ and $\beta_Y \neq 0$. Our purpose in analyzing this model is to understand the impact a linkage between dividends, output, and executive compensation has on the dividends declared. It is reiterated that the linkage between dividends, output, and executive compensation has been empirically observed. So the coefficients for the dividend term and the output term is constrained to be non-zero.

Lemma 1. In the first-best or full information solution L type agent will declare a higher dividend than that declared by the H type agent.

Proof. In the first-best or full information case, the type of the agent will be common knowledge, i.e., there will not be any asymmetric information. Principal will therefore pay every agent the reservation wage and specify the dividend to be paid (or equivalently specify the investment to be made). The principal will then solve the following problem:

$$\underset{D_j}{Maximize}\, D_j + \theta_j \ln(C - D_j) - \omega_0 \forall j$$

The maximand is a concave function of D_j. Therefore the first-order condition will be necessary and sufficient for a global maxima.

The first-order condition would be

$$1 - \frac{\theta_j}{C - D_j^*} = 0 \Rightarrow \quad D_j^* = C - \theta_j \tag{A.1}$$

where D_j^* is the first best level of dividends.

From (A.1) we see that

$$\theta_L < \theta_H \Rightarrow D_L^* > D_H^*$$

∎

Lemma 2. The indifference curves in the (β_Y, β_D) plane for both the H-type and L-type agents are concave and downward sloping.

Proof. For a given value of (β_Y, β_D), an agent solves the following problem.

$$\underset{D_j}{Maximize}\ \beta_D D_j + \beta_Y \theta_j \ln(C - D_j) \text{ for every } j$$

Let $U_j \equiv \beta_D D_j + \beta_Y \theta_j \ln(C - D_j)$

U_j is a concave function of D_j, so first-order condition will give the global optimum. First-order condition is

$$\beta_D - \frac{\beta_Y \theta_j}{C - D_j} = 0$$

$$\Rightarrow \quad D_j = C - \frac{\beta_Y}{\beta_D}\theta_j \tag{A.2}$$

Also

$$\frac{\partial U_j}{\partial \beta_D} = D_j \ and \ \frac{\partial U_j}{\partial \beta_Y} = \theta_j \ln(C - D_j)$$

$\Rightarrow$ Slope of the indifference curve in (β_Y, β_D) plane

$$= \frac{d\beta_D}{d\beta_Y} = \frac{\partial U_j/\partial \beta_Y}{\partial U_j/\partial \beta_D} = -\frac{\theta_j \ln(C - D_j)}{D_j} < 0 \tag{A.3}$$

By taking the total differential of the first-order condition (A.2) with respect to β_D and β_y, we get

$$\left[1 - \frac{\beta_Y \theta_j}{(C - D_j)^2}\frac{\partial D_j}{\partial \beta_D}\right]d\beta_D - \frac{\theta_j}{(C - D_j)}\left[1 + \frac{\beta_Y}{(C - D_j)}\frac{\partial D_j}{\partial \beta_Y}\right]d\beta_Y = 0$$

The left-hand side of the above equation will be zero for all arbitrary and small values for $d\beta_D$ and $d\beta_Y$. Therefore, the coefficients of $d\beta_D$ and $d\beta_Y$ must always be zero. Equating coefficients of $d\beta_D$ and $d\beta_Y$ to zero and simplifying, we get

$$\frac{\partial D_j}{\partial \beta_D} = \frac{(C - D_j)^2}{\beta_Y \theta_j} > 0 \text{ and } \frac{\partial D_j}{\partial \beta_Y} = -\frac{C - D_j}{\beta_Y} < 0$$

$$\frac{d^2 \beta_D(j)}{d\beta_Y^2(j)} = \frac{\theta_j}{D_j^2} \left[\left\{ \frac{D_j}{(C - D_j)} + \ln(C - D_j) \right\} \frac{\partial D_j}{\partial \beta_Y(j)} \right] < 0$$

Therefore the indifference curves for the agents are concave and downward sloping in the (β_Y, β_D) plane. ∎

Corollary 1. In order to induce the first best outcome we must have $\beta_D(j) = \beta_Y(j)$

Proof. This follows from (A.1) and (A.2). ∎

Proposition 1. No pooling contract exists in equilibrium.

Proof. We prove this result by demonstrating that there exists a separating contract which dominates the best-possible pooling contract.

The principal will have to ensure that the contract offered should at least give the agent an ex-ante wage of ω_0 – the reservation wage below which no agent will accept a contract. This is known as the participation constraint.

Consider the contract which will induce first best decisions from the agent. This contract will set $\beta_D(\hat{j}) = \beta_Y(\hat{j}).\beta_0(\hat{j})$ cannot be set to make the participation constraint binding for the H-type because in that case the participation constraint will be violated for the L-type and the contract will not be accepted by the L-type. Therefore $\beta_0(\hat{j})$ will be set in such a way so as to make the participation constraint binding for the L-type agent. We know from Lemma 1 that in this case dividends declared by agents will reveal their types. The first best contract with the participation constraint being binding ex-ante for L will therefore be a separating contract.

Now consider the pooling contract where principal forces the dividend to be D_L^* (recall that dividend is a contractible information), sets $\beta_D(L, H) = \beta_Y(L, H)$ and sets $\beta_0(L, H)$ in such a way so as to make the participation constraint binding ex-ante for L. This is the best pooling contract possible as in this case at least an L type agent can be induced to give the first best output which is not possible for any other pooling contract. In this case the output from H will be less than the first best level. This contract is however dominated by the separating contract where principal forces dividends to belong to $\{D_L^*, D_H^*\}$, sets $\beta_D(L, H) = \beta_Y(L, H)$ and sets $\beta_0(L, H)$ in such a way so as to make the participation constraint binding ex-ante for L – because in this case both L and H will produce at first best levels and H will derive some information rent. ∎

Lemma 3. $\partial D_j / \partial \theta_j < 0$

Proof. By partially differentiating the first-order condition (A.2) with respect to θ_j, we get

$$\frac{\partial D_j}{\partial \theta_j} = -\frac{\beta_Y}{\beta_D} < 0$$

∎

Lemma 4. The indifference curves for L and H in the (β_Y, β_D) plane satisfy the single crossing condition.[3]

Proof. Differentiating the slope of the indifference curve (A.3) partially with respect to θ_j, we see $\frac{\partial}{\partial \theta_j}$ (Slope of the indifference curve)

$$= -\frac{1}{D_j^2} \left[D_j \left\{ \ln(C - D_j) + \frac{\theta_j}{C - D_j} \left(-\frac{\partial D_j}{\partial \theta_j} \right) \right\} \right.$$

$$\left. - \{\theta_j \, \ln(C - D_j)\} \frac{\partial D_j}{\partial \theta_j} \right]$$

$$< 0 \quad \because \frac{\partial D_j}{\partial \theta_j} < 0 \text{ by Lemma 3}$$

From above we know that the sorting condition is satisfied and that at any point in the (β_Y, β_D) plane the indifference curve for H-type is steeper than the indifference curve for L-type passing through the same point. ∎

Lemma 5. The L-type will be offered an inefficient contract such that the ex-ante net expected payment to L-type is equal to the reservation wage ω_0. The contract offered to L would be such that $\beta_D(L)/\beta_Y(L) > 1$ and $\beta_Y(L) < 1$ and $\beta_0(L)$ is such that the ex-ante net gain of agent L is equal to the reservation wage ω_0. The H-type would be offered an efficient contract to induce first-best results. This would be achieved by setting $\beta_D(H) = \beta_Y(H) \cdot \beta_0(H)$ would be set at a level so that the ex-ante net expected payment to H is the same, irrespective of whether he accepts this contract or the contract offered to L.

Proof. The principal's problem can be represented as below

$$\underset{\substack{\beta_0(L),\beta_0(H),\beta_D(L), \\ \beta_D(H),\beta_Y(L),\beta_Y(H), \\ D_L,D_H}}{Maximize} \quad \left[p\left[\{1 - \beta_D(L)\}D_L \right. \right.$$

$$+ \{1 - \beta_Y(L)\} \ \theta_L \ln(C - D_L) - \beta_0(L)\right]$$

$$+ (1 - p)\left[\{1 - \beta_D(H)\}D_H \right.$$

$$+ \left. \left. \{1 - \beta_Y(H)\} \ \theta_H \ln(C - D_H) - \beta_0(H)\right]\right]$$

such that the following incentive constraints, participation constraints, and truth-telling constraints are satisfied.

Incentive constraints

$$D_j = C - \frac{\beta_Y(j)}{\beta_D(j)}\theta_j, j = \text{L}, \text{H} \tag{A.4}$$

$$D_{j\hat{j}} = C - \frac{\beta_Y(\hat{j})}{\beta_D(\hat{j})}\theta_j, j = \text{L}, \text{H}; \hat{j} = \text{L}, \text{H}; j \neq \hat{j} \tag{A.5}$$

Participation constraints

$$\beta_0(j) + \beta_D(j)D_j + \beta_Y(j)\theta_j \ln(C - D_j) \geq \omega_0, j = \text{L}, \text{H} \tag{A.6}$$

where ω_0 is the reservation wage.

Truth telling Constraints

$$E\left[\beta_0(j) + \beta_D(j)D_j + \beta_Y(j)\tilde{Y}|\theta_j, D_j\right]$$

$$\geq E\left[\beta_0(\hat{j}) + \beta_D(\hat{j})D_{j\hat{j}} + \beta_Y(\hat{j})\tilde{Y}|\theta_j, D_{j\hat{j}}\right],$$

$$j = \text{L}, \text{H}; \hat{j} = \text{L}, \text{H}; j \neq \hat{j} \tag{A.7}$$

The maximand is obtained by considering the expected net gain to the principal. Incentive constraints capture the fact that the agent would choose dividend D so as to maximize his/her own expected pay. Incentive constraints are obtained by substituting the first-order conditions (A.2) from the agent's optimization problem. Participation constraints takes account of the fact that agents will not work below a certain minimum wage. Participation constraints are obtained by explicitly writing out the conditional expected compensation. These constraints are derived for cases where agents report their type truthfully. Truth inducing constraints make use of the revelation principle and ensure that in equilibrium agents report their type truthfully. Note that in order to take into account the off-equilibrium behavior, we need to include, in incentive constraints, the choices of agents for those cases where agents send false reports of their types. In equilibrium however agents declare their type truthfully and incentive constraints for the false reporting scenario are not binding.

The solution to this optimization will determine the equilibrium values for the fixed component of compensation offered to each agent $[\beta_0(j), j = L, H]$, the component of compensation linked to the dividend payment $[\beta_D(j), j = L, H]$, the component of compensation linked to the final output $[\beta_Y(j), j = L, H]$, and the amount of dividend declared by each agent $[D_j, j = L, H]$. The principal will choose $[\beta_0(j), \beta_D(j), \beta_Y(j)]$; the agent will choose $D(j|\beta_D(j), \beta_Y(j))$.

We propose to solve this problem by the following method.

Step 1: Find the agent's optimal choice of D for a particular value of the coefficients of the wage function. These can be found from the incentive condition.

Step 2: Substitute the optimum values of D from the incentive conditions in the agent's objective function and the principal's objective function. This will express the agent's objective function and the principal's objective function in terms of the coefficient values.

Step 3: We find the indifference curves for the principal and agent from the expression obtained in Step 2. The indifference curves are drawn in the space (β_Y, β_D).

Step 4: Identify a contract for the lowest type L on the indifference curve corresponding to the binding participating wage ω_0.

Step 5: Given the contract for L, we now identify the space in which the separating contracts for H must lie. We use the *single crossing criterion* (see endnote 3) in order to delineate the contracts in (β_Y, β_D) space.

Step 6: Maximize principal's expected profit in the space identified in Step 5.

The approach can be illustrated by referring to Figs. 1 and 2. In Fig. 1 we have drawn the indifference surfaces for the L-type and the H-type agent. The indifference surfaces are drawn in the space $(\beta_0, \beta_D, \beta_Y)$. Fig. 2 shows the cross-sectional view of the indifference surfaces drawn in Fig. 1, the cross-sectional plane running parallel to the (β_Y, β_D) plane.

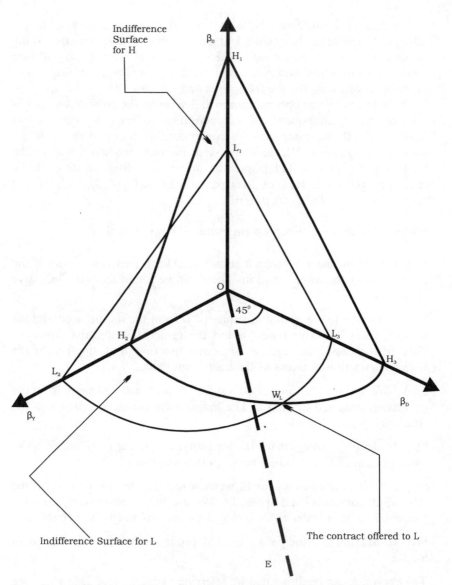

Fig. 1. Indifference Surfaces for the L-Type and the H-Type Agent. The Indifference Surfaces are Drawn in the Space $(\beta_0, \beta_D, \beta_Y)$.

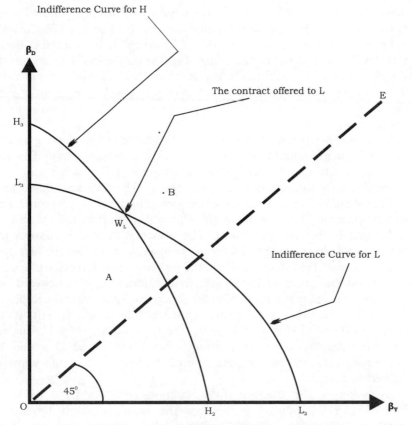

Fig. 2. Cross Sectional View of the Indifference Surfaces for H(igh) type and L(ow) Type Agents – Cross Section by a Plane Parallel to β_D and β_Y.

In Fig. 1, $L_1L_2L_3$ (thin line) is the indifference surface for L for a net expected reservation wage of ω_0. Suppose W_L is the contract offered to L. $H_1H_2H_3$ (thick line) is the indifference surface for H passing through W_L. OE (the dashed line) is the line on the (β_Y, β_D) plane, such that $(\beta_Y = \beta_D)$.

In Fig. 2, L_2L_3 is the section of the indifference surface for L and H_2H_3 is the section of the indifference surface for H. The separating contract offered to H must lie in the area bounded by section $W_L H_2$ and W_LL_2 of the indifference plane (see Fig. 2). Consider a contract represented by point A. If this contract is offered then both L-type and the H-type would prefer the contract W_L to A. Conversely, if contract B is offered, then both L-type and H-type would prefer contract B to contract W_L.

Let ω_H be the value that H would get by accepting the contract offered to L [in Fig. 1 it would be the value obtained on the indifference surface for H]. Clearly H would reject any contract that offers him/her a value less than ω_H. It can be shown that $\omega_H > \omega_0$. The L-type agent is paid the reservation wage, while the H-type agent is paid an information rent equal to $\omega_H - \omega_0$.

Since the H-type is restricted on the indifference surface, having a value ω_H, the principal should rationally extract the first-best output. This can be done by setting $\beta_D(H) = \beta_Y(H)$ and setting $\beta_0(H)$ in such a way so as to make the ex-ante utility to H equal to ω_H. The contract offered to L would be an inefficient contract which would optimize the expected gain to the principal. However, the more efficient the contract offered to L is, the higher is the rent paid to H. The principal therefore balances the efficiency lost by offering an inefficient contract to L against the rent paid to H. The contract offered to H should lie on the indifference surface for H (viz., on the surface $H_1H_2H_3$) and, in addition, it must lie between two planes: one is the plane containing the β_0 axis and passing through points O and W_L; the other is the plane defined by the β_y and β_0 axis. If the contract offered to H is in this space, then L would strictly prefer his/her own contract W_L over the contract offered to H and H would be indifferent between the contract offered to him/her and the contract offered to L.

By looking at the structure of the equations (A.1) and (A.2), we know that H can be induced to achieve the first-best result by setting $\beta_D(H) = \beta_Y(H)$. The principal will design the contract W_L so as to maximize the expected gain to himself/herself. In general, we cannot expect the contract W_L to be such as to induce efficient (first best) decisions for L, because in order to induce efficient decisions, L will also have to be offered a contract with $\beta_D(L) = \beta_Y(L)$. In that case the contract W_L will be on the line OE. However, this means that the rent paid to H (which is determined by the indifference surface for H passing through W_L) will be higher. Therefore, the principal will maintain balance between the rent paid to H and the inefficient decision by L, so as to maximize his/her expected profit.[4] We can also see that the contract W_L will be such that the line joining O and W_L must remain in the region OE and the β_D axis (see Fig. 2). This is because otherwise L would prefer the efficient contract given to H and in the process derive a rent.

This implies that $\beta_D(L)/\beta_Y(L) > 1$. We also note that $\beta_Y(L) < 1$, because otherwise H would prefer the contract W_L as opposed to the efficient contract. ∎

Proposition 2. The H-type agent will declare a smaller dividend than the L-type agent.

Proof.

$$\theta_H > \theta_L$$

$\Rightarrow$ $\theta_H > (\beta_Y(L)/\beta_D(L))\theta_L \because (\beta_Y(L)/\beta_D(L)) < 1$ by Lemma 5

$\Rightarrow$ $C - \theta_H < C - (\beta_Y(L)/\beta_D(L))\theta_L$

$\Rightarrow$ $D_H < D_L \because D_H = C - \theta_H$ and $D_L = C - (\beta_Y(L)/\beta_D(L))\theta_L$

∎

CORPORATE DOWNSIZING AND CEO COMPENSATION

Alexandros P. Prezas, Murat Tarimcilar and Gopala K. Vasudevan

ABSTRACT

Our study examines CEO compensation for firms that announce layoffs during the 1993–2001 period. We find that overall there is a large increase in CEO equity-based compensation in the year prior to and the year of the downsizing. Our sample of downsizing firms has small improvements in operating performance following the announcement. However, these performance improvements manifest themselves in the low but not the high equity-based compensation firms. We find that the announcement period returns are higher for downsizing firms that are larger, hire a new CEO in the year prior to the downsizing, have higher leverage, and better operating performance.

1. INTRODUCTION

In the last decade there has been a substantial increase in the use of incentive-based compensation for CEOs in corporate America. Jensen and Meckling (1976) and Smith and Watts (1982) argue that incentive-based compensation plans can reduce the conflicts of interests between managers

Issues in Corporate Governance and Finance
Advances in Financial Economics, Volume 12, 119–136
Copyright © 2007 by Elsevier Ltd.
ISSN: 1569-3732/doi:10.1016/S1569-3732(07)12006-5

and shareholders and motivate these managers to make value-maximizing decisions. Dial and Murphy (1995) analyze the role of managerial incentives in value creation at General Dynamics. They find that executive compensation plans motivated managers to partially sell off assets and increase firm value even at the expense of their own jobs. Our study is a large sample analysis of the clinical study by Dial and Murphy (1995) and provides evidence across several industries and a large number of firms.

We examine the relationship between corporate downsizing announcements and CEO compensation because this topic has attracted considerable interest in the academic community as well as corporate America. Anderson and Cavanagh (1994) and Sloan (1996) criticize downsizing by arguing that CEOs are firing employees only to increase their own compensation at the expense of the workers. Managers and economists argue that these downsizings are due to declining product demand, or because new technologies have increased worker productivity and hence reduced the demand for labor. Jensen (1993) and Dial and Murphy (1995) suggest that these firms may also need to cut labor costs to succeed in the global markets against foreign companies that have lower labor costs.

There are several reasons why traditional CEO pay practices will not work for a firm that has to downsize to become profitable. First as Healy (1985) suggests, there is a strong relationship between pay and firm size for the traditional firm. Hence, these compensation schemes only provide incentives to grow. Second, Dechow, Huson, and Sloan (1994) indicate that the annual bonuses that managers receive are very closely tied to accounting profitability ratios. Since downsizing typically involves restructuring charges (e.g., severance packages) that can reduce profitability, managers do not have any incentive to downsize. Third, managers also receive non-pecuniary benefits such as power, prestige, and other benefits that can be tied to firm size. This creates another disincentive for these managers to downsize. Fourth, since these managers generally posess skills that are specific to one industry, the downsizing may ultimately cost the managers their own jobs. As Murphy (1995) points out, this may happen because downsizing reduces the number of firms in these industries leading to the need for fewer executives.

We examine the CEO compensation, announcement period returns, and the operating performance for a sample of 133 firms that downsize during the 1993–2001 period. First, we examine the CEO compensation during the 6-year period around the downsizing announcement. Second, we examine the operating performance of the sample firms around the downsizing announcement and its relationship to CEO compensation. Finally, we examine the relationship between announcement period returns and CEO compensation.

Overall, we find that there is a large increase in equity-based compensation (EBC) for firms that make downsizing announcements. Most of the increase in EBC takes place in the year prior to and the year of the downsizing. We subdivide our sample into high and low EBC firms based on whether these firms have EBC higher than or lower than the median EBC in the year prior to the downsizing announcement. We find that the low EBC firms have larger improvements in operating performance in the 3-year period following the downsizing announcements. We find that the abnormal announcement period returns are higher for firms that hire a new CEO in the year prior to the downsizing, have higher leverage, have better operating performance in the year of the downsizing, and are of larger size.

The remainder of the paper is organized as follows: Section 2 summarizes related papers, while Section 3 describes the data and methodology. Section 4 examines CEO EBC during the 6-year period around the downsizing announcement. Section 5 examines the operating performance of the sample firms around the date of the downsizing announcement. Section 6 examines the association of CEO equity-based compensation with the announcement period returns. Section 7 has the summary and conclusions.

2. BACKGROUND

Jensen (1993) and Murphy (1995) argue that CEO compensation in most corporations provides strong incentives to expand but provide few incentives to downsize when there is excess capacity. To motivate CEOs to reduce firm size through asset restructuring and employee layoffs, their compensation contracts have to be structured so that managerial wealth is tied to increases in firm value rather than size or accounting profits.

Smith and Watts (1982) argue that incentive compensation schemes can mitigate the conflict of interest between shareholders and managers. The use of stock options and restricted stock grants can motivate managers to downsize for at least two reasons. First, if the downsizing announcements have a positive impact on the share price, any stock and stock option grants owned by the management become more valuable. Second, if downsizing increases the profitability, and hence the long-term stock price of the firm, it can also increase the value of the stock and stock options held by the managers.

Our study is related to Dial and Murphy (1995). They examine how managerial incentives led to value creation at General Dynamics. They find that during the 1991–1993 period, shareholders realized an increase in their share value of more than 500% due to CEO decisions to downsize and liquidate unprofitable divisions. We examine whether these findings can be generalized by analyzing a large sample of downsizing firms across several industries and through several years.

Our study is also related to Datta, Iskandar- Datta, and Raman (2001) who examine the role of executive compensation on the acquisition policy of firms. They find that the success of acquisitions is related to the EBC of acquiring managers. Specifically, managers of high EBC firms tend to make acquisitions that create more value and the EBC of managers is an important determinant of the post-acquisition stock price performance. Like Datta et al. (2001), we use EBC to explain the success of managerial decisions but, unlike them, we concentrate on corporate downsizings not acquisitions.

Frye (2004) examines the relationship between EBC for employees and firm performance. She finds a strong positive relationship between EBC and Tobin's Q. However, she finds that firms which provide their CEOs with higher EBC tend to have lower levels of accounting performance (as measured by the return on assets) in some future years. This is consistent with our results that high EBC firms tend to have lower operating performance.

Hallock (1998) examines whether the CEOs of downsizing firms have larger increases in compensation when compared to other firms. He finds that the CEOs of firms that announce layoffs typically have larger compensation as well as larger increases in compensation when compared to firms that do not announce layoffs. However, he finds no relationship between these two variables after controlling for other factors such as firm size and CEO age. Finally, he documents a negative stock price reaction to layoff announcements. There are several important distinctions between Hallock (1998) and our study. Hallock's (1998) measure of CEO compensation does not include the stock or stock options granted to CEOs both of which are important components of incentive compensation. Our study includes both these components of CEO compensation. Further, we provide cross-sectional evidence on the relationship between incentive compensation and the stock price reaction to the announcement of the downsizing. Hallock (1998) only reports the announcement period returns for the sample of downsizing firms and does not examine the relationship between CEO compensation and announcement period returns. Finally, we provide evidence on the long-term success of the downsizing, measured by operating performance and its relationship to CEO compensation.

Mehran, Nogler, and Schwartz (1998) examine the role of insider ownership and CEO compensation on the voluntary liquidation decision of 30 U.S. industrial firms. They find that as the percentage of a company's stock held by the CEO or the sensitivity of the CEO's stock options outstanding to share price increases, so does the probability of a voluntary liquidation. Also, firms with more outside board members and lower market to book ratio of equity are more likely to be liquidated. Finally, they find the majority of the CEOs of these firms do not find comparable positions in publicly traded firms for a period of at least 3 years following the liquidation decision.

3. DATA AND METHODOLOGY

We first obtain a sample of layoff announcements from a search of the Wall Street Journal Index between 1993 and 2001 using the keywords "layoffs," "laid off," "downsize," "plant closing," and "downsizing". Our sample meets the following criteria:

(1) We include only the first announcement for each firm.
(2) The firm has compensation data in Standard and Poor's ExecuComp database.
(3) The firm has stock price data in CRSP.
(4) The firm has accounting data for the 2 years prior to, the year of and the 3 years following the downsizing announcement in Compustat.

We initially obtain a sample of 499 announcements through our search of the Wall Street Journal Index. We drop 114 announcements because they are made by the same firm. We lose 167 firms because CEO compensation data is not available in ExecuComp. We lose another 30 firms because accounting data is not available in Compustat and we lose 55 firms because we do not obtain stock price data from CRSP. Our final sample is 133 firms.

Table 1 shows the distribution of the 133 firms by year. The largest number of downsizing announcements (46) takes place in 1994. The next largest number of downsizings (29) takes place in 1996. The smallest number (2) takes place in 1995.

CEO compensation data is obtained from Standard and Poor's ExecuComp database. For each firm the total compensation is the sum

Table 1. Distribution of Downsizing Firms by Calendar Year.

Year	Number of Firms
1993	6
1994	46
1995	2
1996	29
1997	12
1998	20
1999	12
2000	3
2001	3
Total	133

Notes: The sample of 133 firms shown by year. The sample of layoff firms is obtained from the Wall Street Journal Index during the 1993–2001 period. We include a firm only if executive compensation data is obtained from Standard and Poor's ExecuComp database and stock price and accounting data are obtained from CRSP and Compustat. We include only the first announcement for each firm.

of salary, bonus, other annual compensation, the dollar value of restricted stock granted, the value of new stock options granted during the year, the long-term incentives paid out and all other long-term compensation paid to the CEO. We define EBC as the sum of restricted stock granted and the dollar value of options granted as a percentage of total compensation.[1]

Panel A of Table 2 reports the summary compensation statistics for our sample of 133 firms. The statistics are for year −1, the year before the downsizing announcement. The mean CEO salary for our sample is $806,220. On average, CEOs received a bonus of $705,630 and other annual compensation equal to $60,840. The average value of restricted stock granted is $425,440 and the CEOs received stock options worth $186,200. They also received long-term incentive plan payouts worth $294,870, while all other long-term compensation is $334,770. The average total compensation is $5,020,200. The average EBC is 36.26%. The distribution of compensation is quite skewed. The median EBC is 36.14% and the minimum and maximum total compensation is $118,000, for the CEO of Chiquita and $39,935,892 for the CEO of Compaq, respectively. By comparison, Datta et al. (2001) report 29.76% mean EBC for their sample, while Mehran et al. (1998) report 12.7%.

Table 2. Compensation Characteristics of the CEO of the Downsizing Firms.

Panel A: CEO compensation for downsizing firms

Compensation	Mean	Median	Minimum	Maximum
Salary	806.22	757.38	115	3709.84
Bonus	705.63	525.27	0	7086.44
Other annual	60.84	0	0	998.21
Restricted stock granted	425.44	0	0	16293.75
Stock options granted	186.20	61	0	2688.39
Long-term incentive plan payouts	294.87	0	0	5387.39
All other (long-term)	334.77	44.17	0	17819.70
Total compensation	5020.20	2812.81	118.01	39935.89
EBC	36.26%	36.14%	0%	95.26%

Panel B: Total compensation for the 6-year period around the downsizing

Years to Downsizing	−3	−2	−1	0	1	2	3
Median total compensation	2,561	2,569	2,812	3,300	3,915	4,696	4,798
Average total compensation	4,461	4,789	5,021	5,773	8,889	8,574	9,817

Notes: The sample consists of 133 downsizing firms between 1993-2001. All compensation data is obtained from Standard and Poor's ExecuComp database and is reported for the year prior to the downsizing announcement. Total compensation is the sum of salary, bonus, other annual compensation, value of restricted stock granted, value of new options granted during the year, long-term incentive payouts, and all other compensation paid to the CEO. Equity-based compensation (EBC) is the sum of the value of new stock options (using the modified Black-Scholes method) and restricted stock granted to the CEO as a percentage of total compensation paid to them. Except EBC, all figures are in thousands of dollars.

Panel B of Table 2 reports the total compensation for the 6-year period around the downsizing. In the 3 years prior to downsizing, average total compensation increases. The increase is even more pronounced in the 3 years after the downsizing.

We examine the operating performance of the firms over a 6-year period. This includes the 2 years before the downsizing (years −2 to −1), the year of the downsizing (year 0), and the 3-year period following the downsizing (years +1 to +3).

Our measure of operating performance is pretax operating cash flow scaled by the book value of total assets. We define pretax operating cash flow as net sales, minus cost of goods sold, minus selling and administrative expenses, but before deducting interest, depreciation, and amortization expenses (Compustat item no. 13). The book value of total assets is the total value of assets (liabilities and net worth) from the balance sheet (Compustat item no. 6).

We use pretax operating cash flow rather than earnings for two reasons. First, earnings include interest expense, income taxes, and special items that can obscure operating performance. Second, as Barber and Lyon (1996) point out, operating cash flow represents the economic benefits generated by the firm, and as a pretax measure it is unaffected by the changes in capital structure or tax rates that can accompany downsizing. Since the level of these economic benefits depends on the total value of the firm's assets, we scale pretax operating cash flow by the book value of total assets. This gives us a performance measure (henceforth, *operating performance*) we can compare across firms and through time.

Barber and Lyon (1996) argue that using the book value of assets to scale cash flows may be problematic because changes in this variable could create a bias in post-downsizing performance. We address this issue by following each sample firm's performance for 3 years after the downsizing and by examining changes in performance from pre- to post-announcement.

We evaluate both levels of and changes in operating performance based on the performance of a portfolio of control firms matched by size and performance. To determine matched-firm-adjusted performance, we construct a control sample of firms with no downsizing announcement during the 5-year period prior to the sample firm's announcement date using a procedure similar to one used by Barber and Lyon (1996). Specifically, we select all non-downsizing firms (with financial data available) whose size is within 70–130% of the sample firm's book value of total assets and with operating performance within 95–105% of that of the sample firm's in year 0. Then, we subtract the median operating performance of the portfolio of these matching firms from the sample firm's operating performance.

We match firms on operating performance for two reasons. First, it has been documented by Fama and French (1995) that matching on operating performance controls for potential mean reversion in earnings and other operating ratios. Second, Barber and Lyon (1996) conclude that tests using control firms that are not matched on cash flow performance are misspecified if the event firms have either especially good or especially poor prior operating performance. To test for the statistical significance of the levels and changes in operating performance, we conduct Wilcoxon signed-rank tests and parametric *t*-tests.

We examine the stock price reaction to the downsizing announcement using the standard event-study method of Brown and Warner (1985) to compute daily excess returns. Average daily abnormal returns are computed in a two-step procedure, using stock price data from CRSP. The market portfolio proxy is the CRSP equally weighted index.

First, we estimate the parameters of a single-factor market model for each firm. We use the returns from day –255 to day –46 to estimate each firm's alpha and beta coefficients. Second, we compute the excess return by subtracting a firm's expected daily return from its actual return. Cumulative abnormal returns are calculated by summing the abnormal returns over the period from day –1 to day +1, where day 0 represents announcement of the downsizing.

We then regress the announcement period returns against several firm variables such as the leverage of the firm in year –1, the change in employees in year –1, the operating performance in year –1, the log of the book value of assets in year –1 and two dummy variables. The first, a dummy variable set equal to 1 if the CEO has been replaced in year –1 and the second a dummy variable set equal to 1 if the incentive compensation of the CEO is higher than the median EBC in year –1.

We use leverage as an explanatory variable because, as suggested by Jensen (1986), firms with higher leverage will have lower agency costs of equity and hence can be expected to generate more value for their shareholders. We use the change in employees in year –1 as an explanatory variable because larger reductions in employees can lead to a greater reduction in the cost of labor and cost of sales. Hence, the stock price reaction should be more positive for these firms. The third variable we use is the firm's operating performance in year –1. John, Lang, and Netter (1992) find that firms may downsize because of poor performance due to inefficient expansion in the past. We should expect to find that the benefits from downsizing would be highest for those firms with lower operating performance and hence we expect a negative coefficient for this variable.

The fourth variable we use is the firm size given by the log of the book value of assets. As Jensen (1993) points out, if firms downsize because they have grown to be larger than optimal and hence experience deterioration in performance, we should expect to find a negative relationship between the stock price reaction and firm size. The fifth variable we use is a dummy set equal to 1 if there is a new CEO in year –1. We should expect new CEOs to make more drastic changes because they have fewer connections with the current management or its employees. Hence we expect a positive coefficient for this variable. The last variable we use is a dummy, EBC, set equal to 1 if the CEO has incentive compensation higher than the median EBC in year −1. Smith and Watts (1982) argue that CEOs with larger EBC have more incentives to downsize the firm to improve the operating and stock price performance because a larger portion of their income is based on the stock price performance of the firm. Hence we expect a positive coefficient for this variable.

4. CEO COMPENSATION

Table 3 reports the mean and median values of the EBC during the 6-year period around the downsizing announcement. The mean EBC for the overall sample is 0.335 in year −2. This increases to 0.420 in year 0. There is an increase to 0.435 in year + 1 and there are increases in years + 2 and + 3. We

Table 3. EBC for Full Sample, High EBC, and Low EBC in Years −2 through + 3.

Year around downsizing	−2	−1	0	+ 1	+ 2	+ 3
Full sample mean	0.335	0.363	0.420	0.435	0.486	0.472
Full sample median	0.321	0.362	0.427	0.437	0.505	0.486
N (full sample)	95	133	133	133	129	111
High EBC mean	0.383	0.439	0.664	0.505	0.539	0.551
High EBC median	0.375	0.435	0.654	0.578	0.578	0.611
N (high EBC)	54	66	66	66	64	61
Low EBC mean	0.294	0.288	0.133	0.342	0.404	0.413
Low EBC median	0.284	0.237	0.189	0.353	0.423	0.440
N (low EBC)	41	67	67	67	65	50
t-Statistic for the difference between high and low EBC means	1.75	3.17[a]	19.48[a]	3.5[a]	2.82[a]	2.65[a]

Notes: The sample consists of 133 downsizing firms between 1993-2001. All compensation data is obtained from Standard and Poor's ExecuComp database and is reported for the year prior to the downsizing announcement. Total compensation is the sum of salary, bonus, other annual compensation, value of restricted stock granted, value of new options granted during the year, long-term incentive payouts, and all other compensation paid to the CEO. Equity-based compensation (EBC) is the sum of the value of new stock options (using the modified Black-Scholes method) and restricted stock granted to the CEO as a percentage of total compensation paid to them. The EBC for high (low) EBC firms is above (below) the median EBC in year −1.
[a]Significance at the 0.01 level.

then divide the sample into high and low EBC firms and report the EBC for each group over the 6-year window around the downsizing announcement. A firm is characterized as high (low) EBC if the EBC of its CEO is above (below) the median EBC in year −1.

For the high EBC firms the mean is 0.383 in year −2, 0.439 in year −1, and then increases by more than 50% to 0.664 in year 0. The mean EBC decreases to 0.505 in year +1 and it shows small increases in years +2 and +3 following the downsizing. This indicates that the CEO of the high EBC firms is given the highest incentive compensation in the year of the downsizing announcement.

For the low EBC sample, the mean EBC is 0.294 in year −2 and is only 0.133 in year 0. There is a big increase in EBC to 0.342 in year +1 and small increases in years +2 and +3. The differences between the high and low EBC samples are significant in all the years except year −2 of our analysis.

Our analysis indicates that there are substantial changes in the EBC of the downsizing firms. For the high EBC sample the mean incentive compensation increases by more than 50% from year −1 to 0. The median incentive compensation shows a similar increase. For the low EBC firms the mean incentive compensation more than doubles from year 0 to +1. The median incentive compensation also shows a similar trend. The CEOs of the high EBC firms have incentive compensation that is five times the incentive compensation of the low EBC firms in the year of the downsizing announcement.

5. OPERATING PERFORMANCE

We examine the operating performance for the downsizing firms during the 6-year period around the downsizing announcement. This includes the year of the downsizing (year 0) the 2 years prior to the downsizing (years −2 and −1) and the 3 years following the downsizing (years +1, +2, and +3).

Table 4 reports the results. Panel A reports the results for the overall sample. For the overall sample, the mean matched-firm-adjusted performance is 0.011 (significant at the 1% level) in year −2, 0.002 in year −1 (significant at the 1% level) and is zero in year 0. The mean is not significantly different from zero in any of the years following the downsizing.

Panel B reports the results for the high EBC sample. The mean operating performance is not significantly different from zero in year −2. It is positive

Table 4. Operating Performance around Year of Downsizing Based on EBC.

	Year (−2)	Year (−1)	Year (0)	Year (+1)	Year (+2)	Year (+3)
Panel A: Matched-firm-adjusted operating performance for the overall downsizing sample						
Median	0.000	0.000	−0.002	0.002	0.000	−0.002
Mean	0.011[a]	0.002[a]	−0.007	0.003	0.001	−0.005
Standard deviation	0.044	0.003	0.052	0.055	0.067	0.059
N (sample size)	133	133	133	133	126	121
Panel B: Matched-firm-adjusted operating performance for the high EBC downsizing sample						
Median	−0.000	0.001[a]	−0.002	0.001	−0.0026	−0.004
Mean	0.008	0.002[a]	−0.012	−0.004	−0.016	−0.016[c]
Standard deviation	0.046	0.003	0.069	0.062	0.078	0.069
N (sample size)	66	66	66	66	63	60
Panel C: Matched-firm-adjusted operating performance for the low EBC downsizing sample						
Median	0.000	0.001[a]	−0.002	0.002	0.005	0.005
Mean	0.014[a]	0.002[a]	−0.002	0.009[c]	0.017[b]	0.007[b]
Standard deviation	0.044	0.003	0.037	0.044	0.060	0.030
N (sample size)	67	67	67	67	63	61

Notes: Summary statistics for matched-firm-adjusted cash flow to book value ratios for the downsizing sample based on EBC. Only the first downsizing is included per firm per year. Pretax operating cash flow is defined as net sales, minus cost of goods sold, minus selling and administrative expenses, but before deducting interest, depreciation, and amortization expenses. Panel A reports the mean, median, and standard deviation of matched-firm-adjusted cash flow to book value ratio for the overall sample. Panel B reports the statistics for the matched-firm-adjusted cash flow to book value ratio for the high (above-median) EBC firms. Panel C reports the statistics for the matched-firm-adjusted cash flow to book value ratio for the low (below-median) EBC firms. The EBC for high (low) EBC firms is above (below) the median EBC in year −1. Annual matched-firm-adjusted performance subtracts the mean cash flow to book value ratio for the portfolio of non-downsizing matching firms from the downsizing firm's ratio. Non-downsizing matching firms are obtained based on firm size and operating performance of the downsizing firm. Significance levels are based on the parametric *t*-statistic for mean and the Wilcoxon signed-rank test for the median.
[a]Significance at the 0.01 level.
[b]Significance at the 0.05 level.
[c]Significance at the 0.10 level.

and significant in year −1 and zero in year 0. It is zero in years +1 and +2, but it is −.016 (significant at the 10% level) in year +3.

Panel C reports the results for the low EBC sample. The mean matched-firm-adjusted operating performance is 0.014 and 0.002 (both significant at the 1% level) in year −2 and in year −1, respectively, but not significantly different than zero in year 0. The mean matched-firm-adjusted operating

Table 5.   Changes in the Operating Performance around Year
of Downsizing Based on EBC.

	−1 to 0	0 to +1	0 to +2	0 to +3
Panel A: Change in the matched-firm-adjusted operating performance for selected time intervals for full sample				
Median	−0.003	0.007[a]	0.003	0.001
Mean	−0.009[b]	0.009[a]	0.007	0.002
Standard deviation	0.044	0.045	0.070	0.053
N (Sample size)	133	133	126	121
Panel B: Change in the matched-firm-adjusted operating performance for selected time intervals for high EBC firms				
Median	−0.002[c]	0.009	0.001	−0.003
Mean	−0.014[b]	0.008	−0.002	−0.004
Standard deviation	0.049	0.055	0.078	0.061
N (Sample size)	66	66	63	60
Panel C: Change in the matched-firm-adjusted operating performance for selected time intervals for low EBC firms				
Median	−0.003	0.007[a]	0.006[a]	0.003
Mean	−0.003	0.011[a]	0.017[a]	0.008
Standard deviation	0.037	0.032	0.061	0.045
N (Sample size)	67	67	63	61

Notes: Changes in the matched-firm-adjusted performance around the downsizing announcement year for U.S. industrial firms that downsized during the period 1993 to 2001. Only the first
downsizing is included per firm per year. Pretax operating cash flow is defined as net sales,
minus cost of goods sold, minus selling and administrative expenses, but before deducting
interest, depreciation, and amortization expenses. Panel A reports the mean, median, and
standard deviation of the change in the matched-firm-adjusted operating performance for the
full sample. Panel B reports the statistics for the high (above-median) EBC firms, while Panel C
does the same for the low (below-median) EBC firms. Annual matched-firm-adjusted
performance subtracts the mean cash flow to book value ratio for the portfolio of non-
downsizing matching firms from the downsizing firm's ratio. Non-downsizing matching firms
are obtained based on firm size and operating performance of the downsizing firm. Significance
levels are based on the parametric *t*-statistic for mean and the Wilcoxon signed-rank test for the
median.
[a]Significance at the 0.01 level.
[b]Significance at the 0.05 level.
[c]Significance at the 0.10 level.

performance is positive and significantly different from zero in years +1,
+2, and +3.

Table 5 reports the operating performance changes for the overall sample,
as well as the high and low EBC sub-samples. Panel A reports the results

for the overall sample. The mean matched-firm-adjusted operating performance change from year −1 to 0 is negative, −0.009, and statistically significant at the 5% level. The mean operating performance change from year 0 to 1 is 0.009 and is significant at the 1% level. The operating performance changes from years 0 to +2 and 0 to +3 are not statistically significant. Our results indicate that for the overall sample there is a small decline in operating performance from year −1 to 0, and a small improvement from year 0 to +1.

Panel B reports the results for the high EBC sample. The mean change from year −1 to 0 is negative, −0.014, and significant at the 5% level. The mean changes from year 0 to +1, 0 to +2, and 0 to +3 are not significantly different from zero.

Panel C reports the changes in operating performance for the low EBC sample. The mean change from year −1 to 0 is not significantly different from zero. The mean change from year 0 to +1 is positive, 0.011, and significant at the 1% level. The mean change from year 0 to +2 is also positive, 0.017, and significant at the 1% level. The mean change from year 0 to +3 is not significantly different from zero.

Our results on operating performance show that overall downsizing firms have small improvements in operating performance following the downsizing. Once we partition the sample into high and low EBC firms, our results show operating performance improvements for the low EBC firms but not for the high EBC firms. These findings are not consistent with the results in Dial and Murphy (1995) which show that tying managerial compensation to shareholder wealth can create higher value for the shareholders. Our result that high EBC firms tend to have lower future operating performance is consistent with Frye (2004) who finds that greater use of EBC leads to lower levels of accounting return in some later periods.

6. ANNOUNCEMENT PERIOD RETURNS

Table 6 reports the regressions relating the abnormal announcement period returns to firm characteristics for our sample of downsizing firms. The coefficient of leverage is positive, 0.193, and significant at the 1% level. This implies that the announcement period returns are larger for firms that have larger amounts of debt. The coefficient of the change in employees in year −1 is not significantly different from zero. The coefficient of the operating performance is positive, 0.330, and significant at the 1% level. This implies that the announcement period returns are larger for firms that have better

Table 6. Regression of Abnormal Announcement Period Returns
on Firm Characteristics.

Independent Variables	
Intercept	−0.258[a]
	(−5.16)
Leverage	0.193[a]
	(3.41)
Change in employees in year −1	−0.000
	(0.61)
EBITDA/ASSETS in year −1	0.330[a]
	(3.05)
Firm size	0.019[a]
Log of the book value of assets	(3.70)
CEONEW	0.078[a]
Dummy set equal to 1 if there is a new CEO in year −1	(2.68)
EBC	−0.010
Dummy set equal to one if this is a high EBC firm	(−0.54)
N	119
Adjusted R^2	0.26
F	7.98[a]

Notes: Estimates of weighed least squares regressions relating the abnormal returns and firm variables for 133 U.S. industrial firms that downsized during the 1993 to 2001 period. The dependent variable is the cumulative abnormal returns from day −1 to +1, where day 0 is the announcement of the acquisition. The weight variable is the reciprocal of the variance of the market model cumulative abnormal return. The independent variables are: the leverage of the firm calculated as the debt/total assets, the change in employees in year −1 (in thousands), the operating performance (defined as EBITDA of the firm in year −1 scaled by the book value of assets), the log of the book value of assets in year −1, the dummy variable CEONEW set equal to 1 if there is a change in the CEO in year −1 and the dummy variable EBC set equal to 1 if the firm has an EBC greater than the median EBC in year −1. *t*-statistics are in parentheses.
[a]Significance at the 0.01 level.

operating performance in the year prior to the downsizing announcement. This is contrary to our expectations. The coefficient of firm size is positive, 0.019, and significant at the 1% level. This implies that the market expects more value to be created by larger firms. This is consistent with our expectations. The coefficient of the high EBC dummy is not significantly different from zero. This implies that the market does not believe that high incentive compensation creates more value among downsizing firms. This is again contrary to our earlier expectation that incentive compensation can potentially motivate CEOs to increase shareholder wealth by downsizing. One potential explanation for this finding is provided by John et al. (1992) who suggest that the problems faced by these companies may be due to other factors such as poor industry conditions or foreign competition. The CEOs may not be able to turn around these firms by doing a superior job. The coefficient of the CEONEW dummy is positive, 0.078, and significant at the 1% level. This implies that firms that hire a new CEO in the year prior to the downsizing and then announce their downsizing potentially create more value. A possible explanation for the higher announcement period return is that a new manager makes more drastic changes when compared to an entrenched manager who may have potentially created the problems at the firm in the first place. The R^2 of the regression is 26% and the F-value is 7.98, significant at the 1% level.

7. SUMMARY AND CONCLUSIONS

During the last decade, we have witnessed a substantial increase in the use of incentive-based compensation for CEOs in corporate America. Jensen and Meckling (1976) and Smith and Watts (1982) argue that incentive-based compensation plans can reduce the conflicts of interests between managers and shareholders and can motivate these managers to make value maximizing decisions. Dial and Murphy (1995) analyze the role of managerial incentives in value creation at General Dynamics. They find that executive compensation plans motivated managers to partially sell off assets and substantially increase firm value. Our study is a large sample analysis of the clinical study by Dial and Murphy (1995) and provides evidence across several industries and a large number of firms.

Overall, we find that in the year prior to the downsizing there is a large increase in the equity-based CEO compensation for our sample of 133 firms during the 1993–2001 period. The sample firms show improvements in operating performance in the year following the downsizing announcement. Nevertheless, we find that these improvements exist only for the low EBC firms but not the high EBC firms. Our cross-sectional regressions relating the abnormal announcement period returns to firm variables indicate that the announcement period returns are higher for downsizing firms with better operating performance, more leverage, and bigger size. We also find that the announcement period returns are larger when the incumbent CEO is replaced in the year prior to the downsizing announcement. We do not find any relationship between CEO incentive compensation and announcement period returns. Our results indicate that incentive-based compensation schemes do not necessarily lead to long-term improvements in firm value and operating performance.

ACKNOWLEDGMENTS

We are thankful for comments received from Kose John, Anil Makhija, Craig Rennie, Emery Trahan, participants of the 2006 FMA Annual Meeting and the 2006 International Conference on Business, Economics, Management and Marketing. Remaining errors are our responsibility.

REFERENCES

Anderson, S., & Cavanagh, J. (1994). *Workers lose, CEOs win.* Washington, DC: Institute for Policy Studies.

Barber, B. M., & Lyon, J. D. (1996). Detecting abnormal operating performance: The empirical power and specification of test statistics. *Journal of Financial Economics, 41,* 359–399.

Brown, S. J., & Warner, J. B. (1985). Using daily stock returns: The case of event studies. *Journal of Financial Economics, 14,* 3–31.

Datta, S., Iskandar- Datta, M., & Raman, K. (2001). Executive compensation and corporate acquisition decisions. *Journal of Finance, 56,* 2299–2336.

Dechow, P., Huson, M., & Sloan, R. (1994). The effect of restructuring charges on executives' cash compensation. *Accounting Review, 69,* 138–156.

Dial, J., & Murphy, K. (1995). Incentives, downsizing and value creation at General Dynamics. *Journal of Financial Economics, 37,* 261–314.

Fama, E., & French, K. (1995). Size and book-to-market factors in earnings and returns. *Journal of Finance, 45,* 1045–1068.

Frye, M. (2004). Equity-based compensation for employees: Firm performance and determinants. *The Journal of Financial Research, 27,* 31–54.

Hallock, K. F. (1998). Layoffs, top executive pay, and firm performance. *American Economic Review, 88,* 771–793.

Healy, P. (1985). The effect of bonus schemes on accounting decisions. *Journal of Accounting and Economics, 7,* 85–107.

Jensen, M. (1986). The agency costs of free cash flow, corporate finance, and the market for takeovers. *American Economic Review, 76,* 323–329.

Jensen, M. (1993). The modern industrial revolution, exit and the failure of internal control systems. *Journal of Finance, 48,* 831–876.

Jensen, M., & Meckling, W. (1976). Theory of the firm: Managerial behavior, agency costs and ownership structure. *Journal of Financial Economics, 3,* 305–360.

John, K., Lang, H. P., & Netter, J. (1992). The voluntary restructuring of large firms in response to performance decline. *Journal of Finance, 47,* 891–918.

Mehran, H., Nogler, G. E., & Schwartz, K. B. (1998). CEO incentive plans and corporate liquidation policy. *Journal of Financial Economics, 50*, 319–349.

Murphy, K. J. (1995). Politics, economics and executive compensation. *University of Cincinnati Law Review, 63*, 713–748.

Sloan, A. (1996). The hit men. *Newsweek* (February 26), 44–48.

Smith, C., & Watts, R. (1982). Incentive and tax effects of U.S. executive compensation plans. *Australian Management Journal, 7*, 117–161.

THE EXTERNAL MONITORING BODIES' VIEW OF THE BOARD INDEPENDENCE IN THE NEW PUBLIC FAMILY FIRMS

Imants Paeglis and Dogan Tirtiroglu

ABSTRACT

Some commentators suggest that the Wall Street views family firms with scepticism. The appointment of independent directors to form a majority on a firm's board of directors should constitute a strong signal to the market of a family firm's willingness to be monitored objectively and thus should alleviate Wall Street's scepticism. This is likely to be more important for the newly public family firms than for mature family firms since outsider-domination on the board pre-dates the involvement of other outsiders, such as underwriters, financial analysts, or institutional investors. Whether the presence of an independent board alleviates the market's scepticism may be evident in the responses of various external monitoring entities to the newly public family and non-family firms. Using a hand-collected sample of newly public firms, we cast brand-new light on whether an independent board provides any advantage to the newly public family firms in underwriter reputation, analyst coverage, and investment by institutional investors over newly public non-family firms. We find that independence of board of directors is overall a positive signal and that

Issues in Corporate Governance and Finance
Advances in Financial Economics, Volume 12, 137–164
© 2007 Published by Elsevier Ltd.
ISSN: 1569-3732/doi:10.1016/S1569-3732(07)12007-7

while the independence of board is more important than the independence of management for underwriters and financial analysts, the reverse is the case for institutional investors.

1. INTRODUCTION

Of late, there has been an increasing interest in studying the influence of the founding family on family firms' financial performance (see, e.g. Anderson & Reeb, 2003; Villalonga & Amit, 2006). Recent papers, without exception, choose their samples from large, mature, and index-listed family firms and focus their attention almost entirely on the valuation differential between these firms and non-family firms with similar characteristics. So far, empirical results indicate a value premium for the family firms. In this literature, Anderson and Reeb (2004) is the only paper that examines empirically the role of the board of directors (BOD henceforth) in the context of family firms. They find that only family firms with a majority of independent directors on their BOD are trading at a premium.

Our paper considers the role of BOD in newly public family firms. It differs from previous family firm papers, including Anderson and Reeb (2004), in a number of fundamental ways. First, it appears that, in spite of the recently documented value premium for family firms, the Wall Street views these firms with scepticism (Stein, 2001). Jerome Kohlberg (2005) of KKR indicates that extensive extraction of firm resources for private consumption by family members was a main reason for the discount in family firms and for his company's focus on management buy-outs in the 1980s. The value premium for the mature, large, and index-listed family firms may be an outcome of a survival bias. In particular, these firms were born as family firms and survived the time's tests, including the management buy-outs of the 1980s. Over time, they have built a self-identity that has become independent of the family's name and reputation. Also, being listed in either the S&P 500 Index or the Fortune 500, these firms are not in need of the nurture and care of the founding family anymore; they are under the tight scrutiny and monitoring of the financial markets. Even if the family ownership vanishes completely today, it is unlikely to have any material effect on the firm and its direction.

Newly public family firms, however, are more likely to need the nurture and care of the founding family and to be without the scrutiny and monitoring received by firms listed on the market-wide indices. Therefore, the Wall Street's scepticism is much more likely to be apparent in the newly public family firms than mature, large, and index-listed family firms. Thus, we focus our attention on the sample of newly public family and non-family firms. They face considerable asymmetric information and uncertainty, but offer potential of fast growth. In addition, the founding family members own a larger percentage of the equity, at least initially, in the newly public family firms than in mature, large, and index-listed family firms.

Second, outsider-domination on BOD of the newly public firms pre-dates the involvement of other outsiders, such as financial analysts and institutional investors. This offers very useful insights about the prospects of an IPO-issuing firm.[1] The appointment of independent directors to form a majority on a firm's BOD should constitute a strong signal to the market of its willingness to be monitored objectively.[2] Whether the presence of an independent BOD alleviates the market's scepticism may be evident in the responses of various external monitoring entities to the newly public family and non-family firms. Thus, we ask the following specific questions:

1. Does the presence of an independent BOD lead to any difference in the reputation of IPO underwriters between family and non-family firms?
2. Does the presence of an independent BOD lead to any difference in the post-IPO analyst coverage between family and non-family firms?
3. Does the presence of an independent BOD lead to any difference in the post-IPO percentage of shares held by institutional investors between family and non-family firms?

We also conduct further empirical tests on the following sub-samples: (1) family firms with and without an independent BOD and (2) family firms with an independent BOD and non-family firms with an insider-dominated BOD. These tests unearth evidence about the importance of an independent BOD only in the context of family firms and about the external monitoring establishments' preferences between board independence and managerial independence. To our knowledge, no evidence is presently available on any of these questions for the newly public firms.

Third, going public is a crucial step not only in the evolution of a family firm into a public corporation, but also in the separation of ownership and control (Schwert, 1985; Brennan & Franks, 1997). Focusing on the IPO and post-IPO stages allows us to recognize *separately* the unseasoned influence of: (1) an owner-founder chief executive officer and the chairperson of the BOD (FCC henceforth), (2) an owner-founder chief executive officer (FCEO henceforth), or (3) an owner-founder chairperson of BOD (FCHAIR henceforth), on various characteristics of IPOs, as put forth in the questions above. Holding ownership constant, each of the above three categories represents a different degree of owner-founders' involvement in the management and governance of their firms.[3] It is likely that the importance of board independence will vary with the degree of the owner-founders' involvement in the management and governance of the firm. Consequently, each category is likely to exhibit its own distinct differences not only from the non-family firms, but also from one another. We are the first to identify explicitly and study empirically family firms with a FCC, a FCEO, or a FCHAIR at the time of going public.

We find that: (1) all three external monitoring bodies exhibit a negative response to the newly public family firms, (2) the presence of an independent BOD in newly public family firms serves as a positive signal, (3) while the independence of BOD is more important than the independence of management for IPO underwriters and financial analysts, the reverse is the case for institutional investors.

The rest of the paper is organized as follows. The next section presents empirically testable arguments either in favor or against family firms. Section 3 covers data and sample characteristics. Section 4 offers empirical methodology, variable definitions, and empirical results. Section 5 concludes the paper.

2. FAMILY FIRMS IN THE IPO PROCESS

Below, Section 2.1 considers the board independence in the context of newly public family firms and Section 2.2 presents empirical implications of observing an independent BOD in the newly public firms on underwriter reputation, financial analyst coverage, and post-IPO interest of institutional investors.

2.1. Board Independence and Family Firms in the IPO Process

The rich agency-theoretic literature suggests arguments or presents empirical evidence on whether the presence of an owner-founder in a family firm might be good news or not-so-good news in relation to the presence of a professional manager in a non-family firm. We take the presence of an independent BOD in a newly public family firm as a bonding signal to alleviate market participants' reservations about the presence of an owner-founder in a family firm.

Outsider-domination on BOD of the newly public firms pre-dates the involvement of other outsiders, such as financial analysts and institutional investors. In the presence of an owner-founder in a family firm in the IPO process, the appointment of independent directors to form a majority on its

BOD is one of the ways for it to signal strongly and credibly to the market of its willingness to be monitored directly and objectively. Overall, the market participants should prefer family firms with an independent BOD over family firms with an insider-dominated BOD. Whether the market participants would prefer family firms with an independent BOD over non-family firms with an independent BOD depends on their view of the abilities of a founder-manager relative to those of a professional manager. This is an empirical matter. Finally, a comparison of family firms with an independent BOD against non-family firms with an insider-dominated BOD reflects the market participants' preference for the independence of either BOD or the management. Once again, this is an empirical matter.

We expect to observe distinct differences not only between family and non-family firms, but also among family firms with various degrees of owner-founder involvements (i.e., with FCC, FCEO, or FCHAIR). The posited positive bonding effect of an independent BOD should be more pronounced for the newly public family firms with a FCC than those with a FCEO or a FCHAIR.[4] The dual role of a FCC in the absence of an independent BOD may, in itself, be seen as a negative signal. Yermack (1996) finds higher market valuation of firms with separated roles of CEO and chair of BOD (see also Jensen, 1993). Hence, a FCC's choice to establish an independent BOD, as opposed to an insider-dominated one, signals credibly his/her confidence in his/her managerial abilities, skills, and hard work. In the case of a family firm with a FCEO, the separation of the roles of the CEO and the chair of the board, in itself, may be seen as a positive signal; this suggests that the need for monitoring by an independent BOD should be lower for family firms with a FCEO relative to that for family firms with a FCC. Finally, the role of BOD in a newly public family firm with a FCHAIR is somewhat different from that in a newly public family firm, in which an owner-founder still has an active managerial role. The role of BOD in such a firm is to monitor a professionally employed CEO, not the owner-founder. Whether the monitoring of a professional CEO by an independent BOD will be stronger than that by an insider-dominated BOD does not appear to have a clear cut answer.[5] The most likely explanation for observing a FCHAIR in a newly public family firm without a venture capital backing is that the key founding individual has decided on his/her own to leave the FCEO role and to hire a professional manager. Overall, giving up the FCEO or the FCC role is a candid acknowledgement by the owner-founder of his/her limited managerial skills and/or experience. This should send a positive signal to the market. But, the market's preference for either an insider- or an independent BOD in a family firm with a FCHAIR remains an empirical question.

2.2. External Monitoring Bodies and Independence of BOD in Newly Public Firms

Our first question concerns the reputation of IPO underwriters. Since the reputation of an IPO underwriter is one of its most important assets and is attained over a long period of time, it is natural to expect highly reputable IPO underwriters to be more selective in choosing firms they bring public. They are likely to seek the business of better firms that are characterized by, among other things, a lower level of asymmetric information (see, e.g. Chemmanur & Fulghieri, 1994). If the presence of an independent BOD is a credible and objective positive signal, holding all else constant, we expect family firms with an independent BOD to attract more reputable IPO underwriters (relative to family firms without an independent BOD). The question of whether more reputable IPO underwriters would prefer non-family firms with an insider-dominated BOD over family firms with an independent BOD pits the independence of management against the independence of governance. Empirical results will shed light on this question.

Our second question concerns financial analyst coverage of firms after going public. Asymmetric information about a firm's prospects is a hindering and fundamental source of uncertainty for investors and renders them hesitant or withdrawn to inject capital into it. Increased financial analyst coverage is crucial for firms to increase their liquidity and reduce their cost of capital (Amihud & Mendelson, 2000; Das, Guo, & Zhang, 2006). The amount and continuity of financial analyst coverage depends on a number of factors, including costs of information production, analysts' own personal reputation and their business interests in the potential clients.

If the presence of an independent BOD is a credible and objective signal, then, holding all else constant, we expect: (1) that financial analyst coverage will be more for family firms with an independent BOD than those family firms without an independent BOD, (2) that financial analyst coverage for non-family firms with an independent BOD will be more than family firms, and (3) that financial analyst coverage of non-family firms with an insider BOD vis-a-vis family firms with an independent BOD will be, once again, an empirical matter.

Our third and final question concerns the post-IPO investment position of institutional investors in family and non-family firms. The institutional investors are likely to be more informed than individual investors. They tend to take up large ownership positions in a firm and become forceful owners to keep the management of the firm transparent and focused, as much as possible, on shareholder wealth maximization. In addition, the presence of institutional investors may be crucial for, especially newly public, firms' success and survival (see, e.g. Field & Lowry, 2004). Meanwhile, given that intergenerational transfer of managerial control is a stated objective of most family firms, it is likely that there may not be a fluid chemistry between institutional investors and the members of the family unless the institutional investors prefer to be 'silent' providers of capital.[6] Whether the presence of an independent BOD may remove institutional investors' reservations about family firms remains an empirical question. Overall, we expect institutional investors to prefer (1) non-family firms to family firms, especially those with an insider BOD and (2) family firms with an independent BOD to family firms with an insider-dominated BOD.

3. DATA AND SAMPLE CHARACTERISTICS

The data for this study come from several different databases. The list of IPOs of common equity between 1993 and 2000 is from the SDC/Platinum New Issue database. We eliminate REITs, closed-end funds, unit offerings, equity carve-outs, financial (all firms with SIC codes between 6000 and 6999) and foreign firms. This screening leaves us with a sample of 2,764 firms. We then exclude previous leveraged buyouts and roll-ups. There are 19 firms, which are not found in the Center for Research in Security Prices (CRSP) database. For an additional six firms, the CRSP and the SDC databases show different first dates of trading. Eliminating these 25 firms leaves a total of 2,613 firms in our sample, as shown in Panel A of Table 1. 722 out of these 2,613 firms are non-venture-backed firms and constitute the final sample for this study. The data on the presence of founding family, shareholdings of CEOs, the number of shares outstanding, and book values of firms' equity, as well as various corporate governance measures are hand collected from the prospectuses of firms going public. Stock prices necessary to calculate IPO underpricing are from CRSP. The number of institutional shareholders and the percentage of the shares held by them after the IPO are from the Compact D database. The number of analysts is from the IBES.

Table 1 provides a distribution of the sample by year and the presence of founding family. Of the 722 firms in our sample, 67 firms (9.3%) have a FCEO, 371 firms (51.4%) have a FCC, and 57 firms (7.9%) have a FCHAIR. Thus, the owner-founders are actively involved in either the management, or the governance, or both of 495 firms, comprising 68.5% of the final sample.

Table 1. Number of IPOs by Year, Type of Founding Family Presence, and Pre-IPO Institutional Backing Type.

	1993	1994	1995	1996	1997	1998	1999	2000	Total
Common stock issues	615	516	539	792	473	307	498	376	4,116
Units	91	108	86	122	26	11	2	3	449
Carve-outs	98	69	40	64	36	26	42	30	405
LBO	40	12	11	15	3	0	3	5	89
Financial	48	29	31	62	72	67	44	10	363
Foreign	10	4	19	27	3	1	34	37	135
CRSP NA	3	4	1	4	3	2	1	1	19
Unclear	0	2	0	1	0	2	0	1	6
Roll-ups	0	0	2	11	9	10	4	1	37
Venture-backed	200	165	247	350	200	136	323	270	1,891
Final sample	**125**	**123**	**102**	**136**	**121**	**52**	**45**	**18**	**722**
Non-family	33	35	35	43	41	20	15	5	227
FCC	76	68	49	72	54	22	21	9	371
FCEO	10	12	9	10	16	5	5	0	67
FCHAIR	6	8	9	11	10	5	4	4	57

Panel A of Table 2 reports summary statistics on the independent and dependent variables. Panel B of Table 2 shows not only the means and medians, but also the test results for the mean and median differences in various firm characteristics between family and non-family firms. We find that family firms are smaller and younger than non-family firms. We also find that family firms are less likely to be listed on NYSE. Finally, family and non-family firms are equally likely to belong to the technology sector.

Panel C of Table 2 exhibits the correlations between independent variables. Correlation coefficients indicate no potential for multi-co linearity for our empirical tests.

4. EMPIRICAL METHODOLOGY AND RESULTS

In Section 4.1, we discuss the variables used in our empirical tests; in Section 4.2, we report the univariate results of the tests of the differences in the degree of board independence between non-family and various types of family firms; from Section 4.3 onwards, we report empirical results.

Table 2. Summary Statistics.

Panel A: Summary statistics

	Min.	Mean	Median	Max.	SD
FAMILY	0	0.6856	1	1	0.4646
FAM_ODOM	0	0.2078	0	1	0.4060
LNBVA	12.0639	16.7201	16.8337	23.6529	1.5273
LFAGE	0	2.4220	2.3979	4.9767	0.9308
ODOMB	0	0.3338	0	1	0.4719
NCOM	1	2.0429	2	17	1.0074
CEOA	0	0.3132	0.2682	1	0.2321
NYSE	0	0.0845	0	1	0.2783
NASDQ	0	0.7604	1	1	0.4271
HOT	0	0.0873	0	1	0.2824
DTECH	0	0.2313	0	1	0.4220
RRANK	1	6.1136	7	9	2.4762
LNUM	0	0.4605	0	2.8332	0.7275
INSTP	0	0.1318	0.1138	0.6266	0.1096

Panel B: Differences in various firm characteristics between family and non-family firms

	Non-Family		Family		Difference	
	Mean	Median	Mean	Median	Mean	Median
LNBVA	16.9209	17.0391	16.6280	16.7355	0.2929 (2.40)**	0.3036 (2.37)**
LFAGE	2.5490	2.4849	2.3638	2.3979	0.1852 (2.49)**	0.0870 (1.96)**
NYSE	0.1145	0	0.0707	0	0.0438 (1.97)**	0.0000 (1.96)**
NASDQ	0.7225	1	0.7778	1	−0.0553 (−1.62)	0.0000 (−1.62)
DTECH	0.1938	0	0.2485	0	−0.0547 (−1.62)	0.0000 (1.62)

Table 2. (*Continued*)

Panel C: Correlations between independent variables

	1	2	3	4	5	6	7	8	9	10	11
FAMILY	1										
FAM_ODOM	0.6442	1									
LNBVA	-0.0855	-0.0329	1								
LFAGE	-0.0894	-0.1402	0.2274	1							
ODOMB	-0.128	0.4886	0.0447	-0.1482	1						
NCOM	-0.0341	0.0849	0.3979	-0.0639	0.2202	1					
CEOA	0.2721	-0.0113	-0.0321	0.1203	-0.3559	-0.153	1				
NYSE	-0.101	-0.0938	0.3625	0.169	-0.0666	0.1644	0.0098	1			
NASDQ	0.0739	0.0951	0.0686	-0.011	0.1328	0.1103	-0.0344	-0.5849	1		
HOT	0.0134	0.0838	0.1359	-0.1901	0.2018	0.4857	-0.1234	-0.09	0.1725	1	
DTECH	0.0103	0.0299	-0.0418	-0.0909	0.1117	0.1912	-0.0983	-0.1213	0.1417	0.3433	1

Notes: The sample consists of 722 non-venture-backed initial public offerings between 1993 and 2000. FAMILY is a dummy variable that takes on a value of one if the founder of the firm is either CEO (FCEO), chairman of the board (FCHAIR), or both (FCC), and zero otherwise. ODOMB is a dummy variable that takes on a value of one if the firm's board of directors is dominated by outsiders, and zero otherwise. FAM_ODOM is a product of FAMILY and ODOMB. LNBVA is the natural logarithm of the book value of the firm's assets at the time of going public. LFAGE is the natural logarithm of one plus firm age, where firm age is defined as the number of years between the year of incorporation or start of operations (whichever is earlier), and the time of going public. NCOM is the number of co-managing underwriters. HOT is a dummy variable that takes on a value of one if the firm went public in 1999 and 2000, and zero otherwise. DTECH is a dummy variable that takes on a value of one if the firm is in a technology-related industry (as defined by Loughran & Ritter, 2004), and zero otherwise. CEOA is the percentage of the shares outstanding held by the CEO after the IPO. NYSE is a dummy variable that takes on a value of one if the firm is listed in the NYSE, and zero otherwise. NASDQ is a dummy variable that takes on a value of one if the firm is listed on NASDQ, and zero otherwise. RRANK is the lead underwriter's reputation as measured by Loughran and Ritter (2004). INSTP is the percentage of the shares outstanding held by institutional investors at the end of the first quarter after the IPO. LNUM is the natural logarithm of one plus the number of analysts following the firm one quarter after the IPO. The results of *t*-tests for the difference in means and non-parametric Wilcoxon signed rank tests for the difference in medians are reported in parenthesis.

***Significance at the 1% level.

**Significance at the 5% level.

*Significance at the 10% level.

4.1. Variable Definitions and Methodology

To study the differences between family and non-family firms, we create a dummy variable, FAMILY. It takes on a value of one if the founder of the firm is either FCEO, FCHAIR, or FCC, and zero otherwise. Our measure of board independence, ODOMB, is a dummy variable with a value of one if BOD is dominated by independent (outside) directors, and zero otherwise. Following Baker and Gompers (2003), we put directors on a firm's BOD into one of three groups: outside, gray, and inside. Outside directors are those, who have neither any affiliation with, nor provide any business services to the firm. This excludes full and part time employees of a firm. Former employees and their family members are all classified as insiders. Gray directors have substantial business ties to the firm and include, among others, lawyers, bankers, and consultants. All others are inside directors. We also generate an interaction variable, FAM_ODOM, between FAMILY and ODOMB to allow for a differential influence of board independence on various IPO characteristics of family and non-family firms.

For each question posed in the Introduction, we report five sets of empirical results, pertaining to five samples that vary in the definition of a family firm. These five samples are: (1) full sample (family firms with a FCC, a FCEO, or a FCHAIR, and non-family firms), (2) sample of family firms with the managerial role of the founder (both FCC and FCEO) and non-family firms, (3) sample of family firms with a FCC and non-family firms, (4) sample of family firms with a FCEO and non-family firms, and (5) sample of family firms with a FCHAIR and non-family firms. The last four samples exclude the types of family firms other than those specified (e.g., in sample (2), we exclude family firms with FCHAIR, while in sample (3) we exclude those with either a FCEO or a FCHAIR).

In addition, for each of Tables 4–6 we report the results of above five specifications for three different samples. The first panel (Panel A) of Tables 4–6 reports results for the full sample. The second panel (Panel B) uses only the family firm sub-sample, and considers a comparison between family firms with independent BOD and those without it. The third panel (Panel C) uses a sample that contains family firms with an independent BOD and non-family firms with an insider-dominated BOD. This allows us to compare the external monitoring establishments' perception of management independence and board independence. Thus, each table provides 15 different estimations reported in three panels.

4.2. Univariate Tests

Table 3 reports the results of univariate tests of the differences in the degree of board independence between non-family and various types of family firms. Family firms with a FCC are less likely to have independent boards than are non-family firms. In particular, while 40% of non-family firms have independent boards, only 27% of family firms with a FCC have independent BOD. The difference is statistically significant at the 1% level. The differences in the board independence between family firms with either a FCEO or a FCHAIR and non-family firms are not statistically significant. Furthermore, the percentage of independent BOD for the family firms with a FCC is statistically significantly (at the 5% level) less than those for both

Table 3. Univariate Tests of Differences in the Proportion of Firms with Outsider-Dominated Boards by the Type of Founding Family Presence.

	Mean	Median
FCC	0.2696	0
FCEO	0.4107	0
FCHAIR	0.4138	0
Non-family	0.4027	0
Differences		
FCC less non-family	−0.1330	0.0000
	(3.40)***	(11.56)***
FCEO less non-family	0.0081	0.0000
	(−0.11)	(0.01)
FCHAIR less non-family	0.0111	0.0000
	(−0.15)	(0.02)
FCC less FCEO	−0.14	0.00
	(2.18)**	(4.74)**
FCC less FCHAIR	−0.1442	0.0000
	(−2.26)**	(5.10)**
FCEO less FCHAIR	−0.0031	0.0000
	(−0.03)	(2.16)

Notes: FCEO, FCC, and FCHAIR refer to founder-CEO, founder-CEO-and-chairman, and founder chairman, respectively. The results of non-parametric Wilcoxon signed rank test for the differences in means and the Pearson χ^2 tests for the differences in medians are reported in parenthesis.
*Significance at the 10% level.
**Significance at the 5% level.
***Significance at the 1% level.

family firms with a FCEO and family firms with a FCHAIR. To summarize, family firms with a FCC are less likely to have an independent BOD relative to both non-family firms and other types of family firms.

4.3. Family Firms and Underwriter Reputation

We examine the potential relationship between the presence of a founder in a firm and the reputation of its IPO underwriters using the following empirical model, estimated by OLS:

$$RRANK_i = \beta_0 + \beta_1 FAMILY_i + \beta_2 FAMILY\_ODOM_i + \beta_3 ODOM_i + \beta_4 LNBVA_i$$
$$+ \beta_5 LFAGE_i + \beta_6 DTECH_i + \beta_7 HOT_i + \beta_8 CEOA_i + \varepsilon_i \qquad (1)$$

RRANK is the Carter and Manaster (1990) ranking, as updated by Loughran and Ritter (2004). FAMILY is a dummy variable with a value of one for a family firm, and zero otherwise. As described above, we consider a total of five different specifications of Eq. (1), with the definition of a family firm varying from one specification to another. For example, in specification (1) FAMILY takes on a value of one if the firm had either FCC, FCEO, or FCHAIR, while in specification (2) it takes on a value of one if the firm had either FCC or FCEO.

The remaining independent variables in Eq. (1) control for various aspects of firm quality. Two common firm quality variables, used in many IPO studies, are firm size and firm age (see, e.g., Ritter, 1984; Michaely & Shaw, 1994). We use the natural logarithm of book value of a firm's assets at the time of going public, LNBVA, as a proxy for firm size. Firm age, LFAGE, is defined as the natural log of one plus the number of years between either the year of incorporation or the start of operations, whichever is earlier, and the time of going public. Following Loughran and Ritter (2004), we also control for industry differences by introducing DTECH, which is a dummy variable with a value of one if the firm is in a technology-related industry, and zero otherwise. Since our sample period includes the hot issue markets of 1999 and 2000, we introduce HOT, a dummy variable that takes on a value of one if a firm went public either in 1999 or 2000, and zero otherwise. Finally, we use a CEO's post-IPO ownership position, CEOA, as a control variable.

Table 4 presents the empirical results on the relationship between family firms and underwriter reputation. In Panel A, we observe three pertinent results. First, the coefficient estimates for ODOMB across all samples are statistically significant. The market receives the independence of BOD, for

Table 4. The Relationship between the Presence of a Founding Family, Board Independence, and Underwriter Reputation.

	(1) Full sample	(2) FCEO & FCC	(3) FCC	(4) FCEO	(5) FCHAIR
Panel A: Results for the full sample					
FAMILY	−0.072	−0.218	−0.124	−0.959	0.947
	(0.37)	(1.08)	(0.61)	(2.10)**	(2.53)**
FAM_ODOM	−0.141	−0.045	−0.221	1.126	−1.056
	(0.48)	(0.15)	(0.70)	(1.74)*	(2.16)**
ODOMB	0.482	0.471	0.445	0.547	0.548
	(2.10)**	(2.04)**	(1.93)*	(2.30)**	(2.32)**
LNBVA	1.052	1.042	1.060	1.066	1.107
	(17.13)***	(16.18)***	(16.77)***	(12.89)***	(16.55)***
LFAGE	−0.009	−0.020	−0.057	−0.116	−0.166
	(0.09)	(0.21)	(0.60)	(1.03)	(1.60)
DTECH	0.832	0.864	0.899	0.511	0.504
	(4.93)***	(4.88)***	(4.91)***	(1.87)*	(1.89)*
HOT	0.407	0.518	0.651	0.132	0.124
	(1.70)*	(2.01)**	(2.45)**	(0.34)	(0.33)
CEOA	−0.075	0.201	0.072	0.267	0.123
	(0.24)	(0.62)	(0.22)	(0.63)	(0.28)
Constant	−11.741	−11.615	−11.804	−11.722	−12.261
	(12.49)***	(11.78)***	(11.97)***	(9.17)***	(11.21)***
Adj. R^2	0.40	0.40	0.41	0.45	0.49
N	718	661	606	280	282
Panel B: Results for the family firm sub-sample					
ODOMB	0.348	0.433	0.242	1.325	−0.456
	(1.81)*	(2.07)**	(1.08)	(2.26)***	(0.96)
LNBVA	1.020	1.002	1.019	0.847	1.097
	(11.61)***	(10.49)***	(10.19)***	(2.62)**	(6.38)***
LFAGE	0.144	0.150	0.186	0.099	0.031
	(0.96)	(0.96)	(1.16)	(0.21)	(0.07)
DTECH	0.932	0.984	1.027	1.161	0.513
	(4.58)***	(4.53)***	(4.33)***	(2.05)**	(0.83)
HOT	0.438	0.616	0.663	1.227	−0.481
	(1.55)	(1.96)*	(1.86)*	(2.12)**	(0.73)
CEOA	−0.210	0.126	0.379	−0.755	0.349
	(0.53)	(0.28)	(0.76)	(0.48)	(0.14)
Constant	−11.630	−11.576	−12.048	−8.858	−11.614
	(9.31)***	(8.53)***	(8.38)***	(1.96)*	(4.34)***
Adj. R^2	0.36	0.35	0.36	0.28	0.43
N	492	436	371	65	56

Table 4. (*Continued*)

	(1) Full sample	(2) FCEO & FCC	(3) FCC	(4) FCEO	(5) FCHAIR
Panel C: Results for the sub-samples of family firms with an independent BOD and non-family firms with an insider-dominated BOD					
ODOMB	0.307	0.235	−0.001	0.974	0.551
	(1.35)	(0.93)	(0.00)	(2.13)**	(1.61)
LNBVA	1.107	1.089	1.092	1.085	1.133
	(17.22)***	(16.32)***	(15.66)***	(13.28)***	(13.36)***
LFAGE	0.007	−0.020	−0.008	−0.086	−0.071
	(0.07)	(0.17)	(0.07)	(0.71)	(0.59)
DTECH	0.944	1.044	1.155	0.323	0.275
	(3.45)***	(3.52)***	(3.78)***	(0.74)	(0.71)
HOT	0.194	0.359	0.513	−0.093	−0.244
	(0.49)	(0.79)	(1.11)	(0.09)	(0.36)
CEOA	0.211	0.263	0.478	0.486	0.285
	(0.50)	(0.58)	(1.03)	(0.88)	(0.51)
Constant	−12.810	−12.465	−12.611	−12.142	−12.937
	(12.12)***	(11.32)***	(10.94)***	(8.89)***	(9.09)***
Adj. R^2	0.49	0.47	0.50	0.48	0.53
N	284	260	237	158	159

Notes: The dependent variable is lead underwriter's reputation, as measured by Loughran and Ritter (2004). FAMILY is a dummy variable that takes on a value of one if the founding family is present in the firm at the time of the IPO, and zero otherwise. The reported regression splits the sample by the type of the founding-family presence, with the definition of FAMILY in each regression indicated at the top of the column. FCEO is founder-CEO, FCHAIR is founder-chairman, and FCC is founder-CEO-and-chairman. ODOMB is a dummy variable that takes on a value of one if the firm's board of directors is dominated by outsiders, and zero otherwise. FAM_ODOM is a product of FAMILY and ODOMB. LNBVA is the natural logarithm of the book value of the firm's assets at the time of going public. LFAGE is the natural log of one plus firm age, where firm age is defined as the number of years between the year of incorporation or start of operations (whichever is earlier), and the time of going public. DTECH is a dummy variable that takes on a value of one if the firm is in a technology-related industry (as defined by Loughran & Ritter, 2004), and zero otherwise. HOT is a dummy variable that takes on a value of one if the firm went public in 1999 or 2000, and zero otherwise. CEOA is the percentage of shares outstanding held by CEO after the IPO. Heteroskedasticity-adjusted (White) standard errors are used in calculation of *t*-statistics.
***Significance at the 1% level.
**Significance at the 5% level.
*Significance at the 10% level.

non-family as well as for all types of family firms, as a positive and important signal. Second, the coefficient estimates for FAM_ODOM are statistically significantly positive for firms with a FCEO (column (4)) and negative for firms with a FCHAIR (column (5)). IPO underwriters of family firms with a FCEO and an independent BOD have better reputation than those of family firms with a FCEO and insider-dominated BOD, and non-family firms. The reverse is the case for family firms with a FCHAIR. Third, the coefficient estimates for FAMILY are statistically significantly negative for firms with a FCEO (column (4)) and positive for firms with a FCHAIR (column (5)). IPO underwriters of non-family firms have better reputation than those of family firms with a FCEO. The reverse is the case for family firms with a FCHAIR.

The results for family firms with a FCEO indicate that, as expected, the presence of an independent BOD serves as a positive signal, attracting more reputable underwriters to family firms with a FCEO and an outsider-dominated BOD. We find that monitoring of professionally employed CEOs is stronger in family firms with a FCHAIR and insider-dominated BOD than in firms with a BOD dominated by outsiders without significant ownership stakes. This is consistent with the idea that families maintain sufficiently large ownership positions and have the incentives to be constructively vigilant in their monitoring activities.

Our results are also economically significant. For example, the presence of a FCEO in a family firm reduces the underwriter reputation by about 13.4% of the average firm's underwriter reputation. The presence of a FCHAIR in a family firm, however, increases it by about the same percentage. The magnitude of the coefficient estimates for FAM_ODOM is also economically meaningful. The difference, both in the FCEO and the FCHAIR sub-samples, in the underwriter reputation between family firms with an insider-dominated BOD and non-family firms with an independent BOD is around 15% of average firm's underwriter reputation.

Results in Panel B of Table 4 are for the sub-sample of family firms and reflect IPO underwriters' differential reaction to board independence only in these firms. ODOMB attains a positive and statistically significant (at the 5% level) estimate for the FCEO sample.[7] The coefficient estimate for FCHAIR sample is negative, but insignificant. Clearly, IPO underwriters distinguish between family firms with and without an independent BOD. This is consistent with our expectations that the presence of an independent BOD would be a positive signal of the owner-managers' willingness to be monitored objectively and rigorously.

Results in Panel C of Table 4 are based on the samples of family firms with an independent BOD and non-family firms with an insider-dominated

BOD. This is an interesting comparison to establish evidence on whether IPO underwriters take independence of management more seriously than independence of board. The coefficient estimate for ODOMB for the FCEO sub-sample in Panel C of Table 4 is positive and significant at the 5% level. This indicates that the appointment of an independent board is an important positive signal to the IPO underwriters and that they prefer independence of BOD over independence of management.

4.4. Family Firms and Post-IPO Analyst Coverage

We examine the potential relationship between a founder's presence in a firm and the extent of post-IPO analyst coverage using the following empirical model, estimated by OLS:

$$\text{LNUM}_i = \beta_0 + \beta_1\text{FAMILY}_i + \beta_2\text{FAMILY\_ODOM}_i + \beta_3\text{ODOM}_i + \beta_4\text{LNBVA}_i$$
$$+\beta_5\text{LFAGE}_i + \beta_6\text{DTECH}_i + \beta_7\text{HOT}_i + \beta_8\text{XRR}_i + \beta_9\text{UNDERPR}_i$$
$$+\beta_{10}\text{NYSE}_i + \beta_{11}\text{NASDQ}_i + \beta_{12}\text{NCOM}_i + \varepsilon_i \qquad (2)$$

LNUM is the natural logarithm of one plus the number of analysts, who provide coverage of a given firm. In addition to the control variables used in the previous sub-section, we incorporate several additional variables, which have been found to influence analyst coverage. First, since underwriter reputation can also influence the extent of analyst coverage of the firm after its IPO, we use the underwriter reputation not explained by the presence of founding family, XRR (i.e., residuals from the regressions reported in Table 4) as a control variable. Second, since higher underpricing can generate higher analyst interest (see, e.g. Chemmanur, 1993; Rajan & Servaes, 1997), we incorporate UNDERP, defined as the closing price on the first day of trading less the offer price, divided by the offer price. Third, the exchange, on which a firm is listed, may influence the extent of analyst coverage (see, e.g. Hong, Lim, & Stein, 2000). We control for this possibility by introducing two new dummy variables. NYSE (NASDQ) takes a value of one if a firm is listed on the New York Stock Exchange (NASDAQ), respectively, and zero otherwise. Finally, we also control for the number of co-managing underwriters, NCOM, which is defined as the number of lead and co-managers involved in the IPO.[8] As before, we consider five different specifications of Eq. (2).

Table 5 presents the empirical results on the relationship between the presence of a founding family and financial analyst coverage.[9] We note at the

Table 5. The Relationship between the Presence of a Founding Family, Board Independence, and the Post-IPO Analyst Coverage.

	(1) Full sample	(2) FCEO & FCC	(3) FCC	(4) FCEO	(5) FCHAIR
Panel A: Results for the full sample					
FAMILY	−0.107	−0.122	−0.108	−0.275	0.084
	(1.45)	(1.65)	(1.45)	(2.13)**	(0.52)
FAM_ODOM	0.141	0.136	0.126	0.201	0.020
	(1.14)	(1.08)	(0.97)	(0.83)	(0.08)
ODOMB	0.012	0.012	0.006	0.039	0.041
	(0.12)	(0.12)	(0.06)	(0.38)	(0.39)
LNBVA	0.019	0.017	0.020	0.056	0.095
	(0.82)	(0.70)	(0.78)	(1.63)	(2.33)**
LFAGE	−0.056	−0.065	−0.076	−0.142	−0.156
	(1.59)	(1.75)*	(1.98)**	(2.63)***	(2.94)***
XRR	0.024	0.023	0.014	0.016	0.004
	(1.67)*	(1.56)	(0.86)	(0.61)	(0.16)
UNDERP	0.110	0.129	0.194	0.020	0.195
	(0.85)	(0.99)	(1.44)	(0.09)	(0.68)
NYSE	−0.098	−0.107	−0.185	−0.241	−0.443
	(0.64)	(0.67)	(1.13)	(0.92)	(1.70)*
NASDQ	−0.029	−0.002	0.002	−0.142	−0.247
	(0.34)	(0.03)	(0.02)	(0.89)	(1.44)
DTECH	0.089	0.095	0.089	−0.016	−0.033
	(1.27)	(1.33)	(1.20)	(0.13)	(0.26)
HOT	0.091	0.021	−0.031	0.079	0.152
	(0.75)	(0.17)	(0.24)	(0.41)	(0.81)
NCOM	0.109	0.112	0.168	0.075	0.097
	(2.91)***	(2.98)***	(3.75)***	(2.61)***	(1.36)
Constant	0.074	0.113	−0.027	−0.132	−0.728
	(0.22)	(0.32)	(0.07)	(0.26)	(1.28)
Adj. R^2	0.04	0.04	0.05	0.03	0.04
N	718	661	606	280	282
Panel B: Results for the family firm sub-sample					
ODOMB	0.166	0.165	0.188	0.043	0.041
	(2.24)**	(2.07)**	(2.11)**	(0.21)	(0.18)
LNBVA	−0.019	−0.026	−0.035	−0.034	0.039
	(0.69)	(0.92)	(1.04)	(0.45)	(0.27)
LFAGE	0.042	0.037	0.029	0.102	0.012
	(0.99)	(0.81)	(0.57)	(0.74)	(0.08)
XRR	0.027	0.026	0.022	0.040	0.052
	(1.65)*	(1.53)	(1.19)	(0.73)	(0.76)
UNDERP	0.072	0.090	0.103	0.146	−0.315
	(0.48)	(0.59)	(0.63)	(0.36)	(0.32)
NYSE	0.134	0.145	0.120	0.472	−0.528
	(0.75)	(0.77)	(0.57)	(0.84)	(0.62)
NASDQ	0.032	0.070	0.109	−0.126	−0.704
	(0.35)	(0.75)	(1.01)	(0.44)	(1.12)
DTECH	0.140	0.160	0.114	0.483	−0.183
	(1.68)*	(1.85)*	(1.28)	(1.51)	(0.53)
HOT	0.130	0.029	−0.004	−0.224	0.641
	(0.91)	(0.19)	(0.03)	(0.39)	(1.55)

Table 5. (*Continued*)

	(1) Full sample	(2) FCEO & FCC	(3) FCC	(4) FCEO	(5) FCHAIR
NCOM	0.109	0.115	0.110	0.245	0.082
	(2.52)**	(2.56)**	(2.63)***	(1.46)	(0.53)
Constant	0.295	0.375	0.509	0.256	0.344
	(0.75)	(0.91)	(1.08)	(0.22)	(0.19)
Adj. R^2	0.06	0.06	0.05	0.06	−0.08
N	492	436	371	65	56

Panel C: Results for the sub-samples of family firms with an independent BOD and non-family firms with an insider-dominated BOD

ODOMB	0.047	0.026	0.018	0.006	0.119
	(0.48)	(0.25)	(0.16)	(0.03)	(0.66)
LNBVA	0.018	0.013	0.009	0.084	0.077
	(0.42)	(0.29)	(0.19)	(1.66)*	(1.46)
LFAGE	−0.079	−0.083	−0.111	−0.122	−0.154
	(1.36)	(1.40)	(1.80)*	(1.65)	(2.08)**
XRR	0.030	0.037	0.032	0.017	−0.022
	(1.28)	(1.54)	(1.22)	(0.49)	(0.58)
UNDERP	0.187	0.207	0.235	0.461	0.616
	(0.95)	(1.04)	(1.16)	(1.10)	(1.51)
NYSE	0.085	0.036	−0.005	−0.161	−0.041
	(0.33)	(0.13)	(0.02)	(0.49)	(0.12)
NASDQ	−0.103	−0.067	−0.022	−0.157	−0.092
	(0.79)	(0.50)	(0.16)	(0.80)	(0.45)
DTECH	0.019	0.012	0.020	0.037	0.044
	(0.16)	(0.10)	(0.16)	(0.21)	(0.26)
HOT	0.247	0.120	0.096	0.123	0.352
	(1.26)	(0.59)	(0.47)	(0.31)	(1.05)
NCOM	0.167	0.170	0.157	0.108	0.093
	(2.37)**	(2.34)**	(2.09)**	(1.21)	(0.98)
Constant	0.061	0.140	0.274	−0.798	−0.670
	(0.11)	(0.23)	(0.42)	(1.16)	(0.94)
Adj. R^2	0.05	0.04	0.04	0.01	0.05
N	284	260	237	158	159

Notes: The dependent variable is the natural logarithm of one plus the number of analysts following the firm one quarter after the IPO. XRR is the lead underwriter's reputation (as measured by Loughran & Ritter, 2004) not explained by the presence of founding family (i.e., residuals from the regressions reported in Table 4). UNDERP is the first-day return, defined as the closing price on the first day of trading less the offer price, divided by the offer price. NYSE is a dummy variable that takes on a value if the firm is listed on the NYSE, and zero otherwise. NASDQ is a dummy variable that takes on a value of one if the firm is listed on NASDQ, and zero otherwise. NCOM is the number of co-managing underwriters. All other variables are as defined in Table 4. Heteroskedasticity-adjusted (White) standard errors are used in calculation of t-statistics.

***Significance at the 1% level.
**Significance at the 5% level.
*Significance at the 10% level.

outset two broad results. First, the coefficient estimates for FAMILY for the FCEO or FCC sub-samples are negative across all quarters. Second, the coefficient estimates for FAMILY for the FCHAIR sub-sample are positive and insignificant across all quarters. The coefficient estimate for FAMILY for firms with a FCEO is significant at the 5% in the first quarter and becomes persistently and increasingly more negative and more significant over time. Meanwhile, the coefficient estimates for FAM_ODOM for the same firms are increasingly positive across all quarters, but attain statistical significance at the 10% level only in the fourth quarter. These results indicate that although financial analysts prefer, in general, to offer increasingly less coverage of family firms, especially those with a FCEO, than of non-family firms, they take the presence of an independent BOD in family firms with a FCEO as an increasingly positive signal of their credibility.

While all coefficient estimates for FAMILY for firms with a FCC are negative across all quarters, only that for the second quarter is statistically significant at the 10% level. Meanwhile, the coefficient estimates for FAM_ODOM for the same firms are increasingly positive across all quarters, and are statistically significant at the 10% and 5% levels in the third and fourth quarters, respectively. Financial analysts cover, in general, family firms less extensively than non-family firms; they, however, take increasingly the presence of an independent BOD in family firms with a FCC as a positive signal of these firms' credibility. The extent of analyst coverage three and four quarters after the IPO for firms with an independent BOD increases by between 23.76% (21.30%) and 27.78% (25.67%) of average (median) firm's coverage.

The coefficient estimates for FAMILY and FAM_ODOM for family firms with a FCHAIR are not statistically significantly different from zero across quarters. This seems to indicate that financial analysts view presence of independent BOD as an asset in family firms with a FCC or a FCEO, but not in the family firms with a FCHAIR. Thus, financial analysts offer the same amount of coverage, on average, for all professionally managed firms. Finally, the coefficient estimates for ODOMB across all quarters are insignificant. The presence of an independent BOD does not lead to increased financial analyst coverage for the non-family firms, either.

Results in Panel B of Table 5 are for the sample of family firms and reflect financial analysts' differential reaction to board independence only in these firms. ODOMB attains a positive and statistically significant (at the 5% level) estimate for the FCC sample and drives the same estimate's significance for the full sample and the combined sample of FCEO and FCC. The coefficient estimates for FCEO and FCHAIR samples are positive, but not significant.

Our results suggest that financial analysts distinguish between family firms with and without an independent BOD. The presence of an independent BOD in a family firm signals positively to financial analysts the owner-managers' willingness to be monitored objectively and rigorously.

Results in Panel C of Table 5 are based on the samples of family firms with an independent BOD and non-family firms with an insider-dominated BOD. None of the coefficient estimates for ODOMB in Panel C of Table 5 are statistically significant. These results are consistent with the finding in Panel A. Observing an independent BOD in family firms renders financial analysts indifferent between these firms and non-family firms despite the fact that they prefer, overall, non-family firms over family firms, especially those with a FCEO.

4.5. Family Firms and Post-IPO Institutional Interest

We examine the potential relationship between a founder's presence in a firm and the post-IPO institutional interest using the following empirical model, estimated by OLS:

$$INSTP_i = \beta_0 + \beta_1 FAMILY_i + \beta_2 FAMILY\_ODOM_i + \beta_3 ODOM_i + \beta_4 LNBVA_i$$
$$+ \beta_5 LFAGE_i + \beta_6 TECH_i + \beta_7 HOT_i + \beta_8 XRR_i + \beta_9 CEOA_i + \varepsilon_i \quad (3)$$

INSTP is the post-IPO institutional holdings after going public, expressed as a percentage of the shares outstanding.[10] As before, we estimate five different specifications of Eq. (3).[11]

Table 6 presents the empirical results on the relationship between the presence of the founding family and post-IPO institutional interest.[12] Once again, the two broad results we noted at the outset for Table 5 are relevant for Table 6 results. The coefficient estimates for FAMILY for firms with: (1) a FCC are negative and significant at the 5% level across all quarters, except for the third quarter when they are significant at the 10% level; (2) a FCEO are decreasingly negative for the first three quarters, with the first quarter estimate being the only significant one (at the 5% level) and the fourth quarter estimate turning positive; and (3) a FCHAIR are close to zero and insignificant across all quarters. Institutional investors distinguish, over time, between family firms with a FCC and those with a FCEO. Institutional investors prefer persistently non-family firms over family firms with a FCC, but they do not make a visible distinction between non-family firms and family firms with a FCEO beyond the first quarter after the IPO.

Table 6.   The Relationship between the Presence of a Founding Family, Board Independence, and the Post-IPO Institutional Interest.

	(1) Full sample	(2) FCEO & FCC	(3) FCC	(4) FCEO	(5) FCHAIR
Panel A: Results for the full sample					
FAMILY	−0.026	−0.029	−0.027	−0.044	−0.004
	$(2.40)^{**}$	$(2.61)^{***}$	$(2.34)^{**}$	$(2.44)^{**}$	(0.19)
FAM_ODOM	0.019	0.018	0.016	0.030	0.014
	(1.07)	(1.01)	(0.90)	(1.13)	(0.45)
ODOMB	−0.028	−0.027	−0.027	−0.027	−0.027
	$(1.78)^{*}$	$(1.74)^{*}$	$(1.70)^{*}$	(1.63)	(1.58)
LNBVA	0.017	0.018	0.019	0.024	0.023
	$(5.76)^{***}$	$(5.88)^{***}$	$(5.75)^{***}$	$(4.87)^{***}$	$(4.41)^{***}$
LFAGE	−0.003	−0.004	−0.004	−0.013	−0.013
	(0.64)	(0.74)	(0.81)	$(1.94)^{*}$	$(1.84)^{*}$
DTECH	−0.008	−0.009	−0.011	0.001	0.001
	(0.93)	(0.99)	(1.12)	(0.08)	(0.05)
HOT	−0.041	−0.039	−0.039	−0.050	−0.060
	$(3.61)^{***}$	$(3.05)^{***}$	$(2.78)^{***}$	$(2.88)^{***}$	$(3.57)^{***}$
XRR	0.021	0.020	0.019	0.021	0.022
	$(12.10)^{***}$	$(11.26)^{***}$	$(10.01)^{***}$	$(5.77)^{***}$	$(5.36)^{***}$
CEOA	−0.038	−0.032	−0.036	−0.036	−0.027
	$(2.54)^{**}$	$(1.98)^{**}$	$(2.09)^{**}$	(1.28)	(0.90)
Constant	−0.106	−0.120	−0.130	−0.193	−0.177
	$(2.27)^{**}$	$(2.52)^{**}$	$(2.55)^{**}$	$(2.50)^{**}$	$(2.17)^{**}$
Adj. R^2	0.24	0.24	0.22	0.24	0.21
N	718	661	606	280	282
Panel B: Results for the family firm sub-sample					
ODOMB	−0.010	−0.010	−0.010	−0.020	0.015
	(1.17)	(1.12)	(1.01)	(0.76)	(0.56)
LNBVA	0.012	0.013	0.012	0.024	−0.006
	$(3.71)^{***}$	$(3.83)^{***}$	$(3.54)^{***}$	$(2.24)^{**}$	(0.58)
LFAGE	0.006	0.006	0.012	−0.019	0.012
	(1.00)	(0.93)	$(1.83)^{*}$	(1.06)	(0.77)
DTECH	−0.012	−0.013	−0.017	0.029	−0.006
	(1.24)	(1.26)	$(1.67)^{*}$	(0.66)	(0.21)
HOT	−0.035	−0.030	−0.019	−0.121	−0.053
	$(2.62)^{***}$	$(1.91)^{*}$	(1.14)	$(2.91)^{***}$	$(2.17)^{**}$
XRR	0.021	0.020	0.019	0.024	0.031
	$(12.27)^{***}$	$(11.27)^{***}$	$(9.93)^{***}$	$(4.68)^{***}$	$(4.60)^{***}$
CEOA	−0.042	−0.034	−0.031	−0.129	0.313
	$(2.50)^{**}$	$(1.85)^{*}$	(1.58)	(1.65)	$(2.85)^{***}$
Constant	−0.073	−0.093	−0.090	−0.199	0.201
	(1.50)	$(1.86)^{*}$	$(1.70)^{*}$	(1.41)	(1.25)

Table 6. (*Continued*)

	(1) Full sample	(2) FCEO & FCC	(3) FCC	(4) FCEO	(5) FCHAIR
Adj. R^2	0.27	0.26	0.25	0.30	0.32
N	492	436	371	65	56

Panel C: Results for the sub-samples of family firms with an independent BOD and non-family firms with an insider-dominated BOD

ODOMB	−0.038	−0.042	−0.041	−0.056	−0.024
	(2.92)***	(3.25)***	(2.97)***	(2.59)**	(0.90)
LNBVA	0.022	0.022	0.021	0.027	0.028
	(5.11)***	(4.83)***	(4.50)***	(4.45)***	(4.19)***
LFAGE	−0.015	−0.015	−0.014	−0.025	−0.024
	(2.16)**	(2.16)**	(1.84)*	(2.98)***	(2.69)***
DTECH	0.006	0.011	0.015	0.030	0.026
	(0.37)	(0.65)	(0.85)	(1.11)	(1.09)
HOT	−0.036	−0.030	−0.031	−0.041	−0.062
	(2.25)**	(1.69)*	(1.72)*	(1.07)	(2.13)**
XRR	0.024	0.024	0.024	0.029	0.029
	(7.80)***	(7.63)***	(6.70)***	(6.09)***	(5.18)***
CEOA	−0.045	−0.041	−0.041	−0.050	−0.042
	(1.93)*	(1.62)	(1.47)	(1.31)	(1.03)
Constant	−0.164	−0.155	−0.152	−0.222	−0.230
	(2.42)**	(2.22)**	(2.07)**	(2.39)**	(2.28)**
Adj. R^2	0.30	0.31	0.29	0.32	0.28
N	284	260	237	158	159

Notes: The dependent variable is the percentage of shares outstanding held by institutional investors at the end of the first quarter after going public. All independent variables are as defined in Table 4. Heteroskedasticity-adjusted (White) standard errors are used in calculation of *t*-statistics.
***Significance at the 1% level.
**Significance at the 5% level.
*Significance at the 10% level.

The coefficient estimates for FAM_ODOM are insignificant across all quarters and samples.

Our results indicate that independence of BOD does not influence institutional investors' decision to invest in the newly public family firms. To put it differently, they seem to be equally reluctant to invest in family firms with an independent BOD as in family firms with an insider-dominated BOD.

Results in Panel B of Table 6 are for the sample of family firms and reflect institutional investors' differential reaction to board independence only in these firms a quarter after they go public. None of the estimates for

ODOMB is statistically significant. This evidence is overall consistent with our expectations, as indicated in Section 2.2, and confirms that institutional investors exhibit scepticism about family firms in general and that they prefer non-family firms over family firms with or without an independent BOD. Evidently, the independence of management is more important for institutional investors than the independence of corporate governance.

Panel C of Table 6 reports additional evidence on whether institutional investors prefer board independence over independence of management. The results show strongly institutional investors' preference for non-family firms with an insider-dominated board over family firms with an independent board. That is, they prefer an independent management over an independent board. This is not a surprising piece of evidence in spite of the positive signal quality, as observed in our results for the IPO underwriter reputation and financial analyst coverage, of an independent BOD in a family firm. While institutional investors risk their capital in a firm they invest in, financial analysts and IPO underwriters do not. Thus, institutional investors are likely to differ from financial analysts and underwriters when evaluating a firm's signals. For example, institutional investors may not be able to sway the direction of family firms while they may be assertive in non-family firms. Families tend to maintain sufficiently large ownership to control the firm for an intergenerational transfer. This may keep institutional investors away from family firms.

5. SUMMARY AND CONCLUSIONS

Reports suggest that the Wall Street is sceptical about family firms in spite of the value premium documented for family firms listed on the S&P 500 Index or Fortune 500 during the 1990s. The roots of this scepticism are in the agency-theoretic arguments about owner-managers' excessive consumption of firms' resources.

The value premium documented for the mature, large and index-listed family firms by several recent studies may be an outcome of a survival bias. These firms were born as family firms and survived the time's tests. Over time, these firms build a self-identity and reputation that become independent of the family's name and reputation. Also, being listed in either the S&P500 Index or the Fortune 500, they are not in need of the nurture and care of the founding family anymore; they are under the tight scrutiny and monitoring of the financial markets. Even if the family ownership vanishes completely today, it is unlikely to have any material effect on the firm and its direction.

Newly public family firms, however, are more likely to need the nurture and care of the founding family and to be without the scrutiny and monitoring received by firms listed on the market-wide indices. Therefore, the Wall Street's scepticism is much more likely to be apparent in the newly public family firms than in mature, large, and index-listed family firms.

The appointment of an independent board of directors in the newly public family firms pre-dates the presence and attention of any external monitoring entity, such as IPO underwriters, financial analysts, or institutional investors. Thus, the owner-founders of newly public family firms may form an independent BOD to bond themselves in the face of the Wall Street's scepticism. An independent BOD may reveal owner-founders' willingness to be monitored objectively.

This paper tests empirically whether the presence of an independent BOD in a newly public family firm is a positive signal to the external monitoring entities of IPO underwriters, financial analysts, and institutional investors. Using a hand-collected sample of newly public family and non-family firms between 1993 and 2000, we find (1) that all three external monitoring bodies exhibit a negative response to the newly public family firms, (2) that the presence of an independent BOD in the newly public family firms serves as a positive signal, (3) that while the independence of BOD is more important than the independence of management for IPO underwriters and financial analysts, the reverse is the case for institutional investors.

Overall, these results suggest convincingly that the appointment of an independent board of directors is a crucial step for the newly public firms to get and retain the attention of external monitoring entities. This, in turn, may be crucial for the long-run survival and success of these firms.

NOTES

1. Since the literature shows the influence of venture capital on board independence (see e.g., Baker & Gompers, 2003), we exclude newly public firms with any venture capital involvement. This allows us to study empirically the independence of BOD alone.

2. The agency-theoretic framework highlights the importance of internal corporate governance mechanisms in mitigating the likely agency problems in firms characterized by separation of ownership and control (Jensen & Meckling, 1976; Fama & Jensen, 1983, 1985; Milgrom & Roberts, 1992).

3. FCCs are empowered with both the management and governance functions. FCEOs have managerial powers, but do not participate – albeit directly – in their firms' governance while FCHAIRs maintain a visible role in the governance of their firms, but do not assume a managerial role.

4. The set of authorities and responsibilities of a FCC encapsulates that of a FCEO. Hence, all of the not-so-good news implications for the presence of a FCEO in a newly public family firm should fundamentally apply in the same direction, but with a more pronounced intensity, for the presence of a FCC.

5. On the one hand, since the outside directors are more likely to have the relevant knowledge and experience, they can be better at monitoring the management. On the other hand, a significant ownership by a founding family may make the monitoring by a family-dominated BOD more effective than that by a BOD dominated by outsiders without significant ownership stakes in the firm. An outsider-dominated board, however, may have a marginally positive contribution in case of close ties, such as a friendship or a prior business partnership, between the professionally employed CEO and the founding family.

6. Stein (2001, p.125) notes that "…institutional and disgruntled shareholders levy against the family companies: that they are insulated by their relatively secure position and slow to pursue growth opportunities or replace ineffective managers." Furthermore, Stein (2001, p. 128) continues that "Now they could band together at their whim to remove managers who didn't share their vision for how the company should be run. But, one group of companies remained out of reach: those in which the family controlled enough of the voting shares to keep institutional investors on the periphery."

7. It is also driving the full sample and the combined sample of FCEO and FCC to attain statistically significant estimates (at the 5% and 10% levels, respectively).

8. Bradley, Bradford, and Ritter (2003) find that the extent of post-IPO coverage at the end of the quiet period can be predicted by the number of co-managing underwriters. See, however, Bradley, Jordan, Ritter, and Wolf (2004) for alternative evidence.

9. To save space, we report only the results for the first quarter after going public. The results for the subsequent three quarters, which we discuss below, are available from the authors upon request.

10. We also consider Eq. (3) with the alternative dependent variable, LINSTN, defined as the natural logarithm of one plus the number of institutional holders. To save space, we do not report these results. They are consistent with the reported results and are available from the authors upon request.

11. We also estimated these regressions controlling for the float, defined as a ratio of the number of shares offered in the IPO to shares outstanding. The results were qualitatively unchanged. We also used the market capitalization of the firm as an alternative proxy for the firm size. Again, the results were qualitatively unchanged.

12. To save space, we report only the results for the first quarter after going public. The results for the subsequent three quarters, which we discuss below, are available from the authors upon request.

ACKNOWLEDGMENTS

For helpful comments, we thank the participants of the Conference on the Corporate Governance of Closely-Held Firms, Copenhagen, Denmark, Nilanjan Basu, and Harjeet Bhabra. We thank Anna Kaolina, Vishal Patel, and Parianen Veeren for excellent research assistance. Tirtiroglu thanks for the hospitality of the Department of Land Economy, University of Cambridge, UK where parts of this paper were written during his sabbatical leave. We remain solely responsible for any remaining errors.

REFERENCES

Amihud, Y., & Mendelson, H. (2000). The liquidity route to a lower cost of capital. *Journal of Applied Corporate Finance, 12*(4), 8–25.

Anderson, R., & Reeb, D. (2003). Founding-family ownership and firm performance: Evidence from the S&P 500. *Journal of Finance, 58*(3), 1301–1328.

Anderson, R., & Reeb, D. (2004). Board composition: Balancing family influence in S&P 500 firms. *Administrative Science Quarterly, 49*(2), 209–237.

Baker, M., & Gompers, P. (2003). The determinants of board structure at the initial public offering. *Journal of Law and Economics, 46*, 569–598.

Bradley, D., Bradford, J., & Ritter, J. (2003). The quiet period goes out with a bang. *Journal of Finance, 58*, 1–36.

Bradley, D., Jordan, B., Ritter, J., & Wolf, J. (2004). The IPO quiet period revisited. *Journal of Investment Management, 2*(3), 3–13.

Brennan, M., & Franks, J. (1997). Underpricing, ownership and control in initial public offerings of equity securities in the UK. *Journal of Financial Economics, 45*, 391–413.

Carter, R., & Manaster, S. (1990). Initial public offerings and underwriter reputation. *Journal of Finance, 45*(4), 1045–1067.

Chemmanur, T. (1993). The pricing of initial public offerings: A dynamic model with information production. *Journal of Finance, 48*, 285–304.

Chemmanur, T., & Fulghieri, P. (1994). Investment bank reputation, information production and financial intermediation. *Journal of Finance, 49*, 57–79.

Das, S., Guo, R., & Zhang, H. (2006). Analysts' selective coverage and subsequent performance of newly public firms. *Journal of Finance, 61*(3), 1159–1185.

Fama, E., & Jensen, M. (1983). Separation of ownership and control. *Journal of Law and Economics, 26*, 301–325.

Fama, E., & Jensen, M. (1985). Organizational forms and investment decisions. *Journal of Financial Economics, 14*, 101–119.

Field, L., & Lowry, M. (2004). *How is institutional investment in initial public offerings related to the long-run performance of these firms?* Unpublished working paper. Penn State University.

Hong, H., Lim, T., & Stein, J. (2000). Bad news travel slowly: Size, analyst coverage, and the profitability of momentum strategies. *Journal of Finance, 55*(1), 265–295.

Jensen, M. (1993). The modern industrial revolution, exit, and the failure of internal control systems. *Journal of Finance, 48*, 831–880.

Jensen, M., & Meckling, W. (1976). Theory of the firm: Managerial behaviour, agency costs and ownership structure. *Journal of Financial Economics, 3*, 305–360.

Kohlberg, J. (February 10, 2005). Strictly Private. In Day, P. (presenter). *In Business*, BBC-Radio 4.

Loughran, T., & Ritter, J. (2004). Why has IPO underpricing increased over time? *Financial Management, 33*(3), 5–37.

Michaely, R., & Shaw, W. (1994). The pricing of initial public offerings: Tests of adverse selection and signaling theories. *The Review of Financial Studies, 7,* 279–319.

Milgrom, P., & Roberts, J. (1992). *Economics, Organization & Management.* NJ, USA: Prentice Hall.

Rajan, R., & Servaes, H. (1997). Analyst following of initial public offerings. *Journal of Finance, 52*(2), 507–529.

Ritter, J. (1984). The hot issue market of 1980. *Journal of Business, 32,* 215–240.

Schwert, W. (1985). A discussion of CEO deaths and the reaction of stock prices. *Journal of Accounting and Economics, 7,* 175–178.

Stein, N. (2001). The age of the scion: A new generation of leaders takes its place at family-run corporations worldwide. Will the kids be allright? *Fortune, 143*(7), 121–128.

Villalonga, B., & Amit, R. (2006). How do family ownership, control, and management affect firm value? *Journal of Financial Economics, 80,* 385–417.

Yermack, D. (1996). Higher market valuation of companies with small boards of directors. *Journal of Financial Economics, 40,* 185–211.

OWNERSHIP STRUCTURE, FINANCIAL RENT AND PERFORMANCE: EVIDENCE FROM THE MALAYSIAN MANUFACTURING SECTOR

Ei Yet Chu

ABSTRACT

This paper addresses the interaction relationship between debt financing and ownership structure towards firms' value in Malaysia. Two issues are addressed in this study. The study examines whether managers and controlling large shareholders pursue rent-seeking objective through excessive leverage in a firm. Second, the paper examines whether financial restraint policy is effective in enhancing corporate governance. The sample of the study covers a small economy – Malaysia where rent-seeking opportunities prevail. A total 256 manufacturing firms are examined. The hypotheses are set to examine whether rent seeking prevails in firms with high intangible asset and less competitive industries. The findings show that first, financial restraint policy is only effective when managerial equity interest is relatively low. Managers with a higher equity interest hinder the positive effects driven by financial restraint policy. Second, at a higher threshold of equity interest, the use of excessive leverage by managers leads

Issues in Corporate Governance and Finance
Advances in Financial Economics, Volume 12, 165–202
Copyright © 2007 by Elsevier Ltd.
ISSN: 1569-3732/doi:10.1016/S1569-3732(07)12008-9

to a lower firm value, confirming the presence of rent-seeking motive. The presence of the largest shareholder as directors also follows the same conjecture despite at a lower magnitude. Both findings could not be refuted in less competitive industries. Other findings from this paper conclude that a high industrial concentration industry increases firms' value in this economy. Financial institutions can also exert corporate governance on firms in less competitive industries. It is, however, the agency problem mitigates the positive effects brought forth by financial rent in this emerging economy.

1. INTRODUCTION

Among the corporate governance issues, corporate ownership structure is found to have contributed directly to the firms' agency conflicts and moral hazard (e.g. Claessens, Djankov, & Lang, 1999; Johnson, La Porta, Lopez-De-Silanes, & Shleifer, 2000; Mitton, 2002). The standard agency cost theory suggests that increasing controlling owners' equity interest in a firm can reduce asymmetric information and increase monitoring on managers (Shleifer & Vishny, 1986), however, the outcomes are not found to be definite as it also dependent on other institutional factors. For instance, large shareholders could employ leverage (Faccio, Lang, & Young, 2003) and diversification (Claessens, Djankov, Fan, & Lang, 2002) to facilitate expropriation on other minority shareholders. La Porta, Lopez-De-Silanes, and Shleifer (1999) also show that firm value in countries with better shareholder protection is higher than those where such protection is weak.

Generally, firms in East Asian countries tend to borrow excessively to enhance controlling owners' interest which consequently leads to a detrimental in firm value. Deesomsak, Paudyal, and Pescetto's (2004) cross-sectional studies showed that firms established a positive relationship between ownership concentration and leverage for the sample period from 1993 to 2001. However, the positive relationship between debt and the controlling owner do not seem to be consistent with other single nation studies. In Thailand, large shareholders are found to negatively explain debt ratio for the sample period of 1996 (Wiwattanakantang, 1999). Suto (2003) showed that top 10 shareholdings in Malaysia are negatively related to debt ratio for each cross-sectional year study from 1995 to 1999. Pandey (2002) also noted a similar negative relationship between debt ratio and number of outstanding shares for the study for the sample period from 1994 to 2000. It is assumed that larger number of shares imply diffused ownership. The above studies however, do not assess the direct impact of the relationship between ownership structure and debt towards firm value. In contrast, Baek et al. (2002) provide evidence that owner–managers in Korea tend to incur excessive borrowing and have expropriated other investors to maximise their own or the group's welfare during the crisis period.

The inconsistencies in the findings show that there are gaps in the study of ownership structure and leverage. In this study, we test the view of Bebchuk's (1999) rent-seeking hypothesis that controlling owners incur leverage to enhance their private interest, which is more prevalent in environments with higher rent-seeking opportunities. We focus on a single nation so that we can examine corporate ownership structure issues at a level of detail that would be hard to aggregate across countries.

Malaysia provides a number of characteristics that makes it particularly suited to the investigation of the relationship between ownership structure and debt and its effect on firm value. The high debt ratio prior to financial crisis period is always suggested as the factor that leads to a lower firm value in the economy. However, due to the interest tax shield, financial literature generally argues that issuance of debt as a movement towards the optimum of firm value (Miguel, Pindado, & de la Torre, 2005). On the other hand, one notable feature of Malaysian firms is that ownership is heavily concentrated. For instance, La Porta et al.'s (1999) study showed that top three largest shareholders hold 46% of the voting stock in the 10 largest firms. It is generally argued that the tendency for large shareholders to extract private benefits increases in tandem with their controlling interest (Barclay & Holdedrness, 1989; Shleifer & Vishny, 1997). Despite large shareholders and debt prevail in this economy, we are yet to ascertain whether the controlling owners in this economy have intentionally increased debt to enhance their private interest which is subsequently leading to reducing firm value.

There are two issues in this economy leading to the study of this paper. One possible answer to the high debt in an economy could due to Bebchuk's (1999) rent-seeking theory. The theory suggests that controlling owners may use excessive leverage instead of equity financing to finance investments so that their relative equity interests in a firm are not threatened. The theory emphasises that controlling owners tend to protect their controlling interests, especially in the environment where rent-seeking opportunities are prevalent. The firms' size and industrial competition are two factors that could provide opportunities for rent-seeking purposes (Bebchuk, 1999; Bebchuk & Roe 1999). Following Bebchuk's (1999) conjecture, Van der Elst (2004) showed that different shareholders control patterns that are characterised by different industrial sectors, especially when controlling for the country factor, but he found no evidence that a firm's size could influence ownership structure in a large sample of firms involving six European countries. Nonetheless, the study does not specifically control for the characteristics such as industrial competition and type of asset that provide opportunities for rent seeking. An emerging economy, such as Malaysia could provide a platform to address the rent-seeking hypothesis, as generally, rent-seeking opportunities prevail in this economy.

A second explanation to the issue of high leverage is resorting to "financial restraint hypothesis" advocated by Hellmann, Murdock, and Stiglitz (1996). The hypothesis suggests that financial institutions (FIs) in East Asian economies are more inclined to lend, largely due to the financial restraint policy. The financial restraint policy aims at promoting overall economic growth through lending at a lower interest rate with higher volume of loans. The policy creates "financial rent" benefits (excess profit opportunities) which are the incentives for firms and FIs to borrow and prudently monitor their client firms, respectively. Therefore, the financial restraint policy aims at promoting growth in private sectors firms through borrowing while FIs function as a governance mechanism on the firms to stimulate overall economic growth.[1]

Nonetheless, the "financial rent" could provide the chances of controlling owners to incur excessive leverage so as to enhance their controlling interests. On the other hand, FIs in this economy are not effective in monitoring firms which they lend their loans to. FIs in Malaysia were largely relationship based. The implicit and explicit guarantees increase the probability of FIs to shirk monitoring and therefore lead to the increases in the number of financial distressed firms (Bongini, Claessens, & Ferri, 2000). Although the relationship-based banking may work well in an economy where legislation contract are poorly enforced and capital is scarce, it can also trigger misallocation of capital problem when large external capital flows in (Rajan & Zingales, 1998). The problem will be more severe in a weak legislation and financial infrastructure economy as market price would not be able to reflect the costs and benefits of investment and therefore lead to unjustifiable investments.

Aoki, Patrick, and Sheard (1994) point out that the close ties between finance and industry in Japan lead the firms to a high level in the international market. In contrast to Japanese FIs, the Malaysian FIs are not able to intervene in the borrowers' firm management in the event of financial distress as banks do not usually have board representation. Japanese banks have virtually unlimited access to corporation and place their representative in top management positions. Appendix provides further details on the financial restraint policy and factors that explained the ineffectiveness of bank-centred corporate governance in this economy.

Two features distinguish this study from others. First, this study focuses on the interaction effects of controlling owners and excessive debt towards firm value. The result is expected to vary with types of ownership structure. Managers and controlling owners may incur additional leverage so as to enhance their private interests, which could lead to a lower firm value. On the other hand, if financial restraint policy is effective, we may observe a higher firm value. The outcomes of the interaction effects are also largely dependent on the degree of control by controlling owners. By using an interaction approach, it allows us to learn the direct effect of the use of leverage by controlling owner or managers.

Second we set the conditions that rent-seeking opportunities prevail upon the conditional of lower intensity of competition and firm characteristics (Bebchuk, 1999). The absence of the pressure from industrial competition may prompt controlling owners to act imprudently (Bebchuk & Roe, 1999). Firm characteristics, such as intangible assets also provide opportunities for rent seeking especially through excessive leverage (Williamson, 1988). In this regards, Williamson (1988) suggests that the vagueness of intangible assets provide opportunities to controlling owners to expropriate firm value. Williamson (1988) argues that controlling owners tend to utilise debt financing instead of equity financing in firms with a high degree of intangible assets. By incurring debt financing it can increase chances of misappropriation of the controlling shareholders by virtue that debt holders have little control over the managerial action in ensuring resources are utilised efficiently.

The essential contributions from this paper are in the following ways. It provides a new perspective to the policy makers on the issue of corporate governance. The issues of ownership structure as governance mechanism could also take into consideration of institutional economics factors such as FIs, industrial competition and types of asset. The role of managers and controlling owner in enhancing performance can become less effective when financial and industrial policies offer rent-seeking opportunities. On the same note, a manager or controlling owner could hinder the policies on FIs and industrial structure that could enhance overall economic growth and industrial development.

This paper proceeds as follows. Section 2 discusses the literature on the firm value caused by ownership structure and leverage, and both interaction effects. Two ownership structure issues are addressed in this study, the issues of managerial ownership and large shareholders. The perceptions toward leverage level are different between large shareholders and managerial ownership. The section also addresses the prediction of the outcomes under the conditions of low intensity of competition and intangible assets. Section 3 describes data and sample characteristics. In Section 4, we show the results of our empirical analysis. If the aim of controlling owners is to enhance their private interest through excessive leverage, we could have observed a significant decline in firm value. In contrast, if FIs monitoring role prevails, we predict a positive outcome. The findings suggest that the effectiveness of FIs as corporate governance rather than rent-seeking mechanisms prevail when the controlling interest of the managers and large shareholders are relatively low. As the controlling owner's interest increases, the interaction term of ownership concentration and leverage produce a negative value, confirming Bebchuk (1999) proposition. The finding is not refuted under low competition industry. Lastly, Section 5 discusses and summarises the findings of this paper.

2. OWNERSHIP STRUCTURE, LEVERAGE AND FIRM VALUE: HYPOTHESES

The effects of the interaction relationship between controlling owner and debt toward firm value could not be directly predicted. It is largely dependent on the degree of control a controlling owner possessed and also the effects that debt could assert on the controlling owner and the firm's value.

Agency theory is known to explain the influence of ownership structure towards firm value. The standard approach focuses on an incentive alignment mechanism as suggested in Jensen and Meckling's (1976) agency theory, in which any marginal equity of interests owned by managers follows "entrenchment" and "convergence of interest" hypotheses, albeit in a non-linear fashion (Morck, Shelifer, & Vishny, 1988; McConnell & Servaes, 1990). The entrenchment hypothesis suggests that when the controlling managers own a relatively small portion of equity in the firms, they may consume excessive perquisite, shirking and pursue non-value maximisation objectives at the expenses of shareholders. These unscrupulous activities could be mitigated by increasing managerial equity interest in a firm, so that managerial interests could converge with external shareholders thereby reducing the cost of deviating from value maximisation objectives. This argument is essentially focusing on the managers who manage the firms.

A second perspective of the agency conflicts lies between the controlling large shareholders and weak minority shareholders. The presence of large shareholder can exacerbate the exploitation problem. The presence of large shareholders can also come with cost. Large shareholders can inflict substantial costs on other shareholders through outright theft, dilution of external shareholders through share issues to insiders, excessive salaries, and asset sales to themselves or corporations they control at favourable prices (Shleifer & Vishny, 1997).

Under the proposition of Bebchuk's (1999) rent-seeking theory, the relationship between ownership structure and debt is predicted to be positive, as the owner tends to increase debt to protect their rent interest. An alternative argument, however, suggests that debt could also function as corporate governance mechanism (Grossman & Hart, 1980; Jensen, 1986), while Hellmann et al. (1996) argue that FIs (debt holder) could exert the monitoring effect. Therefore, empirically, a priori, the effects of the interaction relationship of managers or controlling owners to incur debt and subsequently on firm value are vague. Moreover, prior studies have generally only examined separately the effect of ownership structure on capital structure or ownership structure on firm value. The effects are largely dependents on managers and the controlling owners' objectives as well as the effectiveness of FIs in an economy to perform the role of corporate governance.

On the positive side of the relationship between ownership structure and debt, managers and controlling owner may incur higher debt for empire building or build up their specific human capital (Jensen & Meckling, 1976). This proposition stems from the view that debt could enhance firm value. Ross (1977) states that debt could be a signal to the quality of firms, as it reflects debt holder's confidence on the capability of firms to generate sufficient cash flow to meet the obligation of repayment. Therefore, a higher debt value level will induce a higher firm value and further insulate managers and controlling owners from being expelled from their positions or become the subject of takeover by other firms (Stulz, 1988). In a similar note, a higher debt level could also enhance managers' compensation and fringe benefits (Short, Keasey, & Duxbury, 2002).

Kim and Sorenson (1986) illustrate that the relationship between debt and managers' controlling interest is positive. The finding indicates that managers may enhance their private interest by transferring the risks to the debt holders especially in high growth and high operating risks firms. Managers or controlling owners may also attempt to alter their bargaining power ex-post. This is shown in Agrawal and Mandelkar's (1987), where the relationship between the equity holdings of managers and the changes in financial leverage between the time period of t and $t-1$ is found to be positive. In this perspective, managers shifted agency cost of equity to debt holders. By this means, firm managers reduce their risk.

In contrast, Grossman and Hart (1980) and Jensen (1986) argue that debt disciplines borrower firms for efficient management via threats of liquidation. A firm's commitment towards debt instalment reduces the chances of managers from committing indiscreet decision, especially in firms with surplus of free cash flows. By increasing debt, managers are bonded with the covenant commitment and the use of the free cash flow for interest and instalment.

The effectiveness of debt as corporate governance mechanism could be observed when an entrenched manager attempts to avoid the stringency of monitoring from FIs. On the negative side, empirical studies show that firms controlled by entrenched managers (a lower market value firm) usually link to lower debt so as to avoid monitoring from the FIs. On the same note, Friend and Lang (1988) assert that a controlling owner with large equity is associated with higher risks and therefore more likely to maintain a lower debt policy in the firm. The motive of the controlling owner is to avoid intervention from debt holder on high-risk portfolios. Agrawal and Nagarajan (1990) also found that managerial shareholdings are significantly greater in all equity firms (firms with zero long term debt) than levered firms (defined as the ratio of long term debt to asset). Along with other findings, Jensen, Solberg, and Zorn (1992) used three-stage least square simultaneous equation to prove that managerial controlled firms choose lower levels of debt and dividend for two cross-sectional firm level sample data in 1982 and 1987. Berger, Ofek, and Yermack (1997) reported a similar finding in their study on 452 industries companies from 1984 to 1991. They show that the entrenched CEOs seek to avoid debt to pursue strategies that benefit their personal interest. In summary, the findings suggest that firms with lower market value (entrenched firms) tend to incur lower debt.

Another strand of argument on the relationship between debt and ownership structure focuses on whether debt could substitute or complement the role of ownership structure as corporate governance mechanism. The empirical findings are found to be inconsistent dependent on the economy and financial system in a country. For instance, Agrawal and Knoeber (1996), in a study of over 500 of the largest US firms find that debt could not efficiently substitute managers. In contrast, in economy such as in Denmark, Dilling-Hansen, Eriksson, Madsen, and Smith (1999) show that debt pressures yield a higher substitutions effect in the dispersed structure where owners exercise less control. The finding suggests that the effectiveness of financial institution as governance mechanism prevails when managers are weak in controlling a firm. In Spain, Miguel et al. (2005) illustrate that managers, debt and dividend complement each other when interests of managers and owners converge. The finding signifies that corporate policies such as debt and dividend policies could complement ownership structure in corporate governance framework.

The locus of the agency theory suggests that as the managers' interest in the firm increases, it eases the agency costs due to the fact that managers tend to align more with external shareholders and convergence of interest occur. Similarly, a large shareholder who owns a large fraction of equity interest could provide valuable monitoring and act as a restraint to opportunistic managerial behaviour (Shleifer & Vishny, 1986). However, as the managers' or large controlling shareholders' interest in a firm become large, the risks they bear also increase correspondingly. In order to reduce the risks which he may have to bear alone, a large shareholder could also emphasis debt so that the risk is shifted to a debt holder. By doing so, it enhances the large shareholder's controlling interest. Moreover, large controlling shareholders are also likely to undertake excessive leverage when there is an opportunity to expropriate (Shleifer & Vishny, 1997).

There are also possibilities of coincidence of interest between large shareholders and managers where large shareholders have other common business that is related to the firm (Pound, 1988). The coincidence interest occurs when there are existing business relationships with other directors, therefore, reducing large shareholders initiative to curb managements' unscrupulous decision making and create conflicts of interest with other minority shareholders. On the same note, the inter-connection trading between large shareholders and managers could further enhance the managers' private interest (Johnson et al., 2000). To protect their private interests in the firms, large shareholders and managers will tend to incur debt to protect their private interest, which may at the expense of minority shareholders. The empirical evidence on this issue has however not particularly consistent. For instance, Baek et al. (2002) show that owner–managers in Korean Chaebol firms borrowed more from the main banks. In Australia, Brailsford, Oliver, and Pua (2002) show that management establish a positive relationship with leverage after the threshold point of 49%. They also illustrate that the significance level of external block shareholders in monitoring the leverage financing diminishing as management share owner-ship increases. The finding show that in a more establish capital market, the presence of large shareholders acts to reduce the positive relationship between debt ratios and managers in the UK (Short et al., 2002), while large shareholders do not seem to alter the negative relationship between managers and capital structure in the US market (Friend & Lang, 1988).

In summary, there are several threads to the argument. Following the argument of agency theory, the relationship between manager and firm value follows a non-linear relationship (first declining and then improving). That is, firms become entrenched when the controlling interest of the managers in the firm is relatively low, as their interests increase, the convergence of interest with external shareholders lead to improvement in firm value. By incurring higher debt they could reduce the entrenchment effect, and improve the firm value. However, when the controlling interests of the managers increase, they may issue debt instead of issuing new equity to protect their equity interests. Moreover, incurring debt could serve as a strategy to pre-empt hostile takeover attempts although it is at the expense of other shareholders which lead to a detriment in firm value.

In the context of Malaysia, due to the financial restraint policy which encourages firms to incur higher leverage, we are therefore uncertain whether managers in this economy incur higher leverage for their own private interest. The effectiveness of debt in corporate governance has also yet to be tested. Following the literature discussed earlier, we conjecture that

H1. The interaction effects between managers and higher leverage on firm value follow a non-linear inverted U relationship (improving initially, and the declining).

Williamson (1988) cites that firms with high asset specificity have higher agency problems. He suggests that this type of firm faces greater uncertainty and severe information asymmetric problems. A highly specific asset is arguably intangible and less deployable due to the difficulties in measuring intangible assets (Jensen et al., 1992). For instance, the controlling owner may appropriate the value of goodwill of the intangible assets so that it could affect the charges in the costs of acquisitions. In addition, Williamson (1988) suggests that firms with high intangible assets should be better financed with equity financing. This is because the debt holder has little control over the managerial action in ensuring resources in firms with high intangible assets are utilised efficiently (Kochhar, 1996). Therefore, debt financing provides opportunities for the controlling shareholder to misappropriate shareholder value. In order to examine whether rent seeking by managers prevail in highly intangible asset firms, we propose that

H2. The utilisation of higher leverage by managers in firms with high intangible assets leads to a lower firm value.

Industries with lower intensity of competition encourage managers to slack and leads to the detriment of firm value (Bebchuk & Roe, 1999; Roe, 2001). In contrast, a greater competition intensity industry could reinforce controlling owner to improve performance. The relationship is nonetheless ambiguous a priori and dependent on the industrial and capital market development. If the financial market is efficient, financial pressure such as debt financing could complement industrial competition in ensuring better performance. Nickell, Nicolitsas, and Dryden (1997) present evidence that industrial competition, debt pressure and ownership control could positively explain firm performance for UK manufacturing firms. In another study, industrial competition is found to complement controlling owners at the threshold of "convergence of interest" and producing value-enhancing performance for manufacturing firms listed in Warsaw Stock Exchange (Grosfeld & Tressel, 2002). However, in the Continental European market where the degree of industrial competition is less intense, the presence of agency conflicts could attenuate the positive effects brought forth by industrial competition. Januszewski, Koje, and Winter (2002) illustrate that the negative interaction effect prevails between industrial competition and highly concentrated ownership structure for the German market which they attribute to the possibilities of pyramid structure in Germany. On the other hand, to examine Bebchuk (1999) rent-seeking hypothesis, Van der Elst (2004) show that controlling owner interest may differ according to type of industries across six European countries, however, they do not provide further evidence that the rent interest could positively affect firm value.

Apparently, the empirical evidence shows that the issue of controlling owner could mitigate the positive effects brought forth by the high competition industry in a market where large shareholders are prevalent. The Malaysian economy is predominated by the issues of protectionism. A recent study by Bhattacharya (2002) shows that the mean of industries concentration ratio in Malaysia was 0.55 in 1996, and only 31% of the manufacturing industries appear to be competitive. In this regard, controlling owners in low competition intensity industries are more inclined to extravagance in their daily operations. Moreover, Bank Negara Malaysia's (1996) Annual Report shows that average debt financing in the Malaysian manufacturing sector was on the average of 72.67%, of which 97% was contributed by the banking system in the economy for the period from 1994 to 1996. Despite this, we are uncertain whether managers and controlling owners intentionally pursue higher debt financing in areas of low intensity of competition in this economy. We follow the argument of Bebchuk and Roe (1999) that an existing controlling ownership structure is more inclined to enhance its private interest through debt in a rent-seeking prevailing environment. To examine whether lack of industrial competition has indulged managers in unscrupulous activities, we conjecture that

H3. The utilisation of higher leverage by managers in industries with low intensity of competition leads to a lower firm value.

Lastly, corporate governance literature on East Asian generally suggests that large shareholders expropriate shareholders (e.g. Faccio et al., 2003). In the view that financial restraint policy prompts firms to increase leverage in this economy, following the rent-seeking theory of Bebchuk's (1999), we could expect that detriments in firms with excessive debt is severe if firms are controlled by large shareholders. The proposition could also prevail in the firms with high level of intangible assets and industries with low intensity of competition. Furthermore, there is likely to be coincidence of interest between managerial and large shareholder that will lead to the declination in firm value.

H4. With the presence of the large shareholders, the utilisation of higher leverage in firms with high intangible asset and in industries with low intensity of competition could lead to a lower firm value.

3. DATA AND MODEL SPECIFICATION

This section describes an empirical model for the determinants of firms' value in the manufacturing industry. The specification of the empirical model is as follows:

$$
\begin{aligned}
\Delta\text{Value} = {} & \alpha_{i,t-1} + \sum_{i=1}^{3}(\gamma_1 + \gamma_3\text{DED}_{i,t-1} + \gamma_5\text{DUM}_{i,t-1})(\text{OS})_{i,t-1} \\
& + \sum_{i=1}^{3}(\gamma_2 + \gamma_4\text{DED}_{i,t-1} + \gamma_6\text{DUM}_{i,t-1})(\text{OS})_{i,t-1}^2 + \gamma_j(\text{DE})_{t-1} \\
& + \gamma_k(\text{CR45}) + \gamma_L(\text{INTAN})_{t-1} + \gamma_M(\text{CR45} \times \text{DED})_{t-1} \\
& + \gamma_N(\text{INTAN} \times \text{DED})_{t-1} + \gamma_o\left(\sum_{i=1}^{N} \textit{Cont. var.}\right)_{i,t-1}
\end{aligned} \tag{1}
$$

Where ΔValue is the difference in Tobin's Q value between t and $t-1$. Tobin's Q is measured as firm market value plus total debt divided by book asset; OS the ownership structure, refers to total manager or insider equity interest (DIR) and DirLarge where it is OS × Large; Large $= 1$ when a large shareholder is present, otherwise $= 0$. Ext $= 1$, the large shareholder is not present as board member, otherwise $= 0$; DED the dummy of excess leverage above each industrial leverage median for 3-digit industries MIC code for each year; DE the debt/equity; DUM the dummy for firms with a high industrial competition ratio (CRD) and high intangible assets (INT), respectively; CRD the dummy equals 1 for each industrial competition ratio above 0.40, otherwise equals 0 for each Malaysian Standard Industrial Classification (MSIC) code; INT the intangible asset dummy equal 1 above each 3-digit MSIC code median, otherwise equals 0; CR45 the industrial competition concentration at 5-digit MSIC code; INTAN the intangible assets measured as intangible asserts divided by fixed assets; and Cont. var. refers to control variables – export, cash flows and standard deviation of the firms' weekly share price.

In Eq. (1), the dependent variable for the firm value of firm i in year t is ΔValue_{it}, refers to changes in Tobin's Q value. The use of Tobin's Q value is widely used in assessing expropriation of shareholder values (e.g. Claessens et al., 1999; Lins & Servaes, 2002). Our measure applies a measure of the annual differences between t and $t-1$ which indicates the changes in firm value. We follow a modified Tobin's Q applied in Chung & Pruitt (1994) and Chen and Ho (2000), defined as market capitalisation plus book value of total debt divided by book value of total assets.

The problem of endogenous problem is likely to influence ownership and performance. The endogeneity problem exists when ownership and performance are contemporarily related and the directional relations between other variables such as leverage, ownership and performance are not easily predicted.[2] Therefore, the use of changes in firm value seem to vanish the simultaneous effect directly. In additional, various studies also applied a lag period to minimise endogeneity problem (e.g. Hermalin & Weisbach, 1991; Palia & Lichtenberg, 1999). All other independent variables are therefore valued at year $t-1$.

Lastly, year effects appear to be an essential issue in the studies that involved East Asian countries. Mitton (2002), for instance shows that expropriation tends to go up as the expected return on investment falls during the crisis. The crisis triggered greater awareness of weaknesses in corporate governance in the region.[3] To check the robustness of our findings, we divide the sample into 1997–1998, and 1999 and 2000 and regress again the main findings. The issue is included in Section 5.

3.1. Main Variables

In this study, we define debt as the leverage ratio of total debt over equity. In order to reflect the influence of financial rent caused by FIs in this economy, we define the debt as short-term and long-term debt that pays explicit interest. We dummied leverage as 1, when the leverage is above industry median at each 3-digit MSIC code each year, otherwise it (DED) equals 0. This approach allows us to capture around 50% of the firms with excessive leverage. A more stringent approach is to reclassify excessive leverage as being those in the top 75% quartile of the industry's leverage. The dummy variable for the excessive leverage (DED) is introduced into the model and it interacts with the ownership structure variable. We do not apply continuous value of leverage (DE) into the interaction term as the influence of leverage towards firm value is a priori uncertain. A higher leverage ratio could possibly signal a firm's capability in managing their cash flow which subsequently increases the firm's value. Likewise, a lower leverage ratio may also reflect a higher value due to the firm capability in generating internal funding. Therefore, by controlling of excessive leverage, we could be certain of the ultimate influence from excessive leverage.

In this study, two aspects of ownership structure are examined empirically. First, we calculate the proportion of all the managers' equity interest (DIR) as a percentage of outstanding shares for each firm. This calculation includes the percentage of shares owned by the chairman, chief executive officers, managing directors and other directors in the firms. Second, the models also incorporate the effects of both large shareholders on the corporate financing decisions and subsequently on firm performance.

To address the influence of the large shareholders on managerial decision making, we follow Short et al. (2002), by creating an interaction term of large shareholders on managerial ownership so that their influence on managers could be captured. A dummy of the largest shareholder (LARGE) equal 1 is given if the largest shareholder holds more than 5% of equity interest in a firm, otherwise equals 0. When the dummy LARGE equals 1, the continuous variable from the interaction term reflects the influences of the large shareholders on managerial ownership. On the same note, the zero value of the interaction term (when LARGE = 0) implies the largest shareholder is unable to exert any influence on the managers.

We apply intangible assets as the proxy for a firm's specific assets. Balakrishnan and Fox (1993) suggest that examples of firms' intangible assets are such as brand names, internally generated goodwill, research and development expenditure and other reputation investments. The value of intangible assets is deflated by total sales. We apply a dummy variable for firms with highly intangible assets when the value is higher than the industrial intangible asset median at each 3-digit MSIC's code, each year. The dummy variable will be interacted with the ownership structure variable and excessive leverage (DED) in order to ascertain whether the controlling owner has utilised excessive leverage to finance any intangible asset.

Industrial market competition has a direct influence on firm value. Generally, industrial economics literature has largely suggested that industrial competition serves to weed out poorly managed firms. However, it is also possible that firms in industries with low intensity of competition boost their performance as a result of the enormous resources and market share they possess and control. In this study, we control for the industry competition factor to further examine whether excessive leverage is prompted by industrial rent. The main variable used to measure industrial competition is the industrial concentration ratio of the four largest firms (CR4). It is defined as the output of the largest four firms divided by total industrial output. In this regard, Bhattacharya (2002) proves that industrial competition based on CR4 in Malaysia is generally a good measurement for market competition. In this study, we could only secure CR4 at the aggregate figure as we are unable to obtain the individual sales figure of the largest four firms to compute Herfindahl index as used in Januszewski et al. (2002). The data on the four largest firms output and total output is obtained from Department of Statistics, Malaysia (Malaysia).

We create a dummy 1 for the industry with industrial concentration ratio more than 0.40 as the threshold for low intensity of competition at 5-digit MSIC code, otherwise equals 0. The level is arbitrary but close to the means of our sample's concentration ratio of 0.41. The dummy variable is interacted with the ownership structure variables in order to ascertain whether a controlling owner has misappropriated firm value in an industry with a higher concentration level.

We also apply the quadratic term on ownership structure to capture entrenchment and convergence of interest effects in a singular framework. The main focus in our model is on the interaction between OS and DED. When a firm incurs excessive leverage (DED takes the value of 1), such an effect is captured as $(\gamma_1 + \gamma_3)$. Similarly, if a non-linear interaction term (OS^2) exists, the total coefficient effect is observed as $\gamma_1 + \gamma_3 + \gamma_2 + \gamma_4$. On the other hand, the effect of firm with no excessive leverage (DED takes value 0) on performance is measured as γ_1 and γ_3 for OS and OS^2, respectively.

The issue of high intangible assets and low intensity of industrial competition is dubbed as DUM, respectively. For instance, when a controlling owner incurs higher debt in a firm with high value of intangible assets, the total effect on firm performance caused by the managers or controlling owners is $\gamma_1 + \gamma_3 + \gamma_5$. A similar approach is applied to low intensity of industrial competition.

3.2. Other Control Variables

We incorporate export concentration measurement (export divided by total industrial output) to capture the impacts of international trade on firm value. The variable is measured at 2-digit of MSIC level, the nearest possible classification for the data available. Hanazaki and Horiuchi (2001) show that it is international competitive market pressure instead of FIs discipline Japanese manufacturing firms. The measurement of export concentration is also applied in the studies by Januszewski et al. (2002) and Koke and Renneboog (2003) in their studies.

Putterman (1993) highlights three dimensions of the nature of the firm: firm size, information asymmetry and risk sharing which could affect the type of ownership structure and firm value. Firm size affects the formation of ownership structure. A dispersed structure with many shareholders can better share the risk of a large sized firm and, vice versa. A larger sized firm encompasses economies of scale and scope and also expected to incur a large scale of debt capital as well as performance. Pandey (2002), for instance found that there is a positive relationship between size and debt ratio in Malaysia due to the fact that larger firms are less prone to bankruptcy and the transaction costs of issuing debt is smaller. Frank and Goyal (2003) show that larger size firms increase their debt in order to support the payment of dividend. To capture the influence of size effect, we apply the logarithm of total assets as the proxy for firm size.

The second dimension is information asymmetry. Due to information asymmetric problems, specific information may not be shared with other shareholders. A larger cash flow firm is generally associated with the problem of information asymmetry. In firms with large asymmetric information problems, higher concentrated shareholding is preferred so that decision can be swiftly reached, thus, reducing opportunities of misappropriation in the firms. In a similar vein, a company with a larger cash flow can reflect a higher firm value because cash flow represents resources, which help boost firm value. Liquidity values such as cash flows, are normally the proxy for information asymmetric problem. Cash flow is defined here as profit before taxation plus depreciation.

Lastly, a bigger sized firm should have a wider spread of shareholders so that a single large shareholder would not be made to bear higher risk. Under this argument, a firm with a singular large shareholder and a high level of risk will tend to be risk adverse. Conversely, a dispersed structure in a larger firm can benefit from a more aggressive investment, as the risks are well spread among shareholders. If the risks to a firm are well spread, we can expect a higher risk level to induce higher return. Reverse effects are also predicted when causation effects from variations in firm performance due to risk variations, lead to variations in shareholdings in a firm. We define risk as the yearly standard deviation of a firm's weekly share price movement from 1994 to 2000, the same definition applied in Gursoy and Aydogan's (2002) empirical work. Therefore, both a very large firm and small size firm could have extracted the most in terms of costs and benefits of the ownership concentration and excessive leverage. However, the inclusions of firms' size (e.g. firms assets) can create significant multicollinearity with the above variables. To control for firm size effect, we restrict the sample size to lie between 5% and 95% of total assets. We address this issue in Section 5.

3.3. Data Sources

Our analysis uses a dataset of unbalanced 256 Malaysian manufacturing corporations (consumer and industrial sectors) listed on Bursa Malaysia. The details of the sample selection are presented in Table 1. The sample period is from 1994 to 2000, including 3 years of pre and post crisis period.

Table 1. Sample Description.

Description	1994	1995	1996	1997	1998	1999	2000
Initial number	182	215	254	294	310	319	335
PN4 Corporation[a]	26	27	29	32	33	33	33
Insufficient data[b]	10	12	15	21	22	30	46
Balance	146	176	210	241	255	256	256
BURSA Malaysia total listing	478	529	621	708	736	757	795
Obs./BURSA's total (%) average = 33.27%	30.54	33.27	33.82	34.04	34.65	33.95	32.33
3-digit MISC code (number of sectors)	27	27	27	27	27	27	27
5-digit MISC code (number of sectors)	51	66	71	71	71	71	71

[a]Accumulating number.

[b]Financial and ownership data were not published for two consecutive years. This included firms just listed in the year and therefore, excluded from the sample. Total number of firms listed in 1993 was 419 firms.

The earlier sample of 332 observations were identified from KLSE Statistics (2001), which reports the listed firms according to their core activities in 2000, in which, the definitions of the core activities is similar to the definition of industries provided by the Malaysian Department of Statistics. Only firms with a full 12 months financial data are included. Thirteen firms change their financial reporting year. Fourty-six firms were excluded because of their ambiguous ownership data or incomplete financial data for two consecutive years. We also excluded 33 PN4 firms from our sample[4] (Table 1).

We used the annual KLSE Hand Book and KLSE ON DISCs as the primary sources for collecting managerial ownership and the largest shareholder ownership data. Financial data is largely drawn from the same sources. We calculated the standard deviation of weekly share price annually for each firm.

4. FINDINGS

4.1. Descriptive Statistics

Table 2 presents the annual averages of the descriptive statistics of all the variables used in the regression models. The maximum value of Tobin's Q (TOBQ) is close to 7, whereas the lowest value is 0.08. The distribution is however, central at the value of 2.25 with the median of 1.95. The difference in t and $t-1$ for Tobin's Q (ΔTOBQ) which is the dependent variable shows a fair distribution between -4.45 and 4.28 with the mean and median at the centre of the distribution (-0.17 and -0.07 respectively). The directors hold an average 39% of outstanding equity interest. The maximum controlling interest is as high as 85%, reflecting that ownership concentration is high in this economy.

The leverage (DE) ratio in Malaysian firms is relatively high with a mean of 1.03 as compared to the equity portion. The firms' intangible asset (INTAN) normalised by fixed assets ranges from 0 to 20.28. The spread of exports is also wide showing different export orientation in different industries. The sample consists of firms from main board and second board which are very different in size. This is reflected in the measurement of total assets. The logarithm of total assets (Log TA), however, illustrates that the dispersion for one standard deviation is relatively small at 1.28.

The last column in the table shows the correlation between dependent variables and independent variables. With the exception of intangible assets (INTAN) and export (EXPORT), most of the variables show significant

Table 2. Descriptive Statistics.

	Mean	Median	Maximum	Minimum	Std. Dev.	Observations	Correlation
TOBQ	2.25	1.95	6.91	0.08	1.64	1,490	−0.0268
ΔTOBQ	−0.17	−0.07	4.28	−4.45	0.57	1,231	1.0000
DIR (%)	35	39	85	0.00	1.25	1,252	−0.0728**
EXT	0.39	0.00	1.00	0.00	0.49	1,252	0.1061***
LARGE	0.61	1.00	1.00	0.00	0.49	1,252	−0.1061***
DE	1.03	0.43	5.00	0.00	1.20	1,320	0.1638***
DED	0.50	1.00	1.00	0.00	0.50	1,320	0.0612**
CR45	0.41	0.35	1.00	0.00	0.26	1,540	0.0538**
CR43	0.27	0.18	0.96	0.01	0.21	1,540	0.0669**
CRD	0.50	1.00	1.00	0.00	0.50	1,540	0.0490**
INTAN	0.20	0.01	20.28	0.00	1.12	1,396	0.0063
INT	0.54	1.00	1.00	0.00	0.50	1,420	−0.0019
EXPORT	0.62	0.39	18.19	0.01	0.98	1,540	−0.0029
CASH	0.06	0.10	1.53	−14.00	0.52	1,540	−0.3767***
STD	7.81	6.79	29.63	−0.09	3.00	1,331	0.0630**
TA ('000)	589,854	148,898	15,669,618	6,696	1,352,706	1,535	0.083**
LOGTA	12.24	11.91	16.57	8.81	1.28	1,535	0.108**

Notes: TOBQ, Tobin's Q value, market value of equity plus book value of debt divided by book value of asset; ΔTOBQ is the difference of TOBQ between t and $t-1$. DIR is defined as total stock ownership (%) by director. EXT the dummy equals 1 when largest shareholder is not presented as board member. LARGE the dummy equals 1 when first largest shareholder presents as board member. DE the debt over equity ratio. DED is the excessive leverage of the firm when DE is above each industrial median, dummy = 1 for each year. CR43 and CR45 are output concentration ratio for four largest firms based on Malaysia Standard Industrial Classification code at 3-digit and 5-digit respectively. CRD the dummy variable equals 1 when CR45 is above 0.40. INTAN is intangible asset normalised by fixed asset; INT the dummy variable equals 1 when intangible asset value is above median for each industry and each year. EXP, export based on 2-digit industrial code; CASH, free cash flow/total sales, free cash flow is calculated as profit before taxation plus depreciation. Std. is the standard deviation of the firms' weekly share price from 1994 to 2000. TA, total asset; LOGTA, logarithm of total asset.
**Denotes significance at the 5% level.
***Denotes significance at the 1% level.

level of association with dependent variable (ΔTOBQ). Managers (DIR) and the dummy for the presence of a large shareholder as board member (LARGE) shows a negative contribution to firm value, showing that a higher ownership concentration could lead to a detriment firm value. It is interesting to note that ΔTOBQ and excessive leverage (DED) establish a positive relationship. The excessive leverage (DED) also has a positive and significant relationship. This poses an interesting question which relates to our hypotheses: how managers (DIR) (which has a negative relationship)

Table 3.   Descriptive Statistics of Insider Ownership.

LARGE	Managerial Ownership (DIR) (%)							
	0–20		20–49		>50		Total (%)	
	LARGE	DIR	LARGE	DIR	LARGE	DIR	LARGE	DIR
DIRLARGE								
N	155	171	465	399	162	202	780 (62.36)	772 (61.66)
Mean	15.26	13.75	34.93	35.81	34.40	57.75		
Median	15.33	14.00	35.39	39.41	51.75	55.74		
EXT								
N	99	119	277	230	96	131	472 (37.64)	480 (38.34)
Mean	15.31	14.00	34.69	39.08	38.59	57.99		
Median	15.81	14.75	33.59	43.26	52.65	55.90		
Total								
N	254	290	742	629	258	333	1,252	1,252
Percentage	20.26	23.16	59.17	50.24	20.57	26.60	(100)	(100)

Notes: DIR refers to equity share based on the dispersion of share (%) owned by directors. LARGE is defined as the largest shareholder who own more than 5% share in a firm. EXT the dummy for largest shareholder not present as board member. DIRLARGE the dummy for the largest shareholders presents as board member.

and leverage (DED and DE) (which has a positive relationship) interact and influenced firm value?

Table 3 presents the breakdown of the sample according to share ownership based on the controlling right of the largest shareholders (LARGE) as compared to that of managerial ownership (DIR). In total, the sample consists of 62.36% of the largest shareholders who control the board (DIRLARGE). Their influences as shown by their voting rights, increases in tandem with the distribution of managerial ownership (DIR). The influences appear to be stronger when managerial ownership (DIR) is less than 50%. In the threshold of 20–49%, the influence of the large shareholder on directors is great at 34.93% of the 35.81% of total managerial ownership (DIR). In the threshold of more than 50%, the largest shareholders hold a mean of 34.40% out of 57.75% of the total managerial ownership (DIR). These two scenarios imply that the probability of expropriation by the largest shareholders to occur is higher in the threshold when managerial ownership (DIR) is less than 50%. In this threshold, the controlling stake of the largest shareholders is too large for other directors to refute if there are any unscrupulous decisions.

Table 4. Descriptive Statistics and Univariate Analysis.

Panel A	Largest	Mean	Panel B	DED	Mean	*F*-Value	*p*-Value
LEVERAGE	<20%	1.6436	DIR	<median	31.5699	17.085	0.000
	20–50%	0.9112		>median	37.7008		
	>50%	0.7435					
TOBQ	<20%	0.3367	TOBQ	<median	2.3971	11.403	0.001
	20–50%	0.2782		>median	2.1117		
	>50%	0.2481					
CR43	<20%	0.2015	CR43	<median	0.2645	1.823	0.177
	20–50%	0.2786		>median	0.2797		
	>50%	0.3089					
CR45	<20%	0.3825	CR45	<median	0.4048	5.514	0.019
	20–50%	0.4185		>median	0.4362		
	>50%	0.4730					

Notes: There are 678 firm-years with excessive leverage, 669 firm-years with below industry leverage median. CR43 and CR45 are calculated as output concentration ratio for four largest firms based on Malaysia SIC code at 3-digit and 5-digit respectively. TOBQ (Tobin's Q value) is measured as, market value of equity plus book value of debt divided by book value of asset. DED is the excessive leverage equals 1, otherwise 0 when DE ratio is above industrial leverage median for each year. LARGE is defined as first largest shareholder who owns more than 5% share in a firm. DIR the total fraction of shares owned by directors of the firms.

Table 4 (Panel A) separates ownership concentration of the largest shareholders (LARGE) into three thresholds to examine their influence on the observed leverage ratio (DE), Tobin's Q and industrial competition (CR43 and CR45). In corresponding to Suto's (2003) and Pandey's (2002) a negative relation between ownership concentration and capital structure ratio, leverage ratio (DE) declines as the largest shareholder (LARGE) equity interest increases in their respective thresholds. The adverse relationship highlights the possibility for largest shareholders to avoid debt financing in this economy. In contrast, managerial ownerships are found to increase debt financing in this economy (Panel B). We also observe that firm value (TOBQ) decreases when industrial concentration – CR43 and CR45 increases. Although the leverage does not seem to increase in line with the equity portion of the largest shareholders (LARGE), the mean concentration of managerial ownership (DIR) is high at 37.70% in excessive leverage firms as compared to 31.57% of equity ownership in low leverage firms. The differences are significant at $p < 0.001$ (Panel B), signifying that managers may use higher leverage to protect their interest as their controlling interest increases.

Rent seeking by the managerial group is also verified because the competition ratio – CR43 (insignificant) and CR45 (significant at $p < 0.05$) is higher when leverage is higher than the median. The findings portray that higher leverage has been employed to protect rent interest, which could be derived from an industry with low competition intensity. Interestingly, firm value appears to be significantly lower with excess leverage. However, we are uncertain of the effects of the utilisation of leverage by the controlling owner on firm value. The following section uses multiple regressions to address this.

4.2. Regression Finding: Managerial Ownership, Excessive Leverage and Firm Value

We initially estimated the equations using ordinary least squares (OLS), however, the results do not show the significant impact of ownership variables on firm value which is largely contributed to the heteroscedasticy problem.[5] We then used the generalised least square (GLS) method, where the variances of the OLS are used to minimise the sum of residual square. Table 5 reports the regression results of the dependent variable – difference of excess Tobin's Q value based on generalised lease square.

Model 1 of Table 5 reports the regression results based on OLS for the purpose of comparison. The remaining models in the study use the GLS model. The regression in model 2, clearly shows improvement in terms of explanatory power as well as t-value. The explanatory power R^2 increases from 4% to 25%. With the exception of the risk variable (STD) and industrial competition (CR45), the signs for the main variables OS and OS^2 remain unchanged. STD is not significant, while the coefficient sign of industrial competition (CR45) changes from positive to negative. The t-value of other variables in the GLS model is also higher than in the model 1. In summary, the use of GLS is more relevant in this study.

Generally in model 2, the relationship between ownership structure and performance follows a U-shaped relationship, which corroborates with the theoretical work of Jensen and Meckling (1976) regarding entrenchment and convergence of interest hypotheses. When director ownership equity interest is relatively low (OS), a 1% increase in managerial ownership (DIR) is able to cause a 0.0068 reduction in ΔTobin's Q. When managerial ownership is relatively high (OS^2), a 1% increase in equity interest could enforce a positive value of 0.00006 improvement in the Tobin's Q value from $t-1$ to t.

In model 3, we address hypothesis H1 where the interaction effects between managerial ownership and higher leverage (DED) on firm value follow a non-linear inverted U relationship. Generally, the relationship of the variables remains unchanged. At the first order of OS, the impacts of

Table 5. Firm Value (ΔTOBQ) Regression Analysis (Managerial Ownership).

Dependent ΔTOBQ	ΔTOBQ				
	Model 1 (DIR)	Model 2 (DIR)	Model 3 (DIR)	Model 4 (DIR)	Model 5 (DIR)
C	−0.20738 (−3.0460)***	−0.04151 (−2.1843)**	−0.02965 (−1.4436)	−0.02234 (−1.1657)	−0.01997 (−1.3192)
Ownership (OS)$_{t-1}$	−0.00656 (−2.6281)***	−0.0068 (−10.7143)***	−0.00642 (−9.5768)***	−0.00833 (−10.1540)***	−0.00624 (−8.6185)***
(OS^2)$_{t-1}$	0.00006 (1.6669)*	0.00006 (5.7618)***	0.00005 (5.4474)***	0.00009 (6.3610)***	0.00005 (5.3834)***
Financial rent (DE)$_{t-1}$	0.05253 (3.1022)**	0.04547 (5.8703)***	0.00732 (0.8769)	−0.00017 (−0.0244)	0.01184 (1.2352)
(OS × DED)$_{t-1}$			0.00314 (5.3666)***	0.00516 (4.5507)***	0.00311 (4.4666)***
(OS^2 × DED)$_{t-1}$			−0.00002 (−2.5969)***	−0.00005 (−3.0692)***	−0.00002 (−2.2814)**
Competition rent (CR45)$_{t-1}$	0.05343 (0.7006)	−0.00874 (−0.4783)	0.04841 (2.6136)***	0.03517 (1.9936)**	0.02928 (1.7445)*
(CR45 × DED)$_{t-1}$					0.03765 (2.1921)**
(OS × CRD)$_{t-1}$					0.00033 (0.5485)
Ownership × rent (OS × DED × CRD)$_{t-1}$					−0.00141
Asset uniqueness (INTAN)$_{t-1}$	0.00887 (0.4681)	0.00923 (2.1213)**	0.00635 (2.5524)***	0.0157 (2.3513)**	
(INTAN × DED)$_{t-1}$				−0.02037 (−2.3379)**	
(OS × INT)$_{t-1}$				0.00091 (1.4507)	
(OS × INT × DED)$_{t-1}$				0.00015 (1.1951)	
Control (EXP)$_{t-1}$	−0.00181 (−0.1857)	−0.0022 (−0.9655)	−0.00616 (−2.3924)**	−0.00707 (−2.4949)**	−0.00547 (−2.4196)**
(CASH)$_{t-1}$	−0.02319 (−0.294)	−0.10464 (−4.3946)***	−0.40638 (−6.6852)***	−0.38745 (−7.2802)***	−0.45962 (−7.0943)***
(STD)$_{t-1}$	0.01374 (3.0647)***	0.00108 (0.9904)	0.00091 (0.6921)	0.00235 (2.0584)**	−0.00016 (−0.1342)

Table 5. (*Continued*)

Dependent ΔTOBQ	ΔTOBQ				
	Model 1 (DIR)	Model 2 (DIR)	Model 3 (DIR)	Model 4 (DIR)	Model 5 (DIR)
R^2	0.04	0.25	0.37	0.53	0.4
Adjusted R^2	0.03	0.24	0.36	0.52	0.39
S.E. of regression	0.53	0.52	0.52	0.51	0.52
F-statistic	4.35	30	41.22	69.64	35.19
Prob. (F-statistic)	0	0	0	0	0
Number of obs.	1,252	1,252	1,252	1,252	1,252

Notes: The table uses regression on unbalanced panel data to estimate firm value as a function of the director ownership. ΔTOBQ is the difference of TOBQ between t and $t-1$. OS (ownership structure) in models 1–5 refers to managerial or director ownership (DIR), percentage of share owned by directors. DE is the debt over equity ratio. DED the excessive leverage of the firm when DE is above each industrial median, dummy equals 1, otherwise 0 for each year. CR45 the output concentration ratio for four largest firms based on Malaysia Standard Industrial Classification code at 5-digit respectively. CRD the dummy variable equals 1 when CR45 is above 0.40. INTAN the intangible asset normalised by fixed asset; INT the dummy variable equals 1 when intangible asset value is above median for each industry and each year. EXP, export based on 2-digit industrial code; CASH, free cash flow/total sales, free cash flow is calculated as profit before taxation plus depreciation. STD is defined as standard deviation of the firms' weekly share price.
*Denotes significance at the 10% level.
**Denotes significance at the 5% level.
***Denotes significance at the 1% level.
t-statistics are in parentheses.

leverage clearly reduced the magnitude of entrenchment effect by 0.00314. This result is consistent with Jensen's (1986) argument that debt is a disciplinary mechanism on entrenched managers, At the other end, when managerial ownership equity interest is relatively large (OS^2), we observe that incurring excessive leverage reduces the positive effects by 0.00002. The negative value is suggestive that firms with large managerial ownership use excessive leverage which is however, at the expense of other shareholders. Therefore, H1 is substantiated.

Model 4 includes the interaction terms of OS, DED and INT, dummy for high intangible assets. Apparently, the presence of intangible assets (INTAN) in a firm illustrates the potential for value added and potential for future growth for the firms. The coefficient is 0.0157 at $p<0.05$. The managers do not entrench firm value through intangible assets (OS × INTAN), as shown in the positive coefficient of 0.00091. Further, management does not seem to use excessive leverage in firms with high intangible assets (OS × DED × INT) for entrenchment purpose. The coefficient is in fact positive but insignificant. Nonetheless, the interaction effect of high intangible assets and excessive leverage (INTAN × DED) reduces firm value by 0.02, supporting Williamson's (1988) argument that intangible assets are best financed by equity.

Model 5 shows the regression results when the dummy for industries with high industrial concentration (CRD) is introduced into the model.[6] Industrial concentration is found to exert a positive influence of 0.029 on the dependent variable. It signifies a positive response from shareholders to firms in industries with lower intensities of competition.[7] The interaction variable between managerial ownership and dummy for low intensity of competition (OS × CRD) is positive, but not significantly different from zero. Interestingly, the interaction variable of industrial competition with excessive leverage (CR45 × DED) establishes a positive impact of 0.0376 on ΔTOBQ. The finding signifies a complementary impact on firms' value as governance from a debt holder is effective, although it is in industries with lower intensity of competition.

Lastly, it is clear from our findings that the presence of management appears to have aligned these complementary effects. Managers are found to use excessive leverage in industries with lower competition intensity, and induce a significant discount impact of 0.0014 on ΔTOBQ. This signifies that the controlling shareholders entrench shareholder value. It is also apparent that the effectiveness of debt as a governance mechanism becomes an instrument to expropriate, instead of governance. We find no evidence of a significant relationship between interaction terms of (OS^2 × DED × CRD), therefore, irrespective of their degree of control, the controlling insider utilises excessive leverage especially in an industry with high competition intensity and further leads to the deterioration in firm value.

4.3. The Influences from Large Shareholder

Table 6 examines whether large shareholders in the position of board members have a greater incentive to monitor management due to their significant investment in the firm. Although the regression result between manager with the presence of large shareholder (DIRLARGE) and performance is suggestive of a U-shaped relationship, the negative coefficient (−0.00012) is lesser than the coefficient in model 3 in Table 5. This signifies

Table 6. Firm Value (ΔTOBQ) Regression Analysis (Effects of Largest Shareholder).

Dependent ΔTOBQ	Model 1 DIRLARGE	Model 2 DIRLARGE	Model 3 DIRLARGE
C	−0.07717	−0.09591	−0.08033
	(−3.2305)***	(−4.4566)***	(−2.8944)***
Ownership			
$(OS)_{t-1}$	−0.00012	−0.0001	−0.00013
	(−6.1329)***	(−6.0534)***	(−6.0412)***
$(OS^2)_{t-1}$	0.00001	0.00001	0.00001
	(5.1635)***	(4.0417)***	(3.5448)***
Financial rent			
$(DE)_{t-1}$	−0.00527	−0.00213	−0.00664
	(−0.6826)	(−0.2799)	(−0.7656)
$(OS \times DED)_{t-1}$	0.00013	0.00011	0.00014
	(6.0709)***	(5.8523)***	(5.9351)***
$(OS^2 \times DED)_{t-1}$	−0.00001	−0.00001	−0.00001
	(−5.0487)***	(−5.2526)***	(−2.4743)**
Competition rent			
$(CR45)_{t-1}$	0.03592	0.06587	0.03503
	(1.6589)*	(3.7796)***	(1.7355)*
$(CR45 \times DED)_{t-1}$			0.03598
			(1.7444)*
$(OS \times CRD)_{t-1}$			0.00005
			(2.4048)**
Ownership × rent			
$(OS \times DED \times CRD)_{t-1}$			−0.00008
			(−3.8708)***
Asset uniqueness			
$(INTAN)_{t-1}$	0.00421	0.01306	−0.0035
	(1.9387)*	(1.4569)	(−0.9586)
$(INTAN \times DED)_{t-1}$		−0.01634	
		(−1.4253)	
$(OS \times INT)_{t-1}$		0.00002	
		(3.0170)***	
$(OS \times INT \times DED)_{t-1}$		0.00001	
		(1.1301)	
Control			
$(EXP)_{t-1}$	−0.00842	−0.00832	−0.00919
	(−2.9511)***	(−2.6548)***	(−3.8129)***
$(CASH)_{t-1}$	−0.40111	−0.51686	−0.41195
	(−6.4958)***	(−10.6913)***	(−6.4291)***
$(STD)_{t-1}$	0.00499	0.00489	0.00469
	(3.7045)***	(4.4913)***	(3.6449)***
R^2	0.33	0.88	0.33
Adjusted R^2	0.32	0.87	0.32
S.E. of regression	0.5	0.51	0.5

Table 6. (*Continued*)

Dependent ΔTOBQ	Model 1 DIRLARGE	Model 2 DIRLARGE	Model 3 DIRLARGE
F-statistic	37.65	413.99	28.93
Prob. (*F*-statistic)	0	0	0
Number of obs.	1,252	1,252	1,252

Notes: ΔTOBQ is the difference of TOBQ between *t* and *t*−1. OS (ownership structure) refers to DIRLARGE–DIR × LARGE where LARGE = 1 when a large shareholder is present, otherwise = 0. DIR is the percentage of share owned by directors, DE the debt over equity ratio. DED the excessive leverage of the firm when DE is above each industrial median, dummy equals 1, otherwise 0 for each year. CR45 the output concentration ratio for four largest firms based on Malaysia Standard Industrial Classification code at 5-digit respectively. CRD the dummy variable equals 1 when CR45 is above 0.40. INTAN the intangible asset normalised by fixed asset; INT the dummy variable equals 1 when intangible asset value is above median for each industry and each year. EXP, export based on 2-digit industrial code; CASH, free cash flow/total sales, free cash flow is calculated as profit before taxation plus depreciation. STD is defined as standard deviation of the firms' weekly share price from 1994 to 2000
*Denotes significance at the 10% level.
**Denotes significance at the 5% level.
***Denotes significance at the 1% level.
t-statistics are in parentheses.

the capability of the large shareholder in monitoring. In this model, the presence of the largest shareholder exerts an effective governance mechanism as interaction terms of ownership and excessive leverage (OS × DED) reduce the detrimental effects by 0.00013. However, as the largest shareholder's controlling interest increases (OS^2), the interaction term of OS^2 × DED shows a negative value, which is also lower than the value in model 3 in Table 5, further confirming that the presence of large shareholder can reduce the agency conflict. In model 2, the presence of the large shareholder does not seem to alter the value of the firm when excessive leverage is applied in firms with high intangible assets. The coefficient signs of other variables do not seem to be different from previous models.

The presence of the large shareholder as director in industries with lower intensity of competition (OS × CRD) can enhance the firm's performance (model 3, Table 6). Higher leverage alike could also complements firms in highly concentrated industries to enhance their performance (CR45 × DED).[8] Nevertheless, the presence of largest shareholder with excessive debt in highly concentrated industries confirms the rent-seeking objectives which reduce the changes in firm value by another 0.00008, which lend support to the hypothesis H4 that the presence of large shareholder could further lead to the declination in firm value.

5. SENSITIVITY ANALYSIS

Furthermore, firm size may exert an influence on ownership structure, leverage and performance. In model 1 (Table 7), we restrict the sample size to lie between 5% and 95% of total assets. This allows us to exclude 76 firm years observation (total assets at lower 5%) and 77 firm years observation (total asset at higher 95%) from the regressions. A total of 55 firms are excluded.[9]

Model 1 (Table 7) also shows that the DE ratio is now positively significant, which demonstrates that firm size does affect the use of debt in a firm.

Table 7. Sensitivity Analysis.

Dependent ΔTOBQ	Model 1 DIR Firms' Size (5–95%)	Model 2 DIR	Model 3 DIR	Model 4 DIR	Model 5 DIR
C	−0.12268	−0.077108	−0.08201	−0.218039	−0.02082
	(−5.0874)***	(−5.8455)***	(−6.0198)***	(−8.1721)***	(−1.1294)
Ownership					
$(OS)_{t-1}$	−0.00012	−0.000176	−0.00017	−0.00016	−0.00014
	(−6.2197)***	(−9.2272)***	(−9.0259)***	(−7.2427)***	(−6.8338)***
$(OS^2)_{t-1}$	0	2.95E−08	0.00000	0.00000	0.00000
	(3.5154)***	(5.4860)***	(5.5105)***	(4.1482)***	(6.6002)***
Financial rent					
$(DE)_{t-1}$	0.01709	0.01040	0.00958	0.02247	0.00492
	(1.6405)*	(2.5132)**	(2.4656)**	(3.1005)**	(1.5355)
$(OS \times DED)_{t-1}$	0.00011	0.00016	0.00015	0.00017	0.00013
	(4.9663)***	(7.5461)***	(7.3216)***	(6.9856)***	(5.7030)***
$(OS^2 \times DED)_{t-1}$	−0.00001	−0.00001	0.00000	0.00000	0.00000
	(−2.0814)**	(−4.1813)***	(−3.9646)***	(−2.9885)**	(−4.4252)***
Competition rent					
$(CR45)_{t-1}$	0.06389	0.02277	0.03251	0.12656	0.02283
	(2.2458)**	(1.1390)	(1.5883)*	(4.1135)***	(0.9459)
$(CR45 \times DED)_{t-1}$	0.0075	0.02639	0.02406	0.01161	0.02639
	(0.2322)	(1.5507)	(1.4231)	(0.6279)	(1.3174)
$(OS \times CRD)_{t-1}$	0.00003	0.00003	0.00003	0.00004	0.00001
	(2.1564)**	(2.1819)**	(2.0104)**	(2.3679)**	(0.6806)
Ownership × rent					
$(OS \times DED \times CRD)_{t-1}$	−0.00006	−0.00004	−0.00004	−0.00008	−0.00003
	(−3.3024)***	(−2.5556)**	(−2.4541)**	(−4.1985)***	(−1.5263)
Asset uniqueness					
$(INTAN)_{t-1}$	0.002	0.00383	0.00405	0.00230	0.00004
	(0.5317)	(0.8667)	(0.8871)	(0.4048)	(0.0201)
Control					
$(EXP)_{t-1}$	−0.00786	Omitted	−0.00379	−0.00695	−0.00787
	(−2.8247)***		(−5.1026)***	(−2.6440)**	(−3.6443)***
$(CASH)_{t-1}$	−0.45099	Omitted	Omitted	Omitted	−0.51645
	(−7.9595)***				(−10.6394)***
$(STD)_{t-1}$	0.00604	Omitted	Omitted	0.00785	Omitted
	(4.2754)***			(6.0549)***	

Table 7. (*Continued*)

Dependent ∆TOBQ	Model 1 DIR Firms' Size (5–95%)	Model 2 DIR	Model 3 DIR	Model 4 DIR	Model 5 DIR
R^2	0.44	0.37	0.476217	0.44	0.36
Adjusted R^2	0.43	0.36	0.469533	0.43	0.36
S.E. of regression	0.52	0.51	0.514917	0.52	0.51
F-statistic	43.12	51.50	71.24717	43.12	41.78
Prob. (*F*-statistic)	0	0.00	0	0	0.00
Number of obs.	1,099	1,252	1,252	1,252	1,252

Notes: ∆TOBQ is the difference of TOBQ between *t* and *t*−1. OS (ownership structure) refers to the percentage of shares owned by directors, DE is the debt over equity ratio. DED the excessive leverage of the firm when DE is above each industrial median, dummy equals 1, otherwise 0 for each year. CR45 the output concentration ratio for four largest firms based on Malaysia Standard Industrial Classification code at 5-digit respectively. CRD the dummy variable equals 1 when CR45 is above 0.40. INTAN the intangible asset normalised by fixed asset; INT the dummy variable equals 1 when intangible asset value is above median for each industry and each year. EXP, export based on 2-digit industrial code; CASH, free cash flow/total sales, free cash flow is calculated as profit before taxation plus depreciation. STD is defined as standard deviation of the firms' weekly share price from 1994 to 2000.
*Denotes significance at the 10% level.
**Denotes significance at the 5% level.
***Denotes significance at the 1% level.
t-statistics are in parentheses.

Ownership variables remain unchanged, the interaction term of CR45 × DED is positive but becomes insignificant. The coefficient of OS × DED × CRD remains qualitatively consistent with previous findings with higher explanatory power.

Generally, the control variables in our earlier findings do conform well to our expectations. The lagged year of export concentration appears to be negatively related to differences in firm value, illustrating the stiff world competition. This finding is in contrast to the industrial concentration ratios (CR45) which consistently show a positive coefficient. The positive value in the industrial concentration ratio also illustrates that shareholders perceive industries with high protectionism policies as having better potential future growth. Although high cash flow should illustrate a positive relationship with the changes in Tobin's Q value, but the negative and significant relationship in our findings highlight the degree of information asymmetric problem in our sample firms. Lastly, with the exception in model 3 (Table 5), risk measured as standard deviation of share prices shows positive and significant influences on the difference in firm value throughout the models.

Nonetheless, cash flows and risk could possibility affect ownership variables as suggested in Putterman (1993). To further examine whether our results are robust, we excluded the control variables jointly and separately from our regression.

From models 2, 3 and 4 and 5 (Table 7), we examine the effects of controlling variables on our empirical findings. In model 2, excluding of controlling variables from our analysis reduced the explanatory power R^2 to 37%. Excluding EXPORT, CASHFLOWS separately and CASHFLOWS and STD jointly do not create any problem for our analysis. However, excluding of risk variable (STD) clearly affect the interaction term of OS × CRD and OS × DED × CRD, both coefficients become insignificant. The finding illustrates that risk variable to some extent influences controlling owners in utilising excessive debt in industries with lower competition.

The second issue that needs to be addressed in our study is year's effect. Although the results from Tables 5 and 6 generally support the hypotheses, we are hesitant to draw strong conclusions from our full sample period, which includes a volatile period of financial crisis as well as post crisis recovery period. After the financial crisis period, various policies on corporate governance have been emphasised and bank financing in the country has become more prudent. We reassess the findings for the 1997–1998 periods as those for the crisis period and the 1999–2000 period as those for the post crisis period (Table 8, models 1 and 2). The findings clearly

Table 8. Sensitivity Analysis.

Dependent ΔTOBQ	Model 1 DIRLARGE 1997–1998	Model 2 DIRLARGE 1999–2000	Model 3 DIRLARGE DED above 75% of Quartile
C	0.00409	0.00836	−0.15792
	(0.1168)	(0.3432)	(−7.2325)***
Ownership			
$(OS)_{t-1}$	−0.00015	−0.00013	−0.00011
	(−7.2333)***	(−5.3550)***	(−7.1976)***
$(OS^2)_{t-1}$	0.00001	0.00001	0
	(1.6808)*	(5.4930)***	(6.3439)***
Financial rent			
$(DE)_{t-1}$	0.00587	−0.00873	0.01483
	(0.4789)	(−1.2255)	(1.7278)*
$(OS × DED)_{t-1}$	0.00013	0.00011	0.00019
	(4.9803)***	(4.4169)***	(−6.1917)***
$(OS^2 × DED)_{t-1}$	−0.00001	−0.00001	0.00001
	(1.7910)*	(−4.0671)***	(−6.1917)***

Table 8. (*Continued*)

Dependent ΔTOBQ	Model 1 DIRLARGE 1997–1998	Model 2 DIRLARGE 1999–2000	Model 3 DIRLARGE DED above 75% of Quartile
Competition rent			
$(CR45)_{t-1}$	−0.02072	−0.0236	0.09863
	(−0.5095)	(−0.9991)	(4.7677)***
$(CR45 \times DED)_{t-1}$	0.01881	0.09451	−0.05266
	(0.5835)	(3.1153)***	(−1.0372)
$(OS \times CRD)_{t-1}$	0.00008	−0.00002	0.0001
	(4.0804)***	(−1.2002)	(3.1214)***
Ownership × rent			
$(OS \times DED \times CRD)_{t-1}$	−0.00006	−0.00002	−0.00007
	(−2.5299)***	(−1.3365)	(−6.7495)***
Asset uniqueness			
$(INTAN)_{t-1}$	0.01266	−0.00652	0.01059
	(3.8901)***	(−1.9664)**	(1.7797)*
Control			
$(EXP)_{t-1}$	−0.01858	−0.01009	−0.00582
	(−14.9693)***	(−4.1785)***	(−2.7794)***
$(CASH)_{t-1}$	−0.41788	−0.32467	−0.1937
	(−4.8017)***	(−6.6539)***	(−4.6105)***
$(STD)_{t-1}$	−0.00248	0.00235	0.00593
	(−0.8529)	(1.8764)*	(4.3799)***
R^2	0.69	0.63	0.55
Adjusted R^2	0.68	0.62	0.54
S.E. of regression	0.53	0.43	0.51
F-statistic	70.33	63.7	70.98
Prob. (*F*-statistic)	0	0	0
Number of obs.	356	396	1252

Notes: ΔTOBQ is the difference of TOBQ between t and $t-1$. OS (ownership structure) in model 5, refers to DIRLARGE–DIR × LARGE where LARGE = 1 when a large shareholder is present, otherwise = 0. Director is the percentage of share owned by directors, DE the debt over equity ratio. DED the excessive leverage of the firm when DE is above each industrial median, dummy equals 1, otherwise 0 for each year. In model 3, DED is defined as those in the top 75% quartile of the industry's leverage. CR45 the output concentration ratio for four largest firms based on Malaysia Standard Industrial Classification code at 5-digit respectively. CRD the dummy variable equals 1 when CR45 is above 0.40. INTAN the intangible asset normalised by fixed asset; INT the dummy variable equals 1 when intangible asset value is above median for each industry and each year. EXP, export based on 2-digit industrial code; CASH, free cash flow/total sales, free cash flow is calculated as profit before taxation plus depreciation. STD is defined as standard deviation of the firms' weekly share price from 1994 to 2000.
*Denotes significance at the 10% level.
**Denotes significance at the 5% level.
***Denotes significance at the 1% level.
t-statistics are in parentheses.

show that controlling large shareholders incurs excessive leverage in industries with lower intensity of competition and lead to a significantly lower firm value. The coefficients involve ownership structure variables and their interaction terms are very similar to the full sample both in signs and significances on all variables. In contrast, the interaction term of the rent-seeking behaviour does not seem to be prevalent in post crisis period.

Finally, we use a more stringent approach to reassess the measurement of excessive leverage. Excessive leverage is reclassified as leverage which is in the top quartile of the debt equity ratio. This approach reduces excessive leverage firms to 25%. In model 3 (Table 8), we readdress the model based on the presence of large shareholder as director (DIRLARGE), as suggested in Bebchuk (1999), large shareholders are more incline to increase debt instead of equity to protect their rent interest. The coefficients are largely unchanged. The overall fit also improves to 55%. The findings show that the reclassification of excessive leverage above the median is consistent with the findings when we raise excessive leverage to above the top quartile.

6. SUMMARY AND CONCLUSIONS

This paper has empirically shown that there is an U-shaped relationship between managers and performance, which is consistent with the effects of management entrenchment and convergence of interest hypotheses. The use of excessive debt by the managers, however, reduces the entrenchment effects when the managerial controlling interest is relatively low, signifying the role of FIs in monitoring firms. The finding is consistent with Nickell et al. (1997) and Dilling-Hansen et al. (1999) that debt financing can reduce entrenchment effects. However, as the controlling interest of the manager grows higher, the monitoring role of FIs seems to diminish. The findings highlight that agency problem overwhelms the effectiveness of the financial restraint policy as a governance mechanism. The objective of using debt is clearly for private interest which lends support to Bebchuk's (1999) rent protection theory, which is especially profound in less competitive industries. The presence of largest shareholder as director to monitor follows a non-linear relationship. As their equity interest increases, incurring excessive leverage also lead to a reduction in firm value. It is obvious that the marginal benefits from rent seeking are higher than the marginal cost of monitoring when rent-seeking benefits are prevalent in this economy.

There are two policies implications that we can draw from this study. First, agency problem is found to be severe in this economy which reduces the effectiveness of governance by FIs. The FIs in this economy are able to exert corporate governance at the lower threshold of managerial equity interest, but directors are able to overwhelm the FIs monitoring effects when the controlling managerial equity interest exceeds a certain threshold. In order to increase the effectiveness of governance from FIs, more regulatory power should be offered to FIs so that they can assert a more effective governance effort. Second, in contrast to standard economics argument, our findings suggest that firms in less competitive industries exert a positive impact on the firm value, signifying industrial rent value does reflect into market value in this economy. The findings also show that FIs are able to govern firms, especially in industries with lower intensity of competition. Nonetheless, managers and large shareholders are found to erode the monitoring effects by FIs, confirming rent-seeking hypothesis in this economy. These findings suggest that the issues of poor performance of Malaysian manufacturing firms are due to rent-seeking behaviour rather than the government's protectionism policy in the economy.

Lastly, there are possibilities that causation and endogeneity problem prevail among ownership structure, leverage, market competition and form performance. Although our research design includes a method to reduce the endogeneity problem, it cannot be claimed to be eliminated fully.

NOTES

1. Hanazaki and Horiuchi (2001) conduct a study on whether financial restraint policy could effectively enhance management in the Japanese corporate governance framework. They find that the market competition, instead of financial restraint policy has consistently contributed to the efficiency of corporate management in Japan's manufacturing firms.

2. Many variables related to ownership structure, leverage and performance are likely to be determined simultaneously. This causes endogenous problem as the regressors are correlated with the error term, which leads to inconsistency as the figures do not approach true values of the population when sample size increases (Wooldridge 2000).

3. Rajan and Zingales (1998) suggest that the relationship-based economy work well when an economy is performing well, since investors did not have information on the appropriation of their investments. The crisis triggered investors to become aware of weaknesses in relationship-based system and led them to withdraw their funds drastically.

4. PN4 firms are firms that are in the process of restructuring their capital. The firms are basically trade with restriction. Generally, these firms face the problems of dormant account, negative shareholder funds and are under financial distress. Failing which to restructure, the firms will be delisted from KLSE listing.

5. The heteroscedasticy problem is identified through the process of Park test. First, we obtained the residual of OLS from model 1. Then, we regress the logarithm of the square of the residual on each logarithm of the independent variables separately. Three variables: director ownership (DIR), industrial competition (CR45) and market risk (STD) indicate the presence of heteroscedasticy problem. Generalised least square (GLS) could minimize the unequal variances among variables.

6. We also reclassified CRD based on the measurement of CR43, the regression findings do not seem to differ from CR45. Therefore, we only report the findings based on CR45, which can closely reflect the activities of firms in our sample.

7. This finding is in contrast to the general believed in Anglo-Saxon economies that a less competitive industry will lead to lower firm value. However, it is not surprising in a rent-seeking prevailing environment because most of the shareholders view that industrial rent can further expedite their capital gains.

8. The finding differs from Nickell et al. (1997) as they have shown that highly competitive market and debt pressure could further enhance firm performance. Our study uses the dummy of low intensity of competition instead. The earlier findings also suggest that industrial concentration is positively related to firm value. Taken all together, it implies that FIs in Malaysia are able to complement a lower competitive industry to enhance firm value.

9. For simplicity purpose, in Table 7, we only readdress the issue on the ownership structure based on managerial or director ownership. In Table 8, we readdress year's effect and alternative measurement of excessive leverage on the ownership structure where large shareholders present as directors.

REFERENCES

Agrawal, A., & Knoeber, C. R. (1996). Firm performance and mechanisms to control agency problems between managers and shareholders. *Journal of Financial and Quantitative Analysis, 31*(3), 377–397.

Agrawal, A., & Mandelker, G. (1987). Managerial incentives and corporate investment and financing decisions. *Journal of Finance, 42*(4), 823–837.

Agrawal, A., & Nagarajan, N. J. (1990). Corporate capital structure, agency costs and ownership control: The case of all-equity firms. *Journal of Finance, XLV*(4), 1325–1331.

Aoki, M., Patrick, H., & Sheard, P. (1994). *The role of the main bank in the corporate governance structure in Japan. The Japanese main bank system: Its relevance for developing and transforming economics.* Oxford: Oxford University Press.

Baek, J., Kang, J., & Park, K. (2004). Corporate governance and firm value: Evidence from the Korean financial crisis. *Journal of Financial Economics, 71*(2), 265–314.

Balakrishnan, S., & Fox, I. (1993). Asset specificity, firm heterogeneity and capital structure. *Strategic Management Journal, 14*, 3–16.

Bank Negara Malaysia. (1996). Annual Report. Kuala Lumpur.

Barclay, M. J., & Holdedrness, C. (1989). Private benefits from control of public corporation. *Journal of Financial Economics, 25*, 861–878.

Bebchuk, L. A. (1999). *A rent protection theory of corporate ownership and control.* NBER Working Paper 7203.

Bebchuk, L. A., & Roe, M. J. (1999). A theory path dependence in corporate governance and ownership. *Stanford Law Review, 52*, 127–170.

Berger, P., Ofek, E., & Yermack, D. L. (1997). Managerial entrenchment and capital structure decisions. *Journal of Finance, 52*(4), 1411–1438.

Bhattacharya, M. (2002). Industrial concentration and competition in Malaysian manufacturing. *Applied Economics, 34*, 2127–2134.

Bongini, P., Claessens, S., & Ferri, G. (2000). *The political economy of distress in East Asian financial institutions.* Working Paper No. 2265. World Bank.

Brailsford, T. J., Oliver, B. R., & Pua, S. L. (2002). On the relation between ownership structure and capital structure. *Accounting and Finance, 42*, 1–26.

Chen, S. S., & Ho, K. W. (2000). Corporate diversification, ownership structure and firm value. The Singapore evidence. *International Review of Financial Analysis, 9*, 315–326.

Chung, K. H., & Pruitt, S. W. (1994). A simple approximation of Tobin's Q. *Financial Management, 23*(3), 70–74.

Claessens, S., Djankov, S., Fan, J., & Lang, L. (2002). Disentangling the incentive and entrenchment effects of large shareholdings. *Journal of Finance, 57*, 2741–2770.

Claessens, S., Djankov, S., & Lang, L. H. (1999). *Expropriation of minority shareholders: Evidence from East Asia.* Working Paper Series No. 2088. World Bank.

Dilling-Hansen, M., Eriksson, T., Madsen, S., & Smith, V. (1999). *The influence of competition and ownership structure on the performance of Danish manufacturing firms.* Working Paper series 99-9. Aarhus School of Business – Department of Economics.

Deesomsak, R., Paudyal, K., & Pescetto, G. (2004). The determinants of capital structure: Evidence from the Asia Pacific region. *Journal of Multinational Financial Management, 14*, 387–405.

Faccio, M., Lang, L., & Young, L. (2003). *Debt and expropriation.* SSRN Working Paper No. 239724. EFMA-2001 Lugano Meetings.

Frank, M. Z., & Goyal, V. (2003). Testing the pecking order theory of capital structure. *Journal of Financial Economics, 67*, 217–248.

Friend, I., & Lang, L. H. (1988). An empirical test of the impact of managerial self-interest on corporate capital structure. *Journal of Finance, 43*(2), 271–281.

Grosfeld, I., & Tressel, T. (2002). Competition and ownership structure: Substitutes or complements? Evidence from the Warsaw Stock Exchange. *Economics of Transition, 10*(3), 525–551.

Grossman, S., & Hart, O. (1980). Takeover bids, the free-rider problem and the theory of the corporation. *Bell Journal of Economics, 11*(4), 42–64.

Gursoy, G., & Aydogan, K. (2002). Equity ownership structure. Risk taking and performance: An empirical investigation in Turkish listed companies. *Emerging Market Finance and Trade, 38*(6), 6–25.

Hanazaki, M., & Horiuchi, A. (2001). *Can the financial restraint hypothesis explain Japan's post war experience?* CEI Working Paper Series No. 2001-12.

Hellmann, T., Murdock, K., & Stiglitz, J. (1996). Financial restraint: Toward a new paradigm. In: M. Aoki, H. -K. Kim & M. Okuno-Fujiwara (Eds), *The role of government in East Asian economic development* (pp. 342–372). Oxford: Clarendon Press.

Hermalin, B., & Weisbach, M. (1991). The effects of board composition and direct incentives on financial performance. Rochester Business Finance Research. 9F02.

Januszewski, S. I., Koke, J., & Winter, J. K. (2002). Product market competition, corporate governance and firm performance: An empirical analysis for Germany. *Research in Economics, 56*, 299–332.

Jensen, G. R., Solberg, D. P., & Zorn, T. S. (1992). Simultaneous determination of insider ownership, debt and dividend policies. *Journal of Financial and Quantitative Analysis, 27*(2), 247–263.

Jensen, M. C. (1986). Agency costs of free cash flow, corporate finance and takeovers. *AEA Papers and Proceedings, 76*(2), 659–665.

Jensen, M. C., & Meckling, W. H. (1976). Theory of the firm: Managerial behaviour, agency costs and ownership structure. *Journal of Financial Economics, 3*, 305–360.

Johnson, S., La Porta, R., Lopez-De-Silanes, F., & Shleifer, A. (2000). Tunneling. *American Economic Review, 90*(2), 22–27.

Khan, M. H. (2000). Rents, efficiency and growth. In: M. H. Khan & J. Kwame Sundram (Eds), *Rents, rent-seeking and economic development* (pp. 21–69). Cambridge: Cambridge University Press.

Kim, W., & Sorenson, E. (1986). Evidence on the impact of the agency costs of debt on corporate debt policy. *Journal of Financial and Quantitative Analysis, 21*(2), 131–144.

Koke, J., & Renneboog, L. (2003). *Do corporate control and product market competition lead to stronger productivity growth? Evidence from market-oriented and blockholder-based governance regimes.* Working Paper No. 14/2003. European Corporate Governance Institute.

KLSE. (2001). KLSE statistics. Kuala Lumpur: KLSE.

KLSE Hand Book. (Various years). Kuala Lumpur: KLSE.

KLSE ON DISCs. (Various years). Kuala Lumpur: KLSE.

Kochhar, R. (1996). Explaining firm capital structure: The role of agency theory vs. transaction cost economics. *Strategic Management Journal, 17*(9), 713–728.

La Porta, R., Lopez-De-Silanes, F., & Shleifer, A. (1999). Corporate ownership around the world. *Journal of Finance, LIV*(2), 471–517.

Lins, K., & Servaes, H. (2002). Is corporate diversification beneficial in emerging markets. *Financial Management, 31*(2), 5–32.

Malaysia. (Various years). External trade statistics. Kuala Lumpur: Department of Statistics.

McConnell, J., & Servaes, H. (1990). Additional evidence on equity ownership and corporate value. *Journal of Financial Economics, 27*(2), 595–612.

Miguel, A., Pindado, J., & de la Torre, C. (2005). How do entrenchment and expropriation phenomena affect control mechanisms? *Corporate Governance: An International Review, 13*(4), 505–516.

Mitton, T. (2002). A cross-firm analysis of the impact of corporate governance on the East Asian financial crisis. *Journal of Financial Economics, 64*, 215–241.

Morck, R., Shelifer, A., & Vishny, R. (1988). Management ownership and corporate performance: An empirical analysis. *Journal of Financial Economics, 20*, 293–315.

Nickell, S., Nicolitsas, D., & Dryden, N. (1997). What makes firms perform well? *European Economic Review, 41*, 783–796.

Palia, D., & Lichtenberg, F. (1999). Managerial ownership and firm performance: A re-examination using productivity measurement. *Journal of Corporate Finance, 5*, 323–339.

Pandey, I. M. (2002). Capital structure and market power interaction: Evidence from Malaysia. *Capital Market Review, 10*(1), 23–40.

Pound, J. (1988). Proxy contests and the efficiency of shareholder oversight. *Journal of Financial Economics, 20*, 237–265.

Putterman, L. (1993). Ownership and the nature of the firm. *Journal of Comparative Economics, 17*, 243–263.

Rajan, R., & Zingales, L. (1998). Which capitalism? Lessons from the East Asian crisis. *Journal of Applied Corporate Finance, 11*, 40–48.

Roe, M. J. (2001). Rents and their corporate consequences. *Stanford Law Review, 53*, 1463–1496.

Ross, S. (1977). The determinants of financial structure: The incentive signaling approach. *Bell Journal of Economics, 8*, 23–40.

Shleifer, A., & Vishny, R. W. (1986). Large shareholders and corporate control. *Journal of Political Economy, 94*(3), 461–488.

Shleifer, A., & Vishny, R. W. (1997). A survey of corporate governance. *Journal of Finance, LII*(2), 737–783.

Short, H., Keasey, K., & Duxbury, D. (2002). Capital structure, management ownership and large external shareholders: A UK analysis. *International Journal of the Economics of Business, 9*(3), 375–399.

Stulz, R. M. (1988). Managerial control of voting rights financing policies and the market for corporate control. *Journal of Financial Economics, 27*, 143–164.

Suto, M. (2003). Capital structure and investment behavior of Malaysian firms in the 1990s: A study of corporate governance before the crisis. *Corporate Governance: An International Review, 11*(1), 25–39.

Van der Elst, C. (2004). Industry-specificities and size of corporations: Determinants of ownership structures. *International Review of Law and Economics, 24*(4), 425–446.

Williamson, O. (1988). Corporate finance and corporate governance. *Journal of Finance, XLIII*(3), 567–591.

Wiwattanakantang, Y. (1999). An empirical study on the determinants of the capital structure of Thai firms. *Pacific Basin Finance Journal, 7*, 371–403.

Wooldridge, J. (2000). *Introductory econometrics: A modern approach.* Cincinnati, OH: South-Western Publication.

APPENDIX. FINANCIAL RESTRAINT POLICY

Hellmann, Murdock, and Stiglitz (1996) elucidate the financial restraint theory which emphasises the government's intervention in the financial sector to facilitate overall economic growth, especially in East Asian economies during the 1990s. The underlying of the theory is on the government through a set of financial policies that create rent opportunities in the private sector. Generally, the government sets the deposit rate below the market equilibrium level. Through this policy, the financial system increases the supply of loans through better deposit security and facilities which exceed the demand of the loans. This allows FIs to lend loans at a lower rate of interest than the market equilibrium rate in the financial market. Hence, firms are better off as they obtain a greater volume of loans at a lower rate of interest and at greater volume. Firms capture the difference of the new lower interest rate and market equilibrium rate as financial rent, while FIs capture the difference of the new lower interest rate and deposit rate as financial rent. The policy therefore allows FIs to lend more at a lower interest rate, while still maintaining the banks' profitability. The theory assumes that rent is the incentive for FIs to prudently monitor firms. Khan (2000) points out that this rent acts as a monitoring and management rent, and may be efficient if it induces efficient monitoring of credit portfolios by FIs. The financial restraint policy could therefore, enhance firm value if FIs participate in corporate governance, if only, FIs could enjoy additional financial rent value under the condition of less competitive environment.

Nonetheless, the role of FIs in corporate governance in Malaysia is limited due to the following reasons: first, over surplus of domestic FIs. In 1996, there were 36 commercial banks and 28 non-bank FIs in Malaysia. The competition among FIs dilutes the advantages of rent value, which is the monitoring incentive of banks. Second, the FIs in the country are characterised as relationship-based banking. In 1996, out of 66 FIs, 13 were government linked and 36 were family connected (Bongini et al., 2000). This causes implicit guarantee by the government or other relationship in project financing which often exaggerates the degree of leverage. The relationship-based banking has an adverse effect on firm value when a bank suffers from a decreased ability to lend, especially during the shock period. Thirdly, the powers of FIs to exert control on restructuring the illiquid firms are not well established. This reason is largely contributed by the country's Banking and Financial Act (BAFIA), 1989, which prohibits FIs from holding any management role or board directorship. Combining all these factors, the role of FIs in corporate governance in the country is very limited. Therefore, firms tend to borrow unscrupulously and subsequently affect firms' value.

BOARD OF DIRECTOR CONFIGURATIONS IN MUTUAL FUND SPONSORS: EARLY EVIDENCE OF BOARD-LEVEL PERFORMANCE ☆

Scott Besley, Steve P. Fraser and Christos Pantzalis

ABSTRACT

We examine the relationship between how mutual fund sponsors configure their board(s) of directors and the performance of the funds under a particular board's purview. Fund sponsors utilize either one board to oversee all the funds within a fund family or multiple boards that oversee one fund or a subset of the family's funds. Our results suggest that fund families – that is, sponsors – that use multiple boards have significantly higher objective-adjusted board-level weighted excess returns. But, there are no significant differences in the objective-adjusted board-level weighted excess expenses. These results are consistent with the argument that multiple boards provide superior monitoring.

☆ The views expressed in this article are those of the author and do not reflect the official policy or position of the United States Air Force, Department of Defense, or the U.S. Government.

Issues in Corporate Governance and Finance
Advances in Financial Economics, Volume 12, 203–236
Published by Elsevier Ltd.
ISSN: 1569-3732/doi:10.1016/S1569-3732(07)12009-0

This study examines whether the manner in which boards of directors of mutual fund sponsors are configured is associated with fund performance. Our analysis is based on the premise that any cross-sectional variation of board of directors' structures does not represent an equilibrium outcome determined by the relative costs and benefits of the alternatives given the economic circumstances. We believe this to be a realistic assumption because mutual fund board structures are not dynamic ("sticky") in the sense that re-organizing board structures is prohibitively expensive. It follows that boards of directors can affect fund performance in two ways. First, boards directly affect performance through their approval of the level of fees paid to investment advisors each year. Second, boards can affect performance indirectly through their ongoing monitoring function.

The Investment Company Act of 1940 (the Act) and the Securities and Exchange Commission (SEC) regulate the structure and operation of mutual funds. Under the Act, boards have fiduciary duties to the fund and its shareholders. Boards are "expected to exercise sound business judgment, establish procedures, and undertake oversight and review of the performance of the investment advisor and others that perform services for the fund."[1] One of the most important responsibilities of the board is to select the fund's investment advisor and approve the annual fees paid to this advisor. Generally, boards simply hire the fund's sponsor as its advisor. For this reason, critics argue that this practice results in cases where boards are nothing more than token symbols of governance.

Today we see two prominent board governance configurations in the mutual fund industry. Sponsors utilize either one board to govern all of the mutual funds offered by the sponsor (single-board configuration) or multiple boards, each of which is responsible for governing one or more funds (i.e., a cluster of) offered by the sponsor (multiple-board configuration, MBC). Cogent arguments can be made for the existence of both of these board configurations. Proponents of the single-board configuration argue that the bulk of a board's responsibilities are the same, no matter the number of funds it oversees. As a result, the use of a single board to oversee multiple funds should capture economies of scale through elimination of redundant activities, which should result in lower relative expenses. Furthermore, there is the potential for the board to gain leverage in negotiations with the investment advisor. In other words, in the case of a single-board configuration, the board's ability to negotiate lower fees might be enhanced because the number of funds and the amount of assets under management are greater than with a MBC – that is, a greater number of funds and assets under management significantly enhance a board's negotiating position. However, boards do more than simply approve fees. Directors also have an ongoing responsibility to monitor the performance of the fund(s) they oversee. Therefore, critics of the single-board configurations, argue that the board has to evaluate the average performance of the investment advisor for all the funds under management, which might not be in the best interests of shareholders of the individual funds. It follows that MBCs might be better designed for providing monitoring that protects the interests of investors.

The role that the board of directors plays in mutual fund performance remains an unsettled question. At the most basic level, the performance of a mutual fund is a function of the returns of the assets held in the fund and the expenses associated with managing and administering the portfolio. Previous research has shown that management fees directly affect net returns generated by mutual funds.[2] In addition, the board's monitoring function might have an impact on the fund's performance. Although the board holds the ultimate authority to fire an advisor, this action (often dubbed "the nuclear deterrent") is virtually never exercised, which makes the board's ongoing oversight role even more important.[3] Even though the board does not directly hire and fire fund managers, the board can influence the investment advisor who does make those decisions. It is therefore possible that better oversight results in better objective-adjusted performance, either through ongoing interactions with the advisor, lower expenses, or both. This is an empirical question that has not been explored to date. In this study, we examine the relationship of several board governance factors with a board-level return measure comprised of the objective-adjusted excess returns of the individual funds in the board's portfolio of funds. In addition to board composition and other board structure variables, we investigate whether board configuration is associated with higher board-level excess returns. The results of this research will provide indirect evidence as to whether board configuration can improve fund governance. The remainder of the study is organized as follows: Section 1 discusses the role of the board of directors and the mutual fund arena. Section 2 describes the methodology, Section 3 presents the results, and Section 4 concludes.

1. THE BOARD OF DIRECTORS AND THE AGENCY RELATIONSHIP

Although there is a vast body of empirical research relating to corporate governance, Hermalin and Weisbach (2003) suggest that there is a vacuum of formal theory with respect to the board of directors. They note, however, that this void has neither prohibited researchers from contributing to the literature on board relationships nor changed the fact there is much more to learn. One area of governance literature includes research that attempts to determine whether the degree of a board of directors' independence (the ratio of the number of independent directors to the number of total directors on the board) is related to such factors as firm value or executive compensation.[4] Boards with low levels of independence are thought to be more influenced by the managing officers, and therefore might not be effective monitors. Some argue, however, that insiders are more knowledgeable of the firm's operations, and therefore might be in a better position to identify problems before they adversely affect firm operations. Although the empirical evidence concerning the effectiveness of boards as monitors is mixed (see Hermalin & Weisbach, 1991; Agrawal & Knoeber, 1996; and Yermack, 1996, among others), it can be generally concluded that smaller and more independent corporate boards are associated with higher firm values. Unfortunately, examining governance factors within the context of the mutual fund environment is not necessarily a simple extension of the corporate case.

The nature of the mutual fund environment requires the analysis of the agency problem to be examined in a different context.

> In theory, a mutual fund is owned by its shareholders who hire independent directors to run it. The directors, in turn, select various service providers, including an investment advisor, to manage the fund. In reality, a mutual fund is usually created, sponsored, and operated by the advisor. It is the investment advisor's services, not the directors, that investors buy.[5]

This apparent difference between theory and reality raises many points of interest for mutual fund research and specifically the impact of the board of directors.

The same firm that creates or sponsors a mutual fund selects the *original* board of directors that governs the fund and attempts to attract investors. The individual fund itself has no employees per se because the board hires separate entities to handle the investment management, distribution, and custodial functions required for each fund. Most often, a fund's board of directors simply hires subsidiary units of the fund sponsor to provide the services shown in Fig. 1, which means that the investment advisor has a business relationship with the fund sponsor. A mutual fund board has as many different shareholder groups as the number of funds it oversees, and

Panel A: Typical Fund Structure

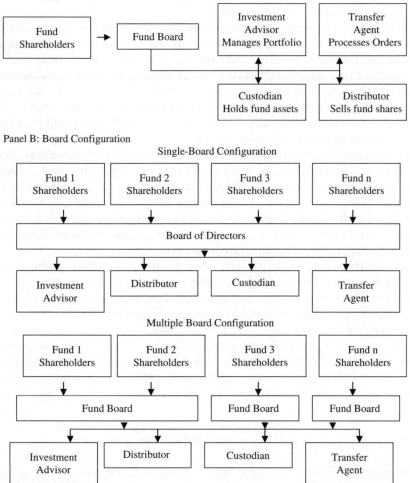

Panel B: Board Configuration

Fig. 1. Mutual Fund Structure & Board Configuations. Panel A Outlines the Basic Structure Common to Mutual Funds. Boards Hire Separate Entities to Handle the Investment Advisory, Distribution, Custodial, and Transfer Agent Functions. Most Often these are all Subsidiary Organizations of the Sponsor Organization. Panel B Depicts the Single and MBCs. In Panel B, a Single Board Oversees all Funds within the Complex or Family, and Multiple Boards Provide Governance over Differing Number of Funds within the Family.

therefore there might be times when the interests of the different fund shareholder groups are not the same.

Mitigating the agency problem for mutual funds can be more difficult than for corporations. For example, corporations often use performance-based compensation packages for senior executives. In the case of mutual funds, the Investment Advisors Act[6] restricts the use of performance fees for advisors. Performance fees, also called incentive fees, exist when the advisor receives a base fee plus a bonus for exceeding a specified benchmark. The advisor's compensation can, however, be based on a fulcrum fee arrangement, whereby the base fee is increased when performance exceeds a predetermined benchmark and is decreased when performance falls short of the benchmark. Das and Sundaram (1999) find that investors actually might be better off from a welfare standpoint under asymmetric incentive fee arrangements. Most investment advisor compensation arrangements are fee-based – that is, advisors receive fees as a percentage of the total assets under management. As a result, when fees rise without improved performance, the board's agency concerns increase.

Monitoring management is also used to mitigate agency problems. In addition to the board, large corporations generally have institutional stockholders who monitor management. For mutual funds, the funds themselves are the institutional investors who monitor corporations. Although ownership in any one firm is limited, the role of mutual funds as shareholder activists – that is, monitors of corporations – is gaining interest.[7] In essence, the board provides the primary monitoring mechanism of a mutual fund advisor. As a result, mutual fund shareholders should be concerned with how well a mutual fund board performs its monitoring responsibilities.

1.1. The Mutual Fund Board

The ability of a mutual fund board to monitor and thus mitigate agency problems depends on the relationship with, and the characteristics of, the organization that sponsors the individual fund. An important factor that should be considered when evaluating the board's monitoring effectiveness is the numbers and types of funds the board oversees. There is no unified agreement among the courts, investment professionals, regulators, or academicians as to whether the interests of mutual fund shareholders are better served by a single-board configuration or a MBC. Although a majority of sponsors utilize a single board to oversee all of their funds, a number of sponsors choose some variation of the MBC.

Clearly the board of directors plays an extremely important role in the governance of mutual funds. Unfortunately, we have little evidence as to why fund sponsors choose different board configurations when creating mutual funds. One reason is because much of the early research on mutual funds focused on individual funds. Most of the research examined the relationships between fund performance and fund manager turnover,[8] the characteristics of fund managers,[9] the relationship between various board characteristics and fund fees,[10] and a fund's choice of investment advisor.[11] More recent research has examined mutual funds from the sponsor level. For example, Khorana and Servaes (1999) find that sponsors that perform better, offer a wider range of products, and start more funds relative to the competition also have higher market shares. Similarly, Siggelkow (2002) and Ciccotello, Miles, and Walsh (2002) find that mutual funds offered by sponsors with more focused strategies generally outperform similar funds offered by less-focused sponsors. Finally, Sirri and Tufano (1998) find that membership in a large fund complex is an important determinant of fund flows, and they caution that future research must recognize that structure and organization of an industry affect investors' decisions. Our study addresses this concern.

A major factor that needs to be considered when examining mutual fund board configurations is the number of funds the board governs. At the most basic level, the number of funds that a board can effectively oversee involves a trade-off between the marginal workload associated with the addition of a fund to the board's portfolio versus the marginal benefit derived from the effect of any economies of scale that result in a reduction in relative administration costs. There is clearly disagreement as to the nature of this tradeoff. On the one hand, critics suggest that a single-board configuration might not be as efficient as a MBC because it is difficult, if not impossible, for a single board to appropriately monitor individual funds if it is responsible for overseeing a large number of funds.[12] For example, a board that oversees 50 funds that are managed by one investment advisor might evaluate the average aggregate performance of the funds rather than the performances of each of the funds. In this case, there is a tendency for the board to overlook the poor performances of a few funds if most of the funds perform very well. As a result, the board is not acting in the best interests of investors in the individual funds that perform poorly.

On the other hand, proponents of a single-board configuration argue that the primary role of mutual fund directors is to hire and negotiate the fees of the investment advisor, and the more funds that a board oversees, the greater negotiating leverage it has when reviewing the advisory contract.

In this case, the benefit is from economies of scale at the sponsor level. Latzko (1999) examines mutual fund costs and finds that mutual fund expenses increase less than proportionately with fund assets, which implies that economies of scale do exist. Chen, Hong, Huang, and Kubik (2004) find that fund performance declines with fund size yet increases with the size of other funds in the fund family. The latter finding is consistent with the economy argument; although neither of these studies considers board-level performance. Each investigates performance at the individual fund level.

Directors of a single-board configuration have as many different sets of shareholders as the number of funds the board oversees, although all the shareholders may not have identical interests. When the board negotiates the advisory contract, it is safe to assume that all shareholders would like the board to set expenses so as to maximize expected returns. With respect to the monitoring responsibility, it is not clear that all shareholders of all the different funds have the same priorities for the board. Tate (2000) notes that one such occurrence is where the board provides oversight of the advisor's use of soft dollars.[13] The more diverse the type of funds governed by a board, the less likely the research will benefit each fund equally. The end result might be that certain mutual fund board structures actually *add* to the agency problem that they actually are expected to mitigate.

Diversity of fund objectives can also be a contributing factor. Often a sponsor establishes an individual board to cover general categories of funds – that is, one board each for equity funds, bond funds, or money market funds. It is reasonable to assume the scope of oversight is different for a board that oversees a few Treasury bond funds versus one that oversees several aggressive growth funds. It is understandable that the two boards might benefit from having different cores of expertise available from its members. Another factor to consider is the type of management involved or required for each type of fund. Boards that oversee funds that are passively managed funds – that is, index funds – will likely have fewer monitoring responsibilities than boards that oversee actively managed funds. All else equal, we might expect that a board that oversees passively managed funds is able to handle more funds than a board that oversees actively managed funds. An interesting consequence of the single-board configuration is whether the structure affects the "independence" of independent directors. Carter (2001) highlights a recent court case where the independence of directors is called into question simply by the structure of the boards used by the mutual fund sponsor. These factors are controlled for in this study.

1.2. Mutual Fund Returns and Expenses

The research into mutual fund returns and expenses is considerably more developed than that for mutual fund governance. Only recently has there been progress in the area of linking mutual fund returns and expenses to the boards that oversee the activities of the funds. Most mutual fund performance literature deals with the question of market efficiency; more specifically, whether actively managed funds perform better than unmanaged indices or benchmarks. Unfortunately, the empirical evidence is mixed.[14]

There are also studies that examine the relationship of mutual fund boards of directors and the fees that boards approve for investment advisors. Melms (1994) finds a significant inverse relationship between the percentage of independent directors and a fund's expense ratio – that is, boards with greater independence exhibit lower expense ratios. Tufano and Sevick (1997) examine whether there is any relationship between board composition and the shareholder fees that boards approve each year. They conclude: (1) there exist economies of scale (fees are inversely related to fund size); (2) there is little evidence that *prior* fund performance (12, 24, or 36 months) is related to fund fees; (3) funds with a larger percentage of independent directors have lower fees; and (4) the percentage of sponsor assets a director oversees is negatively related to fund fees. This last result suggests that boards are not "captured" by the sponsors. The finding that is important to this study is that boards do not reward sponsors based on past performance when setting fees. Previously, Elton, Gruber, and Blake (1996) find that expenses account for only a portion of the differences in performances across funds. Thus, there must be factors that affect performance that are not manifested in the fund's expense ratio.

Elton and Gruber (1997) note that in an efficient market we would expect some funds to outperform and other funds to under perform a passive benchmark or strategy, and the difference should be strictly random. They highlight however, that if superior management exists, and unless performance is reflected in higher fees, we might find persistence in performance. Because we know that mutual funds do not raise fees to reflect performance, (Tufano & Sevick, 1997), and that fees are lower for higher performing funds (Carhart, 1997), superior management should be reflected in persistence of fund performance. If the claims that mutual fund returns demonstrate persistence are true, it is possible that superior management exists as well.

In one of the first studies to investigate board characteristics and fund performance, Dowers (1997) finds no relationship between the size of a board or its percentage of independent directors and a fund's abnormal performance. Using various measures of abnormal performance, including different asset pricing methods similar to those used by Carhart (1997), he also finds limited evidence that boards with a greater percentage of independent directors have lower fees. In this study, we extend Dowers (1997) work by introducing board-level performance as a proxy for board monitoring. Although there may exist a relationship between board composition and fund-level performance, any relationship suggests little about how the board of directors might perform their monitoring role as a "board" – that is, the board's performance across all funds within its purview. As a result, the purpose of this study is to examine the monitoring function of a mutual fund board of directors.

2. METHODOLOGY

A mutual fund sponsor generally uses one of two types of configurations when creating a board. The single-board configuration (SBC) consists of a single board of directors that is responsible for overseeing multiple investment funds. The MBC consists of more than one board, where each board is responsible for overseeing a single investment fund (or a cluster of funds). Although boards have many duties and responsibilities, ultimately they are charged with monitoring the investment advisor to ensure that the best interests of the investors in each fund are pursued. Prior research shows board *composition* (the number of directors and percent of those that are non-interested or independent) is associated with the board's primary responsibility of selecting and approving the fees paid to the investment advisor. Earlier studies suggest smaller and more independent boards are associated with lower fees. However, boards have an ongoing monitoring function as well, and we know little as to how effectively they serve in this capacity. Here, we examine the monitoring ability of individual boards by investigating the relationships of board composition and configuration with board-level performance. Eq. (1) shows this relationship.

$$BXR = F(BCV; CONTROL) \tag{1}$$

BXR is a board's excess return, a board-level performance measure. This value captures the aggregate relative performance of a board's portfolio of funds with respect to the individual fund's investment category. BCV is the board configuration variable, which is set equal to one for a MBC board and zero otherwise. CONTROL is the series of board composition, board portfolio, and board-level, fund-derived vectors of control variables. Eq. (1) is designed to provide evidence as to whether board configuration leads to improved monitoring.

Using a cross-sectional sample of fund complexes within the largest 25 mutual fund sponsors at year-end 2000, we investigate the relationship between board-level performance and board configuration in two general frameworks. First, we analyze the sample based on the type of board configuration. In this framework we conduct simple difference-in-means tests to determine whether there is any evidence of differing levels of performance between boards overseeing all of a sponsor's funds (boards in a SBC) and those overseeing some subset of the sponsor's funds (boards in a MBC).

Second, we conduct an ordinary least squares (OLS) regression analysis to identify whether board configuration is associated with better performance when controlling for variables that have been identified as affecting mutual fund returns. The general regression framework is depicted in Eq. (2).

$$BXR = \alpha_0 + \alpha_1 BCV + \alpha_j CONTROL + \varepsilon \tag{2}$$

We examine the relationship of BXR and board configuration (BCV) with each of the control vectors. Each of the models utilizes robust standard errors to correct for the presence of heteroschedasticity.

2.1. Variable Discussion

2.1.1. Variables of Interest
The variables for this cross-sectional study are shown in Table 1. Variables are grouped according to their role in the analysis. Panel A contains the specific variables of interest, BXR and BCV.

Panel B shows the control variables separated according to those that represent board composition, board portfolio characteristics, and board-level fund-derived control variables that are derived form the individual funds in the board's portfolio.

The excess return value BXR is calculated similar to the sponsor performance variable formulated by Khorana and Servaes (2002).

$$BXR = \sum_{i=1}^{N} \left[w_i \left(R_i - \sum_{j=1}^{M_i} w_{ij} R_{ij} \right) \right] \tag{3}$$

where w_i is the weight of the Fund i within all funds of board's portfolio; w_{ij} the weight of Fund j within all funds in the sample with the same objective

Table 1. Variable List.

Variable	Identifier	Source
Panel A: Variables of interest		
Board excess return (Obj.)	BSEXRET	Calculated – Lipper fund analyzer*
Board excess return (Maj. Obj.)	BMSEXRET	Calculated – Lipper fund analyzer
Board configuration	BCV	Dummy – fund SAIs
Panel B: Control variables		
Board composition controls		
Number of directors	NODIRS	Fund SAIs
Percent independent directors	BIND	Calculated – fund SAIs
Board portfolio controls		
Number of funds	BFDS	Fund SAIs
Board focus – by objective	BFOC	Calculated – fund SAIs
Board area – equity vs. Debt	BAREA	Calculated – fund SAIs
Fund-derived board-level controls		
Board TNA ($Mil) *Ln*	BTNA *Ln*	Calculated – Lipper fund analyzer
Board's use of loads	BLDRT	Calculated – Lipper fund analyzer
Board's use of 12b-1 *Ln*	B12B1 *Ln*	Calculated – Lipper fund analyzer
Board's use of multiple share classes	BMSC	Dummy – Lipper fund analyzer
Board turnover	BTURN	Calculated – Lipper fund analyzer
Board win–% of funds w/+ BXR	BWIN	Calculated – Lipper fund analyzer
Board expenses (Obj.)	BEXEXP	Calculated – Lipper fund analyzer
Board expenses (Maj. Obj.)	BMEXEXP	Calculated – Lipper fund analyzer

Notes: The following table describes the variables required for this research. The variable and source of the information are listed in the table. SAIs – Statements of additional information – Part B of a mutual fund's prospectus. Required to be filed annually with SEC and available to investors.

*Lipper fund analyzer -a Lipper product providing individual fund data such as returns and expense ratios. Special thanks to Heritage Asset Management for their generous use of the Lipper Fund Analyzer.

as fund i; R_i the return of the individual fund (1-year cumulative total return); R_{ij} the return of the Fund j in Fund i's objective category, used to compute weighted-average; M_i the number of funds in objective category of Fund i, used to compute weighted-average; and N the number of funds in a board's portfolio.

To compute this measure, we first compute the weighted-average return of all funds with the same investment objective as Fund i, where the weight (w_{ij}) is the relative size of Fund j within all funds in the sample (across all sponsors) with the same objective as Fund i. Then, for each Fund i we subtract the weighted-average return for its objective category from the fund's return. This process provides an excess return measure (XR) for each fund in the sample – that is the fund's return in excess of its objective's weighted-average return. Finally, for each board, we compute the weighted-average of these excess returns across all funds governed by the specific board, where the weight (w_i) is the relative size of each fund within all funds assigned to the board. Following Khorana and Servaes (2002) and Ciccotello et al. (2002), we standardize each of the BXR variables by dividing the investment objective (or major objective) weighted-average by the standard deviation of the returns within the classification scheme used.

2.1.2. Control Variables

The CONTROL series consists of vectors (board composition, board portfolio, and board-level fund-derived controls) designed to account for different aspects of mutual fund operations. Each of the vectors contains variables that have been either hypothesized or demonstrated to influence mutual fund returns either directly or indirectly through expenses as discussed previously. The first vector of control variables captures the composition of the board in terms of the number of directors who sit on the board (NODIRS), and the degree of independence of the board, measured as the ratio of non-interested directors to total directors (BIND). These measures are the variables of interest in much of the governance literature. They are included here primarily as controls, but also to investigate their relationship with a board's excess returns as suggested by prior studies. As discussed earlier, there is no clear evidence as to whether the degree of independence is associated with fund performance, whereas there is evidence that boards with greater independence are associated with lower fees (Tufano & Sevick, 1997). Dowers (1997) does not find evidence to suggest that the degree of board independence is related to fund returns at the individual fund level. In the corporate arena, Lipton and Lorsch (1992) recommend limiting the size of boards because greater numbers of directors might prevent meaningful dialogue in the boardroom. Jensen (1993) recommends that boards limit the inside directors to only the CEO. Yermack (1996) finds evidence that smaller boards are associated with higher firm values as measured by Tobin's Q.

The variables in the board portfolio control vector provide different methods to measure the scope of monitoring responsibilities required of the board. The first variable is the number of funds (BFDS) a board oversees. The number of funds overseen by a board involves a trade-off between the potential benefits from economies of scale (possibly lower expenses) and the marginal increase in the monitoring activity workload. A significant positive relationship implies that the benefits from any scale economies outweigh a higher monitoring workload for directors, and vice versa.

Another attribute of boards that describes the scope of monitoring is related to the investment objectives of the funds a board oversees. If a board oversees several funds in one objective category, the board members will in all likelihood better understand details of individual fund operations than if the board oversees funds with several objectives. Here, we compute two variables designed to capture the breadth of the investment objectives of the funds that are overseen by a particular board. The first variable measures the concentration of investment objectives in the board's portfolio (BFOC). BFOC is a Herfindahl index defined as follows:

$$\text{BFOC} = \frac{\sum_{i=1}^{N}(\text{Number of funds in major objective})_i^2}{(\text{Number of funds})^2} \qquad (4)$$

The degree of focus of the funds offered by a sponsor appears to matter; funds that belong to more focused families outperform similar funds offered by more diversified providers (Siggelkow, 2002). Khorana and Servaes (2002) find families that offer a wider range of products have greater market share. Ciccotello et al. (2002) find more focused families have a larger percentage of winning funds (those where the fund's performance is above the median for the objective category). Therefore, BFOC could proxy for the level of knowledge a board possesses about fund operations; greater knowledge implies greater monitoring capabilities. As a result, all else equal, the degree of concentration of the funds a board oversees should be positively related to the board's excess return. A second measure we use takes into account the *types* of investment objectives of the funds in a board's portfolio as opposed to the range of objectives. This measure, BAREA, captures the simple percentage of funds in a board's portfolio that are designated as equity funds. Following Deli (2002), volatility of fund returns can proxy for the difficulty of monitoring advisor actions. And, Khorana (1996) shows that returns for equity funds are more volatile than returns for fixed income funds.

The final vector of control variables accounts for factors associated with the board's individual fund operations. The first variable captures the effect of expenses. At the most basic level, mutual fund expenses come in three basic forms – one-time sales charges (loads), ongoing management expenses (advisory and administrative costs), and marketing and distribution expenses (Rule 12b-1 fees). We address each of these components.

Loads are sales charges that investors pay simply to acquire or dispose of shares of the fund (commissions). To the extent that these loads are simply transaction costs similar to the brokerage charge incurred by investors purchasing a stock or bond, they need not be specifically considered. However, sponsors often view mutual fund expenses in total – that is, as a combination of sales loads as well as management expenses and 12b-1 fees. For this reason, loads will be accounted for by measuring the percentage of funds in the board's purview that have loads (BLDRT).

The second type of expense is management expense, which is comprised of advisory and other fees. Advisory fees are those fees paid to the advisor for the day-to-day management of the fund, which includes such expenses as research costs. Costs in the "other" category include administrative costs and other services contracted for the fund by the board – that is, custodian, transfer agent functions, and so forth. All these expenses are reported as part of a fund's expense ratio. Similar to the method used to calculate a board's excess return (BXR) in Equation (3), we calculate a board's excess expense ratio (BXP). Each fund has an excess expense value (XP) that is used to form a board's BXP.[15]

The final type of expense is marketing and distribution fees, or 12b-1 fees. Rule 12b-1 allows funds to use assets to make continuing payments to those who sell and distribute the funds. These 12b-1 fees must be approved by a majority of the independent directors of the fund's board. Because 12b-1 fees are charged as a percentage of assets, the board-level variable B12B1 captures the total value of 12b-1 fees by summing the product of a fund's 12b-1 charge by the value of the assets for each fund that charges a 12b-1 fee.

We also use a fund-derived control variable to capture the instances where a board utilizes a multiple share class (MSC) structure. To capture this attribute, we introduce a dummy variable to identify the presence of a MSC structure. Commercial data sources treat each class of a MSC fund as an individual fund. Here, we consider each share class contained in a fund as a separate fund for fund-level analysis, but as a single fund for board-level analysis. For example, if a sponsor offers 10 funds, each with four classes, fund-level analysis utilizes 40 observations, whereas board-level investigations consider the family to be comprised of 10 funds.

The third fund-derived control variable captures the size of a fund under management by measuring the fund's total net asset (TNA) value. The board-level TNA is simply the sum of the TNA values of all the funds a board oversees (BTNA). Because most advisory contracts are based on the value of assets under management, the more assets an advisor manages, the more the fund sponsor collects in fees. If fund assets grow simply because of increases in the prices of the securities held by the fund, it is likely there will be little or no increase in the advisory effort, and thus economies do exist. In contrast, if a fund's asset base grows simply due to inflows of new money and accounts, such benefits will not be on the same scale as if prices of assets in the portfolio rose. Sirri and Tufano (1998) find higher inflows go to funds with higher performance. As discussed earlier, many argue that there exist potential economies of scale in the advisory compensation agreements that can be passed on to investors. In the case where a sponsor utilizes multiple boards, the size of the assets overseen by one board relative to the size of the assets overseen by other boards might capture a board's level of leverage with the sponsor. If economies exist at all levels, more assets under management should lead to lower overall expenses and potentially higher returns.

Because fund management approaches are often classified as active or passive, the fourth fund-derived control variable that we use to examine a board's monitoring function is portfolio turnover. Turnover captures the management approach a particular fund uses to obtain its investment objective. The level of analysis and skill of security selection performed by the manger of a fund that tracks the S&P 500 index is not nearly the same as for an aggressive growth fund that tries to identify the next Microsoft or Dell. Those funds with high turnovers involve more buying and selling of securities, which suggests the funds are not passively managed. In the Lipper database, turnover is only reported on equity funds. To capture the effect of turnover at the board level, we calculate a board's turnover measure as follows:

$$\text{BTURN} = \left[\frac{\text{TURNTNA}}{\text{BTNA}}\right] \times \left[\sum_{j=1}^{n}\left(\frac{\text{TNA}_j}{\text{TURNTNA}}\right) \times \text{TURNOVER}_j\right] \quad (5)$$

Here TURNTNA is the sum of a board's TNA values for funds with TURNOVER reported. BTNA is the sum of the TNA values for j funds within a board's purview, and TURNOVER is the turnover rate reported by Lipper. Carhart (1997) finds an inverse relation between turnover and fund performance and Malhotra and McLeod (1997) and Deli (2002) find higher turnover leads to higher expenses. On the other hand, Ippolito (1989) finds turnover is not related to fund performance.

The final variable included in the vector of board-level fund-derived controls measures the percentage of funds within a board's purview that have positive excess returns. The rationale for including this variable is to examine whether a board's return is driven by the strong performance of one or a small number of the funds the board oversees. If the board-level return is driven by a single or small percentage of funds the board oversees, the return might come at the expense of other funds in the board's portfolio. If a board's governance practices are similar across all funds, a greater percentage of top performing funds should lead to higher board-level performance.

2.2. The Sample

The sample includes fund complexes offered by the largest 25 mutual fund groups at year-end 2000 as included in Pozen (2002).[16] At that time, these fund complexes represented approximately 71% of mutual fund market.[17] In this study, a fund complex, or family of funds, is one in which funds are offered and marketed under a common name. Although the fund sponsor normally uses a single advisor for all of the funds within a sponsor family, at times outside investment advisors are employed. Often, the outside advisors act as sub-advisors to the sponsors' primary investment advisors. Very seldom does a fund select an outside advisor to act as the primary advisor. In this study, a fund is considered part of the family under whose name the fund is marketed to the public. For example, if Merrill Lynch is an advisor for a Vanguard fund but the fund is marketed by Vanguard, the fund is considered part of the Vanguard family of funds.

The data for this study come from a variety of sources. The Lipper Directors' Analytical Data report (LDAD First Edition 2002) provides basic board information (numbers of directors and compensation) for fund complexes, and the Lipper Fund Analyzer (LFA) provides return data and various fund characteristics (expenses, loads, turnover, and so forth). Return data are total cumulative returns based on changes in net asset values (NAVs) assuming all distributions are reinvested. A fund's NAV is simply the market value of the securities held by the fund divided by the number of shares outstanding. The expense ratio includes all expenses charged with the exception of sales loads. Loads are designated as front-end, back-end, level, or institutional load. The LFA also reports the maximum 12b-1 fees (if in place) a fund can charge as indicated in the fund prospectus. Because the actual expense incurred from the 12b-1 is charged daily, it is reflected in the fund's NAV and therefore the impact is contained within the fund's return. It is important to note that brokerage fees and transaction costs are not included in a fund's expense ratio. Similar to the 12b-1 fees, these costs are accounted for prior to the fund calculating its daily NAV. The LFA also reports the specific objective of each fund.

Neither the LDAD nor the LFA provides sufficient information to match a specific board of directors with the fund or funds that a board might oversee. This can only be accomplished by a review of the Statement of Additional Information (SAI) for each fund. For each family, we generate a list of open-end mutual funds from the LFA, and then collect the most recent SAI (dated in 2001 or the first half of 2002) for all funds in the sample from the sponsors or the SEC. From the SAIs, we determine the composition of the board of each fund, including the number of total directors and the number of non-interested directors. For each unique combination of non-interested directors, we establish a unique board identifier. In cases where a fund family has more than one unique board, we classify the sponsor as utilizing a MBC. Conflicts between the various sources are clarified by contacting the fund sponsor directly.[18]

2.3. Board-Level Analysis (Ex Money Market Funds)

One concern of the board-level analysis involves the role that money market funds play in overall performance. Many studies of mutual funds specifically exclude money market funds either due to data limitations or by design (Ciccotello et al., 2002). Because the board is the primary level of analysis, money market funds are specifically included in this study, even though they can constitute a large portion of the assets governed by a board. However, not all boards oversee investments in money market funds. One reason is that the sponsor does not offer money funds. Another reason, and more of a concern to the focus of this study on board configuration, is that some boards do not oversee money market funds *because* of the board configuration used by the sponsor. If a sponsor offers money market funds and uses a single board, then the single board will oversee those funds *by design*. In contrast, those sponsors that use more than one board might only use one board to oversee its money market funds. In an effort to evaluate whether the main results of this research are driven by the returns of a board's money market funds, we construct a separate sample that specifically excludes money market mutual funds. If the assets held in money market funds drive the primary results, the findings from this analysis should differ from those results found using the full sample.

3. RESULTS

The evaluation of the relationship between board configuration and board-level performance suggests boards operating within a multiple board configuration (MBC) have significantly higher board-level objective-adjusted excess returns than boards operating in a SBC. The review of sponsor documentation and Statements of Additional Information (SAIs) for the largest 25 mutual fund sponsors provided sufficient information to match individual funds with a specific board for 23 fund complexes, which included nearly 1500 funds that had greater than $3.25 trillion in assets under management at year-end 2001. Table 2 shows the summary statistics for the sample used in our study. The average fund family included $141.5 billion in assets under management. With an average size equal to nearly $150 billion, sponsors using a single-board configuration (65% of the sample) offered as few as 11 funds and as many as 229 funds; with an average size equal to nearly $127 billion, sponsors using a MBC offered as few as 29 funds and as many as 103.

The MBC sample includes 41 individual boards. As a result, when combined the SBC sample, the full sample consists of 56 board-level observations. Panel B in Table 2 shows summary statistics for all of the variables for the 56 sample boards. The average board has 9.5 directors, 74% of whom are designated non-interested parties. This is a particularly interesting finding given the recent emphasis to increase board independence. Prior to a new SEC rule that requires boards to be comprised of a majority of independent directors, boards were only required to have 40% non-interested directors. Only one of the boards included in the sample has less than 60% independent directors (57%), which suggests that the new rule might do little more than formalize what is already practiced. Alternatively, the findings might indicate fund sponsors anticipated the SEC's action and already increased the percentage of non-interested directors accordingly.[19] In either case, all boards within this study contain a majority of non-interested directors. The average board oversees 26 funds with nearly $60 billion in assets under management. Almost half (49 percent) of an average board's funds (at the individual class-level) have positive excess returns. Both excess return and excess expense values, regardless of whether they are measured against the individual specific objective or at the major objective level, are positive at the board level. Boards either have a greater proportion of assets in funds generating positive excess returns or those funds with positive excess returns and fewer assets have much greater relative excess

Table 2. Summary Statistics – Sponsors and Boards.

Variable		Mean	Std. Dev.	Min.	Max.
Panel A: Sponsor summary					
Number of sponsor funds	SPFDS	64.4	46.5	11	229
Size of sponsor assets ($Bil)	SPTNA	141.5	177.2	0.7	739.5
Sponsor focus	SPFOC	0.18	0.11	0.06	0.44
Number of boards	NOBRDS	2.43	3.16	1	13
$n = 23$					
Single-board configurations					
Number of sponsor funds	SPFDS	59.6	55.3	11	229
Size of sponsor assets ($Bil)	SPTNA	149.3	213.2	0.7	739.5
Sponsor focus	SPFOC	0.23	0.11	0.11	0.44
Number of boards	NOBRDS	1	0	1	1
$n = 15$					
Multiple-board configurations					
Number of sponsor funds	SPFDS	73.5	23.6	29	103
Size of sponsor assets ($Bil)	SPTNA	126.9	86.2	67.4	329.6
Sponsor focus	SPFOC	0.09	0.03	0.06	0.14
Number of boards	NOBRDS	5.1	4.3	2	13
$n = 8$					
Panel B: Board summary					
Excess return – objective	BSEXRET	0.03	0.56	−1.32	1.22
Excess return – major object	BMSEXRET	0.07	0.64	−0.94	2.23
Board size	NODIRS	9.5	2.7	3	16
Board independence	BIND	0.74	0.09	0.57	0.90
Number of funds	BFDS	26.5	36.7	1	229
Board focus	BFOC	0.47	0.34	0.11	1
Percent equity	BAREA	0.63	0.34	0	1
Board TNA ($Bil)	BTNA	58.1	122.2	0.004	739.5
Board load rate	BLDRT	0.83	0.30	0	1
Board turnover	BTURN	38.8	32.2	0	133.3
Board 12b-1	B12B1	111.1	193.8	0	985.7
Percent winning funds	BWIN	0.49	0.29	0	1
Excess expense – objective	BEXEXP	0.06	0.19	−0.46	0.64
Excess expense – major object	BMEXEXP	0.10	0.24	−0.45	0.74
$n = 56$					

Notes: This table provides summary statistics for the 23 sponsors and 56 individual boards in the sample. Panel A provides statistics on sponsors for the full sample as well for those that utilize a single-board configuration (SBC) and those that use a multiple-board configuration (MBC). Panel B describes the 56 boards in the sample.

returns than the other funds in the board's portfolio, which is also the case for excess expenses. Whereas boards on average have positive excess returns, it is not clear that these returns are sufficient to cover their positive excess expenses.

3.1. Difference-in-Means Tests

The first level of analysis involves the comparison of the means between SBC boards and MBC boards. The results are shown in Panel A of Table 3. The most notable finding is that both of the excess return measures (BXRs) are *negative* for SBC boards, and are *positive* for the MBC boards, and that the differences in means are statistically significant at the 10% level. On the other hand, the excess expense measures (BXPs) are positive for both board configurations, and the differences in means are not statistically significant.

There is little difference in board composition between the two board configurations. Although SBC boards are larger and more independent than their MBC counterparts, the differences are not statistically significant. There are, however, significant differences between control variables contained within the board portfolio and board-level fund-derived control vectors of variables. Within the board portfolio controls, MBC boards are significantly more focused (BFOC) than SBC boards. Sponsors with multiple boards appear to align boards at least partially by fund objective, perhaps attempting to match specific director expertise with a fund type. Within the fund-derived controls, it is not surprising that total board assets (BTNA) and board-level 12b-1 fees (B12B1) are significantly different given that the number of funds overseen by SBC and MBC boards is significantly different. The difference in the percentage of funds with positive excess returns within a board's portfolio (BWIN) is also significant, which is expected because there is a high correlation between BWIN and the return variable BSEXRET. In general, evaluation of the excess return and expense measures suggests that returns at the board-level are more than simply a function of expenses.

There is a further delineation of performance within the MBC sample. MBC boards monitor as few as one fund and as many as 48 funds. Within this group, approximately 40% of the boards (16 of 41) oversee fewer than three funds. Panel B in Table 3 presents the results from difference-in-means tests between the two sub-samples of MBC boards for the Board Composition and Board Portfolio variables. Those boards who oversee

Table 3.   Difference-in-Means Tests.

Panel A: Full sample

Variable	SBC Boards ($n=15$)		MBC Boards ($n=41$)		Diff.	P Value
	Mean	Std. dev.	Mean	Std. dev.		
Board excess returns (BXRs)						
Excess return (BSEXRET)	−0.30	0.52	0.15	0.53	−0.45	0.008
Excess return (BMSEXRET)	−0.14	0.51	0.15	0.66	−0.29	0.094
Board composition controls						
Board size (NODIRS)	10.1	3.2	9.3	2.5	0.8	0.395
Board independence (BIND)	0.77	0.08	0.73	0.09	0.04	0.114
Board portfolio controls						
Number of funds (BFDS)	59.6	55.3	14.3	15.0	45.3	0.007
Board focus (BFOC)	0.23	0.11	0.55	0.35	−0.32	0.000
Board equity (BAREA)	0.63	0.19	0.63	0.39	0.01	0.924
Board-level						
Fund-derived controls						
Board TNA ($Bil) (BTNA)	149.3	213.2	24.8	19.6	124.5	0.040
Board load rate (BLDRT)	0.74	0.34	0.85	0.28	−0.11	0.261
Board turnover (BTURN)	49.8	28.2	34.9	33.0	14.9	0.105
Board 12b1 ($Bil) (B12B1)	0.246	0.326	0.061	0.071	0.184	0.046
Percent winning funds (BWIN)	0.32	0.16	0.55	0.30	−0.23	0.001
Excess expense (BEXEXP)	0.05	0.20	0.06	0.19	−0.01	0.809
Excess expense (BMEXEXP)	0.08	0.24	0.10	0.24	−0.01	0.853

Panel B: MBC sample

Variable	MBC Boards – Small (≤ 3) Funds ($n=16$)		MBC Boards – Large (>3) Funds ($n=25$)		Diff.	P Value
	Mean	Std. dev.	Mean	Std. dev.		
Board excess returns (BXRs)						
Excess return (BSEXRET)	0.37	0.64	0.01	0.39	−0.35	0.060
Board composition controls						
Board size (NODIRS)	10.4	2.39	8.6	2.40	−1.8	0.024
Board independence (BIND)	0.72	0.06	0.73	0.10	0.01	0.745
Board portfolio controls						
Number of funds (BFDS)	1.75	0.58	22.4	14.2	20.65	0.000
Board focus (BFOC)	0.91	0.20	0.33	0.21	−0.58	0.000
Board equity (BAREA)	0.72	0.45	0.56	0.34	−0.16	0.245

Notes: This table depicts the mean and standard deviation for each board-level variable for single-board configuration (SBC) and multiple-board configuration (MBC) sponsors. Differences-in-means, SBC mean−MBC mean, and *P* values are reported following each variable.

fewer than three funds have significantly higher excess returns than those MBC boards that oversee more than three funds. Not surprisingly, these MBC boards monitor significantly more focused portfolios as well. Interestingly, MBC boards with fewer than three funds are significantly larger.

3.2. Configuration Regression Analysis

Regression analysis is used to determine what relationship exists between a board's excess return measure and the particular board configuration, controlling for variables within the board composition, board portfolio, and board-level fund-derived control vectors. The results are shown in Table 4. The BXR depicted in the Table 4 regressions is BSEXRET – the board-level excess return utilizing excess objective-average returns standardized by the standard deviation of the returns within each objective. A simple regression of board returns on the BCV variable confirms the earlier result from the means difference test. Models (i) and (ii) regress BXR against the board composition and board portfolio controls respectively. In each case, BCV is positive and significant, suggesting MBC boards are associated with higher board-level excess returns.

Recall that the primary competing arguments for the two mutual fund board configurations are the benefit of potential economies of scale for SBC boards versus less identity with the sponsor (more independence) and more identity with fund shareholders for MBC boards. If there are fundamental underlying differences in the way the boards operate, then board portfolio characteristics might affect the two board types differently. As a result, we introduce a series of interaction variables to assess the impact of the portfolio controls on each of the separate board configurations. Model (iii) shows the relationship of the board portfolio controls together with the interaction terms. The use of interaction variables changes the interpretation of the coefficients. The interaction terms estimate the extent to which the effect differs by configuration. The most notable observation is the differing relationship between the number of funds in a board's portfolio and the board's BXR. The data suggest that the number of funds a board oversees affects each board type differently. The relationship between the numbers of funds a SBC board oversees and BXR is significant and positive, which is consistent with the economies of scale argument for SBC boards. For MBC boards, the coefficient is *negative* and significant suggesting the benefit of an additional fund for MBC boards is lower than for SBC boards.[20]

Table 4. Configuration OLS Regression Results.

Variable	(i)	(ii)	(iii)	(iv)	(v)	(vi)	(vii)	(viii)	(ix)
BCV	0.469*** (2.82)	0.406* (1.94)	0.704* (1.73)	0.415* (1.88)	0.721* (1.74)	0.616*** (3.73)	0.223** (2.13)	0.564*** (3.31)	0.194 (1.59)
NODIRS	0.018 (0.71)			0.012 (0.43)	0.005 (0.19)			-0.007 (-0.21)	0.016 (0.66)
BIND	0.107 (0.18)			0.099 (0.14)	-0.004 (-0.01)			-0.012 (-0.01)	0.165 (0.29)
BFDS		0.001 (0.63)	0.003** (2.13)	0.001 (0.57)	0.003** (2.08)			-0.001 (-0.27)	-0.002 (-1.28)
BFOC		0.315 (1.34)	1.399 (0.48)	0.307 (1.27)	1.461 (0.49)			0.079 (0.18)	-0.319 (-1.27)
BAREA		0.122 (0.82)	-0.592 (-0.61)	0.103 (0.58)	-0.597 (-0.56)			0.029 (0.07)	0.173 (0.74)
LnBTNA						-0.027 (-0.29)	-0.004 (-0.08)		
BEXEXP						-0.832** (-2.31)	0.017 (0.06)	-0.738* (-1.73)	-0.056 (-0.18)
BCV*BFDS			-0.015** (-2.21)		-0.015** (-2.23)			-0.018 (-0.13)	
BCV*BFOC			-1.495 (-0.51)		-1.558 (-0.51)				0.003 (0.05)

BAREA	0.765 (0.77)		0.763 (0.73)						
BLDRT						0.512 (1.22)	0.215 (1.11)	0.476 (1.01)	0.331 (1.30)
LnB12B1						0.083 (1.42)	0.047 (1.59)	0.085 (1.03)	0.029 (0.58)
BMSC						−0.614* (−1.73)	−0.471** (−2.01)	−0.605 (−1.45)	−0.542** (−2.14)
BTURN						−0.000 (−0.13)	−0.001 (−0.95)	−0.001 (−0.17)	−0.003 (−1.28)
BWIN							1.509*** (8.27)		1.577*** (8.15)
R^2	0.14	0.17	0.17	0.23	0.23	0.29	0.74	0.29	0.77
N	56	56	56	56	56	55	55	55	55

Notes: BXR = F(BCV; CONTROL). BXR is a board's excess return (BSEXRET). BCV is the board configuration variable and CONTROL represents the series of control variables defined in Section II and shown in Table I. Models (iii)–(v) include interaction variables of BCV with Board Portfolio controls illustrating the differing relationship between board configuration types (*t*-statistics are reported in parentheses).

*Indicate significance at the 10% levels.

**Indicate significance at the 5% levels.

***Indicate significance at the 1% levels.

Models (iv) through (v) combine the board composition and board portfolio controls (with interaction terms). The results from these tests show the BCV to be positive and significantly related to BXR when introduced to the respective model. The number of funds overseen by a board continues to appear to be associated differently for each board type, and there remains no relationship between the board composition variables and BXR. Model (vi) examines the relationship between the board-level fund-derived control variables, board configuration, and BXR. Board-level excess expenses and the presence of MSCes are both significantly related to board-level excess returns. BCV remains positive and significant at the 1% level.

An additional variant of the board-level fund-derived control vector is the percentage of funds within a board's portfolio that generated positive excess returns (BWIN). This control seeks to account for those instances where a board's BXR might be driven by the performance of a single fund, perhaps where a board has a single large fund that dominates the board's BXR. The results are shown in Model (vii). As expected, the higher the percentage of funds with positive excess returns, the higher BXR. Including BWIN in the model results in a substantial increase in the R^2 values. This is not surprising, because BWIN and BSEXRET are highly correlated. All aspects of the above analysis are combined in Models (viii) through (ix). BCV remains positive in the full models. Only when BWIN is included, is the significance of BCV diminished.

In general, the regression analysis of board-level excess returns and board configuration suggests that MBC boards are associated with higher BXR. There is no consistent significant relationship between the board composition, board portfolio, and board-level fund-derived control variables and BXR. This entire analysis is repeated using BMSEXRET as the dependent variable BXR, which measures a board's excess return based on a fund's *major-objective* average (as opposed to the specific individual objective average). The major-objective category combines a much wider array of fund types into a single group. The results of this analysis are consistent with those described earlier, with two notable exceptions. First, although it is still positive and significant, the significance of BCV is diminished. Second, due to the greater variability of the returns in the wider asset classifications, the percentage of a board's funds that are equity funds (BAREA) becomes significant. Boards with a greater percentage of equity funds are associated with a higher BXR.

The results in Table 4 suggest that board configuration matters. However, it is not clear exactly what aspect of governance is captured by the configuration variable. One possibility is that use of multiple boards provides a board with more autonomy, or greater independence, from the sponsor. To examine this possibility, three different proxies of the BCV variable are tested in the full regression model used earlier (Model (viii) in Table 4). The first measure is FUNDRAT, the ratio of the number of funds overseen by a board to the number of funds offered by the sponsor.[21] A lower ratio is associated with greater independence in the context used here. The second measure is the number of boards a sponsor utilizes to govern its funds. A larger number of boards is associated with greater independence. Finally, we use BLEV, the ratio of assets under management for a particular board to the total assets in the sponsors' fund complex. Similar to FUNDRAT, a lower ratio implies greater independence from the sponsor. The results of these analyses are shown in Table 5. Model (i) is simply Model (viii) from Table 4 replicated for comparison. In each instance, when the new proxies are added, the signs on the coefficients are significant and the signs are consistent with the notion that separation from the sponsor is associated with higher board-level excess returns.

An alternative explanation for the significance of the BCV variable is that MBC boards have directors who are more specialized. Recall that there is a significant difference in the focus variable (BFOC) between the two board configuration types. The concentration of objectives for MBC boards is significantly higher than the concentration of objectives for SBC boards. As such, sponsors using an MBC structure might form their boards by matching the particular skills or experience of a board member with a particular mutual fund objective type. This matching of director skills might lead to better monitoring as indicated by higher board-level excess returns.

3.3. Board-Level Analysis (Ex Money Market Funds)

We mentioned earlier that board-level returns might be more sensitive if a particularly large proportion of assets under management are found within a board's money market funds. Excluding money market funds from the analysis does not change the initial conclusions. MBC boards continue to have significantly higher board-level objective-adjusted excess returns than SBC boards. Four of the boards in the sample have money market assets that comprise greater than 50% of their total portfolio; whereas 36 of the 56 boards have no money market assets. This is not surprising, because a fund sponsor that uses a single board and offers any money market funds will, *by design*, have such funds in its board's portfolio of funds. However, in a

Table 5. Configuration OLS Regression Results with Independence Proxies.

	(i)	(ii)	(iii)	(iv)	(v)	(vi)	(vii)
BCV	0.564***		0.238		0.321		0.179
	(3.31)		(0.99)		(1.56)		(0.41)
LnFUNDRAT		−0.332***	−0.259				
		(−2.89)	(−1.66)				
NOBRDS				0.073***	0.051*		
				(2.89)	(1.69)		
BLEV						−0.759***	−0.563
						(−3.25)	(−0.97)
CONTROLS[a]							
Board composition	Included	Included	Included	Included	Included	Included	Included
Board portfolio	Included	Included	Included	Included	Included	Included	Included
Board-level fund-derived	Included	Included	Included	Included	Included	Included	Included
R^2	0.29	0.34	0.35	0.31	0.34	0.31	0.31
N	55	55	55	55	55	55	55

Notes: BXR = F (BCV; CONTROL). BXR is a board's excess return (BSEXRET). BCV is the board configuration variable and CONTROL represents the series of control variables defined in Section II and shown in Table I. LnFUNDRAT, NOBRDS, and BLEV are independence proxies as defined in Section II. (*t*-statistics are reported in parentheses.)
*Indicate significance at the 10% levels.
**Indicate significance at the 5% levels.
***Indicate significance at the 1% levels.
[a]In each model, the control variables for board composition, board portfolio, and board-level fund-derived returns are included the same as in the models shown in Table 4.

MBC sponsor, perhaps only one of the sponsor's boards will oversee money market assets, especially if the sponsor forms boards based on fund objectives.

In the ex-money fund sample, the average sponsor size is reduced by approximately $30 billion ($42 billion for SBC boards and $17 billion for MBC boards), and each sponsor offers an average of 10 fewer funds. Table 6 shows the results from the difference-in-means tests. As stated earlier, MBC boards have significantly higher excess return values. Similar to the full sample, there are significant differences in the values for BFDS, BFOC, and BWIN. The configuration regression analyses (results not reported) show a similar pattern in terms of significance of the configuration variable as well as those associated with the various control vectors. BCV remains significant and positively associated with excess returns, suggesting that MBC boards have higher board-level excess returns than SBC boards.

Table 6. Difference-in-Means Tests (Money Market Funds Excluded).

Variable	SBC Boards $n=15$		MBC Boards $n=41$		Diff.	*P* Value
	Mean	Std. dev.	Mean	Std. dev.		
Board excess returns (BXRs)						
Excess return (BSEXRET)	−0.31	0.54	0.16	0.53	−0.48	0.007
Excess return (BMSEXRET)	−0.19	0.54	0.18	0.64	−0.37	0.040
Board composition controls						
Board size (NODIRS)	10.1	3.2	9.3	2.5	0.8	0.395
Board independence (BIND)	0.77	0.08	0.73	0.09	0.04	0.115
Board portfolio controls						
Number of funds (BFDS)	50.0	44.8	12.5	13.5	37.5	0.006
Board focus (BFOC)	0.26	0.10	0.58	0.33	−0.32	0.000
Board equity (BAREA)	0.70	0.16	0.66	0.38	0.04	0.574
Board-level fund-derived controls						
Board TNA ($Bil) (BTNA)	107.3	166.5	21.4	18.4	85.9	0.066
Board load rate (BLDRT)	0.74	0.35	0.88	0.28	−0.14	0.199
Board turnover (BTURN)	60.93	22.92	38.11	32.86	22.81	0.006
Board 12b1 ($Bil) (B12B1)	0.213	0.300	0.057	0.068	0.156	0.065
Percent winning funds (BWIN)	0.32	0.16	0.56	0.30	−0.24	0.000
Excess expense (BEXEXP)	0.07	0.25	0.08	0.21	−0.00	0.972
Excess expense (BMEXEXP)	0.13	0.30	0.10	0.26	0.03	0.764

Notes: This table depicts the mean and standard deviation for each board-level variable for single-board configuration (SBC) and multiple board configuration (MBC) sponsors. Differences-in-means, SBC mean-MBC mean, and *P*-values are reported following each variable.

4. CONCLUSIONS

This study examines whether the configurations of mutual funds boards of directors affect the performance of the funds. Boards of directors can affect fund performance in two ways. First, performance is directly affected through the fees that are paid to the investment advisor, which are approved each year by the board. Second, boards can affect performance indirectly through the ongoing monitoring function with which they are charged. The results from the analysis suggest that when a board is responsible for overseeing a single investment fund (or a cluster of funds) – referred to as a MBC – it has significantly higher board-level objective-adjusted excess returns than the case where a single board is responsible for overseeing all funds for a sponsor – referred to as a SBC.

We find that two-thirds of 23 fund complexes offered by the largest 25 fund sponsors that we studied utilize SBC boards. We find that MBC boards have significantly higher board-level objective-adjusted excess returns (BXR) than SBC boards. The regression analysis suggests that BXR is not related to board composition, board portfolio, or board-level fund-derived control variables. The results of our analysis suggest that boards with greater degrees of independence provide better monitoring environments as suggested by higher board-level excess returns.

An alternative explanation is that the configuration variable is a proxy for the manner in which sponsors form boards. Specifically, fund sponsors that use multiple boards might better match the skills and experience of directors with the funds they monitor. If MBC sponsors can effectively match the right directors with appropriately focused portfolios of funds, the combination might result in higher board-level performance. Here, MBC boards are found to have significantly more focused portfolios than SBC boards. This interpretation is consistent with Siggelkow (2002) who finds that mutual funds that belong to more focused fund providers (sponsors) outperform similar funds offered by more diversified providers.

Certainly an important component of the configuration decision by a sponsor is the number of funds offered by a sponsor. For sponsors that offer just a few or a relatively small number of funds, a single board is perhaps the appropriate choice due to the cost and administrative burden of implementing more than one board. The ability to attract qualified board members can also factor into this choice. However, as is the case in this sample, the board configuration decision might be a key determinant of returns generated for fund shareholders for large sponsors with many funds. The data suggest that the impact of the number of funds within a board's portfolio differs for each configuration. For the MBC boards, the data suggest that performance measured at the board level suffers as the number of funds increases, which is consistent with the notion that more funds involve greater, more costly monitoring. For SBC boards, it appears there is some support for the economies of scale position in that board-level performance is higher for boards that oversee a greater number of funds. Although Chen et al. (2004) find individual fund performance is not improved by individual fund size, they do find funds benefit from membership in a large family. Our results support this notion while introducing the model that board configuration is equally important.

Taken together, the evidence presented here supports the assertion that monitoring involves more than the simple approval of fees. Board-level excess expenses are neither significantly different between MBC and SBC boards nor significant in explaining board-level excess returns. MBC boards are associated with higher objective-adjusted excess returns, and such boards might be described as boards that: (1) "identify" less with the sponsor, (2) are less "captured" by the sponsor, or (3) are more "independent" from a sponsor in that the sponsor must interact with more than one board. Alternatively, MBC boards allow directors to specialize, and such an approach improves monitoring and performance.

This examination of board configuration is important for researchers, fund sponsors, regulators, and investors. For the finance field, this research moves the analysis to the board-level of mutual fund governance and introduces the investigation of board configuration as a governance factor. For fund sponsors, any evidence that might lead to better fund performance is of special interest. The findings here provide evidence against the argument made in the popular press that fund boards are no more than "rubber stamps" for the investment advisor. For individual investors, this research suggests investors might consider reviewing the back cover of a fund's annual report to determine how the fund is governed when selecting a particular mutual fund.

NOTES

1. Investment Company Institute, Mutual Fund Factbook, 2002, p. 2.
2. For example, Malkiel (1995) finds limited evidence that a negative relationship exists between the total expense ratio of a fund and its *net* performance, but he finds no relationship between *gross* investment returns and expenses. Carhart (1997) finds mutual funds on average do not recoup their investment costs and suggests expenses have at least a one-for-one negative impact on fund performance. Given that the board affects funds performance through the fees it approves, it might be concluded that a particular board configuration – that is, either a single-board configuration or a multiple board configuration – would be preferred.
3. One viewpoint as to why boards do not replace sponsors is because board members often feel some level of identity with, or are "captured" by the sponsor. The sponsor initially creates the fund hoping to profit from its operation, and selects the initial slate of directors to oversee it. Critics argue directors essentially feel obligated to serve the sponsor, because the sponsor is responsible for the directors' initial position on the board. Further, directors might be reluctant to fire the advisor if the sponsor has a very reputable and marketable name, an established distribution network, or a research capability that might benefit their portfolio of funds in the future. These factors suggest directors might use methods other than simply the threat of replacing the investment advisor in performing their ongoing monitoring role.
4. In this study, the terms independent, outside, and non-interested are used interchangeably when describing director affiliation. An independent director cannot be an employee of the investment advisor, a family member of an employee, an employee or a 5% shareholder of a broker-dealer, or affiliated with the fund's legal

counsel. *Understanding the Role of Mutual Fund Directors*, Investment Company Institute, 1999.

5. Sturms (1999), p. 104.

6. Similar to the requirement of mutual funds to register as a "Registered Investment Company" under the Investment Company Act of 1940, the Investment Advisors Act of 1940 provides regulatory guidance for advisors.

7. Josh Friedman, "Vanguard to Turn More Activist in Proxy Voting," *Los Angeles Times*, August 22, 2002. Vanguard stated it would withhold votes for non-independent directors who serve on audit, compensation, or nominating committees of a board and would not vote for any directors whose election would make the majority of the board made up of insiders.

8. See Khorana (1996).

9. See Chevalier and Ellison (1999).

10. See Tufano and Sevick (1997).

11. See Deli (2002).

12. SEC document "The Role of the Independent Investment Company Directors" – Part 2, February 23 and 24, 1999, contains a comprehensive discussion.

13. Soft dollars are what results when an advisor's pays higher than market commission rates to a brokerage firm that executes the portfolio's trades in exchange for research products.

14. Notable earlier studies of mutual fund performance are Ippolito (1989) and Hendricks, Patel, and Zeckhouser (1993). More recently, Malkiel (1995) finds that mutual funds tend to underperform the market, not only after management expenses have been deducted, but also gross of all reported expenses except load fees. He concludes that it appears investors do not get their money's worth from investment advisory expenditures. Carhart (1997) shows a strong relationship between performance and size, expense ratios, turnover, and load fees, which suggest that mutual funds on average do not recoup their investment costs through higher returns. He argues that persistence in expense ratios explains any persistence in mutual fund performance.

15. Both BXR and BXP take two forms. Both are calculated at the *objective* and *major objective* level.

16. Due to mergers of fund sponsors, the largest sponsors include over 30 individual fund families or complexes. For example, AIM Funds and INVESCO Funds are considered two separate fund families in this research, while each is a unit of AMVESCAP PLC, considered a single sponsor.

17. Pozen notes the 2000 figures include assets held by mutual fund products available through variable annuity assets. While annuity assets are specifically excluded here as they are not readily available to all investors and must usually be purchased as part of an insurance contract, these fund sponsors represent the majority of mutual fund assets. The largest 25 fund sponsors represented 76% of the market in 1990 and did not include annuity assets.

18. Common disconnects between data sources occur due to fund mergers, fund name changes, or apparent conflicts due to the timing of the fund documentation. Some sponsors use one SAI to cover multiple funds while others use a single SAI for each fund. Depending on the fiscal years of the individual funds and how the sponsor organizes its fund documentation, matching a fund to a board can be a considerable

challenge. Where possible, confirmation of the configuration used in this study was sought from fund sponsor representatives.

19. Just a few years ago (2001), the Securities and Exchange Commission (SEC) imposed a rule that required the boards of mutual funds to be comprised of a majority of independent directors. In 2004, the SEC passed a rule that requires at least 75% of each mutual fund's board to be independent. The rule, which went into effect at the end of 2005, also requires that the chair of the board to be an independent board member. Clearly, the SEC's actions illustrate the importance of independent governance in mutual funds. Neither of these SEC rules affects this study, because we examine mutual funds prior to when either of the independent director rules was in effect. Because our data are free from these requirements, the results of our study better indicate the effects of governance on mutual fund performance.

20. We also run separate regressions for each configuration of boards. The coefficient on BFDS is significant and positive for SBC boards, but significant and negative for MBC boards. However, due to the limited number of observations for SBC boards, such results must be interpreted with caution.

21. The log of FUNDRAT is used due to skewness of the variable.

ACKNOWLEDGMENTS

Special thanks are due to James Pappas, Ninon Sutton, and the staff at Heritage Funds.

REFERENCES

Agrawal, A., & Knoeber, C. R. (1996). Firm performance and mechanisms to control agency problems between managers and shareholders. *Journal of Financial and Quanitative Analysis, 31,* 377–397.

Carhart, M. M. (1997). On persistence in mutual fund performance. *The Journal of Finance, LII,* 57–82.

Carter, D. J. (2001). Mutual fund boards and shareholder action. *Villanova Journal of Law and Investment Management, 3,* 6–39.

Chen, J., Hong, H., Huang, M., & Kubik, J. D. (2004). Does fund size erode mutual fund performance? The role of liquidity and organization. *American Economic Review, 94,* 1276–1302.

Chevalier, J., & Ellison, G. (1999). Are some mutual fund managers better than others? Cross-sectional patterns in behavior and performance. *Journal of Finance, 54,* 875–899.

Ciccotello, C. S., Miles, J. A., & Walsh, L. S. (2002). *Does focus matter? A study of mutual fund families.* Working paper. Pennsylvania State University.

Das, S. R., & Sundaram, R. K. (1999). *Fee speech: Signalling and the regulation of mutual fund fees.* Working paper. Harvard University.

Deli, D. N. (2002). Mutual fund advisory contracts. *The Journal of Finance, LVII,* 109–133.

Dowers, M. (1997). *Corporate governance in the mutual fund industry: Board structure and director compensation.* Dissertation. State University of New York at Buffalo, 39.

Elton, E. J., & Gruber, M. J. (1997). Modern portfolio theory, 1950 to date. *Journal of Banking and Finance, 21*, 1743–1759.

Elton, E. J., Gruber, M. J., & Blake, C. R. (1996). The persistence of risk-adjusted mutual fund performance. *The Journal of Business, 69*, 133–157.

Hendricks, D., Patel, J., & Zeckhauser, R. (1993). Hot hands in mutual funds: Short-run persistence of performance in relative performance, 1974–1988. *Journal of Finance, 48*, 93–130.

Hermalin, B. E., & Weisbach, M. S. (1991). The effects of board composition and director incentives on firm performance. *Financial Management, 20*.

Hermalin, B. E., & Weisbach, M. S. (2003). Boards of directors as an endogenously determined institution: A survey of the economic literature. *FRBNY Economic Policy Review* (April).

Ippolito, R. A. (1989). Efficiency with costly information: A study of mutual fund performance, 1965–1984. *The Quarterly Journal of Economics, CIV*, 1–23.

Jensen, M. C. (1993). Presidential address: The modern industrial revolution, exit, and the failure of internal control systems. *The Journal of Finance, 48*, 831–880.

Khorana, A. (1996). Top management turnover: An empirical investigation of mutual fund managers. *Journal of Financial Economics, 40*, 403–427.

Khorana, A., & Servaes, H. (1999). The determinants of mutual fund starts. *The Review of Financial Studies, 12*, 1043–1074.

Khorana, A., & Servaes, H. (2002). *What drives market share in the mutual fund industry?* Working paper. Georgia Institute of Technology.

Latzko, D. A. (1999). Economies of scale in mutual fund administration. *The Journal of Financial Research, 22*, 331–339.

Lipton, M., & Lorsch, J. (1992). A modest proposal for improved governance. *The Business Lawyer, 48*, 59–77.

Malhotra, D. K., & McLeod, R. W. (1997). An empirical analysis of mutual fund expense. *The Journal of Financial Research, XX*, 175–190.

Malkiel, B. G. (1995). Returns from investing in equity mutual funds 1971–1991. *The Journal of Finance, L*, 549–572.

Melms, G. G. (1994). *Board of Director composition and other agency cost control mechanisms in the investment company industry.* Working paper. University of Oregon.

Mutual Fund Factbook. (2002). Investment Companies Institute.

Pozen, R. C. (2002). *The mutual fund business.* Boston: Houghton Mifflin Company.

Siggelkow, N. (2002). *Why focus? A study of intra-industry focus effects.* Working paper. University of Pennsylvania.

Sirri, E. R., & Tufano, P. (1998). Costly search and mutual fund flows. *The Journal of Finance, LIII*, 1589–1623.

Sturms, D. (1999). Enhancing the effectiveness of independent directors: Is the system broken, creaking or working. *Villanova Journal of Law and Investment Management, 1*, 97–127.

Tate, S. (2000). *The role of independent directors in mutual fund governance.* Working paper. Harvard Law School.

Tufano, P., & Sevick, M. (1997). Board structure and fee-setting in the US mutual fund industry. *Journal of Financial Economics, 46*, 321–355.

Yermack, D. (1996). Higher market valuation of companies with a small board of directors. *Journal of Financial Economics, 40*, 185–211.

EXPROPRIATION, WEAK CORPORATE GOVERNANCE AND POST-IPO PERFORMANCE: CHINESE EVIDENCE

Peng Cheng, Jean Jinghan Chen and Xinrong Xiao

ABSTRACT

This study provides evidence that Chinese initial public offerings (IPOs) report better operating performance than industry peers in the pre-IPO period, and worse performance in post-IPO period compared to the pre-IPO level. We find that related party transactions (RPTs) with controlling shareholders have significant effects on the long-run performance of IPO firms. Controlling shareholders structure a large percentage of operating (non-loan) RPTs to artificially boost revenues and/or profits of their IPO subsidiaries in the pre-IPO period. However, in the post-IPO period, controlling shareholders discontinue this RPT-based earnings manipulation practice and begin to expropriate IPO subsidiaries by obtaining a large percentage of cash loans, primarily in return for profits and/or resources transferred into the IPO subsidiaries in the pre-IPO period. Finally, we find that state-controlled IPO firms with a highly concentrated ownership structure and a less independent board of directors are more likely to be expropriated by controlling shareholders in the post-IPO period through related loans.

Issues in Corporate Governance and Finance
Advances in Financial Economics, Volume 12, 237–267
Copyright © 2007 by Elsevier Ltd.
All rights of reproduction in any form reserved
ISSN: 1569-3732/doi:10.1016/S1569-3732(07)12010-7

237

1. INTRODUCTION

Prior studies show that US initial public offering (IPO) firms exhibit a decline in the post-issue operating performance relative to the pre-IPO level, both before and after industry adjustments (Jain & Kini, 1994; Mikkelson, Partch, & Shah, 1997). The international evidence also obtain the same findings, including Holland (Roosenboom, Goot, & Gerard, 2003), Japan (Kutsuna, Okamura, & Cowling, 2002), Thailand (Kim, Kitsabunnarat, & Nofsinger, 2004), China's A-share market (Wang, Xu, & Zhu, 2001; Chen & Shih, 2004; Wang, 2005) and China's B- and H-share market (Aharony, Lee, & Wong, 2000; Huang & Song, 2003).[1]

One of possible explanations for the decline is that pre-issue operating performance may have been exaggerated. Teoh, Welch, and Wong (1998) and Roosenboom et al. (2003), by examining the US and Dutch IPO firms, find that pre-IPO reported earnings are artificially manipulated through accounting accruals. Discretionary accruals, which are under the control of managers and proxy for accrual-based earnings management, are high before the IPO relative to those of non-issuers, and issuers with higher discretionary accruals have poorer performance in the subsequent 3 years. Similarly, Aharony et al. (2000) also find that Chinese B- and H-share IPO firms are likely to accelerate credit sales (specific accrual item) to manipulate reported earnings in the pre-IPO period.

In this research, we extend prior research by focusing on the effects of related party transactions (RPTs) with controlling shareholders on the long-run performance of IPO firms. We hypothesize that IPO firms may abuse the use of RPTs for opportunistic purposes, which may have a significant effect on IPO long-run performance. Controlling shareholders could use their influential relationship over their affiliated companies to structure transactions in a way that allows resources to be transferred, or profits to be shifted between the two parties. In the pre-IPO period, controlling shareholders may structure transactions to artificially boost revenues and/or profits of pre-IPO subsidiaries, primarily because IPO firms with better historical earnings performance would normally be easier to float on the Chinese stock market, and probably offer the stocks with a higher IPO price, if investors do not see through the earnings manipulative schemes. However, in the post-IPO period, controlling shareholders lose interest in structuring transactions to benefit listed subsidiaries; furthermore, controlling shareholders are likely to expropriate their listed subsidiaries in return for economic resources transferred to the subsidiaries in the pre-IPO period (Jian & Wong, 2004).

This study provides empirical evidence based on Chinese A-share IPO market, since Chinese firms use a large amount of RPTs with their controlling shareholders before and/or after the IPO. In prior literature, Wang et al. (2001), Chen and Shih (2004) and Wang (2005) have studied Chinese A-share IPOs, and found that public listing is associated with a sharp deterioration in operating performance for up to 6 years after the IPO year. Wang et al. (2001) and Wang (2005) argue that the deterioration in operating performance is associated with concentrated ownership structure and weak corporate governance. However, the question 'how concentrated ownership and weak governance structure affect the IPO long-term operating performance in China' has not been explored. We further argue that IPO firms with a highly concentrated ownership and a board of directors less independent from controlling shareholders are more likely to engage in this pre-IPO RPT-based earnings management and post-IPO RPT-based expropriation. So, in this sense, RPTs with controlling shareholders would affect long-run operating performance of Chinese IPOs.

The remainder of the paper is organized as follows: Section 2 presents the literature review and an introduction to Chinese laws and regulations. Section 3 introduces the hypotheses and variables. Section 4 describes the data, and discusses the findings. Section 5 comes to the conclusion.

2. LITERATURE REVIEW

2.1. Related Party Transactions, Earnings Management and Expropriation

A related party transaction is *"a transfer of resources, services, or obligations between related parties, regardless of whether a price is charged, and Parties are considered to be related if one party has the ability to control the other party or to exercise significant influence or joint control over the other party in making financial and operating decisions"* (International Accounting Standards, IAS 24, p. 9). RPTs among group members can be cost-effective, because they help reduce transaction costs and enhance the enforcement of property rights and contracts (Coase, 1937). However, controlling shareholders and/or corporate executives may abuse these related dealings for opportunistic purposes. For example, if the transactions are structured at a price other than the market price, and then the profits would be shifted between group members, however the consolidated earnings remain generally unaffected (Thomas, Herrmann, & Inoue, 2004). Coca-Cola once uses the influential relationship with its bottlers, in which Coca-Cola has large ownership and board seats, to charge a higher price for the concentrate sold to bottlers and eventually boost its profits (McKay, 2002).

Further, RPTs may be associated with the expropriation of the listed subsidiaries by controlling shareholders. Recent US corporate scandals have highlighted the extensive misuse of RPTs and the opportunities to expropriate resources out of related parties. In the example of Adelphia, the company engaged in extensive RPTs so that the controlling family members' dealings with the listed company have *"looted Adelphia on a massive scale, using the company as the Rigas family's personal piggy bank, at the expense of public investors and creditors"* (Feeney, 2002, p. 1).[2]

2.2. Expropriation, Corporate Governance and Concentration Ownership

Expropriation is *"the process of using one's control powers to maximize own welfare and redistribute wealth from others"* (Claessens, Djankov, Fan, & Lang, 1999, p. 2). It is highly associated with legal protection of minority investors, because investor protection makes expropriation technology less efficient (La Porta, Lopez-de-Silanes, Shleifer, & Vishny, 1997, 1998, 2000, 2002). Strong corporate governance is likely to restrain the magnitude of expropriation. However, the transition economies, due to weak regulations and enforcements, provide rich settings for considering the importance of investor protection. Indeed, the term 'tunneling', as noted in Johnson, La Porta, Lopez-De-Silanes, and Shleifer (2000), signifies the idea that majority shareholders can employ various means to transfer the assets and profits out of firms for their personal benefit through RPTs in many ways. For example, loans on preferential terms; or a transfer of assets from the listed company to other companies under their control (Cheung, Rau, & Stouraitis, 2006b).

Recent literature also shows the relationship between ownership concentration and expropriation. With poor investor protection, ownership concentration becomes a substitute for legal protection (La Porta et al., 1998). Particularly in emerging markets, the emergence of concentrated block shareholders does not appear to be synonymous with the provision of monitoring services (Berglof, 1995), mainly because large shareholders might need to own a high percentage of shareholdings to exercise their control rights and thus expropriate wealth from minority shareholders. Minority investors, when poorly protected, might request a very low demand for corporate shares, which would indirectly stimulate ownership concentration (La Porta et al., 1998).

2.3. Overview: China's IPO Market

Since the early 1990s, public listing on the stock exchanges is the China's strategy to privatize its state-owned enterprises (SOEs). However, China's economic reform is often called as *"one-third privatized"* policy (Green, 2003), since Chinese SOEs initially only sell around one third of their equities to public investors, and still retain control. The government agencies ultimately keep 47.9% of total shares for the entire market (CSRC, 2004). Institutional shareholdings, held by mutual funds and QFIIs,[3] account for a small percentage of 4% of the overall ownership by 2003 (HKEx, 2004). Since the ownership structure is highly concentrated, minority shareholders may be on the verge of being expropriated.

The corporate governance is still to be well functional in China. Executive members of listed firms often hold a position in controlling shareholders' entity simultaneously, or previously. The board is strongly dominated by the members representing controlling shareholders, and there is no independent director in the board before the promulgation of the Code of Corporate Governance in 2002 (CSRC, 2002),[4] which requires one third of board members to be independent by June 30, 2003. However, a survey (CNINFO, 2006) shows that the enforcement for the code is weak, and more than 15% of listed firms do not comply with the code yet by the end of 2005. Moreover, independent directors are too small to fight against the state-owned controlling shareholders, who normally have extensive political connections with the governments. Chen and Cheng (2007) further argue that there is no open recruitment procedure in China to appoint an independent director, and many independent directors are nominated by controlling shareholders and/or executive directors of the companies, so that the true nature of independent directors may be jeopardized.

Furthermore, property rights are one of the most important aspects of good governance (Dollar & Kraay, 2000). However, there were no constitutional safeguards for private property in China, until Chinese Constitution was amended in 2004. China's new Constitution (Constitution of China, 2004, Article 17.1) shows that private property is inviolable and the government protects the legitimate rights of citizens to private property and its inheritance. However, it also makes clear that the State may expropriate or requisition private property for its use and shall make compensation for the private property expropriated or requisitioned (Article 17.3). Obviously, Chinese rules are really weak in protecting private property.

Empirically, Cheung, Jing, Rau, and Stouraitis (2006a) further use a sample of mainland Chinese firms to investigate RPTs between listed firms and their state-owned shareholders and show how resources are expropriated from minority shareholders of the firm to the State. They find that the expropriation is concentrated in firms with the highest state ownership and controlled by local governments. They argue that median value loss for these firms represents 45% of the value of RPTs, suggesting that the results are economically significant.

3. RPT PRACTICES IN CHINA AND HYPOTHESIS DEVELOPMENT

3.1. RPT Disclosures in China

From 1998 onwards, Chinese listed firms have been required to publish transactions between related parties on their annual reports, including the nature of the related party relationship as well as the amount of the transactions. Since then, corporate disclosures show a huge amount of transactions between listed companies and their controlling shareholders, mainly because of the 'special bond' between the two parties. Most Chinese listed firms originated from one profitable unit of their parent SOEs, and they do not even have an independent marketing and distribution network and supply chains, so that they have to sell (or purchase) products (or raw materials) to (or from) their controlling shareholders, and then controlling shareholders re-sell the products to a third party. In other cases, listed firms sell semi-finished goods and products to their controlling shareholders, and then controlling shareholders further develop these semi-finished goods into finished goods.

Based on our observations, we categorize all types of transactions between controlling shareholders and Chinese listed firms reported at corporate annual reports into two different groups: operating RPTs (or say, non-loan RPTs) and loan RPTs. Table 1 defines the two different types of RPTs.

(1) Operating items: This category consists of trade relationship and some other sources of transactions, such as the sales of non-monetary assets, leases, franchises, and administrative overheads (water and electricity supply etc.) and so on. Trade relationship is the main source of RPTs between controlling shareholders and listed firms, consisting of the sales and/or purchases of goods, products and services.

(2) Non-operating items: The second category represents loan transactions, such as cash loans and loans guarantees. In China, a non-financial

Table 1.   Seven Types of Related Party Transactions Widely used in China.

	Types	Description
Operating items	1. Goods and services (trade relationship)	Sales/purchases of goods, products, and services between controlling shareholder and its listed subsidiary
	2. Sales/acquisitions of non-monetary assets	Sales/acquisitions of non-monetary assets between controlling shareholder and its listed subsidiary, such as tangible and intangible assets
	3. Overhead assigned (administrative services)	Overhead costs paid from controlling shareholder (or its listed subsidiary) to its listed subsidiary (or the controlling shareholder) for obtaining administrative services and the use of facilities
	4. Royalties and franchises	Patents, permits and franchises between controlling shareholder and its listed subsidiary; normally controlling shareholder acts as the franchisor
	5. Leases	The operating and financial leases between controlling shareholder and its listed subsidiary
Non-operating items	6. Cash loans	The loans of cash between controlling shareholder and its listed subsidiary
	7. Loan guarantees	The loan guarantees provided for listed company using controlling shareholder's assets as collateral, or provided for controlling shareholder using listed firm's assets as collateral

Note: Based on the RPT observations disclosed on corporate annual reports of Chinese companies.

company is normally not allowed to act as a financial service lender and engage in the business of making customers cash loans. However, loans offered to related parties are legal. It is reported that more than 54% of Chinese firms make cash loans to their controlling shareholders and the aggregate amount of cash loans reaches Chinese ¥57.7 billion by the end of 2003 (Xinhua Net, 2005). These related loans are often made with preferential terms, and usually interest free, or at an interest rate lower than the market level. So, in this sense, related loans by listed firms to controlling shareholders are often associated with the expropriation of listed firms.

Loan guarantee is not a real transfer of economic resources from one party to the other, so that it would not have a significant effect on corporate operating performance, unless the debtor is not able to return the funds to the lending institution. In this case, the guarantor will have to repay it to the creditor, and the operating performance of the guarantor's entity may suffer from this activity.

3.2. Hypotheses

In this study, we extend prior literature and investigate the effects of RPTs between IPO firms and their controlling shareholders on the long-term IPO performance.

3.3. Pre-IPO RPT-based Earnings Management

In the pre-IPO period, controlling shareholders have incentives to boost the revenues and/or profits of their subsidiaries, primarily because IPO firms with good historical earnings performance are more likely to qualify for equity offerings. Earnings manipulation may sometimes lead to a higher IPO price, if investors are deceived by the manipulative schemes and are willing to pay a higher price (Teoh et al., 1998). We hypothesize that operating transactions with their controlling shareholders might boost the pre-IPO earnings figures of IPO firms. For example, IPO subsidiaries may sell goods, products and services to their controlling shareholders, at a higher selling price other than the fair price, and/or purchase raw materials from controlling shareholders at a lower price, so that profits can be shifted from controlling shareholders to IPO firms. In this sense, the pre-IPO operating performance may be inflated through transactions with controlling shareholders.

So, we test the following hypothesis:

H1. *In the pre-IPO period, reported operating performance of IPOs is associated with the aggregate operating RPTs between controlling shareholders and IPO subsidiaries.*

3.4. Post-IPO Payback

However, once IPO subsidiaries get listed, controlling shareholders lose interest in continuingly propping up their listed subsidiaries. Furthermore, controlling shareholders may expect future payback for what they have contributed in the pre-IPO period. One common way for controlling shareholders to benefit from pre-IPO contributions is probably to sell the shares in the market after the IPO event is completed. However, in Chinese A-share market, the shares held by controlling shareholders are categorized as non-tradable shares, which cannot be traded publicly on the stock exchanges. Controlling shareholders are only allowed to sell these non-tradable shares in a large sum (Block Trade) off stock exchanges by seeking a prospective buyer on their own, when a 3-year lock-up period ends up. So, a more likely way for controlling shareholders to gain payback is to expropriate listed subsidiaries in the post-IPO period by siphoning cash and/or other economic resources back from the listed firms, in return for the assets and/or profits surrendered by controlling shareholders in the pre-IPO period.

For example, controlling shareholders may obtain cash loans from their listed subsidiaries with the terms preferential to controlling shareholders. Since IPO firms normally keep a large amount of unused IPO proceeds in their bank accounts, they are able to make loans to their controlling shareholders without running short of working capitals, unless those loans are extraordinarily larger than IPO firms can comfortably afford. Of course, controlling shareholders may also expropriate their listed subsidiaries through some other ways, like charging a higher price for selling goods and non-monetary assets to their subsidiaries, and paying a lower price for buying goods and non-monetary assets from their subsidiaries. However, it is important to recognize that expropriations through cash loans are more likely than expropriations through other RPTs. For example, expropriations through trade relationship and/or non-monetary assets are less likely to be adopted, because a loss will be immediately recognized into profit and loss accounts of listed subsidiaries to write off the difference between the trading price and the fair price. As a result, controlling shareholders and listed subsidiaries may both suffer from the collapse of stock prices, triggered by the decline in reported earnings of listed subsidiaries. So, we expect that expropriation through cash loans is the main way for controlling shareholders to expropriate listed firms after the IPO event, and, in this research, the extent of loans is the proxy for the magnitude of expropriation.

One may argue that prospect of expropriation may discourage participation of public investors in the IPOs. However, it is important to recognize that Chinese IPOs are offered at a great discount to attract investors. Chan, Wang, and Wei (2004) find that Chinese IPOs are highly underpriced and the average underpricing[5] for Chinese A-share IPOs (1993–1998) is 178%. As a result, the demand for Chinese IPOs is extremely high, and all the Chinese

IPOs have been enthusiastically oversubscribed usually by 100 times or more. Even if investors expect controlling shareholders to expropriate IPO firms in the post-IPO period, investors may not turn away from participation in the IPOs.

We, then, will test the following hypothesis below:

H2. *Controlling shareholders are likely to expropriate IPO subsidiaries in the post-IPO period via related loans; the post-IPO operating performance is negatively associated with the amount of such loans.*

As soon as controlling shareholders expropriate their listed subsidiaries in the post-IPO period via related loans, stock prices are also expected to drop, because public investors, when poorly protected, might be willing to buy corporate shares only at a lower price (La Porta et al., 1998). Such loans may significantly impact corporate operating performance and stock performance, when they are considerably large. So, our third hypothesis is:

H3. *In the post-issue period, the size of loans by IPO firms to controlling shareholders is negatively associated with the post-IPO stock performance.*

One may argue that when a controlling shareholder obtains cash loans from the listed subsidiary for its own benefits, the stock price may go down and the controlling shareholder would lose money in the stock market. Although the controlling shareholder expropriates its subsidiary through cash loans, they lose money in the stock market so as to end up with nothing in the end. However, the shares held by controlling shareholders are categorized as non-tradable shares, which can only be traded off stock exchanges on a negotiation basis. So, controlling shareholders do not necessarily care much about the ups and downs of their stock prices on the exchanges, if they have no plan for a second equity offering.

4. EMPIRICAL RESULTS

4.1. Data Collection and Sample Distribution

This research uses the IPOs offered in Chinese A-share market, whose first trading day on stock exchange is between 1st January 1999 and 31st December 2000. The sample IPOs should have accounting figures and RPT disclosures available from 1 year before till 4 years after, and data for stock returns available up to 4 years after the IPO. As a result, 239 IPO cases are included into our final research sample.

Firstly, we choose IPOs offered in the period (1999–2000), because China made a major GAAP change towards IAS/IFRS in 1998 (CMOF, 1998). Since then, disclosures of the related party relationships and transactions are required in full details as a separate section on the footnotes of financial statements. So, data on RPTs between controlling shareholders and IPO firms can be easily distinguished and manually collected from firms' IPO prospectuses and/or their annual reports.

Secondly, we only investigate the 6-year operating performance of these IPOs, including 1 year before the IPO year and 4 years after the IPO year, because accounting data, particularly RPT data, in prior years are not available. IPO firms are only required to publish RPT transactions in the 1 year prior to the IPO. Accounting performance and stock performance figures are provided by China Securities Info Co. Ltd. and GreatWise Info Co. Ltd. respectively.

Panel A of Table 2 describes sample distribution by industry sectors. The sample firms are segregated into 13 industry groups (1-digit), by using the CSRC's Standard Industry Classification (CSRC, 2001 – SIC, 2001), which is currently the only official system to classify Chinese listed firms. We further break the group C into nine sub-groups (2-digit), because most of sample firms (62%) are categorized into manufacturing Group (Group C). So, in this research, sample firms are divided into these 21 industry (sub-) sectors, and matched publicly traded firms are those which come from the same industry (sub-)sectors and went public prior to 1998.

Panel B presents descriptive statistics of sample firms in comparison to the contemporaneous figures of the whole market, in terms of sales, total assets, EBITDA, return on assets and asset-scaled cash flow from operation. Sample firms are of a magnitude similar to the whole market by means of operation scales and profitability. Sales figures of the sample firms are Chinese ¥ 1.44 billion (mean value) and 0.70 billion (median value) respectively, and the figures for the market are ¥ 1.90 billion and 0.62 billion respectively. The mean and median values of EBITDA for sample companies are Chinese ¥ 0.21 billion and ¥ 0.09 billion respectively, and ¥ 0.27 billion and ¥ 0.08 billion for the entire market. We further conducted the mean and median tests (not reported here), showing that the differences between sample firms and the market are not statistically significant.

4.2. Long-term IPO Operating Performance

In this research, ROA (EBITDA divided by lagged (-1) total assets) and CFO (net cashflow from operation divided by lagged (-1) total assets) are

Table 2. Data Description.

Panel A: Sample companies distributed by industry

SIC (2001)	Sample	Whole Market[a]
A. Agriculture, forestry, and fishing	10	30
B. Mining	5	20
C. Manufacturing	153	742
C0 Foods and beverages	14	58
C1 Textiles, suits and leathers	16	56
C2 Wood products and furniture	1	2
C3 Papers, stationery, sporting, musical instruments	4	24
C4 Petroleum refining, chemicals and allied products	27	136
C5 Electronic, electric components and home appliances	5	39
C6 Mineral products and metal products	27	117
C7 Equipments and machineries	35	194
C8 Drugs and biologic products	24	82
D. Water, electricity, and gas	9	52
E. Construction	4	25
F. Transport and public utilities	13	55
G. Information technology	12	79
H. Wholesale and retail trade	10	96
I. Finance and insurance	2	10
J. Real estate	1	45
K. Service	12	41
L. Publishing, media, and allied services	1	11
M. Miscellaneous products and services	7	81
Total	239	1,287

Panel B: Sample statistics (unit: billion Chinese RMB Yuan)

	Mean	Median	Minimum	Maximum
Sales				
Sample	1.44	0.70	0.03	15.63
Market	1.90	0.62	0.00	417.19
Total assets				
Sample	5.19	1.50	0.43	279.30
Market	4.94	1.34	0.02	503.89
EBITDA				
Sample	0.21	0.09	−0.22	1.95
Market	0.27	0.08	−1.07	63.01
EBITDA on total assets				
Sample	7.27%	6.84%	−13%	30%
Market	8.52%	7.12%	−68%	205%
Operating cashflow on total assets				
Sample	6.89%	5.47%	−15%	88%
Market	5.37%	4.84%	−90%	268%

Source: Standard Industry Classification of China (2001) promulgated by the CSRC.
[a]Ending at year 2003.

employed as the operating performance indicators, since they are widely used in prior literature to evaluate the efficiency in making profits. Furthermore, the IPO firms' operating performance is examined after industry adjustment, in order to control for the industry shock. The industry-adjusted operating performance figures are obtained by deducting the median contemporaneous ROA (or CFO) figures of the same 2-digit publicly traded firms (Mikkelson et al., 1997).

Panel A of the Table 3 shows the industry-adjusted ROA figures from Y (-1) year to $Y(+4)$ year. It is clear that IPO firms report significantly better earnings performance than industry peers in the pre-IPO year by 12.71% (t-statistic = 10.39) in mean value and 10.18% (z-statistic = 8.43) in median value respectively. IPO firms continue to outperform their industry peers in terms of ROA figures in the IPO year, but this abnormally high earnings performance is reduced to 7.06% (mean value, t-statistic = 4.76) and 3.40%

Table 3. Industry-Adjusted Operating Performance around the IPO.

	$Y(-1)$	IPO	$Y(+1)$	$Y(+2)$	$Y(+3)$	$Y(+4)$
Panel A: ROA						
Median	10.18%***	3.40%***	−0.79%	−0.07%	−0.82%	−1.08%
(z-statistic)	(8.43)	(6.20)	(0.87)	(0.45)	(1.07)	(1.43)
Mean	12.71%***	7.06%***	0.09%	0.10%	−0.44%	−0.65%
(t-statistic)	(10.39)	(4.76)	(0.11)	(0.13)	(−0.72)	(−0.91)
Maximum	80.40%	119.00%	43.02%	20.74%	17.26%	21.91%
Minimum	−8.30%	−9.10%	−18.01%	−24.95%	−18.73%	−20.82%
Standard deviation	0.121	0.146	0.076	0.071	0.060	0.070
Panel B: CFO						
Median	2.54%***	−2.26%	1.09%*	1.12%*	0.13%	−0.91%
(z-statistic)	(3.81)	(1.37)	(1.70)	(1.70)	(0.03)	(0.53)
Mean	6.74%***	−0.41%	1.72%	2.55%**	−0.28%	−0.70%
(t-statistic)	(2.79)	(−0.17)	(1.45)	(2.08)	(−0.35)	(−0.78)
Maximum	179.36%	176.52%	59.23%	83.99%	24.13%	22.10%
Minimum	−29.26%	−42.59%	−45.60%	−19.33%	−24.73%	−28.25%
Standard deviation	0.23	0.23	0.12	0.14	0.07	0.08

Notes: Return of assets (ROA) is the EBITDA divided by the lagged (-1) total assets less the median contemporaneous ROA figures of the same 2-digit publicly traded firms. Cash flow from operations (CFO) is net cash flows from operations divided by the lagged (-1) total assets less the median contemporaneous CFO figures of the same 2-digit publicly traded firms.
*Denotes significance (2-tailed) at 0.10 level.
**Denotes significance (2-tailed) at 0.05 level.
***Denotes significance (2-tailed) at 0.01 level.

(median value, z-statistic = 6.20) respectively. This abnormally high earnings performance fades away from Y (+1) year onwards. Panel B reports industry-adjusted cashflow performance from $Y(-1)$ year to $Y(+4)$ year. It shows that IPO firms report significantly higher CFO figures than industry peers by 6.74% (mean value, t-statistic 2.79) and 2.54% (median value, z-statistic = 3.81) respectively in $Y(-1)$ year. However, from the IPO year onwards, the industry-adjusted CFO figures report no significant out-performance, and fluctuate around the zero point.

Table 3 shows that, in terms of both ROA and CFO figures, IPO firms report extraordinarily better operating performance in the pre-IPO period, however, the abnormal outperformance fades away in the pre-IPO period. This finding is consistent with prior research that Chinese IPOs experience a sharp deterioration in operating performance from pre-IPO level to post-IPO level (Wang et al., 2001; Chen & Shih, 2004; Wang, 2005). However, our results indicate that the deteriorating performance is formed, primarily because IPO firms abnormally outperform the industry peers in terms of operating performance in the pre-IPO period, and this abnormally out-performance disappears after the IPOs are successfully listed. We conjecture that the pre-IPO performance figures may have been significantly inflated.

4.3. Descriptive Statistics: RPT Variables

Table 4 reports the six line-item RPTs between controlling shareholders and their IPO subsidiaries in terms of actual amount scaled by lagged (−1) total assets. The first line item describes the loan transactions between the two parties, which is measured as the loans by controlling shareholders to IPO subsidiaries net of the loans offered by listed companies to their controlling shareholders. The remaining line items demonstrate non-loan operating transactions, which cover trade relationships, non-monetary transactions, administrative services, royalties and leases etc.

As a whole, the total amount of RPTs scaled by lagged (−1) total assets starts at 24.18% in the $Y(-1)$ year, and reaches a peak of 30.17% in the IPO year. However, it declines to 20.12% in the $Y(+1)$ year, and then remains stable from that year on. The first two line items in Table 4, which include net loans and trade relationship, show the most active transactions between controlling shareholders and IPO subsidiaries. Trade relationship is the largest type of RPTs: the percentage in $Y(-1)$ year is 19.49%, and rises to 21.48% in the IPO year. It significantly declines to 13.86% in $Y(+1)$ year and fluctuates in a range from 12.77% to 15.27% subsequently.

Table 4.   Related Party Transactions Before and After the IPO.

Items	$Y(-1)$	IPO	$Y(+1)$	$Y(+2)$	$Y(+3)$	$Y(+4)$
Loan RPTs						
Net_loan	0.45%	−3.73%***	−3.24%***	−2.23%***	−2.83%***	−1.84%**
(*t*-statistic)	(0.81)	(−4.32)	(−4.21)	(−3.50)	(−3.95)	(−3.15)
Operating RPTs						
Trade_relationship	19.49%***	21.48%***	13.86%***	15.27%***	12.78%***	14.94%***
(*t*-statistic)	(5.21)	(5.54)	(5.58)	(5.58)	(5.35)	(4.46)
Non_monetary_asset	0.70%	2.01%**	1.54%***	1.76%***	0.82%***	2.10%***
(*t*-statistic)	(1.50)	(2.25)	(3.73)	(2.84)	(3.33)	(3.21)
Administrative_service	0.65%***	0.46%***	0.27%***	0.50%***	0.33%***	0.38%***
(*t*-statistic)	(4.39)	(5.00)	(5.46)	(3.51)	(2.82)	(3.00)
Royalty	0.02%	0.02%	0.00%	0.00%	0.06%	0.02%
(*t*-statistic)	(1.00)	(1.00)	(1.00)	(1.00)	(1.00)	(1.00)
Lease	0.00%	0.00%	0.01%	0.01%**	0.00%**	0.00%**
(*t*-statistic)	(1.00)	(1.00)	(1.48)	(2.38)	(2.30)	(1.92)
Total amount	24.18%***	30.17%***	20.12%***	22.14%***	17.88%***	21.71%***
	(5.92)	(6.74)	(7.29)	(7.42)	(7.16)	(5.68)

Notes: This table describes line-item related party transactions between controlling shareholders and listed subsidiaries over the 6 years. Net_loan is the difference between loans provided by controlling shareholders to their listed subsidiaries and loans provided by listed subsidiaries to their controlling shareholders (loans guarantees should not be included, if not executed). Trade_relationship is the sales and/or purchases of goods, products, and services between controlling shareholders and their listed subsidiaries. Non_monetary_asset is the sales and/or acquisitions of non-monetary assets between controlling shareholders and their listed subsidiaries, such as tangible and intangible assets. Administrative_service is the expenses paid from controlling shareholders (or listed subsidiaries) to listed subsidiaries (or controlling shareholders) for obtaining administrative services and the use of private resources. Royalty is the annual expenses paid for the use of patents, permits and Franchises between controlling shareholders and listed subsidiaries. Lease is the annual expenses paid for operating and financial leases between controlling shareholders and listed subsidiaries. Total amount denotes the aggregate amount of absolute related party transactions, which includes all the six types of transactions above. All the numbers in the table are the actual amounts scaled by the lagged (−1) total assets.
**Denotes significance (2-tailed) at 0.05 level.
***Denotes significance (2-tailed) at 0.01 level.

Net loans begin at 0.45% in $Y(-1)$ year, and soon turn to be a negative figure (−3.73%) in the IPO year. It shows that IPO firms start to make loans to controlling shareholders as soon as getting listed. From $Y(+1)$ year onwards, the percentage remains to be negative, and the absolute value seems to narrow down steadily from 3.24% in $Y(+1)$ year to 1.85% in $Y(+4)$ year.

Table 4 shows that trade relationship between controlling shareholders and IPO subsidiaries significantly decrease from the pre-IPO period to the post-IPO period. It is expected that controlling shareholders discontinue those artificial trade relationship to benefit IPO subsidiaries in the post-IPO period. Moreover, IPO subsidiaries begin to make cash loans to controlling shareholders as soon as the IPO event is completed. An IPO is expected to make ownership structure more diversified and improve the quality of corporate governance from before to after the IPO, since listed firms have to abide by the CSRC's regulations, particularly those requirements for corporate governance. However, Table 4 shows that the improvement in ownership structure and corporate governance resulting from the IPO does not seem to make expropriation difficult, and cash loans by IPO firms to controlling shareholders become more in the post-IPO period. One of the possible reasons is that controlling shareholders retain a large percentage of ownership and fully dominate the boardrooms, so that the quality in corporate governance is not substantially improved in the post-IPO period.

From Table 4, it seems that there is a likely relation between pre-IPO RPTs and post-IPO RPTs. So, Table 5 presents loan RPTs (net loans) between listed firms and controlling shareholders over the 6 years from $Y(-1)$ year to $Y(+4)$ year segregated by pre-IPO non-loan RPTs quartiles. The pre-IPO non-loan RPTs is measured as the aggregate amount of assets-scaled RPTs (other than loan transactions) between $Y(-1)$ year and the IPO year.

In Table 5, the last column shows the average of net loans between listed subsidiaries and controlling shareholders over the 5 years from the IPO year to $Y(+4)$ year in the four quartile portfolios. The mean value of net loans in the first quartile portfolio (Q1), which reports the lowest non-loan RPTs in the pre-IPO period, is -0.89% (t-statistic $= -2.21$), and the figure for the second smallest portfolio (Q2) is -2.82% (t-statistic $= -3.86$). The same percentage for the third smallest portfolio (Q3) rises a bit to -2.99% (t-statistic $= -2.61$), and the portfolio (Q4) with the largest non-loan RPTs in the pre-IPO period reports the largest net loans of -4.38% (t-statistic $= -2.65$). It is indicated that the more controlling shareholders structure non-loan transactions to benefit their subsidiaries in the pre-IPO period, the more controlling shareholders receive loans from their listed subsidiaries in the post-IPO period.

Table 5 shows that there is a positive relation between pre-IPO non-loan RPTs and post-IPO cash loans by listed subsidiaries to controlling shareholders. If controlling shareholders structure more pre-IPO non-loan RPTs with their listed subsidiaries, they are likely to take more cash loans

Table 5. Loan RPTs Segregated by Pre-IPO Operating RPTs Quartiles.

Quartiles	Tests	$Y(-1)$	$Y(0)$	$Y(+1)$	$Y(+2)$	$Y(+3)$	$Y(+4)$	Post-IPO Average
Q1 (smaller)	Mean	0.00%	−1.66%*	−0.60%	−0.13%	−0.41%	−1.33%*	−0.89%**
	(t-statistic)	(0.21)	(−2.00)	(−1.33)	(−0.41)	(−1.16)	(−2.00)	(−2.21)
Q2	Mean	0.84%	−2.26%	−3.94%***	−3.58%***	−3.14%***	−1.79%*	−2.82%***
	(t-statistic)	(0.65)	(−1.63)	(−2.81)	(−3.24)	(−3.30)	(−1.99)	(−3.86)
Q3	Mean	1.19%	−4.49%**	−2.85%**	−2.38%*	−3.36%**	−1.88%	−2.99%**
	(t-statistic)	(0.75)	(−2.24)	(−2.32)	(−1.69)	(−2.44)	(−1.29)	(−2.61)
Q4 (larger)	Mean	−0.23%	−6.61%***	−4.36%**	−3.68%*	−4.52%*	−2.56%*	−4.38%**
	(t-statistic)	(−0.28)	(−2.95)	(−2.12)	(−1.73)	(−1.89)	(−1.57)	(−2.48)
One-way ANOVA	F-statistic	0.383	4.60***	1.16	1.54	2.15*	0.77	2.65*
	(significance)	(0.76)	(0.00)	(0.32)	(0.20)	(0.09)	(0.51)	(0.05)

Notes: This table describes loan transactions between controlling shareholders and listed subsidiaries over the 6 years in four quartile portfolios segregated by pre-IPO operating RPTs. Pre-IPO operating RPTs is the aggregate amount of related party transactions other than loan RPTs between the $Y(-1)$ year and the IPO year scaled by the lagged (-1) total assets. Post-IPO average is the mean amount of asset-scaled net loans between the IPO year and the $Y(+4)$ year.

*Denotes significance (2-tailed) at 0.10 level.
**Denotes significance (2-tailed) at 0.05 level.
***Denotes significance (2-tailed) at 0.01 level.

from their listed subsidiaries in the post-IPO period. It implies that controlling shareholders receive cash loans from their listed subsidiaries in the post-IPO period, probably in return for profits and/or resources transferred into the subsidiaries in the pre-IPO period.

4.4. OLS Cross-sectional Analysis

We then use an OLS cross-sectional regression analysis to investigate the relationship between IPO operating performance and the size of RPTs. We use the two RPT variables: 'Net_loan' and 'Operating_items', as defined previously. The industry-adjusted ROA and CFO figures are regressed on the two line-item RPT variables for each of the 6 years. We also include a set of control variables, including firm size (total assets at the beginning of the year), age (difference between the establishment year and the IPO year), capital expenditure (asset-scaled capital investment adjusted for depreciation charges in a given year) and government subsidy (asset-scaled governmental subsidy received, including tax refunds, and project-specific government grants in a given year).

Table 6a presents the regression results, when ROA is regressed on RPT variables. The first two models explain 21.5 and 18.3% (R^2) of the variation of the dependent variable respectively. The estimated coefficients of variable 'Operating_items' in the first two models are found to be strongly positive (0.071 and 0.105 respectively) and highly significant (at 5 and 1% level respectively), indicating that operating RPTs significantly contribute to the IPO earnings performance between $Y(-1)$ year and the IPO year. The coefficients of variable 'Net_loan' are positive (0.146 and 0.163 respectively) as to the first 2 years, but none is found statistically significant. Further, for the remaining four models, the R^2 values increase a little, ranging from 20.1% to 31.8%. The estimated coefficient of 'operating_items' decreases to 0.076 (at 5% level) for $Y(+1)$ year. It continues to decrease (0.036, 0.033 and 0.030 respectively) in the subsequent years, but the relationship is not significant. It shows that non-loan RPTs become a less significant contributing factor to the earnings performance from $Y(+1)$ year onwards. However, in $Y(+1)$ year, the coefficient of 'Net_loan' is strongly positive (0.311) and significant at 1% level. Between $Y(+2)$ year and $Y(+3)$ year, it slightly declines to 0.305 (at 1% significance level) and 0.194 (at 5% significance level) respectively, indicating that 'Net_loan' is positively associated with the post-IPO earnings performance. As shown in Table 4, 'Net_loan' turns to be negative figures in the post-IPO period, so that loan

Table 6a. OLS Regression Models on Related Party Transactions.

	Coefficients					
	$Y(-1)$	$Y(0)$	$Y(+1)$	$Y(+2)$	$Y(+3)$	$Y(+4)$
Intercept	0.148***	0.045	0.012	−0.012	−0.012	−0.028**
(*t*-statistic)	(6.74)	(1.43)	(0.88)	(−0.76)	(−1.09)	(−2.10)
RPT variables						
Net_loan	0.146	0.163	0.311***	0.305***	0.194**	0.082
(*t*-statistic)	(0.60)	(0.95)	(3.25)	(2.74)	(2.57)	(0.77)
Operating_items	0.071**	0.105***	0.076**	0.036	0.033	0.030
(*t*-statistic)	(2.32)	(2.94)	(2.53)	(1.41)	(1.45)	(1.60)
Control variables						
Size	−0.002*	−0.001	−0.001	−0.000	−0.000	−0.000
(*t*-statistic)	(−1.70)	(−0.90)	(−0.99)	(−0.43)	(−0.05)	(−0.24)
Age	−0.010**	−0.006	−0.003	−0.003	−0.005**	−0.004
(*t*-statistic)	(−2.00)	(−1.03)	(−1.00)	(−0.89)	(−2.05)	(−1.50)
Capital_expenditure	0.044	0.127**	0.375	0.201**	0.317***	0.367***
(*t*-statistic)	(0.57)	(2.07)	(0.94)	(2.61)	(4.09)	(5.50)
Government_subsidy	−0.468	0.601	−1.354	1.122	−0.757	0.406
(*t*-statistic)	(−0.54)	(0.74)	(−1.05)	(0.67)	(−0.92)	(0.31)
R^2	21.5%	18.3%	20.1%	20.6%	30.5%	31.8%
Adjusted R^2	13.5%	12.9%	14.8%	15.3%	25.9%	27.3%
F-statistic	2.62	3.40	3.81	3.93	6.65	7.07

Notes: Table 6 presents regression results that operating performance (ROA and CFO) is regressed on the two RPT variables 'Net_loan' and 'Operating_items'. Net_loan is measured as the difference between loans by controlling shareholders to listed subsidiaries and loans by listed subsidiaries to controlling shareholders scaled by lagged (−1) total assets in a particular year. Operating_items is the aggregate RPTs other than loans scaled by lagged (−1) total assets in a particular year. Size is the beginning-year total assets (billion Chinese ¥). Age is the difference between the establishment year and the IPO year. Capital_expenditure is the capital investment (adjusting for depreciation charges) scaled by lagged (−1) total assets in a particular year. Governmental_subsidy is the governmental subsidy received, including tax refunds, and project-specific government grants scaled by lagged (−1) total assets in a particular year.

Model 1:

$$\text{ROA}_i = \beta_0 + \beta_1 \times \text{Net\_loan}_i + \beta_2 \times \text{Operating\_items}_i + \beta_3 \times \text{Size}_i + \beta_4 \times \text{Age}_i$$
$$+ \beta_5 \times \text{Capital\_expenditure}_i + \beta_6 \times \text{Government\_subsidy}_i + \varepsilon_i$$

*Denotes significance (2-tailed) at 0.10 level.
**Denotes significance (2-tailed) at 0.05 level.
***Denotes significance (2-tailed) at 0.01 level.

transactions by IPO firms to controlling shareholders have a negative effect on post-IPO earnings performance.

Table 6b further provides regression results, when the dependent variable 'ROA' is replaced with 'CFO'. Table 6b further confirms the findings

Table 6b. Regression Models on Related Party Transactions.

	Coefficients					
	Y (−1)	Y (0)	Y (+1)	Y (+2)	Y (+3)	Y (+4)
Intercept	0.035	−0.016	0.012	0.004	−0.028*	0.010
(t-statistic)	(0.79)	(−0.31)	(0.52)	(0.16)	(−1.86)	(0.50)
RPT variables						
Net_loan	0.908	0.664**	0.348**	0.185*	0.044	0.077
(t-statistic)	(0.87)	(2.43)	(2.28)	(1.91)	(0.42)	(0.51)
Operating_items	0.106*	0.109*	0.110**	0.095*	0.104	0.002
(t-statistic)	(1.73)	(1.91)	(2.28)	(1.97)	(1.36)	(0.82)
Control variables						
Size	−0.000	−0.000	−0.000	−0.000	−0.000	0.000
(t-statistic)	(−0.14)	(−0.02)	(−0.19)	(−0.27)	(−0.28)	(0.49)
Age	−0.004	−0.006	−0.002	−0.000	−0.004**	−0.010***
(t-statistic)	(−0.37)	(−0.63)	(−0.40)	(−0.51)	(−1.26)	(−2.82)
Capital_expenditure	0.389**	0.061	0.778	0.123	0.293***	0.182*
(t-statistic)	(2.50)	(0.62)	(0.22)	(0.88)	(3.12)	(1.90)
Government_subsidy	−0.045	1.898	0.818	−1.443	0.066	0.243
(t-statistic)	(−0.02)	(1.46)	(0.31)	(−0.47)	(0.05)	(0.13)
R^2	10.8%	12.6%	14.8%	11.0%	16.7%	13.0%
Adjusted R^2	4.9%	6.8%	9.2%	6.9%	10.2%	7.2%
F-statistic	1.83	2.18	2.62	2.31	2.67	2.26

Model 2:

$$CFO_i = \beta_0 + \beta_1 \times Net\_loan_i + \beta_2 \times Operating\_items_i + \beta_3 \times Size_i$$
$$+ \beta_4 \times Age_i + \beta_5 \times Capital\_expenditure_i + \beta_6 \times Government\_subsidy_i + \varepsilon_i$$

*Denotes significance (2-tailed) at 0.10 level.
**Denotes significance (2-tailed) at 0.05 level.
***Denotes significance (2-tailed) at 0.01 level.

presented in Table 6a. The estimated coefficients of variable 'Operating_items' in the first two models are found to be positive (0.106 and 0.109 respectively) at 10% significance level, indicating that non-loan RPTs significantly contribute to the IPO cashflow performance in the $Y(-1)$ year and the IPO year. However, the positive relationship between non-loan RPTs and cashflow performance grows weaker in $Y(+3)$ year, and fades away thereafter. In $Y(-1)$ year, the estimated coefficient of variable 'Net_loan' is positive (0.908) but statistically insignificant. However, from the IPO year to $Y(+2)$ year, the coefficients of 'Net_loan' are 0.664, 0.348 and 0.185 (at 5, 5 and 10% significance level) respectively, indicating that 'Net_loan' is positively associated with the post-IPO cashflow performance.

Table 6 provides evidence that operating performance of IPO firms, in terms of earnings performance and cashflow performance, is highly related to RPTs between controlling shareholders and IPO firms. Non-loan RPTs, particularly trade relationship, show an abnormally large figure in the $Y(-1)$ year and IPO year, and the size of non-loan RPTs is positively associated with pre-IPO operating performance. This positive relationship fades away, when the firms are listed for more than 3 years. Simultaneously, we further find that IPO firms significantly make cash loans to their controlling shareholders from the IPO year onwards, and the size of such loans has a negative effect on post-IPO operating performance.

In short, we argue that operating non-loan RPTs with controlling shareholders are responsible for the operating outperformance of IPO firms in the pre-IPO period. The reasons for the decline in the post-IPO operating performance relative to the pre-IPO level are twofold: (1) controlling shareholders used to structure a large amount of non-loan transactions beneficial to their IPO subsidiaries in the pre-IPO period; however, in the post-IPO period, controlling shareholders structure less non-loan RPTs beneficial to IPO firms. (2) Controlling shareholders begin to expropriate IPO subsidiaries in the post-IPO period, for example obtaining a large amount of cash loans.

4.5. RPTs and Stock Returns

Then, we further investigate the association between post-IPO stock performance and the size of RPTs. The two stock performance measures, buy-and-hold returns (BAHRs) and cumulative abnormal returns (CARs), are used to evaluate the aftermarket abnormal performance of Chinese IPOs, since both of them are widely used in prior literature to identify long-term abnormal performance (Teoh et al., 1998; Roosenboom et al., 2003), but neither of them is always preferred (Gompers & Lerner, 2003). BAHRs and the CARs for an IPO firm i during the period between the first trading day and the fiscal year-end t ($t = 0, 1, 2, 3, 4$) are calculated as:

$$\text{BAHR}_{i,t} = \prod_{s=1}^{t}(1 + R_{i,s}) - \prod_{s=1}^{t}(1 + R_{m,s})$$

$$\text{CAR}_{i,t} = \sum_{s=1}^{t}(R_{i,s} - R_{m,s})$$

$R_{i,s}$ represents the stock return of stock i in Y (s) year ($s = 0, 1, 2, 3, 4$); $R_{m,s}$ is the benchmark return in Y (s) year ($s = 0, 1, 2, 3, 4$), which is the Shanghai Composite Index return at the same period. The compounded BAHRs and CARs are inclusive of dividends and other distributions.So, we sort the stocks into four quartile portfolios by the average amount of post-IPO net loans (between the IPO year and Y ($+4$) year) scaled by the lagged (-1) total assets. Table 7 presents the results.

Panel A of Table 7 shows the median benchmark-adjusted BAHRs in four portfolios: the portfolio (Q4) with the largest negative loans in the post-IPO period does not underperform the market and/or the other three IPO portfolios (Q1, Q2 and Q3) over a 2-year period. However, over a 3-year period or longer, it seems that portfolio Q4 appears to underperform the market; and the other three quartile portfolios (Q1, Q2 and Q3) perform much better than Q4, and are not likely to underperform the market. In panel B, it shows the median CARs in four portfolios: portfolio Q4 with the largest negative loans in the post-IPO period clearly underperforms the market and/or the remaining three portfolios (Q1, Q2 and Q3) particularly over 3 years or longer.

Table 7 presents some evidence that IPO firms involved with large cash loans to controlling shareholders in the post-IPO period are underperforming the market and/or the other IPO firms, over a 3-year period or longer. It indicates that post-IPO loan transactions are likely to have a negative impact on long-term stock performance of IPO firms in the long run.

4.6. RPTs Segregated by Ownership and Governance Characteristics

Finally, we further examine the ownership structure and corporate governance of IPO firms involved with RPT practices, aiming to find out the effects of firm characteristics on the likelihood of pre-IPO earnings manipulation and post-IPO expropriation practices. We hypothesize that an IPO subsidiary with a concentrated ownership structure is more likely to make transactions with its controlling shareholder, when corporate governance is weak. With poor investor protection, ownership concentration becomes a substitute for legal protection (La Porta et al., 1998). In this circumstance, the controlling shareholder is more likely to engage in RPT-based earnings management in the pre-IPO period, and expropriate the IPO subsidiary in the post-IPO period in return for profits and/or resources transferred into the subsidiaries around the IPO. Sound corporate governance practices may be able to protect the subsidiary from being

Table 7. Market Reaction to Post-IPO Loan-Based Expropriation.

Panel A: Long-run BAHRs

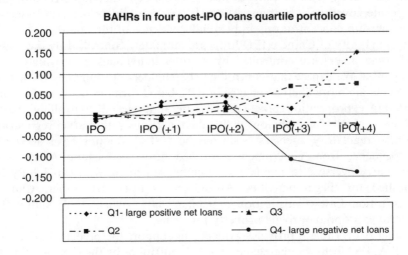

Panel B: Long-run CARs

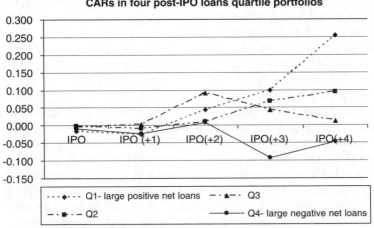

Notes: This table presents long-run stock performance (in terms of benchmark-adjusted BAHRs and CARs) of Chinese IPOs in four quartile portfolios segregated by post-IPO loan RPTs (The aggregate amount of asset-scaled net loans between the IPO year and the $Y(+4)$ year). BAHRs (and CARs) in four portfolios are the median value of market-adjusted BAHRs (and CARs) of a given quartile portfolio starting from the first trading day to a particular fiscal year-end less the contemporaneous market return (Shanghai Composite Index return).

expropriated. However, with weak corporate governance, this is not the case.

In this section, we investigate three aspects of ownership structure and corporate governance characteristics: (1) type of ultimate owner; (2) degree of ownership concentration; and (3) independence of the board.

The majority of Chinese IPO firms are ultimately controlled by the State, and some others are controlled by wealthy individuals or privately held companies. We expect that controlling shareholders, if ultimately owned by the State, are more likely to engage in RPT-based earnings management and post-IPO expropriation practices, because state-owned controlling shareholders generally have obvious political connections with market regulators. Chinese regulatory agencies, such as the CSRC, do not have adequate independence from government-controlled firms, and cannot work as a third-party overseer to regulate state-controlled firms, who can hardly be punished for illegal activities. Moreover, as discussed earlier, China's Constitution Law (Constitution of China, 2004, Article 17.3) allows the State to expropriate private property for its use.

Panel A of Table 8 provides evidence to support the predicted effect. In Panel A, IPO firms are segregated into two portfolios by the type of ultimate owner at the end of the IPO year. In the pre-IPO period, the 39 non state-controlled firms report smaller pre-IPO non-loan RPTs (8.87% in $Y(-1)$ year) than the 200 state-controlled firms (23.21% in $Y(-1)$ year). In the post-IPO period, the 39 non state-controlled IPO firms report much smaller negative loans (ranging from -0.43% to -1.88%) than the 200 state-controlled IPO firms (ranging from -2.13% to -3.57%). Panel A shows that state-controlled IPO firms are more likely to engage in RPT-based earnings management in the pre-IPO period, and get expropriated by controlling shareholders through cash loans in the post-IPO period.

We expect that a diversified ownership structure of IPO firms is likely to constrain RPT-based earnings management and expropriation practices, since minority shareholders may be on the verge of being expropriated, if controlling shareholders retain strong voting power. It is believed that the ownership structure is less concentrated, if the controlling shareholder holds a percentage of 30% ownership or less. However, once the percentage by the controlling shareholder reaches 50% or above, the ownership structure of the IPO firm is considered to be highly concentrated and the controlling shareholder has gained the absolute power to control shareholders' meetings.

Then, in Panel B, IPO firms are segregated into three portfolios by the percentage of ownership held by controlling shareholders at the end of the

Table 8. Related Party Transactions Segregated by Firm Characteristics.

Portfolios	Stock Counts	Types of RPTs	$Y(-1)$	IPO	$Y(+1)$	$Y(+2)$	$Y(+3)$	$Y(+4)$
Panel A: State-controlled vs. non state-controlled								
Non state-controlled	39	Net loans	1.71% (0.71)	-0.69% (-0.77)	-1.39% (-1.35)	-0.85% (-1.10)	-1.88%** (-2.24)	-0.43% (-1.46)
		Non-loan RPTs	8.87%*** (3.13)	13.03%** (2.09)	8.56%*** (3.47)	13.25%** (2.31)	7.47%** (2.61)	5.04%*** (3.69)
State-controlled	200	Loans	0.22% (0.47)	-4.35%*** (-4.30)	-3.57%*** (-4.03)	-2.47%*** (-3.36)	-3.06%*** (-3.55)	-2.13%*** (-3.02)
		Non-loan RPTs	23.21%*** (5.00)	26.46%*** (5.49)	16.96%*** (5.83)	18.33%*** (5.67)	15.25%*** (5.34)	19.88%*** (4.89)
Panel B: Ownership concentration								
Ownership ≤30% (least concentrated)	9	Net loans	-0.55% (-1.45)	-1.52% (-1.37)	-1.15%* (-2.02)	-0.67%* (-2.01)	-0.17% (-0.73)	-0.17% (-0.71)
		Non-loan RPTs	2.15% (1.53)	1.90% (1.31)	1.25% (1.11)	0.70% (1.89)	11.77% (1.03)	2.53% (1.28)
30% < Ownership < 50%	31	Loans	3.36% (1.15)	-0.22% (-0.16)	-4.63% (-1.40)	-2.21% (-1.46)	-2.36%* (-1.84)	-0.07% (-0.13)
		Non-loan RPTs	14.81%* (1.95)	7.57%** (2.41)	6.01%** (2.32)	5.28%** (2.25)	4.16%** (2.22)	8.93%* (2.11)
Ownership ≥ 50% (most concentrated)	199	Net loans	0.09% (0.17)	-4.37%*** (-4.35)	-3.10%*** (-3.98)	-2.27%*** (-3.16)	-3.07%*** (-3.59)	-2.20%*** (-3.13)
		Non-loan RPTs	22.67%*** (4.97)	27.80%*** (5.70)	17.69%*** (6.12)	20.11%*** (6.05)	15.55%*** (5.46)	19.43%*** (4.80)
Panel C: Independence of the board of directors								
Percentage ≤30% (more independent)	88	Net loans	0.52% (0.65)	-0.71% (-0.96)	-1.74%* (-1.72)	-1.05% (1.56)	-1.30%* (1.98)	-0.94%* (1.86)
		Non-loan RPTs	10.99%** (2.71)	12.75%*** (3.17)	7.86%*** (3.97)	13.23%*** (3.71)	7.41%*** (3.58)	6.05%*** (4.16)

Table 8. (*Continued*)

Portfolios	Stock Counts	Types of RPTs	$Y(-1)$	IPO	$Y(+1)$	$Y(+2)$	$Y(+3)$	$Y(+4)$
30% < Percentage < 50%	65	Loans	1.41%	−2.15%	−1.47%**	−2.15%*	−2.54%**	−2.57%*
			(1.04)	(−1.58)	(−2.19)	(−1.94)	(−2.12)	(−1.99)
		Non-loan RPTs	24.08%**	21.86%***	15.64%***	16.26%***	15.77%***	25.06%**
			(2.55)	(3.34)	(3.63)	(3.16)	(3.03)	(2.75)
Percentage ≥ 50% (less independent)	86	Loans	−0.32%	−8.11%***	−6.07%***	−3.43%**	−4.74%***	−2.24%*
			(−1.00)	(−4.37)	(−3.55)	(−2.50)	(−2.82)	(−1.87)
		Non-loan RPTs	28.55%***	37.98%***	23.51%***	22.86%***	19.35%***	23.32%***
			(4.05)	(4.06)	(4.28)	(3.88)	(3.84)	(3.78)

Notes: This table examines the firm characteristics of Chinese IPOs that are more likely to be expropriated by controlling shareholders. In Panel A, IPOs are segregated in two portfolios: non state-controlled and state-controlled, which represent the IPO firms that are ultimately controlled by the individuals and the State respectively at the end of the IPO year. In Panel B, IPO firms are segregated in three portfolios by the ownership concentration, which is measured as the percentage of shares held by the controlling shareholder in the listed firm at the end of the IPO year. In Panel C, IPO firms are further segregated in three portfolios by board composition, which denotes the proportion of board members (at the end of the IPO year) who represent the controlling shareholder and hold a senior position in the controlling shareholder's entity simultaneously.

*Denotes significance (2-tailed) at 0.10 level.
**Denotes significance (2-tailed) at 0.05 level.
***Denotes significance (2-tailed) at 0.01 level.

IPO year. Panel B shows that only nine IPO firms have a less concentrated ownership structure ($\leqslant 30\%$), and they report the smallest pre-IPO non-loan RPTs (2.15%) in Y (-1) year and the smallest post-IPO loans with a range between -0.17% and -1.52%. However, the majority of firms (199 in total) report a highly concentrated ownership structure ($\geqslant 50\%$) and show the largest pre-IPO non-loan RPTs (22.67%) in Y (-1) year and the largest loan RPTs to controlling shareholders in the post-IPO period (with a range between -2.20% and -4.37%). Panel B shows that IPO firms with a highly concentrated ownership structure are more likely to engage in RPT-based earnings management in the pre-IPO period, and get expropriated by controlling shareholders through cash loans in the post-IPO period.

We then expect that a board independent from controlling shareholders is likely to constrain RPT-based earnings management and expropriation practices conducted by controlling shareholders, primarily because a balanced and independent board of directors is likely to effectively monitor the operating activities and financial reporting practices of the firm. The independence of the board is essential to the effectiveness of corporate governance of the company, and each company should be headed by an effective board. However, once the independence of the board is jeopardized, the effectiveness of the monitoring is questionable. China did not officially bring independent directors into the board, until the promulgation of the Code of Corporate Governance in 2002. Traditionally, the board is fully occupied by the representatives from major shareholders. It is expected that the monitoring of the board is weak, when most directors are representing controlling shareholders.

The sample firm is then segregated into three portfolios by the percentage of directors in the board who hold a senior position in controlling shareholders' entity at the end of the IPO year (cutting point: 30 and 50%). Panel C shows that the 88 firms with an independent board (30% or less) report the smallest pre-IPO non-loan RPTs (10.99%) in Y (-1) year and the smallest post-IPO loan RPTs to controlling shareholders (ranging from -0.94% to -1.74%). The 86 firms with a highly dependent board (more than 50%) show the largest pre-IPO non-loan RPTs (28.55%) in Y (-1) year and the largest loan RPTs to controlling shareholders in the post-IPO period (ranging from -2.24% to -8.11%). Panel C shows that IPO firms with a board less independent from the controlling shareholder are more likely to engage in RPT-based earnings management in the pre-IPO period, and be expropriated via related loans by the controlling shareholder in the post-IPO period.

5. CONCLUSION, IMPLICATION AND LIMITATION

5.1. Concluding Remarks

This study examines the operating performance of Chinese IPOs, and the effects of RPTs between IPO firms and their controlling shareholders on the pre- and/or post-IPO performance. We find that Chinese IPOs significantly outperform the industry peers in terms of operating performance (ROA and CFO) in the pre-IPO period, but the outperformance disappears in the post-IPO period.

We argue that the deterioration in performance is partly because operating performance of IPO firms may be inflated through RPTs in the pre-IPO period. Controlling shareholders structure a large percentage of non-loan RPTs with IPO firms in the pre-IPO year, which are positively associated with the operating performance of IPO firms. In the post-IPO period, controlling shareholders do not prop up their listed subsidiaries through non-loan RPTs, and the positive relation between operating performance of IPO firms and the size of non-loan RPTs fades away in the long run.

Furthermore, controlling shareholders begin to expropriate listed subsidiaries via cash loans from the IPO year onwards, in return for profits and/or resources transferred into the subsidiaries around the IPO event. The size of such loans is negatively associated with the operating performance of IPO firms in the post-IPO period. We further investigate the long-run stock performance of Chinese IPOs, and find that the long-run stock performance, in terms of market-adjusted BAHRs and CARs, is negatively associated with the size of post-IPO loan-based expropriation in the long run.

Finally, we have explored firm characteristics of IPOs involved with RPTs. We find that state-controlled IPO firms with a highly concentrated ownership and a board of directors less independent from the controlling shareholder are more likely to be expropriated by controlling shareholders in the post-IPO period via related loans.

5.2. Implication

Our findings have important implication for investors willing to participate in Chinese A-share IPO market. We have found that Chinese IPO firms are likely to abuse the use of RPTs around the IPO. So, investors may need to be cautious about these transactions disclosed on IPO prospectuses and corporate financial statements, before making investment decisions. On the other hand, this research may be of use to market regulators in the financial sector. It urges regulators to improve rules and regulations, particularly in corporate governance rules and disclosure regulations. Of course, enforcing these rules and regulations is as equally important as developing these rules and regulations.

5.3. Limitation

In this study, we can only observe the data of RPT practices disclosed on public sources, such as IPO prospectuses and corporate financial statements. We assume that firms produce their financial reports in accordance with the CSRC's regulations and disclose their RPT practices whenever required. However, if firms fail to perform their responsibilities of public disclosures and report their RPT practices improperly, RPT variables, as a result, may be inappropriately determined.

NOTES

1. A shares market is the main market for domestic investors; however, B shares market is designed for overseas investors, and B shares stocks are traded in foreign currencies, either US Dollars or Hong Kong Dollars.
2. US Postal Inspector.
3. Qualified Foreign Institutional Investors.
4. China Securities Regulatory Commission, Chinese securities authority.
5. Underpricing rate is calculated as the return on the first day of trading (relative to the offering price).

REFERENCES

Aharony, J., Lee, C. W. J., & Wong, T. J. (2000). Financial packaging of IPO firms in China. *Journal of Accounting Research, 38*, 103–126.
Berglof, E. (1995). *Corporate governance in transitional economies: The theory and its policy implications. Issue in corporate governance in transitional economies: Insider control and the role of banks*. Washington: World Bank.
Chan, K., Wang, J. B., & Wei, K. C. (2004). Underpricing and long-term performance of IPOs in China. *Journal of Corporate Finance, 10*, 409–430.
Chen, C., & Shih, H. (2004). *Initial public offering and corporate governance in china's transitional economy. NBER-EAST Asia seminar on economics (Vol. 12)*. Chicago, IL: University of Chicago Press.
Chen, J. J., & Cheng, P. (2007). Corporate governance and accounting harmonisation with IFRS – Evidence from China. *Corporate Governance: An International Review, 15*, 286–296.

Cheung, Y., Jing, L. Rau, P. R., & Stouraitis, A. (2006a). *How does the grabbing hand grab? Tunneling assets from Chinese listed companies to the state*. Working Paper. City University of Hong Kong.

Cheung, Y., Rau, P. R., & Stouraitis, A. (2006b). Tunneling, propping and expropriation evidence from connected party transactions in Hong Kong. *Journal of Financial Economics*, *82*, 343–386.

Claessens, S., Djankov, S., Fan, J., & Lang, L. (1999). *Expropriation of minority shareholders in East Asia*. Working Paper No. 2088. Work Bank.

CMOF (Chinese Ministry of Finance). (1998). *Accounting system for joint stock limited companies: Accounting and financial statements*. (Chinese version), Beijing: Finance Press of China.

CNINFO (China Securities Info. Co. Ltd.). (2006). Surveys on the Board of Directors in China (Chinese version). May be available on: http://www.cninfo.com.cn/default.htm

Coase, R. H. (1937). *The firm, the market and the law*. New York: University of Chicago Press.

Constitution of China. (2004). English version. May be available on Helpline Law: http://www.helplinelaw.com/law/constitution/china/china01.php

CSRC (China Securities Regulatory Commission). (2001). The Standard Industrial Classification for Listed Companies. May be available on CSRC's Website: http://www.csrc.gov.cn/tj.html

CSRC (China Securities Regulatory Commission). (2002). Code of Corporate Governance for Listed Companies in China. May be available on CSRC's Website: http://www.csrc.gov.cn/en/homepage/index_en.jsp

CSRC (China Securities Regulatory Commission). (2004). China's Securities and Futures Markets (yearly report). May be available on CSRC's Website: http://www.csrc.gov.cn/en/homepage/index_en.jsp

Dollar, D., & Kraay, A. (2000). *Growth is good for the poor*. Washington: World Bank.

Feeney, T. (2002). Bail Set For Adelphia Execs. May be available on CBS News Online: http://www.cbsnews.com/stories/2002/09/23/national/main522992.shtml

Gompers, P., & Lerner, J. (2003). The really long-run performance of initial public offerings: The pre-Nasdaq evidence. *Journal of Finance*, *58*, 1355–1392.

Green, S. (2003). *Two-thirds privatisation: How China's listed companies are finally privatised*. London: The Royal Institute of International Affairs.

HKEx (Hong Kong Exchanges and Clearing). (2004). Institutional Investors in Mainland China (Research Paper), May be available on HKEx's Website: http://www.hkex.com.hk/research/r-papers/IIMC.pdf

Huang, S., & Song, F. (2003). *The Financial and operating performance of China's newly listed H-firms*. Working Paper. University of Hong Kong.

IAS 24 (International Accounting Standards 24). Related Party Disclosures. May be available on Deloitte IAS Plus: http://www.iasplus.com/standard/ias24.htm

Jain, B. A., & Kini, O. (1994). The post-issue operating performance of IPO firms. *Journal of Finance*, *49*, 1699–1726.

Jian, M., & Wong, T. J. (2004). *Earnings management and tunneling through related party transactions: Evidence from Chinese corporate groups*. Working Paper. Hong Kong University of Science and Technology.

Johnson, S., La Porta, R., Lopez-De-Silanes, F., & Shleifer, A. (2000). Tunneling. *The American Economic Review*, *90*, 22–27.

Kim, K. A., Kitsabunnarat, P., & Nofsinger, J. R. (2004). Ownership and operating performance in an emerging market: Evidence from Thai IPO firms. *Journal of Corporate Finance, 10,* 355–381.

Kutsuna, K., Okamura, H., & Cowling, M. (2002). Ownership structure pre- and post-IPOs and the operating performance of JASDAQ companies. *Pacific-Basin Finance Journal, 10,* 163–181.

La Porta, R., Lopez-de-Silanes, F., Shleifer, A., & Vishny, R. (1997). Legal determinants of external finance. *Journal of Finance, 52,* 1131–1150.

La Porta, R., Lopez-de-Silanes, F., Shleifer, A., & Vishny, R. (1998). Law and finance. *Journal of Political Economy, 106,* 1113–1155.

La Porta, R., Lopez-de-Silanes, F., Shleifer, A., & Vishny, R. (2000). Investor protection and corporate governance. *Journal of Financial Economics, 58,* 3–28.

La Porta, R., Lopez-deSilanes, F., Shleifer, A., & Vishny, R. (2002). Investor protection and corporate valuation. *Journal of Finance, 57,* 1147–1170.

McKay, B. (2002). Coca-Cola: Real thing can be hard to measure. *Wall Street Journal* (January 23) C[4].

Mikkelson, W. H., Partch, M. M., & Shah, K. (1997). Ownership and operating performance of companies that go public. *Journal of Financial Economics, 44,* 281–307.

Roosenboom, P., Goot, T., & Gerard, M. (2003). Earnings management and initial public offerings: Evidence from the Netherlands. *International Journal of Accounting, 38,* 243–266.

Teoh, S. H., Welch, I., & Wong, T. J. (1998). Earnings management and the long-run market performance of initial public offerings. *Journal of Finance, 53,* 1935–1974.

Thomas, W., Herrmann, D., & Inoue, T. (2004). Earnings management through affiliated transactions. *Journal of International Accounting Research, 3,* 1–25.

Wang, C. (2005). Ownership and operating performance of Chinese IPOs. *Journal of Banking and Finance, 29,* 1835–1856.

Wang, X., Xu, L. C., & Zhu, T. (2001). *Is public listing a way out for state-owned enterprises? The case of China.* Working Paper. City University of Hong Kong.

Xinhua Net. (2005). Cash Loans to Controlling Shareholders (News Release). May be available at: http://news.xinhuanet.com/fortune/2005-04/05/content_2786775.htm

PART II:
OTHER ISSUES IN FINANCE

BLACK–SCHOLES–MERTON, LIQUIDITY, AND THE VALUATION OF EXECUTIVE STOCK OPTIONS

Don M. Chance and Tung-Hsiao Yang

The principal deficiency in using the Black–Scholes–Merton model to value executive stock options is that the model assumes that the option is liquid while executive stock options are essentially illiquid. Models that account for liquidity are typically based on utility functions and require personal information about the executive. We show that the differences between the Black–Scholes–Merton model and utility-based models are largely captured by moneyness, volatility, and time to expiration and not by the specialized factors required by the utility-based models. We propose and test a variation of the Black–Scholes–Merton model that incorporates an artificial dividend yield to adjust the model price downward, thereby moving it much closer to the utility model value.

Since I don't believe Black-Scholes provides an accurate picture of the financial condition of our company, how can I certify our financial results using it to guesstimate the cost of options?

Craig Barrett, CEO
Intel
The Wall Street Journal
April 23, 2003

I've bought and sold options for 40 years and know their pricing to be highly sophisticated. It's far more problematic to calculate the useful life of machinery, a difficulty that makes

Issues in Corporate Governance and Finance
Advances in Financial Economics, Volume 12, 271–310
ISSN: 1569-3732/doi:10.1016/S1569-3732(07)12011-9

the annual depreciation charge merely a guess. No one, however, argues that this imprecision does away with a company's need to record depreciation expense. Likewise, pension expense in corporate America is calculated under widely varying assumptions and CPAs regularly allow whatever assumption management picks.

Warren Buffett
The Washington Post
April 9, 2002

One of the most controversial issues in the corporate world today is the valuation and expensing of options awarded to executives and employees for compensation and incentives. These options were used for decades with no explicit requirement that their costs be expensed. Consequently little attention was paid to what these options were worth to their holders or what they cost their issuers. In recent years, U.S. and global accounting authorities have invoked new requirements that companies expense these options. Thus, there has been an increase in the number of studies focused on valuation and expensing of these instruments.

Naturally practitioners, academics, and regulators have looked at the celebrated Black and Scholes (1973) and Merton (1973) models, hereafter referred to as Black–Scholes–Merton for an understanding of what these instruments are worth. But the Black–Scholes–Merton fails to capture many of the salient characteristics of executive stock options. Thus, direct application of the model is normally questionable if relatively precise values are required. While executive stock options are typically exercisable early (i.e., American-style) and have vesting periods, the most fundamental difference between Black–Scholes–Merton options and executive stock options is that the former are assumed to be liquid, while the latter clearly are not. The absence of liquidity is assumed, quite correctly, to be an important factor in the valuation of executive stock options. These options are generally thought to be worth less, and perhaps considerably less, than Black–Scholes–Merton or tradeable options.

Valuation models of these illiquid executive stock options certainly exist. They can be classified into three general categories: utility-based models, exogenous exercise models, and adjustments to Black–Scholes–Merton models. Utility-based models use a utility function to obtain an option value and can be further classified into two sub-groups. The first group, which we shall refer to as *static utility models*, assume that the option holder, hereafter referred to as an executive (though it could be simply an employee), has a portfolio of non-option wealth and also options awarded by the company. The portfolio can consist of bonds, stock of the company in question, and/or other stock or indices. The executive accepts the portfolio as static and values the option using a utility function to arrive at the certainty equivalent value. This approach was pioneered by Lambert, Larcker, and Verrechia (1991) and subsequently used by Huddart (1994), Kulatilaka and Marcus (1994), Aboody (1996), Hall and Murphy (2000, 2002), and Rubinstein (1995) among others.

The second group, which we shall call *dynamic utility models*, assumes that the executive optimizes the overall portfolio, a process that simultaneously values the option. These models have been developed by Cao and Wei (2007), Detemple and Sundaresan (1999), Henderson (2005), Ingersoll (2006), Jain and Subramanian (2004), and Kadam, Lakner, and Srinivasan (2002). These models vary in their assumptions related to portfolio composition, availability of hedging instruments, choice of utility function, and liquidity of the component instruments.

In a paper that falls indirectly into the classification of a utility model, Meulbroek (2001) combines the Black–Scholes–Merton model with the continuous-time capital asset pricing model to value executive stock options. Her focus is on valuing the options as part of a highly undiversified portfolio. Her model essentially assumes that holders of these options would require a risk premium to compensate for the lack of diversification and amounts to the assumption that for a manager to be indifferent between this type of option and a standard option, there would have to be a return for bearing unsystematic risk. Given that the CAPM is based on utility maximization, her model should be classified indirectly as a (dynamic) utility-based model.

Exogenous exercise models employ what essentially amounts to a barrier option approach to reflect the tendency of these options to be exercised early. These models have been developed by Carr and Linetsky (2000) and Raupach (2003) among others. Carpenter (1998) compares exogenous exercise models with static utility model and shows that the former give similar results at lower cost.

Another family of models adjusts the Black–Scholes–Merton or binomial frameworks to accommodate features of executive and employee stock options. Finnerty (2002), for example, treats the risk of forfeiture and early exercise as non-priced risks and shows how the Black–Scholes–Merton model can then be calibrated using empirical data on exercise and forfeiture. Hull and White (2004) take a similar approach using a trinomial tree implementation.

The most important and near-unanimous finding of these studies is that standard European option valuation techniques significantly overstate the values of these options. Although these options are all American and are frequently exercised early, their values are considerably less than the Black–Scholes–Merton model values, primarily due to the inability to trade the option. The differences vary widely depending on the models and inputs used but a range of 20–30% is fairly reasonable. The 30% figure may have arisen because of studies of discounts on illiquid stock, such as Silber's (1991) finding of an average discount of about a third for 69 private placements over the period 1981–1988. A study by Brenner, Eldor, and Hauser (2001) comparing the value of illiquid options that traded simultaneously side-by-side with comparable liquid options revealed a difference of about 21%.

While the accounting profession and many economists make a distinction between the value and cost of an executive stock option, this distinction is a subtle one. Consider a company that offers an executive an option with a Black–Scholes–Merton value of $5. Suppose that, due to illiquidity, the executive values the option at only $2. Is the cost to the company $5 or $2? The majority view seems to be that $5 is the correct answer. But if the cost is really $5, the situation is not Pareto-optimal. The company could sell the option to an outsider and give the executive the $5. The company would be no worse off, as $5 remains the cost, but the executive is better off. An alternative strategy would be for the company to buy the option in the open market for $5 and give it to the executive. The cost is the same, but the executive is happier than if he had been granted a standard executive stock option. Another alternative would be to give the executive $5 in cash.

In all three scenarios, the cost remains at $5, the same alleged cost of the executive stock option but the executive is happier. The difference between these scenarios and the executive stock option, however, is that the executive is not incentivized with the former while he is with the latter. For the three alternative scenarios, the executive either holds no options or holds a tradeable option; hence, there is no incentive to remain with the company. The $3 difference between the value of a traded option and the value of the executive stock option is precisely the value to the company of the incentives it grants the executive.

Unfortunately conventional accounting practice does not permit the firm to capitalize the value of incentives. To do so would double count because the benefits of incentives pay off later in increased cash flows. Thus, we might think of $2 as the net economic cost to the company and $5 as the accounting cost.

But this argument does not mean that the value of the option to the executive is unimportant. Understanding how executives value options is the essence of understanding the incentives. Options that executives value more highly presumably provide greater incentives. Moreover, executive stock option valuation forms at least the starting point for determining what motivates executives to take such actions as working harder, leaving the firm, or exercising their options early.

As noted, this paper focuses on the impact of liquidity on the valuation of executive stock options. We focus exclusively on the Black–Scholes–Merton model. For standard European options, little is gained by using the binomial model. The binomial option value is known to converge to the Black–Scholes–Merton option value for an infinite number of time periods. If improvements can be made to the Black–Scholes–Merton model, it follows that further refinements can be implemented using the binomial model. We leave those refinements to future research. We also focus exclusively on the question of how liquidity affects the value of the option. Vesting, forfeiture, volatility, and dividend estimation over a long period of time and several other factors make valuation of executive stock options more difficult than valuation of standard options. Nonetheless, we believe the primary issue of concern is the liquidity of the options.

This paper examines the question of whether the liquidity discount that is inherent in executive stock options can be incorporated into the Black–Scholes–Merton model. We begin by examining and comparing alternative benchmark models. These models provide the basis for assessing a benchmark value for an executive stock option. We proceed by examining the characteristics of differences between values produced by the Black–Scholes–Merton and benchmark models. We find that those characteristics are relatively invariant with respect to the factors captured in the utility models that are not captured in the Black–Scholes–Merton model. With this information, we then propose a variation of the Black–Scholes–Merton model by introducing an artificial dividend yield. We estimate how this pseudo-yield is affected by moneyness, time to expiration, and volatility. This process serves to capture the utility-specific factors in an indirect manner. We then use a hold-out sample of options to test whether the adjusted Black–Scholes–Merton model can reduce the differences between it and the utility-based models. In short, this study introduces a pseudo-yield parameter to calibrate the Black–Scholes–Merton model to utility-based models and thereby implicitly adjust for liquidity.

In Section 1 we provide an overview of the central issue of how liquidity affects the valuation of options in general and executive stock options in particular. Section 2 examines the utility model benchmark we use, exploring the model's sensitivity to input parameters. Section 3 examines the time series and cross sectional valuation errors of the Black–Scholes–Merton model to the utility benchmark.[1] It answers the question of whether zero is a better estimate of the true option value than the Black–Scholes–Merton value. It also examines the properties of how the errors in Black–Scholes–Merton values relative to the benchmark value decrease over time. Section 4 documents characteristics of these errors and uses them to develop a modified version of the Black–Scholes–Merton model that calibrates it to the utility benchmark. Section 5 provides our conclusions.

1. LIQUIDITY AND OPTION VALUE

In some contexts, this illiquidity of executive stock options is referred to as non-transferability. In others, the problem is cast in terms of the highly concentrated portfolios that managers hold, an implication of which is that managers could not trade the options to diversify. The notion of option liquidity usually conjures up images of trading pits at the Chicago Board Options Exchange or other exchanges. The existence of an active trading pit gives a powerful visual image of liquidity, but, as evidenced by the success of electronic options exchanges such as New York's International Securities Exchange and Frankfurt's EUREX, a trading pit is hardly a requirement for liquidity. The existence of a guaranteed market for standardized options as implied by options exchanges (whether pit-based or electronic) further gives a misleading appearance of high liquidity. There is also a very large market for customized over-the-counter options. It is a misconception to think that these options are not liquid when they are simply not standardized. If an investor can create a highly customized long position in an option, that investor should be able to create a highly customized short position in the same option at a later date before expiration. If both options are created through the same dealer, they will usually be treated as an offset, as they would if they were standardized options clearing through a clearinghouse. If the two transactions are not with the same dealer, they would both remain alive, but the market risks would offset. Only the credit risk, a factor we ignore in this paper, would remain. Hence, these seemingly illiquid options are, for all practical purposes, liquid.[2]

The statement that Black–Scholes–Merton does not apply to executive stock options because they cannot be traded is technically incorrect. The model does not apply to executive stock options, but the reason is not because the options cannot be traded. The Black–Scholes–Merton model technically does not require trading. Let the standard Black–Scholes–Merton assumptions apply such that a tradeable European call option value is given as c, the Black–Scholes–Merton value. Consider a firm that offers an executive a cash award of c dollars. Suppose the executive would prefer an option, however, so he simply takes the c dollars and purchases either an exchange-listed option, a customized over-the-counter option, or $N(d_1)$ shares of unrestricted stock and $N(d_2)$ bonds paying X at expiration, where $N(d_1)$ and $N(d_2)$ are the familiar Black–Scholes–Merton pseudo-probabilities. The exchange-listed and customized over-the-counter options would be liquid and would have a value given by the Black–Scholes–Merton formula. Under the third alternative, $N(d_1)$ and $N(d_2)$ change over time, and the executive would be required to continuously adjust the holdings of stock and bonds. At expiration, this combination would pay $\text{Max}(0, S_T - X)$ where S_T is the stock price at expiration and X is the exercise price. Clearly this combination of unrestricted stock and bonds would replicate the option. Hence, the option must be worth c.

But if the executive's circumstances or needs change during the life of the option, he might wish to sell it. He could, of course, sell the exchange-listed option, or he could create an offsetting position in the over-the-counter option. He could liquidate the combination of stocks and bonds. He could not, however, liquidate the actual executive stock option. This point initially seems to suggest a fallacy in the Black–Scholes–Merton model. By the above replicating arguments, the model seems to value the executive stock option correctly, but it fails to recognize a significant difference between the replicating instruments and the option itself.

Because it is preference-free, however, the Black–Scholes–Merton framework is incapable of accommodating any motivation to sell an option. In the Black–Scholes–Merton model, the only motivations for selling an option (or *buying* one) are to exploit an arbitrage opportunity or to adjust a dynamic hedge or replicating strategy. Selling to improve one's expected utility is not motivated within the model.

This apparent weakness in the model is reconciled, however, by remembering that the stock and risk-free bonds are perfect substitutes for the option. An executive who holds an option that he desires to sell can substitute the sale of unrestricted stock (and purchase of bonds). If the executive holds a sufficient number of unrestricted shares, the sale of stock can be accomplished by disposing of existing unrestricted shareholdings. Whether executives can do this, however, depends on their holdings of unrestricted stock relative to the number of options the executive desires to sell. That is an empirical question that we leave to future research.

Another means of selling the necessary shares is by selling short shares. But Section 16(c) of the Securities Exchange Act of 1934 prohibits executives from doing this. A third means of hedging the option would be by creating a short position in an identical option, perhaps through an over-the-counter options dealer. A fourth method would be by creating a short call by selling short a put and unrestricted stock and buying a risk-free bond. The Securities Exchange Act of 1934 permits executives to hedge stock positions, but by 17 C.F.R. 240.16c-4, they can do so only if the size of the options position does not exceed that of the underlying stock. Thus, an executive could use a covered call or protective put only to hedge a stock position and only if the number of options does not exceed the number of shares of stock. Hence, the executive could not legally sell calls or buy puts for the purpose of selling executive stock options.[3]

Within the Black–Scholes–Merton framework, the holder of the option can do any of these transactions. So it is not the inability to trade the option that makes the Black–Scholes–Merton model inapplicable to executive stock options. That the option is non-transferable is irrelevant. It is the inability to engage in synthetic sales of stock or other derivatives to offset the option.[4] Hence, it is a legal rather than an economic constraint that renders the Black–Scholes–Merton model problematic for valuing executive stock options.

In spite of the inability to directly apply the Black–Scholes–Merton model to executive stock options, we cannot rule out the possibility that the model can be altered in some way to make it applicable. But to determine if the model gives good values, whether adjusted or not, requires that we have a benchmark for the true value of the option.

2. A BENCHMARK MODEL

As noted in the introductory section, there are two types of utility models that can serve as a benchmark. Static utility models take the manager's personal portfolio as given and proceed to derive the option value. Dynamic utility models take the manager's portfolio as amenable to change, derive the optimum portfolio, and simultaneously value the option. Although a dynamic model would seem to be more general, there are reasonable arguments for using a static model. A static model is much simpler: the static model takes the manager's portfolio as given and determines the value of the option in the context of the existing portfolio. Dynamic utility models are considerably more demanding, both in terms of model complexity and information requirements. Static models have been widely used in the literature to address the problem of valuing executive stock options.

2.1. Selection of a Static Utility Benchmark Model

As noted, the first application of a static model in the context of executive stock options was Lambert et al. (1991). There have been a number of variations of the model since that time, each based on different assumptions about portfolio composition. We choose the version used by Hall and Murphy (2000, 2002) and provide an explanation here.

Hall and Murphy assume an executive with wealth of W consisting of B dollars invested in risk-free bonds at the rate r, q shares of stock priced at S, and n options expiring at T with exercise price X. Terminal wealth W_T, conditional on the stock price, S_T, is given as

$$W_T = B(1 + r)^T + qS_T + n\text{Max}(0, S_T - X)$$

The manager's utility is given by the power function

$$U(W_T) = \frac{W_T^{1-\lambda}}{1 - \lambda}$$

where λ is the coefficient of relative risk aversion. Hall and Murphy then propose that instead of being granted n options, the manager is given an amount of cash v. The terminal wealth from this compensation package is

$$W_T^v = (B + v)(1 + r)^T + qS_T$$

The value of the option is the amount v such that the cash compensation package has the same expected utility as the option compensation package:

$$\int_0^\infty U(W_T^v)\text{f}(S_T)\text{d}S_T = \int_0^\infty U(W_T)\text{f}(S_T)\text{d}S_T$$

Hall and Murphy assume that the stock return is distributed lognormally with expected return given by the capital asset pricing model. They then solve the above equation for v by a numerical integration scheme.

This model accounts for the illiquidity of the option but does not consider forfeiture or early exercise. Forfeiture, the risk that options will be abandoned because an executive is fired or resigns before the options are vested, is an extremely difficult factor to incorporate into valuation. Others have attempted to adjust option values to reflect the risk of forfeiture, but as Rubinstein (1995) points out, these adjustments assume that all parties are neutral toward this risk, which is hardly the case.[5] There is no obvious solution to the forfeiture problem in this model or any of the other models, so like most other models we do not address this factor here. Hall and

Murphy do not consider early exercise in this model, opting to evaluate only liquidity considerations. They do consider early exercise later in their paper.

Early exercise can be easily incorporated into a binomial utility model, as shown in Huddart (1994) and Kulatilaka and Marcus (1994). At node ij where i is state i and j is time j, the holder of the option decides whether the expected utility at time $j+1$, conditional on exercising in state i at time j is greater than the expected utility at time $j+1$, conditional on not exercising in state i at time j. If the expected utility from exercising is greater, the exercise value of the option is designated as the value of the option in state ij. Hall and Murphy take this approach later in their paper, but their primary results are based on the assumption of no early exercise, wherein the differential between the Black–Scholes–Merton and benchmark values would be completely accounted for by the liquidity assumption. Interestingly, if early exercise were incorporated into the benchmark model and not into the Black–Scholes–Merton model, the difference between the two models would appear to be less. The Black–Scholes–Merton model value will normally be higher than the benchmark value because the benchmark value does not permit trading. Since the Black–Scholes–Merton model cannot accommodate early exercise and since early exercise raises the value of an option, the Black–Scholes–Merton value would be closer to the benchmark value if we incorporated early exercise into the latter. The adjustment would appear to be an improvement, but it is a misleading one. The gap between the two values is due to liquidity, because it would exist even if the option were European-style. If the gap is narrowed because we allowed early exercise into the benchmark, we may be misled into thinking that the gap is smaller than it really is. Therefore, by omitting early exercise from the benchmark model, we can focus on the value differential due to liquidity and not bias our results.

On the surface, the static utility model appears to suffer from another limitation not noted by its authors. Suppose an executive is given a choice of compensation package A, which consists of an illiquid European-style call option expiring in T years, and compensation package B, which consists of a share of stock and a loan at the risk-free rate r maturing in T years. Which package would the executive choose?

The payoff of package A is $\max(0, S_T - X)$. The payoff of package B is $S_T - X$. Package A clearly dominates package B, because its payoff is zero in the state in which $S_T < X$, while package B pays off $S_T - X$, which is negative in that state. If package A is valued more, then it must be worth at least $S_t - X(1 + r)^{-T}$. Hence, package B establishes a basis for determining the minimum value of the option. Students of derivatives will recognize this result as simply the lower bound of a European call. Yet a few simple side calculations using Hall and Murphy's examples (see, e.g., Fig. 1, p. 11) show numerous violations of this rule. What seems puzzling is that trading is not required to establish the lower bound rule. We showed that an executive would value package *A* at least as high as package *B*, with no trading at the grant date or during the life of the option. Thus, the Hall–Murphy static utility model would seem to be inconsistent with rational preferences.

To resolve this conundrum, it must be assumed that the stock in package *B* is illiquid. Hence, it should be either restricted or illiquid stock or stock that the manager simply chooses not to sell. Thus, the static utility model can value either options or restricted stock.[6]

It is tempting to wonder if a static utility model could recover the Black–Scholes–Merton version if conditions were right. As Henderson (2005) has noted, however, static utility models do not recover the Black–Scholes–Merton model for risk neutral investors ($\lambda = 0$). This result occurs, however, because even risk neutral investors require liquidity. The illiquidity of these options is built into the expected utility analysis. A properly specified dynamic expected utility model would recover the Black–Scholes–Merton value, even for risk averse investors, provided the options are liquid, but of course, we wish to study illiquid options.[7]

2.2. Testing the Benchmark Model

Having chosen the Hall–Murphy model as a benchmark candidate, we proceed to examine some properties of the model. The model requires the standard six inputs specified by the Black–Scholes–Merton model: stock price, exercise price, risk-free rate, time to expiration, stock volatility, and dividend yield.[8] The Hall–Murphy model also requires six additional inputs: the market risk premium, the stock beta, the number of options granted, the executive's total wealth not counting the options, the percentage of the executive's wealth invested in stock, and the coefficient of relative risk aversion.[9] Some of these variables are easy to measure. The stock price, exercise price, risk-free rate, time to expiration, and the number of options granted are straightforward. The dividend yield, the executive's wealth, and the percentage of wealth invested in stock are somewhat more difficult to obtain but should be measurable with high accuracy. The market risk premium, stock beta, volatility, and coefficient of relative risk aversion are, however, subject to considerable measurement error. A worthwhile starting point is to examine the errors in the benchmark that could occur if these variables are measured with error.

In this paper, we select a standard case of a risk-free rate of 6%, a market risk premium of 6.5%, a beta of 1.0, a volatility of 30%, 5000 options granted, executive wealth of $5 million, and 50% of wealth invested in stock. Corresponding with the approach taken elsewhere in the literature, we assume no dividends. These input values are those used by Hall and Murphy, though we choose a different exercise price, $50 versus $30 in their paper. Hall and Murphy examine relative risk aversions of 2 and 3, while we use a value of 2.5.

As a criterion for examining the robustness of the benchmark, we assume that there is a true value of the option based on these input parameters. We then allow one parameter at a time to be entered incorrectly into the model. We calculate the value of the option using both the utility model and the Black–Scholes–Merton model. We compare the valuation error using the utility model relative to the benchmark, with the error using the Black–Scholes–Merton model relative to the benchmark. If the utility model is a good benchmark, we should not find that errors in the inputs move the Black–Scholes–Merton model closer to the true value of the option than the utility model. Although not a sufficient condition for a good benchmark model, it is almost surely a necessary one. As noted we vary the inputs that are potentially subject to error, which are the volatility, the relative risk aversion, the market risk premium, and the beta.

Panel A of Table 1 contains four sections that show the difference in the absolute values of the percentage Black–Scholes–Merton error minus the absolute value of the percentage error for the power utility model, with all errors relative to the benchmark, assuming these four inputs are measured separately with error. Because of consistent results and to conserve space we show only the cases of options at-the-money and 50% in- and out-of-the-money, as well as options with 10, 5, and 1 year to expiration. We do not show the results for in- and out-of-the-money options at 10 years since these options, for all practical purposes, never exist. Positive values indicate that the Black–Scholes–Merton model is further from the true value than the utility model. Negative values are cause for alarm for they indicate that input errors make the utility model further away from the true value than the Black–Scholes–Merton model.

In all cases in which we vary an input not associated with the Black–Scholes–Merton model (relative risk aversion, market risk premium, and beta), the utility model is closer to the true value than is the Black–Scholes–Merton model. This is a particularly interesting result, because we injected

Table 1. Sensitivity of the Utility Benchmark Model to Input Parameters.

		Time to Expiration (years)				
	10	5	1	10	5	1
Panel A: True value is power utility						
			σ (true) = 30%			
		σ (used) = 20%			σ (used) = 40%	
50% ITM	NA	−9.60	−2.16	NA	29.20	3.99
ATM	−20.78	−11.46	2.01	88.62	73.31	58.88
50% OTM	NA	−4.68	0.00	NA	321.71	717.07
			λ (true) = 2.5			
		λ (used) = 2			λ (used) = 3	
50% ITM	NA	36.30	9.64	NA	39.64	9.93
ATM	78.01	53.34	19.26	87.02	58.59	20.23
50% OTM	NA	125.46	74.46	NA	138.79	81.15
			RP (true) = 6.5%			
		RP (used) = 5%			RP (used) = 8%	
50% ITM	NA	45.04	12.32	NA	44.37	12.30
ATM	94.16	65.87	24.52	91.94	64.69	24.34
50% OTM	NA	151.15	91.74	NA	148.06	90.26
			β (true) = 1.00			
		β (used) = 0.75			β (used) = 1.25	
50% ITM	NA	44.22	12.03	NA	43.43	12.01
ATM	92.78	64.86	24.03	90.27	63.47	23.82
50% OTM	NA	149.76	90.73	NA	146.13	89.00
Panel B: True utility is negative exponential with absolute risk aversion of 0.0000005						
			λ (true) = 2.5			
		λ (used) = 2			λ (used) = 3	
50% ITM	NA	40.85	9.34	NA	972.66	279.67
ATM	137.52	64.36	18.38	449.03	197.95	48.96
50% OTM	NA	224.25	81.75	NA	114.72	23.69

Notes: The following inputs are used for the standard case: exercise price = $50; risk-free rate = 6%; time to expiration = 10, 5, 1; volatility (σ) = 30%; dividend yield = 0%; executive wealth = $5,000,000; percentage of executive wealth in stock (%W) = 50%; number of options = 5000; market risk premium (RP) = 6.5%, beta (β) = 1.0; relative risk aversion (λ) = 2.5. Some of these values are varied as indicated. The true value of the option is obtained using a power utility model with the standard inputs, except as noted in Panel B. The percentage indicated is the absolute value of the percentage difference between the Black–Scholes–Merton and the true value minus the absolute value of the percentage difference between the utility model with erroneous inputs and the true value. Positive (negative) errors indicate that the utility (Black–Scholes–Merton) model with erroneous inputs is closer to the true option value. ITM, ATM, OTM refer to "it-the-money", "at-the-money," and "out-of-the-money".

errors into the utility model and none into the Black–Scholes–Merton model and yet the utility model gave option values closer to the true value than did the Black–Scholes–Merton model. When we change volatility, however, we do see some cases in which the Black–Scholes–Merton model now moves closer to the true value than the utility model. These cases occur when the volatility used is lower than the true volatility. This finding suggests that, as sensitive as the Black–Scholes–Merton model is known to be to the volatility, the utility model may be even more sensitive. This result probably occurs because the volatility has a positive effect on the payoff of the option but also affects the expected return of the stock. Thus, it enters into the utility model in two places, so it has more potential for causing errors. Later we shall see that low volatility is the source of a critical problem in valuing executing stock options.

For errors in the variables not included in the Black–Scholes–Merton model, there is a consistent pattern of attenuation over time, which means that the Black–Scholes–Merton model converges more rapidly to the true value over time. The accuracy also changes consistently with respect to moneyness. The higher the stock price, the lower is the difference. For volatility errors, the patterns are not as consistent. For high volatility, the errors are greater the longer the time to expiration and the lower the stock price. For low volatility, the errors are greater the longer the time to expiration, but the moneyness effect is difficult to judge. Clearly volatility exerts an erratic impact, which will return as an important issue later in the paper.

Nonetheless, the benchmark model seems relatively robust to input errors, particularly errors in its own input values that are not associated with Black–Scholes–Merton. Even when volatility is measured with error, the utility model is not necessarily worse than the Black–Scholes–Merton model.

Now let us consider what happens if we use the wrong utility model. A reasonable alternative utility model is the negative exponential of the form:

$$U(W_T) = -\frac{1}{\gamma}e^{-\gamma W_T}$$

where γ is now the coefficient of absolute risk aversion.[10] Suppose the true utility function is the negative exponential, but we mistakenly employ the power utility function. As a benchmark, let us calibrate the negative exponential model to the power utility model. For the power utility model, we assumed a coefficient of relative risk aversion of 2.5 and a level of executive wealth of $5 million. These values imply a level of absolute risk aversion of 2.5/$5,000,000 = 0.0000005. As noted, in the negative exponential utility model, γ is the coefficient of absolute risk aversion. Therefore, let us use a value of γ of 0.0000005.[11] So now we assume that the true utility function is the negative exponential with $\gamma = 0.0000005$. We solve the integral equation for the certainty equivalent value of the option. We then compare the error in using the Black–Scholes–Merton model to the error in using the power utility model with errors in the coefficient of risk aversion. Panel B of Table 1 presents these results.

We see that even when using the wrong utility function, we still obtain better estimates of the true value of the option using the utility model than using the Black–Scholes–Merton model. The errors monotonically reduce over time. For low risk aversion, we observe a lower difference the higher the stock price; for high risk aversion, we observe a lower difference the lower the stock price.

It is impossible to provide an incontrovertible verification of a benchmark model. As long as the true value is not observable, any choice of a benchmark to estimate the value will almost surely contain error. The analysis here shows that at the very least, the static power utility benchmark model is likely to be closer to the true value than the Black–Scholes–Merton model even with input errors or an erroneous utility function. Of course, that result in no way completely validates the benchmark model, but a failure to pass this test would certainly invalidate it. The literature is replete with benchmark models that take their values as given. Here we have chosen one benchmark model, provided a sensitivity analysis, and observed reasonably stable performance of the model. We now have a more confident basis for evaluating the accuracy of the Black–Scholes–Merton model.

3. AN ANALYSIS OF BLACK–SCHOLES–MERTON VALUATION ERRORS

With the benchmark established, we can now proceed to examine the properties of Black–Scholes–Merton errors over time. One of the first questions of interest is whether valuation with the Black–Scholes–Merton model is better than assuming a value of zero. Such an argument has been used to support the notion that not expensing options is better than expensing them. We can examine this issue by calculating the absolute value of the percentage difference of the Black–Scholes–Merton value to the benchmark value. If this number exceeds 100%, the Black–Scholes–Merton model is further from the true value than is zero.[12]

3.1. Black–Scholes–Merton is Better than Zero?

When the question of whether not expensing is better is raised, the information is based on the value of the option at the time it is granted. Thus, we address the question using a 10-year option. Since all options are issued at-the-money, we consider only at-the-money options. Table 2 provides the percentage errors for a wide range of inputs.[13]

In Panel A, we use the Black–Scholes–Merton model with the full maturity of 10 years. We see that there is a basis for the case that zero is closer to the true value than is the Black–Scholes–Merton model. For the standard set of inputs, the error is 110%. When varying these inputs, the error is still frequently over 100%. The error is larger, the lower the risk-free rate, the lower the beta, the higher the volatility, the higher the percentage of wealth invested in stock, the lower the market risk premium, and the higher the relative risk aversion.

The Financial Accounting Standards Board now encourages the use of the expected expiration of the option as the time to expiration when using the Black–Scholes–Merton model to expense options. In Panel B we examine the percentage errors using a time to expiration of 5.8 years, the average used by Carpenter (2000) taken from a sample of actual option exercises over the period 1979–1994. In this case, we see that most of the values are below 100%. In the most extreme cases, however, the values exceed 100%. But for a typical stock (as Hall and Murphy's inputs are supposed to represent), the error is less than 100%. Thus, the Black–Scholes–Merton model does seem to give a value closer to the true value than zero for most reasonable cases.

The relative errors in Table 2 are quite large, however and suggest more generally that the Black–Scholes–Merton model could be a poor method of valuing executive stock options. Recall that these errors are at the grant date. We know that at expiration, the Black–Scholes–Merton model will value the option correctly at its exercise value. Thus, the errors must reduce over time, though that reduction might not be monotonic and it might occur slowly. Let us take a look at how the Black–Scholes–Merton errors reduce over time.

Table 2. Black–Scholes–Merton versus a Value of Zero Relative to the Benchmark.

Panel A: Using maturity of 10 years in the Black–Scholes–Merton model (standard case % = 110.71)

$r=4\%$	$r=8\%$
126.04	98.79
$\beta=0.75$	$\beta=1.25$
156.46	74.95
$\sigma=20\%$	$\sigma=40\%$
10.07	364.71
$\%W=33\%$	$\%W=67\%$
38.59	240.41
$RP=5\%$	$RP=7\%$
152.51	77.41
$\lambda=2$	$\lambda=3$
58.79	176.14

Panel B: Using maturity of 5.8 years (average time to exercise) in the Black–Scholes–Merton model (standard case % = 85.71)

$r=4\%$	$r=8\%$
92.63	78.73
$\beta=0.75$	$\beta=1.25$
116.81	59.32
$\sigma=20\%$	$\sigma=40\%$
7.70	258.32
$\%W=33\%$	$\%W=67\%$
29.66	175.49
$RP=5\%$	$RP=7\%$
114.13	61.14
$\lambda=2$	$\lambda=3$
45.89	134.16

Notes: The following inputs are used for the standard case: exercise price $(X)=\$50$; risk-free rate $(r)=6\%$; time to expiration $=10$, 5, 1; volatility $(\sigma)=30\%$; dividend yield $=0\%$; executive wealth $=\$5,000,000$; percentage of executive wealth in stock $(\%W)=50\%$; number of options $=5000$; market risk premium $(RP)=6.5\%$, beta $(\beta)=1.0$; relative risk aversion $(\lambda)=2.5$. Some of these values are varied as indicated below. The true value of the option is obtained using a power utility model with the standard inputs. The percentage indicated is the absolute value of the percentage difference between the Black–Scholes–Merton and benchmark values. Percentages larger than 100% indicate that zero is closer to the true option value than is the Black–Scholes–Merton model.

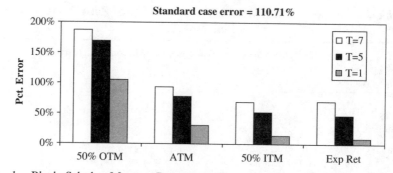

Fig. 1. Black–Scholes–Merton Percentage Error by Time and Moneyness for Standard Case. *Note:* The Following Inputs are Used for the Base Case: Exercise Price = $50; Risk-Free Rate = 6%; Time to Expiration = 7, 5, 1; Volatility = 30%; Dividend Yield = 0%; Executive Wealth = $5,000,000; Percentage of Executive Wealth in Stock (%W) = 50%; Number of Options = 5000; Market Risk Premium (RP) = 6.5%, Beta = 1.0; Relative Risk Aversion (λ) = 2.5. The Cases Examined are Options 50% out-of-the-Money, at-the-Money, 50% in-the-Money, and the Condition that the Stock has Grown at its Expected Return. The Percentage Indicated is the Absolute Value of the Percentage Difference between the Black–Scholes–Merton and the Benchmark Value.

3.2. Black–Scholes–Merton Errors Over Time

Fig. 1 shows the percentage difference between the Black–Scholes–Merton value and the benchmark value for the base case, using the standard inputs discussed above and the full 10-year maturity in the Black–Scholes–Merton model. The base case error value, which refers to the error of the 10-year at-the-money option, is 110.71%. The series illustrated show the percentage errors for 7, 5, and 1 year to expiration for options 50% out-of-the-money, at-the-money, 50% in-the-money, and the case in which the stock price has moved at its expected return. We see for all cases the rate of descent of the Black–Scholes–Merton value toward the benchmark value. The errors are the largest for out-of-the-money options. Options that are at-the-money and 50% in-the-money give similar results. The error decay is somewhat slow at the start, but does seem to drop off rapidly, but this result should be interpreted with caution because the differences in time increments are not equal.

Figs. 2–6 show the same graph while varying the inputs. In all cases, a consistent pattern is revealed. The errors decline monotonically through time, but the rate of reduction is somewhat slow at the start. The results for

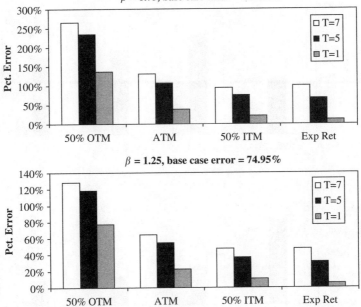

Fig. 2. Black–Scholes–Merton Errors with Different Betas. *Note:* The Following Inputs are used: Exercise Price = $50; Risk-Free Rate = 6%; time to Expiration = 7, 5, 1; Volatility = 30%; Dividend Yield = 0%; Executive Wealth = $5,000,000; Percentage of Executive Wealth in Stock = 50%; Number of Options = 5000; Market Risk Premium = 6.5%, Relative Risk Aversion = 2.5. The Cases Examined are Options 50% out-of-the-Money, at-the-Money, 50% in-the-Money, and the Condition that the stock has Grown at its Expected Return. The Percentage Indicated is the Absolute Value of the Percentage Difference between the Black–Scholes–Merton and the Benchmark Value. The Base Value Error is for Options Issued at-the-Money with 10 Years to Expiration Given the Beta Indicated.

the case when the stock moves at its expected return are very similar to those for the case of options that are 50% at-the-money. The errors are quite large for options 50% out-of-the-money. The errors are so much larger for those options, because their values are often very close to zero, where percentage errors are somewhat magnified. We also observe that the errors are particularly sensitive to the volatility, the percentage of executive wealth, and the risk aversion. The errors are somewhat less sensitive to the beta and the market risk premium, though even in those cases, they have a significant degree of sensitivity.

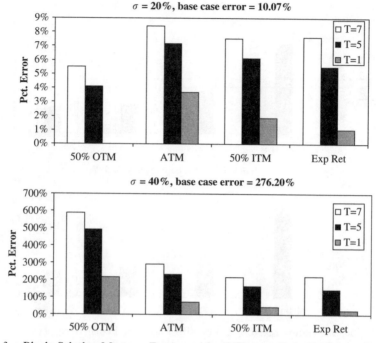

Fig. 3. Black–Scholes–Merton Errors with Different Volatilities. *Note:* The Following Inputs are Used: Exercise Price = $50; Risk-Free Rate = 6%; Time to Expiration = 7, 5, 1; Dividend Yield = 0%; Executive Wealth = $5,000,000; Percentage of Executive Wealth in Stock = 50%; Number of Options = 5000; Market Risk Premium = 6.5%, Beta = 1.0; Relative Risk Aversion = 2.5. The Cases Examined are Options 50% out-of-the-Money, at-the-Money, 50% in-the-Money, and the Condition that the Stock has Grown at its Expected Return. The Percentage Indicated is the Absolute Value of the Percentage Difference between the Black–Scholes–Merton and the Benchmark Value. The Base Value Error is for Options Issued at-the-Money with 10 years to Expiration Given the Volatility Indicated.

Although the Black–Scholes–Merton model will eventually converge to the true option value over time, the rate of convergence seems relatively slow at the start. For example, for the base case, the error is over 110% at the start, about 94% at year seven, almost 79% at year five, and 30% with but one year to go. The errors seem exceptionally large for high volatility stocks, low beta stocks, high executive wealth percentage, and high risk aversion.

Table 3 provides details for the base case results with a wide degree of moneyness and by varying volatility from 20% to 30% to 40%. We observe

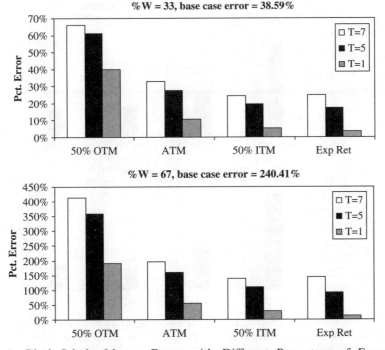

Fig. 4. Black–Scholes–Merton Errors with Different Percentage of Executive Wealth Invested in Stock. *Note:* The Following Inputs are Used: Exercise Price = $50; Risk-Free Rate = 6%; Time to Expiration = 7, 5, 1; Volatility = 30%; Dividend Yield = 0%; Executive Wealth = $5,000,000; Number of Options = 5000; Market Risk Premium = 6.5%, Beta = 1.0; Relative Risk Aversion = 2.5. The Cases Examined are Options 50% out-of-the-Money, at-the-Money, 50% in-the-Money, and the Condition that the Stock has Grown at its Expected Return. The Percentage Indicated is the Absolute Value of the Percentage Difference between the Black–Scholes–Merton and the Benchmark Value. The Base Value Error is for Options Issued at-the-Money with 10 Years to Expiration Given the Wealth Percentage Indicated.

an interesting pattern. In all cases, the errors are larger, the longer the time to expiration. For volatilities of 30% and 40%, the errors are larger the lower the stock price and the larger the volatility. For a volatility of 20%, however, there is no apparent relationship between moneyness and the errors. Moreover, the errors are not greater the greater is the volatility, when the 20% case is considered compared to the 30% case. Further examination reveals that this unusual effect at 20% volatility arises because it is at

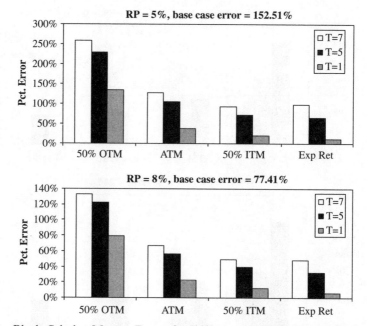

Fig. 5. Black–Scholes–Merton Errors for Different Market Risk Premiums. *Note:*
The Following Inputs are Used for the Base Case: Exercise Price = $50; Risk-Free
Rate = 6%; Time to Expiration = 7, 5, 1; Volatility = 30%; Dividend Yield = 0%;
Executive Wealth = $5,000,000; Percentage of Executive Wealth in Stock = 50%;
Number of Options = 5000; Beta = 1.0; Relative Risk Aversion = 2.5. The Cases
Examined are Options 50% out-of-the-Money, at-the-Money, 50% in-the-Money,
and the Condition that the Stock has Grown at its Expected Return. The Percentage
Indicated is the Absolute Value of the Percentage Difference between the Black–
Scholes–Merton and the Benchmark Value. The Base Value Error is for Options
Issued at-the-Money with 10 Years to Expiration Given the Wealth Percentage
Indicated.

approximately that point that the Black–Scholes–Merton value falls below
the benchmark value. For all other combinations, that is, while varying all
other input variables, we see a clear pattern that the percentage errors are
greater the longer the time to expiration, the lower the stock price, and the
greater the volatility. The time to expiration and volatility effects seem the
strongest, but the moneyness effect is also strong, except when volatility is
low. These relationships can be exploited in explaining the errors in the
Black–Scholes–Merton model relative to the benchmark.

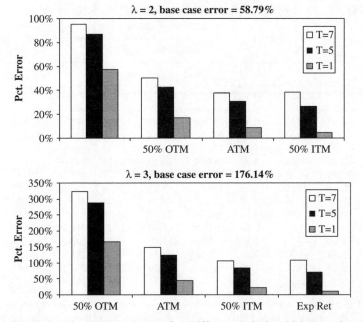

Fig. 6. Black–Scholes–Merton Errors for Different Relative Risk Aversions. *Note:* The Following Inputs are Used: Exercise Price = \$50; Risk-Free Rate = 6%; Time to Expiration = 7, 5, 1; Volatility = 30%; Dividend Yield = 0%; Executive Wealth = \$5,000,000; Percentage of Executive Wealth in Stock = 50%; Number of Options = 5000; Market Risk Premium = 6.5%, Beta = 1.0. The Cases Examined are Options 50% out-of-the-Money, at-the-Money, 50% in-the-Money, and the Condition that the Stock has Grown at its Expected Return. The Percentage Indicated is the Absolute Value of the Percentage Difference between the Black–Scholes–Merton and the Benchmark Value. The Base Value Error is for Options Issued at-the-Money with 10 Years to Expiration Given the Relative Risk Aversion Indicated.

4. CALIBRATING THE BLACK–SCHOLES–MERTON MODEL TO THE BENCHMARK

As noted above, the percentage errors seem related to the time to expiration and are usually related to the moneyness. They are also usually related to the volatility, except that this relationship is somewhat different at low volatility. But these errors could also be related to the variables that are not

Table 3.   Percentage Difference between Black–Scholes–Merton and
Benchmark Values.

S/X	$\sigma = 20\%$			$\sigma = 30\%$			$\sigma = 40\%$		
				Time to expiration					
	10	5	1	10	5	1	10	5	1
0.40	−4.63	−0.13	0.00	257.74	224.07	152.90	882.71	652.02	310.67
0.50	−7.58	−4.13	0.00	203.91	169.44	104.49	689.38	492.04	215.31
0.60	−9.03	−6.06	−4.21	170.54	136.21	75.97	571.80	396.51	160.36
0.70	−9.73	−6.94	−4.90	148.04	114.19	57.74	493.46	333.81	125.54
0.80	−10.03	−7.27	−4.76	131.96	98.68	45.42	437.86	289.87	101.95
0.90	−10.11	−7.30	−4.28	119.96	87.28	36.74	396.53	257.57	85.17
1.00	−10.07	−7.19	−3.70	110.71	78.60	30.44	364.71	232.94	72.80
1.10	−9.97	−6.99	−3.16	103.39	71.82	25.76	339.51	213.62	63.41
1.20	−9.83	−6.77	−2.70	97.48	66.40	22.23	319.10	198.10	56.13
1.30	−9.68	−6.54	−2.34	92.61	61.99	19.52	302.27	185.38	50.38
1.40	−9.53	−6.32	−2.07	88.55	58.34	17.41	288.17	174.81	45.77
1.50	−9.39	−6.12	−1.86	85.11	55.29	15.76	276.20	165.89	42.02
1.60	−9.25	−5.93	−1.70	82.18	52.71	14.45	265.93	158.28	38.93

Notes: The following inputs are used for the standard case: exercise price $(X) = \$50$; risk-free rate $(r) = 6\%$; dividend yield $= 0\%$; executive wealth $= \$5,000,000$; percentage of executive wealth in stock $(\%W) = 50\%$; number of options $= 5000$; market risk premium $(RP) = 6.5\%$, beta $(\beta) = 1.0$; relative risk aversion $(\lambda) = 2.5$. Some of these values are varied as indicated. The true value of the option is obtained using a power utility model with the standard inputs. The value shown is the Black–Scholes–Merton value minus the benchmark value divided by the benchmark value.

included within the Black–Scholes–Merton model. Let us examine the effect of varying these inputs.

Table 4 contains separate panels showing the value of the option as provided by the benchmark model for a broad range of values of the six variables that are not associated with the Black–Scholes–Merton model: the number of options granted, the level of executive wealth, the percentage of wealth invested in stock, the beta, the market risk premium, and the relative risk aversion. The standard values of these inputs are 5000 options granted, $5 million executive wealth, 50% of executive wealth invested in stock, beta of 1, market risk premium of 2.5, and relative risk aversion of 2.5. We use the standard set of Black–Scholes–Merton variables, which produces a Black–Scholes–Merton value of $27.58. Thus, we examine the table values for cases in which the benchmark value is below $27.58.

Table 4. Benchmark Model Values for a Range of Values of Variables not in the Black–Scholes–Merton Model.

Value of Input	Benchmark Value of Option
Panel A: Number of options	
1	13.46
5,000	13.09
50,000	10.63
100,000	8.93
Panel B: Level of executive wealth	
$1,000,000	11.83
$5,000,000	13.09
$50,000,000	13.42
$100,000,000	13.44
Panel C: Percentage of wealth invested in stock	
10%	**36.77**
20%	27.56
33%	19.90
50%	13.09
67%	8.10
90%	2.94
Panel D: Beta	
0.50	8.73
1.00	13.09
1.50	18.80
2.00	26.09
2.50	**35.17**
Panel E: Market risk premium	
1%	6.41
5%	10.92
9%	17.35
12%	23.67
15%	**31.45**
Panel F: Relative risk aversion	
1.0	**32.13**
1.5	23.40
2.0	17.37
2.5	13.09
3.0	9.99

Notes: The following inputs are used for the standard case: exercise price $(X) = \$50$; risk-free rate $(r) = 6\%$; time to expiration $= 10$; volatility $(\sigma) = 30\%$; dividend yield $= 0\%$; executive wealth $= \$5,000,000$; percentage of executive wealth in stock $(\%W) = 50\%$; number of options $= 5000$; market risk premium $(RP) = 6.5\%$, beta $(\beta) = 1.0$; relative risk aversion $(\lambda) = 2.5$. Some of these values are varied as indicated. The true value of the option is obtained using a power utility model with the standard inputs. Under these assumptions, the Black–Scholes–Merton value is $27.58. Benchmark values that exceed this value are indicated in bold.

In Panel A, we see that the value of the input is somewhat insensitive to the number of options granted. The option is worth $13.46 if a single option is granted, $13.09 if 5000 options are granted, $10.63 if 50,000 options are granted, and $8.93 if 100,000 options are granted. Thus, the benchmark value of the option changes very slowly with the number of options granted. More importantly, however, the benchmark value of the option seems incapable of exceeding the Black–Scholes–Merton value. In Panel B, we see that the benchmark value is not very sensitive to the level of executive wealth. At $50 million, the option is worth only $13.42 and increases to only $13.44 at $100 million of wealth. In Panel C, we do see a significant sensitivity of the benchmark value to the percentage of wealth invested in stock. At 20%, the benchmark value is approximately the Black–Scholes–Merton value, and at 10%, the benchmark value exceeds the Black–Scholes–Merton value. In practice, however, such levels of executive wealth invested in the stock are unlikely to be observed. In Panel D, we see that the benchmark value is directly related to the beta and exceeds the Black–Scholes–Merton value at a beta a little over 2. Again, in practice, such betas are not commonly seen.[14] In Panel E, we see that the benchmark value is directly related to the market risk premium and exceeds the Black–Scholes–Merton value for a risk premium of more than 12%. Again, this value seems unreasonable in light of historical stock market performance. In Panel F, the benchmark value is seen to be inversely related to the relative risk aversion, but a risk aversion of less than 1.5 is required for the benchmark value to exceed the Black–Scholes–Merton value. Most economists agree that relative risk aversion should be in the range of 2–3.

The results of Table 4 seem to suggest that the variables not contained within the Black–Scholes–Merton model do not explain how the Black–Scholes–Merton value can be below the benchmark value, at least not for reasonable ranges of these variables. Now let us see how the Black–Scholes–Merton variables are related to the condition that the Black–Scholes–Merton value is below the benchmark value. These variables are contained within both models and can contribute to the Black–Scholes–Merton value being relatively low and/or the benchmark value being relatively high.

The variables of interest to us are the moneyness (which jointly reflects the stock price and exercise price), the volatility, and the time to expiration. In keeping with most other studies, we do not assume any dividends (their effect being equivalent to a lower stock price). The risk-free rate imparts a very mild effect on the Black–Scholes–Merton value and the benchmark value. Experiments reveal no risk-free rate that can generate a Black–Scholes–Merton value below the benchmark value, except by altering other variables.

Table 5 shows the difference between the Black–Scholes–Merton value and the benchmark value (negative values indicate the Black–Scholes–Merton value is smaller) for different combinations of moneyness, time to expiration, and volatility and more granularity in the moneyness and time to expiration. Unlike Table 4 where the Black–Scholes–Merton value is constant, the Black–Scholes–Merton values vary in this table. The numbers in the table show the difference between the Black–Scholes–Merton value and the benchmark value. Negative values are cases in which the Black–Scholes–Merton value falls below the benchmark value. We see that this condition occurs only when the volatility is 20%. Most of the negative cases are for options that are at- or in-the-money, but some cases occur for options out-of-the-money, particularly if the time to expiration is long.

Given this aberrant behavior when the volatility is 20%, we need to look further at how even lower volatilities would affect these results. In Table 6 we examine the differences for volatilities of 10%, 15%, and 20%, for maturities of 10, 7, 5, 3, and 1 year, and various degrees of moneyness. We see that the lower the volatility, the more negative this number becomes, the longer the time to expiration, the more negative is the number, and the larger is the stock price, the more negative is the number.

A further analysis with finer variations in volatility reveals that this effect starts at around 21%. Thus, in adjusting the stock price, we must find a way to account for these relationships when the volatility is 20–21% or lower. We should also account for the moneyness and time to expiration, which could affect the model's performance differently for low volatilities.[15]

So far our findings suggest that it may be possible to adjust the Black–Scholes–Merton value based on these variables. Although such an adjustment would seem arbitrary, there may be a strong basis for doing so. Anecdotal evidence suggests that professional option traders frequently adjust the volatility to account for biases in the model. The volatility smile is one such adjustment. Volatility is unique. It cannot vary, what more vary across options differing only by exercise price. But traders seem to know that certain options should be more or less expensive than others, and they adjust the volatility accordingly.

The models of Ingersoll (2006) and Detemple and Sundaresan (1999) derive a utility maximizing value for an executive stock option, and show that factors beyond those included in the Black–Scholes–Merton model manifest in the form of an artificial dividend yield. Ordinarily a dividend yield adjusts the stock price by reducing it by the present value of the

Table 5.   Difference between Black–Scholes–Merton and Benchmark
Option Values for Different Values of Variables Included in the
Black–Scholes–Merton Model.

	Moneyness (S/X)						
	0.25	0.50	0.75	1.00	1.25	1.50	1.75
$\sigma = 20\%$							
1 year	0.00	0.00	−0.03	−0.21	−0.40	−0.53	−0.62
3 years	0.00	−0.01	−0.22	−0.68	−1.14	−1.52	−1.84
5 years	0.00	−0.06	−0.52	−1.21	−1.89	−2.49	−3.04
7 years	0.01	−0.16	−0.87	−1.79	−2.67	−3.47	−4.22
10 years	0.04	−0.43	−1.51	−2.72	−3.87	−4.95	−5.97
$\sigma = 30\%$							
1 year	0.00	0.03	0.54	1.71	2.96	3.85	4.64
3 years	0.03	0.81	2.77	5.16	7.50	9.67	11.69
5 years	0.24	2.11	5.09	8.28	11.38	14.34	17.20
7 years	0.65	3.52	7.24	11.02	14.70	18.26	21.74
10 years	1.49	5.54	10.04	14.49	18.83	23.08	27.27
$\sigma = 40\%$							
1 year	0.00	0.22	1.55	3.87	6.37	8.66	10.69
3 years	0.22	2.25	5.97	10.39	14.94	19.43	23.79
5 years	0.89	4.63	9.82	15.49	21.24	26.96	32.61
7 years	1.78	6.84	13.05	19.58	26.16	32.72	39.23
10 years	3.17	9.69	16.96	24.40	31.84	39.27	46.66

Notes: The following inputs are used for the standard case: exercise price (X) = $50; risk-free
rate (r) = 6%; dividend yield = 0%; executive wealth = $5,000,000; percentage of executive
wealth in stock (%W) = 50%; number of options = 5000; market risk premium (RP) = 6.5%,
beta (β) = 1.0; relative risk aversion (λ) = 2.5. Some of these values are varied as indicated. The
true value of the option is obtained using a power utility model with the standard inputs. The
value shown is the Black–Scholes–Merton value minus the benchmark value. Negative values
indicate options in which the benchmark value is greater.

dividends. In the context of the Ingersoll and Detemple–Sundaresan models,
however, their adjustment is dependent on variables not included within the
Black–Scholes–Merton model, particularly the utility function.

We believe that any adjustment to the Black–Scholes–Merton model or
any alternative model that requires variables specific to a utility function is
not likely to provide a practical solution for valuing executive stock options.
Nonetheless, such variables are, as we have demonstrated above, relevant
to the valuation of these options. Thus, it is worthwhile to determine if the
relationships induced by these variables can be captured by variables

Table 6. Difference between Black–Scholes–Merton and Benchmark Option Values for Different Values of Variables Included within the Black–Scholes–Merton Model for Low Volatilities.

	Moneyness (S/X)						
	0.25	0.50	0.75	1.00	1.25	1.50	1.75
$\sigma = 10\%$							
1 year	0.00	0.00	−0.04	−1.90	−2.95	−3.54	−4.14
3 years	0.00	−0.03	−2.40	−6.82	−9.16	−11.03	−12.87
5 years	0.00	−0.82	−6.97	−12.29	−15.84	−19.06	−22.25
7 years	−0.01	−3.45	−12.05	−18.15	−23.02	−27.68	−32.32
10 years	−0.41	−9.61	−19.89	−27.64	−34.25	−41.77	−48.78
$\sigma = 15\%$							
1 year	0.00	0.00	−0.10	−1.07	−1.84	−2.26	−2.64
3 years	0.00	−0.09	−1.47	−3.76	−5.50	−6.81	−8.00
5 years	0.00	−0.72	−3.63	−6.79	−9.30	−11.44	−13.44
7 years	−0.05	−1.97	−6.11	−9.98	−13.24	−16.17	−18.99
10 years	−0.39	−4.54	−10.07	−14.95	−19.31	−23.45	−27.51
$\sigma = 20\%$							
1 year	0.00	0.00	−0.03	−0.21	−0.40	−0.53	−0.62
3 years	0.00	−0.01	−0.22	−0.68	−1.14	−1.52	−1.84
5 years	0.00	−0.06	−0.52	−1.21	−1.89	−2.49	−3.04
7 years	0.01	−0.16	−0.87	−1.79	−2.67	−3.47	−4.22
10 years	0.04	−0.43	−1.51	−2.72	−3.87	−4.95	−5.97

Notes: The following inputs are used for the standard case: exercise price (X) = $50; risk-free rate ($r$) = 6%; dividend yield = 0%; executive wealth = $5,000,000; percentage of executive wealth in stock (%W) = 50%; number of options = 5000; market risk premium (RP) = 6.5%, beta (β) = 1.0; relative risk aversion (λ) = 2.5. Some of these values are varied as indicated. The true value of the option is obtained using a power utility model with the standard inputs. The value shown is the Black–Scholes–Merton value minus the benchmark value. Negative values indicate options in which the benchmark value is greater.

associated only with the Black–Scholes–Merton model. We propose that a continuous factor ψ be applied to the stock price as though it were a continuously compounded dividend yield.

Suppose we specify that the Black–Scholes–Merton value of an option is given as the function $C_{BS}(S,X,r,T,\sigma)$, and that the true value of the option, as given by the utility model, is specified as $C(S,X,r,T,\sigma,\Omega)$ where Ω reflects the additional variables required by the utility model over and above those required by the Black–Scholes–Merton model.[16] Suppose we now add a variable to the Black–Scholes–Merton formulation such that the price is given as $C_{BS}(S,X,r,T,\sigma,\psi)$. If we can find a value of this variable ψ that can capture the effects of the variables Ω, we may be able to make the Black–Scholes–Merton model behave like the utility model. Thus, we propose that the new variable be used like a dividend yield, such that it adjusts the stock price to the value $Se^{-\varphi T}$.

Consider a specific option. Suppose we solve for the value ψ that forces equivalence of the Black–Scholes–Merton value to the utility model value. In this way, we are solving for a measure that behaves in a manner roughly equivalent to the implied volatility:

$$C_{BS}(S, X, r, T, \sigma, \psi) = C(S, X, r, T, \sigma, \Omega)$$

Using a sample of options spanning a wide range of input parameters, we can obtain a sample of cases with an implied value ψ. We may then be able to capture the properties of ψ by examining its relationship with the key inputs. We noted that the Black–Scholes–Merton errors are related to moneyness, volatility, and time to expiration. We propose that we run a regression of ψ on measures of moneyness, volatility, and time to expiration:

$$\psi = b_0 + b_1(S/X) + b_2 T + b_3 \sigma + e$$

If reliable coefficients can be estimated, we can then obtain a value of ψ to apply to each option to adjust the Black–Scholes–Merton model for the effects of the variables required by the utility function.

To develop the model under the most rigorous conditions, we create a sample of options that vary widely in terms of moneyness, time to expiration, and volatility, but do not vary in terms of the variables that ψ is designed to capture. This characteristic imposes the heaviest demands on the ability of ψ to capture these additional variables that do not appear in the Black–Scholes–Merton model. The estimation process does not allow variation in these non-Black–Scholes–Merton variables. The application of the model does allow variation in these variables.

The sample contains our standard set of inputs (exercise price of $50, risk-free rate of 6%, executive wealth of $5 million, the percentage of executive wealth invested in stock of 50%, beta of 1.0, market risk premium of 6.5%, and relative risk aversion of 2.5). We vary the moneyness from 0.40 to 1.60 in increments of 0.02, use times to expiration of 10, 7, 5, 3, and 1 years, and volatilities of 20%, 30%, and 40%. We estimate the regression for the full sample and use the coefficients to adjust the stock price to see if the accuracy of the Black–Scholes–Merton model can be improved. We obtained extremely promising results except for the case of volatility of 20%, which does not come as a surprise. We then undertake separate regressions for two groups, which we call high volatility and low volatility. The high volatility case consists of volatilities of 30% and 40%. The low volatility case consists of volatilities of 10%, 15%, and 20%.

Note again that this combination of variables does not vary the inputs whose effects we are attempting to capture in ψ. This would seem to be a problem but only if we perform in-sample tests. But what we shall do is use the coefficients estimated from this regression on a different sample that does allow variation in these other variables.

Alternative versions of the regression were tested, omitting certain variables, and trying log values of variables, but no worthwhile improvements were found. Thus, the basic regression was supported. Diagnostic tests revealed a high level of confidence in the coefficients, which is not surprising. We used a large sample and the relationships are not particularly noisy. The results are as follows, with all coefficients significant at probability levels less than 0.0001:

Volatility of 20% or below

$$\Psi = -0.07394 + 0.37215\sigma \quad -0.00561(S/X) - 0.00021T + e$$
$$R^2 = 89.1\% \qquad\qquad N = 915$$

Volatility of 30% or above

$$\Psi = -0.14099 + 0.79270\sigma \quad -0.0209(S/X) - 0.00397T + e$$
$$R^2 = 96.7\% \qquad\qquad N = 610$$

The results show a very high degree of explanatory power. For both samples, the volatility adjustment is quite large. For the high volatility sample, the intercept sets the value of ψ to start at approximately -0.14. The volatility adjustment moves it up by a factor of approximately 0.79. For a volatility of 21% (ignoring moneyness and expiration), this adjustment would set ψ to about 0.026, which would lower the stock price and thus, lower the Black–Scholes–Merton value, bringing it down and closer to the benchmark value. The higher the volatility, the larger will be the value of ψ and the greater the downward adjustment of the Black–Scholes–Merton value. The moneyness and time to expiration adjustments have a small effect on top of the volatility adjustment. For the low volatility sample, the intercept is about -0.07. With a volatility of 20%, the value of ψ would then be adjusted to almost 0.0. For volatilities lower than 20% (where the Black–Scholes–Merton value tends to be lower than the benchmark value), the value of ψ would tend to be negative, which would raise the stock price and raise the Black–Scholes–Merton price, pushing it up toward the benchmark value. Then the moneyness and time to expiration would make a slight additional adjustment. In both samples, however, the moneyness and time to expiration effect is small relative to the volatility adjustment.

For the low volatility case, the signs are all the same as in the high volatility case but are of smaller magnitude. The intercept and volatility adjustments are only about half their magnitudes for the high volatility sample. The moneyness adjustment is about a fourth of its magnitude in the high volatility sample. The time to expiration adjustment is only about 5% of its magnitude in the high volatility case.

The real test of these adjustments, however, is whether the values obtained with the adjusted Black–Scholes–Merton model are noticeably closer to the benchmark values. We previously reported the percentage differences for a broad range of input parameters using 30% volatility as the standard case. We shall continue to use 30% volatility as the standard case for the high volatility sample. For the low volatility sample, however, we need a new standard case, which we shall create using 15% volatility.

Tables 7 and 8 show the percentage errors for the high and low volatility cases respectively. In parentheses is the percentage error for the unadjusted model. For the 10-year options, only the at-the-money cases are shown. For the high volatility case, the adjustment results in a substantial decrease in the percentage error for almost all combinations of inputs. For the standard case at 10 years, the error is 110.71%. The stock price adjustment reduces that error to 17.18%. The at-the-money case for a percentage of wealth of 33% shows a small increase for the five-year case and a large increase for the one-year case. But in all other cases, the adjustment leads to a reduction and usually a rather large one. In some cases, the errors are still large after the adjustment, but in most cases, the errors are smaller and often considerably smaller.

For the low volatility case (Table 8) the results are almost as good. The weakest improvement is in the low beta case, where we do observe one case with a slightly larger error after the adjustment. But other than those cases, the errors are lower with the adjustment, and in many cases, substantially lower. For the standard case, using 15% as the base volatility for the low volatility group, the error before the adjustment is 39.39%. The error after the adjustment is 1.62%.

Before the adjustment we found a distinctive pattern according to moneyness, volatility, and time to expiration. Of course, we exploited those patterns in building the model to adjust the stock price. After the adjustment, these patterns no longer exist. One consequence of this effect is that the percentage errors need not diminish over time. Given the

Table 7. Percentage Errors for the Adjusted Black–Scholes–Merton Model for the High Volatility Sample.

A: Different betas

	β=0.75			β=1.00			β=1.25		
	T=10	T=5	T=1	T=10	T=5	T=1	T=10	T=5	T=1
50% ITM	NA	17.00 (74.63)	2.80 (20.24)	NA	4.05 (55.29)	1.03 (15.76)	NA	6.98 (38.83)	4.61 (11.58)
ATM	42.63 (156.46)	12.94 (107.05)	1.61 (39.38)	17.18 (110.71)	2.58 (78.60)	4.90 (30.44)	2.70 (74.95)	15.38 (55.13)	10.81 (22.34)
50% OTM	NA	20.11 (235.45)	6.38 (137.10)	NA	3.52 (169.44)	8.26 (104.49)	NA	21.76 (118.52)	20.56 (77.07)

B: Different volatilities

	σ=30%			σ=40%		
	T=10	T=5	T=1	T=10	T=5	T=1
50% ITM	NA	4.05 (55.29)	1.03 (15.76)	2.33 (165.89)	2.33 (42.02)	NA
ATM	17.18 (110.71)	2.58 (78.60)	4.90 (30.44)	4.66 (232.94)	2.63 (72.80)	14.68 (364.71)
50% OTM	NA	3.52 (169.44)	8.26 (104.49)	6.28 (492.04)	14.69 (215.31)	NA

C: Different % of stock wealth

	%W=33%			%W=50%			%W=67%		
	T=10	T=5	T=1	T=10	T=5	T=1	T=10	T=5	T=1
50% ITM	NA	19.90 (19.55)	9.77 (5.53)	NA	4.05 (55.29)	1.03 (15.76)	NA	39.79 (108.64)	9.19 (27.72)
ATM	22.92 (38.59)	30.51 (27.39)	19.41 (10.54)	17.18 (110.71)	2.58 (78.60)	4.90 (30.44)	89.31 (240.41)	41.61 (159.61)	12.92 (54.89)
50% OTM	NA	42.38 (60.93)	37.27 (39.81)	NA	3.52 (169.44)	8.26 (104.49)	NA	64.14 (358.38)	30.99 (191.96)

Table 7. (Continued)

	T=10	T=5	T=1	T=10	T=5	T=1	T=10	T=5	T=1
D: Different market risk premiums									
	RP=5%			RP=6.5%			RP=8%		
50% ITM	NA	15.93	2.50	NA	4.05	1.03	NA	6.19	4.34
		(73.03)	(19.89)		(55.29)	(15.76)		(40.00)	(11.89)
ATM	40.43	11.64	1.09	17.18	2.58	4.90	1.34	14.48	10.37
	(152.51)	(104.66)	(38.66)	(110.71)	(78.60)	(30.44)	(77.41)	(56.78)	(22.94)
50% OTM	NA	18.06	5.15	NA	3.52	8.26	NA	20.51	19.68
		(229.73)	(134.37)		(169.44)	(104.49)		(121.99)	(79.02)
E: Different risk aversion									
	λ=2			λ=2.5			λ=3		
50% ITM	NA	12.55	6.74	NA	4.05	1.03	NA	23.37	5.09
		(30.51)	(9.08)		(55.29)	(15.76)		(84.12)	(22.92)
ATM	11.69	22.23	14.47	17.18	2.58	4.90	53.57	21.80	5.91
	(58.79)	(42.58)	(17.32)	(110.71)	(78.60)	(30.44)	(176.14)	(123.28)	(45.27)
50% OTM	NA	32.99	29.45	NA	3.52	8.26	NA	39.10	19.67
		(87.14)	(57.26)		(169.44)	(104.49)		(288.50)	(166.74)

Notes: The following inputs are used for the standard case: exercise price (X) = $50; risk-free rate ($r$) = 6%; dividend yield = 0%; executive wealth = $5,000,000; percentage of executive wealth in stock (%W) = 50%; number of options = 5000; market risk premium (RP) = 6.5%, beta (β) = 1.0; relative risk aversion (λ) = 2.5. Some of these values are varied as indicated. The true value of the option is obtained using a power utility model with the standard inputs. The value shown is the absolute percentage difference between the Black–Scholes–Merton and the benchmark values. The Black–Scholes–Merton value is obtained using the adjusted stock price, obtained by estimating the coefficients in a regression of the adjustment factor on volatility, moneyness, and time to expiration. For comparative purposes, the unadjusted percentage error is shown in parentheses. ITM, ATM, OTM refer to "in-the-money", "at-the-money", and "out-of-the-money".

Table 8. Percentage Errors for the Adjusted Black–Scholes–Merton Model for the Low Volatility Sample.

A: Different betas

	β=0.75			β=1.00			β=1.25		
	T=10	T=5	T=1	T=10	T=5	T=1	T=10	T=5	T=1
50% ITM	NA	13.20 (12.60)	3.10 (4.00)	NA	0.54 (23.26)	0.67 (7.51)	NA	11.40 (31.64)	4.18 (10.78)
ATM	23.74 (23.76)	15.13 (18.88)	6.63 (10.48)	1.62 (39.39)	4.06 (32.40)	3.58 (19.05)	20.23 (50.85)	18.78 (42.77)	12.33 (26.39)
50% OTM	NA	34.55 (32.86)	0.00 (0.00)	NA	11.42 (55.80)	0.00 (0.00)	NA	39.56 (69.84)	0.00 (0.00)

B: Different volatilities

	σ=10%			σ=15%			σ=20%		
	T=10	T=5	T=1	T=10	T=5	T=1	T=10	T=5	T=1
50% ITM	NA	1.66 (33.62)	0.06 (11.30)	NA	0.54 (23.26)	0.67 (7.51)	NA	2.09 (6.12)	0.29 (1.86)
ATM	1.97 (55.42)	1.09 (48.47)	2.15 (34.09)	1.62 (39.39)	4.06 (32.40)	3.58 (19.05)	2.48 (10.07)	0.47 (7.19)	0.59 (3.70)
50% OTM	NA	12.64 (89.32)	0.00 (0.00)	NA	11.42 (55.80)	0.00 (0.00)	NA	3.57 (4.13)	0.00 (0.00)

C: Different % of stock wealth

	%W=33%			%W=50%			%W=67%		
	T=10	T=5	T=1	T=10	T=5	T=1	T=10	T=5	T=1
50% ITM	NA	7.62 (28.72)	2.96 (9.65)	NA	0.54 (23.26)	0.67 (7.51)	NA	7.06 (17.39)	1.69 (5.31)
ATM	13.96 (46.99)	14.04 (39.43)	9.53 (24.04)	1.62 (39.39)	4.06 (32.40)	3.58 (19.05)	12.31 (30.80)	7.16 (24.50)	2.82 (13.68)
50% OTM	NA	31.58 (65.86)	0.00 (0.00)	NA	11.42 (55.80)	0.00 (0.00)	NA	13.13 (43.55)	0.00 (0.00)

Table 8. (Continued)

	T = 10	T = 5	T = 1	T = 10	T = 5	T = 1	T = 10	T = 5	T = 1
D: Different market risk premiums									
	RP = 5%			RP = 6.5%			RP = 8%		
50% ITM	NA	11.40	2.80	NA	0.54	0.67	NA	10.63	3.92
		(14.04)	(4.28)		(23.26)	(7.51)		(31.04)	(10.54)
ATM	21.48	13.46	5.78	1.62	4.06	3.58	18.98	17.77	11.70
	(25.16)	(20.06)	(11.19)	(39.39)	(32.40)	(19.05)	(50.08)	(42.06)	(25.86)
50% OTM	NA	30.11	0.00	NA	11.42	0.00	NA	37.83	0.00
		(35.07)	(0.00)		(55.80)	(0.00)		(68.98)	(0.00)
E: Different risk aversion									
	λ = 2			λ = 2.5			λ = 3		
50% ITM	NA	5.50	2.16	NA	0.54	0.67	NA	4.66	0.84
		(27.08)	(8.90)		(23.26)	(7.51)		(19.24)	(6.10)
ATM	10.86	10.97	7.39	1.62	4.06	3.58	8.48	3.48	0.44
	(45.08)	(37.27)	(22.25)	(39.39)	(32.40)	(19.05)	(33.16)	(27.09)	(15.67)
50% OTM	NA	26.16	0.00	NA	11.42	0.00	NA	6.62	0.00
		(63.15)	(0.00)		(55.80)	(0.00)		(46.79)	(0.00)

Notes: The following inputs are used for the standard case: exercise price (X) = \$50; risk-free rate (r) = 6%; dividend yield = 0%; executive wealth = \$5,000,000; percentage of executive wealth in stock (%W) = 50%; number of options = 5000; market risk premium (RP) = 6.5%, beta (β) = 1.0; relative risk aversion (λ) = 2.5. Some of these values are varied as indicated. The true value of the option is obtained using a power utility model with the standard inputs. The value shown is the absolute percentage difference between the Black–Scholes–Merton and the benchmark values. The Black–Scholes–Merton value is obtained using the adjusted stock price, obtained by estimating the coefficients in a regression of the adjustment factor on volatility, moneyness, and time to expiration. For comparative purposes, the unadjusted percentage error is shown in parentheses. ITM, ATM, OTM refer to "in-the-money", "at-the-money", and "out-of-the-money".

substantial reduction in the error at year 10, however, the feature of diminishing over time is less critical. Indeed in nearly all cases, the error with 5 years remaining is small and with one year remaining is extremely small.

The results we obtained here appear quite promising. Because they are based on two mathematically specified models across a broad range of inputs, these relationships will hold over time. In other words, this adjustment is not a sample-specific empirical finding that could be less accurate if estimated at some later date over a different sample.

5. SUMMARY

The Black–Scholes–Merton model is criticized for its failure to accommodate illiquid options, but the problem is not attributable to a shortcoming of the model. The problem is due to the regulatory constraint that prohibits an executive from synthetically selling options by short selling stock, selling calls, or buying puts. In other words, there is nothing inherently flawed with the model that assumes a liquid market for the instrument. Replication is the essence of Black–Scholes–Merton valuation, and it is only from restrictions on alternative strategies that the model breaks down.

Models for the valuation of executive stock options are either based on stopping points, expected utility maximization, or adjustments to the Black–Scholes–Merton model. We propose a version of the Black–Scholes–Merton model that adjusts the model to account for the illiquidity. Using a utility-based model as a benchmark, we find that the discount is not particularly related to the variables that the utility model captures that are not in the Black–Scholes–Merton model. As such, we find that the Black–Scholes–Merton model can be adjusted by an artificial dividend yield that is related to moneyness, time to expiration, and volatility. This adjustment greatly reduces the difference between values given by the Black–Scholes–Merton model and the utility benchmark model.

This research is limited by our focus only on European-style options. American-style options mitigate the liquidity problem somewhat inasmuch as early exercise serves as a surrogate for selling the option. Hence, the liquidity discount should be less. By ignoring early exercise in this paper, our adjustment had a greater distance to overcome. Vesting and the possibility of forfeiture also affect the value of an executive stock option and are not accounted for in the standard Black–Scholes–Merton model. We intentionally withheld these factors at this point, but they suggest issues for further research.

NOTES

1. By "cross-sectional errors" we refer to a comparison of errors given differences in moneyness and input variables other than the time to expiration.

2. We make no implication that the bid-ask spreads are small in these circumstances, but there is no guarantee that the bid-ask spread is small for standardized options as well.

3. For a good explanation of these rules, see Schizer (2000).

4. It is possible that while executives cannot legally engage in these types of transactions, employees could. In fact, an employee could easily and probably legally sell an option on the employer's stock, though due to likely limitations on the average employee's wealth and bargaining power, the option would probably have to be a standardized instrument on the options exchange, resulting in a less-than-perfect hedge.

5. From the perspective of the issuing firm, it may be reasonable to assume that forfeiture is diversifiable risk. From the perspective of the executive, forfeiture can hardly be viewed as diversifiable or non-priced risk.

6. Even dynamic utility models can produce values that are less than the lower bound so this problem would not be solved by using a dynamic model. Examples from Ingersoll (2002), Henderson (2005), and Cao and Wei (2007) can be easily constructed.

7. Henderson (2005), Ingersoll (2002) and Cao and Wei (2007) develop dynamic utility models that incorporate a portfolio that can serve as a hedging instrument for the option. In the extreme case, in which a perfect hedge of the option can be obtained using the hedging portfolio, the illiquidity of the option becomes irrelevant and the Black–Scholes–Merton model is recovered for any risk aversion.

8. The dividends can either be specified as stochastic with a known constant yield or as discrete deterministic cash payments. When positive dividends are assumed, all previous research on executive stock options has used a constant yield. Most papers in this line of research assume no dividends, which is potentially the preferred approach given that dividends can induce early exercise for reasons altogether unrelated to the unique properties of executive stock options.

9. Technically, the market risk premium and beta could be condensed into a single variable, the expected return on the stock (also reflecting the risk-free rate).

10. The negative exponential model has been the primary alternative model to the power utility model in examining the valuation of executive stock options. See Kadem et al. (2002) and Henderson (2005).

11. It is worth noting that calibrating the models does not give the same option value, but does serve to put the models on similar footing, i.e., with equivalent absolute and relative risk aversion.

12. In most cases, the Black–Scholes–Merton value exceeds the benchmark value. Thus, if the former exceeds the latter by more than 100%, an estimate of zero would be closer to the benchmark value. In those cases in which the Black–Scholes–Merton value is less than the benchmark value, it cannot be more than 100% less.

13. We do not vary the number of options awarded as it has only a minor impact on the results.

14. We estimated betas for all firms in the CRSP combined NYSE-AMEX-Nasdaq data base using one year of daily data and the CRSP value-weighted portfolio as the index. In 2000, 8.2% of the firms had betas greater than 2. In 2001, 7.3% of the firms had betas greater than 2. In 2002, 3.4% of the firms had betas greater than 2.

15. Although we have to estimate a different model for low volatility stocks, we should note that volatilities of 20% or less are fairly uncommon. Using the CRSP data base of NYSE-AMEX-Nasdaq stocks, we estimated the volatilities of the continuously compounded returns using one year of daily data. For the year 2000, about 5.7% of the stocks had volatilities below 20%. For the year 2001, 6.8% had volatilities below 20%. For 2002, 8.2% had volatilities below 20%.

16. These variables are specifically the stock beta, the manager's wealth, the percentage of the manager's wealth invested in the company's stock, the number of options granted, and the measure of relative risk aversion.

ACKNOWLEDGMENTS

Earlier versions of this paper were presented at the 2004 Portuguese Finance Network, the University of Southern Mississippi, and Rutgers University-Camden. The authors thank Ana Lacerda for helpful comments.

REFERENCES

Aboody, D. (1996). Market valuation of employee stock options. *Journal of Accounting and Economics, 22,* 357–391.

Black, F., & Scholes, M. (1973). The pricing of options and corporate liabilities. *Journal of Political Economy, 81,* 637–659.

Brenner, M., Eldor, R., & Hauser, S. (2001). The price of options illiquidity. *The Journal of Finance, 56,* 789–805.

Cao, M., & Wei, J. (2007). Incentive stocks and options with trading restrictions – not as restricted as we thought. *Research in Finance* (forthcoming).

Carpenter, J. N. (1998). The exercise and valuation of executive stock options. *Journal of Financial Economics, 48,* 127–158.

Carpenter, J. N. (2000). Does option compensation increase managerial risk appetite? *The Journal of Finance, 55,* 2311–2331.

Carr, P., & Linetskey, V. (2000). The valuation of executive stock options in an intensity-based framework. *European Finance Review, 4,* 211–230.

Detemple, J., & Sundaresan, S. (1999). Nontraded asset valuation with portfolio constraints: A binomial approach. *The Review of Financial Studies, 12,* 835–872.

Finnerty, J. D. (2002). *Extending the Black–Scholes–Merton model to value employee stock options.* Working paper. Analysis Group/Economics.

Hall, B. J., & Murphy, K. J. (2000). Optimal exercise prices for executive stock options. *American Economic Review, 90,* 209–214.

Hall, B. J., & Murphy, K. J. (2002). Stock options for undiversified investors. *Journal of Accounting and Economics, 33,* 3–42.

Henderson, V. (2005). The impact of the market portfolio on the valuation, incentives and optimality of executive stock options. *Quantitative Finance, 5,* 35–47.

Huddart, S. (1994). Employee stock options. *Journal of Accounting and Economics, 18,* 207–231.

Hull, J., & White, A. (2004). Accounting for employee stock options. *Financial Analysts Journal, 60*(January–February), 114–119.

Ingersoll, J. E., Jr. (2006). The subjective and objective evaluation of incentive stock options. *The Journal of Business, 79,* 453–487.

Jain, A., & Subramanian, A. (2004). The intertemporal exercise and valuation of employee stock options. *The Accounting Review, 79,* 705–743.

Kadam, A., Lakner, P., & Srinivasan, A. (2002). *Optimal exercise and valuation of executive stock options.* Working paper. University of Michigan.

Kulatilaka, N., & Marcus, A. J. (1994). Valuing employee stock options. *Financial Analysts Journal, 50*(November–December), 46–56.

Lambert, R. A., Larcker, D. F., & Verrechia, R. E. (1991). Portfolio considerations in valuing executive compensation. *Journal of Accounting Research, 29,* 129–149.

Merton, R. C. (1973). Theory of rational option pricing bell. *Journal of Economics and Management Science, 4,* 141–183.

Meulbroek, L. K. (2001). The efficiency of equity-linked compensation: Understanding the full cost of awarding executive stock options. *Financial Management, 30,* 5–20.

Raupach, P. (2003). *The valuation of executive stock options – how good is the standard.* Working paper. Goethe University.

Rubinstein, M. (1995). On the accounting valuation of employee stock options. *The Journal of Derivatives, 3*(fall), 8–24.

Schizer, D. M. (2000). Executives and hedging: The fragile legal foundation of incentive compatibility. *Columbia Law Review, 100,* 440–504.

Silber, W. L. (1991). Discounts on restricted stock: The impact of illiquidity on stock prices. *Financial Analysts Journal, 47*(July–August), 60–64.

UNOBSERVED HETEROGENEITY AND THE TERM-STRUCTURE OF DEFAULT

Koresh Galil

ABSTRACT

This paper estimates the conditional hazard baseline (term-structure) of the hazard rate to default at the time of bonds' issuance by using two hazard models–one ignoring and another allowing unobserved heterogeneity (UH) in the hazard rate. Following Diamond (1989) one can predict a declining hazard rate to default due to adverse selection and moral hazard. After controlling for UH caused by adverse selection and time-series shocks, the hazard rate shows to be increasing over time and hence the moral hazard effect cannot be confirmed.

1. INTRODUCTION

Credit risk is one of the major financial risks faced by commercial banks and portfolio managers. However, credit risk was not as thoroughly explored as market risk. While we know much about the properties of market risk, we know very little about properties of credit risk. One of the major reasons for that is the curse of rare events. The frequency of defaults or bankruptcies is

Issues in Corporate Governance and Finance
Advances in Financial Economics, Volume 12, 311–344
Copyright © 2007 by Elsevier Ltd.
ISSN: 1569-3732/doi:10.1016/S1569-3732(07)12012-0

too low to enable empirical investigation in the same scale of investigations regarding market risk. One consequence of this phenomenon is a lack of stylized facts. For example, when evaluating theoretical or empirical models concerning market risk, the phenomena of fat tails and negative skewness can be used as validating facts. However similar stylized facts hardly exist when discussing credit risk models.

This study attempts to investigate one aspect of credit risk, which is the term-structure of the hazard rate to default. The estimation of the term-structure has an importance in providing additional insight toward a better understanding of the properties of default risk. Asquith, Mullins, and Wolff (1989) point out that traditional studies of high-yield bonds have not properly considered the aging of the bonds, i.e. default rates are not stationary through time but rise with bonds' age. Altman (1989), employing an aging concept as well as other corrections, provides higher default rates than what was achieved before. This upward correction in default rates reduces the credit risk premium that is observed in corporate bonds.

This study can also shed light on some properties of bond markets. Diamond (1989), shows that in a debt market with heterogeneous credit quality of borrowers, the hazard rate to default should decline over time. This result has two deriving forces. The first, firms with lower credit quality tend to go bankrupt faster, and hence the remained population tends to become safer over time. The second, the lenders that know that the remained population is safer demand lower interest and hence the borrowers who have gained reputation (an intangible asset that cannot be liquidated in the case that the firm goes bankrupt) tend to invest in less risky assets. Therefore, according to Diamond (1989), both the adverse selection and the moral hazard phenomena will bring to a declining term-structure of hazard rate.

Though Diamond's model discusses the evolution of a firm's credit quality starting its first issuance of debt, the conclusions can be extended to other ages as well. The diminishing adverse selection within each rating category should exist in any age level and good credit history should create valuable reputation, no matter the age of the firm. The two market failures – adverse selection and moral hazard should be present in any age.

Gorton (1996) brings evidence on one of the consequences of Diamond (1989) theory, i.e. firms with shorter (or no) credit history pay higher interest rate. However, this result cannot be traced to the two deriving forces described in Diamond (1989), which are the diminishing adverse selection and the moral hazard.

Fons (1994) and Carty (2000) estimate the term-structure of the hazard rate itself. Fons, using average cumulated default rates shows that for higher graded firms, the hazard rates first increases over time and only then it decreases. He also shows that low-graded firms (firms having a Moody's rating of Ba) have a decreasing hazard rate to default. Carty (2000) however, once controlling for particular annual macroeconomic shocks and industrial classification and some other possible heterogeneities, shows that the hazard rate first increases and then decreases even for low-graded firms (such as firms graded Baa by Moody's). Duffie, Saita, and Wang (2005) estimate a multi-period default model that allows the default term-structure to vary across firms and through time. They do not focus on the estimation of the term-structure but illustrate their results on one company and show how its term-structure can have different shapes – upward sloping, downward sloping, or hump-shaped.

The appearance of a positive slope in the term-structure of the hazard rate, suggests that Diamond's model ignores relevant forces. A possible force might be the accessibility to cash (cash-flow effect). After raising new funds, a firm can experience several years of low default risk due to the new reserves of cash. However, as these reserves diminish after a while, the firm becomes more vulnerable to a possibility of default.

The empirical investigation in this study employs two types of hazard models. The first model follows a duration model introduced by Prentice and Gloeckler (1978). In this model, the hazard rate is proportional, i.e. the term-structure is separable from other factors that affect the hazard risk, and the time measure is discrete. This model is semi-parametric and can be estimated using a maximum likelihood approach. However the model does not contain any source of noise in the hazard rate and hence it does not allow unobserved heterogeneity (UH).[1] Therefore, ratings, when used as explanatory variables are assumed to be the absolute measure of the firm's credit risk.

The second model follows Meyer (1990) and allows both covariates and noise. On assuming this noise to be Gamma distributed, it is possible to draw the likelihood function and to estimate the hazard function using a maximum likelihood approach. This model is suitable for the case that there are other (omitted) variables that affect the hazard rate. By adding covariates as well as noise, the model allows both cross-sectional and time-series UH.

Shumway (2001) shows that hazard models are more appropriate than single-period models in bankruptcy prediction. While Shumway (2001) considers a monotonic aging effect through using ln(age) as an explanatory variable, the discrete-time feature of the models employed in this study allow estimation of an unrestricted term-structure.

A simple and naive calculation of the hazard rate to default, using cumulated historical default probabilities leads the observer to suspect that the hazard rate of default increases in the first years after issuing a new bond and then decreases again to a level close to the one immediately after issue. However, such a calculation might be misleading. Lancaster (1990) points out that in a wide group of popular duration models ignoring the UH would lead to downward estimates of all coefficients of the hazard rate function, including the term-structure.[2] The intuition behind this can be easily illustrated using a simple example. Consider a population that consists of two equal-sized groups of firms that differ in their constant hazard rate of default, with 8 and 6% respectively. The observed (average) hazard rate would be 7% at the beginning. Over time the remained population would consist of firms with lower default risk, and therefore, the observed average hazard rate would tend to decrease toward 6%. However, conditioning on the information available at the time of rating, the hazard rate to default for each type is constant over time.

This effect of UH can to some extent be controlled for by using a transition matrix in calculating the implied hazard rate. A transition matrix is a common way to describe the stochastic process of the credit quality of the firm and is used in reduced form models (such as Jarrow, Lando, & Turnbull, 1997) for pricing of credit spreads. The matrix describes not only the annual probability of default for each rating classification but also the probability of transition to other rating classifications. Hence, the matrix takes into account existence of UH. Yet, according to S&P methodology, the ratings aim to look through the cycle, and hence the transition matrix only slightly takes into account possible heterogeneity.

The term-structure of the hazard rate to default derived from the transition matrix is shown to be increasing over time for most rating classifications. This exercise shows that on controlling for adverse selection, there is almost no diminishing moral hazard effect visible. Though such an effect might still exist, it seems to be overshadowed by another effect that induces increasing hazard rate over time (possibly cash-flow effect).

The term-structure of default is also estimated by using a panel database. A list of 10,000 new corporate bonds issued in the US during the years 1983–1993 is merged with lists of default occurrences during the years 1983–2000, obtained mainly from *Moody's Investor Services* publications. After eliminating financial corporations, multiple issues by single issuers within a calendar year, a database with 2,596 bonds of 1,013 issuers is left. The long-term horizon that features the survival analysis enables 235 cases of default by 155 firms to be identified. However, this methodology also uses each year of exposure to default risk as an individual observation. Therefore the total number of observation in the sample is 27,906 of which 235 are observation of default.

Both Fons (1994) and Carty (2000) use ratings as a of measure of credit quality while Duffie et al. (2005) use a Merton-type distance to default based on Merton (1974). Loeffler (2004) shows that market-based measures are not necessarily superior over ratings in investment management. Bharath and Shumway (2005) show that a Merton-type model performs worse than other simplified forecasting measures when used in hazard models. Rating are also commonly and freely used while distance to default involves complex calculations. Therefore, this study uses ratings as explanatory variable and hence the paper's results should be compared to those of Fons (1994) and Carty (2000).

Fons (1994) estimates the term-structure at the start of each calendar year, Carty (2000) at the first issuance of rating by Moody's and Duffie et al. (2005) estimate the term-structure for each month. On assuming that the debt issuance itself affects the term-structure, it is more suitable to condition the estimation on the date of issuance, rather than at an arbitrary point of time. This study uses ratings at the time of bond issuance, and term-structure is estimated at this time.

The estimation of the term-structure, while ignoring UH within each rating category reveals similar results to those when using Standard and Poor's statistics for cumulated frequencies of default. The term-structure appears to be first increasing, and then decreasing. This term-structure appears to be significant. Yet, on allowing UH, the decreasing pattern of the term-structure is replaced with a slightly increasing pattern. The hazard rate in the year following issue is still significantly low and from the second year and on, it is slightly increasing. The noise-variance is significant, and therefore the case of absence of UH is rejected.

The UH in this study is only partly introduced by introducing noise at the date of issuance to reflect cross-sectional UH and year dummies to reflect time-series UH. It is likely that introduction of other variables, such as firm-level accounting and market variables and specific macrolevel covariates (as done in Duffie et al., 2005) would strengthen the results.

An interesting observation (yet not significant) is a drop in the hazard rate in the years 4, 6, 8, and 11 from the time of issue. These drops might further support the cash-flow effect thesis. Since firms tend to issue new bonds in intervals of 3, 5, 7, and 10 years, then we can expect their default risk to drop in the respective following years (i.e. 4, 6, 8, and 11). Nevertheless, this correlation of the term-structure of the hazard rate to default with the time to maturity of the bonds is not the driving force of the results but only an indicator for the relevance of the cash-flow effect.

The remainder of the paper is organized as follows. Section 2 provides an analysis based on aggregate data. Section 3 describes the methodology used in the microanalysis. Section 4 describes the data and Section 5 the results. Section 6 contains the conclusions.

2. AGGREGATE DATA OBSERVATION

2.1. Using Cumulative Default Probabilities

Table 1 shows the historical average cumulative default probabilities of the main rating categories up to 15 years after issue as documented by S&P.[3] Let $F_r(t)$ denote the average cumulative probability of default of rating r, t years after assigning the rating. Panel b describes $f_r(t) = F_r(t) - F_r(t-1)$ – the average probability of default of rating r between time $t-1$ and time t and Table 1-c shows $\theta_r(t) = f_r(t)/[1 - F_r(t-1)]$ – the average hazard rate of default between time $t-1$ and time t.

Fig. 1 shows $\theta_r(T)$ for each rating category up to 15 years after assigning the rating. These tables and figures suggest that the average hazard rate first increases over time and then decreases. The lower the rating, the faster the hazard rate reaches its maximum.

2.2. Using Transition Matrix

Suppose $S \in \{1, \ldots k\}$ represents a firm's rating at some period, where 1 is the highest rating (the lowest default risk) and $k-1$ the lowest rating (the highest default risk but not default) and k represents the state of default. Suppose the rating of the firm follows a Markovian process that can be specified by the following $k \times k$ transition matrix,

$$
Q = \left\{
\begin{array}{cccc}
q_{11} & q_{12} & \cdots & q_{ik} \\
q_{21} & q_{22} & \cdots & q_{2k} \\
\vdots & & & \\
q_{k-1,1} & q_{k-1,2} & \cdots & q_{k-1,k} \\
0 & 0 & \cdots & 1
\end{array}
\right\}
$$

where $q_{rs} \geq 0$ for all $r,s, r \neq s$ and $q_{rr} = 1 - \sum_{s=1, s \neq r}^{k} q_{rs}$ for all r. q_{rs} represents the probability of a change from rating r to rating s in 1 year. It is assumed

Table 1. The Term-Structure of Average Hazard Rate using S&P Historical Average Cumulative Default Probabilities.

Rating	Years from Rating														
	1	2	3	4	5	6	7	8	9	10	11	12	13	14	15
Panel A: Average cumulative default rate – $F_r(t)$															
AAA	0.00	0.00	0.03	0.06	0.10	0.18	0.26	0.40	0.45	0.51	0.51	0.51	0.51	0.51	0.51
AA	0.01	0.04	0.09	0.16	0.25	0.37	0.53	0.63	0.70	0.79	0.85	0.92	0.96	1.01	1.07
A	0.04	0.11	0.19	0.32	0.49	0.65	0.83	1.01	1.21	1.41	1.56	1.65	1.70	1.73	1.83
BBB	0.22	0.50	0.79	1.30	1.80	2.29	2.73	3.10	3.39	3.68	3.91	4.05	4.22	4.37	4.48
BB	0.98	2.97	5.35	7.44	9.22	11.11	12.27	13.35	14.29	15.00	15.65	16.00	16.29	16.36	16.36
B	5.30	11.28	15.88	19.10	21.44	23.20	24.77	26.01	26.99	27.88	28.48	28.96	29.34	29.68	29.96
CCC	21.94	29.25	34.37	38.24	42.13	43.62	44.40	44.82	45.74	46.53	46.84	47.21	47.66	48.29	48.29
Investment grade	0.08	0.19	0.31	0.51	0.72	0.95	1.17	1.37	1.54	1.71	1.84	1.93	2.00	2.06	2.14
Speculative grade	4.14	8.34	11.93	14.67	16.84	18.64	19.98	21.09	22.05	22.85	23.46	23.88	24.22	24.45	24.58
Panel B: Average probability of default – $f_r(t)$															
AAA	0.00	0.00	0.03	0.03	0.04	0.08	0.08	0.14	0.05	0.06	0.00	0.00	0.00	0.00	0.00
AA	0.01	0.03	0.05	0.07	0.09	0.12	0.16	0.10	0.07	0.09	0.06	0.07	0.04	0.05	0.06
A	0.04	0.07	0.08	0.13	0.17	0.16	0.18	0.18	0.20	0.20	0.15	0.09	0.05	0.03	0.10
BBB	0.22	0.28	0.29	0.51	0.50	0.49	0.44	0.37	0.29	0.29	0.23	0.14	0.17	0.15	0.11
BB	0.98	1.99	2.38	2.09	1.78	1.89	1.16	1.08	0.94	0.71	0.65	0.35	0.29	0.07	0.00
B	5.30	5.98	4.60	3.22	2.34	1.76	1.57	1.24	0.98	0.89	0.60	0.48	0.38	0.34	0.28
CCC	21.94	7.31	5.12	3.87	3.89	1.49	0.78	0.42	0.92	0.79	0.31	0.37	0.45	0.63	0.00
Investment grade	0.08	0.11	0.12	0.20	0.21	0.23	0.22	0.20	0.17	0.17	0.13	0.09	0.07	0.06	0.08
Speculative grade	4.14	4.20	3.59	2.74	2.17	1.80	1.34	1.11	0.96	0.80	0.61	0.42	0.34	0.23	0.13

Table 1. (Continued)

Rating	Years from Rating														
	1	2	3	4	5	6	7	8	9	10	11	12	13	14	15
Panel C: Average hazard rate of default – $\theta_r(t)$															
AAA	0.00	0.00	0.03	0.03	0.04	0.08	0.08	0.14	0.05	0.06	0.00	0.00	0.00	0.00	0.00
AA	0.01	0.03	0.05	0.07	0.09	0.12	0.16	0.10	0.07	0.09	0.06	0.07	0.04	0.05	0.06
A	0.04	0.07	0.08	0.13	0.17	0.16	0.18	0.18	0.20	0.20	0.15	0.09	0.05	0.03	0.10
BBB	0.22	0.28	0.29	0.51	0.51	0.50	0.45	0.38	0.30	0.30	0.24	0.15	0.18	0.16	0.12
BB	0.98	2.01	2.45	2.21	1.92	2.08	1.30	1.23	1.08	0.83	0.76	0.41	0.35	0.08	0.00
B	5.30	6.31	5.18	3.83	2.89	2.24	2.04	1.65	1.32	1.22	0.83	0.67	0.53	0.48	0.40
CCC	21.94	9.36	7.24	5.90	6.30	2.57	1.38	0.76	1.67	1.46	0.58	0.70	0.85	1.20	0.00
Investment grade	0.08	0.11	0.12	0.20	0.21	0.23	0.22	0.20	0.17	0.17	0.13	0.09	0.07	0.06	0.08
Speculative grade	4.14	4.38	3.92	3.11	2.54	2.16	1.65	1.39	1.22	1.03	0.79	0.55	0.45	0.30	0.17

Notes: Panel a describes the historical average cumulative default rates (in percent) of the main rating categories as documented by S&P. Denoted by $F_r(t)$ the average cumulative probability of default of rating r from time of rating till time t. Panel b describes $f_r(t) = F_r(t) - F_r(t-1)$ – the average probability of default of rating r between time $t-1$ and time t. Panel c describes $\theta_r(t) = f_r(t)/[1 - F_r(t-1)]$ the average hazard rate of default between time $t-1$ and time t.

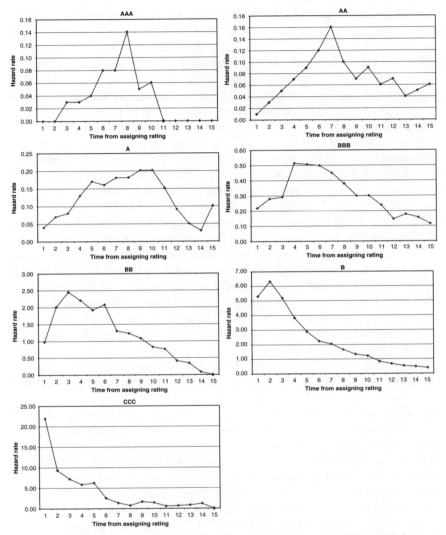

Fig. 1. The Term-Structure of Average Hazard Rate using S&P Historical Average Cumulative Default Probabilities. These Figures Describe the Average Hazard Rate of Default for Each Rating Category as a Function of Time from Rating. These Figures are Based on Average Cumulative Default Probability as Documented by S&P ("Ratings Performance 2000", Standard & Poor's). Let $F_r(t)$ Denote the Average Cumulative Probability of Default of Rating r, t years after Assigning the Rating. Then $f_r(t) = F_r(t) - F_r(t-1)$ Denote the Average Probability of Default of Rating r between Time $t-1$ and Time t and $\theta_r(t) = f_r(t)/[1 - F_r(t-1)]$ the Average Hazard Rate of Default between Time $t-1$ and Time t.

that the lowest grade (the state of default) is an absorbing state, so that the probability of a change from a state of default to a non-default rating is $q_{kr}=0$ for all r and $q_{kk}=1$. Note that the k-th column of the matrix Q represents the annual probability of default for all rating classes. However, for estimation of the term-structure of the hazard rate to default, it is necessary to take into account that the rating evolves over time.

Let $q_{rs}(0,t)$ denote the probability of transition from rating r at time 0 to rating s at time t. The t-years $k \times k$ transition matrix, $Q_{0,t}$ whose (r,s) entry is $q_{rs}(0,t)$ satisfies $Q_{0,t}=Q^t$. The k-th column represents the set of the cumulated probabilities of default till time t. Let $F_r(t) \equiv q_{rk}(0,t)$, then the probability of default at time t of a firm rated r at time 0 can be calculated by $f_r(t) \equiv F_r(t) - F_r(t-1)$ and the hazard rate to default at time t of a firm rated r at time 0 can be also calculated by $\theta_r(t) \equiv f_r(t)/[1-F_r(t)]$.

Panel a in Table 2 shows an S&P annual transition matrix.[4] The category of RW resembles cases that the rating is withdrawn. Carty (1997) shows that 92% of the rating withdrawals by Moody's were because the issues had matured or had been called. Assuming that S&P's withdrawals of ratings follow the same reason, it is reasonable to add the cases of withdrawals to cases that the rating was unchanged. Panel b shows the transition matrix when the cases of withdrawals are added to the cases that the rating was unchanged and the cases of default are assumed to be terminal (bonds that default do not recover).

Fig. 2 shows the term-structure of the hazard rate to default for each of the rating categories computed using the transition matrix. The hazard rate to default for ratings AA, A, BBB, BB, and B show to be monotonically increasing. Rating AAA appears to be increasing to a pick at years 6 and 7 after issue and then slightly decreasing. The decreasing patterns in the term-structure of default that appear in this figure disappear in the ratings AA, A, BBB, BB, and B, and weaken in the case of AAA. In the case of CCC, the term-structure remains declining. It should be noted that the transition matrix approach would always exclude a case of monotonically increasing term-structure of default for the lowest non-default rating category.

The results' differences might be attributed to the effect of adverse selection. The first approach totally ignores existence of UH. The transition matrix, however, allows for UH. While the 1 year default probability for each rating category is homogeneous, the transition probabilities induce heterogeneous probabilities of default over time for each rating category. It should be noted that S&P ratings follow the rule of 'looking through the cycle'[5] and therefore the transition matrix still does not take into the account the entire heterogeneity in default probabilities.

Table 2. The Average S&P 1-Year Rating Transition Matrix, 1981–1996.

Panel A: Average S&P 1-year transition matrix with state of rating withdrawal (RW)

Rating	AAA	AA	A	BBB	BB	B	CCC	D	RW
AAA	88.5	8.1	0.7	0.1	0.1	0.0	0.0	0.0	2.6
AA	0.6	88.5	7.6	0.6	0.1	0.1	0.0	0.0	2.4
A	0.1	2.3	87.6	5.0	0.7	0.2	0.0	0.4	3.6
BBB	0.0	0.3	5.5	82.5	4.7	1.0	0.1	0.2	5.7
BB	0.0	0.1	0.6	7.0	73.8	7.6	0.9	1.0	8.9
B	0.0	0.1	0.2	0.4	6.0	72.8	3.4	4.9	12.2
CCC	0.2	0.0	0.3	1.0	2.2	9.6	53.1	19.3	14.2

Panel B: Average S&P 1-year transition matrix, where rating withdrawal (RW) is assumed as a non-change in rating and default is assumed as a terminal state

Rating	AAA	AA	A	BBB	BB	B	CCC	D
AAA	91.1	8.1	0.7	0.1	0.1	0.0	0.0	0.0
AA	0.6	90.9	7.6	0.6	0.1	0.1	0.0	0.0
A	0.1	2.3	91.2	5.0	0.7	0.2	0.0	0.4
BBB	0.0	0.3	5.5	88.2	4.7	1.0	0.1	0.2
BB	0.0	0.1	0.6	7.0	82.7	7.6	0.9	1.0
B	0.0	0.1	0.2	0.4	6.0	85.0	3.4	4.9
CCC	0.2	0.0	0.3	1.0	2.2	9.6	67.3	19.3
D	0.0	0.0	0.0	0.0	0.0	0.0	0.0	100.0

Notes: Panel a describes the average S&P 1-year transition matrix during the years 1981–1996. Panel b describes the corresponding S&P 1-year transition matrix when withdrawal of rating is assumed to be a no-change in the rating and default is considered to be a terminal state.
Source: Standard & Poor's (1997), "Rating Performance: Stability and Transition. Special Report".

3. METHODOLOGY FOR A MICROANALYSIS

Assume that all firms that are exposed to default risk experience default at some time in future. Let i denote an observation on a firm issuing a new bond. Let T_i^D denote the time till the first time the firm defaults, and $\theta(t)$ denote the hazard rate to default at time t (the probability to default at time t conditioned on survival till time t). Now consider two alternative structures of the hazard rate function:

$$\theta(t; x_{it}) = k(x_{it}, t) \tag{1}$$

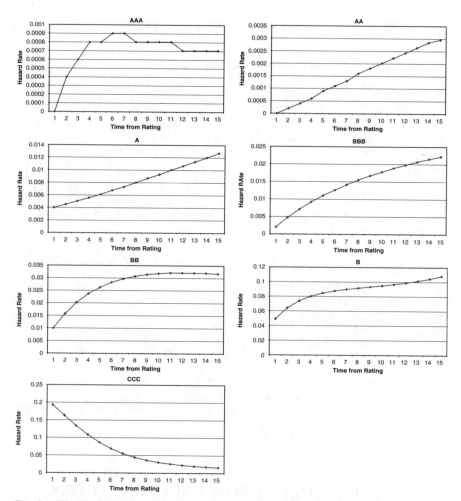

Fig. 2. The Term-Structure of the Average Hazard Rate using 1-Year S&P Ratings Transition Matrix. This Figure Shows Term-Structures of the Hazard Rate to Default Computed by using the S&P 1-Year Rating Transition Matrix During the Years 1981–1996. Suppose the Rating of the Firm Follows a Markovian Process that can be Specified by a $k \times k$ Transition Matrix Q where Each $0 \le q_{rs} \le 1$ is the Probability of Transition from Rating r to Rating s Within 1 Year. The t-Years Transition Matrix, $Q_{0,t}$ whose (r,s) Entry is $q_{rs}(0,t)$ Satisfies $Q_{0,t} = Q^t$. The k-th Column Represents the Set of the Cumulated Probabilities of Default till Time t. Let $F_r(t) \equiv q_{rk}(0,t)$, then the Probability of Default at Time t of a Firm Rated r at Time 0 can be Calculated by $f_r(t) \equiv F_r(t) - F_r(t-1)$ and the Hazard Rate to Default at Time t of a Firm Rated r at Time 0 can be also Calculated by $\theta_r(t) \equiv f_r(t)/[1 - F_r(t)]$.

and

$$\theta(t; x_{it}) = k(x_{it}, t, v_i) \tag{2}$$

where x_{it} is a vector of variables, whether describing the firm or its industry or the economy at time t, and v_i is noise. v_i resembles the affect of cross-sectional omitted variables on the exact realization of T_i^D. Both these models allow covariates, while the second model only is a mixture model (introduces noise). Appendix follows Prentice and Gloeckler (1978), Lancaster (1990), and Meyer (1990) to describe in detail how these two types of models can be estimated by using discrete-time transformation.

For the purpose of this study, two specifications are considered:

$$\theta(t; x_{it}) = \exp(x'_{i0}\beta) \times k_2(t) \tag{3}$$

$$\theta(t; x_{it}) = \exp(x'_{it}\beta) \times k_2(t) \times v_i \tag{4}$$

where $k_2(t)$ is a function describing the term-structure of the hazard rate to default. The model in Eq. (3) assumes that the entire hazard-rate curve is set at the time of issue and depends on x_{i0}, the variables describing the firm or its industry or the economy at time of issue, The model described in Eq. (4) adds to the previous model by introducing UH (at the time of issue) through the addition of noise v_i and covariates x_{it}. Prentice and Gloeckler (1978) show how by defining the integrated hazard rate

$$h(t) = \int_{t-1}^{t} \theta(u)\mathrm{d}u \tag{5}$$

and defining the integrated (discrete) term-structure

$$\gamma(t) \equiv \ln\left[\int_{t-1}^{t} k_2(u) \times \mathrm{d}u\right] \tag{6}$$

it is possible to estimate the integrated hazard rate function

$$h(t; x_{i0}) = \exp\left(x'_{i0}\beta + \gamma(t)\right) \tag{7}$$

Using this term, it is easily possible to estimate the parameters β and $\{\gamma(t)\}$ where $\{\gamma(t)\}$, the set of parameters describing the term-structure of default is the subject of this empirical investigation.

For estimating the second model, it is typical to assume a shape for the distribution of the noise v_i. A convenient distribution for v_i is the gamma distribution with unit mean (normalized) and variance $1/\eta$. Adopting this assumption and using the same definitions of the integrated hazard rate $h(t)$

and discrete term-structure $\gamma(t)$ as before, Meyer (1990) shows that the associated survival function has an explicit form and therefore the parameters β, $\{\gamma(t)\}$, and η can also be estimated.

The significance of the variance and the covariates in the second model would confirm the presence of UH. The comparison of the estimated term-structure $\{\gamma(t)\}$ once ignoring the UH (the first model) and once allowing for (the second model), would teach us on the effect of the UH on the estimated term-structure.

4. DATA

4.1. Database

The database is based on three sources. A list of more than 10,000 corporate bonds issued during the years 1983–1993 was obtained from the *Capital Division of Federal Reserve*.[6] Each issue in this database is detailed with name of issuer, date of issue, S&P and Moody's rating at date of issue, and other characteristics of the bond. A list of default events was mainly obtained from *Moody's Investor's Service* publications.

After combining these sources and eliminating financial corporations, multiple issues within each year, companies with no S&P rating, 2,596 bonds of 1,013 non-financial corporations remained. Of which 235 bonds belong to 155 firms that default at some point after appearance of their issues in the sample. Many corporations issued more than one bond during the sample period. For the estimation of the term-structure of the hazard function each year of exposure to default risk is defined as an observation. Hence the total number of observations (exposures to default risk) is 27,906 of which 235 are observations of default.

4.2. Data Definition

First, T_i the time that firm i has been exposed to default risk since the issue is calculated. This period depends not only on the time to maturity of a bond issued at this time but also on bonds issued before and after. For example, if the time of maturity of a bond issued at year 1991 is year 1999 and the time of maturity of the bond issued at time 1992 is 1998, then it is clear that the firm has been exposed to default risk since 1991 through time 1992 till 1999. Therefore, and unless default occurred before 1999, for the issuance of 1991,

$T_i = 8$ and for the issue of 1992, $T_j = 7$. If the firm defaulted during this period then the final period T_{it} was calculated from its date of issue till date of default. In such a case (and only in such case) the observation is considered to be uncensored ($\delta_i = 1$). For all observations, where the period of exposure to default risk has not ended with default, the observation is considered to be censored ($\delta_i = 0$). An observation is also considered censored if the time of exposure to risk is beyond year 2000. The reason for that is that it is not known at what exact time (after year 2000) the firm defaults.

The observations are taken over 11 years (1983–1993). Some firms appear in the sample several times since they issued bonds in several different years, while other firms only appear in the sample once. Since this paper focuses on estimation of the term-structure of default conditioned on the information at the time of issuance, each year of issue by the same firm is considered as a

Table 3. Distribution of Annual Observations of Exposure to Default Risk by the Number of Years from Issue and Default.

Year from Issue	Not Default	Default	Total
1	2,584	12	2,596
2	2,545	38	2,583
3	2,508	37	2,545
4	2,483	22	2,505
5	2,455	27	2,482
6	2,414	19	2,433
7	2,386	23	2,409
8	2,108	16	2,124
9	1,787	10	1,797
10	1,556	9	1,565
11	1,315	5	1,320
12	1,139	7	1,146
13	957	5	962
14	718	3	721
15	408	2	410
16	205	0	205
17	103	0	103
Total	27,671	235	27,906

Notes: This table presents the distribution of annual observations of exposure to default risk according to the number of years past from the issue and the occurrence of default in that year. Note that the number of issues is 2,596, from which 235 ended with default during the subsequent 17 years. Since in most cases the time to default was larger than one, the number of years of exposure to default risk is 27,906 and exceeds the number of issues.

separate observation. It should be noted that this is a common practice in reports concerning default experience.

4.3. Data Description

Table 3 shows the distribution of annual observation of exposure to default risk by the number of years passed from issue. It shows that as expected, the longer is the distance from the time of issue; the lower is the number of annual observations. This is due to the censorship and the defaults that occur over time. A special attention should be paid to the number of defaults (which does not have to be necessarily decreasing over time). The number of defaults is especially low after 8 years. There are no cases of defaults at years 16 and 17. Therefore it is not possible to estimate the term-structure at years 16 and 17.

Table 4 shows the distribution of the annual observations of exposure to default risk by rating of the bond at the time of issue. The number of defaults for the higher rated bonds is quite low. However, it should be noted that rating is used here just for controlling and the coefficients of the rating dummy variables are not the target of this paper. This table also shows that the sample is quite diverse and includes both investment graded and speculative graded bonds.

Table 4. Distribution of Annual Observations of Exposure to Default
Risk by Rating at Issue and Default.

Rating at Issuance	Not Default	Default	Total
AAA	1,073	1	1,074
AA	4,710	9	4,719
A	7,999	10	8,009
BBB	5,761	24	5,785
BB	1,979	21	2,000
B	5,404	137	5,541
CCC	740	30	770
CC	5	3	8
Total	27,671	235	27,906

Notes: This table presents the distribution of annual observations of exposure to default risk by the rating at the issue and the occurrence of default during that year. Note that the number of issues is 2,596, from which 235 ended with default during the subsequent 17 years. Since in most cases the time to default was larger then one, the number of years of exposure to default risk is 27,906 and exceeds the number of issuances.

Table 5. Estimation of the Hazard Function.

Explanatory Variable	Ignoring Unobserved Heterogeneity		Allowing for Unobserved Heterogeneity	
	Coefficient	t-Statistic	Coefficient	t-Statistic
Term structure (years from issuance)				
1	-3.822^{***}	-11.610	-3.384^{***}	-3.200
2	-2.642^{***}	-11.630	-1.944^{*}	-1.720
3	-2.627^{***}	-11.440	-1.758	-1.530
4	-3.116^{***}	-11.600	-2.090^{*}	-1.770
5	-2.887^{***}	-11.450	-1.607	-1.350
6	-3.210^{***}	-11.410	-1.603	-1.310
7	-2.996^{***}	-11.300	-1.145	-0.920
8	-3.217^{***}	-10.810	-1.117	-0.870
9	-3.511^{***}	-9.910	-0.902	-0.680
10	-3.526^{***}	-9.560	-0.761	-0.560
11	-3.931^{***}	-8.280	-1.161	-0.820
12	-3.465^{***}	-8.460	-0.786	-0.550
13	-3.585^{***}	-7.530	-0.987	-0.670
14	-3.727^{***}	-6.180	-1.191	-0.780
15 or 16 or 17	-4.091^{***}	-5.600	-1.543	-0.950
Calendar year				
1985	–	–	-0.135	-0.120
1986	–	–	0.536	0.490
1987	–	–	0.384	0.350
1988	–	–	-0.943	-0.840
1989	–	–	-0.464	-0.420
1990	–	–	0.095	0.090
1991	–	–	0.523	0.480
1992	–	–	-0.933	-0.830
1993	–	–	-1.216	-1.080
1994	–	–	-2.491^{**}	-2.070
1995	–	–	-1.405	-1.240
1996	–	–	-2.468^{**}	-2.070
1997	–	–	-2.147^{*}	-1.820
1998	–	–	-1.780	-1.520
1999	–	–	-1.448	-1.240
2000	–	–	-1.081	-0.920
Rating				
AAA	-3.829^{***}	-3.770	-4.492^{***}	-3.970
AA	-3.094^{***}	-8.220	-3.781^{***}	-6.360
A	-3.529^{***}	-9.770	-4.184^{***}	-7.170
BBB	-2.340^{***}	-8.720	-2.903^{***}	-5.740
BB	-1.401^{***}	-5.020	-1.893^{***}	-3.950
B	-0.546^{***}	-2.820	-0.741^{**}	-2.210

Table 5. (*Continued*)

Explanatory Variable	Ignoring Unobserved Heterogeneity		Allowing for Unobserved Heterogeneity	
	Coefficient	*t*-Statistic	Coefficient	*t*-Statistic
Unobserved heterogeneity Variance	–	–	2.924**	1.827
No. of observations	27,906		27,906	
Log likelihood	−1181.762978		−1116.062604	

Notes: The table contains results of two regressions for estimation of the survival function. The first model (ignoring unobserved heterogeneity) assumes that the hazard function is proportional with the form $\theta(t, x_{it}) = \exp(x'_{it}\beta) \times k_2(t)$. The second model (allowing unobserved heterogeneity) also assumes that the hazard rate is proportional but with the form $\theta(t, x_{it}) = \exp(x'_{it}\beta) \times k_2(t) \times v_i$ where v_i is Gamma distributed with unit mean. The parameters β, γ (a set of parameters which each integrates $k_2(t)$ the term-structure-component of the hazard rate), and the variance of v_i (in the second model) are estimated using a maximum likelihood approach. In these regressions x_{it} includes only dummy variables indicating the issue's rating at the time of issue (x_{it} can be notated x_i).
*Denotes significance at the 10% level.
**Denotes significance at the 5% level.
***Denotes significance at the 1% level.

5. RESULTS

Table 5 shows the results of estimations of the two models using the micro data; one ignoring UH and the other does not. The significance of the variance of the Gamma distributed noise in the second model, leads to the rejection of the hypothesis of absence of cross-sectional UH. An *F*-test also rejects the hypothesis of no time-series heterogeneity in hazard rates.[7]

Fig. 3 describes the estimated term-structure for each model. When ignoring UH, the estimated term-structure is quite similar to the one generally observed when looking at the aggregate cumulated frequencies of default. When ignoring UH, the term-structure is low at the year following the issue, increasing to a maximum and then decreasing slowly over time to a level close to the one in the first year following the issue. However, the control for UH makes clear changes. All coefficients are larger than in the first model. This result is expected in presence of UH. The hazard rate to default is still smaller in the first year following the issue compared to the

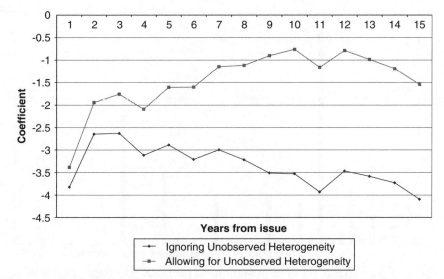

Fig. 3. The Estimated Term-Structure of the Hazard Rated to Default. This Figure Shows the Estimated Term-Structures of Two Hazard Models (See Table 4). The First Model (Ignoring Unobserved Heterogeneity) Assumes that the Hazard Function is Proportional with the Form $\theta(t, x_{it}) = \exp(x'_{it}\beta) \times k_2(t)$. The Second Model (Allowing Unobserved Heterogeneity) also Assumes that the Hazard Rate is Proportional but with the Form $\theta(t, x_{it}) = \exp(x'_{it}\beta) \times k_2(t) \times v_i$ where v_i is Gamma Distributed with Unit Mean (Standardization). This Figure Shows the Estimates for γ – A Set of Parameters which Each Integrates $k_2(t)$ the Term-Structure-Component of the Hazard Rate within Each Year.

following years. Then the term-structure shows an increasing pattern. The gap created between the two graphs widens.

The effect of the UH on the estimated term-structure is consistent with Diamond (1989). However, after controlling for the adverse selection (by introducing UH), the term-structure does not show a declining pattern. This result is not consistent with Diamond (1989) that predicts that the accumulation of reputation by the issuer should weaken the problem of moral hazard and encourage the firms to take less risky investments.

An interesting result is the correlation between the pattern of the term-structure to default and the time to maturity of the issues that were used for creating the estimation sample. Fig. 4 shows the frequencies of the time to maturity of 2,596 bonds. The highest frequencies (in the horizon of 15 years) are time to maturities of 10 years (27.9%), 7 years (7.6%), 5 years (6.8%), 15 years (6.4%), 12 years (5.5%), and 3 years (2.4%). Excluding the year 15,

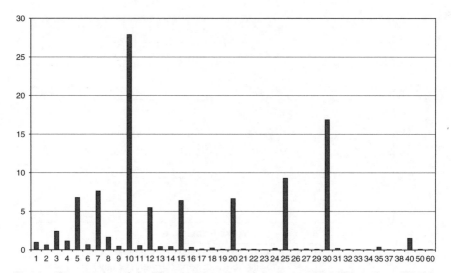

Fig. 4. Frequencies of the Time to Maturity of the Issues. The Figure Describes the Frequency (in Percent) of the Time to Maturity a Sample of 2,596 Bonds that were used to Create the Estimation Sample.

in all these years the hazard rate to default is slightly higher than the year before and the year after. Significant drops are in the years 4 and 11. These drops might reflect existence of a cash-effect. Yet, the general pattern of the term-structure as reflected in the model allowing UH cannot be explained by the time to maturity of the bonds. As an example, while the frequencies of bonds of 1 year to maturity is 1.0% and 11 years to maturity is 0.5%, the hazard rate to default at year 11 is significantly higher than at year 1.

To address the question of the significance of the term-structure, it is necessary to group the dummy variables. As it was shown in Table 3, the number of observations for the 9th year from the issue and later is relatively small. Fig. 3 shows that the term-structure has a small slope from starting year 2. Hence, for easing the significance tests, it is desirable to group the dummy variables for the term-structure into four dummy variables – 1 year after issue, 2 or 3 years after issue, 4–8 years from issue, and 9–17 years from issue. The results of estimation of the two models when using such dummy variables are reported in Table 6.

Table 7 shows the *t*-statistics for the differences between the dummy variables for the time from issue. The term-structure in model 1 (ignoring UH) induces the hazard rate to be significantly lower in year 1 compared to

Table 6. Estimation of the Hazard Function with Grouping of Age.

Explanatory Variable	Ignoring Unobserved Heterogeneity		Allowing for Unobserved Heterogeneity	
	Coefficient	*t*-Statistic	Coefficient	*t*-Statistic
Term structure (years from issuance)				
1	−3.818***	−11.600	−3.488***	−3.360
2 or 3	−2.630***	−13.350	−2.088*	−1.890
4–8	−3.068***	−16.220	−2.054*	−1.820
9–17	−3.624***	−16.120	−1.821	−1.500
Calendar year				
1985	–	–	−0.146	−0.130
1986	–	–	0.507	0.470
1987	–	–	0.278	0.260
1988	–	–	−0.963	−0.860
1989	–	–	−0.448	−0.410
1990	–	–	0.099	0.090
1991	–	–	0.571	0.530
1992	–	–	−0.812	−0.730
1993	–	–	−1.008	−0.910
1994	–	–	−2.223*	−1.880
1995	–	–	−1.082	−0.980
1996	–	–	−2.124*	−1.820
1997	–	–	−1.774	−1.550
1998	–	–	−1.379	−1.220
1999	–	–	−0.984	−0.880
2000	–	–	−0.646	−0.580
Rating				
AAA	−3.834***	−3.780	−4.171***	−3.840
AA	−3.101***	−8.250	−3.454***	−6.670
A	−3.535***	−9.790	−3.857***	−7.600
BBB	−2.346***	−8.740	−2.604***	−6.030
BB	−1.408***	−5.040	−1.654***	−3.980
B	−0.551***	−2.840	−0.653**	−2.270
Unobserved heterogeneity				
Variance	–	–	1.653*	1.350
No. of observations	27,906		27,906	
Log likelihood	−1183.3783		−1121.9761	

Notes: The table contains results of two regressions for estimation of the survival function. The first model (ignoring unobserved heterogeneity) assumes that the hazard function is proportional with the form $\theta(t, x_{it}) = \exp(x'_{it}\beta) \times k_2(t)$. The second model (allowing unobserved heterogeneity) also assumes that the hazard rate is proportional but with the form $\theta(t, x_{it}) = \exp(x'_{it}\beta) \times k_2(t) \times v_i$ where v_i is Gamma distributed with unit mean (standardization). The parameters β, γ (a set of parameters which each integrates $k_2(t)$ the term-structure-component of the hazard rate), and the variance of v_i (in the second model) are estimated using a maximum likelihood approach. In these regressions x_{it} includes dummy variables indicating the issue's rating at the time of issuance and dummy variables indicating the year of observation of exposure to default risk. In these regressions, the years from issuance are grouped into dummy variables for, 1 year after issuance, 2–3 years from issuance, 4–8 years from issuance and 9–17 years from issuance.
*Denotes significance at the 10% level.
**Denotes significance at the 5% level.
***Denotes significance at the 1% level.

Table 7. Statistics for Differences between Years from Issue.

Years after Issuance	1	2 and 3	4–8
A: Ignoring unobserved heterogeneity			
2 and 3	14.590**		
4–8	6.070*	8.440**	
9–17	0.350	26.160**	9.160**
B: Allowing unobserved heterogeneity			
2 and 3	16.960**		
4–8	13.130**	0.030	
9–17	8.700**	0.400	0.560

Notes: The table shows the *t*-statistics for the differences between the parameters describing the term structure of the hazard rate to default. The statistics are based on estimation of two models (reported in Table 5), where the first model (ignoring unobserved heterogeneity) assumes that the hazard function is proportional with the form $\theta(t, x_{it}) = \exp(x'_{it}\beta) \times k_2(t)$. The second model (allowing unobserved heterogeneity) also assumes that the hazard rate is proportional but with the form $\theta(t, x_{it}) = \exp(x'_{it}\beta) \times k_2(t) \times v_i$ where v_i is Gamma distributed with unit mean (standardization). The parameters γ (a set of parameters which each integrates $k_2(t)$ the term-structure-component of the hazard rate) are estimated using a maximum likelihood approach. In these regressions, the years from issuance are grouped into dummy variables for, 1 year after issuance, 2–3 years from issuance, 4–8 years from issuance and 9–17 years from issuance.
*Denotes significance at 5% level.
**Denotes significance at 1% level.

years 2 and 3 and 4–8 but not so comparing with years 9–17. The hazard rate during the years 2 and 3 is significantly higher comparing to years 4–8 and 9–17. And the hazard rate during the years 4–8 is also significantly higher than the years 9–17.

The *t*-statistics for the second model (allowing UH and AS) show that only the hazard rate of 1 year after issue is significantly lower compared to years 2 and 3, 4–8, and 9–17. And the hazard rates during the years 2–17 are not significantly different from each other. It should be emphasized that the models are estimated using the same sample and with identical variables. Furthermore, it should be noted that adding the noise does not only make the difference between years 2 and 17 insignificant but also the default risk at year 1 becomes significantly different from the one in years 9–17. Therefore, the change in the estimated term-structure cannot be only regarded to the increased standard deviation of the coefficients. Fig. 5 illustrates again the change in the term-structure of default between the two models.

The additional cross-sectional UH can be related both to adverse selection within each rating category and to heterogeneity of the term-structure across

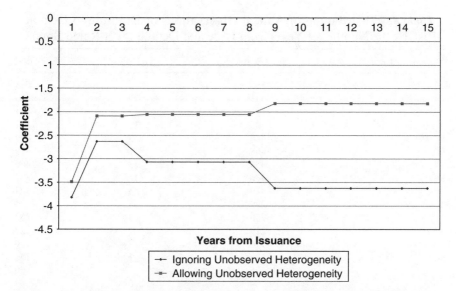

Fig. 5. The Estimated Term-Structure of the Hazard Rated to Default when Using Grouped Dummy Variables for the Year from Issuance. This Figure Shows the Estimated Term-Structures of Two Hazard Models (see Table 6) when the Dummy Variables for the Year from Issuance are Grouped into Four Dummy Variables – 1 Year, 2 or 3 Years, 4–8 Years, and 9–17 Years from Issuance. The First Model (Ignoring Unobserved Heterogeneity) Assumes that the Hazard Function is Proportional with the Form $\theta(t, x_{it}) = \exp(x'_{it}\beta) \times k_2(t)$. The Second Model (Allowing Unobserved Heterogeneity) also Assumes that the Hazard Rate is Proportional but with the Form $\theta(t, x_{it}) = \exp(x'_{it}\beta) \times k_2(t) \times v_i$ where v_i is Gamma Distributed with Unit Mean (Standardization). This Figure Shows the Estimates for γ – A Set of Parameters which Each Integrates $k_2(t)$ the Term-Structure-Component of the Hazard Rate within Each Year.

rating categories. In order to verify the effect of the UH on the term-structure of each rating category, it is necessary to repeat the estimation using sub-samples for each rating category. Table 4 reveals that the there are not enough default observations in order to estimate the default term-structure for each rating category. The only rating category that might have sufficient observations is B. However, this rating category embeds a very low-credit quality and therefore it might not be associated with significant adverse selection. Yet, we should at least expect time-series UH. Table 8 shows the distribution of annual observation of exposure to default risk by

Table 8. Distribution of Annual Observations of Exposure to Default Risk by the Number of Years from Issue and Default for B-Rated Bonds.

Year from Issue	Not Default	Default	Total
1	556	8	564
2	531	25	556
3	512	19	531
4	500	12	512
5	480	19	499
6	468	11	479
7	453	13	466
8	386	11	397
9	319	5	324
10	299	4	303
11	250	3	253
12	219	2	221
13	176	3	179
14	129	1	130
15	75	1	76
16	34	0	34
17	17	0	17
Total	5,404	137	5,541

Notes: This table presents the distribution of annual observations of exposure to default risk according to the number of years past from the issue and the occurrence of default in that year for B-rated bonds. Note that the number of issues is 564, from which 137 ended with default during the subsequent 17 years. Since in most cases the time to default was larger than one, the number of years of exposure to default risk is 5,541 and exceeds the number of issues.

the number of years passed from issue. There are obviously less cases of defaults within each year after issue. Therefore, it is necessary again to group the years from issue to a small number of dummy variables.

Table 9 shows the results of estimation of the two models using this subset. It appears now that the variance in the second model is statistically insignificant. However, an *F*-test results with the rejection of the null hypothesis that the coefficients of the time-series shocks are zero.[8] Therefore, this estimation also affirms the presence of UH within a single rating category.

Fig. 6 illustrates again the effect of the UH on the estimated term-structure. Once again, the estimated term-structure ignoring the UH appears to be first increasing and then decreasing. Allowing for UH makes the slope more positive and less negative.

Table 9. Estimation of the Hazard Function for B-Rated Issues.

Explanatory Variable	Ignoring Unobserved Heterogeneity		Allowing for Unobserved Heterogeneity	
	Coefficient	*t*-Statistic	Coefficient	*t*-Statistic
Term structure (years from issuance)				
1	−4.248***	−12.020	−4.266***	−6.540
2 or 3	−3.186***	−21.130	−3.075***	−5.040
4–8	−3.560***	−28.920	−3.167***	−4.740
9–17	−4.387***	−19.120	−3.469***	−3.850
Calendar year				
1986	–	–	0.912	1.300
1987	–	–	0.177	0.240
1988	–	–	−0.282	−0.390
1989	–	–	−0.511	−0.700
1990	–	–	0.294	0.430
1991	–	–	0.880	1.280
1992	–	–	−0.485	−0.620
1993	–	–	−0.423	−0.560
1994	–	–	−1.298	−1.590
1995	–	–	−0.946	−1.240
1996	–	–	−1.262	−1.540
1997	–	–	−1.478*	−1.680
1998	–	–	−0.550	−0.710
1999	–	–	−0.469	−0.610
2000	–	–	0.109	0.150
Unobserved heterogeneity				
Variance	–	–	0.973	0.514
No. of observations	5,541		5,541	
Log likelihood	−629.48029		−599.0997	

Notes: The table contains results of two regressions for estimation of the hazard rate function for B-rated issues. The first model (ignoring unobserved heterogeneity) assumes that the hazard function is proportional with the form $\theta(t, x_{it}) = \exp(x'_{i0}\beta) \times k_2(t)$. The second model (allowing unobserved heterogeneity) also assumes that the hazard rate is proportional but with the form $\theta(t, x_{it}) = \exp(x'_{it}\beta) \times k_2(t) \times v_i$ where v_i is Gamma distributed with unit mean (standardization). The parameters β, γ (a set of parameters which each integrates $k_2(t)$ the term-structure-component of the hazard rate), and the variance of v_i (in the second model) are estimated using a maximum likelihood approach.

Table 10 shows the *t*-statistics for the significance of the term-structure. Ignoring UH, the statistically significant term-structure is of an increasing term-structure from the first year to years 2 and 3 and then a falling hazard rate to the years 9–17. Allowing for UH, only the upward sloping from the first year remains statistically significant.

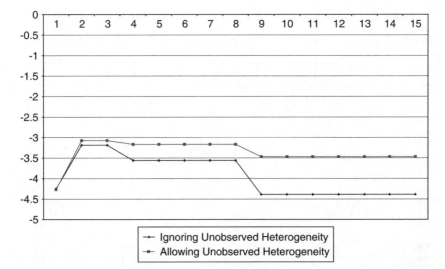

Fig. 6. The Estimated Term-Structure of the Hazard Rated to Default for B-Rated Issues. This Figure Shows the Estimated Term-Structures of Two Hazard Models for B-Rated Issues (See Table 9) when the Dummy Variables for the Year from Issuance are Grouped into Four Dummy Variables – 1 Year, 2 or 3 Years, 4–8 Years, and 9–17 Years from Issuance. The First Model (Ignoring Unobserved Heterogeneity) Assumes that the Hazard Function is Proportional with the Form $\theta(t, x_{it}) = \exp(x_{it}'\beta) \times k_2(t)$. The Second Model (Allowing Unobserved Heterogeneity) also Assumes that the Hazard Rate is Proportional but with the Form $\theta(t, x_{it}) = \exp(x_{it}'\beta) \times k_2(t) \times v_i$ where v_i is Gamma Distributed with Unit Mean (Standardization). This Figure Shows the Estimates for γ – A Set of Parameters which Each Integrates $k_2(t)$ the Term-Structure-Component of the Hazard Rate within Each Year.

6. CONCLUSIONS

This paper focuses on one aspect of credit risk – the term-structure of default. It shows that ignoring the UH (i.e. the fact that ratings are merely noisy signals) can bring to biased results; i.e. a downward biased term-structure of default. The paper affirms the presence of both cross-sectional and time-series UH in models that rely on ratings in prediction of long-term default. The paper also shows that the hazard rate to default is significantly lower in the first year following issue of bonds and that the appearance of downward sloping term-structure in the subsequent years can be related to the UH. The cross-sectional UH can be interpreted as adverse selection.

Table 10. Statistics for Differences between Years from Issue for B-Rated Issues.

Years after Issuance	1	2 and 3	4–8
A: Ignoring unobserved heterogeneity and annual shocks			
2 and 3	7.640***		
4–8	3.390*	3.680*	
9–17	0.110	19.120***	10.100***
B: Allowing unobserved heterogeneity			
2 and 3	8.570***		
4–8	4.600**	0.090	
9–17	0.880	0.320	0.370

Notes: The table shows the *t*-statistics for the differences between the parameters describing the term structure of the hazard rate to default for B-rated issues. The statistics are based on estimation of two models (reported in Table 9), where the first model (ignoring unobserved heterogeneity) assumes that the hazard function has the form $\theta(t, x_{it}) = \exp(x'_{it}\beta) \times k_2(t)$. The second model (allowing unobserved heterogeneity) assumes that the hazard rate has the form $\theta(t, x_{it}) = \exp(x'_{it}\beta) \times k_2(t) \times v_i$ where v_i is Gamma distributed with unit mean. The parameters γ (a set of parameters which each integrates $k_2(t)$ the term-structure-component of the hazard rate) are estimated using a maximum likelihood approach.

With this respect, the results are consistent with Diamond (1989) that predict a downward sloping term-structure of default due to adverse selection. However, the other conjecture of Diamond (1989) that moral hazard also causes decreasing hazard rate to default, is not confirmed. On controlling for adverse selection by allowing for UH, no further significant negative slope in the term-structure is observed. It can be concluded that adverse selection and another effect (possibly cash-flow effect) determine the term-structure of the default risk.

From the methodological point of view, the results teach us that hazard models in prediction of default should be carefully designed. Such models should allow unrestricted term-structure. It is also important to allow covariates or at least annual shocks in the hazard function. Introduction of noise in the hazard rate is also necessary, especially when using a small number of explanatory variables.

The paper presents a comprehensive framework for studying default risk, but several enhancements are still possible and even desired. For example, it is interesting to try other distributions than the Gamma distribution. In the current state of the research in default risk, a Gamma distribution is as legitimate as others. However, it was employed in this research merely due to its convenient properties and not due to its fit to previous observations or theoretical insights. Another desired enhancement is introduction of heteroscedasticity. It is reasonable that the larger the distance from the rating assignment, the lower its relevance and the greater the UH in the default risk. Allowing heteroscedasticity might show that the term-structure of default is significantly non-decreasing or even significantly increasing.

Implementation of the methodology presented in this paper with a larger sample, can shed a light on many open questions. For example, it would be possible to estimate the term-structure of the hazard rate for each rating category and to test the separability of the hazard rate function (as assumed in this paper and others). It would also be possible to identify the covariates that determine a firm's hazard rate to default including macroeconomic variables. The adjustment of ratings to business cycles and the declining quality in the credit markets can be also tested by using this framework.

NOTES

1. Prentice and Gloeckler's (1978) original model allows covariates that can stand for unobserved heterogenity. Since the goal of this study is to show the effect of unobserved heterogeneity on the estimation of the term structure, the implemented model does not allow covariates but only ratings at the date of issue.

2. See pages 64–65 in Lancaster (1990).

3. See "Ratings Performance 2000", Standard and Poor's. These statistics are based on all bonds rated by S&P during the years 1981–2000.

4. See Standard & Poor's (1997), "Rating Performance: Stability and Transition. Special Report". These statistics are based on changes in ratings of all S&P-rated bonds during the years 1981–1996.

5. A temporary change in the credit quality of the firms does not necessarily lead to a change in its rating.

6. This dataset is used by Guedes and Opler (1996).

7. The F-statistics is 103.17.

8. The F-statistics is 56.16. Testing for the significance of the time-series shocks in the framework of a model without noise (the first model using dummy variables for each calendar year as covariates) also produces similar results. The time-series shocks are statistically significant (F-statistics of 58.24).

REFERENCES

Altman, E. I. (1989). Measuring corporate bond mortality and performance. *Journal of Finance*, *44*(4), 909–922.

Asquith, P., Mullins, D. W., & Wolff, E. D. (1989). Original issue high yield bonds: Aging analysis of defaults, exchanges, and calls. *Journal of Finance*, *44*, 923–952.

Bharath, S. T., & Shumway, T. (2005). *Forecasting default with the KMV-Merton Model*, Memo.

Carty, L. V. (1997). *Moody's rating migration and credit quality correlation.* Moody's Special Report July.

Carty, L. V. (2000). Corporate credit-risk dynamics. *Financial Analysts Journal, 56*(4), 67–81.

Cox, D. R. (1972). Regression models and life tables. *Journal of the Royal Statistical Society B, 34*, 187–220.

Diamond, D. W. (1989). Reputation acquisition in debt markets. *Journal of Political Economy, 97*(4), 828–862.

Duffie, D., Saita, L., & Wang, K. (2005). Multi-period corporate default prediction with stochastic covariates, Working paper, Standford University.

Fons, J. S. (1994). Using default rates to model the term structure of credit risk. *Financial Analysts Journal* (Sept./Oct.), 25–32.

Gorton, G. (1996). Reputation formation in early bank note markets. *The Journal of Political Economy, 104*(2), 346–397.

Guedes, J., & Opler, T. (1996). The determinants of the maturity of corporate debt issues. *Journal of Finance, 51*, 1809–1833.

Jarrow, R. A., Lando, D., & Turnbull, S. (1997). A Markov model for the term structure of credit risk spreads. *Review of Financial Studies, 10*(2), 481–523.

Lancaster, T. (1990). *The econometric analysis of transition data, Econometric Society Monograph No. 17*. Cambridge: Cambridge University Press.

Loeffler, G. (2004). Ratings versus market-based measures of default risk in portfolio governance. *Journal of Banking and Finance, 28*, 2715–2746.

Merton, R. C. (1974). On the pricing of corporate debt: The risk structure of interest rates. *Journal of Finance, 29*, 449–470.

Meyer, B. D. (1990). Unemployment insurance and unemployment spells. *Econometrica, 58*(4), 757–782.

Prentice, R. L., & Gloeckler, L. A. (1978). Regression analysis of grouped survival data with application to breast cancer data. *Biometrics, 34*, 57–67.

Shumway, T. (2001). Forecasting bankruptcy more accurately: A simple hazard model. *Journal of Business, 74*(1), 101–124.

APPENDIX. ESTIMATION OF THE TERM-STRUCTURE OF THE HAZARD RATE

This appendix shows how the term-structure of the hazard rate can be estimated in two frameworks – one not allowing noise in the hazard function (Prentice and Gloeckler (1978)) and one allowing (mixture model). The estimation procedure is described first for the general models and then for special specifications.

A Discrete-Time Model for Default Occurrence with no Unobserved Heterogeneity

General Discrete-Time Hazard Model with Covariates

Assume that all firms that are exposed to default risk experience default at some time in future. Let i denote an observation on a firm issuing a new bond. Let T_i^D denote the time till the first time the firm defaults, and $\theta(t)$ denote the hazard rate to default at time t (the probability to default at time t conditioned on survival till time t). x_{it} is a vector of variables, whether describing the firm or its industry or the economy at time t. Suppose that the time is observed in discrete intervals. It is possible to integrate the hazard rate over the time interval $(t-1,t]$. The integrated hazard rate is

$$h(t; x_{it}) = \int_{t-1}^{t} \theta(u; x_{it}) \mathrm{d}u \qquad (A.1)$$

Note that this is not the discrete hazard rate. Now $\bar{F}(t; x_{i1}, ..., x_{it})$, the associated survivor probability till time t is

$$\bar{F}(t; x_{i1}, ..., x_{it}) \equiv \exp\left(-\int_0^t \theta(u; x_{iu})\mathrm{d}u\right) = \exp\left(-\sum_{s=1}^{t} h(s; x_{is})\right)$$

$$= \prod_{s=1}^{t} \exp[-h(s; x_{is})] \qquad (A.2)$$

The probability to survive till time t conditional on surviving till time $t-1$ is

$$\mathrm{prob}(T_i^D \geq t; T_i^D \geq t - 1, x_{i1}, ..., x_{it}) = \frac{\bar{F}(t; x_{i1}, ..., x_{it})}{\bar{F}(t - 1; x_{i1}, ..., x_{it-1})} \qquad (A.3)$$

Incorporating Eq. (A.2), it can be rephrased,

$$\mathrm{prob}(T_i^D \geq t; T_i^D \geq t - 1, x_{i1}, ..., x_{it}) = \exp[-h(s; x_{it})] \qquad (A.4)$$

And the hazard rate for the discrete time t is,

$$\text{prob}(T_i^D \leq t; T_i^D \geq t-1, x_{i1}, ..., x_{it}) = 1 - \exp[-h(s; x_{it})] \tag{A.5}$$

Define T_i as the period during which the firm i is known to have been exposed to default risk. Each period can end whether due to default, or censorship (when T_i^D is not observed due to a maximum length of observation or lack of information on availability of outstanding bonds). Let $\delta_i = 1$ in the case the period T_i ended with default $(T_i = T_i^D)$, and $\delta_i = 0$ otherwise $(T_i < T_i^D)$. Then the likelihood function for a sample of N observation is,

$$l(.) = \prod_i^N \left\{ \prod_{s=1}^{T_i-1} \exp[-h(s; x_{is})] \right\} \times \left\{ 1 - \exp[-h(s; x_{it})] \right\}^{\delta_i} \tag{A.6}$$

Proportional Hazard Function (Prentice & Gloeckler, 1978)

For estimating the model, it is needed to fully or partially parameterize the hazard rate. Following Cox (1972), assume that the hazard function is of the proportional hazard form and has the following construction

$$\theta(t; x_{it}) = k_1(x_{it}) \times k_2(t) \tag{A.7}$$

This construction assumes that term-structure of the hazard rate $k_2(t)$ is separable from $k_1(x_{it})$. The Cox (1972) is a semi-parametric model, which enables estimating the first component $k_1(x_{it})$ without parameterizing the term-structure of the hazard rate, $k_2(t)$. On assuming that x_{it} is constant during the interval $(t-1, t]$, the integrated hazard at the discrete time t, $h(t; x_{it})$, has the following form

$$h(t; x_{it}) = \int_{t-1}^{t} \theta(u; x_{it}) du = k_1(x_{it}) \times \exp(\gamma(t)) \tag{A.8}$$

where $\gamma(t) \equiv \ln\left[\int_{t-1}^{t} k_2(u) \times du\right]$. On incorporating this equation in the survival function presented in Eq. (A.2), the survival function will be

$$\bar{F}(t; x_{i1}, ..., x_{it}) = \prod_{s=1}^{t} \exp[-k_1(x_{is}) \times \exp(\gamma(s))] \tag{A.9}$$

And the probability to survive till time t conditional on surviving till time $t-1$ is

$$\text{prob}(T_i^D \geq t; T_i^D \geq t-1, x_{i1}, ..., x_{it}) = \exp[-k_1(x_{it}) \times \exp(\gamma(t))] \tag{A.10}$$

Hence, the hazard rate to default at the discrete time t (the probability to default at the discrete time t conditional on surviving till time $t-1$) is

$$\text{prob}(T_i^D \leq t; T_i^D \geq t - 1, x_{i1}, ..., x_{it}) = 1 - \exp[-k_1(x_{it}) \times \exp(\gamma(t))] \quad \text{(A.11)}$$

Therefore this likelihood function in the case of Cox (1972) proportional hazard model, can be written as

$$l(.) = \prod_i^N \left\{ \prod_{s=1}^{T_i-1} \exp[-k_1(x_{is}) \times \exp(\gamma(s))] \right\} \times \left\{ 1 - \exp\left[-k_1(x_{iT_i}) \times \exp(\gamma(T_i))\right] \right\}^{\delta_i}$$

$$\text{(A.12)}$$

This approach enables estimating the parameters of $k_1(x_{it})$, the first component of the hazard function, and a vector of parameters, $\gamma = [\gamma(0), \gamma(1), ...]$, describing the term-structure of the hazard rate without parameterizing $k_2(t)$, the baseline of the hazard function. A simple and common case is where $k_1(x_{it})$ is linear. In such a case, $k_1(x_{it}) = \exp(x_{it}'\beta)$ where β is a vector of parameters corresponding to x_{it}. The hazard function for the continuous term in such a case is

$$\theta(t; x_{it}) = \exp(x_{it}'\beta) \times k_2(t) \quad \text{(A.13)}$$

And the integrated hazard at the discrete time t, is

$$h(t; x_{it}) = \exp\left(x_{it}'\beta + \gamma(t)\right) \quad \text{(A.14)}$$

The probability to survive till time t is $\bar{F}(t; x_{i1}, ..., x_{it}) = \prod_{s=1}^{t} \exp\left[-\exp(x_{is}'\beta + \gamma(s))\right]$. And the corresponding likelihood function for estimating Eq. (A.14) is

$$l(\beta, \gamma) = \prod_i^N \left\{ \prod_{s=1}^{T_i-1} \exp\left[-\exp(x_{is}'\beta + \gamma(s))\right] \right\} \times \left\{ 1 - \exp\left[-\exp\left(x_{iT_i}'\beta + \gamma(T_i)\right)\right] \right\}^{\delta_i}$$

$$\text{(A.15)}$$

Note that the formation of the hazard function allows for the determinants of the hazard rate to vary over time. However, it is also possible to assume constant variables over time. This case draws a special attention since it enables to estimate the hazard function conditioned on information available only at the time of rating. In such a case the vector x_{it} in Eqs. (1), (A.14), and (A.15) has to be simply replaced by the vector x_i.

A Mixture Model for Default Occurrence

General Model

The introduction of the random variable in the hazard rate function enables considering UH among firms and the possibility of stochastic hazard rate due to unexpected changes in the economy or unexpected changes in the creditworthiness of the issuer itself. Let $\theta(t;x_{it},v_i)$ denote the hazard rate to default at time t where v_i is a random variable with density $\mu(v)$. v_i resembles the affect of all omitted variables or unexpected events on the exact realization of T_i^D. The integrated survival function till time t can be constructed by conditioning on the unobserved v_i

$$\bar{F}(t; x_{i1}, ..., x_{it}) \equiv \int_v \exp\left(- \int_0^t \theta(u; x_{iu}, v)\mathrm{d}u \right) \mathrm{d}\mu(v) \qquad (A.16)$$

The likelihood function for the sample is

$$l(.) = \prod_{i=1}^N \left\{ \begin{array}{l} \delta_i \times \left[\bar{F}(T_i - 1; x_{i1}, ...x_{iT_i-1}) - \bar{F}(T_i; x_{i1}, ...x_{iT_i}) \right] \\ +(1 - \delta_i) \times \left[\bar{F}(T_i; x_{i1}, ...x_{iT_i}) \right] \end{array} \right\} \qquad (A.17)$$

It is possible to write (A.17) differently:

$$l(.) = \prod_{i=1}^N \{ \bar{F}(T_i; x_{i1}, ...x_{iT_i}) - \delta_i \times \bar{F}(T_i - 1; x_{i1}, ...x_{iT_i-1}) \} \qquad (A.18)$$

Now, incorporating Eq. (A.16), it will have the following form:

$$l(.) = \prod_{i=1}^N \int_v \exp\left(- \int_0^{T_i} \theta(u; x_{iu}, v)\mathrm{d}u \right) \mathrm{d}\mu(v) - \delta_i \times \int_v \exp\left(- \int_0^{T_i-1} \theta(u; x_{iu}, v)\mathrm{d}u \right) \mathrm{d}\mu(v)$$
$$(A.19)$$

The Case of Proportional Hazard Rate (Meyer, 1990)

Assume again that the hazard rate has a proportional form $\theta(t;x_{it})=k_1(x_{it}) \times k_2(t) \times v_i$. Then the survival function (A.15) can be written as,

$$\bar{F}(t; x_{i1}, ..., x_{it}) \equiv \int_v \exp\left(- \int_0^t k_1(x_{iu}) \times k_2(u) \times v \times \mathrm{d}u \right) \mathrm{d}\mu(v) \qquad (A.20)$$

On observing discrete times (where a discrete time t is the time-interval $(t-1,t]$), and assuming again that x_i is constant during the time-interval

$(t-1,t]$, the likelihood function is:

$$\bar{F}(t; x_{i1}, ..., x_{it}) \equiv \int_v \exp\left(-v \times \sum_{u=0}^{t} k_1(x_{iu}) \times \exp[\gamma(u)]\right) d\mu(v) \qquad \text{(A.21)}$$

where again $\gamma(t) = \ln\left[\int_{t-1}^{t} k(u) \times du\right]$. In the linear case where $k(x_j) = \exp(x'_{it}\beta)$, the survival function has the following form

$$\bar{F}(t; x_{i1}, ..., x_{it}) \equiv \int_v \exp\left(-v \times \sum_{u=0}^{t} \exp[x'_{it}\beta + \gamma(u)]\right) d\mu(v) \qquad \text{(A.22)}$$

For estimation of a duration model using Eq. (A.22), it is typical to assume a shape for the distribution $\mu(v)$. A convenient and commonly used distribution for v is the gamma distribution with unit mean (normalized) and variance $1/\eta$. This distribution gives a closed form expression for the likelihood function, avoiding numerical integration. Meyer (1990) shows that under such conditions $\bar{F}(t; x_{i1}, ..., x_{it})$ – the survival probability till time T can be denoted as:

$$\bar{F}(t; x_{i1}, ..., x_{it}) = \left[1 + \frac{1}{\eta} \times \sum_{u=0}^{t} \exp\{x'_{iu}\beta + \gamma(u)\}\right]^{-\eta} \qquad \text{(A.23)}$$

And the likelihood function of the sample is

$$l(\beta, \gamma, \eta) = \prod_{i=1}^{N} \left\{ \begin{array}{l} \left[1 + \frac{1}{\eta} \times \sum_{u=0}^{T_i} \exp\{x'_{iu}\beta + \gamma(u)\}\right]^{-\eta} \\ -\delta_i \times \left[1 + \frac{1}{\eta} \times \sum_{u=0}^{T_i-1} \exp\{x'_{iu}\beta + \gamma(u)\}\right]^{-\eta} \end{array} \right\} \qquad \text{(A.24)}$$

FINANCIAL SECTOR DEVELOPMENT AND SUSTAINABLE ECONOMIC GROWTH IN REGIONALLY CO-INTEGRATED EMERGING MARKETS

Ritab S. Al-Khouri

This paper presents new evidence of the relationship between financial market development (banking sector) and economic growth for a set of seven Middle East and North African economies over the period 1965–2002. We find evidence that in six of the seven countries, banking-sector development Granger causes increases in economic growth. However, in three of those six countries, economic growth also Granger causes banking development. Our co-integration analysis reveals that there is a stable long-run equilibrium relationship between banking-sector development and economic growth for all our countries. However, based on vector error-correction models, there is limited evidence that banking-sector development boosts economic growth in the short run.

Issues in Corporate Governance and Finance
Advances in Financial Economics, Volume 12, 345–360
ISSN: 1569-3732/doi:10.1016/S1569-3732(07)12013-2

1. INTRODUCTION

In the last decade researchers have become increasingly interested in the relationship between financial development and economic growth. Demirguc-Kunt and Maksimovic (1998) show that firms in countries with better functioning banks and equity markets grow faster than predicted by individual firm characteristics. According to Gertler (1988), Levine (1997), and Bencivenga and Smith (1991), financial institutions can reduce risk, improve corporate governance, mobilize savings, reduce transaction and information costs, and promote specialization.

An important issue that has not received much attention is the direction of causality in the relationship between financial development and economic growth. Does financial development lead to greater economic growth, or does economic growth leads to greater financial development? This is an important issue for many developing economies. For example in the Middle East and North Africa (MENA), many of the countries have pursued reform programs suggested by international organizations such as the International Monetary Fund (IMF) and the World Bank. These programs require countries to invest considerable resources into improving the operation and the efficiency of their financial markets and institutions to help bring about sustained economic growth. Due to the limited resources of these countries, this huge investment in the financial sector led to a significant reduction in the amount of funds directed to other sectors within their economies. If financial development does not lead to increased economic growth then these countries' valuable financial resources are not being allocated optimally.

This paper presents new evidence of the relationship between financial market development and economic growth for a set of seven Middle East and North African economies over the period 1965–2002, using Granger causality tests, cointegration techniques, and vector error-correction models.

We use three proxies for banking-sector development, the credit extended to the private sector as a percentage of GDP, the ratio of deposits to broad money (M1), and the money supply (M2) as a percentage of GDP. Based on our proxies for banking-sector development we find evidence that for six of the seven countries, after controlling for other important macroeconomic factors, improvements in banking-sector development Granger cause increases in economic growth. However, for three of those six countries we find evidence that economic growth also Granger causes banking-sector development.

Further, we find evidence of a cointegrating relation between GDP per capita and our proxies for banking-sector development. However, this relation is sensitive to both the lag length and the choice of proxy for banking-sector development. Overall, the results of our cointegration analysis indicate that there appears to be a long-term stable equilibrium relationship between banking-sector development and economic growth for all of the countries in our sample.

The co-integration analysis combined with the Granger causality tests provide strong evidence that there is a long-run equilibrium relationship between banking-sector development and economic growth, and that improvements in the banking sector should boost economic growth in the long run. To analyze the impact that banking-sector development has on economic growth in the short run we estimate vector error-correction models. We find limited evidence that banking-sector development boosts economic growth in the short run. For one proxy of banking-sector development our results are statistically significant, but for the remaining two proxies we find that the coefficients are correctly signed, but not significant. Thus we conclude that none of our sample countries should rely on banking-sector development to promote economic growth in the short term.

The outline for the rest of the paper is as follows. In Section 2 we briefly review the literature related to our study. In Section 3 we describe our data and outline our methodology. Section 4 presents the main results, while section five concludes.

2. LITERATURE REVIEW

In the last decade researchers have become increasingly interested in the relationship between financial development and economic growth. Demirguc-Kunt and Maksimovic (1998) show that firms in countries with better functioning banks and equity markets grow faster than predicted by individual firm characteristics, while Gertler (1988), Levine (1997), and Bencivenga and Smith (1991), find that more developed financial institutions can reduce risk, improve corporate governance, mobilize savings, reduce transaction and information costs, and promote specialization.

King and Levine (1993b), find that various measures of financial development are strongly associated with both current and future rates of economic growth, while Atje and Jovanovic (1993) present a cross-country study of stock markets and economic growth for 40 countries and find a significant correlation between growth and the value of the stock market. Levine and Zervos (1998) find stock market liquidity to be positively and significantly correlated with current and future rates of economic growth, capital accumulation, and productivity growth. Moreover, they find that the level of banking development is positively related to growth.

An important issue that has not received much attention is whether financial development leads to greater economic growth, or whether economic growth leads to greater financial development. Endogenous growth theory suggests that steady-state growth is a function of three parameters: the level of technology, the proportion of savings available to be invested, and the saving rate. This implies that financial development could influence economic growth by increasing capital productivity, by improving the allocation of resources across investment projects, by lowering intermediation costs, or by increasing the saving rate. In other words, an improvement in financial development should have a positive effect on economic growth rates. If this is true then developing countries should invest resources improving their financial infrastructure.

However, it is also possible that financial development may not lead to economic growth, but rather that economic growth stimulates financial development. Economic growth increases banking activity and profits, and promotes the entry of more banks. Therefore, economic growth may create a demand for financial intermediation. The entry of more banks facilitates regional specialization and in the process lowers the cost of financial intermediation, which in turn boosts investment and growth.

Few researchers investigate whether financial development leads to greater economic growth, or whether economic growth leads to greater financial development. Jung (1986) investigates the casual and temporal behavioural relationship between financial development and economic growth in 56 countries over the period 1950–1980. Using the Granger causality test, he finds that the direction of the casual relationship in less-developed countries (LDCs) runs from financial development to economic growth, while the reverse is true for developed countries.

Demetriades and Hussein (1996) test for causality between financial development and real per capita gross domestic product (GDP) for 16 countries over the period 1960–1990. They find little support for the view that finance is a leading sector in the process of economic development. In contrast, Rousseau and Wachtel (1998), using co-integration and vector error-correction models (VECM), find that improvements in financial intermediation Granger–cause positive changes in real per capita GDP. In addition, Luintel and Khan (1999) examine the long-term causal relationship between financial development and economic growth using vector autoregressions (VAR). They find that shocks to the the level of per capita real income, and the real interest rate, have a significant positive impact on financial development.

3. DATA AND METHODOLOGY

Our sample covers seven countries in the MENA; Algeria, Jordan, Turkey, Egypt, Tunisia, Morocco, and Israel. We obtain data on these countries for the period 1965–2002 from the International Financial Statistics database and the World Development Indicator database. To enable comparison between our results and previous research, we define economic growth rate to be the real per capita growth rate in GDP.

To assess the relationship between economic growth and banking development, we need to create proxies for the level of banking-sector development within each country. We propose three different proxies:

1. *Financial Depth Ratio (FDR)*. The FDR, or the monetization ratio, is measured by dividing the stock of broad money (M2) by GDP. This variable, calculated as M2/GDP, measures the overall size of the banking sector. A higher M2/GDP ratio indicates a larger financial sector.
2. *Bank Credit Ratio (BCR)*. As King and Levine (1993a) note, the financial depth ratio does not capture whether the liabilities are those of banks, the central bank, or other financial intermediaries. Nor does it identify how the financial system allocated capital. The Bank Credit Ratio, calculated as the credit provided by the financial intermediaries to the private sector (BC) divided by GDP, measures the magnitude of the banking sector. The Bank Credit Ratio improves upon the financial depth ratio measure of banking development by separating credit offered by banks to the private sector, as opposed to that offered to governments or other financial intermediaries. Therefore, the higher ratio of credit offered to the private sector as a percent of GDP, the greater the development of the financial sector.
3. *Demand Deposit to Money Supply (DMS)*. The third measure for banking development is the ratio of demand deposit to the Narrow Money (M1). Vogel and Buser (1976) argue that this measure represents the complexity of the financial sector. A high ratio indicates a higher degree of sophistication and diversification of the financial institutions.

To evaluate the relation between bank development and economic growth it is necessary to control for other macroeconomic variables that researchers have found to be associated with economic growth. These factors include:

1. *Government Consumption Ratio.* Barro and Sala-I-Martin (1995) argue that government consumption (GC) as a percentage of GDP proxies for political corruption, non-productive public expenditures or taxation. In addition, changes in the government size could be important given the fact that governments in developing countries play a crucial role in influencing economic activities within their country.
2. *The Degree of Openness of an Economy.* The more open an economy is to trade the more likely it is that foreign investors will be attracted to that country. In turn this should stimulate economic growth. Bekaert and Harvey (1997, 2000), and Levine and Zervos (1998) measure the openness of trade as the sum of exports and imports divided by GDP.
3. *Exchange rate (Exch).* The exchange rate is also necessary to control for the possible effects of external shocks.

The specific empirical technique that we use to examine the relation between economic growth and financial sector development is cointegration. Cointegration analysis tells us that any two non-stationary time series processes, which are integrated to the same order, are co-integrated if a linear combination of the two processes exists which is stationary. If this is the case then the non-stationarity in one series offsets the non-stationarity in the other, and a long run relationship is established between the two variables.

In order to test co-integration we follow the procedure first introduced by Engle and Granger (1987). The first step before we can test for co-integrating relationship is to test for the non-stationarity of the time series being considered. Both the time series under consideration need to be integrated of order d, denoted I(d), before we can conduct the co-integration study.

We test for unit roots using the Augmented Dickey Fuller (ADF) test and the Phillips–Perron (PP) test. The Phillip Perron test, is similar to the ADF test but it allows for mild assumptions concerning the distribution of the errors. The errors can be weakly dependent and heterogeneously distributed. We use these tests to identify the order of integration for the two processes, economic growth and financial sector development.

If both processes are integrated of the same order we can proceed to test the null hypothesis of no co-integration. We adopt the approach suggested by Johansen and Juselius (1990). We estimate a VAR model which includes differences as well as levels of the non-stationary variables,

$$\Delta Y_t = \Gamma_1 \Delta Y_{t-1} + \ldots + \Gamma_{k-1} \Delta Y_{t-k+1} + \Pi Y_{t-k} + \Phi D_t + \varepsilon_t \qquad (1)$$

where Y_t is a vector of p stochastic variables (i.e. GDP, FDR, BCR, and DMS), ε_t is a vector of Gaussian random variables, and D_t is a vector of exogenous variables. Γ_1 and Π are matrices of parameters estimated using OLS as described in Johansen (1988). The matrix Π contains information regarding the long-run properties of the system described by the model. For example, if the rank of the matrix Π is 0 then no series of the variables can be expressed as a linear combination of the remaining series. Thus, if the rank of Π is 0 then we are unable to reject the null hypothesis of no co-integration. However, if the rank of the matrix Π is 1 or greater, then there exists one or more co-integrating vectors. This indicates that a long run relationship exists between the variables.

We evaluate the rank of the the matrix Π by using the method proposed by Johansen (1988). We use a likelihood ratio test to test the null hypothesis that the number of co-integrating vectors is r against the alternative hypothesis that the number of co-integrating vectors is $r+1$. In this framework we are only interested whether there exists at least one co-integrating vector.

An important implication of co-integration is given by the Granger representation theorem (Engle & Granger, 1987) which shows that if two or more I(1) variables are co-integrated then there must exist an error-correction representation governing their dynamic evolution,

$$\Delta GDP = \alpha + \sum_{i=1}^{m} \beta_i \Delta GDP_{t-i} + \sum_{j=1}^{n} \gamma_j \Delta X_{t-j} + \sum_{k=1}^{o} \delta D_{t-k} + \varphi Z_{t-1} + \varepsilon_t \qquad (2)$$

where X_{t-j} denotes each of the financial market development. One lag of the residuals, z_{t-1}, obtained from the long-term co-integration relation is added to the model that contains stationary variables. These residuals are called the error-correction term. The coefficient on the error-correction term describes how economic growth, GDP, adjusts back towards its equilibrium value in the current period. According to Granger and Lin (1995), the error-correction term provides another channel through which Granger-Causality can occur, in addition to the traditional channel through lagged independent variables. The error-correction term represents long-term Granger Causality, while the traditional channel reflects short-term Granger-Causality.

Therefore, the VECM representation allows us to differentiate between the short-term and the long-term dynamic relationships.

In this model, the absence of Granger-Causality requires the additional condition that the coefficient on the error-correction term be equal to zero. If this is the case then there is no long-run equilibrium relationship, and our model is incorrect.

4. EMPIRICAL RESULTS

In Table 1 we report the results of unit root tests for all the variables used in our study. We are unable to reject the null hypothesis of a unit root process for the log of per capita GDP growth for all of the countries in our sample. However, the results of the ADF and PP tests on the first difference of log per capita GDP growth strongly reject the hypothesis of a unit root in the log of GDP indicating that the log of GDP growth follows an I(1) process.[1] The results of the ADF and PP tests for unit roots on the other financial development indicators are also reported in Table 1. The evidence suggests that financial development indicators also follow an I(1) process. Thus we can proceed to investigate whether a co-integrating relationship exists.

Table 2 Panel A shows the results of co-integration tests between economic growth and each of the financial development variables. We run the analysis on lag lengths of 1–4. The lags based on Swartz Criterion are given by L in the table. We use the likelihood ratio test (Johansen & Juselius, 1990) to test the null hypothesis that $r = 0$ against the alternative hypothesis that $r = 1$. In other words we test whether there is at least one co-integrating relationship.

We find that we are unable to reject the null hypothesis that there is no co-integrating relationship between GDP and BCR for Egypt. For all the other countries we find evidence of one co-integrating relationship for at least one lag length. We obtain similar results when we use FDR as our proxy of banking-sector development rather than BCR. There is at least one co-integrating relationship for all countries except for Turkey. Finally, when we test for a co-integrating relationship between economic growth and the final proxy for banking-sector development, DMS, we find evidence of a co-integrating relationship for only Tunisia and Morocco.

Table 2 Panel B shows the co-integration relationship between financial market development indicators and economic growth after adding the control variables, the GC ratio, the degree of openness of an economy, and the exchange rate. In this panel we just show the number of co-integrating

Table 1. Augmented Dickey–Fuller and Phillips–Perron Tests for Unit Roots.

Variables	Countries													
	Algeria		Egypt		Israel		Jordan		Morocco		Tunis		Turkey	
	ADF	PP	ADF	PP	ADF	PP	ADF	PP	ADF	PP	ADF	PP	ADF	PP
In level														
Log(DepM1)	−3.2**	−3.8*	−2.28	−2.77	−3.4**	−4.57*	−2.13	−2.31	−1.96	−2.55	−2.86	−4.11*	−2.66	−2.63
Log(CrGDP)	−3.1**	−3.92*	0.336	−0.951	−0.93	−0.85	−1.77	−2.67	−1.74	−1.46	−0.14	−0.35	−0.77	−2.59
Log(M2GDP)	−0.87	−0.53	−2.51	−4.02*	−1.08	−1.03	−1.36	−1.69	−1.50	−0.989	−0.137	−0.59	−2.15	−1.87
Log(GDP)	−1.73	−1.74	−0.76*	−0.393	−1.87	−1.11	−1.26	−1.27	−2.09	−3.76	−2.10	−1.92	−1.29	−1.58
Log(GOVEX)	−0.86	−1.48	−1.75	−1.72	−1.54	−1.99	−2.33	−2.44	−1.88	−1.95	−2.59	−3.07	−1.2	−0.98
Log(OPEN)	−0.123	−2.42	−1.61	−1.28	−0.44	−0.729	−1.13	−1.29	−1.05	−1.69	−1.77	−1.92	−0.057	−0.497
In First difference														
Log(DepM1)	−5.44*	−8.26*	−4.35*	−6.63*	−5.46*	−10.3*	−4.31*	−6.53*	−5.65*	−10.3*	−5.29*	−9.85*	−5.00*	−8.17*
Log(CrGDP)	−8.16*	−12.8*	−3.75*	−3.97*	−3.3**	−4.64*	−6.5*	−12.4*	−6.61*(2)	−7.24*	−5.03*	−8.46* (2)	−4.32* (2)	−5.38* (2)
Log(M2GDP)	−4.47*	−7.16*	−6.80*	−12.8*	4.43*	−6.02*	−6.63*	−11.9*	−3.80*	−6.18*	−3.1**	−5.66*	−6.28* (2)	−10.4* (2)
Log(GDP)	−6.27*	−11.0*	−4.58*	−4.39*	−5.44*	−4.82*	−6.13* (2)	−4.89*	−14.5*	−13.2*	−3.91*	−5.11*	−6.63*	−11.9*
Log(GOVEX)	−4.45*	−6.90*	−4.48*	−5.12*	−5.88*	−6.60*	−7.69* (2)	−5.41*	−3.61*	−4.68*	−4.48*	−6.08*	−4.28*	−9.60*
Log(OPEN)	−5.89*	−6.34*	−4.58*	−4.22*	−3.99*	−6.21*	−4.24*	−6.16*	−5.56	−8.00*	−4.04*	−6.38*	−4.38*	−4.66*

(2) Refers of order 2

*Significance at 5% level.

**Significance level at 10%.

Table 2. Johansen Co-integration Tests Based on Maximum Eigenvalues.

Panel A

Variables	GDP and CrGDP				GDP and M2GDP				GDP and depM1			
Hypotheses	H0:r=0 vs H1:r=1				H0:r=0 vs H1: r01				H0:r=0 vs H1: r01			
Countries	K=1	K=2	K=3	K=4	K=1	K=2	K=3	K=4	K=1	K=2	K=3	K=4
Algeria	–	–	–	–	5.07	5.27	17.77*L	7.53	–	–	–	–
Egypt	8.47	13.35L	10.68	7.66	8.86	10.64	16.25*L	7.06	13.35L	8.47	10.47	7.66
Israel	11.28	14.28	28.4**L	8.73	10.57	16.19**	27.95**L	13.61	–	–	–	–
Jordan	13.8	19.65*L	18.43*	24.69**	8.50	13.98	12.17L	19.14*	10.05	10.46	8.26	10.41
Morocco	5.49	111.4**L	27.39**	9.25	23.26**	24.63**	176.3**L	14.18	14.66	9.16	23.45**L	14.66
Tunis	10.95	13.44	16.48*L	14.79	11.59	14.06	16.78*L	16.72*	20.14*L	28.36**L	17.15*	24.09**
Turkey	11.89	15.54*L	12.04	10.21	12.78	13.61	11.81L	11.98	10.17	9.55	11.9L	9.81

Panel B

Variables	GDP CrGDP GOVEX OPEN and EXCH	GDP M2GDP GOVEX OPEN and EXCH	GDP DepM1 GOVEX OPEN and EXCH
Countries	K=1	K=1	K=1
Algeria	–	(2)*	–
Egypt	(1)*	(2)**	(1)*
Israel	(1)*	(1)*	–
Jordan	(2)*	(2)**	(1)*
Morocco	(1)*	(1)*	(1)*
Tunis	(1)*	(2)*	(1)*
Turkey	(1)*	(1)*	(1)**

K= indicates the test based on the number of lags (k). Numbers in brackets are the number of co-integration relations. The lag length based on AIC suggest one lag for the models with four variables in all countries except in thee case of Jordan and Morocco (2) lags suggested. L indicates the optimal lag length based on AIC.
*Significant at 5% level.
**significant at 10% level.

relationships between brackets. Since our sample is small, we confine our analysis to only one lag, so as not to loose the power of our tests. The results of the table show that co-integration exists between economic growth and FDR for all countries after including the the control variables in our tests. For the remaining two proxies for financial development we find evidence of co-integration between the proxies and economic growth for the majority of countries, but the results are not as strong as they are for the proxy FDR. Overall, the results in Table 2 indicate that there is a co-integrating relationship between economic growth and financial development.

Before considering the results from our VECM, we first test for causality using the Granger-Causality Test. Table 3 reports the results of the Granger Causality test between economic growth and each of our financial development indicators separately. For Egypt, Israel, Jordan, and Morocco, the BCR has strong predictive power for GDP, so the hypothesis that BCR does not Granger cause economic growth is strongly rejected. For Algeria and Turkey, we find a bidirectional relationship between GDP and BCR. For Algeria, economic growth has strong predictive power for DMS and FDR, while these two variables have little predictive power for GDP and we are unable to reject the hypothesis of no Granger-Causality. In contrast, for Turkey, both the DMS and FDR Granger-cause economic growth.

To examine how shocks to the long-run equilibrium relationship between economic growth and banking-sector development are corrected in the short run we use a VECM,

$$\Delta GDP = \alpha + \sum_{i=1}^{m} \beta_i \Delta GDP_{t-i} + \sum_{j=1}^{n} \gamma_j \Delta X_{t-j} + \sum_{k=1}^{o} \delta \Delta GOVEX_{t-k}$$

$$+ \sum_{l=1}^{p} \phi \Delta OPEN_{t-l} + \sum_{s=1}^{q} \nu \Delta EXCH_{t-s} + \varphi Z_{t-1} + \varepsilon_t \qquad (2)$$

where X is our proxy of banking-sector development, GOVEX, OPEN, and EXCH are control variables, and Z is the error-correction term.

The results, in Table 4, indicate that the error-correction term is an important channel of influence for Israel, Jordan, Morocco, Tunisia, and Turkey. When we proxy financial sector development using BCR the parameter estimates are significantly negative for all the countries in our sample. This supports the presence of a co-integrating relationship between financial sector development and economic growth in all countries. The results obtained when we use the DMS and FDR as proxies for banking-sector development are not as robust. While the parameter estimates are

Table 3. Granger Causality Test.

Country		Lags	F statistics	Probability
Algeria	GDP does not Granger cause CrGDP	(2)	8.224*	0.0014
	CrGDP does not Granger cause GDP	(2)	11.22*	0.0002
	GDP does not Granger cause DepM1	(3)	3.16*	0.056
	DepM1 does not Granger cause GDP	(3)	0.48	0.622
	GDP does not Granger cause M2GDP	(3)	3.14*	0.057
	M2GDP does not Granger cause GDP	(3)	0.43	0.654
Egypt		(1)	1.72	0.195
	GDP does not Granger cause CrGDP	(1)	7.169*	0.002
	CrGDP does not Granger cause GDP	(4)	0.496	0.614
	GDP does not Granger cause DepM1	(4)	0.537	0.590
	DepM1 does not Granger cause GDP	(1)	3.37*	0.047
	GDP does not Granger cause M2GDP	(1)	0.707	0.501
	M2GDP does not Granger cause GDP	(1)	0.693	0.435
Israel	GDP does not Granger cause CrGDP	(2)	1.51	0.237
	CrGDP does not Granger cause GDP	(2)	2.465**	0.101
	GDP does not Granger cause DepM1	(2)	0.006	0.994
	DepM1 does not Granger cause GDP	(2)	0.161	0.852
	GDP does not Granger cause M2GDP	(2)	1.53	0.232
	M2GDP does not Granger cause GDP	(2)	2.45**	0.102
Jordan	GDP does not Granger cause CrGDP	(2)	1.08	0.37
	CrGDP does not Granger cause GDP	(2)	3.51*	0.028
	GDP does not Granger cause DepM1	(2)	0.078	0.925
	DepM1 does not Granger cause GDP	(2)	1.21	0.312
	GDP does not Granger cause M2GDP	(4)	1.03	0.367
	M2GDP does not Granger cause GDP	(4)	1.26	0.297
Morocco	GDP does not Granger cause CrGDP	(3)	1.86	0.16
	CrGDP does not Granger cause GDP	(3)	40.4*	0.0001
	GDP does not Granger cause DepM1	(2)	0.542	0.66
	DepM1 does not Granger cause GDP	(2)	40.2*	0.000
	GDP does not Granger cause M2GDP	(2)	24.68*	0.00
	M2GDP does not Granger cause GDP	(2)	2.22**	0.10
Tunis	GDP does not Granger cause CrGDP	(2)	2.72*	0.08
	CrGDP does not Granger cause GDP	(2)	1.84	0.17
	GDP does not Granger cause DepM1	(2)	6.450*	0.004
	DepM1 does not Granger cause GDP	(2)	.057	0.945
	GDP does not Granger cause M2GDP	(2)	3.11*	0.051
	M2GDP does not Granger cause GDP	(2)	1.579	0.222
Turkey	GDP does not Granger cause CrGDP	(2)	2.82**	0.074
	CrGDP does not Granger cause GDP	(2)	5.146*	0.011
	GDP does not Granger cause DepM1	(2)	.006	0.994
	DepM1 does not Granger cause GDP	(2)	2.669**	0.085
	GDP does not Granger cause M2GDP	(2)	1.82	0.178
	M2GDP does not Granger cause GDP	(2)	2.59**	0.10

Table 4. Granger Causality Regression Results from Error Correction Models with Change in GDP as Dependent variable.

Country	Algeria	Egypt	Israel		Jordan		Morocco			Tunis			Turkey
Reg	3	3	1	3	1	3	1	2	3	1	2	3	1
Indep. Var.													
C	0.227 (1.81)	0.027 (4.16)*	0.025 (2.49)*	0.02 (2.35)*	0.012 (.97)	0.012 (.95)	0.074 (.48)	0.033 (.226)	0.162 (1.06)	0.038 (4.51)*	0.033 (4.11)*	0.027 (3.37)*	-0.02 (-.62)
GDP(-1)	-0.436 (-1.64)	0.016 (.137)	0.279 (1.85)	0.296 (1.99)*	0.199 (1.20)	0.211 (1.18)	0.171 (.93)	0.184 (1.0)	0.125 (.70)	0.048 (.30)	0.122 (.739)	0.123 (.703)	-0.222 (1.40)
CrGDP(-1)			-0.009 (-.66)		-0.017 (-.64)		-0.71 (-0.507)			-0.092 (-1.74)			
DepM1(-1)								0.267 (0.07)			-0.014 (-0.173)		0.269 (2.75)*
M2GDP(-1)	0.080 (0.36)	-0.003 (-1.13)		0.0004 (0.03)		-0.001 (-0.04)			-1.78 (-1.63)			-0.068 (-0.91)	
OPEN	0.076 (0.088)	-0.190 (-3.17)*	-0.02 (-0.16)	-0.004 (-0.03)	-0.05 (-0.49)	-0.05 (-0.045)	0.525 (0.377)	0.605 (0.44)	0.52 (0.39)	-0.115 (-1.56)	-0.126 (-1.52)	-0.08 (-0.96)	-0.136 (-0.83)
EXCH	-0.047 (-1.24)	-0.075 (-1.50)	-0.008 (-.44)	-0.03 (-.78)	-0.24 (-1.42)	-0.26 (-1.44)	-0.06 (-0.25)	-0.04 (-0.17)	0.438 (0.30)	-0.052 (-0.722)	-0.121 (-1.66)	-0.089 (-1.15)	-0.089 (-0.97)
GOVEX	-0.137 (-2.06)*	-0.226 (-3.07)*	-0.003 (-2.01)*	-0.003 (-2.08)*	0.005 (1.52)	0.189 (1.05)	-1.59 (-0.91)	-1.61 (-0.93)	-1.49 (-0.90)	-0.122 (-1.60)	-0.118 (-1.41)	-0.117 (-1.46)	-0.013 (-0.85)
(Z_{t-1}) or ECT(-1)	-0.069 (-0.91)	-0.04 (-1.43)	-0.159 (-3.26)*	-0.179 (-3.18)*	-0.169 (-2.11)*	-0.136 (-1.56)	-1.35 (-4.87)*	-1.36 (-4.9)*	-1.31 (-4.96)*	-0.065 (-2.04)*	0.0002 (0.69)	-0.069 (-1.28)	-0.539 (-2.85)*
R2	0.34	0.55	0.38	0.39	0.35	0.28	0.60	0.61	0.64	0.39	0.266	0.31	0.48
SE of equation	0.51	0.03	0.03	0.39	0.06	0.07	0.77	0.77	0.73	0.03	0.03	0.03	0.09

1 refers to the regression GDP on lag difference of CrGDP, 2 is the regression GDP on lag difference M2GDP, 3 refers to the regression GDP on lag difference DepM1 on lag difference M2GDP.
*Significance at 5% level.

negative, they are not statistically significant for the majority of countries, suggesting that the impact of an improvement in banking-sector development may not have a significant impact on economic growth in the short run for all the countries in our sample.

The results in Tables 2–4 are of considerable interest to policy makers at international organisations such as the IMF, as well as developing countries. Overall our results indicate that while there is a stable long run equilibrium relationship between banking-sector development and economic growth, developing countries should not rely on banking-sector developments to promote or boost economic growth in the short run.

5. CONCLUSION

In the last decade researchers have become increasingly interested in the relationship between financial development and economic growth. An important issue that has not received much attention is the direction of causality in the relationship between financial development and economic growth. Does financial development lead to greater economic growth, or does economic growth lead to greater financial development? This is an important issue for many developing economies. For example in the MENA, many of the developing countries have pursued reform programs suggested by international organizations such as the IMF and the World Bank, which involve investing considerable resources to improve the operation and the efficiency of their financial markets and institutions with the aim of achieving sustained economic growth.

This paper presents new evidence of the relationship between financial market development and economic growth for a set of seven Middle East and North African economies over the period 1965–2002, using co-integration techniques, Granger causality tests, and VECM.

We use three proxies for banking-sector development, the credit to the private sector as a percentage of GDP, the ratio of Deposits to broad money (M1), and the money supply (M2) as a percentage of GDP. Based on our proxies for banking-sector development we find evidence that for six of the seven countries, improvements in banking-sector development Granger cause increases in economic growth. However, for three of those six countries we find evidence that economic growth also Granger causes banking-sector development.

The results of our co-integration analysis reveal that there is evidence of a co-integrating relation between GDP per capita and our proxies for banking-sector development. In other words, there appears to be a significant stable long-run equilibrium relationship between banking-sector development and economic growth for all of countries in our sample. To analyze the impact that banking-sector development has on economic growth in the short run we estimate VECM. We find limited evidence that banking-sector development will boost economic growth in the short run. For one proxy of banking-sector development our results are statistically significant, but for the remaining two proxies we find that the coefficients are correctly signed, but not significant. Thus we conclude that there is a stable long run equilibrium relationship between economic growth and banking-sector development, none of our sample countries can confidently rely on banking-sector development to deliver economic growth in the short-run.

NOTE

1. The results for Jordan were mixed, while ADF did not reject the hypothesis of unit root with first difference, the results of PP on the first difference strongly reject the hypothesis of unit root.

ACKNOWLEDGMENT

This research was done during my research stay in Germany, and was financed by the Alexander von Humboldt Stiftung. I thank the AvH for its support, and Prof. Dr. W. Bühler, Lehrstuhl für Finanzierung, for his generous hospitality and valuable comments. I also appreciate valuable suggestions made by Professor Anil Makhija and Phil Davies from Ohio State University.

REFERENCES

Atje, R., & Jovanovic, B. (1993). Stock markets and development. *European Economic Review*, *37*(2/3), 632–640.
Barro, Y., & Sala-I.-Martin. (1995). *Economic growth*. New York: McGraw-Hills.
Bekaert, G., & Harvey, C. R. (1997). Emerging equity market volatility. *Journal of Financial Economics*, *43*, 29–78.
Bekaert, G., & Harvey, C. R. (2000). Foreign speculators and emerging equity markets. *Journal of Finance*, *55*, 565–613.
Bencivenga, V. R., & Smith, B. D. (1991). Financial intermediation and endogenous growth. *Review of Economic Studies*, *58*(2), 195–209.

Demetriades, P., & Hussein, K. (1996). Does financial development cause economic growth? Time series evidence from 16 countries. *Journal of Development Economics, 51*, 387–411.

Demirguc-Kunt, A., & Maksimovic, V. (1998). Law, finance and firm growth. *Journal of Finance, 53*(6), 2107–2131.

Engle, R. F., & Granger, C. W. J. (1987). Co-integration and error correction: Representation, estimation and testing. *Econometrica, 55*, 251–276.

Gertler, M. (1988). Financial structure and aggregate economic activity: An overview. *Journal of Money, Credit and Banking, 20*, 25–50.

Granger, C., & Lin, J-I. (1995). Causality in the long run. *Econometric Theory, 11*(3), 530–536.

International Monetary Fund. (2002). *International Financial statistics Fact Book*. D.C: International Monetary Fund, Washington, USA.

Johansen, S. (1988). Statistical analysis of cointegration vectors. *Journal of Economic Dynamics and Control, 12*, 231–254.

Johansen, S., & Juselius, K. (1990). Maximum likelihood estimation and inference on cointegration – with application to the demand for money. *Oxford Bulletin of Economics and Statistics, 52*, 169–210.

Jung, W. S. (1986). Financial development and economic growth: International evidence. *Economic Development and Cultural Change, 34*, 333–344.

King, R., & Levine, R. (1993a). Finance, entrepreneurship, and growth: Theory and evidence. *Journal of Monetary Economics, 32*.

King, R., & Levine, R. (1993b). Finance and growth: Schumpeter might be right. *Quarterly Journal of Economics, 108*(3).

Levine, R. (1997). Financial development and economic growth: Views and agenda. *Journal of Economic Literature, 35*(2).

Levine, R., & Zervos, S. (1998). Stock markets, banks, and economic growth. *American Economic Review, 88*.

Luintel, K. B., & Khan, M. (1999). A quantitative reassessment of the finance–growth nexus: Evidence from a multivariate VAR. *Journal of Development Economics, 60*, 381–405.

Rousseau, P., & Wachtel, P. (1998). Financial intermediation and economic performance: Historical evidence from five industrial countries. *Journal of Money, Credit, and Banking, 30*(4).

Vogel, R., & Buser, S. (1976). Inflation, financial repression, and capital formation in Latin Americans. In: R. McKinnon (Ed.), *Money and finance in economic growth and development*. New York, NY: Marcel Dekker, Inc.

THE LONG-TERM RISK EFFECTS OF THE GRAMM-LEACH-BLILEY ACT (GLBA) ON THE FINANCIAL SERVICES INDUSTRY

Vijay Gondhalekar, C.R. Narayanaswamy and Sridhar Sundaram

ABSTRACT

We examine whether systematic risk of the financial services industry (banks, finance, insurance, and real-estate sectors) declined after the passage of GLBA. This study differs from prior work in that we examine changes over a long period of time (5 years before and 5 years after the Act) and we use the Carhart (1997) four-factor model for assessing changes in risks. The study finds that banks, insurance, finance, and real-estate segments load on the market, size, and value factors before as well as after GLBA (the real-estate segment loads on the value factor only after GLBA). Except for finance companies, betas decline significantly for all the other segments after the GLBA. In the case of banks even their loadings on the size and value factors decline after the GLBA, while in the case of finance and real-estate companies the loadings on the momentum factor exhibits reduction in risk after the Act. Overall, the GLBA had a risk reducing impact on the financial services industry.

Issues in Corporate Governance and Finance
Advances in Financial Economics, Volume 12, 361–377
Copyright © 2007 by Elsevier Ltd.
All rights of reproduction in any form reserved
ISSN: 1569-3732/doi:10.1016/S1569-3732(07)12014-4

1. INTRODUCTION

The Gramm-Leach-Bliley Act (GLBA, also known as Financial Services Modernization Act) was legislated and signed into law by President Clinton on November 12, 1999. The primary objective of the GLBA was to remove the regulatory barriers for banks, insurance companies, and securities firms and enable them to do business under one entity called a 'financial holding company.' It was hoped that the removal of regulatory barriers would allow these industries to benefit from economies of scale and scope (like other unregulated industries). Such changes could naturally affect the pervasive risks of companies in the financial services industry and that is the focus of our study.

Although GLBA was considered a landmark legislation for liberalizing the financial services industry, opinions on its impact on the industry are divided. For example, Feldman and Schmidt (2000) and Wirtz (2000) claim the GLBA was only a formalization of the long evolving process in the banking industry and therefore was not likely to change the industry significantly. They argue that banks were allowed to do securities business under 'section 20 subsidiaries' and even to some extent the insurance business for several years before GLBA. Furthermore, the extent of securities business that banks have been allowed to pursue has gradually increased over the years (from 10% to 25% of the revenues for Section 20 subsidiaries). Therefore, this evolution would render the Act a mere formality. In contrast to these conjectures, empirical research (e.g., Carrow & Heron, 2002; Akhigbe & Whyte, 2001; Mamun, Hassan, & Maroney, 2005) indicates that the market responded favorably to the introduction of GLBA.

The GLBA is purported to enable having the banking, insurance, and securities business jointly under one roof. This could increase the profitability of the financial services industry (banks, insurance companies, finance companies, and even real-estate companies) due to cost efficiency and synergies from cross product offerings. The favorable market response is certainly consistent with this story. There could, however, be another reason behind the favorable market response. Diversification of income streams from banking, insurance, and securities business could reduce earnings volatility of companies in the financial services industry. This may partially be responsible for the favorable market response. Several studies have examined whether riskiness of companies in the financial services industry changed around the passage of GLBA. The results are mixed, however. While some studies report an increase in betas for banks and insurance companies (e.g., Akhigbe & Whyte, 2004; Yu, 2002; Geyfman, 2005), the study by Mamun et al. (2005) claims that betas of banks actually decreased after the Act (detailed literature review is in the next section). Typically, these studies use daily data spanning about a year before and after GLBA.

We differ from prior studies in that we take a long-term view of the situation for the following reason. It is likely that GLBA caused fundamental changes in the scope and mission of companies in the financial services industry. For example, the provisions of GLBA amended Section 4(k)(4)(E) of the Bank Holding Company Act, allowing a bank holding company or a foreign bank to become a financial holding company that may engage in securities underwriting, dealing, and market-making activities. As a result several BHCs converted to the financial holding company structure with the intent to operate subsidiaries engaged in the business of securities and insurance activities. Such changes take time and their impact on earnings volatility may take even longer (the incompatibility of some operations and culture clashes could become apparent only with time). Short-term analysis may therefore not provide the true picture of shifts in risk characteristics of companies due to the passage of GLBA. We therefore use monthly data (instead of daily data typical in extant studies) spanning 5 years before and after the passage of GLBA (extant studies usually examine a year or so before and after GLBA) for assessing the risk characteristics of companies in the financial services industry. This has not been done in prior research.

The most important difference between this study and prior studies is that we use the Carhart (1997) four-factor model for assessing changes in risk around GLBA. Prior studies typically use a market factor and an interest rate factor for assessing whether the 'beta' of the industry changed after the GLBA. Fama and French (1993, 1995, 1996), among others, make a compelling argument that the non-diversifiable risk of stocks is multi-dimensional. They provide extensive empirical evidence in support of the view that for fully capturing pervasive risk in equity returns, one should not only account for the sensitivity of equity returns to the market (i.e., beta) but also account for the sensitivity of equity returns to risk factors related to size and book-to-market equity of firms. Fama and French (1995) claim that the latter two factors are related to earnings distress of companies and are therefore driven by the fundamentals of companies. Carhart (1997), on the basis of evidence pertaining to the momentum effect in stock returns (i.e., winners and losers stay their course in the short term, see Jegadeesh & Titman, 1993, 2001), adds a fourth factor to the Fama-French prescription in order to account for this pervasive effect in stock returns. This four-factor model is widely used in empirical research and is recognized as legitimate application of available research on asset pricing (see Fama & French, 2004).

The GLBA is likely to impact the volatility of earnings, i.e., earnings distress of companies in the financial services industry. Plus, the provisions of the Act may present different opportunity sets to the winners (prior to the passage) relative to the losers in the industry. Using the Carhart (1997) four-factor model would therefore provide a comprehensive assessment of changes in the risk of the financial services industry after the passage of the GLBA. This has not been done in prior research and so we fill this gap. We use the 5 years 1993–1997 as the pre-GLBA period and the 5 years 2000–2004 as the post-GLBA period in our analysis. Some of the prior studies group banks into important subgroups (money center banks (MCBs), super regional banks (SRBs), banks that had Section 20 subsidiaries, and banks without Section 20 subsidiaries) in their examination of risk changes around GLBA. We do this as well.

The main findings of this study are as follows. All the four segments of the financial services industry (banks, insurance, finance and real-estate companies), in addition to loading on the market factor also load on the size and value factors before as well as after the passage of the GLBA (the real-estate segment does not load during the pre-GLBA period). Betas decline significantly after the GLBA for banks, insurance, and real-estate companies. For banks, even the loadings on size and value factors decline after GLBA (the difference is not significant for other segments). None of the segments load on the momentum factor prior to GLBA, but the finance and real-estate segment load negatively on this factor after the passage of the Act. These findings indicate that the risk of the financial services industry declined substantially after the GLBA primarily from the decline in sensitivity to the market. Earnings distress (related to the size and value factors) declines only for banks, while finance and real-estate companies exhibit a decline in risk after GLBA because of reduced sensitivity to the momentum effect in stocks.

The rest of the study is organized as follows: Section 2 discusses the extant literature pertaining to the changes in risk of the financial services industry. Section 3 presents the data and methodology used in this study. Section 4 deals with the empirical findings and the conclusions are in Section 5.

2. RISK EFFECTS OF THE GLBA AND EXPANSION INTO NON-BANKING ACTIVITIES BY BHCs

In this section we document the key findings of prior literature examining the changes in the systematic risk of banks, insurance companies, finance companies, and real-estate companies since the passage of the GLBA. Prior studies have examined this issue using daily data over short time horizons – ranging from 1 to 2 years before and after the act.

Boyd, Graham, and Hewitt (1993) simulate mergers between BHCs and firms in non-banking financial industries. They find the BHCs merging with life insurance and property/casualty insurance firms may reduce risk but that merger with securities firms or real-estate firms would likely increase risk. Akhigbe and Whyte (2001) analyze daily returns data for the year 1999 for a sample of 92 financial institutions comprising banks (42), insurance companies (26), and brokerage firms (24). Using a two-factor model with market index and an interest rate factor, they find the beta of the portfolios of banks and insurance companies increased, while securities firms experience a decrease in beta following the passage of the GLBA.

Yu (2002) also uses a two-factor model, with the market index and an interest rate factor, to show that the systematic risk of banks as well as insurance companies increased in the post-GLBA time period. Yu's sample consists of 620 firms (434 banks, 37 insurance companies, and 148 securities firms) and daily stock returns from the end of 1998–2000. Geyfman (2005) examined a sample of BHCs with and without Section 20 subsidiaries to test for differential in market-based risk measures. She finds that BHCs that expanded into securities activities exhibited significantly lower total and unsystematic risk but a higher systematic risk. Stiroh and Rumble (2006) examine a sample of financial holding companies from 1997 to 2002 and report that diversification gains from shifting toward activities that generate fees, trading revenue, and other non-interest income, are more than offset by the costs of increased exposure to such volatile activities.

Neale and Peterson (2005) examine the impact of GLBA on insurance industry. They consider the 250-day period prior to January 9, 1997 to represent the pre-GLBA period and the 250-day period after November 5, 1999 as the post-GLB period. Using daily returns for these two time periods, they conclude that the beta of the insurance industry decreased from 0.630 to 0.408 after the GLBA. Mamun et al. (2005) investigate the impact of the GLBA on the stocks of banks. They analyze a sample of 343 banks using two different classification schemes. First, they group the stocks into three categories namely, MCBs (3), SRBs (4), and other banks (336). In the second classification scheme, they subdivide the sample into banks with Section 20 subsidiaries (17), banks that never had Section 20 subsidiaries but obtained a financial subsidiary since GLBA (13), and all other banks (313). They use daily returns data for the January 1998–December 2000 time period. Mamun et al. find that the systematic risk decreased for various categories of banks after the passage of the GLBA.

3. DATA AND METHODOLOGY

The passage of the GLBA was long drawn and there were several events in this regard that lead to the eventual passage of the Act on November 12th, 1999. To make the sample data free from influence of the events related to the passage of the law, we removed the data from January 1998 until December 2000 in our analysis. This eliminates almost a year's returns prior to the reintroduction of the Financial Services Reform Bill in Congress in 1998 and a year's returns after the legislation was signed into law in November 1999. We define the 5-year period from 1993 to 1997 as the pre-GLBA period and the period from 2001 to 2005 as the post-GLBA period. This allows us to use 60 monthly returns for the pre as well as the post-GLBA periods.

In the first part of the empirical analysis, we consider shifts in the risk measures of the four major segments of the financial services industry – banks, insurance, finance, and real-estate companies. We downloaded the returns data for these segments from the website made publicly available by Professor Kenneth French of Dartmouth College. The website indicates that the sample size of firms within each of the four sectors (computed on an annual basis) varies substantially during the period 1993–2005. Even a quick look at the lower and higher end of the sample size during the period 1993–2005 for each of the four sectors illustrates this point – banks (361–642), insurance companies (148–225), real-estate companies (22–35), and finance companies (86–519).

Banks form the largest sector of the financial services industry. Further, banks can also easily be categorized into subgroups depending on their scope and mission. In the second part of our analysis we focus on a few important subgroups of banks. The important subgroups and the sample size for each group we investigate are as follows: banks with Section 20 subsidiaries (31), banks that never had Section 20 subsidiaries (13), SRBs (5), and MCBs (6). These subgroups of banks are likely to be affected differently by GLBA. MCBs and SRBs are the largest banks in the economy. Therefore, it is useful to know whether the GLBA had any effect on their risk characteristics. Banks that had Section 20 subsidiaries had experience in securities business before the GLBA and one would be interested in examining whether these banks were affected differently by the GLBA compared to the banks that did not have Section 20 subsidiaries, but started securities business after the GLBA. These groups of banks were investigated by Mamun et al. (2005) for a shorter time frame. We examine changes in the risk of the same subgroups of banks in the long term.

We use the Carhart (1997) four-factor model for assessing the measures of non-diversifiable risk before and after the passage of GLBA. For applying this model, we estimate the following time series regression

$$
\begin{aligned}
R_{jt} - R_{ft} = A_j + B_j \left[R_{mt} - R_{ft} \right] + S_j \left[\text{SMB}_t \right] + H_j \left[\text{HML}_t \right] \\
+ U_j \left[\text{UMD}_t \right] + E_t
\end{aligned} \tag{1}
$$

Where R_{jt} is the return on a financial services sector or bank subgroup, t = monthly return either during 1993–1997 or 2001–2005; $R_{mt} - R_{ft}$ the return on VW market index minus the return on one month T-Bill; SMB_t the difference between the return on small and big stocks; HML_t the difference between the return on low and high book/market stocks; A_j the intercept; and E_t the error term.

Data on R_{ft}, $R_{mt} - R_{ft}$, SMB_t, HML_t, and UMD_t are from Professor French's website (the website provides various details about the definition and computation of these variables).

We estimate Eq. (1) for the pre-GLBA period (1993–1997) and the post-GLBA period (2001–2005) for assessing whether the excess return on a given sector or bank subgroup loads significantly on any of the four factors (market premium, SMB, HML, and UMD). Eq. (1) is again estimated in a modified form using the entire length of data (1993–1997 + 2001–2005). Here each of the four explanatory variables and the intercept are multiplied by the term (1 + dummy variable), where the dummy variables takes a value of one for the post-GLBA period and zero otherwise. Using this standard econometric technique, we examine whether a given slope coefficient (i.e., a given risk measure in this case) is different across periods. Thus, the methodology is intended to examine whether a given financial services sector loads on any of the four risk factors and if the loading changes before and after GLBA.

4. EMPIRICAL FINDINGS

Table 1 reports the returns on the T-Bills, market, and the various segments of the financial services industry. The annual average risk-free rate (as measured by the return on the 1-month T-Bill) declined from 4.57% to 2.14%. The return on the market portfolio (value weighted-NYSE-NASDAQ-index from CRSP) declined from an average of 19.59% to 4.27%. This is no surprise because the post-GLBA period roughly matches the post dot.com bust period. The return on the financial services industry (with the exception of the real-estate segment) also exhibits a decline in the post-GLBA period, but even a cursory look at the results indicate that the financial services industry actually performed much better than the market index.

Table 1. Average Returns before and after GLBA.

	Pre-GLBA (%)	Post-GLBA (%)
Panel A: Average annual return		
Return on a 1-month T-Bill	4.57	2.14
Return on VW market portfolio	19.59	4.27
Insurance companies	21.16	18.32
Finance companies	32.73	22.41
Real-estate companies	14.20	25.09
Banks (all)	35.75	25.75
Money center banks	25.50	10.50
Super regional banks	31.98	4.81
Banks with Section 20 subsidiaries	32.28	9.88
Banks without Section 20 subsidiaries	33.83	14.12
Panel B: Annual risk premiums		
VW market return$-R_f$	14.35	2.19
SMB	−1.64	9.80
HML	5.50	9.25
UMD	11.12	2.99

Notes: The Gramm-Leach-Bliley Act (GLBA) was signed into law on November 12, 1999, but the process was set in motion years earlier. The 5-year period January 1993 through December 1997 is taken as the pre-GLBA period and the 5-year period January 2000 through December 2004 is taken as the post-GLBA period. The data on sector returns for bank (all), insurance, finance, and real estate as well as the data on risk premiums [VW market return$-R_f$, SMB, HML, and UMD] are from Kenneth French's website. The sample of money center banks, super regional banks, banks with Section 20 subsidiaries, and banks that never had Section 20 subsidiaries is from Mamun et al. (2005) and the returns are from CRSP.

Although there was an overall decline in the average return in the financial services industry, the average abnormal returns increased during the same time period. Table 2 provides results from the regression of the excess returns on banks, insurance companies, finance companies, and the real-estate companies on the four factors suggested by Carhart (1997). The intercept terms in these regressions quantify the average return in excess of the required return. The intercept terms were positive and significant at the 5% level for banks and finance companies before and after the GLBA. Further, for both banks and finance companies, the average excess returns increased in the post-GLBA period. For banks, the increase was from 0.7016 to 1.009 and for finance companies, the increase was from 0.6773 to 0.8749.

Although the intercept term was significant and increased for banks as a whole, it was not significant for some important subgroups of banks. For MCBs and SRBs, as reported in Table 3, the intercept terms were not statistically different from zero before and after the passage of the GLBA. This result is in contrast to the findings by Mamun et al. (2005) that both MCBs and SRBs had statistically significant abnormal returns after the passage of GLBA. The results pertaining to other subgroups, namely banks with Section 20 subsidiaries and those that did not have Section 20 subsidiaries, are also similar. Banks with Section 20 subsidiaries had more experience with non-banking activities prior to the GLBA and therefore Mamun et al. hypothesize that these banks could gain more from the GLBA and they find the data to support this hypothesis. In contrast, we find (as reported in Table 4) no significant gain for banks with Section 20 subsidiaries. We have to note, however, that our study measures long-term impact, whereas Mamun et al. focus on the announcement effect in the short-term.

4.1. Changes in the Risk Characteristics of Financial Services Industry

We use the four-factor model proposed by Carhart (1997) to obtain the risk profile. The four factors are: market, size, value, and momentum. Our empirical analysis indicates that among the four factors, all except momentum are generally significant in the pre- and post-GLBA time periods for the four sectors of the financial services industry. In the first set of regressions for the four financial sectors – banks, insurance, finance companies, and real-estate companies, the regression coefficients for size and value factors and the beta coefficient (regression coefficient for the

Table 2.   Changes in Risk Measures of Banks, Insurance, Finance, and
Real-Estate Sectors: Pre- vs. Post-GLBA.

	Banks	Insurance Companies	Finance Companies	Real-Estate Companies
Panel A: Time-series regressions				
Beta	0.9204	0.8910	0.8429	0.9888
Pre-GLBA	$(0.00)^a$	$(0.00)^a$	$(0.00)^a$	$(0.00)^a$
Beta	0.3066	0.6734	0.8027	0.3255
Post-GLBA	$(0.00)^a$	$(0.00)^a$	$(0.00)^a$	$(0.04)^b$
Size factor	0.5258	0.5497	0.4937	0.6330
Pre-GLBA	$(0.00)^a$	$(0.00)^a$	$(0.00)^a$	$(0.01)^a$
Size factor	0.4979	0.5493	0.5098	0.5895
Post-GLBA	$(0.00)^a$	$(0.00)^a$	$(0.00)^a$	$(0.00)^a$
Value factor	0.8624	0.4643	0.6844	0.3315
Pre-GLBA	$(0.00)^a$	$(0.00)^a$	$(0.00)^a$	(0.22)
Value factor	0.3849	0.5185	0.2489	0.7171
Post-GLBA	$(0.00)^a$	$(0.00)^a$	$(0.02)^b$	$(0.00)^a$
Momentum factor	0.0464	0.1039	0.0914	0.0992
Pre-GLBA	(0.67)	(0.25)	(0.45)	(0.68)
Momentum factor	−0.0862	0.0395	−0.1832	−0.2286
Post-GLBA	(0.14)	(0.41)	$(0.00)^a$	$(0.07)^c$
Intercept	0.7016	−0.0211	0.6773	−0.7182
Pre-GLBA	$(0.01)^a$	(0.92)	$(0.03)^b$	(0.23)
Intercept	1.009	0.2838	0.8749	0.6547
Post-GLBA	$(0.00)^a$	(0.18)	$(0.00)^a$	(0.24)
Sample size N	120	120	120	120
Adjusted R^2	0.74	0.81	0.80	0.39
Panel B: Differences in risk measures before and after GLBA				
Beta	0.6138	0.2176	0.0402	0.6633
Pre minus post	$(0.00)^a$	$(0.03)^b$	(0.76)	$(0.01)^a$
Size factor	0.0279	0.0004	−0.0161	0.0435
Pre minus post	$(0.00)^a$	(0.99)	(0.92)	(0.88)
Value factor	0.4774	−0.0542	0.4355	−0.3856
Pre minus post	$(0.00)^a$	(0.68)	$(0.01)^a$	(0.27)
Momentum factor	0.1327	0.064	0.2746	0.3178
Pre minus post	(0.28)	(0.53)	$(0.05)^b$	$(0.03)^b$
Intercept	−0.3072	−0.3049	−0.1976	−1.3728
Pre minus post	(0.42)	(0.33)	(0.63)	$(0.10)^c$

Notes: Monthly excess returns for each of the four sectors: banks, insurance, finance, and real-estate companies (taken as the sector return minus the yield on 1-month T-Bill) are regressed against excess market return, SMB, HML, and UMD (momentum factor). The data on the sector returns and the four explanatory factors are from Kenneth French's website. The 60 months from January 1993 through December 1997 are taken as the pre-GLBA period and the 60 months from January 2000 through December 2004 are taken to comprise the post-GLBA period. *p*-values are in parentheses.
[a]Denotes significance at the 1% level.
[b]Denotes significance at the 5% level.
[c]Denotes significance at the 10% level.

Table 3. Changes in Risk Measures of Money Center Banks and Super Regional Banks: Pre- vs. Post-GLBA.

	Money Center Banks	Super Regional Banks
Panel A: Time-series regressions		
Beta	1.4738	1.5188
Pre-GLBA	$(0.00)^a$	$(0.00)^a$
Beta	0.7949	0.9406
Post-GLBA	$(0.00)^a$	$(0.00)^a$
Size factor	−0.2334	−0.4106
Pre-GLBA	(0.20)	$(0.05)^b$
Size factor	−0.0442	−0.0247
Post-GLBA	(0.77)	(0.99)
Value factor	0.7421	0.6143
Pre-GLBA	$(0.00)^a$	$(0.02)^b$
Value factor	0.1503	0.5151
Post-GLBA	(0.39)	$(0.02)^b$
Momentum factor	0.0422	−0.0691
Pre-GLBA	(0.83)	(0.75)
Momentum factor	−0.3199	−0.2529
Post-GLBA	(0.00)	$(0.03)^b$
Intercept	−0.4469	−0.0519
Pre-GLBA	(0.37)	(0.92)
Intercept	0.6651	−0.1428
Post-GLBA	(0.15)	(0.78)
Sample size N	120	120
Adjusted R^2	0.65	0.60
Panel B: Differences in risk measures before and after GLBA		
Beta	0.6789	0.5782
Pre minus post	$(0.00)^a$	$(0.02)^b$
Size factor	−0.1892	−0.3859
Pre minus post	(0.43)	(0.16)
Value factor	0.5919	0.0992
Pre minus post	$(0.04)^b$	(0.76)
Momentum factor	0.3621	0.1838
Pre minus post	(0.11)	(0.47)
Intercept	1.1119	0.0909
Pre minus post	$(0.10)^c$	(0.90)

Notes: Equally weighted return on money center banks and super regional banks are computed for each month during the periods January 1993–December 1997 (pre-GLBA) and January 2000–December 2004 (post-GLBA). Monthly excess returns on money center and super regional banks (equally weighted return minus the yield on 1 month T-Bill) are regressed on the excess market return, SMB, HML, and UMD (momentum factor). The data on banks are from CRSP and that on the four explanatory factors are from Kenneth French's website. *p*-values are in parentheses.
[a]Denotes significance at the 1% level.
[b]Denotes significance at the 5% level.
[c]Denotes significance at the 10% level.

Table 4. Changes in Risk Measures of Banks with and without Section 20 Subsidiaries: Pre- vs. Post-GLBA.

	Banks with Section 20 Subsidiaries	Banks without Section 20 Subsidiaries
Panel A: Time-series regressions		
Beta	1.1941	1.2294
Pre-GLBA	(0.00)[a]	(0.00)[a]
Beta	0.7577	0.4701
Post-GLBA	(0.00)[a]	(0.00)[a]
Size factor	−0.1845	−0.0896
Pre-GLBA	(0.14)	(0.56)
Size factor	0.1007	0.3365
Post-GLBA	(0.32)	(0.01)[a]
Value factor	0.6084	0.7792
Pre-GLBA	(0.00)[a]	(0.00)[a]
Value factor	0.4501	0.3120
Post-GLBA	(0.39)	(0.03)[b]
Momentum factor	0.0919	0.0008
Pre-GLBA	(0.50)	(0.99)
Momentum factor	−0.1271	−0.0177
Post-GLBA	(0.08)[c]	(0.84)
Intercept	0.1925	0.2427
Pre-GLBA	(0.57)	(0.58)
Intercept	0.1415	0.4018
Post-GLBA	(0.65)	(1.04)
Sample size N	120	120
Adjusted R^2	0.73	0.57
Panel B: Differences in risk measures before and after GLBA		
Beta	0.4364	0.7592
Pre minus post	(0.00)[a]	(0.00)[a]
Size factor	−0.2851	−0.4261
Pre minus post	(0.08)[c]	(0.03)[b]
Value factor	0.1583	0.4672
Pre minus post	(0.42)	(0.05)[b]
Momentum factor	0.2191	0.0185
Pre minus post	(0.15)	(0.92)
Intercept	0.0510	0.1591
Pre minus post	(0.91)	(0.78)

Notes: Equally weighted return on banks with Section 20 subsidiaries and those that never had Section 20 subsidiaries are computed for each month during the periods January 1993–December 1997 (pre-GLBA) and January 2000–December 2004 (post-GLBA). Monthly excess returns on Section 20 and non-Section 20 banks (equally weighted return minus the yield on 1 month T-Bill) are regressed on the excess market return, SMB, HML, and UMD (momentum factor). The data on banks are from CRSP and that on the four explanatory factors are from Kenneth French's website. *P*-values are in parentheses.
[a]Denotes significance at the 1% level.
[b]Denotes significance at the 5% level.
[c]Denotes significance at the 10% level.

market index) are significant at the 5% level for both the pre- and post-GLBA time periods. (The exception was for real-estate companies for the value factor for the pre-GLBA period.) Momentum factor is significant only for finance companies during the post-GLBA period at the 5% level.

Our analysis indicates that the beta of the equally weighted portfolio of all banks has substantially decreased since the passage of the GLBA. It has decreased from 0.9204 to 0.3066 (a decrease of almost 67%). The change is statistically significant at the 1% level. The betas of other sectors (segments) of the financial services industry have also decreased during this period. We find the betas of insurance companies decreased substantially from 0.8910 to 0.6734 – a decrease of about 24%. In their study on the effect of GLBA on insurance companies, Neale and Peterson (2005) also find that betas of insurance companies declined. In contrast, Akhigbe and Whyte (2001) and Yu (2002) find the betas of insurance companies have increased since GLBA. Similar to banks and insurance companies, we find that the betas of real-estate companies also went down post-GLBA. However, the betas of finance companies did not change much.

The size factor was significant for all the sectors in both the time periods. However, the changes in the factor sensitivities were not substantial (as in the case of betas) and were not statistically significant except for banks. Sensitivity to value factor was significant for all the sectors in both time periods but only banks and finance companies exhibit a significant decline after the passage of GLBA. Finally, the table indicates that finance and real-estate companies exhibit a significant decline in the sensitivity to the momentum factor. This suggests that their riskiness has declined after the GLBA. Taken together, the findings in Table 1 indicate that the systematic risk of all the four segments of the financial services industry has declined after GLBA especially for banks. This suggests that banks have benefited the most from the passage of GLBA (in terms of risk reduction), but this does not appear to come at the expense of other segments of the financial services industry.

4.2. Changes in Risk Characteristics of Subcategories of Banks

In the previous section we reported estimates of the beta for the pre- and post-GLBA time periods for banks as a whole and other sectors of the financial services industry. In this section we report the results of our empirical study on the subgroups of banks. The subcategories we considered are MCBs, SRBs, banks that had Section 20 subsidiaries and banks that never had a Section 20 subsidiary but now have a finance subsidiary. MCBs are the largest of the banks with national and international operations. SRBs come next in size in their range of operations. Mamun et al. argue that these two groups, because of their size and scope of business operations, were better prepared to exploit the liberalization opportunities made available by the GLBA. This, they claim should decrease their beta. Similarly, they argue that banks that had Section 20 subsidiaries were better prepared to do securities business than other banks. They argue that their prior experience in this line of business should enable these banks to perform better than the ones that got into the business without prior experience. In this section we report changes in the risk measure of these four important subgroups in the banking industry in the long term and compare our results with the findings of Mamun et al.

We first estimated the pre- and post-GLBA risk profiles for the MCBs and SRBs. Results are shown in Table 3 (panel A). The betas for MCBs and SRBs were 1.47 and 1.52 respectively before the GLBA. Mamun et al. report the beta for these two subgroups of banks pre-GLBA to be 1.31 and 1.19. They report post-GLBA figures for MCBs and SRBs to be 0.78 and 0.74 compared to our estimates of 0.79 and 0.94 respectively. The differences between their findings and ours are likely to stem from the fact that we take a long-term view and we use the four-factor model. Like Mamunn et al., we find that the betas of MCBs and SRBs are much higher than the beta for the bank sector in the pre as well as post-GLBA period. This could partly be due to their greater exposure to the national and international economic and financial conditions compared to the small and medium sized banks.

Panel B of Table 3 indicates that betas of MCBs and SRBs declined substantially from the pre-GLBA period to the post-GLBA period. The beta for MCB decreased from 1.4738 to 0.7949 and that of SRB decreased from 1.5188 to 0.9406. Thus, our findings indicate that the systematic risk of MCBs and SRBs declined substantially after GLBA – more so in the case of MCBs than SRBs. The decrease in betas is 46% for MCBs and 38% for SRBs (Mamun et al. report that the beta for the pre-GLBA as 1.307 and 1.193 for MCBs and SRBs, respectively, and 0.778 for MCBs and 0.739 for SRBs for the post-GLBA period). In contrast, the beta for the bank sector as a whole decreased by 67%. Our results therefore indicate that the systematic risk of mid-size and small banks must have decreased a lot more than the larger banks and so in this sense the Act has benefited mid-size and small banks more than large banks.

Recall from Table 2 that the sensitivity of the bank sector to the size factor and the value factor declined after the Act. For MCBs, the size factor was not significant before and after the GLBA. For SRBs, the size factor was significant and negative before the GLBA but became insignificant from zero after the GLBA. Value factor was significant for MCBs as well as SRBs before the GLBA and the magnitude and significance decreased later. For MCBs and SRBs, the momentum factor was not significant prior to the GLBA but became significant (with a negative sign) during the post-GLBA period.

The second classification scheme of banks – those that had Section 20 subsidiaries and those that never had a finance subsidiary – exhibit the same pattern as the MCBs and SRBs. Results for these subgroups are in Table 4. The beta of banks that had Section 20 subsidiaries is 1.19 before GLBA and 0.76 after GLBA. Corresponding figures for banks that did not have Section 20 subsidiaries are 1.23 and 0.47. The change in betas was significant at the 1% level for both groups. Although the betas decreased for both types of banks, our estimates indicate that the decrease was more for banks that had no Section 20 subsidiaries (62%) compared to Section 20 banks (37%). This could imply that the banks that started a new finance subsidiary after the passage of GLBA were aggressive in taking advantage of the Act and diversified much more than the banks that already had a Section 20 subsidiary.

Reduction in the betas for Section 20 and non-Section 20 banks after GLBA, although consistent with prior literature, is not the whole story. As panel B of Table 4 indicates, both these subgroups surprisingly load more on the size factor after GLBA (relative to pre-GLBA). What complicates things further is that the loading on the value factor decreases for the non-Section 20 subgroup after GLBA. Thus, our findings suggest that one should be cautious about inferring a decline in the systematic risk of Section 20 and non-Section 20 banks after GLBA as has been done in extant research.

5. CONCLUSIONS

In contrast to existing literature, our study takes a long-term perspective in examining changes in the risk characteristics of firms in the financial services industry – particularly banks. Further, we use the four-factor model that consists of the market index, size, value and momentum, which has not been done by others.

Our analysis shows that the risk characteristics of the four sectors of the financial services industries – banks, insurance companies, finance companies, and real-estate companies – have generally come down in the post-GLBA time period. For the four main subgroups of banks we investigated: MCBs, SRBs, banks with Section 20 subsidiaries and those that did not have these subsidiaries, the systematic risk declined substantially and significantly, even after accounting for size, value, and momentum. Size does not seem to be important for these subgroups. But most of these banks, if not all, are large banks and therefore likely did not have any significant relationship to this factor. Value factor, on the other hand, generally was found significant for most of the subgroups but its impact and significance declined in the post-GLBA time period.

REFERENCES

Akhigbe, A., & Whyte, A. M. (2001). The market's assessment of the Financial Service Modernization Act of 1999. *The Financial Review, 36*, 119–138.

Akhigbe, A., & Whyte, A. M. (2004). The Gramm-Leach-Bliley Act of 1999: Risk implications for the financial services industry. *The Journal of Financial Research, 27*, 435–446.

Boyd, J., Graham, S. L., & Hewitt, R. S. (1993). Bank holding company mergers with nonblank financial firms: Effects on the risk of failure. *Journal of Banking and Finance, 17*, 43–63.

Carhart, M. (1997). On persistence in mutual fund performance. *Journal of Finance, 52*(1), 57–82.

Carrow, K. A., & Heron, R. (2002). Capital market reactions to the passage of the Financial Services Modernization Act of 1999. *The Quarterly Review of Economics and Finance, 42*, 465–485.

Fama, E., & French, K. (1993). Common risk factors in the returns on stocks and bonds. *Journal of Financial Economics, 33*(1), 3–56.

Fama, E., & French, K. (1995). Size and book-to-market factors in earnings and returns. *Journal of Finance, 50*(1), 131–155.

Fama, E., & French, K. (1996). Multifactor explanation of asset pricing anomalies. *Journal of Finance, 51*(1), 55–84.

Fama, E., & French, K. (2004). The capital asset pricing model: Theory and evidence. *Journal of Economic Perspectives, 18*(3), 25–46.

Feldman, R., & Schmidt, J. (2000). Is financial modernization anything new? *Federal Reserve Bank of Minneapolis, Fedgazette, 12*(2), 20–21.

Geyfman, V. (2005). *Banks in the securities business: Market-based risk implication of Section 20 subsidiaries.* Working Paper No. 05–17, Federal Reserve Bank of Philadelphia.

Jegadeesh, N., & Titman, S. (1993). Returns to buying winners and selling losers: Implications for stock market efficiency. *Journal of Finance, 48*(1), 65–91.

Jegadeesh, N., & Titman, S. (2001). Profitability of momentum strategies: An evaluation of alternative explanations. *Journal of Finance, 56*(2), 699–720.

Mamun, A., Hassan, M. K., & Maroney, N. (2005). The wealth and risk effects of the Gramm-Leach-Blailey Act (GLBA) on the US banking industry. *Journal of Business and Accounting, 32*(1), 351–388.

Neale, F. R., & Peterson, P. P. (2005). The effect of the Gramm-Leach-Bliley Act on the insurance industry. *Journal of Economics and Business, 57*(4), 317–338.

Stiroh, K. J., & Rumble, A. (2006). The dark side of diversification: The case of US financial holding companies. *Journal of Banking and Finance, 30*, 2131–2161.

Wirtz, R. (2000). Financial evolution, not revolution. *Federal Reserve Bank of Minneapolis, The Region*, pp. 7–9 and 56–57.

Yu, L. (2002). *On the wealth and risk effects of the Glass-Steagall Overhaul: Evidence from the stock market*. Working paper. Department of Finance, Leonard N. Stern School of Business, New York, NY.

HOW DO SMALL FIRMS IN DEVELOPING COUNTRIES RAISE CAPITAL? EVIDENCE FROM A LARGE-SCALE SURVEY OF KENYAN MICRO AND SMALL-SCALE ENTERPRISES ☆

Christopher J. Green, Peter Kimuyu, Ronny Manos and Victor Murinde

ABSTRACT

We utilize a unique comprehensive dataset, drawn from the 1999 baseline survey of some 2000 micro and small-scale enterprises (MSEs) in Kenya. We analyze the financing behavior of these enterprises within the framework of a heterodox model of debt-equity and gearing decisions. We also study determinants of the success rate of loan applications. Our results emphasize three major findings. First, MSEs in Kenya obtain debt

☆The interpretations and conclusions expressed in this paper are entirely those of the authors and should not be attributed in any manner to either DFID or any other institutions with which the authors are associated.

Issues in Corporate Governance and Finance
Advances in Financial Economics, Volume 12, 379–404
ISSN: 1569-3732/doi:10.1016/S1569-3732(07)12015-6

from a wide variety of sources. Second, debt-equity and gearing decisions by MSEs and their success rates in loan applications can all be understood by relatively simple models which include a mixture of conventional and heterodox variables. Third, and in particular, measures of the tangibility of the owner's assets, and the owner's education and training have a significant positive impact on the probability of borrowing and of the gearing level. These findings have important policy implications for policy makers and entrepreneurs of MSEs in Kenya.

1. INTRODUCTION

It is generally agreed that the development of micro and small-scale enterprises (MSEs) can be a key ingredient in poverty reduction (Sen, 1980). However, MSEs generally suffer from a range of problems in their establishment and development. Among these problems, we would argue that finance is perhaps the most central. A World Bank study found that about 90% of small enterprises surveyed stated that credit was a major constraint to new investment (Parker, Riopelle, & Steel, 1995). A priori, it might seem surprising that finance should be so important. Requirements such as identifying a product and a market, acquiring any necessary property rights or licenses, and keeping proper records are all in some sense more fundamental to running a small enterprise than is finance. However, potential providers of finance, whether formal or informal, are unlikely to commit funds to a business which they view as not being on a sound footing, irrespective of the exact nature of the unsoundness. Lack of funds may therefore be the immediate reason for a business failing to start or to progress, even when the more fundamental reason lies elsewhere. In this sense therefore, we would argue that finance is the "glue" that holds together all the diverse aspects involved in a small business start-up and development.

Almost all extant research on finance for MSEs is concerned with the industrial countries (Cook & Nixson, 2000). This literature suggests that MSEs rely heavily on insider finance, including both private debt and private equity (Berger & Udell, 2002). By their very nature, most MSEs suffer particularly from information asymmetries as between provider and user of funds. This creates a strong preference for internal over external finance and implies that MSEs are typically dependent on "relationship lending" for the bulk of their external finance. Relationship lending is characterized by Berger and Udell (1995, 2002) as lending based largely on proprietary information about the firm and its owner acquired by the lender through contacts over time. They argue that such lending is more easily done by smaller, possibly privately owned financial institutions, in which lines of communication are short, and principal-agent conflicts are minimized within the lending institution as well as between lender and borrower. Evidence on the importance of relationship lending is reasonably well-established (Cole, 1998), but its implications for financing type are less well-established. For example, one would expect that firms which are a member of a group would prefer borrowing from other group members than from unassociated external sources. However, Watson and Wilson (2002) found that group debt was actually lower down the pecking order of financing sources than were other forms of external debt in a sample of UK MSEs.

There is much less literature on MSEs in developing countries, in part because basic data availability is sparser. In poorer countries, one would expect the information asymmetries associated with external finance to assume even greater importance. Following the argument of Berger and Udell (2002), this should generate demand particularly for relationship borrowing, which in turn should give an advantage to smaller financial institutions especially co-operatives, Rotating Credit Societies (ROSCAs) and other microfinance institutions. However, Cook and Nixson (2000) note that little in fact is known about the relationships between MSEs and lenders in developing countries, even as to their broad characteristics of ownership, size, and performance.

In this paper we take up the question of how the provision of finance is related to other aspects of small business in a developing economy. Specifically, we study the determinants of probably the most important financial decision of MSEs, that of how to raise capital for the business, distinguishing between the initial capital and any follow-up capital acquired for expansion or restructuring. We examine this decision in the context of a large sample of MSEs in Kenya. Kenya's small enterprise sector forms an important part of the economy and available data suggests that, in the recent past, it has grown faster than the larger organized sector (Aboagye, 1986). Small enterprises also tend to be more labor-intensive than large enterprises (Snodgrass & Biggs, 1995). Thus, a lot is expected of Kenya's MSEs in the fight against poverty and there is considerable interest in research that can enlarge the pool of information to help inform policy towards MSEs. In our research, we seek to identify *first*, the factors which lead Kenyan MSEs to borrow, whether from formal or informal sources, as against using equity; *second*, the determinants of the gearing rate which they actually employ; and *third*, the determinants of their success rate in applying for loans.

To analyze the financing behavior of small enterprises in Kenya we set up and test an eclectic but heterodox empirical model of the capital structure and financial decisions of MSEs. The model is heterodox because it includes a wide range of variables not typically included in conventional financial models. See Prasad, Green, and Murinde (2001) for a survey of such conventional models. In the *first* part of the analysis, we use the full sample of firms in our dataset to investigate the determinants of MSEs' debt-equity decisions, which we study using a binary choice model. We hypothesize that heterodox factors will be important in determining whether or not MSEs are able to get a loan to start up their business, and further that heterodox factors may decrease in importance as the business gets established and seeks further capital. Heterodox factors include inter alia variables representing ownership, the market, and the education, property rights, and book-keeping skills of the owners and managers. Thus the analysis also explores the relationship between the "glue" of finance and the component parts of the businesses which we conjecture are held together by this glue.

In the *second* part of the analysis we use the full sample of data to examine the determinants of gearing, i.e., the ratio of outstanding debt to debt-plus-equity. In theory, we would expect these determinants to be broadly similar to those of the gearing decisions for initial and additional capital examined in the first part of the analysis.

Third, we turn more specifically to debt decisions. It transpires that only a small number of MSEs in the dataset (about 100) did in fact apply for a loan to finance their capital in the recent past. We therefore study this sub-sample directly, and model the determinants of firms' success rate in the debt market, i.e., the ratio of the loan received by a firm to the amount for which it applied.[1] We interpret this as a reduced-form model of screening which describes the outcome of loan applications as a function of firm characteristics.

Our dataset permits a much broader analysis of these issues than is usually possible. We rely on a unique comprehensive dataset, which contains a vast amount of information about the financing behavior of MSEs in Kenya. Drawn from the 1999 baseline survey of MSEs in Kenya, the dataset consists of 2000 businesses, which form the basis for the analysis reported in this paper. The data, which we describe in more detail below, consist of answers to a wide range of qualitative and quantitative questions put to MSEs during 1999. The data do not include detailed accounting information, but they do include numerous other indicators of the nature of each business and its financial, operating, and ownership characteristics.

In summary, this paper includes a number of important innovations. First, in the dataset we use; second, in the application of a heterodox model of financial decisions; third, in the examination of the differences in decision making between new and established businesses; and fourth, in a systematic study of the determinants of the success rates of loan applications by small businesses.

The rest of the paper is organized as follows. In Section 2 we briefly describe the MSE sector in Kenya and the survey data which we use in our analysis. Section 3 sets out the model and the empirical methods we use to analyze these data. Section 4 contains the main empirical results. Concluding remarks appear in Section 5.

2. KENYA'S MICRO AND SMALL ENTERPRISE SECTOR

2.1. MSEs in Kenya

Early research treated small enterprises as peripheral survival mechanisms whose developmental impact was marginal (Ongile & McCormick, 1996). This view was changed by an International Labour Organisation report that demonstrated the significant employment and wealth creation potential of the burgeoning, and often informal, small enterprise sector (ILO, 1972). Since the ILO report, the general outlook towards MSEs has shifted dramatically. Benign neglect has been replaced by a recognition that the sector could be the lynchpin for improving economic prospects in the developing world (King, 1996). However, there has also been a heightened realization that, in many developing countries, the small enterprise sector enjoyed a high and rising share of industrial employment. Previous slanting of government policies towards promotion of large, capital-intensive industry meant that the potential for inducing more efficient use of capital and improving income distribution lay in more neutral policies. MSEs also link closely with agriculture so that their promotion could also be part of an agriculture-led development strategy. As compared with large enterprises, MSEs are invariably more labor-intensive and often more efficient. Indeed, labor-intensive production tends to be more efficient where labor is plentiful and capital scarce, which is frequently the case in developing countries

(Snodgrass & Biggs, 1995). MSEs promote more equitable distribution of income because they are more labor-intensive than larger enterprises, and because owners of small businesses are more likely to be poorer than the owners of large businesses. Small enterprises also nurture entrepreneurs who may eventually expand their firms and move to higher value adding activities.

The Kenyan MSE sector is a mixture of self-employment outlets and small enterprises involved in an array of activities that are concentrated in urban areas but are also evident in rural Kenya. There are about 1.3 million establishments employing 2.3 million individuals and generating as much as 14% of GDP (Mullei & Bokea, 1999). In the recent past, employment growth in the small enterprise sector has outpaced growth in the modern sector (Aboagye, 1986). A majority of small enterprises are sole proprietorships; a third of them operate from homes; and one half are female-owned. Female-owned small enterprises are more likely to be informal, usually start smaller, use less start-up capital, grow slower if at all, have more limited access to credit and more often operate from less permanent premises and homes (Parker & Torres, 1994; Kimuyu & Omiti, 2000).

Through the small enterprise sector, unskilled rural migrants acquire skills needed for survival in an urban environment. The sector also attracts skilled persons retrenched from formal sector jobs, and is often regarded as a second-best option for those unable to find or to keep jobs in the modern sector. The size of an MSE's total labor force varies widely across business establishments and activities. However, the two key components of the labor force are entrepreneurs and apprentices. Informal garages absorb appreciably more apprentices and workers than the formal service sector that is dominated by sole proprietors. Although most small enterprises are younger than the large ones, their ages vary across locations and activities. For informal, the first 2 years are critical for survival since mortality rates are highest around this age. In many sectors, lack of entry barriers creates severe competition that leads to the demise of the less efficient and poorly managed enterprises. Exceptions include construction and vehicle garages where higher capital and skill requirements act as entry barriers and reduce competition accordingly.

2.2. The 1999 Baseline Survey

This paper uses data from the 1999 baseline survey of micro and small-scale enterprises in Kenya. The baseline survey was based on the Central Bureau of Statistics' National Sample Survey and Evaluation Programme (NAS-SEP) III sampling frame. The selection of clusters followed a primary stratification that distinguished between different households based on economic and demographic characteristics. The Kenya Government (1993) reports information about the 1993 survey. Results from this survey were used to determine sample sizes in each stratum while area maps were used to determine the enumeration areas. Overall, a total of 1500 households were sampled. All adult members of the households on the survey sites were interviewed using a structured questionnaire and the module for information on enterprises administered on households with non-agricultural businesses. These procedures generated a sub-sample of about 2000 businesses whose data are used in the analysis reported in this paper.

The survey gives separate *categorical* information about the main source of the initial capital for the business and any additional capital. It does not give quantitative data on the main source of capital by category. It does provide quantitative data on total initial capital and total additional capital, but there is no categorical data on total capital, only the main source is categorized. As shown in Table 1, responses to the questions, "What was the main source of initial (or additional) capital [for the enterprise]?" were classified into equity (family or own funds) or one of 10 categories of debt. There are some ambiguities in the coding of these and other responses. For example, there may be missing observations either because MSEs did

Table 1. MSEs: Main Source of Capital (Number of Firms).

Main Source of Capital	Initial Capital	Additional Capital
Equity		
Family or own funds	1,591	365
Debt		
Loan from family/friends (not free)	125	28
Money-lender	8	1
Bank	13	8
Non-bank credit institutions	13	5
Rotating credit societies	12	5
Government	3	3
NGOs	2	3
Formal/informal co-operatives	21	6
Trade credit	4	3
Other	3	27
Missing observations	162	1,503
Total	1,957	1,957

not require any start-up or additional capital or because of a non-response to the question. We can draw two conclusions from these data. First, MSEs have borrowed from a variety of external sources, particularly from smaller financial organizations such as co-operatives, as we hypothesized. Second, relatively few MSEs have borrowed at all to finance their capital, and fewer still have used lenders outside the family for this purpose: just 4% of all firms raised their initial capital in the form of debt from outside the family; and 3% raised additional capital this way, although only about 25% of firms are identified as having raised any additional capital at all.

Table 2 summarizes the main quantitative data on the overall gearing rates of firms in the sample. Gearing is defined as the ratio of total debt to total debt-plus-equity, where the total is defined to include both initial and additional capital. There is an ambiguity in the gearing measure in that it is not clear from the context of the questions whether firms would necessarily include loans taken out in the last 12 months within their debt total. This would depend in part on when the last accounts were struck from which, formally or informally, firms were reporting the value of their debt and equity. As can be seen from Table 2, adding in recent loans to the debt total (GEAR1) makes some difference to the distribution of the gearing rates. Fewer firms had a diversified capital structure according to the GEAR2 measure (excluding recent loans) than according to GEAR1. Therefore we separately analyzed both measures of gearing and compared them with one another and with the binary model of debt-equity decisions. Overall though, Table 2 confirms the information in Table 1 that relatively few Kenyan MSEs have borrowed to raise capital. In contrast, Berger and Udell (2002) show that the capital of small firms in the USA is derived almost equally from outside debt and equity,[2] suggesting (if tentatively) that external finance may be harder to obtain in Kenya than in the US.

Table 2.   MSEs: Capital Structure (Number of Firms).

	GEAR1	GEAR2
GEAR = 0	1,441	1,492
GEAR = 1	168	166
0 < GEAR < 1	118	67
All firms	1,727	1,725

Notes: GEAR = Total debt/(total debt + total equity); total debt or equity = initial capital + additional capital.
GEAR1: Loans received in previous year added to debt data.
GEAR2: Loans received in previous year assumed to be included in debt data.

Table 3 shows the success rates of those firms which did apply for a loan during the year preceding the survey. Two points are worth noting from these data. First, it would appear that where credit rationing occurs, there are almost as many instances of "all-or-nothing" rationing as there are of partial rationing: 20 enterprises got no credit, while 22 received some credit, but not all they had applied for. The theory of credit rationing generally suggests that a reduction in the size of the loan (rather than an outright refusal) is an effective screening device for lenders (see Freixas & Rochet, 1998 for a review). Of course, the enterprises which were refused credit may also have had insufficient collateral or other observable characteristics leading to refusal of the loan. A second tentative conclusion is that borrowers had more success with co-operatives than with any other form of institutional lender. It is particularly noteworthy that applicants to

Table 3. MSEs: Main Source of Credit Applied for and Success Rate of Applications (Number of Firms).

Main Source of Credit Applied for During Preceding Year	Success Rate of Application			All Firms
	None	Partial	Full	
Family/friends	1	1	3	5
Money-lender	1	1		2
Bank	1	6	4	11
Non-bank credit institutions	4	3	9	16
Rotating credit societies	1	3	5	9
Government	1		3	4
NGOs	5	4	20	29
Formal/informal co-operatives		2	10	12
Trade credit			3	3
Other		2	2	4
Missing observations	6			6
Total	20	22	59	101

Notes:

1. Success rate of application

   None: credit refused by lender.

   Partial: credit granted but amount less than that applied for.

   Full: credit granted equal to that applied for.

2. For one business, there is data on the source of credit applied for but not on the amounts applied for or received. This business applied to a bank for credit, and for the purpose of this table it is assumed that the success rate of this business was "none". However, when modelling the determinants of the success rate, this business is excluded from the sample.

ROSCAs had a lower success rate. ROSCAs are usually thought of as having particularly good knowledge about their members. These data suggest that there may be important differences in credit-granting capabilities and policies among different micro-credit institutions. See Morduch (1999) for a review of these issues. However, we would re-emphasize that this sample is too small for us to draw more than tentative conclusions at this stage.

3. THE MODELS

3.1. Debt vs. Equity

In a recent survey of the literature on capital structure in developing economies, Prasad et al. (2001) evaluate a range of competing models for studying capital structure issues. In the light of these models and in view of the features of MSEs in Kenya, we specify the following general model:

$$y_n = \sum_k \beta_k X_{kn} + \varepsilon_n \qquad (1)$$

The endogenous variable, y_n $(n = 1,...,N)$, is a measure of the main source of capital of the nth MSE. The X_{kn} $(k=1,...,K)$ are company-specific explanatory variables, and ε_n is the error term. The endogenous variable is binary and is defined as:

$$y_n = \begin{cases} 1 \text{ if main capital is debt} \\ 0 \text{ if main capital is equity} \end{cases}$$

As shown in Table 1 "equity" is defined as own or non-interest-bearing family funds; "debt" includes all other sources of funds. Thus the model seeks to explain the debt-equity decision by MSEs; and Eq. (1) could be interpreted loosely as a (binary) demand function for debt. We set up our heterodox model with explanatory variables (X_k) discussed below. Eq. (1) was then estimated twice: first to explain the initial capital decision, and second to explain the decision on additional capital. To economize on space we call these the IC and AC regressions, respectively. At the first stage, we used the same explanatory variables in the two regressions. We then used t-tests and likelihood ratio tests to compare the coefficients in the two regressions, and to test the hypothesis that there would be differences between the factors determining the IC decision and those determining the AC decision. We also tested down to delete insignificant variables wherever possible. Since y_n is a binary variable, we used the probit method to estimate Eq. (1).

The explanatory variables of the model are shown in Table 4, together with their definitions and hypothesized signs in the regression. Although most of the variables in the regression are heterodox in nature, many can be given an interpretation in terms of the standard corporate finance and credit rationing literatures. Therefore, in explaining the rationale for these variables and for their hypothesized signs, we do not attempt to present a new theory or theories. Instead, we seek wherever possible to place them in the context of conventional theory, and to discuss the ways in which they depart from conventional theory.

AGE is a standard measure of reputation. As a firm ages, it establishes itself as a continuing business and it therefore increases its capacity to take

Table 4. Explanatory Variables of the Debt-Equity Model and their Hypothesized Signs.

Mnemonic	Explanatory Variables	Type of Variable[1]	Hypothesized Sign
AGE	Age of business	cont	$\pm/+$
WFEMALE	Female working owner, aged 18+ years	1-0	$\pm$
WOWNER	Working owner, aged 18+ years	1-0	$\pm$
WUAGE	Working owner aged 5-17 years	1-0	$-?$
WFUAGE	Female working owner aged 5-17 years	1-0	$-?$
EDUC	Owner has secondary education	1-0	$+?$
TRAIN	Owner has trade certificates or above	1-0	$+?$
FAMILYB	Ownership type = family	1-0	$\pm$
SOLEP	Ownership type = sole proprietor	1-0	$\pm$
OWNLAND	Business owns land	1-0	$\pm$
PERM	Business housed in permanent structure	1-0	$\pm$
FORMAL	Business is a formal enterprise	1-0	$+?$
BUSREGLA	Business is a regular business	1-0	$+?$
URBAN	Business is urban-based	1-0	$+/\pm$
INC	Log of net income from business	cont	$-/\pm$
SIZE	Log of number of employees	cont	$-/\pm$
GOOD	Performance self-assessed as above average	1-0	$+?$
POOR	Performance self-assessed as below average	1-0	$-?$
KEEP	Business keeps a complete set of accounts	1-0	$+$
PRIMARY	Main economic activity is primary	1-0	$\pm/+$

Notes: Type of variable: cont = continuous; 1-0 = binary variable, equal to 1 when the condition specified for the explanatory variable is met, and 0 otherwise.

on more debt; hence age is positively related to debt. See Wiwattanakantang (1999). In our data however, all MSEs started up at AGE = 0 by construction. Therefore a positive sign may be likely in the AC regression, but in the IC regression, AGE is a retrospective variable whose sign is uncertain.

The next group of variables (WFEMALE, WOWNER, WUAGE, WFUAGE) are those which give the basic ownership characteristics of gender, participation, and age. These are included in the model to control for these basic characteristics of MSEs. There is little theoretical guidance as to the likely signs of the specifically gender-related variables. The estimated signs may provide a hint about possible discrimination, but since it is generally established in the literature that women in developing countries generally make active use of informal financial schemes, such as ROSCAs, even this hypothesis is not very sharp. See Matin, Hulme, and Rutherford (1999). However, it would seem likely that under-age owners would have more difficulty obtaining credit than their older competitors, especially from outside the family, and we therefore suggest that WUAGE and WFUAGE are both likely to have a negative sign.

EDUC and TRAIN are educational variables and we would expect these to be positively related to debt on the grounds that better-educated owners would find it easier to present a plausible case for a loan to an outside body. This would be particularly important if the owner had no book-keeping knowledge.

FAMILYB and SOLEP are ownership variables. The corporate finance literature is inconclusive about the influence of ownership on gearing. On the one hand, agency theory would suggest that family owners and owner-managers prefer lower gearing to reduce the risk of their portfolios in the firm; on the other hand, monitoring costs are lower in the presence of relatively few large shareholders, and this should increase gearing. The empirical evidence is also inconclusive (see Prasad et al., 2001).

In the Kenyan context, OWNLAND and PERM are likely to have an important impact on any MSE's ability to borrow. Indeed, these variables can be interpreted within the corporate finance literature as measures of asset tangibility reflecting an enterprise's ability to provide collateral. However, it could also be argued that ownership of or ability to rent tangible assets is an indicator of wealth. Arguably, more wealthy individuals would be more likely to use their own equity, at least to start a business, possibly borrowing on their tangible assets when seeking additional capital. Thus the anticipated signs of OWNLAND and PERM are ambiguous.

FORMAL and BUSREGLA are indicators of the extent to which the business is an ongoing enterprise and not for example someone who makes irregular appearances by the roadside to wash car windscreens or a seasonal vendor of vegetables. As for OWNLAND and PERM, these variables may indicate an established business which is more easily able to borrow, or a business which is established because of the owner's wealth and which therefore has less need to borrow. On balance though, the former appears more plausible in this case, implying a possibly positive sign.

URBAN is included to check for the possibility that it is easier to obtain credit in urban areas. This would give a positive sign for URBAN, and would be consistent with Liedholm (2002) who reports that African MSEs in urban areas have higher survival rates than do those in rural areas. However, we have no prior theoretical beliefs about this and the hypothesized sign is therefore ambiguous.

INC and SIZE can be interpreted as conventional corporate finance variables. Theory is again ambiguous in its guidance on the signs of these variables. Larger and more prosperous firms are probably more diversified and less risky (respectively) than smaller and less-prosperous firms. This suggests they should use more debt and less equity, ceteris paribus. However, it is also argued that large firms are less transparent and therefore their borrowings cannot be monitored so easily, implying a lower debt ratio. High income may reflect high growth opportunities and may therefore also be associated with a lower debt ratio to reduce the risk that profitable investments may have to be passed over. See Prasad et al. (2001) on these points. In the MSE context these are relatively abstract points. However, there does exist the same ambiguity as before in that INC and SIZE could reflect *either* ability to borrow (high: suggesting a positive sign) *or* need to borrow (low: suggesting a negative sign).

GOOD and POOR provide more distinctively heterodox performance measures, judged not by income (which is not available for all companies in the sample), but by the owner's self-assessment. Since this assessment has much to do with the owner's view about whether (s)he is likely to be able to obtain a loan, we tentatively expect a positive sign on GOOD and negative on POOR.

KEEP refers to book-keeping. Proper book-keeping will almost certainly improve the chances of the owner being able to borrow, and is a necessity for dealing with a formal financial institution. We could again interpret this variable in a corporate finance context as reflecting transparency. On either interpretation, the expected sign is positive.

Finally we control for the general type of activity in which the business is engaged. The survey provides a distinction between businesses engaged in primary activities (agriculture, forestry, and fishing) and those in secondary (manufacturing and services). PRIMARY is a dummy for all businesses engaged in primary activities. The traditional literature would suggest that firms with less specialized capital are more able to borrow because they have lower bankruptcy costs. However, it is difficult to apply this idea directly to the relatively coarse classification available. We tentatively suggest that, in poor countries, capital in primary activities is likely to be more adaptable and have higher liquidation value than that in secondary activities. This would suggest a positive coefficient, but one could equally well argue that the reverse may be true.

3.2. Gearing

In the second part of the analysis we study the determinants of firms' gearing. Gearing is defined as the ratio of debt to debt-plus-equity outstanding at the time of the sample survey. It is important to re-emphasize that gearing as measured here is not simply an elaboration of the binary-dependent variable in the debt vs. equity regressions. The model of Section 3.1 refers to the *main* source of a firm's capital. For this, we have categorical data, but not quantitative data. In this section we are concerned with a firm's *total* capital. For this we have quantitative data but not categorical data. See the discussion in Section 2.2.

The model to be estimated has the same form as Eq. (1), except that y_n is now to be interpreted as one of the gearing measures shown in Table 2, and is not a binary variable. The independent variables are the same as before since we expect the same factors to influence gearing as influence the binary debt-equity decision. However, it is clear from Table 2 that the gearing of MSEs is heavily concentrated at unity and (more particularly) at zero. Fewer than 7% of the sample firms have both debt and equity outstanding according to the GEAR1 measure; fewer than 4% according to GEAR2. To take account of the heavy weights at zero and unity, we used the two-limit Tobit model with truncation at zero and unity to estimate Eq. (1). Maximum likelihood estimation was used. The likelihood function and its properties are set out in several standard texts, such as Maddala (1983, Ch. 6).

3.3. Success Rates of Loan Applications

In the third part of the analysis we concentrate on the 100 firms which applied for a loan during the 1 year prior to that in which the survey was undertaken. Specifically, we use the same explanatory variables as before to model the determinants of the "success rate" in the debt market, i.e. the ratio of the loan received by a firm to the amount applied for. The general empirical set-up is the same as Eq. (1), except that y_n is now the success ratio (SUCCR). However, as is the case for gearing, a substantial proportion of the observations on y_n in this sample are equal to either zero or unity (78% in total; see Table 3). To take this into account, we again estimate the model using the two-limit Tobit estimator, with the limits set at zero and unity.

The SUCCR equation has to be interpreted somewhat differently from the four debt equations which we estimate (IC, AC, GEAR1, and GEAR2), even though the postulated explanatory variables are the same in all the equations. The debt equations might each be interpreted as demand functions for debt by individual firms, or perhaps as reduced-form estimates of the debt decision. However, the success rate of firms in the loan market depends in large part on the lender, although as we have argued and the literature emphasizes, lenders' decisions depend in their turn on the observable and inferred characteristics of borrowers (Freixas & Rochet, 1998). Thus we interpret the SUCCR equation as a (reduced-form) screening equation which describes loan outcomes as a function of firm characteristics. The anticipated signs of the coefficients are the same as in the debt equations because we postulate that the debt decision for MSEs will be intimately related to their chances of success in the loan market.

4. EMPIRICAL RESULTS

We followed the same broad strategy in estimating the three models. First we estimated a general model, and then we tested down to a simplified model, deleting insignificant variables. Given the qualitative nature of most of the data, we adopted a relatively cautious critical region of 25% for both the t-tests and the likelihood ratio tests.[3] Moreover, for the IC and AC equations we tested down two different routes, as we explain in Section 4.1 below. Table 5 gives the results of estimating the general model for all five equations: the debt-equity decision (IC and AC), gearing (GEAR1 and

Table 5.   Estimates of General Models.

| | Probit Models | | Two-Limit Tobit Models | | |
| | Debt-equity decision | | Gearing | | Success rate |
	IC	AC	GEAR1	GEAR2	SUCCR
Constant	−1.434***	−3.077***	−4.343***	−6.840***	3.438*
	(−3.74)	(−5.61)	(−3.63)	(−3.29)	(1.95)
AGE	−0.009	0.004	0.012	0.001	−0.043
	(−1.44)	(0.65)	(0.76)	(0.04)	(−1.31)
WFEMALE	0.015	0.029	0.201	0.145	0.082
	(0.18)	(0.27)	(0.84)	(0.36)	(0.20)
WOWNER	−0.149	0.265	−0.133	−0.451	
	(−0.69)	(0.80)	(−0.20)	(−0.41)	
WUAGE	−0.361	0.007	−1.059	−2.109	−2.819*
	(−0.93)	(0.02)	(−0.99)	(−1.09)	(−1.75)
WFUAGE	0.612	−0.333	2.118*	3.505	2.159
	(1.36)	(−0.56)	(1.68)	(1.56)	(1.00)
EDUC	0.139	−0.035	0.302	0.451	−0.252
	(1.59)	(−0.31)	(1.23)	(1.08)	(−0.58)
TRAIN	0.049	0.206*	0.308	0.392	0.031
	(0.53)	(1.77)	(1.20)	(0.90)	(0.07)
FAMILYB	−0.225	0.110	−0.485	−1.292	−0.982
	(−1.39)	(0.51)	(−1.03)	(−1.62)	(−1.03)
SOLEP	−0.071	0.022	−0.215	−0.573	−0.876
	(−0.49)	(0.11)	(−0.51)	(−0.81)	(−0.95)
OWNLAND	−0.013	0.147	0.106	0.166	0.558
	(−0.12)	(1.09)	(0.35)	(0.32)	(0.98)
PERM	−0.135	0.108	−0.060	−0.232	0.994*
	(−1.34)	(0.876)	(−0.22)	(−0.49)	(1.91)
FORMAL	0.355***	0.003	0.691**	1.319**	−0.300
	(2.93)	(0.02)	(1.97)	(2.20)	(−0.50)
BUSREGLA	0.029	−0.039	−0.152	−0.125	−0.623
	(0.28)	(−0.28)	(−0.52)	(−0.25)	(−1.04)
URBAN	0.059	0.061	0.116	0.206	0.168
	(0.69)	(0.52)	(0.47)	(0.49)	(0.38)
INC	0.040	0.128***	0.162*	0.242	−0.089
	(1.14)	(2.76)	(1.66)	(1.42)	(−0.58)
SIZE	0.075	0.066	0.275	0.509	−0.032
	(0.90)	(0.61)	(1.17)	(1.28)	(−0.08)
GOOD	−0.202*	−0.424***	−0.688**	−1.197**	0.516
	(−1.85)	(−2.84)	(−2.24)	(−2.23)	(0.90)
POOR	0.036	−0.138	0.020	0.058	0.097
	(0.40)	(−1.18)	(0.08)	(0.14)	(0.22)
KEEP	−0.022	−0.332	−0.353	−0.962	−0.781
	(−0.10)	(−1.09)	(−0.60)	(−0.93)	(−0.94)
PRIMARY	0.033	0.268	0.004	0.458	−2.504**
	(0.19)	(1.33)	(0.01)	(0.59)	(−2.34)

Table 5. (*Continued*)

	Probit Models		Two-Limit Tobit Models		
	Debt-equity decision		Gearing		Success rate
	IC	AC	GEAR1	GEAR2	SUCCR
Std. deviation	–	–	3.101***	4.958***	1.378***
			(11.47)	(8.47)	(4.98)
No. of observations	1833	1833	1727	1725	96
R^2	0.02	0.02			
LR test	$\chi^2(20) =$	$\chi^2(20) =$	$\chi^2(20) =$	$\chi^2(20) =$	$\chi^2(19) =$
	37.54**	31.78**	34.79**	34.68**	20.49

Notes:

1. Figures in parentheses are t statistics.
2. WOWNER is excluded from the SUCCR regression as its parameter is unidentified. Of the 96 firms included in the SUCCR regression, there are four with WOWNER = 0; and in all these cases, the success rate is "full" (SUCCR = 1).
3. The LR test is a likelihood ratio test for the null hypothesis that all slope coefficients are zero, distributed as $\chi^2(20)$. Critical values for $\chi^2(20)$ are: 28.41 (10%), 31.41 (5%), and 37.57 (1%). Exceptionally, the LR test is distributed as $\chi^2(19)$ in the SUCCR regression (see note 2). Critical values for $\chi^2(19)$ are: 27.20 (10%), 30.14 (5%), and 36.19 (1%).

*Significant at 10% level.
**Significant at 5% level.
***Significant at 1% level.

GEAR2), and the success rate equation. Only about one-sixth of the coefficients are significant in any of the equations, although this is to be expected given the rather general nature of the model, and that most of the variables are 1-0 dummies. FORMAL and GOOD appear to be significant in several of the models. Nevertheless, we can see from the likelihood ratio tests in Table 5 that, notwithstanding the low *t* statistics and correlation coefficients, each model as a whole does contribute significantly to explaining MSEs' financial decisions: debt-equity, gearing, and loan success rates. We therefore turn next to hypothesis testing which we discuss on a model-by-model basis.

4.1. Debt vs. Equity

The first step in hypothesis-testing was to examine how far decisions on initial capital could be differentiated from those on additional capital.

We proceeded by testing the equality of coefficients on any given explanatory variable as between the IC and AC equations using t-tests. We then used the likelihood ratio to test groups of coefficients accepted as being pairwise equal by the t-tests. To keep the presentation compact, Table 6 just shows the results of the likelihood ratio tests. Given the rather low explanatory power of the initial regressions, it is perhaps not surprising that 15 out of 20 slope coefficients will accept an equality restriction as

Table 6. Hypothesis Tests on Debt-Equity Decisions.

Restrictions	χ^2	Likelihood Ratio	Significance
Impose acceptable equality restrictions between the IC and AC equations *then* delete insignificant coefficients from the combined model			
Initial capital vs. additional capital			
BUSREGLA, URBAN, SIZE	$\chi^2(3)$	0.1586	0.98
PRIMARY, OWNLAND, KEEP	$\chi^2(3)$	2.8768	0.41
WFEMALE, WOWNER, WUAGE, WFUAGE	$\chi^2(4)$	3.0981	0.54
TRAIN, SOLEP	$\chi^2(2)$	1.3276	0.51
INC, GOOD, POOR	$\chi^2(3)$	3.5009	0.32
Tests on parameters of combined model			
WOWNER$_R$, BUSREGLA$_R$, EDUC$_A$, FORMAL$_A$, SOLEP$_R$, WFEMALE$_R$, POOR$_R$, AGE$_A$, OWNLAND$_R$, WUAGE$_R$, WFUAGE$_R$, KEEP$_R$, URBAN$_R$, FAMILYB$_A$, SIZE$_R$, PRIMARY$_R$	$\chi^2(16)$	5.2495	0.99
Delete insignificant coefficients from the IC and AC equations separately, *then* impose acceptable equality restrictions between the simplified IC and AC equations			
Tests on parameters of individual equations			
WUAGE$_A$, FORMAL$_A$, KEEP$_I$, SOLEP$_A$, OWNLAND$_I$, PRIMARY$_I$, WFEMALE$_I$, WFEMALE$_A$, BUSREGLA$_I$, BUSREGLA$_A$, EDUC$_A$, POOR$_I$, URBAN$_A$, SOLEP$_I$, TRAIN$_I$, SIZE$_A$, WFUAGE$_A$, AGE$_A$, WOWNER$_I$, URBAN$_I$, FAMILYB$_A$, WOWNER$_A$, SIZE$_I$, WUAGE$_I$, KEEP$_A$, PERM$_A$, WFUAGE$_I$, POOR$_A$, PERM$_I$, PRIMARY$_A$	$\chi^2(30)$	14.1614	0.99
Initial capital vs. additional capital			
INC$_R$, GOOD$_R$	$\chi^2(2)$	3.0299	0.22

Notes: The subscripts indicate the following: $_R$ = the equality of the pairwise coefficients in the IC and AC models was imposed; $_I$ = the coefficient relates to the IC model; $_A$ = the coefficient relates to the AC model.

between the IC and AC equations. Only AGE, EDUC, FAMILYB, PERM, and FORMAL have a different effect on the IC and AC decisions. The result for AGE is reassuring as we did hypothesize a difference because of the ambiguity involved in interpreting its effect on IC. For other variables we had few prior beliefs about possible differences between IC and AC. We then tested down from the joint model of IC and AC decisions and, as shown in Table 6, were able to delete 12 of the 15 variables restricted to the same parameter values in the IC and AC equations and a further four variables from the AC equation (EDUC, FORMAL, AGE, and FAMILYB). Thus the data will accept a total of 31 restrictions.

Of course, it is possible to test down by a different route, by first simplifying each equation separately and then testing the equality of coefficients on any given explanatory variable as between the separately simplified IC and AC equations. Proceeding in this way, a total of 32 restrictions are accepted, as shown in Table 6. While this methodology is likely to (and does) yield two slightly different models, the differences between them give an indication of the robustness of the underlying results. The coefficient estimates for the two simplified versions of the IC and AC equations are shown in columns 1 and 2 of Table 7.

In fact, an important feature of Table 7 is that there are few major differences between the two versions of the debt-equity model, simplified along two different paths. The coefficients remaining in the model after simplification are surprisingly well-determined and tell a clear and interesting story about the determinants of the capital-raising decisions of Kenyan MSEs. In both models, AGE appears to have a negative influence on the probability of incurring debt in the IC equation, and no impact in the AC equation. Since AGE is a retrospective variable in the IC equation, this implies that older firms were more likely to raise their initial capital in the form of equity. This suggests that borrowing has become a more viable option for firms established in the more recent past, in other words, that the availability of credit for small businesses has improved over time. EDUC is positively signed as expected, implying that more educated owners do have greater possibilities of borrowing. This is also true for TRAIN, although there are some differences between the two models as between IC and AC. Overall, the level of education appears to have an important positive impact on MSEs' debt-raising capacities. FAMILYB tends to be negatively associated with debt. Although this variable could have either sign, it is perhaps not surprising to find that small family-owned businesses are more likely to avoid debt. Of course, it could be argued that monitoring a family business could be less costly for informal financial institutions, such as

Table 7. Simplified Models.

	Probit Models: Debt-Equity Decision				Two-Limit Tobit Models		
	1. Model from test route 1 (see Table 6)		2. Model from test route 2 (see Table 6)		Gearing		Success rate
	1		2		3	4	5
	IC	AC	IC	AC	GEAR1	GEAR2	SUCCR
Constant	-1.825*** (-8.75)	-2.331*** (-10.78)	-1.843*** (-8.91)	-2.373*** (-10.86)	-4.561*** (-5.54)	-7.683*** (-4.98)	2.087*** (3.84)
AGE	-0.009 (-1.45)		-0.009 (-1.53)				-0.039 (-1.41)
WUAGE							-2.789** (-2.14)
WFUAGE					1.096 (1.54)	1.600 (1.31)	2.045 (1.15)
EDUC			0.129 (1.56)		0.274 (1.16)	0.536 (1.35)	
TRAIN	0.107 (1.52)	0.107 (1.52)		0.208* (1.91)	0.320 (1.26)		
FAMILYB	-0.165* (-1.65)		-0.175* (-1.76)			-0.812* (-1.68)	
OWNLAND				0.182 (1.46)			0.571 (1.12)
PERM	-0.137 (-1.40)	0.163 (1.46)					0.639 (1.54)
FORMAL	0.337*** (2.90)		0.303*** (2.71)		0.737** (2.22)	1.388** (2.45)	
BUSREGLA							-0.680 (-1.27)
INC	0.077*** (2.98)	0.077*** (2.98)	0.080*** (3.14)	0.080*** (3.14)	0.167* (1.85)	0.265* (1.69)	
GOOD	-0.269*** (-3.41)	-0.269*** (-3.41)	-0.272*** (-3.44)	-0.272*** (-3.44)	-0.715*** (-2.59)	-1.256*** (-2.59)	

KEEP			-1.009 (-1.576)	-2.090^{**} (-2.278)
PRIMARY				1.406^{***} (4.98)
Std. deviation	3.111^{***} (11.47)	4.975^{***} (8.47)		
No. of observations	1833	1727	1725	96
R^2	0.03	0.03		
LR test1	See upper part of Table 6 $\chi^2(10)=102.94^{***}$	See lower part of Table 6 $\chi^2(9)=101.96^{***}$		
LR test2	$\chi^2(14)=5.486$ $\chi^2(6)=29.31^{***}$	$\chi^2(14)=5.88$ $\chi^2(6)=28.80^{***}$		$\chi^2(11)=3.6208$ $\chi^2(8)=16.87^{**}$

Notes:

1. Figures in parentheses are t statistics.
2. LR test1 is a likelihood ratio test for the null hypothesis that the zero restrictions imposed in comparison with the general model are acceptable.
3. LR test2 is a likelihood ratio test for the null hypothesis that all (remaining) slope coefficients are zero.
4. The degrees of freedom (k) and critical values of the $\chi^2(k)$ statistic are as follows:

Equation	LR Test1/2	Degrees of Freedom	Critical Values for χ^2		
			10%	5%	1%
1	2	10	15.99	18.31	23.21
2	2	9	14.68	16.92	21.67
3,4	1	14	21.06	23.68	29.14
3,4	2	6	10.64	12.59	16.81
5	1	11	17.28	19.68	24.73
5	2	8	13.36	15.51	20.09

*Significant at 10% level.
**Significant at 5% level.
***Significant at 1% level.

co-operatives, but possibly more costly for banks. Indicators of tangibility (OWNLAND and PERM) are clearly important, and firms with these attributes are, as expected, generally more likely to incur debt, but for AC rather than IC where PERM has a counter-intuitive negative sign. It is noteworthy that FORMAL contributes positively to debt in the IC equation, but not in the AC equation. This suggests that if an enterprise is not yet up and running, it is less likely to borrow if it is not constituted as a formal business, but once it is up and running, its formal status is immaterial to the debt decision. Finally, INC and GOOD are clearly very significant, with higher-income businesses more likely to incur debt, but firms which are self-assessed as above-average being less likely to incur debt. It is interesting that these two variables have opposite signs in all the equations. This suggests that there may be an important difference between MSEs' perceptions of their own relative performance and their actual absolute performance. Firms which are large in some absolute sense, measured by high net income, may have more debt. But, firms which perceive that they are performing well relative to their peers, have less debt.

Overall, variables which are indicative of the permanence of the business, the level of education of the owner, and general performance of the business seem to be most important in determining MSEs' debt-equity decisions, both for initial capital and additional capital. Clearly, there are quantitative differences between the coefficients in the IC and AC equations, but there are no sign differences, although some variables do appear in one equation but not the other. This suggests that there are relatively few substantive qualitative differences among financing decisions, as between MSEs' business start-ups and established MSEs. If there are problems involved in start-ups, these results would suggest that, in general, they are also likely to be present for established businesses.

4.2. Gearing

Columns 3 and 4 of Table 7 show the two simplified models of gearing. It is very striking and reassuring that almost all the same variables which are significant in the IC and AC models are also significant in the gearing models. Moreover, all these variables have the same signs in the gearing models as they do in the IC and AC models: EDUC, TRAIN, FAMILYB, FORMAL, INC, and GOOD. This strongly suggests that the model and the underlying influence of these variables on debt-equity and gearing decisions are both very robust. There are some differences. WFUAGE does not appear in the IC and AC models but it is present in the gearing model, and with a positive sign. This is hard to rationalize and may just be an anomaly in the data. OWNLAND and PERM are in the IC and AC models, but do not appear in the gearing model. This is more reasonable as it suggests that tangibility is a factor in the debt-equity decision but not in the exact level of gearing which is decided on by the MSE. The non-appearance of AGE in the gearing equation is consistent with its non-appearance in the AC equation.

4.3. Loan Applications and Decisions

Finally, column 5 of Table 7 gives the results of the screening equation for loans. With some exceptions, the coefficients are plausibly signed and significant. The positive impact of OWNLAND and PERM reinforces the tangibility argument made earlier. The negative impact of AGE is consistent with general corporate finance arguments, although it is perhaps surprising that there is therefore no effect of AGE on AC or on gearing. The negative effect of underage ownership (WUAGE) is also consistent with our hypotheses. Other signs are harder to rationalize however: the positive sign on WFUAGE, and the negative signs on BUSREGLA and on KEEP. The negative sign on PRIMARY is contrary to our tentative hypothesis, but this hypothesis was tentative and the negative sign may suggest that credit agencies view primary production as more risky than manufacturing.

Evidently there are some important similarities and differences as between the screening equation and the debt equations. OWNLAND and PERM are significant in SUCCR as well as in the debt-equity decision, suggesting that conventional tangibility factors are important in all aspects of debt decisions, from the point of view of both borrower and lender. It is also interesting that EDUC, TRAIN, and INC are important in the overall debt-equity decision but not in the SUCCR equation. This, combined with the counter-intuitive signs on BUSREGLA and on KEEP in the SUCCR equation, suggests that there may be an element of self-selection in loan applications. If in general, some education and book-keeping are regarded as a sine qua non for making a loan application, the decision as to whether to grant the loan and for how much, may depend on other factors. Alternatively, educated owners keeping regular accounts may be over-confident in their loan applications and apply for more than they can reasonably expect. Less well-educated owners with less formal businesses may be more cautious, and therefore enjoy a better success rate. Clearly there is more work to be done on this topic.

5. CONCLUDING REMARKS

We emphasize four main findings from our results. First, MSEs in Kenya obtain debt from a wide variety of sources especially family and friends, but including also co-operatives, banks, ROSCAs, and other financial institutions. Second, the debt-equity and gearing decisions of MSEs and their success rates in loan applications can be understood by relatively simple models which include a mixture of conventional and heterodox variables. Third, there is some tentative evidence that the availability of credit for small business may have improved over time. Finally, the main key determinants of debt and loan success rates are a mixture of conventional and heterodox variables. Among the conventional variables, measures of the tangibility of the owner's assets, and objective and subjective measures of income are particularly important, both in the debt and in the screening decisions. Among the more heterodox variables, the level of education and training of the owners have a significant positive impact on the probability of borrowing and of the resultant gearing level. A comparison between the screening regression and the debt regressions would suggest that there may be some degree of self-selection in the loan application process. The evidence concerning relationship lending is more ambiguous. The signs on variables reflecting education levels could be consistent with a story about the development of borrower–lender relationships. However, variables associated with the age or permanence of the enterprise were mostly either not significant or signed inconsistently with a story about relationship lending. Overall, these findings are an important step in analyzing the financing decisions of MSEs in developing countries with potentially important policy implications for MSEs in Kenya. Clearly, further research on these issues is necessary.

NOTES

1. By "recent past" we mean the 1 year preceeding that in which the survey questions were asked. The success-rate data are confined to those firms which applied for a loan during that period.

2. The Berger–Udell data are not precisely comparable with ours because they report capital by amount rather than by number of firms. The average firm size is also substantially larger. However, the difference in external debt proportions is still worth noting.

3. The t tests were set up as two-tailed tests, and the χ^2 tests as one-tailed tests.

ACKNOWLEDGMENT

Useful comments on a preliminary version of this paper were received from Adrian Wood, Dominique Gross, and participants at the International Conference on Finance and Development, Evidence and Policy Issues, held in Nairobi on July 10–11 2001, and funded by The Kenya Institute for Public Policy Research (KIPPRA) and The Department for International Development (DFID); and the International Conference on Finance for Growth and Poverty Reduction: Experience and Policy, held in Manchester on April 10–12 2002, and funded by DFID. We thank DFID for funding the research for this paper under the "Finance and Development Research Programme", Contract No. RSC106506.

REFERENCES

Aboagye, A. A. (1986). *Informal sector employment in Kenya: A survey of informal sector activities in Nairobi, Kisumu and Mombasa*. Addis Ababa: International Labour Office, Jobs and Skills Programme for Africa.

Berger, A. N., & Udell, G. F. (1995). Relationship lending and lines of credit in small firm finance. *Journal of Business, 68*, 351–382.

Berger, A. N., & Udell, G. F. (2002). Small business credit availability and relationship lending: The importance of bank organizational structure. *Economic Journal, 112*(477), F32–F53.

Cole, R. (1998). The importance of relationships to the availability of credit. *Journal of Banking and Finance, 22*, 959–977.

Cook, P., & Nixson, F. (2000). *Finance and small and medium-sized enterprise development*. Working Paper Series, No. 14 (April). Finance and Development Research Programme.

Freixas, X., & Rochet, J.-C. (1998). *Microeconomics of banking*. Cambridge: MIT Press.

International Labour Organisation. (1972). *Kenya: Employment, income and inequality*. Geneva: ILO.

Kenya Government. (1993). *Economic survey*. Nairobi: Central Bureau of Statistics.

Kimuyu, P., & Omiti, J. (2000). *Institutional impediments to access to credit by micro and small scale enterprises in Kenya*. Discussion Paper, No. DP/026, Nairobi. Institute of Policy Analysis and Research.

King, K. (1996). *Jua Kali Kenya: Change and development in an informal economy. 1970–1995*. Nairobi: East African Educational Publishers.

Liedholm, C. (2002). Small firm dynamics: Evidence from Africa and Latin America. *Small Business Economics, 18*(1-3), 227–242.

Maddala, G. S. (1983). *Limited-dependent and qualitative variables in econometrics.* Cambridge: Cambridge University Press.

Matin, I., Hulme, D., & Rutherford, S. (1999). *Financial services for the poor and poorest: Deepening understanding to improve provision.* Finance and Development Research Programme Working Paper, No. 9, October.

Morduch, J. (1999). The microfinance promise. *Journal of Economic Literature, 37*(4), 1569–1614.

Mullei, A., & Bokea, C. (1999). *Micro and small enterprises in Kenya: An agenda for improving the policy environment.* Nairobi: International Center for Economic Growth.

Ongile, G., & McCormick, D. (1996). Barriers to small enterprise growth: Evidence from Nairobi's small garment industry. In: D. McCormick & P. O. Perderson (Eds), *Small enterprise: Flexibility and networking in an African context.* Nairobi: Longhorn.

Parker, R., Riopelle, R., & Steel, W. (1995). *Small enterprises adjusting to liberalisation in five African countries.* World Bank Discussion Paper, No. 271, African Technical Department Series. Washington DC: The World Bank,

Parker, J., & Torres, T. (1994). *Micro and small enterprises in Kenya: Results of a 1993 National Baseline Survey.* GEMINI Technical Report, No. 75, Nairobi.

Prasad, S., Green, C. J., & Murinde, V. (2001). *Company financing, capital structure, and ownership.* SUERF Study No. 12, Vienna: SUERF.

Sen, A. (1980). Labor and technology. In: J. Cody, H. Hughes & D. Wall (Eds), *Policies for industrial progress in developing countries.* Oxford: Oxford University Press.

Snodgrass, D. R., & Biggs, T. (1995). *Industrialization and the small firms: Patterns and policies.* San Francisco, CA: International Centre for Economic Growth and the Harvard Institute for International Development.

Watson, R., & Wilson, N. (2002). Small and medium size enterprise financing: A note on some of the empirical implications of a pecking order. *Journal of Business Finance and Accounting, 29*(3-4), 557–578.

Wiwattanakantang, Y. (1999). An empirical study on the determinants of the capital structure of Thai firms. *Pacific-Basin Finance Journal, 7*(3-4), 371–403.

UNITED STATES VENTURE CAPITAL FINANCIAL CONTRACTING: FOREIGN SECURITIES

Douglas J. Cumming

ABSTRACT

U.S. venture capital financings of U.S. entrepreneurial firms with up to 213 observations are consistent with the proposition that convertible preferred equity is the optimal form of venture capital finance. This paper introduces new evidence from 208 U.S. venture capital financings of Canadian entrepreneurial firms. In contrast to U.S. venture capital investments in U.S. entrepreneurial firms, U.S. venture capitalists finance Canadian entrepreneurial firms with a variety of forms of finance. The differences between domestic and international U.S. venture capitalist financing structures are not attributable to differences in the definition of the term 'venture capital'. The data point to the importance of institutional determinants of venture capitalist capital structures within the U.S. and abroad. Among other things, the data indicate that U.S. venture capitalists often do not choose convertible preferred shares in the absence of tax considerations in favor of that financing vehicle.

Issues in Corporate Governance and Finance
Advances in Financial Economics, Volume 12, 405–444
Copyright © 2007 by Elsevier Ltd.
ISSN: 1569-3732/doi:10.1016/S1569-3732(07)12016-8

1. INTRODUCTION

Perhaps the most well ingrained proposition in the venture capital (VC) finance literature involves the apparent optimality of convertible preferred securities. U.S.-based research has consistently and repeatedly asserted the proposition that convertible preferred equity is the optimal form of VC finance. Empirical research on forms of finance used by U.S. venture capitalists (VCs) financing entrepreneurial firms located in the U.S. is supportive, based on data with up to 213 observations (see, e.g., Tykvová, 2007a, for a survey). This paper introduces new data that show the literature on the optimality of convertibles is not robust, even among financings by U.S. VCs themselves. By exploring U.S. VC transactions in non-U.S. firms, this paper offers a new and innovative contribution to the literature on the optimality of different securities in VC finance.

In the spirit of research on international differences in VC finance (see, e.g., Tykvová, 2003, 2006; Tykvová & Walz, 2007; Mayer, Schoors, & Yafeh, 2005; Schweinbacher, 2001, 2002; Jeng & Wells, 2000; Black & Gilson, 1998), this paper shows U.S. VCs financings of non-U.S. entrepreneurial firms typically involve the use of a variety of securities other than convertible preferred equity. Although not consistent with U.S.-based theoretical and empirical work, the evidence in this paper is consistent with the observation that a variety of forms of finance are used among non-U.S. VCs (see, e.g., Cumming, 2005, for evidence from Canada; see Bascha & Walz, 2001b for evidence from Germany; see Parhankangas & Smith, 2000, for evidence from Finland; Schweinbacher, 2001, 2002; Cumming, 2003; Landier & Thesmar, 2006; and www.evca.com for other European evidence; see Lerner & Schoar, 2005, for evidence from developing countries; there is also similar evidence from Asia[1]). Furthermore, the evidence in this paper is consistent with recent and innovative theoretical work in VC finance (Garmaise, 2000; Yung, 2002; Landier & Thesmar, 2006; DeBettignies, 2003; Kanniainen & Keuschnigg, 2003, 2004; Keuschnigg, 2004; Keuschnigg & Nielsen, 2001, 2004).

There are at least four possible explanations for these differences across countries. First, U.S. VCs are more sophisticated than their foreign counterparts. If so, foreign VCs will likely adopt contractual forms that more closely resemble those used in the U.S. as they become more sophisticated. Second, VCs in different countries face different types of restrictive covenants that affect their investment decisions, including restrictions on the use of debt (see Gompers & Lerner, 1996, for covenants in the U.S.). Third, exit is relatively more difficult and uncertain in different countries, which has implications for the selected financial contract (see Black & Gilson, 1998;

Smith, 2005; Schweinbacher, 2001, 2002; Bascha & Walz, 2001a). Fourth, taxation in the U.S. may be the primary reason why U.S. VC backed companies are financed with convertible preferred equity (Gilson & Schizer, 2003), and such tax benefits may not exist in other countries.

This paper introduces a new dataset comprising 208 U.S. VC investments financing Canadian entrepreneurial firms. This new dataset is similar to the data considered in related prior work in so far as they comprise roughly the same number of observations from VC funds in the U.S. However, this new dataset differs from all those datasets previously considered in that previous research has not considered the financing differences among domestic versus foreign U.S. VC investments. This is important because the vast literature on the optimality of convertible preferred securities in VC finance is based exclusively on datasets from U.S. VCs financing of U.S. entrepreneurial firms.

That the VC funds are based in the U.S. but the entrepreneurial firms are based in Canada in our data is important for three primary reasons. First, a VC fund that does invest in foreign securities likely faces a different set of restrictive covenants than one that does not invest in foreign securities. Second, it may be relatively more difficult for a U.S. VC to exit an invest-ment located in Canada. Third, and possibly most importantly, there are differences in taxation. These three unique institutional features enable a study of the relatively more important aspects of VC financial contracting theory based on data from sophisticated U.S. VCs.

The data indicate that, unlike their capital structure decisions for U.S. entrepreneurial firms, U.S. VCs finance entrepreneurial firms in Canada with a heterogeneous mix of forms of finance. In particular, between 1991 and 2000, U.S. VCs financing entrepreneurial firms in Canada used common equity in 34.62% of the investments, convertible preferred equity in 21.15% of the investments, straight preferred equity in 15.38% of the investments, straight debt in 12.02% of the investments, convertible debt in 12.02% of the investments, and mixes of straight debt and/or straight preferred equity and common equity in 4.81% of the investments. The data also indicate changes over time in the intensity of use of different forms of finance employed by U.S. VCs in financing Canadian entrepreneurial firms (see Figs. 1(a) and (b)).

The data in this paper are not combined with previous datasets. The data are not combined with a sample of Canadian VCs because Canadian VCs may have different attributes than U.S. VCs, as discussed below in Section 3. Because one cannot abstract from U.S. tax laws and other institutional factors when examining a sample of VCs financing U.S.

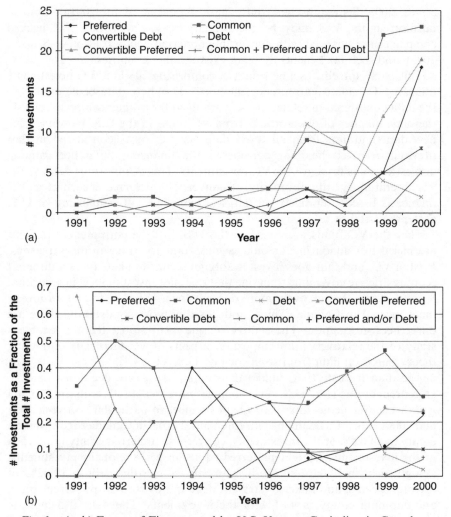

Fig. 1. (a, b) Forms of Finance used by U.S. Venture Capitalists in Canada.

entrepreneurial firms, it is also inappropriate to combine a Canadian sample with a U.S. sample. Moreover, the question of whether U.S. VCs and Canadian VCs use the same financing choice is outside the scope of this paper. This paper focuses on the very narrow question of whether sophisticated U.S. VCs use convertible preferred equity when investing in entrepreneurial firms based in Canada. To bring in other data and to introduce other empirical tests not related to this question would significantly detract from the narrow and fundamental question addressed herein.

U.S. VCs finance a wide variety of Canadian entrepreneurial firms (at different stages of development, high-tech and otherwise, etc.). The transactions in the data herein are more heterogeneous than those considered in studies of U.S. VCs financing U.S. entrepreneurial firms. Importantly, however, the use of a wide variety of forms of finance by U.S. VCs financing Canadian entrepreneurs is not attributable to the definition of venture capital. The results hold for every possible subsample in the data (for every definition of the term 'venture capital' see Tables 1 and 2).[2]

The empirical tests support the conjecture that, given the institutional context, U.S. VC capital structure decisions depend on the characteristics of the entrepreneurial firm and the nature of the financing transaction. The evidence from U.S. VCs investing in Canadian entrepreneurial firms in part parallels evidence from a study of Canadian VCs investing domestically in Canadian entrepreneurial firms (Cumming, 2005). The data herein, however, enable a first look at cross-border financings from sophisticated U.S. VCs to get at the importance of institutional factors such as taxation in the selection of the financing vehicle. That U.S. VCs change their capital structure decisions depending on the country in which the entrepreneurial firm is located enables a new and compelling account of the important aspects of VC capital structure decisions. The evidence points to the importance of institutional determinants of capital structure choice among VCs. The evidence is also consistent with the proposition that U.S. VC contracts mitigate the expected agency problems associated with financing the wide variety of different types of Canadian entrepreneurial firms, within the given institutional context.

Why would U.S. VC investments in Canadian entrepreneurial firms involve forms of finance unlike U.S. VC investments in U.S. entrepreneurial firms? Gilson and Schizer (2003) show U.S. tax law is the primary explanation for the use of convertible securities in the U.S. They state (page 2) that "[a] firm that issues convertible preferred stock to VCs is able to offer more favorable tax treatment for incentive compensation paid to the entrepreneur and other portfolio employees..." In contrast, Canadian tax law does not appear to bias the selection of capital structure in VC;[3] see, for example, Sandler (2001). This difference in taxation is thus capable of explaining why U.S. VCs use convertible preferred equity in the U.S. and not in Canada. It suggests that, when tax considerations do not favor the use of convertible preferred equity, U.S. VCs often do *not* choose convertible

Table 1.   Characteristics of the 55 United States Venture Capital Funds Investing in Canadian Entrepreneurial Firms.

Fund Number	Preferred Equity No. of Inv.	Common Equity No. of Inv.	Conv. Pref. Equity No. of Inv.	Debt No. of Inv.	Conv. Debt No. of Inv.	Start-Up No. of Inv.	Expansion No. of Inv.	Buyout No. of Inv.	Turnaround No. of Inv.	Fund's Min. Inv. ($000)	Fund's Avg. Inv. ($000)	Fund's Max. Inv. ($000)
1	1	0	0	0	0	1	0	0	0	50	50	50
2	0	2	1	0	0	3	0	0	0	333	333	334
3	0	0	1	0	1	2	0	0	0	363	363	363
4	0	1	0	0	0	0	0	0	0	488	488	488
5	0	1	1	1	0	0	1	0	0	500	500	500
6	1	2	0	21	0	4	8	0	2	20	657	1,850
7	0	2	0	0	0	4	0	7	0	80	694	2,208
8	0	0	1	0	0	1	0	0	0	750	750	750
9	0	0	0	0	0	0	0	0	0	750	750	750
10	0	0	0	0	0	1	0	0	0	750	750	750
11	1	0	0	0	0	1	0	0	0	827	827	827
12	2	0	0	0	0	2	0	0	0	975	975	975
13	0	0	1	0	0	0	1	0	0	1,124	1,124	1,124
14	0	1	0	0	0	0	1	0	0	1,142	1,142	1,142
15	0	1	1	0	1	2	1	0	0	500	1,425	3,150
16	0	5	1	0	1	2	4	0	1	192	1,482	4,397
17	0	0	0	0	0	0	0	0	0	1,850	1,850	1,850
18	0	1	2	0	0	0	3	0	0	600	2,039	4,500
19	3	0	0	0	0	1	3	0	0	591	2,171	3,750
20	0	1	1	0	0	0	1	0	0	2,200	2,200	2,200
21	0	0	0	0	0	0	0	0	0	2,250	2,250	2,250
22	1	0	0	0	0	1	0	0	0	2,381	2,381	2,381
23	3	0	0	0	0	3	3	0	0	1,000	2,583	3,750
24	2	1	1	0	0	1	0	0	0	700	2,675	3,500
25	0	1	0	0	0	0	1	0	0	3,000	3,000	3,000
26	0	1	0	0	1	0	0	0	0	900	3,075	5,250
27	0	0	1	0	0	0	1	0	0	3,500	3,500	3,500
28	0	0	0	0	0	1	0	0	0	3,700	3,700	3,700
29	0	2	0	0	1	0	2	0	0	1,000	3,807	12,420
30	2	7	2	3	3	10	4	0	0	250	4,140	19,150

	Pref. eq.	Common eq.	Conv. pref. eq.	Debt	Conv. debt	Start-up	Expansion	Buyout	Turnaround	Min.	Avg.	Max.
31	1	2	1	1	0	1	4	0	0	200	4,581	10,000
32	0	1	0	0	0	1	0	0	0	4,650	4,650	4,650
33	0	0	1	1	0	1	0	0	0	3,500	4,650	5,800
34	1	0	0	0	0	0	2	0	0	222	4,936	9,649
35	0	9	4	0	0	8	4	0	0	500	5,527	24,500
36	0	1	0	2	11	0	1	0	1	6,000	6,000	6,000
37	14	31	15	0	0	32	30	1	30	80	7,315	43,000
38	0	0	1	0	0	1	0	0	0	7,500	7,500	7,500
39	0	0	0	0	0	0	0	0	0	7,500	7,500	7,500
40	1	1	1	0	0	1	1	0	1	1,500	7,750	14,000
41	0	1	0	0	0	0	2	0	2	6,000	9,125	12,250
42	0	0	0	0	0	0	1	0	1	10,395	10,395	10,395
43	1	1	0	0	0	1	0	0	0	10,500	10,500	10,500
44	0	0	0	0	0	0	2	0	0	12,000	12,000	12,000
45	0	0	2	0	0	0	2	0	2	6,000	12,500	19,000
46	0	0	2	0	0	0	2	0	2	6,000	12,500	19,000
47	0	1	0	1	1	1	0	0	0	12,250	13,625	25,000
48	0	0	0	0	0	0	1	0	0	14,500	14,500	14,500
49	0	0	0	0	0	0	0	0	1	17,000	17,000	17,000
50	0	0	0	0	0	1	1	0	0	17,400	17,400	17,400
51	0	0	0	1	1	0	0	0	1	18,750	18,750	18,750
52	0	0	1	0	0	0	0	0	0	18,750	18,750	18,750
53	1	0	0	0	0	2	2	0	2	10,150	22,325	34,500
54	0	2	0	0	0	0	0	0	0	5,000	25,000	45,000
55	1	0	0	0	0	1	0	4	0	41,250	41,250	41,250
Total[a]	38	82	44	29	25	100	89	7	4	270,363	367,709	538,753
Maximum	14	31	15	21	11	32	30	7	2	41,250	41,250	45,000
Minimum	0	0	0	0	0	0	0	0	0	20	50	50
Average	0.69	1.49	0.80	0.53	0.45	1.82	1.62	0.13	0.07	4,916	6,686	9,796
Std. Dev.	1.98	4.38	2.10	2.86	1.55	4.52	4.20	0.94	0.33	7,298	7,848	11,183

Notes: This table presents the number of investments across each venture capital fund by type of security (preferred equity, common equity, convertible preferred equity, debt, convertible debt), and by the stage of development of the entrepreneurial firm (start-up, expansion, buyout, turnaround). Each fund's minimum, average, and maximum dollar investments are also reported. Stages of investment do not sum to 208 because an "other investment stage" category is not reported.

[a] Forms of finance sum to 218 because 10 transactions involved more than one form of finance (see Table 2).

Table 2. Number of Investments with Alternative Forms of Finance used by United States Venture Capitalists in Canada from 1991 to 2000.

Forms of Finance	Total No. of Inv.	No. of Inv. Start-Up	No. of Inv. Expan-sion	No. of Inv. Buy-out	No. of Inv. Turn-around	No. of Inv. Deal <$1m	No. of Inv. $1m <Deal <$5m	No. of Inv. Deal >$5m	No. of Inv. U.S. VC $ Capital/Total Entrepreneurial $ Capital<0.33	0.33<U.S. VC $ Capital/Total Entrepreneurial $ Capital<0.67	No. of Inv. U.S. VC $ Capital/Total Entrepreneurial $ Capital > 0.67	No. of Inv. New	No. of Inv. Syndication	No. of Inv. Hi-Tech	No. of Inv. <50 Employees
Common	72	33	33	0	1	15	30	27	23	19	30	28	57	67	32
Straight preferred	32	22	7	0	1	14	13	5	14	16	2	8	32	31	11
Convertible preferred	44	20	24	0	0	22	12	10	24	13	7	10	43	40	14
Straight debt	25	7	10	6	2	17	7	1	7	16	2	13	24	18	8
Convertible debt	25	16	8	0	0	12	4	9	7	12	6	4	24	24	12
Debt and common	3	1	1	1	0	1	1	1	0	3	0	2	3	1	0
Preferred and common	6	1	5	0	0	4	2	0	4	1	1	4	6	5	3
Preferred +debt +common	1	0	1	0	0	0	0	1	1	0	0	0	1	1	0
Total	208	100	89	7	4	85	69	54	80	80	48	69	190	187	80

Notes: This table presents the number of investments by form of finance (common equity, preferred equity, convertible preferred equity, debt, convertible debt, debt and common equity, preferred and common equity, debt and preferred and common equity), for start-ups, expansion stage firms, buyout transactions, turnaround investments, deals of less than $1 million, deals between $1 million and $5 million, U.S. venture capitalist $ capital contributions/total entrepreneurial firm capital raised, new investments (as, opposed to follow-on investments), syndicated investments, and investments in entrepreneurial firms with fewer than 50 employees. Mixes of preferred and common are treated as convertible preferred in the empirical tests in Tables 5–10. Mixes of debt with common and common and preferred are treated as convertible debt in the empirical tests in Tables 5–10.

preferred shares. Moreover, the evidence in light of tax laws suggests that it is particularly important to examine the financing situation in countries *other than* the U.S. to fully understand the determinants of security choice in VC finance.

This paper is organized as follows. Section 2 describes the data. Section 3 considers competing explanations for the observed data. Empirical tests are provided in Section 4 and the appendix. Concluding remarks follow in Section 5.

2. DATA: WHAT ARE THE DIFFERENCES?

The data herein comprise 208 investments in 124 Canadian portfolio firms by 55 U.S. limited partnership venture capital funds between 1991 and 2000. Coincidentally, the data are extremely similar in scope to U.S. studies of VC investments in U.S. portfolio firms.[4] The data herein are from Macdonald & Associates, Ltd. (Toronto), the leading tracker of VC investments in Canada (see www.canadavc.com) (Macdonald Associates Limited, 1991–2000; Macdonald, 1992). The data indicate that, in contrast to U.S. VC fund investments in U.S. entrepreneurial firms (including the funds in this sample),[5] U.S. VC financings of entrepreneurial firms located in Canada involve the use of a heterogeneous mix of forms of finance.

Table 1 details the financing characteristics of each U.S. VC fund in the sample.[6] The funds are sorted from the smallest to largest average dollar capital contribution. The evidence across the funds indicates that 10% of the funds in the sample use only convertible preferred equity (11 funds, 13 investments). Either just one or two investments are observed in the sample among those funds that only use convertible preferred equity; similarly, some of the other U.S. funds that financed only one or two Canadian firms used other securities.

MacDonald & Associates, Limited (Toronto) and the Canadian Venture Capital Association (CVCA) consider all of the funds in the data to be part of the definition of 'venture capital' (as did the U.S. respondents to their survey of VC financial information), so all of the funds in the data are included in this study. However, some of the funds in the database may not be considered part of the definition of venture capital by others, depending on, for example, the size of the capital contributions. For example, one definition of venture capital may restrict investments levels to be between $500,000 and $7,500,000 in 'start-up' and 'expansion stage' investments (stages of development are defined below).

Regardless, this does not change the observation that forms of finance other than convertible preferred equity are observed. Of the remaining 26 funds in the sample (funds numbered 5, 8–15, 17–28, 32, 33, 36, 38, 39 in Table 1), convertible preferred equity is exclusively used by 8 of the funds, and a variety of forms of finance are observed among the other funds. Table 1 also indicates the use of a heterogeneous mix of forms of finance by U.S. VCs and Canadian entrepreneurs is observed for other more restrictive definitions of 'venture capital'.

The use of a heterogeneous mix of forms of finance by U.S. VCs is also not uniquely attributable to the definition of venture capital by the type of Canadian entrepreneurial firm financed, the amount of capital committed, or whether or not the transaction was syndicated and/or a new or staged investment (see Table 2). The data are summarized by the following mutually exclusive entrepreneurial firm development stages (see Table 2, and Figs. 2(a) and (b)):

- Start-up: The entrepreneurial firm may be based on a concept without a product or any marketing, or it may have a product being developed, but not yet sold commercially.
- Expansion: The entrepreneurial firm requires significant capital for plant expansion and marketing to initiate full commercial production and sales.
- Buyout: The operating management of the entrepreneurial firm wants to acquire a product line, a division, or a company.
- Turnaround: The entrepreneurial firm was once profitable but now is earning less than its cost of capital.

In addition to the mutually exclusive entrepreneurial firm development stages, Table 2 also summarizes the data by the following non-mutually exclusive entrepreneurial firm characteristics:

- Capital requirements: The amount of financing; indicated in Table 2 by the total amount provided by the U.S. VC, and by the amount provided by the U.S. VC divided by the total amount of capital raised by the entrepreneurial firm up to and including the capital provided by the U.S. VC.
- Employees: The number of employees working for the entrepreneurial firm.
- Technology: Firms in technology industries (e.g., biotechnology, communications, electronics, energy, environmental, medical) have characteristics that are distinct from traditional industries (e.g., manufacturing, industrial).

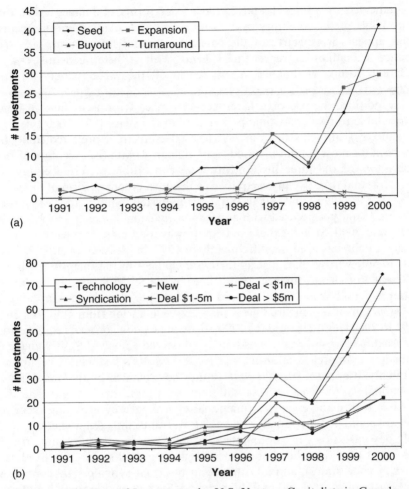

Fig. 2. (a, b) Typs of Investments by U.S. Venture Capitalists in Canada.

- New investment: The entrepreneurial firm has not previously received VC financing (i.e., not "follow-on" financing in subsequent rounds of staged financing).
- Syndicated investment: More than one VC firm finances the entrepreneurial firm.

As indicated in Tables 1 and 2, the use of forms of finance other than convertible preferred equity by U.S. VCs among Canadian entrepreneurial firms appears irrespective of the particular type of transaction. U.S. VCs finance Canadian entrepreneurial firms with a heterogeneous mix of different forms of finance across each of the wide variety of firm characteristics and transaction types.

In addition, the use of a heterogeneous mix of forms of finance is not attributable to particular time periods within the years 1991–2000 (see Figs. 1(a) and (b)). In each year from 1991 to 2000, convertible preferred equity has not been the most commonly used form of finance (with the exception of 1991 where two of the three investments were convertible preferred equity; see Figs. 1(a) and (b)). Common equity was the most common form of finance in 1992, 1993, 1999, and 2000. Straight preferred equity and convertible preferred equity were used with approximately equal intensity in 1992, 1997, 1998, and 2000. Straight preferred equity was used most frequently in 1994. Straight debt was used most frequently in 1997, but least frequently in 2000.

It is noteworthy that, just as there are changes in the intensity of use of different forms of finance over time by U.S. VCs among Canadian entrepreneurial firms (Figs. 1(a) and (b)), there are also changes in the types of Canadian entrepreneurial firms that receive financing from U.S. VCs from 1991 to 2000 (Figs. 2(a) and (b)). The following section considers explanations for the differences in financing structures observed among U.S. VCs financing Canadian entrepreneurial firms, relative to U.S. VCs financing U.S. firms.

Finally, it appears that the data cannot be explained by the possibility of functional equivalence across different securities. In this dataset, it is possible to test the extent of functional equivalence by grouping securities that are could be functionally equivalent: warrants and common equity (that only pay cash flows in good states), straight preferred equity and straight debt (that provide control and pay cash flows in bad states, and fixed cash flows in good states), and all other securities (that provide state contingent differences in control and cash flow rights). Such categories may be inferred from the presentation of the data in Tables 1 and 2, as well as Figs. 1(a) and (b). (They are not presented explicitly to avoid an excessive number of tables and figures. Similarly, empirical tests with aggregated classes of securities are available upon request from the authors.) The data indicate that the securities are not functional equivalents.

This result is consistent with Canadian VC investments in Canadian entrepreneurial firms.[7]

In sum, in contrast to prior theory (see, e.g., Sahlman, 1990; Berglöf, 1994; Trester, 1998; Bergmann & Hege, 1998; Repullo & Suarez, 2004;

Gompers & Lerner, 2001; Casamatta, 2003; Schmidt, 2003; Bascha & Walz, 2001a; and many others) and evidence (see, e.g., Sahlman, 1990; Gompers, 1997; Bergmann & Hege, 1998; Kaplan & Strömberg, 2003), U.S. VCs financing Canadian entrepreneurial firms do not use convertible preferred equity most frequently, regardless of the definition of venture capital. The next section offers a variety of explanations for such differences.

3. THEORY: WHAT EXPLAINS THE DIFFERENCES?

The primary question addressed herein is: what explains the fact that while U.S. VCs finance U.S. entrepreneurial firms with convertible preferred equity, U.S. VCs employ a variety of forms of finance for Canadian entrepreneurial firms? Seven plausible explanations are canvassed: (1) restrictive covenants, (2) sophistication, (3) Canadian conventions, (4) the dearth of other financial institutions in Canada to balance an entrepreneurial firm's capital structure, (5) legal and institutional differences including taxation and securities regulation, (6) differences in exit potential, and (7) agency costs. Importantly, note that these explanations are not mutually exclusive. As discussed herein, it is quite likely that a mix of these factors has given rise to the data described above in Section 2.

3.1. Restrictive Covenants

One explanation of the puzzle for the use of different securities by U.S. VCs for Canadian entrepreneurial firms is that different VCs face different types of restrictive covenants. Gompers and Lerner (1996) have documented the fact that U.S. VCs are often prohibited from, among other things,[8] using debt (66.7% of the time in 1978–1982, 72.1% of the time in 1983–1987, 95.6% of the time between 1988 and 1992). The constraints on debt typically limit the VCs ability to borrow debt or to guarantee the debt of their portfolio firms. For VCs that do not face such constraints, debt securities for their entrepreneurial investees may be relatively more attractive (e.g., to better match cash flows in and out of the fund). That the constraint on debt is used, and that the frequency of use of the constraint on debt financing changes over time, suggests that the constraint is binding on at least some U.S. VCs.

In addition to restrictions on the use of debt, Gompers and Lerner (1996) show that U.S. VCs face covenants relating to the management of the fund (the size of investment in any one firm, coinvestment by the VCs earlier or later funds, and reinvestment of partnership's capital gains), restrictions relating to the activities of general partners (coinvestment by general partners, fundraising by general partners, other actions by general partners, and addition of general partners), and restrictions on the types of investment (investment in other VC funds, investment in public securities, investment in LBOs, investment in foreign securities, and investments in 'other' asset classes).

While previous empirical research on U.S. VCs' financial contracts with U.S. entrepreneurial firms (see, e.g., Sahlman, 1990; Gompers, 1997; Bergmann & Hege, 1998; Kaplan & Strömberg, 2003) has not explicitly considered restrictive covenants faced by the VCs, the homogeneous nature of those investments previously considered (by transaction types and entrepreneurial firm characteristics) suggests the presence of similar types of restrictive covenants explicitly documented by Gompers and Lerner (1996). As with data on U.S. VC investments in U.S. entrepreneurial firms (see, e.g., Sahlman, 1990; Gompers, 1997; Bergmann & Hege, 1998; Kaplan & Strömberg, 2003), the data in this paper from U.S. VCs financing Canadian entrepreneurial firms does not explicitly indicate the types of restrictive covenants faced by the VCs.

We may nevertheless infer that the U.S. VCs investing in Canada in the data herein face fewer restrictive covenants (or at least different restrictive covenants) than the U.S. VCs investing in the U.S. VCs considered in previous research for three primary reasons. First, the entrepreneurial firms are located in Canada, which indicates that none of the funds are prohibited from investing in foreign securities. Second, turnaround and buyout investments are observed, which suggests that there are relatively few restrictions on the types of investments. Third, debt financing is used (and used most frequently in some years), which is suggestive that these VCs are not prohibited from using debt. As discussed above, Gompers and Lerner (1996) show that these three types of restrictions are typically present among U.S. VCs. That these restrictions are not present in this data is interesting because it gives rise to a less restricted contracting and investing environment, and the possibility that different types of financial contracts will be selected.

3.2. Sophistication

A second reason for the observed heterogeneity in capital structure choices described in Section 2 is that U.S. VCs that finance entrepreneurs in Canada are not as sophisticated as U.S. VCs that finance entrepreneurs in the U.S. The level of sophistication cannot be conclusively 'measured' for U.S. VCs considered in this paper. Nevertheless, the empirical tests in the appendix herein are consistent with the view that the U.S. VCs in this data are quite successful at mitigating problems of adverse selection associated with capital structure decisions for Canadian entrepreneurial firms (and more successful than a sample of Canadian VCs; see Cumming, 2005). This is suggestive (albeit not conclusive) evidence of sophisticated U.S. VCs in the data herein.

That the U.S. VCs use forms of finance other than convertible preferred equity for Canadian entrepreneurial firms is not de facto evidence that the U.S. VCs investing in Canada are unsophisticated. The capital structure literature generally (outside the realm of the VC literature) has never suggested a single unique optimal form of finance; rather, optimal capital structure is context dependent. For example, when an investor is more sophisticated and better informed about a project than an entrepreneur, theoretical academic research indicates the use of forms of finance other than convertible preferred equity (Garmaise, 2000).

Do sophisticated U.S. VCs sometimes use forms of finance other than convertible preferred equity for U.S. entrepreneurial firms? While industry associations such as Venture Economics have not collected industry-wide data on forms of finance in the U.S., one may explore the VCs' web pages to investigate further.[9] The PricewaterhouseCoopers MoneyTree™ Survey (http://www.pwcmoneytree.com/) of U.S. VC financings indicates: *Debt is very often part of a venture capital deal* [emphasis added].[10] There are other specific examples. First, Benchmark Capital from Menlo Park, CA, is one of 15 VCs for which the Venture Capital Resource Library indicates: "The venture capital firms listed below include the top names in the industry, firms that have driven the hi-tech economy to new heights".[11] Benchmark Capital states (see www.benchmark.com): "*Raising debt funding is a recent phenomenon for venture-backed start-ups and such funding can be a valuable source of capital*" [emphasis added.] Second, St. Paul Venture Capital, which tends to invest $1 million–$15 million over the course of an investing relationship, states the following under their web page (http://www.stpaulvc.com/): *Our involvement is frequently weighted toward the front end in our later stage deals, structuring mutually beneficial multi-party financings and developing equity and debt structures to fit a company's unique circumstances* [emphasis added.] Third, Northwest Venture Associates (http://nwva.com/), a VC that finances entrepreneurial firms only in the Pacific Northwest region of the U.S., states "*The preferred size of our* *investment ranges from $250,000 to $7,500,000, in the form of common or convertible preferred stock"* [emphasis added.]

Finally, that it may be that U.S. VCs investing in Canada have become more sophisticated over time (possibly as they learn and acquire more VC investing skills; see, e.g., Chan, Siegel, & Thakor, 1990). Note, however, the evolution of contracts over time is not suggestive of a trend towards a single unique form of finance (see Figs. 1(a), (b), 2(a) and (b), discussed above in Section 2).

In sum, we may reasonably expect the level of sophistication among U.S. VCs not to differ all that much depending on whether their investee entrepreneurial firms are located in the U.S. or in Canada. As such, a lack of sophistication does not appear to be a compelling explanation for observed differences in U.S. VC capital structure decisions for entrepreneurial firms located in different countries.

3.3. Canadian Conventions

It may be that U.S. VCs operating in Canada adopt Canadian VC financing practices. That is, because Canadian VCs use a mix of forms of finance (Cumming, 2005), U.S. VCs have decided to also offer a mix of forms of finance. For example, the financial contract used by one syndicated investor is not independent of the financial contract used by another syndicated investor (Admati & Pfleiderer, 1994).

The strength of this argument, however, is weakened by the fact that the data indicate forms of finance other than convertible preferred equity are used where investments are not syndicated (see Section 2 above). Table 2 indicates that 15 of the 18 non-syndicated investments by U.S. VCs involved common equity. Syndication with Canadian VCs does not account for the use of forms of finance other than convertible preferred equity.

3.4. Dearth of other Financial Institutions to Balance the Entrepreneurial Firm's Capital Structure

The variety of forms of finance observed for Canadian entrepreneurial firms by U.S. VCs may be explained by the comparative shortage of other financial institutions in Canada that would round out an entrepreneurial firm's capital structure. For example, there may be a shortage of bank financing for entrepreneurs within Canada's highly concentrated banking industry.[12] In response, VCs that finance Canadian entrepreneurial firms may have adopted 'one-stop' financing – including debt, preferred equity, common equity, and convertible securities – for their entrepreneurial investee firms.

As discussed above (Section 3.2), debt is regarded by top U.S. VCs as a valuable source of capital for venture-backed start-ups, and the advantages of at least some leverage are widely recognized in the finance literature. If the terms available from other institutions to provide such financing are not as favorable as that which could be provided by a VC, it is natural that a VC would offer alternative forms of finance to fit a firm's unique circumstances (as long as the VC is not constrained by restrictive covenants; see Section 3.1 above).

Note, however, that this explanation does not by itself appear to be able to account for the use of a variety of forms of finance by U.S. VCs for Canadian entrepreneurial firms. Although the data do not indicate the forms of finance for the firm from other sources of capital, the data (see Table 2 discussed above) do indicate all forms of finance are used for any size of U.S. VC capital contribution relative to the total amount of capital raised by the entrepreneurial firm (the categories of less than 0.33, 0.33–0.66, and more than 0.66 are provided in Table 2).

3.5. Securities Regulation and Taxation

MacIntosh (1994; 178 pp.) and subsequently others (see, e.g., Halpern, 1997; Cumming & MacIntosh, 2003; Sandler, 2001) have considered legal and institutional factors that give rise to differences in the U.S. and Canadian VC markets (more generally, see Black & Gilson, 1998, and Jeng & Wells, 2000, for a comparative analysis that includes other countries). Only a brief review is provided herein.

Lockout periods are a very important part of securities regulation that affects VC finance (MacIntosh, 1994). Lockout periods significantly affect the VCs' disposition after an initial public offering. Lockout periods for bonds and preferred equity are significantly shorter than that for common equity in Canada (MacIntosh, 1994, p. 107). As such, if lockout periods were a significant determinant of the selected form of finance by a VC, then common equity would be used least frequently in Canada. Interestingly, however, U.S. VCs use common equity most frequently for Canadian entrepreneurial firms (Figs. 1(a) and (b); and Tables 1 and 2). Because common equity is used most frequently, there are likely more compelling explanations for the observed financing patterns for Canadian entrepreneurial firms.

Gilson and Schizer (2003) explain the primary role of U.S. tax law in the use of convertible securities in the U.S.[13] Convertible preferred equity lowers the value of the entrepreneurs' common equity, and therefore lowers the strike price for employee stock options. Tax is deferred until the incentive compensation is sold. In contrast, Canadian tax law does not appear to bias the security choice in Canada; see Sandler (2001).[14] This difference in taxation is thus capable of explaining why U.S. VCs use convertible preferred equity in the U.S. and not in Canada. It suggests that, when tax considerations do not favor the use of convertible preferred equity, U.S. VCs often do *not* choose convertible preferred shares. It also suggests that it is particularly important to examine the financing situation in countries *other than* the U.S. in order to test theories of financial contracting. Further international research is warranted.

There have been significant changes in the intensity of use of different forms of finance over time by U.S. VCs for Canadian entrepreneurial firms (Figs. 1(a) and (b); Tables 1 and 2; see also Cumming, 2005, Fig. 1). There have not been comparable changes in legislation that may explain such changes over time (see, e.g., MacIntosh, 1994; Halpern, 1997; Cumming, 2005; Sandler, 2001). This suggests that factors other than legal and institutional changes probably explain the observed use of a heterogeneous mix of forms of finance in Canada. One possible alternative explanation for the changes in the intensity of use of different forms of finance over time in Canada (Figs. 1(a) and (b)) is the changes in the different types of firms being financed (Figs. 2(a) and (b)), as considered further in Section 3.7.

3.6. Exit Potential

In the U.S., contracting is closely related to exit strategies (see, e.g., Barry, Muscarella, Peavy, & Vetsuypens, 1990; Megginson & Weiss, 1991; Black & Gilson, 1998; Smith & Smith, 2000; Smith, 2005; Schweinbacher, 2001, 2002; Bascha & Walz, 2001a). Relative to the less regulated and more liquid U.S. market, exit in other markets (e.g., Canada) is typically more difficult and uncertain as a result of more onerous securities regulation and a comparative dearth of strategic acquirors (Cumming & MacIntosh, 2003; see also Black & Gilson, 1998; Jeng & Wells, 2000, for international differences in VC across a broader range of countries).

If financial contracting is less closely related to more regulated and uncertain exit strategies in Canada, then capital structure decisions are likely to be more focused on the agency problems that are most pronounced in the particular financing context depending on the type of entrepreneurial firm. The agency problems associated with different types of entrepreneurial firms are considered in the following subsection.

3.7. Agency Costs

In most VC contracting environments there exists bilateral agency problems between the VC and the entrepreneur, as well as agency problems as between syndicated VCs (Sahlman, 1990; Amit, Brander, & Zott, 1998). Start-up, expansion stage, and high-tech investments have been the traditional subject of the theoretical VC literature. This literature has consistently suggested that convertible preferred equity minimizes the expected agency problems associated with start-up and expansion stage investments (see, e.g., Sahlman, 1990; Berglöf, 1994; Lerner, 1994; Gompers, 1995, 1997; Kaplan & Strömberg, 2003; Cornelli & Yosha, 2003; Trester, 1998; Bergmann & Hege, 1998; Repullo & Suarez, 2004; Gompers & Lerner, 2001; Schmidt, 2003; Bascha & Walz, 2001a; and others). The typical arguments that convertible preferred equity minimizes agency costs implicit in VC contracts are as follows. Convertible preferred equity provides the VC with a stronger claim on the liquidation value of the firm in the event of bankruptcy, thereby shifting the risk from the VC(s) to the entrepreneur. At the same time, convertible preferred equity reduces the entrepreneur's dilution of ownership relative to straight common equity financing. Convertible preferred shares also enable a greater amount of funds to be raised relative to straight debt as the VC has some equity participation. In the context of staged financing, convertible preferred equity mitigates window dressing problems and ensures that most positive expected NPV projects continue to receive financing (Cornelli & Yosha, 2003). Similarly, convertible securities may be used with fixed-fraction contracts to mitigate agency problems between syndicated VCs (Admati & Pfleiderer, 1994). Convertible preferred shares have also been argued to facilitate the conversion of illiquid holdings into cash (Sahlman, 1990), and mitigate problems associated with selling the firm particularly when the incentive effects of trilateral bargaining are considered (Berglöf, 1994). As a null hypothesis, we therefore test the following conjecture.[15]

Hypothesis 1. Start-up, expansion, and high-tech Canadian entrepreneurial firms will be financed by U.S. VCs with the use of convertible securities.

As an alternative hypothesis, we may conjecture that the menu of agency problems is not always the same for all entrepreneurs financing transactions. It may be that different types of entrepreneurial pose different needs for aligning effort incentives (see, e.g., Noe & Rebello, 1996) through the use of securities other than convertible preferred equity. If this is the case, then the selected form of finance likely depends on the characteristics of the firm and the transaction (see, e.g., Hart, 1995; Noe & Rebello, 1996), given the institutional framework (few restrictive covenants, a need for one-stop financing, uncertain and regulated exits, etc.) considered above.

Hypothesis 2. The institutional setting of U.S. VCs financing Canadian entrepreneurial firms gives rise to a variety of different types of firms being financed. The menu of agency problems among U.S. VC financings of this wide array of different Canadian entrepreneurial firms differs depending on the characteristics of the firm (stage of development, type of industry, number of employees) and transaction (new or follow-on investment, syndication, deal size). Therefore, the selected form of finance will differ for different types of transactions, as agency problems are different for different transaction types.

Hypothesis 2 considers the possibility that not all entrepreneurial firm financing transactions are similar enough to warrant the use of the same form of finance, given the wide array of different types of transactions with the institutional context of U.S. cross-border financings of Canadian entrepreneurial firms, discussed above. The mix of financing instruments and the structure of the VC contract is a response to conditions of asymmetric information. Problems of moral hazard and adverse selection may be more pronounced at the (mutually exclusive) stages of the entrepreneurial firm's development (buyout, turnaround, start-up, and expansion). In addition, non-mutually exclusive characteristics may independently affect the selected form of finance: first-time financing, high-tech firms, firms with few employees, and deal size. The empirics in Section 4 below test this alternative proposition (Hypothesis 2) against the null (Hypothesis 1).

Plausible ways in which agency problems may differ across different types of firms, within the given institutional context, are indicated in Table 3. The rankings are primarily based on the groundbreaking research of Gompers and Lerner (1999), which shows differences in VC investing behavior

Table 3. Hypothesized Rankings of the Importance of Expected Agency Problems for Different Entrepreneurial Firm and Financing Transaction Characteristics.

Firm Characteristic	Adverse Selection	Effort-Related Moral Hazard between VC(s) and Entrepreneur		Agency Problems between VCs	Trilateral Bargaining	Hold-Up	Window Dressing
		Entrepreneur Qua Agent	VC(s) Qua Agent				
Mutually exclusive development stages							
Start-up	1	1	1	1	2	1	1
Expansion	3	2	2	2	3	2	2
Buyout	5	1	5	5	5	5	5
Turnaround	1	1	1	1	1	1	1
Non-mutually exclusive firm characteristics							
High-tech	1	1	1	1	1	1	1
Few (<50) employees	2	1	3	3	3	3	2
Non-mutually exclusive characteristics of the financing transaction							
Small VC capital contribution	3	3	2	2	3	5	3
Large VC capital contribution	2	3	4	4	3	1	3
New investment	1	1	1	3	1	1	5
Contemporaneous syndication	5	3	3	1	4	4	4

Notes: This table presents hypothesized rankings of the importance of expected agency problems for each firm characteristic: mutually exclusive development stages (start-up, expansion, buyout, turnaround), non-mutually exclusive firm characteristics (high-tech firms, firms with fewer than 50 employees), and the non-mutually exclusive characteristics of the financing transactions (size of VC capital contribution, new investments – as opposed to follow-on staged investments, and syndication). 1, the expected agency problem is most pronounced; 3, average or neutral; 5, least pronounced. Predicted rankings are primarily based on Gompers and Lerner's (1999) empirical studies on agency problems in venture capital.

depending on expected agency problems, the need for monitoring, etc. Consistent with Noe and Rebello (1996) and other capital structure research, there are a variety of agency problems that may impact upon the selected form of finance. A list of typical agency problems is as follows:

Adverse selection: Adverse selection is likely most pronounced for start-up firms with a short track record, turnaround firms with a poor track record, high-tech firms, and new investments (as opposed to follow-on staged investments). See Stiglitz and Weiss (1981) and DeMeza and Webb (1987, 1992).

Moral hazard: There are typically bilateral moral hazard problems in venture capital, such that the effort of both the VC and the entrepreneur affect the performance of the venture. A possible exception whereby the effort of the VC may be less important is in the case of a buyout financing, where the role of the VC is typically less important. See Sahlman (1990), Gompers and Lerner (1999), Tykvová (2007b), Wright, Hoskisson, Busenitz, and Dial (2001), and Wright and Lockett (2003).

Agency problems between VCs: Agency problems are quite common among syndicated VCs, including free-riding, and misstatement of capital requirements, mispricing of securities, etc. See Sahlman (1990), Admati and Pfleiderer (1994), and Gompers and Lerner (1999).

Trilateral bargaining: Certain firms, particularly firms in financial distress (turnaround firms), may have an incentive to give up control over a firm to lower the cost of capital. See Aghion and Bolton (1992) and Berglöf (1994).

Hold-up: Hold-up is particularly pronounced among new start-up entrepreneurial firms that may face contract renegotiation. See Kirilenko (2001).

Window dressing: Window dressing is most common around the time of staged performance reviews. See Cornelli and Yosha (2003).

The empirical analysis in Section 4 below considers the possibility that not all of these expected agency problems will be the same for the wide variety of financing transactions, and the possibility that different forms of finance will therefore be used for different types of transactions to mitigate the agency problems that are expected to be most pronounced in the particular context.

3.8. Summary

Section 3 canvassed a variety of different explanations for U.S. VCs using a variety of securities for Canadian entrepreneurial firms: (1) restrictive covenants, (2) Canadian conventions, (3) sophistication, (4) a dearth of other financial institutions that round out the entrepreneurial firm's capital structure, (5) legal and institutional differences including taxation and securities regulation, (6) exit potential, and (7) agency costs. Sophistication (Section 3.2) is not directly testable with the data, but inferences may be made from the empirical tests in the appendix below. The 'Canadian conventions' explanation (Section 3.3) is testable in part simply by considering the use of a variety of securities among the syndicated investments. Restrictive covenants (Section 3.1), a shortage of other financial institutions that balance the entrepreneurial firm's capital structure (Section 3.4), legal and institutional factors (Section 3.5), and exit potential (Section 3.6) all suggest a unique contracting environment in Canada relative to the U.S., even though the venture capital investors considered are from the U.S. Within this context, it is possible to test whether the use of different forms of finance by U.S. VCs is more likely depending on the type of transaction and type of Canadian firm that is being financed, as conjectured above in Section 3.7. The empirical tests are provided below.

4. EMPIRICS: DO SYSTEMATIC DIFFERENCES EXIST?

Empirical tests of the hypotheses presented in Section 3.7 are conducted using a multinomial logit model (Theil, 1969). The left-hand-side choice variables include the forms of VC finance as presented in Tables 1 and 2 and Figs. 1(a) and (b): common equity, preferred equity, convertible preferred equity, debt, and convertible debt (other combinations of forms of finance were used much less frequently and therefore are not reported). (Other specifications of the left-hand-side variables, such as grouping securities together, yielded similar results and are available upon request.) The right-hand-side variables include the following characteristics for each investment transaction: the stage of development (start-up, expansion), the number of employees (whether or not less than 50), whether or not the firm is in a technology industry, the U.S. VC $ amount invested, the U.S. VC $ amount invested relative to the total $ entrepreneurial capital raised, whether the firm was a new investee (as opposed to a staged investment), and syndication. *Akaike* and *Schwartz information criteria* were used to confirm the appropriateness of the included variables. Endogeneity was not found to be a problem, as discussed further in the appendix.

Table 4 provides correlation coefficients across the explanatory variables. Due to collinearity among start-up and expansion variables, together with the dearth of buyout and turnaround investments in the data, only one stage

Table 4. Correlations across Explanatory Variables.

	Start-Up	Expansion	Buyout	Turnaround	Deal Size	New	Syndication	Technology	Emp. < 50
Start-up	1.0000								
Expansion	-0.8322	1.0000							
Buyout	-0.1796	-0.1614	1.0000						
Turnaround	-0.1347	-0.1211	-0.0261	1.0000					
Deal size	-0.0414	0.1489	-0.1385	-0.1111	1.0000				
New	0.1395	-0.1553	0.1516	-0.0987	-0.1601	1.0000			
Syndication	-0.0119	0.0243	0.0574	0.0431	-0.0395	-0.1463	1.0000		
Technology	0.0350	0.0318	-0.1144	-0.0693	0.2275	-0.1367	0.0104	1.0000	
Employees < 50	0.3469	-0.3442	0.0169	0.0332	-0.2949	-0.0113	0.2082	0.0681	1.0000

Notes: This table presents correlation coefficients for the explanatory variables used in Tables 5 and 6. The explanatory variables include dummy variables for the stages of entrepreneurial firm development (start-up, expansion, buyout, and turnaround), the dollar amount of the venture capitalist capital contribution, and dummy variables for new investments (as opposed to follow-on staged investments), syndicated investments, high-tech firms, and firms with fewer than 50 employees.

of development variable could be included in the econometric specification at a time.

Table 5 provides the multinomial logit regressions with the start-up stage variable; Table 6 provides the regressions with the expansion stage variable.

Table 4 also indicates significant collinearity among the variable measuring the total $ U.S. VC capital contribution divided by the total $ capital raised by the entrepreneurial firm, and the variables for the total $ U.S. VC contribution and the dummy variable for syndication. Therefore, regressions with the variable measuring the total $ U.S. VC capital contribution divided by the total $ capital raised by the entrepreneurial firm are presented in Table 7 (with the start-up variable and without the expansion stage variable) and Table 8 (with the expansion variable and without the start-up variable). These regressions are discussed in Section 4.2. after discussing the regressions in Tables 5 and 6 in Section 4.1.

4.1. Regressions with the Total $ U.S. VC Capital Contribution and Syndication Variables: Tables 5 and 6

Table 5 indicates that Canadian start-up investments are most likely to be financed by U.S. VCs with straight preferred equity (see Eqs. (1), (5), and (6)) and convertible debt (see Eqs. (4) and (10)). Eq. (7) indicates that straight preferred equity is more likely than convertible debt; however, the coefficient is not statistically significant. To the extent that convertible debt is functionally equivalent with convertible preferred equity, the convertible debt result is consistent with previous venture capital research cited above (see Hypothesis 1 and accompanying text).

There are two possible explanations for the straight preferred equity results for start-ups in Table 5. First, Cumming (2005) suggests that straight preferred equity may mitigate mispricing of securities and misstatement of capital requirements among lead and follow-on syndicated VC investors and facilitate optimal continuation. The intuition is straightforward: if the initial lead ('inside') VC's payoff is independent of the entrepreneur's equity share and effort, then the inside VC does not have an incentive to misprice securities to the 'outside' VC (follow-on investor) to maximize the entrepreneur's effort and the inside VC's payoff. The resolution of agency problems between syndicated VCs, however, introduces a cost: the inside VC does not have any upside potential. Therefore, this contractual structure is efficient only if the resolution of agency problems between syndicated VCs is more important than the need to provide the inside VC with upside

Table 5. Multinomial Logit Estimates of Forms of Venture Capital Finance.

Eqn.	Dependent Variable	Constant	Start-Up	Deal Size	New Investee	Syndication	Technology	Emp. < 50
(1)	$\text{Log}_e (P_{\text{Common}}/P_{\text{Preferred}})$	32.4128 (0.00002)	-1.6789 (-3.1644)***	0.0000 (0.4301)	0.6093 (1.1597)	-31.0622 (-0.00002)	-0.8311 (-0.7059)	1.5636 (2.7842)***
(2)	$\text{Log}_e (P_{\text{Common}}/P_{\text{Convertible Preferred}})$	2.1651 (1.7224)*	-0.3152 (-0.7193)	0.0000 (0.4299)	0.3841 (0.8911)	-2.8923 (-2.6849)***	0.4062 (0.5606)	0.9925 (2.1057)**
(3)	$\text{Log}_e (P_{\text{Common}}/P_{\text{Debt}})$	1.1094 (0.8920)	0.6894 (1.1286)	0.0002 (2.9485)***	-0.6421 (-1.1884)	-2.4079 (-2.1078)**	0.6015 (0.8189)	1.2493 (1.9954)**
(4)	$\text{Log}_e (P_{\text{Common}}/P_{\text{Convertible Debt}})$	2.1531 (1.6192)	-1.0355 (-1.9859)**	0.0000 (0.4374)	0.9552 (1.7149)*	-2.1930 (-1.9871)**	0.5168 (0.6215)	0.9541 (1.6928)*
(5)	$\text{Log}_e (P_{\text{Preferred}}/P_{\text{Convertible Preferred}})$	-30.2615 (-0.00002)	1.3637 (2.5816)***	0.0000 (-0.0421)	-0.2253 (-0.4148)	28.1837 (0.00002)	1.2373 (1.0737)	-0.5710 (-1.0072)
(6)	$\text{Log}_e (P_{\text{Preferred}}/P_{\text{Debt}})$	-31.3339 (-0.00002)	2.3683 (3.3782)***	0.0002 (2.8003)***	-1.2515 (-1.9388)*	28.6848 (0.00002)	1.4326 (1.2153)	-0.3143 (-0.4376)
(7)	$\text{Log}_e (P_{\text{Preferred}}/P_{\text{Convertible Debt}})$	-30.2762 (-0.00002)	0.6433 (1.0866)	0.0000 (0.0289)	0.3459 (0.5393)	28.8857 (0.00002)	1.3479 (1.1080)	-0.6094 (-0.9717)
(8)	$\text{Log}_e (P_{\text{Convertible Preferred}}/P_{\text{Debt}})$	-1.0557 (-0.6642)	1.0046 (1.5883)	0.0002 (2.8371)***	-1.0262 (-1.8321)*	0.4844 (0.3257)	0.1953 (0.2720)	0.2568 (0.3965)
(9)	$\text{Log}_e (P_{\text{Convertible Preferred}}/P_{\text{Convertible Debt}})$	-0.0120 (-0.0073)	-0.7203 (-1.3565)	0.0000 (0.0689)	0.5711 (0.9838)	0.6993 (0.4783)	0.1105 (0.1364)	-0.0384 (-0.0666)
(10)	$\text{Log}_e (P_{\text{Debt}}/P_{\text{Convertible Debt}})$	1.0437 (0.6320)	-1.7249 (-2.4762)**	-0.0002 (-2.7803)***	1.5973 (2.3909)**	0.2149 (0.1426)	-0.0847 (-0.1005)	-0.2952 (-0.4010)

Notes: This table presents multinomial logit estimates of the likelihood of selection of different forms of finance (common equity, preferred equity, convertible preferred equity, convertible debt, and debt), based on the characteristics of the entrepreneurial firms being financed: stage of development (start-up; dummy variables for the other stages are excluded to avoid collinearity), size of venture capitalist capital contribution, and dummy variables for syndication, high-tech firms, and firms with fewer than 50 employees. Sample period: 1991–2000 (208 investments). U.S. venture capitalist investments in Canadian entrepreneurial firms. Dummy variables for expansion, buyout, and turnaround variables were not included to avoid singular Hessians during Newton iterations in estimation. Convertible preferred equity includes mixes of common equity and preferred equity. Convertible debt includes mixes of debt and common equity.
*Denotes significance at the 10% level (two-sided tests).
**Denotes significance at the 5% level (two-sided tests).
***Denotes significance at the 1% level (two-sided tests).

Table 6. Multinomial Logit Estimates of Forms of Venture Capital Finance.

Eqn.	Dependent Variable	Constant	Expansion	$ Deal Size	New Investee	Syndication	Technology	Emp. < 50
(1)	$\mathrm{Log}_e\ (P_{\mathrm{Common}}/P_{\mathrm{Preferred}})$	30.9119 (0.00002)	1.8823 (3.3229)***	0.0000 (0.2739)	0.6444 (1.2186)	-31.0944 (-0.00002)	-0.8844 (-0.7490)	1.5888 (2.8446)***
(2)	$\mathrm{Log}_e\ (P_{\mathrm{Common}}/P_{\mathrm{Convertible\ Preferred}})$	2.0849 (1.6631)*	-0.0965 (-0.0202)	0.0000 (0.3771)	0.3122 (0.7288)	-2.7952 (-2.5986)***	0.4211 (0.5825)	0.8019 (1.7229)*
(3)	$\mathrm{Log}_e\ (P_{\mathrm{Common}}/P_{\mathrm{Debt}})$	1.2699 (1.0117)	0.3043 (0.5084)	0.0002 (2.9066)***	-0.4505 (-0.8499)	-2.7254 (-2.3261)**	0.5728 (0.7910)	1.6975 (2.7294)***
(4)	$\mathrm{Log}_e\ (P_{\mathrm{Common}}/P_{\mathrm{Convertible\ Debt}})$	1.4005 (1.0892)	0.9890 (1.8506)*	0.0000 (0.2810)	0.9172 (1.6657)*	-2.2952 (-2.0630)**	0.4909 (0.5919)	0.9159 (1.6322)*
(5)	$\mathrm{Log}_e\ (P_{\mathrm{Preferred}}/P_{\mathrm{Convertible\ Preferred}})$	-28.8742 (-0.00002)	-1.9788 (-3.4766)***	0.0000 (0.0707)	-0.3322 (-0.6014)	28.3464 (0.00002)	1.3055 (1.1216)	-0.7869 (-1.3736)
(6)	$\mathrm{Log}_e\ (P_{\mathrm{Preferred}}/P_{\mathrm{Debt}})$	-29.6796 (-0.00002)	-1.5780 (-2.2653)**	0.0002 (2.8120)***	-1.0950 (-1.7487)*	28.4066 (0.00002)	1.4572 (1.2588)	0.1087 (0.1587)
(7)	$\mathrm{Log}_e\ (P_{\mathrm{Preferred}}/P_{\mathrm{Convertible\ Debt}})$	-29.5532 (-0.00002)	-0.8933 (-1.4154)	0.0000 (0.0195)	0.2728 (0.4262)	28.8410 (0.00002)	1.3753 (1.1255)	-0.6728 (-1.0787)
(8)	$\mathrm{Log}_e\ (P_{\mathrm{Convertible\ Preferred}}/P_{\mathrm{Debt}})$	-0.8149 (-0.5092)	0.4008 (0.6623)	0.0002 (2.8123)***	-0.7628 (-1.3857)	0.0697 (0.04631)	0.1517 (0.2143)	0.8956 (1.4090)
(9)	$\mathrm{Log}_e\ (P_{\mathrm{Convertible\ Preferred}}/P_{\mathrm{Convertible\ Debt}})$	-0.6844 (-0.4245)	1.0856 (1.9888)**	0.0000 (-0.0470)	0.6050 (1.0449)	0.5000 (0.34083)	0.0698 (0.0853)	0.1140 (0.1971)
(10)	$\mathrm{Log}_e\ (P_{\mathrm{Debt}}/P_{\mathrm{Convertible\ Debt}})$	0.1306 (0.0806)	0.6848 (1.0127)	-0.0002 (-2.7963)***	1.3677 (2.1127)**	0.4302 (0.2839)	-0.0819 (-0.0995)	-0.7816 (-1.1225)

Notes: This table presents multinomial logit estimates of the likelihood of selection of different forms of finance (common equity, preferred equity, convertible preferred equity, convertible debt, and debt), based on the characteristics of the entrepreneurial firms being financed: stage of development (expansion; dummy variables for the other stages are excluded to avoid collinearity), size of the U.S. venture capitalist $ capital contribution, and dummy variables for syndication, high-tech firms, and firms with fewer than 50 employees. Sample period: 1991–2000 (208 investments). U.S. venture capitalist investments in Canadian entrepreneurial firms. Dummy variables for expansion, buyout, and turnaround variables were not included to avoid singular Hessians during Newton iterations in estimation. Convertible preferred equity includes mixes of common equity and preferred equity. Convertible debt includes mixes of debt and common equity.

*Denotes significance at the 10% level (two-sided tests).
**Denotes significance at the 5% level (two-sided tests).
***Denotes significance at the 1% level (two-sided tests).

Table 7. Multinomial Logit Estimates of Forms of Venture Capital Finance.

Eqn.	Dependent Variable	Constant	Start-Up	$ U.S. VC Deal Size/Total Entrepreneurial Capital	New Investee	Technology	Emp. < 50
(1)	$Log_e (P_{Common}/P_{Preferred})$	-2.3283 (-2.7209)***	-0.3157 (-0.7044)	3.4399 (4.5544)***	0.4925 (1.1302)	0.9055 (1.2321)	0.7266 (1.6063)
(2)	$Log_e (P_{Common}/P_{Convertible\ Preferred})$	-0.0587 (-0.0462)	-1.6880 (-3.1731)***	3.0699 (3.6551)***	0.8143 (1.5765)	-0.4025 (-0.3411)	1.3245 (2.5327)**
(3)	$Log_e (P_{Common}/P_{Debt})$	-2.3282 (-2.5371)**	0.7507 (1.2438)	3.3254 (3.3215)***	-0.5847 (-1.1259)	2.0544 (2.8108)***	0.2531 (0.4379)
(4)	$Log_e (P_{Common}/P_{Convertible\ Debt})$	-0.5283 (-0.5515)	-0.9459 (-1.8790)*	1.1413 (1.5195)	1.0956 (2.0262)**	0.7877 (0.9896)	0.6129 (1.2205)
(5)	$Log_e (P_{Preferred}/P_{Convertible\ Preferred})$	-2.2696 (-1.8791)*	1.3723 (2.5630)**	0.3700 (0.4101)	-0.3218 (-0.5968)	1.3080 (1.1431)	-0.5979 (-1.1140)
(6)	$Log_e (P_{Preferred}/P_{Debt})$	-2.2695 (-1.7923)*	2.4388 (3.5002)***	0.2555 (0.2234)	-1.3991 (-2.2328)**	2.4569 (2.1078)**	-1.0714 (-1.5851)
(7)	$Log_e (P_{Preferred}/P_{Convertible\ Debt})$	-0.4696 (-0.3552)	0.7422 (1.2370)	-1.9286 (-2.0599)**	0.2812 (0.4410)	1.1903 (0.9714)	-0.7116 (-1.2080)
(8)	$Log_e (P_{Convertible\ Preferred}/P_{Debt})$	0.0001 (0.0001)	1.0664 (1.7136)*	-0.1145 (-0.1091)	-1.0773 (-1.9979)**	1.1489 (1.6406)*	-0.4735 (-0.7768)
(9)	$Log_e (P_{Convertible\ Preferred}/P_{Convertible\ Debt})$	1.8000 (1.9210)*	-0.6302 (-1.1694)	-2.2986 (-2.6426)***	0.6030 (1.0345)	-0.1178 (-0.1443)	-0.1136 (-0.2090)
(10)	$Log_e (P_{Debt}/P_{Convertible\ Debt})$	1.7999 (1.7939)*	-1.6966 (-2.4636)**	-2.1841 (-1.9833)**	1.6803 (2.5691)**	-1.2667 (-1.5226)	0.3599 (0.5383)

Notes: This table presents multinomial logit estimates of the likelihood of selection of different forms of finance (common equity, preferred equity, convertible preferred equity, convertible debt, and debt), based on the characteristics of the entrepreneurial firms being financed: stage of development (start-up; dummy variables for the other stages are excluded to avoid collinearity), size of the U.S. venture capitalist $ capital contribution divided by the total capital raised by the entrepreneurial firm, and dummy variables for high-tech firms, and firms with fewer than 50 employees. Sample period: 1991–2000 (208 investments). U.S. venture capitalist investments in Canadian entrepreneurial firms. Dummy variables for expansion, buyout, and turnaround variables were not included to avoid singular Hessians during Newton iterations in estimation. Convertible preferred equity includes mixes of common equity and preferred equity. Convertible debt includes mixes of debt and common equity.

*Denotes significance at the 10% level (two-sided tests).
**Denotes significance at the 5% level (two-sided tests).
***Denotes significance at the 1% level (two-sided tests).

Table 8. Multinomial Logit Estimates of Forms of Venture Capital Finance.

Eqn.	Dependent Variable	Constant	Expansion	$U.S. VC Deal Size/Total Entrepreneurial Capital	New Investee	Technology	Emp. < 50
(1)	$\text{Log}_e(P_{Common}/P_{Preferred})$	-1.6004	1.8993	3.1395	0.8373	-0.5252	1.3952
		(-1.2289)	(3.3033)***	(3.6787)***	(1.6144)	(-0.4452)	(2.6597)***
(2)	$\text{Log}_e(P_{Common}/P_{Convertible\ Preferred})$	-2.2880	-0.1447	3.3893	0.3983	0.9565	0.4880
		(-2.5075)**	(-0.3214)	(4.4892)***	(0.9170)	(1.3020)	(1.0694)
(3)	$\text{Log}_e(P_{Common}/P_{Debt})$	-1.2309	-0.3400	2.1254	-1.4214	1.2330	0.2281
		(-1.1689)	(-0.5218)	(2.0263)**	(-2.2228)**	(1.5076)	(0.3512)
(4)	$\text{Log}_e(P_{Common}/P_{Convertible\ Debt})$	-1.2426	0.8461	1.1314	1.0447	0.7040	0.5650
		(-1.2237)	(1.6503)*	(1.5182)	(1.9469)*	(0.8810)	(1.1275)
(5)	$\text{Log}_e(P_{Preferred}/P_{Convertible\ Preferred})$	-0.6876	-2.0440	0.2498	-0.4390	1.4817	-0.9072
		(-0.5516)	(-3.4899)***	(0.2672)	(-0.8012)	(1.2791)	(-1.6434)*
(6)	$\text{Log}_e(P_{Preferred}/P_{Debt})$	-2.4735	0.5061	3.2567	-0.3766	1.9370	0.7931
		(-2.5269)**	(0.8971)	(3.4335)***	(-0.7299)	(2.6720)***	(1.3899)
(7)	$\text{Log}_e(P_{Preferred}/P_{Convertible\ Debt})$	0.3578	-1.0532	-2.0081	0.2075	1.2292	-0.8302
		(0.2654)	(-1.6294)	(-2.1098)**	(0.3255)	(1.0055)	(-1.4031)
(8)	$\text{Log}_e(P_{Convertible\ Preferred}/P_{Debt})$	-0.8730	-1.3931	0.1172	-1.2139	2.4622	-0.6021
		(-0.6921)	(-2.0523)***	(0.1072)	(-1.9909)**	(2.1525)**	(-0.9288)
(9)	$\text{Log}_e(P_{Convertible\ Preferred}/P_{Convertible\ Debt})$	1.0454	0.9908	-2.2579	0.6465	-0.2526	0.0770
		(1.0409)	(1.7831)*	(-2.5687)***	(1.1101)	(-0.3075)	(0.1392)
(10)	$\text{Log}_e(P_{Debt}/P_{Convertible\ Debt})$	1.2309	0.3400	-2.1254	1.4214	-1.2330	-0.2281
		(1.1689)	(0.5218)	(-2.0263)**	(2.2228)**	(-1.5076)	(-0.3512)

Notes: This table presents multinomial logit estimates of the likelihood of selection of different forms of finance (common equity, preferred equity, convertible preferred equity, convertible debt, and debt), based on the characteristics of the entrepreneurial firms being financed: stage of development (expansion; dummy variables for the other stages are excluded to avoid collinearity), size of the U.S. venture capitalist $ capital contribution divided by the total capital raised by the entrepreneurial firm, and dummy variables for high-tech firms, and firms with fewer than 50 employees. Sample period: 1991–2000 (208 investments). U.S. venture capitalist investments in Canadian entrepreneurial firms. Dummy variables for expansion, buyout, and turnaround variables were not included to avoid singular Hessians during Newton iterations in estimation. Convertible preferred equity includes mixes of common equity and preferred equity. Convertible debt includes mixes of debt and common equity.

*Denotes significance at the 10% level (two-sided tests).
**Denotes significance at the 5% level (two-sided tests).
***Denotes significance at the 1% level (two-sided tests).

potential. The inside VC may be provided with securities that have upside potential in follow-on financing rounds in later development stages (see the other coefficients, discussed below).

There may be a second explanation for the significance of the straight preferred equity coefficients (not mutually exclusive with the first). The comparative dearth of other financial institutions in Canada (see Section 3.4) providing financing to start-ups may give rise to a need to increase the leverage of the entrepreneurial investee. Straight debt is less attractive than straight preferred equity because investors may force the start-up firm into bankruptcy if interest on debt is not paid, unlike preferred dividends.

As mentioned, the expansion stage variable could not be included in the specification in Table 5 due to collinearity with the start-up variable. Table 6 presents the regression results without the start-up and with the expansion stage variable. Each coefficient for the other variables was not materially different (the one exception between Tables 5 and 6 is the new investee coefficient in Eq. (8), which is insignificant in Table 6 but negative and significant at the 10% level in Table 5). Table 6 indicates that expansion stage investments are more likely to be financed with convertible preferred equity (Eqs. (5) and (9)) as expected (see Hypothesis 1 and the supporting research cited in the accompanying text).

In addition to start-up and expansion stages of development, U.S. VCs finance Canadian entrepreneurial firms at the buyout and turnaround stages. Unfortunately, there are relatively few later stage firms in the data (7 buyouts and 4 turnarounds; see Table 2). It was not possible to include variables for these later stage investments in the multinomial logit econometric specification.

For new investments (as opposed to a staged or follow-on investments), the evidence indicates that straight debt is more likely than straight preferred equity and convertible debt (see Eqs. (6) and (10), respectively). The coefficient in Eq. (4) indicates common equity is more likely than convertible debt. New investments are characterized by pronounced adverse selection problems. The use of straight debt mitigates adverse selection problems associated with mean returns, whereas common equity mitigates adverse selection problems associated with the variance in returns (Stiglitz & Weiss, 1981; DeMeza & Webb, 1987, 1992). It appears that U.S. VC investors view some new Canadian investments as characterized by uncertainty in the expected mean returns, and others by uncertainty in the variance of expected returns.

A few of the coefficient estimates are more difficult to explain. The coefficients for syndicated investments only indicate common equity is least likely to be selected (Eqs. (2)–(4)). None of the technology coefficients are significant. For entrepreneurial firms with few employees, common equity is most likely (Eqs. (1)–(4)). That convertible preferred equity (see Hypothesis 1 and accompanying text) is not used is likely related to the institutional factors discussed above in Section 3.

Finally, the estimates in both Tables 5 and 6 indicate the larger the investment, the more likely that securities with upside potential for the U.S. VC are used (Eqs. (3), (8), and (10)), as would be expected (see, e.g., Noe & Rebello, 1996). The impact of the U.S. VC's capital contribution relative to the total amount of capital raised by the entrepreneurial firm is considered below in Tables 7 and 8.

4.2. Regressions with the Total $ U.S. VC Capital/Total Entrepreneurial Capital Variable: Tables 7 and 8

Tables 7 and 8 present regressions with the total $ U.S. VC capital contribution divided by the total $ amount of capital raised by the entrepreneurial firm. Due to collinearity (see Table 4), the syndication dummy variable and the variable measuring the total $ U.S. VC contribution (as in Tables 5 and 6) are not included when the variable – the total $ U.S. VC capital contribution divided by the total $ amount of capital raised by the entrepreneurial firm – is included.

Note that, with only a few exceptions, the tables indicate that the impact of this change in the included variables on the other coefficient estimates is insignificant. The results discussed in Section 4.1 are also quite robust to the inclusion or exclusion of other variables.

The new variable in Tables 7 and 8 – the total $ U.S. VC capital contribution divided by the total $ amount of capital raised by the entrepreneurial firm – does yield interesting coefficient estimates. Larger values for the ratio of the U.S. VC $ capital contribution to the total entrepreneurial firm capital are associated with an increase in the likelihood that common equity and convertible debt will be selected (the relevant coefficient estimates in Eqs. (1)–3 and (9) are significant at the 1% level, and at the 5% level in Eqs. (7) and (10)). As between common equity and convertible debt, the coefficient estimates are suggestive that common equity is more likely than convertible debt the larger the U.S. VC $ contribution relative to total entrepreneurial capital, but this result is on the cusp of statistical significance (p-value is slightly greater than 0.10 in Eq. (4)). The result that common and convertible debt are more likely the larger the U.S. VC capital contribution relative to total entrepreneurial capital raised is consistent with previous theoretical capital structure research (Noe & Rebello, 1996, Propositions 3 and 4).

4.3. Limitations and Future Research

The data on the contracts used by U.S. VCs financing Canadian entrepreneurial firms considered herein provide a first look at cross-border VC financial contracting. There is, however, information that is not available in the data, including security prices, board structure, and specific contractual contingencies (e.g., Gompers, 1997; Kaplan & Strömberg, 2003). Consistent with theoretical research (Cestone, 2000), preliminary evidence from a sample of European VC contracts (Cumming, 2003) indicates the control rights in contracts are complementary to the security selected. Future research could consider, among other things, whether these specific contractual features differ among domestic and cross-border VC financings.

5. CONCLUSION

Previous research has not considered U.S. VC financial contracts among foreign entrepreneurial firms. The data and empirics introduced herein with U.S. VC investments in Canadian entrepreneurial firms give rise to significantly different conclusions relative to empirical studies of U.S. VC contracts with U.S. entrepreneurial firms. The differences we observe point to the importance of institutional factors in explaining forms of finance used by U.S. VCs.

The first important institutional difference is in the absence of certain restrictive covenants among the VCs in the sample. Later stage investments, foreign securities, and the use of debt appear to be permitted among most of the U.S. VCs considered herein, but are typically prohibited among U.S. VCs investing in the U.S. (Gompers & Lerner, 1996).

Second, Canada's banking market is highly concentrated, and there may be a dearth of debt finance available to Canadian entrepreneurial firms. It appears that U.S. VCs financing Canadian entrepreneurial firms offer 'one-stop' financing – that is, a menu of alternative securities – to balance the capital structure of entrepreneurial firms. In the U.S., by contrast, entrepreneurial firms are more likely to receive debt either from a bank, or possibly from a U.S. VC not prohibited from using debt. As documented in Section 3.2, debt is very often part of U.S. VC deals, even within the U.S.

Third, U.S. tax law significantly biases the choice of financing instrument for U.S. entrepreneurial firms (Gilson & Schizer, 2003). Such distortions are not apparent in Canada (see footnote 14; see also Sandler, 2001). The evidence herein suggests that, when tax considerations do not bias the choice of financing vehicle, VCs often do *not* choose convertible preferred shares. This further suggests that it is particularly important to examine the financing situation in countries *other than* the U.S. to fully understand the factors that affect financial contracting in venture capital. Further international research in warranted.

Fourth, when U.S. tax law does not bias the choice of financing vehicle, U.S. VC structure decisions appear to reflect an interest in mitigating the expected agency problems that are most pronounced in the particular financing context. Unlike most U.S. VC investments within the U.S., U.S. VC investments in Canada systematically involve the use of different securities depending on the characteristics of the entrepreneurial firm. While the evidence herein provides some insight in this regard, further theoretical and empirical work, with regard to the institutional structure, is warranted.

NOTES

1. For example, the first venture capital company in Thailand, Business Venture Promotions, Ltd. indicates they use "common stock, preferred stock, and equity links such as convertible debentures and warrants" (see http://www.supertrade.com/bvp/invest.html). More generally, researchers from The Management School at Shanghai Jiaotong University have indicated to the author that venture capitalists in Taiwan use common equity for most investments (see also Songtao, 2000). Lerner (2000) discusses other evidence from Asia. Further international research is warranted.

2. This statement presumes that 'venture capital' is not tautologically defined as entrepreneurial investments in the form of convertible preferred equity. In this paper, debt investments by venture capital funds are not excluded. Regardless, the results herein are not affected by the inclusion or exclusion of "debt-type" investments. The exclusion of debt-type investments does not give rise to, for example, convertible preferred equity being used most frequently. See also footnote 10, *infra*.

3. Sandler (2001) provides a much more complete discussion; see also Section 3.5 and footnote 14, *infra*.

4. For example, Gompers (1997) considers 50 venture capital investment transactions. Kaplan and Strömberg (2003) consider 213 venture capital investment transactions.

5. The particular details on the contracts for U.S. entrepreneurs used by the U.S. VC funds in this sample data are not available (the information is confidential and not revealed to the CVCA or the authors); nevertheless, the funds have indicated their financing practices for U.S. entrepreneurial firms are similar with those of the U.S. VC industry as documented by Sahlman (1990), Gompers (1997), Bergmann and Hege (1998), and Kaplan and Strömberg (2003).

6. See Kanniainen and Keuschnigg (2003, 2004), and Keuschnigg (2004) for the determinants of venture capital portfolio size.

7. Cumming (2005). In a study of venture capital contracts in Europe, Cumming (2003) also finds that the contingencies, and veto and control rights used in venture capital contracts are complementary to the security used (not substitutes), so that different types of securities are in fact functionally distinct. Theoretical research (Cestone, 2000) supports this empirical finding. There does not exist any other empirical paper that considers this issue. Further research with other datasets would be fruitful.

8. Gompers and Lerner (1996) show that U.S. venture capital funds face restrictions relating to the management of the fund, restrictions relating to the activities of general partners, and restrictions on the types of investment. In the 1988–1992 period in their data, most of these covenants were used among more than 50% of the 140 venture capital funds in their sample.

9. Not all U.S. venture capital firms state the use of any particular form(s) of finance on their web page, but we may infer that most use convertible preferred equity, given evidence from Sahlman (1990), Gompers (1997), Bergmann and Hege (1998), and Kaplan and Strömberg (2003).

10. We may infer that the debt portion comes from investors that are not restricted from using debt-type securities (see *supra*, footnote 8 and Section 3.1). Because 'venture capital' is considered to be a subset of 'private equity', investments that are not 'equity' (e.g., common or convertible preferred) are often excluded from the definition of 'venture capital', depending on the conventions in the country under consideration. But defining the term 'venture capital' or 'private equity' by the form(s) of finance used is obviously tautological and begs the question of whether or not a venture capital fund uses a particular security. For example, Liberty Partners (http://www.libertypartners.com), a private 'equity' firm, indicates on their web page that they sometimes use debt.

11. See www.vfinance.com. It is also noteworthy that the Venture Capital Resource Library allows for searches of venture capital firms by the categories: "equity", "sub debt", and "senior debt".

12. Canada has a mere six major banks. In December 1998, two merger proposals were rejected by the Competition Bureau of Canada, partly due to the lack of a competitive market in debt financing for entrepreneurial firms.

13. Similarly, Bratton (2002) explains the institutional factors that affect specific covenants (e.g., control rights) in U.S. venture capital contracts. Gompers (1997) and Kaplan and Strömberg (2003) provide an empirical analysis of the economic determinants of these control rights.

14. It is actually a matter of debate as to whether Canadian tax practice favors any particular security. The authors have consulted lawyers in three different provinces (Alberta, Manitoba, and Ontario), and perceptions are uncertain as to how Revenue Canada would react to U.S.-style low valuations of common equity upon issuance of convertible preferred equity. The market is relatively young, and it is arguable that there is no established tax practice towards convertible preferred securities being used to devalue the common shares in VC financings. Revenue Canada has not released any Policy Statements on this issue.Gilson and Schizer (2003, note 51) indicate there may be a tax bias against preferred dividends in Canada. Note, however, that most VCs look for returns in capital gains upon exit,

not dividends. As well, if the tax treatment of preferred dividends in Canada is determinative of security choice, we would certainly be less likely to observe straight preferred equity being used in Canada. The data (see Section 2), however, clearly indicate straight preferred equity is used quite often.

15. It is noteworthy that U.S. investors are not as geographically proximate to their Canadian entrepreneurial investee firms. U.S. VCs may provide less value added to their Canadian investee firms relative to U.S. investees, and demand a smaller equity share (perhaps terms of conversion that are less favorable) if fewer incentives are required for the U.S. VC qua agent (but this may be offset by additional risk incurred by U.S. venture capitalists investing in Canadian entrepreneurial firms).

ACKNOWLEDGMENT

I owe thanks to the seminar participants at the 10th Annual Conference on the Theories and Practices of Securities and Financial Markets in Kaohsiung, Taiwan (December 2001), Tilburg University (January 2002), the University of Amsterdam (January 2002), the American Law and Economics Association Annual Conference at Harvard Law School (May, 2002), and the Canadian Law and Economics Association Annual Conference at the University of Toronto Law School (September 2003). I owe special thanks to Joe Frankovic, Mary Macdonald, Jeff MacIntosh, and Dmitri Safine for helpful comments and insights into venture capital in Canada. I have also greatly benefited from earlier discussions and correspondence on related research with Varouj Aivazian, Paul Halpern, Mark Huson, Josh Lerner, Ted Liu, Frank Mathewson, Mary Macdonald, Randall Morck, Tom Ross, and especially Ralph Winter. I am grateful for financial support from the University of Alberta SAS Fellowship, University of Alberta Pearson Fellowship, and University of British Columbia Entrepreneurship Research Alliance Scholarship. Macdonald & Associates, Limited (Toronto) generously provided the data.

REFERENCES

Admati, A. R., & Pfleiderer, P. (1994). Robust financial contracting and the role of venture capitalists. *Journal of Finance, 49*, 371–402.

Aghion, P., & Bolton, P. (1992). An incomplete contracts approach to financial contracting. *Review of Economic Studies, 59*, 473–494.

Amit, R., Brander, J., & Zott, C. (1998). Why do venture capital firms exist? Theory and Canadian evidence. *Journal of Business Venturing, 13*, 441–466.

Barry, C. B., Muscarella, C. J., Peavy, J. W., III., & Vetsuypens, M. R. (1990). The role of venture capitalists in the creation of public companies: Evidence from the going public process. *Journal of Financial Economics, 27*, 447–471.

Bascha, A., & Walz, U. (2001a). Convertible securities and optimal exit decisions in venture capital finance. *Journal of Corporate Finance, 7*, 285–306.

Bascha, A., & Walz, U. (2001b). *Financing practices in the German venture capital industry: An empirical assessment.* Working Paper. University of Tübingen.

Berglöf, E. (1994). A control theory of venture capital finance. *Journal of Law, Economics, and Organization, 10*, 247–267.

Bergmann, D., & Hege, U. (1998). Venture capital financing, moral hazard, and learning. *Journal of Banking and Finance, 22*, 703–735.

Black, B. S., & Gilson, R. J. (1998). Venture capital and the structure of capital markets: Banks versus stock markets. *Journal of Financial Economics, 47*, 243–277.

Bratton, W. (2002). *Venture capital on the downside: Preferred stock and corporate control. Michigan Law Review, 100*, 891–945.

Casamatta, C. (2003). Financing and advising: Optimal financial contracts with venture capitalists. *Journal of Finance, 58*, 2059–2086.

Cestone, G. (2000). *Venture capital meets contract theory: Risky claims or formal control?* Working paper. University of Toulouse and Institut d'Analisi Economica, Barcelona.

Chan, Y.-S., Siegel, D. R., & Thakor, A. V. (1990). Learning, corporate control and performance requirements in venture capital contracts. *International Economic Review, 31*, 365–382.

Cornelli, F., & Yosha, O. (2003). Stage financing and the role of convertible debt. *Review of Economic Studies, 70*, 1–32.

Cumming, D. J. (2003). *Contracts and exits in venture capital finance.* Working Paper. Schulich School of Business, York University.

Cumming, D. J. (2005). Capital structure in venture finance. *Journal of Corporate Finance, 11*, 550–585.

Cumming, D. J., & MacIntosh, J. G. (2003). A cross-country comparison of full and partial venture capital exits. *Journal of Banking and Finance, 27*, 511–548.

Davidson, R., & MacKinnon, J. G. (1993). *Estimation and inference in econometrics.* New York: Oxford University Press.

DeBettignies, J.-E. (2003). *Financing the entrepreneurial venture.* Working paper. University of British Columbia.

DeMeza, D., & Webb, D. C. (1987). Too much investment: A problem of asymmetric information. *Quarterly Journal of Economics, 102*, 281–292.

DeMeza, D., & Webb, D. C. (1992). Efficient credit rationing. *European Economic Review, 36*, 1277–1290.

Garmaise, M. (2000). *Informed investors and the financing of entrepreneurial projects.* Working Paper. University of Chicago Graduate School of Business.

Gilson, R., & Schizer, D. (2003). Venture capital structure: A tax explanation for convertible preferred stock. *Harvard Law Review, 116*, 875–916.

Gompers, P. A. (1995). Optimal investment, monitoring, and the staging of venture capital. *Journal of Finance, 50*, 1461–1489.

Gompers, P. A. (1997). *Ownership and control in entrepreneurial firms: An examination of convertible securities in venture capital investments.* Working Paper. Harvard Business School.

Gompers, P. A., & Lerner, J. (1996). The use of covenants: An empirical analysis of venture partnership agreements. *Journal of Law and Economics, 39*, 463–498.

Gompers, P. A., & Lerner, J. (1999). *The venture capital cycle.* Cambridge: MIT Press.

Gompers, P. A., & Lerner, J. (2001). *The money of invention: How venture capital creates new wealth.* Boston, MA: Harvard Business School Press.

Halpern, P. (Ed.) (1997). Financing growth in Canada. Calgary: University of Calgary Press.

Hart, O. (1995). *Firms, contracts, and financial structure.* Oxford: Claredon Press.

Jeng, L. A., & Wells, P. C. (2000). The determinants of venture capital fundraising: Evidence across countries. *Journal of Corporate Finance, 6,* 241–289.

Kanniainen, V., & Keuschnigg, C. (2003). The optimal portfolio of start-up firms in venture capital finance. *Journal of Corporate Finance, 9,* 521–534.

Kanniainen, V., & Keuschnigg, C. (2004). Start-up investment with scarce venture capital support.". *Journal of Banking and Finance, 28,* 1935–1959.

Kaplan, S. N., & Strömberg, P. (2003). Financial contracting theory meets the real world: An empirical analysis of venture capital contracts. *Review of Economic Studies, 70,* 281–315.

Keuschnigg, C. (2004). Taxation of a venture capitalist with a portfolio of firms. *Oxford Economic Papers, 56,* 285–306.

Keuschnigg, C., & Nielsen, S. B. (2001). Public policy for venture capital. *International Tax and Public Finance, 8*(2001), 557–572.

Keuschnigg, C., & Nielsen, S. B. (2004). Start-ups, venture capitalists, and the capital gains tax. *Journal of Public Economics, 88,* 1011–1042.

Kirilenko, A. A. (2001). Valuation and control in venture finance. *Journal of Finance, 56,* 565–587.

Landier, A., & Thesmar, D. (2006). *Contracting with optimistic entrepreneurs: Theory and evidence.* Review of Finance Studies, (forthcoming).

Lerner, J. (1994). The syndication of venture capital investments. *Financial Management, 23,* 16–27.

Lerner, J. (2000). *Venture capital and private equity: A casebook.* New York: Wiley.

Lerner, J., & Schoar, A. (2005). Does legal enforcement affect financial transactions? The contractual channel in private equity. *Quarterly Journal of Economics, 120,* 223–246.

Macdonald & Associates Limited. (1991–2000 editions). Venture capital in Canada: Annual statistical review and directory. Toronto: Canadian Venture Capital Association.

Macdonald, M. (1992). *Venture capital in Canada: A guide and sources.* Toronto: Canadian Venture Capital Association.

MacIntosh, J. G. (1994). *Legal and institutional barriers to financing innovative enterprise in Canada,* monograph prepared for the Government and Competitiveness Project. Discussion Paper pp. 94–10. School of Policy Studies, Queen's University.

Mayer, C., Schoors, K., & Yafeh, Y. (2005). Sources of funds and investment activities of venture capital funds: Evidence from Germany, Israel, Japan and the UK. *Journal of Corporate Finance, 11,* 586–608.

Megginson, W. L., & Weiss, K. A. (1991). Venture capitalist certification in initial public offerings. *Journal of Finance, 46,* 879–903.

Noe, T. H., & Rebello, M. J. (1996). Asymmetric information, managerial opportunism, financing and payout policies. *Journal of Finance, 51,* 637–660.

Parhankangas, A., & Smith, D. G. (2000). *Conflict management in the entrepreneur-venture capitalist relationship: An international comparative study.* Working Paper. Northwestern School of Law of Lewis & Clark College and Helsinki University of Technology.

Repullo, R., & Suarez, J. (2004). Venture capital finance: A security design approach. *Review of Finance, 8,* 75–108.

Sahlman, W. A. (1990). The structure and governance of venture capital organizations. *Journal of Financial Economics, 27*, 473–521.

Sandler, D. (2001). The tax treatment of employee stock options: Generous to a fault. *Canadian Tax Journal, 49*, 259–302.

Schmidt, K. M. (2003). Convertible securities and venture capital finance. *Journal of Finance, 58*, 1139–1166.

Schweinbacher, A. (2001). *Innovation and venture capital exits.* Working Paper. University of Amsterdam.

Schweinbacher, A. (2002). *Venture capital exits in Europe and the United States.* Working Paper. University of Amsterdam.

Smith, D. G. (2005). The exit structure of venture capital. *VCLA Law Review, 53*, 315–356.

Smith, J. K., & Smith, R. L. (2000). *Entrepreneurial Finance.* New York: Wiley.

Songtao, L. (2000). The stage and character of venture capital development in Taiwan. *Asia and Pacific Economics, 3.*

Stiglitz, J., & Weiss, A. (1981). Credit rationing in markets with imperfect information. *American Economic Review, 73*, 393–409.

Theil, H. (1969). A multinomial logit extension of the Linear Logit Model. *International Economic Review, 10*, 251–259.

Trester, J. J. (1998). Venture capital contracting under asymmetric information. *Journal of Banking and Finance, 22*, 675–699.

Tykvová, T. (2003). Venture-backed IPOs: Investment duration and lock-up by venture capitalists. *Finance Letters, 1*(2), 61–65.

Tykvová, T. (2007a). What do economists tell us about venture capital contracts? *Journal of Economic Surveys, 21*, 65–89.

Tykvová, T. (2006). How do investment patterns of independent and captive private equity funds differ? Evidence from Germany. *Financial Markets and Portfolio Management, 20*, 399–418.

Tykvová, T. (2007b). Who chooses whom? Syndication, skills and reputation. *Review of Financial Economics, 16*, 5–28.

Tykvová, T., & Walz, U. (2007). How important is participation of different venture capitalists in German IPOs? *Global Finance Journal, 17*, 350–378.

Wright, M., Hoskisson, R. E., Busenitz, L. W., & Dial, J. (2001). Finance and management buyouts: Agency versus entrepreneurship perspectives. *Venture Capital: An International Journal of Entrepreneurial Finance, 3*, 239–262.

Wright, M., & Lockett, A. (2003). The structure and management of alliances: Syndication in the venture capital industry. *Journal of Management Studies, 40*, 2073–2104.

Yung, C. (2002). *Security design in private markets.* Working Paper, University of Colorado at Boulder.

APPENDIX

Because adverse selection implies different forms of finance may attract different types of entrepreneurial firms, the effects of endogeneity in the econometric tests in Section 4 were tested. Durbin-Wu-Hausman tests are presented in Table A2. Variables indicating the geographic location (Canadian province) of the entrepreneurial firms were used as instruments.

Choice of these instruments was natural: the capital requirements and the number of expansion firms and technology firms may vary by province; however, the province will not be directly related to the forms of financing (see Table A1). Other instruments were considered as well, including dummy variables for the year of the financing, etc. The qualitative conclusions from the endogeneity tests were not affected by the choice of instrument. Sufficient instruments were used for identification; additional instruments were not used to avoid finite sample bias (Davidson & MacKinnon, 1993, Chapter 7).

The insignificant coefficients in Table A2 suggest the absence of systematic endogeneity problems; as such, the standard multinomial logit model is used in Tables 5–8. (Note that the results with the start-up variables are presented in Table A2; the set of estimates with the expansion stage variable is not materially different, and therefore not presented. Similarly, there were no endogeneity problems with the variable measuring the $ amount of VC capital relative to the total entrepreneurial capital.)

Table A1. Correlations across Financing Choices, Canadian Provinces, and Year of Financing.

	Preferred	Common	Convertible Preferred	Debt	Convertible Debt
British Columbia	0.0465	−0.0925	0.1474	−0.0205	−0.0840
Alberta	0.0088	−0.0500	−0.0909	0.2256	−0.0401
Ontario	0.0436	0.0181	0.0476	−0.1036	−0.0318
Quebec	−0.0797	0.1200	−0.1267	−0.1007	0.1690
Newfoundland	−0.0516	−0.0880	−0.0681	0.3273	−0.0487
1991	−0.0516	−0.0033	0.1207	−0.0447	−0.0487
1992	0.0373	0.0453	0.0032	−0.0518	−0.0564
1993	−0.0597	0.0453	0.0032	−0.0518	0.0447
1994	0.1343	−0.1019	0.0032	−0.0518	0.0447
1995	0.0403	−0.0554	−0.0090	−0.0786	0.1191
1996	−0.0958	−0.0218	0.0839	−0.0831	0.1042
1997	−0.1036	−0.0491	−0.1091	0.3020	0.0264
1998	−0.0544	0.0245	−0.1138	0.2687	−0.0888
1999	−0.0754	0.1292	0.0123	−0.0621	−0.0558
2000	0.1841	−0.0552	0.0755	−0.2129	−0.0092

Notes: This table presents correlation coefficients for the entrepreneurial firm location variables (for each province in which U.S. VCs have invested), the year of financing, and the selected form of finance.

Table A2. Durbin-Wu-Hausman Tests.

Eqn.	Dependent Variable	Start-Up	Deal Size	New Investee	Syndication	Technology	Emp. < 50
(1)	Log_e ($P_{Common}/P_{Preferred}$)	−2.5542	0.0004	0.5620	−31.0690	−1.0678	1.7233
		(−0.8605)	(0.8362)	(1.0463)	(−0.00002)	(−0.8921)	(0.5401)
(2)	Log_e ($P_{Common}/P_{Convertible\ Preferred}$)	−5.2220	0.0010	0.3304	−3.0017	0.1802	4.7817
		(−1.4524)	(1.4819)	(0.7461)	(−2.7387)***	(0.2425)	(1.2035)
(3)	Log_e (P_{Common}/P_{Debt})	1.6078	−0.0004	−0.8451	−2.0878	0.2162	−3.1275
		(0.8103)	(−1.1482)	(−1.4411)	(−1.7557)*	(0.2686)	(−1.5594)
(4)	Log_e ($P_{Common}/P_{Convertible\ Debt}$)	−1.3143	0.0003	1.0148	−2.2866	0.7509	2.2735
		(−0.3917)	(0.5313)	(1.8149)*	(−2.0444)**	(0.8736)	(0.6357)
(5)	Log_e ($P_{Preferred}/P_{Convertible\ Preferred}$)	−2.6678	0.0005	−0.2316	28.0977	1.2481	3.0584
		(−0.6479)	(0.7174)	(−0.4194)	(0.00002)	(1.0710)	(0.6722)
(6)	Log_e ($P_{Preferred}/P_{Debt}$)	4.1620	−0.0008	−1.4071	29.0085	1.2840	−4.8508
		(1.3286)	(−1.4818)	(−2.0367)**	(0.00002)	(1.0347)	(−1.4622)
(7)	Log_e ($P_{Preferred}/P_{Convertible\ Debt}$)	1.2399	−0.0001	0.4528	28.8118	1.8187	0.5501
		(0.3127)	(−0.1747)	(0.6893)	(0.00002)	(1.4577)	(0.1291)
(8)	Log_e ($P_{Convertible\ Preferred}/P_{Debt}$)	6.8298	−0.0013	−1.1755	0.9139	0.0359	−7.9092
		(1.8225)*	(−1.9815)**	(−1.8975)*	(0.6009)	(0.0442)	(−1.9346)*
(9)	Log_e ($P_{Convertible\ Preferred}/P_{Convertible\ Debt}$)	3.9077	−0.0007	0.6844	0.7150	0.5707	−2.5082
		(0.8724)	(−0.8122)	(1.1536)	(0.4834)	(0.6761)	(−0.5106)
(10)	Log_e ($P_{Debt}/P_{Convertible\ Debt}$)	−2.9221	0.0007	1.8598	−0.1989	0.5347	5.4010
		(−0.8551)	(1.1369)	(2.5940)***	(−0.1287)	(0.5688)	(1.4929)

Notes: This table presents endogeneity tests based on multinomial logit estimates of the likelihood of selection of different forms of finance (common equity, preferred equity, convertible preferred equity, convertible debt, and debt), and the characteristics of the entrepreneurial firms being financed: stage of development (expansion; dummy variables for the other stages are excluded to avoid collinearity), size of venture capitalist capital contribution, and dummy variables for syndication, high-tech firms, and firms with fewer than 50 employees. Sample period: 1991–2000 (208 investments). U.S. venture capitalist investments in Canadian entrepreneurial firms. Independent variables: residuals from regressing the explanatory variables (Tables 5–8) on the instruments (location variables; other instruments, such as year dummies, etc., did not materially affect the results). Other independent variables are not reported. Dummy variables for expansion, buyout, and turnaround variables were not included to avoid singular Hessians during Newton iterations in estimation. Convertible preferred equity includes mixes of common equity and preferred equity. Convertible debt includes mixes of debt and common equity.
*Denotes significance at the 10% (two-sided tests).
**Denotes significance at the 5% (two-sided tests).
***Denotes significance at the 1% (two-sided tests).

OPERATIONAL HEDGES AND FOREIGN-EXCHANGE EXPOSURE: THE EXPERIENCE OF U.S. MNCs DURING THE ASIAN FINANCIAL CRISIS

Bill Francis, Iftekhar Hasan and Christos Pantzalis

ABSTRACT

This study provides evidence on the importance of operational hedges in foreign-exchange risk management, an issue that has been largely ignored in the literature. One possible reason for the absence of empirical evidence in the literature may be related to the difficulty in devising the appropriate measures of a firm's ability to construct operating hedges. We utilize measures of the structure of an MNC's foreign subsidiary network as proxies of the firm's ability to devise operational hedges and examine their relationship to exposure coefficients computed prior to and during the 1997–1998 Asian currency crisis. Our results show that the mean exposure during the Asian crisis period was significantly higher than the pre-crisis period. In addition, the mean of the absolute change in the exposure of MNCs that only operate in the Asian crisis region was significantly higher than that of MNCs without operations in the crisis region. We find a strong relationship between our proxies for ability to

Issues in Corporate Governance and Finance
Advances in Financial Economics, Volume 12, 445–479
ISSN: 1569-3732/doi:10.1016/S1569-3732(07)12017-X

construct operating hedges and exchange-rate exposure measures both prior to the crisis and during the crisis. An even stronger association between exposure and measures of the MNC network structure is found for the sub-sample of MNCs that have some operations in the Asian crisis region. Similar results are obtained when the relationship is examined separately for "net importers" (MNCs with positive exposures) and "net exporters" (MNCs with negative exposures). Overall, our results are consistent with the notion that operational hedges significantly reduce a firm's exposure to foreign-exchange risk.

1. INTRODUCTION

The use of derivative securities to manage foreign-exchange risk by multinational corporations (hereafter, MNCs) has and continues to draw attention from both academics and practitioners alike. Although corporate risk-management theory argues that both financial and operational hedges are effective tools in managing risk, little empirical evidence exists on the effectiveness of operational hedges in reducing foreign-exchange risk.[1] This study attempts to fill this gap by examining the ability of US-based multinational corporations to construct operational hedges and the impact of this ability on overall firm exposure to foreign-exchange risk prior to and during the Asian financial crisis of 1997–1998.[2]

The Asian financial crisis that broke out in the middle of 1997 created waves that were felt all over the globe. Among the parties affected by this crisis were U.S. MNCs, many of which had operations in the area where the crisis originated. The exposure to currency risk emanating from the Asian crisis is a classic example of economic exposure to foreign-exchange risk. Economic exposure refers to the effect of unexpected changes in exchange rates on firm values. It is comprised of two components: The transaction exposure component, refers to the impact on contractually fixed cash flows, while the operating exposure component refers to the impact on a firm's operating cash flows. While the former is a short-term exposure that is easier to measure and hedge using financial instruments, the latter is more of a long-term exposure that is more difficult to quantify and more costly to implement.

Firms that are faced with a substantial increase in operating exposure, such as U.S. MNCs during the 1997 Asian currency crisis, can manage this exposure by introducing a number of marketing and production initiatives.[3]

Operating hedges entail long-term operating adjustments in the form of operating policies that are implemented within a firm's network of operating units. These policies' adjustments can be implemented, with varying degrees of effectiveness, across different lines of businesses and locations, in order to create a situation where the exposures of cash flows from the firms' different units offset each other. In this study we conjecture that firms that had operations which were dispersed over many currency and business areas, were more insulated from the exposure created by the Asian financial crisis. This is the case, since they have at their disposal a larger set of alternatives that can be used to devise effective operational hedges.

We proxy MNCs' ability to construct operational hedges by different measures of the firms' multinational network of operations. Specifically, we utilize measures that represent the degree of concentration and dispersion of each MNC's network across different countries and/or regions. It is our contention that MNCs with spread-out subsidiary networks are better equipped with the wherewithal to adjust operations thereby effectively managing their foreign-exchange exposure. Conversely, MNCs with networks that are concentrated in few countries and/or regions should be less capable of effectively reducing their currency exposures.

The choice of the Asian crisis as a study period is motivated by the fact that the crisis received a lot of media coverage and anecdotes but did not get rigorous attention from researchers (Stiglitz, 1999). Stiglitz implied that it is imperative for all parties to better understand the possible exposure to risks, ability to reduce those risks, and to make provisions to insulate from the consequences of such risk. In this paper we give attention to one aspect of this crisis by focusing on the importance of operational hedges during periods of heightened uncertainty. Further, the Asian crisis provides us with an opportunity to empirically compare operating hedges' effectiveness across firms with and without operations in the crisis area and to relate firms' exposure to their network structure.

Using a sample of U.S. multinationals, we find that the mean exposure during the Asian crisis period was significantly higher than the pre-crisis period. In addition, the mean of the absolute change in the exposure of MNCs with operations only in the Asian crisis region was significantly higher than that of MNCs without operations in the crisis region. We find a strong relationship between our proxies for MNCs ability to construct operating hedges and exchange-rate exposure measures both prior to and during the crisis. An even stronger association between exposure and measures of the MNC network structure is found for the sub-sample of MNCs that had some operations in the Asian crisis region. Similar results are found when the relationship is examined separately for "net importers" (MNCs with positive exposures) and "net exporters" (MNCs with negative exposures). Overall, our results provide strong evidence that operational hedges significantly reduce a firm's exposure to foreign-exchange risk.

The remainder of the paper is structured as follows. The next section (Section 2) includes a discussion of foreign-exchange exposure and operational hedges. Section 3 provides a description of the data and the empirical methodology. Empirical results are provided in Section 4 and Section 5 contains concluding remarks.

2. OPERATIONAL HEDGES AND FOREIGN-EXCHANGE EXPOSURE

Previous work on the pricing of exchange-rate risk,[4] as well as surveys,[5] and anecdotal evidence, indicates that investors and managers alike are concerned about foreign-exchange risk. Managerial and/or shareholder risk aversion provides an incentive to manage currency risk (Stulz, 1994; Smith & Stulz, 1985). Thus, the growing focus of firms on foreign-exchange risk management and the widespread use of currency derivatives reflects the firms' increasing concern with the impact of ex-ante uncertainty on firm cash flows.

In a world of perfect markets, there would be no need for foreign-exchange risk management (hedging) because individual investors would be able to construct such hedges on their own. Therefore, corporate hedging policy would not add to firm value. However, in the presence of market imperfections, such as the convexity of the tax schedule, financial distress costs, and agency costs corporations have incentives to hedge (see, Stulz, 1994; Shapiro & Titman, 1985; Smith & Stulz, 1985; Froot, Scarfstein, & Stein, 1993; De Marzo & Duffie, 1995).

Foreign-exchange exposure is understood as the impact of unexpected changes in the real exchange rate on firms. We distinguish between two types of economic exposure: *Transaction exposure* is the impact of unexpected changes in the real exchange rate on contractually fixed cash flows, while *operating exposure* is the impact of unexpected changes in the real exchange rate on operational (not contractually fixed) cash flows. While the former is usually a short-term exposure that can be easily hedged using foreign-exchange derivatives, the latter is more of a long-term exposure that can only be managed through the implementation of operational hedges.

For example, consider the case of a firm whose foreign currency cash flows are certain. The sole source of uncertainty from the parent firm's point of view is the exchange rate. Thus, this type of exposure can easily be hedged using forward contracts. However, if in addition to the exchange rate, the quantity of the foreign cash flows is uncertain as well, and not perfectly correlated with the exchange rate, then derivatives cannot effectively eliminate currency risk. The uncertainty in the quantity of foreign currency cash flows can be due to uncertainty of demand conditions for certain products, or uncertainty in the market for inputs.

Because demand uncertainty is larger for longer than for shorter horizons, firms can forecast sales less accurately in the long term. This implies that firms that face demand uncertainty conditions will be unable to manage long-term exposure by using financial hedges and therefore are more likely to rely on operational hedges. For example, they could shift their production in countries where significant sales revenues in the local currency are expected. Thus, the impact of unexpected changes in the exchange rate on the parent country's (domestic) currency value of sales revenues would be offset by similar changes in the value of local production costs.

Chowdhry and Howe (1999) argue that, in effect, operational hedging policies are equivalent to a series of forward contracts whose quantity is contingent upon the level of sales in each foreign location. These operational hedges provide the firm with "self"-insurance against demand uncertainty. Such insurance contracts would not be feasible to construct in the market.[6] Clearly, the costs of implementing operational hedges are much larger than the costs of financial hedges. For one, such operating adjustments are aimed at managing long-term exposure therefore their length of implementation is considerably higher, as are the costs to reverse them. Firms may be required to maintain excess capacity at different production locations so as to be able to shift production to the least cost location after observing exchange-rate movements.[7] However, unlike financial hedging, operational hedges – such as those feasible through production flexibility – are likely to result in positive expected profits (see relevant discussion in Shapiro (1996), and Eiteman Stonehill, and Moffett (1998), and empirical evidence in Allen and Pantzalis (1996), and Doukas, Pantzalis, and Kim (1999)).

An MNC that has established excess capacity in different foreign locations holds a set of real options to switch operations to the least cost locations. This advantage of MNCs over their domestic competitors is often called the MNCs' operating flexibility.[8] The value of the portfolio of real options is increasing in the volatility of the exchange rate. Also, the benefits from operational hedging of volatile cash flows will be higher when the exchange-rate uncertainty is higher. This implies that the firm's ability to manage long-term exposure increases with the firm's operating flexibility. Prior studies have shown that operating flexibility is a function of the structure of the MNC network of foreign operations. In particular, Allen and Pantzalis (1996) have shown that excess market valuation of MNCs over their domestic competitors increases with the *breadth* (a measure of how spread out is the foreign subsidiaries' network) and decreases with the *depth* (a measure of how concentrated is the foreign subsidiaries' network) of the MNC network.

If operating flexibility can be adequately described by the structure of the MNC network, then we should be able to explain cross-sectional differences in foreign-exchange exposure by differences in the structure of the MNC network. Furthermore, since currency exposure increases during periods of uncertainty in the marketplace, we expect this relationship to be more accentuated during such volatile periods. That is, we expect the relationship between foreign-exchange exposure and a MNC's ability to implement operational hedges to come to the forefront, when the uncertainty of future cash flows has increased.

We examine the above issues using a large sample of US-based MNCs around the period of the Asian crisis of 1997–1998. We initially test the relationship between MNC network variables and foreign-exchange exposure prior to the crisis and then we investigate the impact of operational hedges on exposure during the crisis period. We choose the Asian crisis because it provides an ideal natural experiment for the issues we aim to address.

In the next section we describe the sample selection process, the foreign-exchange exposure estimation procedure, and the empirical methodology.

3. DATA AND EMPIRICAL METHODOLOGY

3.1. Sample Selection

The sample we utilize for this study consists of US-based MNCs. The criteria for selection of the MNCs in the sample were:

a) All firms with Foreign Sales ratio ⩾ 10% (MNC classification in accordance with SFAS 14, that requires firms with more than 10% of

foreign sales to report them), and that reportedly paid some foreign taxes.
b) Firms should have SIC codes < 4000 (i.e., all manufacturing, agricultural and mining firms).
c) Firms with a *Compustat* foreign incorporation code "0," i.e., US-based firms.
d) Firms that are not affiliates or subsidiaries of other firms.

This first screen resulted in 664 US based firms. We proceeded by searching in "*Who Owns Whom*" (by Dunn & Bradstreet, 1998 edition, that includes 1997 information) to identify firms that have foreign subsidiaries, and recorded those by country for each MNC. Out of the initial screen sample of 664 MNCs, 94 firms could either not be found in "*Who Owns Whom*" or had no foreign subsidiaries listed *in "Who Owns Whom*," reducing the sample to 570 MNCs for which foreign subsidiaries' information is available.

Computing exchange-rate exposure coefficients further reduced the sample because of unavailability of some firms for the estimation period on CRSP. This further reduced the sample to 529 firms in the pre-crisis sample and 517 firms in the during-crisis sample. Finally, using firms that are present in both the pre-crisis and the post-crisis samples resulted in 506 firms. This is the sample used in Tables 1 and 2 (the descriptive statistics tables for the network structure and the exposure coefficients, respectively).

After excluding firms that had missing information for the requisite financial variables, (extracted from *Compustat*) the sample is reduced to 421 MNCs with complete MNC network, exposure and financial information. This sample is the one utilized in the regression analysis included in Tables 4–6.

3.2. Foreign-Exchange Exposure Estimation

We measure the currency exposure of the sample firms using a two-factor model that relates daily returns of each firm (R_i) to the market portfolio (R_m) and a foreign-exchange factor (R_e). Thus, the time-series regression model that estimated is analogous to that of (Jorion, 1990; Bartov & Bodnar, 1994; Choi & Prasad, 1995; and Laux, Simkins, & Pantzalis, 1999):

$$R_{i,t} = \alpha_i + \beta_i R_{m,t} + \gamma_i R_{e,t} + \varepsilon_{i,t}. \tag{1}$$

Table 1. The Structure of the MNCs' International Operations
Network.

Panel A: Number of foreign subsidiaries per geographic region, number of foreign countries per geographic region and proportion of MNCs with at least one subsidiary in a particular region. Reported are the mean values and the standard deviations (in parentheses). The sample consists of 506 US-based MNCs

Geographic Region	Number of Foreign Countries in the Region	Number of Foreign Subsidiaries in the Region	Proportion of MNCs with Some Presence in the Region
Asian crisis[a]	1.474	2.217	0.496
	(2.157)	(3.914)	(0.500)
NAFTA[b]	0.864	1.830	0.625
	(0.773)	(3.089)	(0.485)
European Union[c]	3.998	12.123	0.870
	(3.478)	(20.949)	(0.337)
Other Asia[d]	0.727	1.492	0.403
	(1.161)	(3.377)	(0.491)
Western Europe (non-EU)[e]	0.429	0.634	0.265
	(0.858)	(1.535)	(0.442)
Eastern Europe[f]	0.026	0.032	0.018
	(0.254)	(0.319)	(0.132)
Central America and Caribbean[g]	0.194	0.221	0.105
	(0.697)	(0.824)	(0.307)
South America[h]	0.575	0.830	0.249
	(1.332)	(2.218)	(0.433)
Africa[i]	0.097	0.109	0.053
	(0.527)	(0.634)	(0.225)

Panel B: Summary statistics for the variables that describe the MNC network. Reported are the means and the standard deviations (in parentheses) for each variable. The univariate statistics are reported for the pooled sample that consists of 506 US-based MNCs, and for the subsample of the MNCs that have some operations in the Asian Crisis region

Variable	Pooled Sample	Sample of MNCs with Some Operations in the Asian Crisis Region
Number of foreign countries (NFC)	8.316	13.458
	(8.749)	(9.614)
Number of regions (NREG)	3.083	4.502
	(2.038)	(1.810)
Herfindahl index #1 (HERF1)[j]	0.396	0.197
	(0.333)	(0.192)
Herfindahl index #2 (HERF2)[k]	0.654	0.473
	(0.269)	(0.176)
Herfindahl index #3 (HERF3)[l]	0.594	0.384
	(0.302)	(0.177)

Table 1. (Continued)

Panel C: Number of foreign subsidiaries per country located in the Asian Crisis region, and proportion of MNCs with at least one subsidiary in a particular country of the Asian Crisis region. Reported are the means for the sample of 251 US-based MNCs with some operations in the Asian Crisis region

Country in Asian Crisis Region	Number of Foreign Subsidiaries in the Country	Number of MNCs with Subsidiary in the Country
Brunei	0.008	2
China	0.096	20
Hong-Kong	1.016	139
Indonesia	0.171	28
Japan	0.936	155
Korea (South)	0.287	59
Macao	0.008	2
Malaysia	0.442	71
Papua-New Guinea	0.036	5
Philippines	0.171	35
Singapore	0.784	121
Taiwan	0.291	64
Thailand	0.215	43
Vietnam	0.008	2

Note: There are nine different geographic regions: Asian Crisis region, NAFTA, European Union, Other Asia region, Western Europe region, Eastern Europe region, Central America and Caribbean, South America, and Africa.

[a]The Asian Crisis region consists of the following countries: Brunei, China, Hong-Kong, Indonesia, Japan, Korea, Macao, Malaysia, Papua-New Guinea, Singapore, Taiwan, Thailand, Vietnam, Phillippines.

[b]The NAFTA region consists of the following countries: Canada and Mexico. The US is of course part of NAFTA, but US subsidiaries are not counted as part of the NAFTA operations of the sample's MNCs because they are domestic rather than foreign subsidiaries of our sample's US-based MNCs.

[c]The European Union region consists of the following EU member countries: Austria, Belgium, Denmark, Finland, France, Germany, Greece, Ireland, Italy, Luxemburg, Netherlands, Portugal, Spain, Sweden, United Kingdom.

[d]The other Asia region includes all Asian countries not accounted for in the Asian Crisis region.

[e]The Western Europe region includes non-EU Western European countries and some Eastern European countries that have recently applied for EU membership and are expected to join the EU in the next expansion round. They are the following: Norway, Switzerland, Cyprus, Hungary, Slovenia, Poland, Czech Republic, and Malta.

[f]The Eastern Europe region includes all remaining former Soviet Block and Socialist countries.

[g]The Central American and Caribbean Regions include all Caribbean nations and all nations north of Colombia and south of Mexico.

[h]The South America region includes all Latin American countries located in the South American continent.

[i]The Africa region includes all countries of the African continent.

[j]HERF1 $= \sum_i (\mathrm{NFS}_i)^2/[\sum_I (\mathrm{NFS}_i)]^2$, where NFS_i is the number of foreign subsidiaries in country i.

[k]HERF2 $= \sum_j (\mathrm{NFS}_j)^2/[\sum_j (\mathrm{NFS}_j)]^2$, where NFS_j is the number of foreign subsidiaries in geographic region j.

[l]HERF3 $= \sum_j (\mathrm{NFC}_j)^2/[\sum_j (\mathrm{NFC}_j)]^2$, where NFC_j is the number of foreign countries in geographic region j.

Table 2. Univariate Tests of Foreign-Exchange Exposure Coefficients.

Sample Period (Year/Month)	Mean (t-Value)	Standard Deviation	Quartiles					[%]⁻	[%]⁺
			Min	q_1	Med	q_3	Max		
Panel A: Cross-sectional distribution of absolute exchange-rate exposure coefficients, $|\gamma_i|$, of all US-based MNCs in the sample (N = 506)[1]									
95/01-96/12 $|\gamma_i|$	0.1976 (22.18)	0.2004	0	0.07	0.14	0.2498	1.4055	64.82	35.18
97/01-98/12 $|\gamma_i|$	0.2838 (8.41)	0.4322	0	0.081	0.179	0.3455	4.3145	53.58	46.42
Panel B: Cross-sectional distribution of absolute exchange-rate exposure coefficients, $|\gamma_i|$, for the subsample of US-based MNCs with some operations in the Asian Crisis region (N = 251)									
95/01-96/12 $|\gamma_i|$	0.1672 (15.45)	0.1837	0	0.055	0.116	0.1912	1.3955	58.65	41.35
97/01-98/12 $|\gamma_i|$	0.2079 (18.83)	0.222	0	0.074	0.143	0.2704	1.9467	50.67	49.35

Panel C: Cross-sectional distribution of absolute difference, δ, between the exchange-rate exposure coefficients of US-based MNCs prior to the crisis $(t = -1)$ and during the crisis $(t = 0)^2$

Mean (t-value)	Standard Deviation	Quartiles				
		Min	q_1	Median	q_3	Max
0.3181 (19.87)	0.3602	0.0024	0.1054	0.2142	0.3977	4.1903

Panel D: Descriptive statistics of absolute exposure coefficients, $|\gamma_{t=-1}|$ and $|\gamma_{t=0}|$, and absolute difference of the exchange-rate exposure coefficients prior to the crisis ($t=-1$) and during the crisis ($t=0$), δ, for different groups of MNCs classified according to the number of geographic regions (NREG) in which they operate. This is done for both the pooled sample of MNCs, and for the sub-sample of MNCs with operations in the Asian Crisis region. Reported are the means and the standard deviations (in parentheses)

1. Pooled sample of MNCs (N = 506)

Sample Period (Year/Month)	Number of Geographic Regions (NREG) the MNC Operates in								
	NREG = 1 (N = 164)	NREG = 2 (N = 85)	NREG = 3 (N = 64)	NREG = 4 (N = 58)	NREG = 5 (N = 53)	NREG = 6 (N = 53)	NREG = 7 (N = 15)	NREG = 8 (N = 12)	NREG = 9 (N = 2)
95/01–96/12	0.2608	0.2409	0.1686	0.1642	0.1291	0.1246	0.1164	0.0834	0.1156
$|\gamma_{t=-1}|$	(0.2461)	(0.2158)	(0.1715)	(0.1592)	(0.1049)	(0.1153)	(0.0869)	(0.0837)	(0.1078)
97/01–98/12	0.2838	0.2744	0.2432	0.1800	0.1763	0.1768	0.1612	0.1849	0.0402
$|\gamma_{t=0}|$	(0.4322)	(0.2789)	(0.3061)	(0.1315)	(0.1827)	(0.1472)	(0.1045)	(0.1295)	(0.0012)
	0.4135	0.3640	0.3049	0.2596	0.2188	0.1890	0.1981	0.2302	0.1559
$\delta=|\gamma_{t=0}-\gamma_{t=-1}|$	(0.4860)	(0.3563)	(0.2959)	(0.2226)	(0.2286)	(0.1535)	(0.1276)	(0.1254)	(0.1066)

2. Subsample of MNCs with operations in the Asian Crisis region (N = 251)

	NREG = 1 (N = 12)	NREG = 2 (N = 26)	NREG = 3 (N = 39)	NREG = 4 (N = 47)	NREG = 5 (N = 46)	NREG = 6 (N = 52)	NREG = 7 (N = 15)	NREG = 8 (N = 12)	NREG = 9 (N = 2)
95/01–96/12	0.5618	0.2082	0.1755	0.1578	0.1335	0.1237	0.1164	0.0834	0.1156
$|\gamma_{t=-1}|$	(0.3834)	(0.1796)	(0.1800)	(0.1583)	(0.1108)	(0.1162)	(0.0869)	(0.0837)	(0.1078)
97/01–98/12	0.3304	0.2603	0.2606	0.1911	0.1826	0.1768	0.1612	0.1849	0.0402
$|\gamma_{t=0}|$	(0.4029)	(0.1977)	(0.3671)	(0.1293)	(0.1921)	(0.1486)	(0.1045)	(0.1295)	(0.0012)
	0.7159	0.3338	0.3424	0.2631	0.2336	0.1859	0.1981	0.2302	0.1559
$\delta=|\gamma_{t=0}-\gamma_{t=-1}|$	(0.5505)	(0.3051)	(0.3301)	(0.2309)	(0.2379)	(0.1533)	(0.1276)	(0.1254)	(0.1066)

Table 2. (*Continued*)

Panel E: Comparisons of Absolute Exposure and Absolute Change in Exposure Measures between Different Subsamples and Time Periods. Reported are the Means and Standard Deviations for each Subsample, as well as the Difference in Means and the Corresponding t-Statistic for the Means Difference Test

		Mean Difference
$\lvert\gamma_{t=0}\rvert^a$	$\lvert\gamma_{t=-1}\rvert^a$	$\lvert\gamma_{t=0}\rvert - \lvert\gamma_{t=-1}\rvert$
Absolute exposure during the crisis	Absolute exposure prior to crisis	
Pooled sample	Pooled sample	[t-statistic]
(N=506)	(N=506)	0.0382
0.2358	0.1976	[2.33]**
(0.3094)	(0.2004)	
$\lvert\gamma_{t=0}\rvert$	$\lvert\gamma_{t=-1}\rvert$	Mean difference
Absolute exposure during the crisis for MNCs in Asian Crisis region	Absolute exposure prior to crisis for MNCs in Asian Crisis region	$\lvert\gamma_{t=0}\rvert - \lvert\gamma_{t=-1}\rvert$
(N=251)	(N=251)	[t-statistic]
0.2079	0.1627	0.0452
(0.2220)	(0.1837)	[2.24]**
$\delta_{ASIA\ CRISIS=1}$	$\delta_{ASIA\ CRISIS=0}$	Mean difference
Absolute change in δ^b of MNCs with operations in Asian Crisis region	Absolute change in δ^b of MNCs with no operations in Asian Crisis region	$\delta_{ASIA\ CRISIS=1} - \delta_{ASIA\ CRISIS=0}$
(N=251)	(N=255)	[t-statistic]
0.2767	0.3589	−0.0818
(0.2804)	(0.4210)	[2.59]***
$\delta_{ASIA\ CRISIS=1,\ NREG=1}$	$\delta_{ASIA\ CRISIS=0}$	Mean difference
Absolute change in δ of MNCs with operations only in Asian Crisis region	Absolute change in δ of MNCs with no operations in the Asian Crisis region	$\delta_{ASIA\ CRISIS=1,NREG=1} - \delta_{ASIA\ CRISIS=0}$
(N=12)	(N=239)	[t-statistic]
0.7159	0.2546	0.4613
(0.5505)	(0.2416)	[2.89]***

$\delta_{ASIA\ CRISIS=1,\ NREG=1}$ Absolute change in δ of MNCs with operations only in Asian Crisis region	$\delta_{ASIA\ CRISIS=0,\ NREG=1}$ Absolute change in δ of MNCs with operations in only one region other than the Asian Crisis region	Mean difference $\delta_{ASIA\ CRISIS=1,NREG=1} - \delta_{ASIA\ CRISIS=0,NREG=1}$
$(N=12)$	$(N=152)$	[t-statistic]
0.7159	0.3896	0.3263
(0.5505)	(0.4744)	[2.00]**

*Significance at the 10% level.
**Significance at the 5% level.
***Significance at the 1% level.

a γs are from the following model, $R_{it} = \alpha_i + \beta_i R_{mt} + \gamma_i R_{et} + \varepsilon_i$, where R_{it} is the rate of return on the ith MNC on day t, R_{mt} is the rate of return on the equally weighted market portfolio on day t, and R_{et} is the change in the trade-weighted exchange rate on day t.

b The absolute change in exposure coefficients, δ, is defined as $|\gamma_{t=0}| - |\gamma_{t=-1}|$, where $\gamma_{t=-1}$ is the exposure coefficient during the estimation period prior to the Asian crisis ($t = -1$, i.e., during 95/01–96/12), and $\gamma_{t=0}$ is the exposure coefficient during the crisis period ($t = 0$, i.e., 97/01–98/12).

1 Panel A reports the mean, standard deviation, and the quartiles for $|\gamma_i|$ from the following model, $R_{it} = \alpha_i + \beta_i R_{mt} + \gamma_i R_{et} + \varepsilon_i$, where R_{it} is the rate of return on the ith MNC on day t, R_{mt} is the rate of return on the equally wieghted market portfolio on day t, and R_{et} is the change in the trade-weighted exchange rate on day t. [%]$^-$ and [%]$^+$ report the percent of MNCs with positive and negative γs, respectively. The sample includes 506 US-based MNCs for which γ could be measured over two time periods, i.e., 1995-1996 and 1997-1998.

2 The absolute difference in exposure coefficients is defined as $\delta_i = |\gamma_{i,t=0} - \gamma_{i,t=-1}|$, where $\gamma_{i,t=-1}$ is the exposure coefficient for firm i during the estimation period prior to the Asian crisis ($t = -1$, i.e., during 95/01-96/12), and $\gamma_{i,t=0}$ is the exposure coefficient for firm i during the crisis period ($t = 0$, i.e., 97/01-98/12).

Where, $R_{i,t}$ is the rate of return on the ith company's common stock on day t, $R_{m,t}$ is the value-weighted market return on day t, $R_{e,t}$ is the rate of change in the exchange-rate index, and $\varepsilon_{i,t}$ is random error term. The coefficient of $R_{e,t}$, γ_i, is our measure of foreign-exchange exposure. In other words, γ_i, measures the association between changes in the value of the dollar and return of stock i, controlling for the impact of the market factor. Note that since the exchange rate is measured as the price of the US dollar in foreign currency, a positive (negative) γ_i indicates that the firm i is a "net importer" (exporter), i.e., firm i's return, $R_{i,t}$, increases as the dollar strengthens (weakens).

For each firm in the sample, γ_i, is measured for the 2 years prior to the Asian crisis, January 1995 to December 1996. This yields a pre-crisis exposure coefficient, $\gamma_i(T = -1)$. γ_i is also estimated for the 24-month period of the Asian crisis starting from January 1997 to December 1998. This yields the crisis period exposure coefficient, $\gamma_i(T = 0)$. We perform these estimations using daily returns on each stock and the equally weighted market portfolio from CRSP, as well as daily changes in the trade-weighted exchange-rate index from the Federal Reserve Bank of Chicago.

3.3. Empirical Methodology

In order to provide empirical evidence regarding the importance of operating hedges in managing foreign-exchange exposure we will employ both univariate and regression analysis. Our first objective is to show that the level of the absolute exposure coefficients, $|\gamma|$, has increased during the crisis relative to the year prior to the crisis. Also $|\gamma|$, as well as the absolute change in the exposure coefficients (δ, computed as the absolute value of the difference of the crisis and pre-crisis γs), should be significantly higher for MNCs which are less adept at establishing operational hedges and/or are active in the Asian crisis region. As mentioned earlier, we employ several variables that describe the MNC's foreign subsidiary network as proxies for the MNC's ability to structure operational hedges. These alternatives measure the extent to which a MNC's foreign subsidiary network is concentrated and/or spread out. We assume that the MNCs with more spread out (concentrated) networks will be more (less) able to adjust operating policies thereby effectively reducing their currency exposure. In the analysis that follows, we test the following hypotheses:

H1. The average foreign exchange exposure of the sample firms for the year prior to the Asian crisis is lower than the average exposure during the year of the crisis.

H2. Firms whose foreign operations are more concentrated in the Asian region have a higher exposure in the year of the crisis than in the previous year.

H3. Firms with foreign operations that are spread out over many countries and/or geographic regions were less affected by the Asian currency crisis.

The relationship between exposure and MNC network variables prior to the crisis is examined using the following regression model:

$$|\gamma_i| = \alpha_0 + \alpha_1 \text{NETWORK}_i + \alpha_2 \text{SIZE}_i + \alpha_3 \text{TAX}_i + \alpha_4 Q_i + \alpha_5 \text{LTD}_i$$
$$+ \alpha_6 \text{FSALEP}_i + \alpha_7 \text{DIV}_i + \alpha_8 \text{INTCOV}_i + \sum_j \alpha_j \text{IND}_{j,i} + \varepsilon_I. \quad (2)$$

Where, $|\gamma_i|$ is the absolute value of the exposure coefficient estimated from model (1) during the year prior to the crisis. We use five alternative measures of the NETWORK variable in model (2). These are the number of foreign countries (NFC), the number of foreign regions (NREG),[9] and the following three alternative Herfindahl measures of the network's degree of concentration:

$\text{HERF1} = \Sigma_i \ (\text{NFS}_i)^2 / [\Sigma_i \ (\text{NFS}_i)]^2$, where NFS_i is the number of foreign subsidiaries in country i;
$\text{HERF2} = \Sigma_j \ (\text{NFS}_j)^2 / [\Sigma_j \ (\text{NFS}_j)]^2$, where NFS_j is the number of foreign subsidiaries in geographic region j;
$\text{HERF3} = \Sigma_j \ (\text{NFC}_j)^2 / [\Sigma_j \ (\text{NFC}_j)]^2$, where NFC_j is the number of foreign countries in geographic region j.

The remaining variables in (2) are used to control for other factors that may impact foreign-exchange exposure. These are the size of the firm, the convexity of the tax schedule (Smith & Stulz, 1985), the firm's growth opportunities (Froot et al., 1993), the probability of financial distress (Smith & Stulz, 1985), the firm's degree of foreign involvement, and the firm's liquidity position (Nance, Smith, & Smithson, 1993). Firm size (SIZE) is measured by total assets. Our proxy for the firm's reduction of taxation via hedging (TAX) is measured by the ratio of taxes paid to total assets. We measure growth opportunities by Tobin's Q, a ratio proxy computed by the method described in Chung and Pruitt (1994). The probability of financial distress is captured by two variables – long-term debt ratio (LTD) and interest coverage ratio (INTCOV). The degree of foreign involvement is measured by the foreign sales ratio (FSALER); the firm's liquidity position is captured by the dividend yield (DIV).[10] In addition to these variables, and in order to control for industry effects, we include a series of two-digit SIC industry dummy variables in (2) as well as in all subsequent regression models.

He and Ng (1998), show that estimates of γ_i exhibit both negative and positive signs. Thus estimating a model where the estimated coefficients are pooled may lead to incorrect inferences. Similar to He and Ng, we investigate whether the independent variables included in (2) display similar effects for firms with positive and negative exposure coefficients, γ_i. This investigation is carried out by estimating the following model:

$$
\begin{aligned}
|\gamma_i| &= \beta_0 D + \beta_1 D \times \text{NETWORK}_i + \beta_2 D \times \text{SIZE}_i + \beta_3 D \times \text{TAX}_i + \beta_4 D \times Q_i \\
&\quad + \beta_5 D \times \text{LTD}_i + \beta_6 D \times \text{FSALEP}_i + \beta_7 D \times \text{DIV}_i + \beta_8 D \times \text{INTCOV}_i \\
&\quad + \beta_{10}(1 - D) + \beta_{1d}(1 - D) \times \text{NETWORK}_i + \beta_{2d}(1 - D) \times \text{SIZE}_i \\
&\quad + \beta_{3d}(1 - D) \times \text{TAX}_i + \beta_{4d}(1 - D) \times Q_i + \beta_{5d}(1 - D) \times \text{LTD}_i \\
&\quad + \beta_{6d}(1 - D) \times \text{FSALEP}_i + \beta_{7d}(1 - D) \times \text{DIV}_i + \beta_{8d}(1 - D) \\
&\quad \times \text{INTCOV}_i + \sum_j \beta_j D \times \text{IND}_{j,i} + \sum_j \beta_{jd}(1 - D) \times \text{IND}_{j,i} + \varepsilon_I. \quad (3)
\end{aligned}
$$

Where, D is a dummy variable that indicates whether the firm's exposure coefficient is positive ($D = 1$) or negative ($D = 0$). In the case of "net importers", the relationship between $|\gamma_I|$ and the independent variables is captured by the coefficients of the interactions of the independent variables with D. For "net exporters", the relationship is captured by the coefficients of the interactions with $(1 - D)$.

One of the hypotheses stated above is that firms with operations that are more spread out over many countries and/or geographic regions will be less affected by the Asian crisis. To test this hypothesis we examine the impact of our MNC network structure proxies on $\delta = |\gamma_{i,t=0} - \gamma_{i,t=-1}|$, using the following regression model:

$$
\begin{aligned}
\delta_i &= \alpha_0 + \alpha_1 \text{NETWORK}_i + \alpha_2 \text{SIZE}_i + \alpha_3 \text{TAX}_i + \alpha_4 Q_i + \alpha_5 \text{LTD}_i \\
&\quad + \alpha_6 \text{FSALEP}_i + \alpha_7 \text{DIV}_i + \alpha_8 \text{INTCOV}_i + \alpha_9 \text{CRISIS}_i \\
&\quad + \sum_j \alpha_j \text{IND}_{j,i} + \varepsilon_I. \quad (4)
\end{aligned}
$$

Where, CRISIS is a dummy variable that takes the value of one if the firm has operations in the following countries that we define as the Asian crisis region, Brunei, China, Hong-Kong, Indonesia, Japan, Korea, Macao, Malaysia, Papua-New Guinea, Singapore, Taiwan, Thailand, Vietnam, and the Philippines and zero otherwise. It should be noted that countries included in our "Asian crisis region" are chosen to capture as broad a representation of the region as possible. A possible drawback of this strategy is that it may bias our results towards the null hypothesis of no significant differences between the Asian crisis region and other regions. Thus, if in fact we find significant differences it would indicate the strength of our results.

Finally, we also examine the separate impact of the independent variables from (4) on δ for "net importers" and "net exporters" using a regression model similar to model (3) described above:

$$
\begin{aligned}
\delta_i = {} & \beta_0 D + \beta_1 D \times \text{NETWORK}_i + \beta_2 D \times \text{SIZE}_i + \beta_3 D \times \text{TAX}_i + \beta_4 D \times Q_i \\
& + \beta_5 D \times \text{LTD}_i + \beta_6 D \times \text{FSALEP}_i + \beta_7 D \times \text{DIV}_i + \beta_8 D \times \text{INTCOV}_i \\
& + \beta_9 D \times \text{CRISIS}_i + \beta_{10}(1 - D) + \beta_{1d}(1 - D) \times \text{NETWORK}_i \\
& + \beta_{2d}(1 - D) \times \text{SIZE}_i + \beta_{3d}(1 - D) \times \text{TAX}_i + \beta_{4d}(1 - D) \times Q_i \\
& + \beta_{5d}(1 - D) \times \text{LTD}_i + \beta_{6d}(1 - D) \times \text{FSALEP}_i + \beta_{7d}(1 - D) \\
& \times \text{DIV}_i + \beta_{8d}(1 - D) \times \text{INTCOV}_i + \beta_9(1 - D) \times \text{CRISIS}_i \\
& + \sum_j \beta_j D \times \text{IND}_{j,i} + \sum_j \beta_{jd}(1 - D) \times \text{IND}_{j,i} + \varepsilon_I.
\end{aligned}
\tag{5}
$$

4. RESULTS

4.1. Univariate Results

Table 1 portrays the MNC's international operation network structure. The first column of Panel A, reports for each geographic region the number of foreign countries where a MNC has subsidiaries, followed by the number of subsidiaries owned by the MNCs in the region in column 2. The third column shows the proportion of the sample's MNCs with presence in each region. Nearly 50% of our sample firms have some operations in the Asian Crisis region, the third most common choice of location after NAFTA and the European Union.

Panel B further describes the MNC foreign subsidiaries' network structure by providing descriptive statistics for all five alternative NET-WORK measures. This is done for both the pooled sample and the sub-sample of MNCs with some operations in the Asian crisis region. The mean values indicate that MNCs in the Asian crisis area are involved in more countries, i.e., are more spread out, with an average of 4.502 compared to the pooled global average of 3.083. Similarly, MNCs with operations in the Asian crisis region on average, have networks with more foreign subsidiaries and lower degrees of concentration than for the pooled sample. Panel C portrays average MNC representation in each of the crisis region's countries. Also reported in Panel C are the number of MNCs with at least one subsidiary, by crisis region country. Japan and Hong Kong lead the group of Asian crisis countries with 155 and 139 MNCs maintaining operations in their respective countries.

Panel A of Table 2 reports the cross-sectional distribution of absolute exchange-rate exposure coefficients, $|\gamma_i|$, of the MNCs. The average of the pre-crisis coefficients is 0.1976 and ranges from 0.00 to 1.4055. This is much lower than the average of 0.2838 (with a range of 0.00–4.3145) during the crisis period. Panel B reports the distributional characteristics of the exposure coefficients of MNCs with operations in the Asian crisis region. For this sub-sample the pre-crisis mean value of 0.1672 is also considerably lower than the value of 0.2079 during the crisis period.[11] The cross-sectional distribution of the absolute difference, δ, between the exchange-rate exposure coefficients of MNCs prior to the crisis and during the crisis is shown in Panel C. The mean value of δ is 0.3181 (standard deviation 19.87), which is significantly larger than zero at conventional significance levels.

Panel D contains the descriptive statistics of $|\gamma_{i,t=-1}|$, $|\gamma_{i,t=0}|$ and δ for different groups of MNCs classified according to the number of geographic regions (NREG)in which they own subsidiaries. The results clearly show that the higher the number of geographic regions included in the MNC network, the lower the exposure. The findings are qualitatively similar for the sub-sample of MNCs with operations in the Asian crisis region.

Finally, Panel E compares the $|\gamma_i|$ and the δ measures between the different sub-samples and time periods. Consistent with our expectations, it shows that on average the exposure coefficients are significantly higher for the crisis period than for the pre-crisis period in both the pooled sample (row 1) and the Asian crisis region sub-sample (row 2). Row 3 shows that the mean value of δ for MNCs with operations in Asian crisis region is significantly lower than for MNCs with no operations in the Asian crisis region. A possible explanation of this finding is that, as documented earlier, MNCs with operations in the Asian crisis region have more spread-out foreign subsidiary networks (see Table 1, Panel B). To control for this effect we therefore compare the mean δ for the sub-sample consisting of MNCs involved solely in the Asian crisis region with that of MNCs with no operations in the Asian crisis region.

We find that the mean δ is significantly higher for the group of MNCs with operations concentrated in the crisis region. A similar result is obtained when we compare the mean δ's of MNCs involved solely in the Asian crisis region with those of MNCs with operations in a single region, other than the Asian crisis region. These results indicate that foreign-exchange exposure increased during the crisis period, especially for MNCs heavily involved in the Asian crisis region. Taken together, these findings provide strong support of hypotheses H1 and H2.

4.2. Multivariate Results

Table 3 reports estimates of the determinants of the absolute exchange-rate exposure, $|\gamma_i|$, using several measures of the MNC network structure as proxies for the MNCs' ability to construct operational hedges.[12] Column 2 contains estimates without the MNC network structure and is included for comparison purposes, while columns 3 and 4 provide evidence as to the impact of the degree of geographic dispersion (as measured by NFC and NREG) on MNCs foreign-exchange exposure. Consistent with our expectations, we find a strong negative relation between exchange-rate exposure and the number of foreign countries, as well as the number of foreign regions. In columns 4 through 6 we present evidence on the relation between exchange-rate exposure and the depth of the MNCs network as proxied by our three Herfindahl variables (HERF1, HERF2, and HERF3). Consistent with a firm's ability to construct operational hedges, we find a positive, statistically significant association between the absolute value of the exposure and each measure of the MNC's depth of operations. It is instructive to compare the models with and without the MNCs network proxies. We see that the adjusted R^2 for the models that include the network proxies increases substantially, and in some cases more than doubles, relative to the model that does not include a network variable. This underscores the importance of the MNCs network structure in explaining foreign-exchange exposure. Further, given that previous studies that addressed this issue did not account for the foreign subsidiaries' network structure, it provides a possible explanation for the relatively low statistical significance that has plagued previous studies.

Looking at the other explanatory variables that are proxying for hedging incentives, we see that the signs of the coefficients are broadly consistent with our expectations. However, the results are somewhat disappointing in that only LTD is statistically significant. A possible explanation is that we

Table 3. Exchange-Rate Exposure and the MNC Network of Foreign Operations Prior to the Asian Crisis.

Variable		NETWORK Variable is Measured by				
		NFC	NREG	HERF1	HERF2	HERF3
Panel A: Results using the pooled sample of MNCs ($N = 421$)						
Intercept	0.2768***	0.3169***	−0.3186***	0.2041***	0.1769***	0.1705***
	(8.82)	(10.00)	(−9.94)	(5.73)	(4.09)	(4.21)
NETWORK		−0.0497***	−0.0251***	0.1298***	0.1277***	0.1411***
		(−4.75)	(−4.46)	(4.04)	(3.31)	(4.04)
SIZE	-19.9×10^{-7}	5.7×10^{-7}	9.3×10^{-7}	-8.2×10^{-7}	-10.1×10^{-7}	-5.3×10^{-7}
	(−1.48)	(0.40)	(0.63)	(−0.60)	(−0.79)	(−0.39)
Q	−0.0170*	−0.0118	−0.0123	−0.0132	−0.0149*	−0.0151*
	(−1.89)	(−1.33)	(−1.39)	(−1.49)	(−1.67)	(−1.70)
LTD	−0.1187*	−0.1166*	−0.1124*	−0.1210*	−0.1126*	−0.1055*
	(−1.88)	(−1.89)	(−1.82)	(−1.95)	(−1.80)	(−1.70)
FSALER	-1.9×10^{-4}	3.8×10^{-4}	2.9×10^{-4}	1.8×10^{-4}	0.4×10^{-4}	1.2×10^{-4}
	(−0.37)	(0.74)	(0.55)	(0.35)	(0.05)	(0.23)
DIV	−0.0074**	−0.0049	−0.0054	−0.0051	−0.0058*	−0.0054
	(−2.10)	(−1.43)	(−1.55)	(−1.47)	(−1.65)	(−1.54)
INTCOV	-0.7×10^{-5}	-1.4×10^{-5}	-1.3×10^{-5}	-1.2×10^{-5}	-1.3×10^{-5}	$-1.4 \times 10^{-5***}$
	(−0.45)	(−0.86)	(−0.82)	(−0.74)	(−0.78)	(−0.44)
Industry dummies	Yes	Yes	Yes	Yes	Yes	Yes
Adjusted R^2	0.0425	0.0922	0.0863	0.0783	0.0662	0.0784
F-value	1.718	2.580	2.470	2.322	2.102	2.323
Panel B: Results using the sample of MNCs with operations in the Asian Crisis region ($N = 219$)						
Intercept		0.4503***	0.4081***	0.1928***	0.1751**	0.1048**
		(8.30)	(7.64)	(3.66)	(2.56)	(1.63)
NETWORK		−0.0793***	−0.0290***	0.4157***	0.2689***	0.4250***
		(−4.38)	(−3.23)	(5.82)	(3.39)	(5.27)

SIZE	14.8×10^{-7}	11.9×10^{-7}	3.7×10^{-7}	-5.4×10^{-7}	7.0×10^{-7}
	(1.06)	(0.82)	(0.29)	(-0.41)	(0.54)
Q	-0.0116	-0.0144	-0.0088	-0.0167	-0.0099
	(-0.85)	(-1.03)	(-0.68)	(-1.22)	(-0.75)
LTD	-0.1306	-0.1394	-0.0979	-0.1501	-0.1075
	(-1.36)	(-1.42)	(-1.05)	(-1.54)	(-1.14)
FSALER	1.2×10^{-4}	1.2×10^{-4}	-1.1×10^{-4}	-2.1×10^{-4}	-1.2×10^{-4}
	(0.16)	(0.16)	(-0.16)	(-0.29)	(-0.16)
DIV	-0.0399***	-0.0420***	-0.0361***	-0.0431***	-0.0356***
	(-3.30)	(-3.39)	(-3.08)	(-3.51)	(-2.98)
INTCOV	1.3×10^{-5}	1.5×10^{-5}	1.1×10^{-5}	0.8×10^{-5}	-0.0×10^{-5}
	(0.70)	(0.79)	(0.62)	(0.43)	(-0.05)
Industry dummies	Yes	Yes	Yes	Yes	Yes
Adjusted R^2	0.1981	0.1634	0.2503	0.1677	0.2295
F-value	3.144	2.695	3.899	2.749	3.585

Notes: This table reports estimates of the determinants of the absolute exchange-rate exposure, γ_i, using several measures of the MNC network structure as proxies of the MNCs' ability to construct operational hedges. The coefficients of the 2-digit industry dummies (IND_j) included in the regression are not reported. Cross-sectional regressions for 1996 are performed using the following model

$$|\gamma_i| = \alpha_0 + \alpha_1 NETWORK_i + \alpha_2 SIZE_i + \alpha_3 Q_i + \alpha_4 LTD_i$$
$$+ \alpha_5 FSALEP_i + \alpha_6 DIV_i + \alpha_7 INTCOV_i + \sum_j \alpha_j IND_{j,i} + \varepsilon_i.$$

NETWORK is measured by one of the following five variables: NFC, number of foreign countries; NREG, number of foreign regions; $HERF1 = \sum_i (NFS_i)^2 / [\sum_i (NFS_i)]^2$, where NFS_i is the number of foreign subsidiaries in country i; $HERF2 = \sum_j (NFS_j)^2 / [\sum_j (NFS_j)]^2$, where NFS_j is the number of foreign subsidiaries in geographic region j; $HERF3 = \sum_j (NFC_j)^2 / [\sum_j (NFC_j)]^2$, where NFC_j is the number of foreign countries in geographic region j. The remaining variables are: SIZE = total assets; Q = Tobin's Q ratio proxy (Chung & Pruitt, 1994); LTD = Long-term debt ratio (book value); FSALER = Foreign sales/Total sales; DIV = dividend yield; INTCOV = Interest coverage ratio.
*Significance at the 10% level.
**Significance at the 5% level.
***Significance at the 1% level.

used daily returns to estimate our measure of exposure. Evidence provided by Bodnar and Wong (2000) and Chow, Lee, and Solt (1997) suggests that measures of exposure coefficients increase in magnitude and significance when the return horizon is lengthened to at least 12 months. Looked at in this vein, the finding of statistical significance of all five measures of network structure and the relatively high adjusted-R^2 is even more remarkable. This is, therefore, very strong evidence in support of the importance of MNCs network structure as a means of hedging foreign-exchange-rate exposure.

Turning to Panel B, which contains results of the Asian sub sample, we find once again statistical significance for all measures of network structure. With regards to the other independent variables, long-term debt ratio, dividend yield and in some cases, Tobin's Q are statistically significant at conventional significance levels with the expected signs.

Table 4 reports estimates of model (2), where the determinants of the positive and negative exchange-rate exposures are examined separately. Consistent with our previous results we find that the geographic dispersion of MNC operations has a negative effect on exchange-rate exposure, whereas concentration in few countries and/or regions increases exposure. This is the case for both "net importers" and "net exporters" with the statistical significance being higher for the "net importers" group. Similar results hold for MNCs with operations in the crisis region.

As noted above, one of the major objectives of this study is to investigate the effectiveness of MNCs network structure in providing operational hedges during periods of heightened exchange-rate volatility. Here we address this issue by examining the impact of our operational hedges proxies on the absolute change of exchange-rate exposure, δ, as depicted in model (4). Results provided in Table 5, columns' 2 and 3 indicate a negative and significant impact of NFC and NREG on δ. Consistent with our expectations, we also find that all three HERF variables have positive and significant coefficients. These results provide strong support for hypothesis H3, i.e., they indicate that firms whose operations were more spread out were affected the least by the Asian crisis, while those MNCs with the most concentrated operations were impacted the most by the Asian financial crisis. Thus, the significance of all five MNC network structure proxies, with the appropriate sign, provides strong evidence of the effectiveness of operational hedges in foreign-exchange risk management. Furthermore, it provides evidence for the first time on the importance of the network structure as a proxy for MNC's ability to hedge foreign-exchange-rate exposure.

Table 4. Exchange-Rate Exposure and the MNC Network of Foreign Operations Prior to the Asian Crisis Examined Separately for MNCs with Positive ("Net Importers") and Negative ("Net Exporters") Exposure Coefficients.

Panel A: Using the Pooled Sample of MNCs ($N = 421$).

(Model #) NETWORK measure	D	$D \times$ NETWORK	$D \times$ SIZE	$D \times Q$	$D \times$ LTD	$D \times$ FSALEP	$D \times$ DIV	$D \times$ INTCOV	$(1-D)$
(1) NFC	0.3263***	−0.0274***	0.00000122	−0.0199	−0.1309*	0.00028	−0.0406***	0.0000001	0.3165***
	(7.34)	(−2.00)	(0.64)	(−1.39)	(−1.68)	(0.38)	(−3.30)	(0.03)	(7.24)
(2) NREG	0.3278***	−0.0117*	0.00000117	−0.0203	−0.1312*	0.00014	−0.0426***	0.000002	0.3202***
	(7.28)	(−1.65)	(0.60)	(−1.42)	(−1.68)	(0.19)	(−3.49)	(0.11)	(7.33)
(3) HERF1	0.2590***	0.0776*	0.00000054	−0.0214	−0.1302*	0.00021	−0.0424***	0.000001	0.1956***
	(4.97)	(1.80)	(0.29)	(−1.49)	(−1.65)	(0.28)	(−3.47)	(0.07)	(3.58)
(4) HERF2	0.2698***	0.0480	0.00000025	−0.0226	−0.1311*	0.000004	−0.0458***	0.000003	0.1354*
	(4.42)	(0.94)	(0.14)	(−1.56)	(−1.65)	(0.01)	(−3.72)	(0.15)	(1.87)
(5) HERF3	0.2522***	0.0715	0.00000058	−0.0222	−0.1217	0.00005	−0.0429***	0.000002	0.1367**
	(4.40)	(1.55)	(0.32)	(−1.54)	(−1.53)	(0.07)	(−3.47)	(0.09)	(2.02)

(Model #) NETWORK measure	$(1-D) \times$ NETWORK	$(1-D) \times$ SIZE	$(1-D) \times Q$	$(1-D) \times$ LTD	$(1-D) \times$ FSALEP	$(1-D) \times$ DIV	$(1-D) \times$ INTCOV	Adjusted - R^2, F-Value
(1) NFC	−0.0642***	0.00000200	−0.0071	−0.00001	0.00011	−0.0006	−0.00007*	0.5383
	(−3.34)	(0.36)	(−0.57)	(−0.32)	(0.15)	(−0.13)	(−1.89)	10.626
(2) NREG	−0.0396***	0.00000470	−0.0069	−0.00002	0.00018	−0.0013	−0.00008**	0.5391
	(−3.63)	(0.84)	(−0.55)	(−0.56)	(0.24)	(−0.29)	(−2.08)	10.654
(3) HERF1	0.1371**	0.00000032	−0.0105	−0.00002	−0.00023	−0.0004	−0.00007*	0.5312
	(2.47)	(0.06)	(−0.83)	(−0.39)	(−0.31)	(−0.09)	(−1.73)	10.352
(4) HERF2	0.1682**	0.00000093	−0.0114	−0.00002	−0.00021	−0.0015	−0.00008**	0.5283
	(2.48)	(0.17)	(−0.91)	(−0.53)	(−0.29)	(−0.31)	(−2.00)	10.244
(5) HERF3	0.1725***	0.00000153	−0.0117	−0.00002	−0.00014	−0.0014	−0.00008**	0.5318
	(2.74)	(0.28)	(−0.94)	(−0.53)	(−0.18)	(−0.29)	(−2.01)	10.378

Table 4. (*Continued*).

Panel B: Using the sub-sample of MNCs with operations in the Asian Crisis region ($N = 219$)

(Model #) NETWORK measure	D	$D \times$ NETWORK	$D \times$ SIZE	$D \times Q$	$D \times$ LTD	$D \times$ FSALEP	$D \times$ DIV	$D \times$ INTCOV	$(1-D)$
(1) NFC	0.4758***	−0.0463*	0.00000165	−0.0341	−0.2882**	−0.00071	−0.0557***	0.000015	0.5177***
	(6.37)	(−1.95)	(0.79)	(−1.61)	(−2.16)	(−0.67)	(−3.61)	(0.81)	(5.78)
(2) NREG	0.4390***	−0.0127	0.00000106	−0.0363*	−0.2863**	−0.00080	−0.0589***	0.000018	0.4396***
	(5.98)	(−1.13)	(0.50)	(−1.67)	(−2.09)	(−0.73)	(−3.73)	(0.93)	(5.12)
(3) HERF1	0.3065***	0.2637***	0.00000091	−0.0299	−0.2595**	−0.00070	−0.0526***	0.000013	0.1252
	(4.23)	(2.81)	(0.47)	(−1.44)	(−1.98)	(−0.67)	(−3.49)	(0.71)	(1.56)
(4) HERF2	0.3291***	0.1196	0.00000029	−0.0368*	−0.2916**	−0.00085	−0.0598***	0.000015	0.0357
	(3.50)	(1.14)	(0.14)	(−1.68)	(−2.11)	(−0.77)	(−3.79)	(0.74)	(0.34)
(5) HERF3	0.2390***	0.2862***	0.0000099	−0.0295	−0.2602*	−0.00060	−0.0511***	0.000006	0.0243
	(2.63)	(2.61)	(0.50)	(−1.38)	(−1.93)	(−0.56)	(−3.26)	(0.30)	(0.25)

(Model #) NETWORK measure	$(1-D) \times$ NETWORK	$(1-D) \times$ SIZE	$(1-D) \times Q$	$(1-D) \times$ LTD	$(1-D) \times$ FSALEP	$(1-D) \times$ DIV	$(1-D) \times$ INTCOV	Adjusted-R^2, F-Value
(1) NFC	−0.1533***	0.00000431	−0.0013	−0.00001	0.00006	−0.0211	0.00005	0.5596
	(−4.77)	(0.75)	(−0.07)	(−0.17)	(0.52)	(−1.02)	(0.07)	7.022
(2) NREG	−0.0709***	0.00000743	−0.0044	−0.00002	0.00092	−0.0120	0.00025	0.5387
	(−4.03)	(1.20)	(−0.22)	(−0.53)	(0.79)	(−0.55)	(0.32)	6.534
(3) HERF1	0.6218***	0.00000188	−0.0022	−0.00001	−0.00010	−0.0199	−0.00009	0.5782
	(5.23)	(0.34)	(−0.12)	(−0.24)	(−0.09)	(−0.98)	(−0.12)	7.497

(4) HERF2	0.4733***	0.00000235	−0.0091	−0.00003	−0.00037	−0.0154	−0.00008	0.5286	6.314
	(3.49)	(0.40)	(−0.45)	(−0.61)	(−0.32)	(−0.70)	(−0.10)		
(5) HERF3	0.5909***	0.00000532	−0.0053	−0.00004	−0.00050	−0.0190	−0.00035	0.5575	6.970
	(4.33)	(0.91)	(−0.27)	(−0.82)	(−0.44)	(−0.91)	(−0.45)		

Notes: This table reports estimates of the determinants of the absolute exchange-rate exposure, $|\gamma_i|$, using several measures of the MNC network structure as proxies of the MNCs' ability to construct operational hedges. This methodology uses the interactions of each variable with two dummy variables, D and $(1-D)$, where $D=1$ represents positive exposure and $D=0$ represents negative exposure. The coefficients of the interactions of the independent variables with D $[(1-D)]$ will capture the impact of the independent variables on positive γs [negative γs]. Cross-sectional regressions for 1996 are performed using the following model:

$$|\gamma_i| = \beta_0 + \beta_1 D \times \text{NETWORK}_i + \beta_2 D \times \text{SIZE}_i + \beta_3 D \times Q_i + \beta_4 D \times \text{LTD}_i + \beta_5 D \times \text{FSALEP}_i$$
$$+ \beta_6 D \times \text{DIV}_i + \beta_7 D \times \text{INTCOV}_i + \beta_{0d}(1-D) + \beta_{1d}(1-D) \times \text{NETWORK}_i + \beta_{2d}(1-D) \times \text{SIZE}_i$$
$$+ \beta_{3d}(1-D) \times Q_i + \beta_{4d}(1-D) \times \text{LTD}_i + \beta_{5d}(1-D) \times \text{FSALEP}_i + \beta_{6d}(1-D) \times \text{DIV}_i$$
$$+ \beta_{7d}(1-D) \times \text{INTCOV}_i + \sum_j \beta_j D \times \text{IND}_{j,i} + \sum_j \beta_{jd}(1-D) \times \text{IND}_{j,i} + \varepsilon_i.$$

NETWORK is measured by one of the following five variables: NFC = Number of foreign countries; NREG = Number of foreign regions; NFS = Number of foreign subsidiaries; HERF1 = $\sum_i (\text{NFS}_i)^2 / [\sum_i (\text{NFS}_i)]^2$, where NFS$_i$ is the number of foreign subsidiaries in country i; HERF2 = $\sum_i (\text{NFS}_i)^2 / [\sum_i (\text{NFS}_i)]^2$, where NFS$_j$ is the number of foreign subsidiaries in geographic region j; HERF3 = $\sum_i (\text{NFC}_i)^2 / [\sum_i (\text{NFC}_j)]^2$, where NFC$_j$ is the number of foreign countries in geographic region j. The remaining variables are: SIZE = Total Assets; Q = Tobin's Q ratio proxy (Chung & Pruitt, 1994); LTD = Long-term debt ratio (book value); FSALER = foreign sales/total sales; DIV = dividend yield; INTCOV = interest coverage ratio.

Table 5. Absolute Change of the Exchange-Rate Exposure and the MNC Network of Foreign Operations.

Variable	NETWORK Variable is Measured by				
	NFC	NREG	HERF1	HERF2	HERF3
Panel A: Results using the pooled sample of MNCs ($N = 421$)[a]					
Intercept	0.5255***	0.5240***	0.3826***	0.3192***	0.3211***
	(9.26)	(9.18)	(5.23)	(3.30)	(3.49)
NETWORK	−0.0834***	−0.0425***	0.1844***	0.1868**	0.2153**
	(−3.38)	(−3.04)	(2.66)	(2.09)	(2.56)
SIZE	-5.8×10^{-7}	0.0×10^{-7}	26.3×10^{-7}	-29.5×10^{-7}	-23.6×10^{-7}
	(−0.23)	(0.00)	(−1.08)	(−1.22)	(−0.96)
Q	−0.0183	−0.0192	−0.0236	−0.0263*	−0.0256*
	(−1.22)	(−1.28)	(−1.59)	(−1.78)	(−1.73)
LTD	−0.1559	−0.1395	−0.1639	−0.1461	−0.1327
	(−1.45)	(−1.29)	(−1.51)	(−1.34)	(−1.22)
FSALER	0.0018*	0.0017*	0.0016*	0.0015	0.0015
	(1.87)	(1.79)	(1.71)	(1.59)	(1.57)
DIV	−0.0488***	−0.0501***	−0.0510***	−0.0517***	−0.0506***
	(−3.14)	(−3.22)	(−3.27)	(−3.30)	(−3.24)
INTCOV	0.00007	0.00008	0.00008	0.00009	0.00008
	(0.91)	(1.00)	(1.06)	(1.09)	(1.04)
CRISIS	0.0762	0.0775	0.0396	0.0391	0.0592
	(1.59)	(1.54)	(0.88)	(0.81)	(1.19)
Industry dummies	Yes	Yes	Yes	Yes	Yes
Adjusted R^2	0.0995	0.0947	0.0897	0.0835	0.0886
F-value	2.657	2.569	2.479	2.367	2.458
Panel B: Results using the sample of MNCs with operations in the Asian Crisis region ($N = 219$)[b]					
Intercept	0.4866***	0.4441***	0.2427***	0.1629*	0.1229
	(6.07)	(6.06)	(3.38)	(1.74)	(1.37)
NETWORK	−0.1028***	−0.0449***	0.3474***	0.2996**	0.4165***
	(−3.19)	(−3.16)	(3.06)	(2.59)	(3.42)
SIZE	-8.7×10^{-7}	-2.1×10^{-7}	-16.3×10^{-7}	-22.2×10^{-7}	-12.9×10^{-7}
	(−0.43)	(−0.10)	(−0.81)	(−1.09)	(−0.64)
Q	−0.0204	−0.0176	−0.0220	−0.0238	−0.0194*
	(−1.36)	(−1.16)	(−1.48)	(−1.59)	(−1.30)
LTD	0.0025	0.0113	−0.0167	−0.0290	0.0087
	(0.02)	(0.09)	(−0.14)	(−0.24)	(0.07)
FSALER	0.0029***	0.0033***	0.0027**	0.0029***	0.0027**
	(2.75)	(3.05)	(2.51)	(2.67)	(2.57)
DIV	−0.0478***	−0.0462***	−0.0480***	−0.0454***	−0.0437***
	(−3.64)	(−3.50)	(−3.65)	(−3.40)	(−3.31)
INTCOV	0.00074***	0.00079***	0.00071***	0.00078***	0.00074***
	(5.11)	(5.51)	(4.76)	(5.34)	(5.09)
CRISIS	0.0015	−0.0044	−0.0111	−0.0128	−0.0095

Table 5. (*Continued*)

Variable	NETWORK Variable is Measured by				
	NFC	NREG	HERF1	HERF2	HERF3
	(0.13)	(−0.41)	(−1.11)	(−1.28)	(−0.95)
Industry dummies	Yes	Yes	Yes	Yes	Yes
Adjusted R^2	0.3013	0.3006	0.2986	0.2890	0.3065
F-value	4.600	4.588	4.553	4.392	4.689

Notes: This table reports estimates of the determinants of the absolute exchange-rate exposure, $\delta = |\gamma_{t=0} - \gamma_{t=-1}|$, using several measures of the MNC network structure as proxies of the MNCs' ability to construct operational hedges. The coefficients of the 2-digit industry dummies (IND_j) included in the regression are not reported. Cross-sectional regressions are performed using the following model:

$$\delta_i = \alpha_0 + \alpha_1 NETWORK_i + \alpha_2 SIZE_i + \alpha_3 Q_i + \alpha_4 LTD_i + \alpha_5 FSALEP_i$$
$$+ \alpha_6 DIV_i + \alpha_7 INTCOV_i + \alpha_8 CRISIS_i + \sum_{ij} \alpha_j IND_{j,i} + \varepsilon_i.$$

δ is measured as the absolute value of the difference between the exposure coefficient during the crisis ($t = 0$) and prior to the crisis ($t = -1$). NETWORK is measured by one of the following five variables: NFC = Number of foreign countries; NREG = Number of foreign regions; HERF1 = $\Sigma_i (NFS_i)^2 / [\Sigma_i (NFS_i)]^2$, where NFS_i is the number of foreign subsidiaries in country i; HERF2 = $\Sigma_j (NFS_j)^2 / [\Sigma_j (NFS_j)]^2$, where NFS_j is the number of foreign subsidiaries in geographic region j. HERF3 = $\Sigma_j (NFC_j)^2 / [\Sigma_j (NFC_j)]^2$, where NFC_j is the number of foreign countries in geographic region j. The remaining variables are: SIZE = Total Assets; Q = Tobin's Q ratio proxy (Chung & Pruitt, 1994); LTD = Long-term debt ratio (book value); FSALER = Foreign Sales/Total Sales; DIV = Dividend yield; INTCOV = Interest coverage ratio.
*Significance at the 10% level.
**Significance at the 5%, level.
***Significance at the 1% level.
[a]CRISIS is a dummy variable indicating involvement in the Asian Crisis region.
[b]CRISIS is a variable that captures the extent of an MNC's involvement in the Asian Crisis region. It is measured by the number of foreign countries in the Asian Crisis region in which the MNC operates.

Examination of the remaining variables indicates that FSALER and DIV (significant in all five equations), and to a lesser extent INTCOV (significant in two of the five equations) are important determinants of the changes in MNCs exposure. The positive coefficients of FSALER and

INTCOV and the negative DIV coefficient suggest that firms having high foreign sales, or high interest coverage, or a low dividend payout ratio were affected the most by the Asian crisis.

Results for the sub-sample of MNCs with operations in the Asian crisis region are reported in Panel B. In general, the results are much stronger than those reported for the full sample in Panel A. This is evidenced by the much larger adjusted R^2 for all five equations, the finding that each network variable is statistically significant at least at the 95% confidence level and that, FSALER, DIV, and INTCOV are all statistically significant in each of the five equations. Additionally, Tobin's Q is significant in two of the five equations. Thus, consistent with our expectations we find that operational hedges were much more effective for MNCs who had subsidiaries in the crisis region.

Table 6 provides estimates of the determinants of the absolute change in exchange-rate exposure, δ, using several measures of the MNC network structure as proxies of the MNCs' ability to construct operational hedges. Following Table 4 (panel B), this methodology uses the interactions of each variable with two dummy variables, D and $(1-D)$, where $D=1$ represents positive exposure ("net importer") and $D=0$ represents negative exposure ("net exporter"). The regression results indicate that the network variables are significant for MNCs with negative exposures. In the regressions using the sub-sample of MNCs in the Asian crisis regions, the coefficients are significant for both the "net exporter" and "net importer" groups, with the former group revealing stronger results. This finding suggests that operational hedges are more effective in reducing foreign-exchange exposure for "net exporters" than for "net importers". In addition, we observe stronger results for the variables interacted with $(1-D)$ as opposed to the interactions with D. A possible explanation for this finding is that during the crisis, the purchasing power of the Asian countries declined significantly. As a result, firms that are "net exporters" were more affected than those that are "net importers." Consequently the ability to construct operational hedges was more important for "net exporters." This is indeed what we find for both the pooled sample of MNCs and for the sample of MNCs with subsidiaries in the Asian crisis region. This suggests that firms in the "core" crisis area were exposed, irrespective of whether they were exporters or importers. Thus again we find strong evidence that the ability of MNCs to construct operational hedges is an important mechanism by which foreign-exchange exposure is reduced.

Table 6. Absolute Change in Exchange-Rate Exposure and the MNC Network of Foreign Operations Examined Separately for MNCs with Positive ("Net Importers") and Negative ("Net Exporters") Exposure Coefficients.

Panel A: Using the Pooled Sample of MNCs (N = 421)[a]

(Model #) NETWORK measure	D	D × NETWORK	D × SIZE	D × Q	D × LTD	D × FSALEP	D × DIV	D × INTCOV	D × CRISIS	(1–D)
(1) NFC	0.3649*** (4.57)	-0.0406 (-1.16)	-0.0000018 (-0.63)	-0.0044 (-0.24)	-0.1358 (-0.95)	0.0025* (1.95)	-0.0579** (-2.16)	-0.000203 (-0.68)	0.0464 (0.68)	0.6642*** (8.59)
(2) NREG	0.3635*** (4.56)	-0.0205 (-1.11)	-0.0000015 (-0.50)	-0.0043 (-0.23)	-0.1317 (-0.92)	0.0025** (1.96)	-0.0602*** (-2.27)	-0.000205 (-0.68)	0.0468 (0.67)	0.6837*** (8.59)
(3) HERF1	0.3310*** (3.11)	0.0286 (0.28)	-0.0000028 (-1.01)	-0.0092 (-0.50)	-0.1445 (-1.01)	0.0024* (1.86)	-0.0641** (-2.42)	-0.000208 (-0.69)	0.0070 (0.11)	0.4115*** (4.13)
(4) HERF2	0.3756*** (2.74)	-0.0279 (-0.22)	-0.0000029 (-1.06)	-0.0106 (-0.59)	-0.1515 (-1.06)	0.0024* (1.85)	-0.0660** (-2.50)	-0.000211 (-0.70)	-0.0126 (-0.18)	0.2683* (1.87)
(5) HERF3	0.3337** (2.57)	0.0197 (0.17)	-0.0000028 (-1.01)	-0.0097 (-0.53)	-0.1439 (-1.00)	0.0024* (1.84)	-0.0646** (-2.45)	-0.000215 (-0.71)	0.0046 (0.07)	0.2542* (1.90)

(Model #) NETWORK measure	(1–D) × NETWORK	(1–D) × SIZE	(1–D) × Q	(1–D) × LTD	(1–D) × FSALEP	(1–D) × DIV	(1–D) × INTCOV	(1–D) × CRISIS	Adjusted-R², F-value
(1) NFC	-0.1197*** (-3.06)	0.0000068 (0.52)	-0.0290 (-1.07)	-0.000016 (-0.37)	0.0015 (0.96)	-0.0535*** (-2.64)	0.000080 (0.94)	0.0782 (1.07)	0.4891, 8.328
(2) NREG	-0.0713*** (-3.00)	0.0000083 (0.62)	-0.0312 (-1.16)	-0.000016 (-0.37)	0.0011 (0.73)	-0.0520** (-2.56)	0.000089 (1.05)	0.1032 (1.31)	0.4885, 8.309
(3) HERF1	0.2834*** (2.83)	-0.0000005 (-0.04)	-0.0329 (-1.22)	-0.000006 (-0.14)	0.0012 (0.79)	-0.0498*** (-2.44)	0.000094 (1.11)	0.0376 (0.55)	0.4855, 8.223
(4) HERF2	0.3635*** (2.70)	0.0000008 (0.06)	-0.0341 (-1.26)	-0.000014 (-0.31)	0.0011 (0.72)	-0.0456** (-2.20)	0.000093 (1.10)	0.0532 (0.75)	0.4845, 8.195
(5) HERF3	0.3975*** (3.10)	0.0000015 (0.12)	-0.0363 (-1.36)	-0.000011 (-0.25)	0.0010 (0.67)	-0.0464** (-2.26)	0.000091 (1.08)	0.0907 (1.21)	0.4877, 8.286

Table 6. (Continued)

Panel B: Using the sub-sample of MNCs with operations in the Asian Crisis region ($N = 219$)[b]

(Model #) NETWORK measure	D	$D \times$ NETWORK	$D \times$ SIZE	$D \times Q$	$D \times$ LTD	$D \times$ FSALEP	$D \times$ DIV	$D \times$ INTCOV	$D \times$ CRISIS	$(1-D)$
(1) NFC	0.4277***	−0.0884**	−0.0000014	−0.0044	−0.0128	0.0026*	−0.0705***	−0.00041	0.0066	0.6038***
	(4.37)	(−2.06)	(−0.60)	(−0.22)	(−0.08)	(1.86)	(−2.49)	(−0.59)	(0.44)	(4.37)
(2) NREG	0.4018***	−0.0436**	−0.0000007	−0.0007	0.0126	0.0030**	−0.0721**	−0.00026	0.0044	0.5051***
	(4.44)	(−2.23)	(−0.31)	(−0.03)	(0.08)	(2.12)	(−2.56)	(−0.36)	(0.31)	(4.15)
(3) HERF1	0.2408***	0.2400	−0.0000020	−0.0082	−0.0372	0.0024*	−0.0745***	−0.00044	−0.0054	0.2100**
	(2.54)	(1.58)	(−0.84)	(−0.41)	(−0.23)	(1.75)	(−2.65)	(−0.62)	(−0.42)	(2.00)
(4) HERF2	0.1287	0.3240**	−0.0000024	−0.0086	−0.0322	0.0025*	−0.0733**	−0.000044	−0.0031	0.1156
	(1.05)	(2.09)	(−0.99)	(−0.43)	(−0.20)	(1.77)	(−2.60)	(−0.61)	(−0.24)	(0.76)
(5) HERF3	0.0701	0.4494***	−0.0000014	−0.00004	0.0132	0.0025*	−0.0645**	−0.00054	−0.0005	0.1234
	(0.58)	(2.78)	(−0.58)	(−0.00)	(0.08)	(1.79)	(−2.28)	(−0.77)	(−0.03)	(0.93)

(Model #) NETWORK measure	$(1-D) \times$ NETWORK	$(1-D) \times$ SIZE	$(1-D) \times Q$	$(1-D) \times$ LTD	$(1-D) \times$ FSALEP	$(1-D) \times$ DIV	$(1-D) \times$ INTCOV	$(1-D) \times$ CRISIS	Adjusted-R^2, F-value
(1) NFC	−0.1512***	0.0000053	−0.0164	−0.000005	0.0028	−0.0446***	0.00072***	0.0176	0.6535
	(−2.67)	(0.48)	(−0.64)	(−0.14)	(1.46)	(−2.76)	(4.35)	(0.79)	9.389
(2) NREG	−0.0535**	0.0000047	−0.0170	−0.00003	0.0030	−0.0394**	0.00081***	0.0011	0.6509
	(−2.26)	(0.42)	(−0.66)	(−0.09)	(1.59)	(−2.45)	(5.12)	(0.06)	9.294
(3) HERF1	0.5964***	0.0000022	−0.0100	−0.000003	0.0019	−0.0427***	0.00067***	0.0066	0.6557
	(3.18)	(0.20)	(−0.39)	(−0.07)	(0.97)	(−2.67)	(3.93)	(0.33)	9.474

(4) HERF2	0.3753*	0.0000022	−0.0123	−0.00008	0.0024	−0.0343**	0.00083***	−0.0042	0.6469
	(1.91)	(0.20)	(−0.46)	(−0.23)	(1.25)	(−2.10)	(5.21)	(−0.22)	9.150
(5) HERF3	0.4765**	0.0000025	−0.0132	−0.00008	0.0019	−0.0357**	0.00079***	0.0005	0.6572
	(2.37)	(0.23)	(−0.51)	(−0.22)	(1.00)	(−2.24)	(4.95)	(0.02)	9.529

Notes: This table reports estimates of the determinants of the absolute change in exchange-rate exposure, $\delta = |\gamma_{t=0} - \gamma_{t=-1}|$, using several measures of the MNC network structure as proxies of the MNCs' ability to construct operational hedges. The explanatory variables' effects on δ are examined separately for MNCs with positive and negative exchange-rate exposures during the crisis, using the methodology of He and Ng (1998). This methodology uses the interactions of each variable with two dummy variables, D and $(1-D)$, where $D=1$ represents positive exposure and $D=0$ represents negative exposure. The coefficients of the 2-digit industry dummies (IND_j) as well as the coefficients of the industry dummies interactions with D and $(1-D)$ included in the regression are not reported. The cross-sectional regressions are performed using the following model:

$$\delta_i = \beta_0 D + \beta_1 D \times NETWORK_i + \beta_2 D \times SIZE_i + \beta_3 D \times Q_i + \beta_4 D \times LTD_i + \beta_5 D \times FSALEP_i$$
$$+ \beta_6 D \times DIV_i + \beta_7 D \times INTCOV_i + \beta_{0d}(1-D) + \beta_{1d}(1-D) \times NETWORK_i + \beta_{2d}(1-D) \times SIZE_i$$
$$+ \beta_{3d}(1-D) \times Q_i + \beta_{4d}(1-D) \times LTD_i + \beta_{5d}(1-D) \times FSALEP_i + \beta_{6d}(1-D) \times DIV_i$$
$$+ \beta_{7d}(1-D) \times INTCOV_i + \sum_j \beta_j D \times IND_{j,i} + \sum_j \beta_{jd}(1-D) \times IND_{j,i} + \varepsilon_i.$$

NETWORK is measured by one of the following five variables: NFC = Number of foreign countries; NREG = Number of foreign regions; HERF1 $= \sum_i (NFS_i)^2 / [\sum_i (NFS_i)]^2$, where NFS_i is the number of foreign subsidiaries in country i; HERF2 $= \sum_j (NFS_j)^2 / [\sum_j (NFS_j)]^2$, where NFS_j is the number of foreign subsidiaries in geographic region j; HERF3 $= \sum_j (NFC_j)^2 / [\sum_j (NFC_j)]^2$, where NFC_j is the number of foreign countries in geographic region j. The remaining control variables are: SIZE = Total Assets; Q = Tobin's Q ratio proxy (Chung & Pruitt, 1994); LTD = Long-term debt ratio (book value); FSALER = Foreign sales/total sales; DIV = Dividend yield; INTCOV = Interest coverage ratio.
[a]CRISIS is a dummy variable that indicates involvement in the Asian Crisis region.
[b]CRISIS is a variable that captures the extent of an MNC's involvement in the Asian Crisis region and it is measured by the number of foreign countries in the Asian Crisis region where the MNC operates.

5. CONCLUSION AND DISCUSSION

This study sheds new light on an issue that has not drawn much attention in prior empirical studies: the importance of operating hedges in foreign-exchange risk management. A possible reason for the absence of empirical evidence may be related to the difficulty in devising the appropriate measures of a firm's ability to construct operating hedges. We use measures of the structure of a MNC foreign subsidiary network as proxies of a MNC ability to devise operational hedges and examine their relationship to currency exposure prior to and during the Asian crisis period of 1997–1998. The Asian currency crisis provides an ideal case for devising an empirical test because the relationship between operating hedges and exposure should be strengthened during periods of extreme volatility.

Utilizing a sample of US MNCs that is approximately equally divided between firms with and without operations in the crisis region, we construct several measures that represent how concentrated/spread-out is the network of its foreign subsidiaries. Employing a model similar to Jorion (1990, 1991), we estimate each MNC's exposures to foreign-exchange risk during the 2-year period preceding the crisis, as well as during the period of the crisis. We then perform univariate tests and regression analysis to investigate the effectiveness of operational hedges in reducing currency risk exposure.

Our results show that the mean exposure during the Asian crisis period was significantly higher than the pre-crisis period. In addition the mean of the absolute change in the exposure of MNCs that only operate in the Asian crisis region was significantly higher than that of MNCs without operations in the crisis region. Additionally, we find a strong relationship between our proxies for the ability to construct operating hedges and exchange-rate exposure measures, both prior to and during the crisis. As expected, an even stronger association between exposure and measures of the MNC network structure is found for the sub-sample of MNCs that have some operations in the Asian crisis region. Consistent with our hypothesis, the regression results indicate that MNCs with spread-out networks of foreign subsidiaries have significantly lower exposures. Furthermore, when the impact of the network variables on exposure is examined separately for "net importers" and "net exporters" we observe some differences between the pre-crisis and crisis regressions. Specifically, prior to the crisis the MNC network variables have a significant impact on exposure for both "net importers" and "net exporters", with the coefficients of the MNC network are substantially higher for the "net exporters".

For the crisis period, the effect is significant for both "net importers" and "net exporters" only for the sub-sample of MNCs with operations in the Asian crisis region. For the overall sample the effect is only significant for "net exporters". This implies that while prior to the crisis operational hedges provided by the operating flexibility of the MNC network effectively reduced exposure for all firms, during the crisis operating hedges were only effective for "net exporters". This result is consistent with the notion that "net exporters" were the firms that were most affected by the crisis, since the Asian crisis resulted in massive devaluations vis-a-vis the dollar in many countries. Therefore, firms exporting in these countries would benefit from the protection provided by a wide spread network that can facilitate effective operational hedges. Thus, overall our results provide strong evidence that a MNC's ability to construct operational hedges significantly reduces its exposure to foreign-exchange risk.

NOTES

1. Examples of theoretical studies of the importance of operational hedges are Flood and Lessard (1986), Logue (1995), and Chowdhry and Howe (1996), among others. To the best of our knowledge, the only study that empirically examines operational hedges and foreign-exchange exposure is that of Laux et al. (1999).

2. The Asian currency crisis started in the first half of 1997 in South East Asia (Malaysia, Indonesia, and Thailand). Large currency devaluations in the countries affected by the crisis exposed banking system inefficiencies and rattled investors' confidence. The crisis quickly spread over to many Asian countries and lasted until the middle of 1998.

3. The following are some of the marketing and production strategies that a firm may choose to implement in response to unanticipated real exchange-rate changes: Market selection, product strategy, pricing strategy, promotional strategy, product sourcing, input mix, plant location, raising productivity.

4. While Jorion (1991) finds that exposure is not significant in the U.S. market, more recent studies have provided evidence of significant exposure coefficients (see for example, Dumas & Solnik, 1995; Bodnar & Gentry, 1993; Bartov & Bodnar, 1994, 1995; Chow & Prasad, 1995; Chow et al. (1997); He & Ng, 1998; and Laux et al., 1999).

5. See Bodnar, Hayt, Marston, and Smithson (1998), Phillips (1995), and Dolde (1993).

6. As Chowdhry and Howe (1999) state, "market insurance for demand uncertainty is not feasible because of the severe moral hazard problem, since sales can be manipulated by the firm."

7. Mello, Parsons, and Triantis (1995) provide a model of optimal financial hedging policy for an MNC with production flexibility in the case of exchange-rate

uncertainty. Chowdhry and Howe (1999) consider the case where there is also uncertainty regarding the quantity of foreign-currency cash flows.

8. For a discussion of MNC operating flexibility see, Kogut and Kulatilaka (1993), and Mello et al. (1995), among others.

9. We divide the globe into nine different geographic regions: Asian Crisis region, NAFTA, European Union, Other Asia region, Western Europe, Eastern Europe, Central America and Caribbean, South America, and Africa.

10. All the control variables are measured similarly to variables found in Geczy, Minton, and Schrand (1997), He and Ng (1998), and Laux et al. (1999).

11. Results of the mean difference significance tests are included in Table 2, Panel E, and are discussed below.

12. The coefficients of the two-digit industry dummies (IND_j) are not reported.

REFERENCES

Allen, L., & Pantzalis, C. (1996). Valuation of the operating flexibility of multinational corporations. *Journal of International Business Studies, 27*(4), 633–653.

Bartov, E., & Bodnar, G. M. (1994). Firm valuation, earnings expectations, and the exchange rate exposure effect. *The Journal of Finance, 44*, 1755–1785.

Bodnar, G. M., & Gentry, W. M. (1993). Exchange rate exposure and industry characteristics: Evidence from Canada, Japan and the USA. *Journal of International Money and Finance, 12*, 29–45.

Bodnar, G. M., Hayt, G. S., Marston, R. C., & Smithson, C. W. (1998). 1998 Wharton survey of financial risk management by U.S. non-financial firms. *Financial Management, 27*(4), 70–91.

Bodnar, G. M., & Wong, M. H. F. (2000). *Estimating exchange rate exposures: Some 'weighty' issues.* NBER Working Paper.

Choi, J. J., & Prasad, A. M. (1995). Exchange risk sensitivity and its determinants: A firm and industry analysis. *Financial Management, 24*, 77–88.

Chow, E. H., Lee, W. Y., & Solt, M. E. (1997). The economic exposure of U.S. multinational firms. *The Journal of Financial Research, 20*(2), 191–210.

Chowdhry, B., & Howe, J. T. B. (1999). Corporate risk management for multinational corporations: Financial and operational hedging policies. *European Finance Review, 2*, 229–246.

Chung, K. H., & Pruitt, S. W. (1994). A Simple approximation of Tobin's Q. *Financial Management, 23*(Autumn), 70–74.

De Marzo, P. M., & Duffie, D. (1995). Corporate incentives for hedging and hedge accounting. *Review of Financial Studies, 8*, 743–771.

Dolde, W. (1993). The trajectory of corporate financial risk management. *Journal of Applied Corporate Finance, 6*, 33–41.

Doukas, J., Pantzalis, C., & Kim, S. (1999). Intangible assets and the network structure of MNCs. *Journal of International Financial Management and Accounting, 10*(1), 1–23.

Dumas, B., & Solnik, B. (1995). The world price of exchange rate risk. *Journal of Finance, 50*(2), 445–479.

Eiteman, D., Stonehill, A., & Moffett, M. (1998). *Multinational business finance* (8th ed.). Addison-Wesley.

Flood, E., & Lessard, D. R. (1986). On the measurement of operating exposure to exchange rates: A conceptual approach. *Financial Management, 15*(1), 25–36.

Froot, K., Scarfstein, D., & Stein, J. (1993). Risk management: Coordinating corporate investment and financing policies. *Journal of Finance, 48*, 1629–1658.

Geczy, C., Minton, B. A., & Schrand, C. (1997). Why firms use currency derivatives. *The Journal of Finance, 52*, 1323–1354.

He, J., & Ng, L. K. (1998). The foreign exchange exposure of Japanese multinational corporations. *The Journal of Finance, 53*(2), 733–753.

Jorion, P. (1990). The exchange rate exposure of U.S. multinationals. *Journal of Business, 63*(3), 331–345.

Jorion, P. (1991). The pricing of exchange rate risk in the stock market. *Journal of Financial and Quantitative Analysis, 26*, 363–376.

Kogut, B., & Kulatilaka, N. (1993). Operating flexibility, global manufacturing, and the option value of a multinational network. *Management Science, 40*(1), 123–139.

Laux, P., Simkins, B. J., & Pantzalis, C. (1999). *Operational hedges and the foreign exchange exposure of U.S. multinational corporations*. Working Paper.

Logue, D. (1995). When theory fails: Globalization as a response to the (hostile) market for foreign exchange. *Journal of Applied Corporate Finance, 8*(3), 39–48.

Mello, A. S., Parsons, J. E., & Triantis, A. (1995). An integrated model of multinational flexibility and hedging policies. *Journal of International Economics, 33*(1/2), 41–56.

Nance, D. R., Smith, C. W., & Smithson, C. W. (1993). On the determinants of corporate hedging. *Journal of Finance, 48*(March), 267–284.

Phillips, A. L. (1995). 1995 derivatives practices and instruments survey. *Financial Management, 24*(2), 115–125.

Pringle, J. J. (1991). Managing foreign exchange exposure. *Journal of Applied Corporate Finance*, 73–82.

Shapiro, A. C. (1996). *Multinational financial management* (5th ed.). Upper Saddle River, NJ: Prentice Hall Inc.

Shapiro, A. C., & Titman, S. (1985). An integrated approach to corporate risk management. *Midland Corporate Finance Journal, 3*(2), 41–56.

Smith, C. W., & Stulz, R. (1985). The determinants of firm's hedging policies. *Journal of Financial Quantitative Analyses, 20*(4), 391–403.

Stiglitz, J. E. (1999). Reforming the global economic architecture: Lessons from recent crises. *Journal of Finance, 54*(4), 1508–1521.

Stulz, R. (1994). Optimal hedging policies. *Journal of Financial and Quantitative Analysis, 19*, 127–140.

SHARE REPURCHASES IN NEW ZEALAND

Hardjo Koerniadi, Ming-Hua Liu and
Alireza Tourani-Rad

ABSTRACT

In this paper, we investigate the New Zealand stock market reactions to both on-market and off-market share repurchase programmes for the period 1995–2004. Share repurchases have become more frequent in New Zealand in recent years, though the size and the number of repurchases are still small by international standards. The main reason appears to be the presence of the dividend imputation system which diminishes the tax consequences of cash dividends compared to capital gains. On the whole, we observe that the market reacts positively and significantly to the share repurchase announcements. The magnitude of average abnormal returns for the on- and the off-market repurchases on the announcement day are 3.25 and 3.12% respectively. We further observe the reasons companies undertake stock repurchase are consistent with the investment and free cash flows agency hypotheses.

Issues in Corporate Governance and Finance
Advances in Financial Economics, Volume 12, 481–498
Copyright © 2007 by Elsevier Ltd.
ISSN: 1569-3732/doi:10.1016/S1569-3732(07)12018-1

1. INTRODUCTION

In the last two decades share repurchases have grown in popularity and importance as a method of returning capital to shareholders. Share repurchases commonly involve cash offers for outstanding shares of common stock. This form of capital delivery has become a contemporary alternative for the historically popular dividend distribution; Grullon and Ikenberry (2000) report that in 1998 for the first time in the US corporations distributed more cash through share repurchases than through dividends. In 1998 share repurchases amounted to US $145 billion versus US $118 billion cash dividends.

Stock repurchases take place when "a public corporation buys its own shares by tender offer, on the open market, or in a negotiated buy back from a large block-holder" (Weston, Chung, & Siu, 1998, p. 491). There are essentially three types of share repurchase methods used in the market: the fixed price tender offer, Dutch-auction tender offer, and open market repurchases.

Fixed price tender offers involve the firm offering a single price to all shareholders for a specific number of shares. This offer is typically valid for a limited time period and may be contingent on a minimum threshold of shares being tendered. Empirical evidence show that the premium paid in a tender offer is around 13–15% (Vermaelen, 1981; Grullon & Ikenberry, 2000).

The Dutch-auction repurchase is also a fixed deal. In this transaction, managers solicit information from shareholders that allows them to form a final price. The actual price level that the repurchase is completed is determined by adding the shares offered starting at the lowest end of management's price range. Lie and McConnell (1998) and Peterson and Peterson (1993) find that there exist no significant differences between fixed price and Dutch auction tender offer repurchases in terms of the announcement period returns, the tender premiums, the expiration day returns, and the earning performance after the repurchase.

Open market share repurchases occur when a corporation buys back its own shares on the open market at the going price just as any other investor might buy the shares. The average cumulative excess return around such an announcement is about 3.5% (Ikenberry, Lakonishok, & Vermaelen, 1995). While the major methods explained above and some others are available to managers, open market repurchases are by far the most popular medium through which shares are repurchased. In terms of the methods employed by repurchasing firms, open market repurchases outweigh alternative methods of repurchasing by approximately 10 to 1 (Weston et al., 1998).

Research concerning why companies buy back stocks and how such transactions affect stock prices continues to evolve. The majority of the studies surrounding share repurchases originate primarily from the US, and more recently, but to a lesser extent, from the U.K. and Australia. These studies have provided insights into the share repurchase phenomena. However, the question remains whether these insights are applicable in other markets around the world. The international evidence regarding repurchases is rather limited. Thus, a degree of scepticism regarding the generalization of the existing evidence on share repurchases is warranted.

As in countries with developed stock markets, share repurchases are an important corporate event and have been announced with increasing frequency in recent years in New Zealand. However, the size and the number of stock repurchases are still far below those of other markets. The total number repurchase programmes during our sample period of about 10 years were less than 100. These numbers are surprisingly small compared to 4,434 open market share repurchase programmes in the US from 1980 to 1997 (Grullon & Michaely, 2004) and 355 on-market share repurchase programmes in Australia from 1997 to July 2003 (Brailsford, Marchesi, & Tutticci, 2004).

Prior to 1994 share repurchases in New Zealand were not possible.[1] However, since July 1994 New Zealand corporations have been able to undertake share repurchase programmes as a means of repatriating capital to their respective shareholders. The situation in New Zealand is of particular interest because the New Zealand stock market has an unusual characteristic: New Zealand companies pay very high dividends. One of the main motivations for investors is that the imputation tax credit regime provides them with a premium over investors in overseas markets. Under this regime, investors can use the imputation credits attached to those dividends to offset other tax liabilities.

In this paper, we seek to use the current theories from the finance literature to explain the share repurchase programme and motives behind them in New Zealand. We further test empirically the stock market reaction to the repurchase announcements and investigate if these returns are influenced by firm-specific characteristics. The rest of the paper is as follows. Next, a legal review of stock repurchase in New Zealand is presented. Further, a selected repurchase literature and its relevance for New Zealand market are analysed. The next two sections contain data and methodology.

In the following section our empirical results are presented and discussed. The final section concludes the paper.

2. LEGAL REVIEW OF NEW ZEALAND SHARE REPURCHASES

The repurchase by a company is essentially a distribution of funds from the company to its shareholders in trade for their shares. Section 2 of the New Zealand Companies Act 1993 recognizes this in the definition of distribution.

To conduct a share repurchase programme, a company must pass two solvency tests. The first test is to ensure that the company's cash flows are sufficient to sustain its solvency after the repurchase. The second test is to ensure that after the repurchase, the value of the firm's assets is greater than all of its liabilities. These restrictions are intended to protect creditors of the company that, after making cash distribution through a share repurchase programme, the company would not become financially insolvent.

There are effectively six ways in which a company can legally buy back its own shares (Fenwick, 1997):

1. Through a pro rata offer to all shareholders

    Pro rata buy backs are off-market repurchases made by a company when it makes an offer to all of its shareholders to repurchase a specified proportion of their shares. This offer, if accepted by all shareholders, would not change the shareholders' voting proportions and their distribution rights. Furthermore, the company must give the shareholders a reasonable opportunity to accept the offer. Under the Companies Act 1993 Section 60 (3) pro rata buy backs require board of directors' resolutions that:
    a. the acquisition is in the best interest of the company; and
    b. the offers terms and the consideration offered are fair and reasonable to the company; and
    c. the board has no material information not disclosed for a share value assessment that would make the terms of the offer and the consideration unfair to shareholders accepting the offer.
2. A selective offer to some shareholders

    Selective offers are off-market repurchases made to specific shareholders. This offers require the consent of all shareholders in writing and the board of directors' resolution (Section 60 (3)).

3. A special offer

Special offers are off-market buy backs made by a company where the offers are expressly permitted by the company's constitution. The offers require special resolutions and oblige the directors who vote in favour of the repurchase to set out in full the reasons to repurchase and sign a certificate attesting the board's resolution (Section 60 (3) above).

4. An on-market acquisition subject to prior notice to shareholders

On-market repurchases with prior notice are repurchases undertaken on the market for not more than a specified number of stocks. The on-market repurchases also require board of directors' resolutions.

5. An on-market acquisition not subject to prior notice

On-market repurchase without prior notice are on-market buy backs made by a company where the number of shares acquired in the preceding 12 months does not exceed 5% of the shares of the same class as at the beginning of the 12-month period. The board of directors' resolutions prior to the offer are also compulsory.

6. By unanimous written agreement executed by all entitled parties

The entitled party here can be a shareholder and a person entitled by the company's constitution conferred any of the rights and powers of a shareholder.

New Zealand on-market repurchases are similar to open market repurchase programme in the US while pro rata off-market repurchases are somewhat similar to the US tender offer repurchases.

As mentioned earlier, New Zealand environment contains dividend imputation tax system which favours cash dividend relative to share repurchase because of tax credit attached to cash dividend. One possible drawback of this system is that companies may prefer to distribute excess cash back to their shareholders rather than to take additional risks to invest in profitable opportunities, a decision which could affect the growth of these companies. Further distinction is that under certain conditions, a share repurchase programme is not taxable. Section CF 3 of the Income Tax Act 1994 states that for pro rata off-market repurchase, a stock repurchase is not taxable if it results in a 15% reduction in capital, or a 10% reduction in capital and the inland revenue is satisfied it is not in lieu of a dividend. For non pro rata off-market repurchase, share repurchase is not taxable if it results in a 15% capital reduction. For on-market repurchase, it is not taxable if it is sourced from the company's subscribed capital. Finally, if shares are purchased as treasury stocks, they must be cancelled or sold within 12 months and sourced from subscribed capital.

3. THE REPURCHASE LITERATURE

While both dividends and share repurchases are mediums of distributing cash to shareholder, Weston et al. (1998) suggest that managers pay dividends out of long run sustainable earnings. A company with stable earnings would thus tend to pay out a higher dividend than an otherwise similar growth firm. Correspondingly, because dividends represent an ongoing commitment and are used to distribute permanent cash flows, firms on the whole are very reluctant to make a dividend increase if they feel they may have to reverse it in the future. Repurchases thus ensure financial flexibility relative to dividends because they do not require the company to commit to future payout ratios.

There are various reasons that companies choose share repurchase as their payout method. The main ones are:

Tax considerations: Share repurchase is preferred to cash dividend because selling shareholders are subject only to capital gains tax which normally is lower than ordinary income tax as in the case of cash dividend (Grullon & Michaely, 2002; Lie & Lie, 1999). Moreover, non selling shareholders benefit from the increase proportion of their ownership in the firm, and pay capital gains tax only when they sell the shares.

Signalling and asymmetric information: Vermaelen (1981) asserts that repurchases are information signals to the market. The logic follows that company managers are probably best situated to recognize when market prices deviate form the company's true underlying value. Thus a frequent explanation of stock repurchases is that they take place when managers deem their stock is undervalued. This view is consistent with the evidence that firms tend to announce programmes following poor stock price performance (Comment & Jarrell, 1991; Stephens & Weisbach, 1998). The asymmetric information phenomenon is highlighted by Ikenberry et al. (1995), Vermaelen (1981), and Dann (1981). They found evidence to suggest that stock prices climb on the announcement of a repurchase programme. In addition, results from Comment and Jarrell (1991) indicated that the abnormal returns observed around the announcement of a repurchase programme were inversely related to recent stock price performance leading up to the repurchase announcement. This is consistent with the notion that asymmetric information is an influential motive for stock repurchases.

Undervaluation: Han, Suk, and Sung (1998) state that firms with a high book to market ratio (value firms) tend to have a higher likelihood of undervaluation in the market. Thus if we are to accept that firms are influenced by undervaluation beliefs, then firms with a high book to market ratio could be more inclined to announce repurchase programmes. Ikenberry et al. (1995) examine US open market stock repurchase announcements from 1980 to 1990. They form equally weighted portfolios of stocks based on their book to market ratio and find that value stocks experience significant abnormal return of 45% over a 4-year period after the announcements. This finding is robust when the sample data is extended to 1996 (Chan, Ikenberry, & Lee, 2004). Using Canadian open market stock repurchase data from 1989 to 1997, Ikenberry, Lakonishok, and Vermaelen (2000) also report similar evidence of positive long-term returns. The post-announcement excess return over a 3-year period is 7% per year. Canadian value firms earn annual 9.1% abnormal returns, which is close to that of the US value firms.

Change in capital structure: The repurchase of shares in a company has the effect of changing the firm's capital structure. Alternatively, when a company has excess capital but does not want to increase its leverage, it can use share repurchase to adjust its debt to equity ratio. A company may also use share repurchase to maintain its desired debt to equity ratio due to the exercise of employee stock option plan (Chan et al., 2004).

Finally, a share repurchase programme may be used as a defensive tool to fend off a hostile takeover. This method was popular in the US during the takeover era in the1980s (Klein & Rosenfeld, 1988; Mikkelson & Ruback, 1991).

4. DATA

Data on the initial announcements of (non financial) companies to buy back their shares and the corresponding companies accounting information were collected from the New Zealand Stock Exchange (NZX) and Datex New Zealand financial database from 1995 to August 2004. Some companies, however, did not announce their intention to conduct on-market share repurchase but directly bought back their shares on the market and reported their buy back activities to the NZX several days after. These repurchases were not included in the sample. The final sample consists of 37 on-market and 20 off-market share repurchase programmes respectively (Table 1).

Table 1.   Firm's Initial Announcements across Years.

Year	On-Market	Off-Market
1995	0	1
1996	1	1
1997	2	3
1998	7	1
1999	3	1
2000	3	2
2001	5	4
2002	9	3
2003	7	5
2004	1	1
Total	37	20

Reviewing the motives put forward by the firms in our sample, we can state that the on-market repurchase programmes are undertaken because of the lack of profitable projects (seven cases), achieving optimal capital structures (five cases), and to stock option plans (five cases). The motives for the rest of the sample were not available in the announcement reports. For the off-market programmes, main motives were acquisition-related repurchases (five cases), having excess cash (five cases), and achieving optimal capital structure (four cases).

Interestingly, when compared to Australia which has similar imputation tax system, the main reasons for undertaking repurchase programmes are different. The main motives for the Australian firms are to signal to the market that the firms' share prices are undervalued and in order to improve earning per share. For off-market buy back the main purposes are to remove particular shareholders and increase EPS (Mitchell & Robinson, 1999; Mitchell, Dharmawan, & Clarke, 2001).

Fig. 1 shows the total values of shares repurchased compared to the total ordinary cash dividends of the repurchasing companies. Total value of shares repurchased increases from only NZ $197,000 in 1995 and NZ $2,382,000 in 1996 to NZ $206,528,000 in 2004. In 1997 Telecom spent NZ $357,000,000 and NZ $643,800,000 to buy back its stocks from the open market. The amounts of money the companies spent for cash dividends are, on average, higher than those spent for share repurchases. As a payout method it seems that cash dividends are much preferred than share repurchase by New Zealand firms.

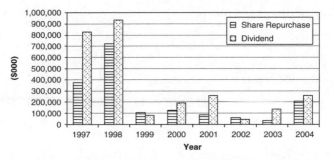

Fig. 1. Share Repurchase and Ordinary Cash Dividend Values.

5. METHODOLOGY

We calculate the market reaction to the announcements of the stock repurchase using a standard event-study methodology in the form of:

$$\hat{R}_{jt} = \hat{\alpha}_j + \hat{\beta}_j R_{mt} \tag{1}$$

$$AR_{jt} = R_{jt} - \hat{R}_{jt} \tag{2}$$

where R_{jt} is the actual return on stock j on day; R_{mt} the return on the market on day t; AR_{jt} the abnormal return on stock j on day t.

The NZSE40 capital index is used as the market index. This index represents more than 90% of the capitalization of the stock market making it a suitable proxy for the market portfolio. The estimation period of the market model is from -220 days to day -21 prior to the announcements. We calculate the profitability over various event windows within the event period -20, 20 by calculating cumulative abnormal returns (CARs) in the form:

$$CAR(t_1, t_2) = \sum_{t=t_1}^{t_2} AR_t \tag{3}$$

When an event causes minor increases in variance of returns, traditional event study methods too frequently commit Type I error, that is, to reject the null hypothesis of zero abnormal return even when the average abnormal return is statistically zero. In order to overcome the bias due to event-induced heteroskedasticity of the abnormal returns, the test for the significance of the abnormal returns is adjusted using a method suggested by Boehmer,

Musumeci, and Poulsen (1991):

$$t\text{-adjusted statistic} = \frac{1/N \sum_{i=1}^{N} SR_{iE}}{\sqrt{1/N(N-1) \sum_{i=1}^{N} SR_{iE} - \sum_{i=1}^{N} \left(SR_{iE}/N\right)^2}}$$

where:

$$SR_{iE} = \frac{A_{iE}}{\hat{s}\sqrt{1 + \frac{1}{T_i} + (R_{mE} - \bar{R}_m)^2 \Big/ \sum_{i=1}^{T_i} (R_{mt} - \bar{R}_m)^2}}$$

N is the number of firms in the sample; A_{iE} the security i's abnormal return on the event day; A_{it} the security i's abnormal return on day t; T_i the number of days in security i's estimation period; R_{mt} the market return on day t; $\bar{R}_m$ the average market return during the estimation period; $\hat{s}_i$ the security i's estimated standard deviation of abnormal returns during the estimation period; SR_{iE} the security i's standardized residual on the event day.

As our sample for both repurchase programmes is quite small, we carried out a further robustness test of the significance of our results by applying the bootstrap methodology. This method was introduced by Efron (1979) and applied in the context of event studies by Foster, Olsen, and Shevlin (1984). The procedure is relatively robust to the problems of non normality, heteroskedasticity, and time dependence of security returns as it avoids many distributional assumptions of parametric tests (Kramer, 2001). This testing was conducted by randomly selecting a replacement firm-date pair from the entire population of companies and dates to match each of the repurchases from our initial sample. The cumulative abnormal returns following each of these random events were then computed for the respective event windows and aggregated. This process was repeated 2,000 times to develop the distribution. The null is rejected at the $\alpha\%$ level if the abnormal return from the repurchase sample exceeds $(1-\alpha) \times 2,000$ simulated values from the empirical distribution.

6. EMPIRICAL FINDINGS

6.1. Announcement Effects

Table 2 presents the average abnormal return during the event window. On average, the on-market share repurchase announcements have a significant average excess return on the event day of 3.25%. The magnitude of this average abnormal return on the announcement day is higher than that of on-market Australian buy backs which is 1.25% (Otchere & Ross, 2002) and comparable to the US findings (Ikenberry et al., 2000; Grullon & Ikenberry, 2000). For the off-market announcements, firms experience significant abnormal return on the event day of 3.12%. This is also higher than that of off-market Australian buy back. Lamba and Ramsay (1999) show that the average abnormal return for Australian off-market repurchase at the event day is 0.6% and statistically insignificant.

Fig. 2 shows the CARs for on-market repurchase jumps from around 0.6% on 1 day before to around 4% on the announcement day, increases to around 5% on the day after the announcements, then stays at around 5–6%. The cumulative abnormal returns for on-market repurchase remain significant for 20 days after the announcement (Table 3, Panel A). It appears that the market under-reacts to the announcement, suggesting price undervaluation. However this conclusion might be premature. Companies undertaking on-market repurchase make subsequent announcements such as details of the programmes, confirmation announcements, and reports of the number of shares bought back to the market. As in on-market repurchase companies are not obliged to buy back shares as stated in their initial announcement, these subsequent announcements may have incremental effects on the stock price. Empirical results on the firm characteristics, reported below, confirm that the post-announcement CAR is not associated with undervaluation.

The CAR for the off-market repurchases increase from −1.65% 1 day before the announcement to 1.47% on the announcement day, peaks at around 5% 5 days after the event, then stays at around 3%. The CAR for the off-market repurchases is however significant only in a short interval around the announcement date (Table 3, Panel B). CAR from −1 to +1 is statistically significant at 1%, but not significant when the event window is extended.[2]

Table 2. Abnormal Returns for On-Market and Off-Market Repurchases.

Day	On-Market			Off-Market		
	t-stat	AAR (%)	CAR (%)	*t*-stat	AAR (%)	CAR (%)
−20	1.23	0.97	0.97	0.56	0.54	0.54
−19	−0.36	−0.22	0.75	−1.42	−0.26	0.29
−18	−0.59	−0.21	0.53	−1.26	−0.90	−0.62
−17	−0.38	0.07	0.60	0.63	0.18	−0.43
−16	1.19	0.02	0.62	−3.04	−1.33	−1.77
−15	0.80	0.40	1.02	0.90	0.67	−1.10
−14	−1.62	−0.42	0.60	−0.30	0.01	−1.08
−13	0.75	0.26	0.86	1.23	0.58	−0.50
−12	−0.11	−0.18	0.68	−0.80	−0.57	−1.08
−11	−1.13	−0.86	−0.18	0.04	0.46	−0.62
−10	1.02	0.26	0.08	−1.36	−0.92	−1.53
−9	0.30	0.46	0.53	1.96	0.73	−0.80
−8	0.59	0.35	0.88	0.26	−0.06	−0.86
−7	1.30	0.38	1.26	−1.61	−1.83	−2.69
−6	−0.44	−0.12	1.14	−1.13	−0.57	−3.25
−5	−0.07	−0.05	1.09	0.39	0.02	−3.24
−4	−0.18	0.03	1.12	−0.63	−0.77	−4.00
−3	−1.30	−0.46	0.66	1.21	0.68	−3.32
−2	−0.19	0.05	0.71	0.36	0.26	−3.06
−1	−0.65	−0.14	0.57	1.83	1.41**	−1.65
0	3.05	3.25***	3.82	2.39	3.12***	1.47
1	2.83	1.58***	5.40	1.36	1.45*	2.92
2	0.39	−0.03	5.37	0.32	0.89	3.81
3	0.33	0.16	5.54	−1.09	−0.41	3.40
4	−0.39	−0.40	5.14	−1.21	−0.71	2.70
5	−0.86	−0.73	4.40	1.01	1.68	4.38
6	−0.68	−0.25	4.16	0.13	0.52	4.89
7	−0.30	0.26	4.42	−0.52	−0.46	4.43
8	0.92	0.44	4.86	−0.86	−0.50	3.93
9	1.29	0.33	5.19	−1.90	−0.38	3.55
10	1.27	0.23	5.42	0.93	0.59	4.14
11	−1.15	−0.26	5.16	−1.10	−0.59	3.54
12	0.17	0.23	5.39	0.68	0.49	4.03
13	−0.29	−0.18	5.21	−0.42	−0.84	3.19
14	−0.84	−0.36	4.86	−2.17	−1.26	1.93
15	0.17	0.20	5.06	0.10	−0.09	1.84
16	3.03	0.89	5.95	0.12	−0.16	1.68
17	−0.34	−0.21	5.73	−0.49	−0.09	1.59
18	−1.48	−0.12	5.61	−0.28	−0.13	1.46
19	1.10	0.37	5.98	0.72	0.32	1.78
20	−0.87	−0.35	5.63	1.05	0.37	2.14

Notes: The estimation period is from −220 to −21 days prior to the announcements. *t*-stat is the heteroskedasticity-adjusted *t*-statistics for the average abnormal return. It tests the null hypothesis that the average abnormal return = 0.
*Denotes significance at 10% level.
**Denotes significance at 5% level.
***Denotes significance at 1% level.

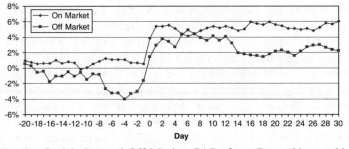

Fig. 2. On-Market and Off-Market CARs from Day −20 to +30.

Table 3. Cumulative Abnormal Returns.

	−1, +1	−10, +10	−20, +20
Panel A: On-market			
CAR	4.69%	5.60%	5.63%
	(3.58)***	(2.66)***	(2.06)**
Panel B: Off-market			
CAR	5.98%	4.75%	2.14%
	(3.26)***	(1.29)	(0.43)

Note: CAR is cumulative abnormal return over the estimated event windows. *t*-statistics are in parentheses.
**Denotes significance at 5% level.
***Denotes significance at 1% level.

6.2. Announcement Effects and Firm Characteristics

In this section we attempt to investigate empirically why New Zealand firms engage in stock repurchase programmes. We regress the cumulative abnormal returns on certain characteristics of the firms and the motives for taking up repurchase programmes.

One of the main reasons firms undertaking open market share repurchase programmes is because the managers believe that their stocks are undervalued (Ikenberry et al., 2000). To investigate this motive, pre-announcement cumulative abnormal return (PRE) is used as a proxy for undervaluation (Comment & Jarrell, 1991; Hatakeda & Isagawa, 2004). The more the stocks are mispriced by the market, the more favourable the market reacts to such announcements. Accordingly PRE is expected to be negatively associated with the abnormal return.

Several studies on share repurchase employ the firm size as a proxy for asymmetric information between management and public investors (Lakonishok & Vermaelen, 1990; Hatakeda & Isagawa, 2004). The smaller the firms the larger the asymmetry problem is to be expected. Company size is then expected to be negatively correlated with the abnormal returns.

Firms with high profitability are expected to have more investment opportunities. When firms have positive net present value investment opportunities, they prefer to invest excess cash in real assets rather than to buy back their stocks. Low profitability firms whose investment opportunities appear to have diminished may find it desirable to repurchase their outstanding shares (Hatakeda & Isagawa, 2004; Grullon & Michaely, 2004). To analyse this motive, return on assets (ROA) is used as a proxy for firms' profitability.

The other main motive for on-market repurchase is to obtain an optimal capital structure. According to the agency cash flows theory, the pre-buy back capital structure is related to the announcement. This is because the higher a firm's leverage, the smaller the agency cost of free cash flows is expected. Thus when a firm initiates a share repurchase programme to increase (reduce) debt (equity), the market should react favourably to the announcement. Therefore debt to asset ratio (D/A) is used as a proxy for the capital structure policy. Eq. (4) analyses the motives for the on-market repurchase:

$$\text{CAR}_{(-1,+1)it} = \alpha_{0it} + \alpha_1 \text{PRE}_{it} + \alpha_2 \text{ROA}_{it} + \frac{\alpha_3 \text{D}_{it}}{\text{A}_{it}} + \alpha_4 \text{Size}_{it} + e_{it} \quad (4)$$

Previous studies find significant correlations between the likelihood of a share repurchase and the firm's excess cash flows (FCF) as well as its pre-buy back level of leverage (Lie, 2000; Vafeas, 1997; Nohel & Tarhan, 1998). When a firm has no positive NPV projects, it is desirable to return the temporary excess cash back to its shareholders (Guay & Harford, 2000). Hence it is expected that the abnormal return is positively related to its cash flows. Eq. (5) examines the off-market share repurchase:

$$\text{CAR}_{(-1,+1)it} = \alpha_{0it} + \alpha_1 \text{Size}_{it} + \alpha_2 \text{ACQ}_{it} + \alpha_3 \text{FCF}_{it} + \frac{\alpha_4 \text{D}_{it}}{\text{A}_{it}} + e_{it} \quad (5)$$

As acquisition was mentioned as a major motive for the off-market repurchases, we include a dummy variable, ACQ, which takes the value of 1 if the buy back is acquisition-related and 0 otherwise.

Panel A of Table 4 presents the relation between the abnormal return surrounding immediately around the announcement and firm characteristics and the motives of share repurchase. Consistent with the investment hypothesis, the coefficient of ROA is negative and statistically significant. Investors perceive that low ROA companies have no or limited profitable investments and prefer the excess funds to be distributed to them. Therefore when these companies announce share repurchase programmes, the investors react favourably to the announcements. The coefficients of PRE and D/A, however, are positive and statistically insignificant which do not confirm the undervaluation and the optimal capital structure hypotheses. The result also shows that although SIZE is negative but not statistically significant.

Panel B of Table 4 shows that excess cash flow is positive and significant as predicted by the agency theory. This result is different from Kharisma, Balachandran, and Skully (2004) who find no evidence for free cash flows hypothesis for Australian off-market buy backs. Size is negative and significantly related to the announcement returns. It also shows that the smaller the firm that announcement of the off-market repurchase, the more

Table 4. Cross-Sectional Model Analysis.

Panel A: On-market

Intercept	Size	D/A	ROA	PRE	Adj. R^2
0.17	−0.01	0.03	−0.30***	0.12	31.12%
(1.65)	(−1.01)	(0.40)	(−2.75)	(0.73)	

Panel B: Off-market

Intercept	Size	D/A	FCF	ACQ	Adj. R^2
0.36	−0.03**	−0.15	0.00***	−0.03	32.16%
(2.88)	(−2.45)	(−1.27)	(3.51)	(−0.76)	

Notes: In Panel A, the dependent variable is CAR from day −1 to day +1. PRE is the cumulative abnormal return from day −20 to −2. Size is approximated by the natural logarithm of total market value of asset. ROA is return on assets computed as net income over total assets. D/A is debt to asset ratio. The number of sample is 37 firm announcements. For Panel B, the dependent variable is CAR from day −1 to day +1. ACQ is a dummy for acquisition-related repurchase. It takes the value of 1 for the merger-related share repurchase and 0 otherwise. FCF is the firm free cash flow and computed following Vafeas (1997): earnings before depreciation, interest and tax-dividend-interest-tax. The number of sample is 20 firm announcements. *t*-statistics are reported in parentheses.

favourable the market reaction to the announcements. This finding is similar to Australian off-market buy backs (Kharisma et al., 2004). The market also reacts favourably to the announcement when companies undertake buy back to increase their leverage. However the effect is not statistically significant.

7. CONCLUSIONS

Share repurchases have become more frequent in the New Zealand in recent years, though the size and the number of them are still quite small by international standards. The main reason appears to be the presence of dividend imputation system. However, evidence suggests that, due to flexibility inherent in share repurchase, share repurchase programmes have been gaining popularity in recent years, along with cash dividends, to distribute transitory cash back to the shareholders.

On average the market reacts positively and significantly to the share repurchase announcements. The magnitude of average abnormal return for the on- and the off-market repurchases on the announcement day are 3.25 and 3.12% respectively.

Further, our evidence supports the investment hypothesis for the on-market repurchases. For the off-market repurchases the evidence is consistent with the agency free cash flows and the information asymmetry hypotheses.

NOTES

1. Although many companies attempted to avoid the prohibition on repurchases through the use of nominee companies and employee share schemes- with varying degrees of success: For an example see NZI Bank Ltd. V Euro-National Corporation Ltd (1992) 3 NZLR 529.
2. Bootstrapping method produce similar results (not reported) for both on-market and off-market abnormal returns.

REFERENCES

Boehmer, E., Musumeci, J., & Poulsen, A. (1991). Event-study methodology under conditions of event-induced variance. *Journal of Financial Economics, 30*(2), 253–272.

Brailsford, T., Marchesi, D., & Tutticci, I. (2004). *Determinants of share repurchased in on-market buy-backs*. Working Paper. University of Queensland Business School.

Chan, K., Ikenberry, D., & Lee, I. (2004). Economic sources of gain in stock repurchases. *Journal of Financial and Quantitative Analysis, 39*(3), 461–479.

Comment, R., & Jarrell, G. A. (1991). The relative signalling power of Dutch auction and fixed-price self-tender offers and open market share repurchases. *Journal of Finance, 46*(4), 1243–1271.

Dann, L. (1981). Common stock repurchases: An analysis of returns to bondholders and stockholders. *Journal of Financial Economics, 39*(2), 113–138.

Efron, B. (1979). Bootstrap methods: Another look at the jackknife. *Annals of Statistics, 7*(1), 1–26.

Fenwick, H. C. (1997). *Share repurchases in New Zealand under the Companies Act 1993*. Unpublished doctoral dissertation. Victoria University, Wellington.

Foster, G., Olsen, C., & Shevlin, T. (1984). Earnings releases, anomalies, and the behavior of security returns. *Accounting Review, 59*(4), 574–603.

Grullon, G., & Ikenberry, D. L. (2000). What do we know about stock repurchases? *Journal of Applied Corporate Finance, 13*(1), 31–51.

Grullon, G., & Michaely, R. (2002). Dividends, share repurchases, and the substitution hypothesis. *Journal of Finance, 57*(4), 1649–1684.

Grullon, G., & Michaely, R. (2004). The information content of share repurchase programs. *Journal of Finance, 59*(2), 651–680.

Guay, W., & Harford, J. (2000). The cash-flow permanence and information content of dividend versus repurchases. *Journal of Financial Economics, 57*(3), 385–415.

Han, K. C., Suk, D. Y., & Sung, H. M. (1998). The evidence of bidders' overpayment in takeovers: The valuation ratios approach. *The Financial Review, 33*(2), 55–68.

Hatakeda, T., & Isagawa, N. (2004). Stock price behavior surrounding stock repurchase announcements: Evidence from Japan. *Pacific Basin Finance Journal, 12*(3), 271–290.

Ikenberry, D., Lakonishok, J., & Vermaelen, T. (1995). Market underreaction to open market share repurchases. *Journal of Financial Economics, 39*(2-3), 181–208.

Ikenberry, D., Lakonishok, J., & Vermaelen, T. (2000). Stock repurchases in Canada: Performance and strategic trading. *Journal of Finance, 55*(5), 2373–2397.

Kharisma, A. B., Balachandran, B., & Skully, M. (2004). *Australian off-market buy-backs: Empirical evidence*. Working Paper. Monash University.

Klein, A., & Rosenfeld, J. (1988). The impact of targeted share repurchases on the wealth of non-participating shareholders. *Journal of Financial Research, 11*(2), 89–97.

Kramer, L. A. (2001). Alternative methods for robust analysis in event study applications. *Advances in Investment Analysis and Portfolio Management, 8*, 109–132.

Lakonishok, J., & Vermaelen, T. (1990). Anomalous price behaviour around repurchase tender offers. *Journal of Finance, 45*(2), 455–477.

Lamba, A., & Ramsay, I. (1999). *Share buy-backs: An empirical investigation*. Working Paper. University of Melbourne.

Lie, E. (2000). Excess funds and agency problems: An empirical study of incremental cash disbursements. *Review of Financial Studies, 13*(1), 219–247.

Lie, E., & Lie, H. (1999). The role of personal taxes in corporate decisions: An empirical analysis of share repurchases and dividends. *Journal of Financial and Quantitative Analysis, 34*(4), 533–552.

Lie, E., & McConnell, J. J. (1998). Earnings signal in fixed-price and Dutch auction self-tender offers. *Journal of Financial Economics, 49*(2), 161–186.

Mikkelson, W., & Ruback, R. S. (1991). Targeted repurchases and common stock returns. *Rand Journal of Economics*, *22*(4), 544–561.

Mitchell, J. D., Dharmawan, G. V., & Clarke, A. W. (2001). Managements' views on share buy-backs: An Australian survey. *Accounting and Finance*, *41*(1/2), 93–129.

Mitchell, J. D., & Robinson, P. (1999). Motivations of Australian listed companies effecting share buy-backs. *Abacus*, *35*(1), 91–119.

Nohel, T., & Tarhan, V. (1998). Share repurchases and firm performance: New evidence on the agency cost of free cash flows. *Journal of Financial Economics*, *49*(2), 187–222.

Otchere, I., & Ross, M. (2002). Do share buy back announcements convey firm-specific or industry-wide information? A test of the undervaluation hypothesis. *International Review of Financial Analysis*, *11*(4), 511–531.

Peterson, D. R., & Peterson, P. P. (1993). Dutch auction versus tender offers: Do firms overpay in fixed price tender offers? *Journal of Financial Research*, *16*(1), 39–48.

Stephens, C., & Weisbach, M. (1998). Actual share reacquisitions in open market repurchases programs. *Journal of Finance*, *53*(1), 313–333.

Vafeas, N. (1997). Determinants of the choice between alternative share repurchase methods. *Journal of Accounting, Auditing and Finance*, *12*(2), 101–125.

Vermaelen, T. (1981). Common stock repurchases and market signalling: An empirical study. *Journal of Financial Economics*, *9*(2), 138–183.

Weston, J. F., Chung, K. S., & Siu, J. A. (1998). *Takeovers, restructuring, and corporate governance*. New Jersey: Prentice Hall.

SET UP A CONTINUATION ORDER TODAY!

Did you know that you can set up a continuation order on all Elsevier-JAI series and have each new volume sent directly to you upon publication? For details on how to set up a **continuation order**, contact your nearest regional sales office listed below.

To view related series in Business & Management, please visit:

www.elsevier.com/businessandmanagement

The Americas
Customer Service Department
11830 Westline Industrial Drive
St. Louis, MO 63146
USA
US customers:
Tel: +1 800 545 2522 (Toll-free number)
Fax: +1 800 535 9935
For Customers outside US:
Tel: +1 800 460 3110 (Toll-free number).
Fax: +1 314 453 7095
usbkinfo@elsevier.com

Europe, Middle East & Africa
Customer Service Department
Linacre House
Jordan Hill
Oxford OX2 8DP
UK
Tel: +44 (0) 1865 474140
Fax: +44 (0) 1865 474141
eurobkinfo@elsevier.com

Japan
Customer Service Department
2F Higashi Azabu, 1 Chome Bldg
1-9-15 Higashi Azabu, Minato-ku
Tokyo 106-0044
Japan
Tel: +81 3 3589 6370
Fax: +81 3 3589 6371
books@elsevierjapan.com

APAC
Customer Service Department
3 Killiney Road #08-01
Winsland House I
Singapore 239519
Tel: +65 6349 0222
Fax: +65 6733 1510
asiainfo@elsevier.com

Australia & New Zealand
Customer Service Department
30-52 Smidmore Street
Marrickville, New South Wales 2204
Australia
Tel: +61 (02) 9517 8999
Fax: +61 (02) 9517 2249
service@elsevier.com.au

30% Discount for Authors on All Books!

A 30% discount is available to Elsevier book and journal contributors on all books (except multi-volume reference works).

To claim your discount, full payment is required with your order, which must be sent directly to the publisher at the nearest regional sales office above.